Imperial Portugal in the *A*

MW00834500

As the British, French, and Spanish Atlantic empires were torn apart in the Age of Revolutions, Portugal steadily pursued reforms to tie its American, African, and European territories more closely together. Eventually, after a period of revival and prosperity, the Luso-Brazilian world also succumbed to revolution, which ultimately resulted in Brazil's independence from Portugal. The first of its kind in the English language to examine the Portuguese Atlantic World in the period from 1770 to 1850, this book reveals that, despite formal separation, the links and relationships that survived the demise of empire entwined the historical trajectories of Portugal and Brazil even more tightly than before. From constitutionalism to economic policy to the problem of slavery, Portuguese and Brazilian statesmen and political writers labored under the long shadow of empire as they sought to begin anew and forge stable post-imperial orders on both sides of the Atlantic.

GABRIEL PAQUETTE is an assistant professor of history at The Johns Hopkins University. He is the author of *Enlightenment, Governance, and Reform in Spain and its Empire, 1759–1808* (2008), editor of *Enlightened Reform in Southern Europe and its Atlantic Colonies*, c. *1750–1830* (2009), and co-editor of *Connections after Colonialism: Europe and Latin America in the 1820s* (2013).

Imperial Portugal in the Age of Atlantic Revolutions

The Luso-Brazilian World, c. 1770–1850

Gabriel Paquette

The Johns Hopkins University

CAMBRIDGE
UNIVERSITY PRESS

CAMBRIDGE
UNIVERSITY PRESS

University Printing House, Cambridge CB2 8BS, United Kingdom

Cambridge University Press is part of the University of Cambridge.

It furthers the University's mission by disseminating knowledge in the pursuit of education, learning and research at the highest international levels of excellence.

www.cambridge.org
Information on this title: www.cambridge.org/9781107640764

© Gabriel Paquette 2013

First published 2013
Reprinted 2013
First paperback edition 2014

A catalogue record for this publication is available from the British Library

Library of Congress Cataloguing in Publication data
Paquette, Gabriel B., 1977– author.
  Imperial Portugal in the age of Atlantic revolutions : the
  Luso-Brazilian world, c. 1770–1850 / Gabriel Paquette, The Johns
  Hopkins University.
    pages cm
  Includes bibliographical references and index.
  ISBN 978-1-107-02897-5 (hardback)
  1. Portugal–Relations–Brazil.   2. Brazil–Relations–
  Portugal.   3. Portugal–Relations–Africa,   Portuguese-speaking.
  4. Africa, Portuguese-speaking–Relations–Portugal.
  5. Portugal–Colonies–History.   6. Imperialism–History.
  7. Revolutions–History.   8. Decolonization–History.
  9. Political culture–Portugal–History.   10. Political
  culture–Brazil–History.   I. Title.
  DP557.B7P37 2013
  909´.0971246907–dc23
  2012036034

ISBN 978-1-107-02897-5 Hardback
ISBN 978-1-107-64076-4 Paperback

Contents

Figures

Acknowledgments

In the preface to an article entitled "Politics and Political Economy of Portugal," published in 1835, the editor of the *London Review* noted that "a book concerning that country would have few readers; and the fewer, perhaps, if it were copious in detail and methodical in generalization. All that the subject will bear is desultory sketches and remarks."[1] I encountered this quotation when I began my research in Lisbon nearly a decade ago. I am grateful that so many fellow historians and funding bodies, to say nothing of Cambridge University Press, refused to reach the same conclusion as the *London Review*. The unflagging encouragement and unstinting generosity I received emboldened me to persevere, to write this book, and to hope that it might find its way into the hands of more than a few readers.

I acknowledge with gratitude the material support furnished by the following institutions which made possible long stints in foreign archives and uninterrupted periods of writing: The Johns Hopkins University; Trinity College, University of Cambridge; the British Academy; the Faculty of History, Cambridge; the Managers of the Smuts Memorial Fund, Cambridge; the Centre for History and Economics, Harvard University; the Brazil Studies Program, Harvard University; the Portuguese Fulbright Commission; the Lilly Library, Indiana University at Bloomington; the John Carter Brown Library; the National Endowment for the Humanities; and the University of Notre Dame Institute for Advanced Study (NDIAS).

I wish to thank several historians without whose example, encouragement, criticism, and letters of support this book would never have been completed: David Armitage, Chris Bayly, Tim Blanning, David Brading, John H. Elliott, Brian Hamnett, Ken Maxwell, Tony McFarlane, Nuno G. Monteiro, John Robertson, and Emma Rothschild. I wish to record my special debt of gratitude to Richard Drayton, who, with characteristic acuity and foresight, persuaded me to study Portuguese and go

---

[1] *London Review*, vol. I, no. 2 (July 1835), p. 371.

viii

to Portugal well before I had written a single word of my dissertation, which he supervised, on eighteenth-century Spain.

The following friends (and colleagues) either read draft chapters of this book or helped me work through certain ideas in the course of conversation: Matthew Brown, José Luís Cardoso, Manuel Lucena Giraldo, Christopher Schmidt-Nowara, John Shovlin, and David Todd. I thank each of them for their comradeship and intellectual generosity. In addition, I wish to acknowledge the following scholars, mainly but not exclusively historians, whose support, conversation, criticism, and scholarship proved crucial to the development of the book: Jeremy Adelman, Tomás Amorim, Ken Andrien, Jesús Astigarraga, Derek Beales, Ted Beatty, Francisco Bethencourt, Harald Braun, Roberto Breña, Angus Burgin, Nicholas Canny, Pedro Cardim, Nathan Connolly, Jordana Dym, Richard Elphick, Javier Fernández Sebastián, Josep Fradera, Carrie Gibson, Karen Graubart, James Green, Patrick Griffin, Boyd Hilton, Jamie Hood, Vittorio Hösle, Maurizio Isabella, Maya Jasanoff, Charles Jones, Richard Kagan, Francis King, Franklin Knight, Thomas Kselman, Paul Lay, Philippa Levine, John Lonsdale, Inga Huld Markan, John Marshall, the late Sabine MacCormack, Adriana Méndez Rodenas, William Nelson, Marcy Norton, William O'Reilly, Paul Ocobock, Vijay Pinch, Pedro Ramos Pinto, Philip Pomper, Txema Portillo, Eduardo Posada-Carbó, Sophus Reinert, Lucy Riall, Mónica Ricketts, John Robertson, Ricardo Roque, the late John Russell-Wood, Neil Safier, Ricardo Salazar-Rey, Peter Sarris, Todd Shepard, Hamish Scott, Carolyn Sherman, Ana Cristina Nogueira da Silva, Marcio Siwi, Ricardo Soares de Oliveira, Koen Stapelbroek, Donald Stelluto, Robert Sullivan, Vasileios Syros, Lauri Tähtinen, Ben Vinson III, Jim Weinstein, Ted Widmer, and Reuben Zahler. In addition to those named, all of the participants at the two conferences held at Trinity College, Cambridge (December 2007 and May 2009, respectively) influenced my thinking. I thank the contributors to the resulting volumes (the second of which was co-edited with Matthew Brown). A monograph seems poor recompense for the many kindnesses bestowed by these colleagues. But if, as Robert Southey wrote toward the end of his monumental *History of Brazil*, "the value of a historical work be in proportion to the facts which it has first embodied, to the fidelity with which they are recorded, and to the addition thereby made to the stores of general knowledge,"[2] then I hope that they judge this effort to have contributed to our common scholarly enterprise.

[2] Southey 1822, vol. III, p. 879.

My colleagues at The Johns Hopkins University, particularly the successive chairmen of the History Department (William Rowe, Ronald Walters, and Philip Morgan, respectively), graciously and generously granted me leave to finish this book soon after my arrival in Baltimore. I also thank the KSAS Deans' Office for approving my research leave. In addition to my current colleagues, I extend my gratitude to my past institutions for their support of my research. In particular, I thank the Master and Fellows of Trinity College, Cambridge; the Department of History, the Committee on History and Literature, the Center for History and Economics, and the David Rockefeller Center for Latin American Studies, all at Harvard University; and the Department of History at Wesleyan University.

I benefited from sharing my work-in-progress with audiences in the following places: Liverpool, Cambridge, Vadstena (Sweden), Helsinki, New York City, Tempe (Arizona), Baltimore, Lisbon, Bristol, Azcoitia (País Vasco), Santander, Seville, Boston, Middletown (Connecticut), Providence, Notre Dame, Mexico City, Medford (Massachusetts), Princeton, and New Orleans. I thank my interlocutors, critics, and collaborators on those occasions for asking hard questions which improved the book and propelled it toward completion. I also benefited from discussing these topics in seminars and tutorials with perspicacious undergraduates at Wesleyan, Cambridge, Harvard, and Johns Hopkins. Though they are too numerous to name individually, I have learned much from my students. I hope that these printed pages capture some of the enthusiasm and intellectual excitement of our seminars and tutorials.

Turning the manuscript into a book was a daunting task, one made much less so by the expert guidance of Michael Watson at Cambridge University Press. I thank him for commissioning this book and for working with me during the process culminating in publication. I express my gratitude to the Press's Syndics and to the two anonymous reviewers whose sound suggestions and perspicacious insights improved the analysis immeasurably. I thank the John Carter Brown Library, Brown University's Hay Library, and Harvard College Library's Map Collection for permission to reproduce images of the prints, lithographs, and maps held in their rich collections.

I wish to record my gratitude for the personal debts incurred during the course of this project to Robin Baird-Smith, Ben Block, Duk Blakaj, Fred Boll, Edith Bukovics, Lucie Campos, Rob Creswell, Danny Forster, Matty Goldstein, Sara Gonçalves, Janet Gunter, Evelyn Lincoln and Brian Shure, Kelly Land, Grant Lindsay, Tyler Luttman, Cristina Miguel (and her entire family in Queluz-Belas),

Jason Nebenzahl, Ana Pereira, Bill and Dru Sampson, Richard Stanton Schwartz, Jack Shamblin, Rupert Shortt, Avi Spivack, Don Andres Jayhawk Toebben, Chris Warnes, and Chris Wuthrich.

I wish to add a more-than-customary-and-perfunctory message of thanks to my parents, Gregory and Kathy, and to my brother, Jonah. My parents took me to Portugal when I was a very young boy and they have encouraged my love of History and travel ever since, even when I pursued those passions to counterproductive extremes. Jonah, during Augusts spent in childhood on Cape Cod, never let Portugal slip from my mind, devouring *malasadas* with me in Provincetown and insisting that our family whale-watch aboard the *Portuguese Princess*. Toward the end of this project, I had the great fortune of entering into a second family. Pamela and Dean Richlin, together with Sara, Eli, Sabrina, and Dalia, have been more enthusiastic about my esoteric endeavors than any non-blood relation deserves.

This book is dedicated to Johanna Bard Richlin. While this project began before we met, it never would have been completed without her. With due respect to Clio, I can imagine neither a future book nor any other pursuit without her inspiration and love.

Abbreviations

AC   Academia das Ciências (Lisbon, Portugal)
ACM   Arquivo Central da Marinha (Lisbon, Portugal)
ADB   Arquivo Distrital de Braga [Arquivo do Conde da Barca] (Braga, Portugal)
AHI   Arquivo Histórico do Itamaraty (Rio de Janeiro, RJ, Brazil)
AHM   Arquivo Histórico Militar (Lisbon, Portugal)
AHP   Arquivo Histórico Parlamentar (Lisbon, Portugal)
AHU   Arquivo Histórico Ultramarino (Lisbon, Portugal)
AMC   *Annaes Maritimos e Coloniaes*
AMI   Arquivo do Museu Imperial (Petrópolis, RJ, Brazil)
ANTT   Arquivos Nacionais / Torre do Tombo (Lisbon, Portugal)
ANRJ   Arquivo Nacional (Rio de Janeiro, RJ, Brazil)
APBAC   *Annaes do Parlamento Brazileiro: A Assembléia Constituinte de 1823*
APEC   Arquivo Público do Estado do Ceará (Fortaleza, CE, Brazil)
APEJE   Arquivo Público Estadual Jordão Emerenciano (Recife, PE, Brazil)
APEM   Arquivo Público do Estado do Maranhão (São Luís, MA, Brazil)
APEP   Arquivo Público do Estado do Pará (Belém, PA, Brazil)
B.Aj.   Biblioteca da Ajuda (Lisbon, Portugal)
BCM   Biblioteca Central da Marinha (Lisbon, Portugal)
BNL   Biblioteca Nacional de Lisboa [Reservados] (Lisbon, Portugal)
BNRJ   Biblioteca Nacional (Rio de Janeiro, RJ, Brazil)
Bod.Ox.   Bodleian Library, University of Oxford (Oxford, UK)
Boe.C.   Boehrer Collection. Spencer Research Library, University of Kansas (Lawrence, KS, USA)

BPBL	Biblioteca Pública "Benedito Leite" (São Luís, MA, Brazil)
BPMP	Biblioteca Pública Municipal do Porto (Porto, Portugal)
Cod.	Códice
CT	Colección Torrijos. Hispanic Society of America (New York, NY, USA)
Cx.	Caixa
DC	*Diário das Cortes*
DCSDNP	*Diário da Câmara do Senhores Deputados da Nação Portugueza*
Hay	John Hay Library, Brown University (Providence, RI, USA)
Houghton	Houghton Library, Harvard University (Cambridge, MA, USA)
IAHGP	Instituto Arqueológico, Histórico e Geográfico Pernambucano (Recife, PE, Brazil)
IHGAl.	Instituto Histórico e Geográfico de Alagoas (Maceió, AL, Brazil)
IHGB	Instituto Histórico e Geográfico Brasileiro (Rio de Janeiro, RJ, Brazil)
JCBL	The John Carter Brown Library (Providence, RI, USA)
Lill.L.	Lilly Library. Indiana University (Bloomington, IN, USA)
Mç.	Maço
Newberry	The Newberry Library (Chicago, IL, USA)
PBDP	*Portugal-Brazil: Debates Parlamentares*
SGL	Sociedade de Geografia de Lisboa (Lisbon, Portugal)
TNA	The National Archives (Kew [London], UK)

Map of the Portuguese Atlantic world *c.* 1800

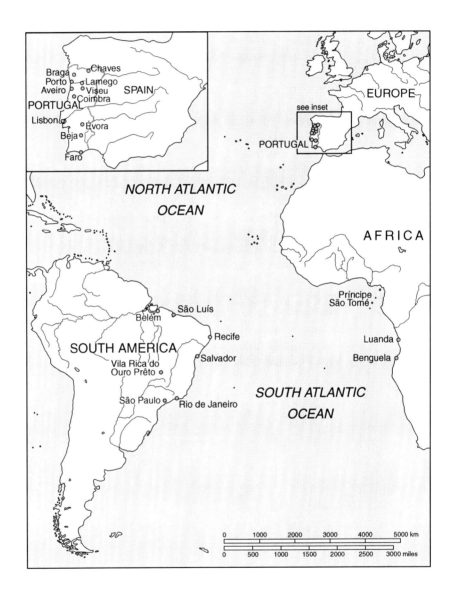

Introduction

This book traces the history of Portugal and its overseas dominions from approximately 1770 until just before 1850. Historians generally refer to this period as the "Age of Revolution(s)," when the imperial institutions, non-state networks, and commercial circuits knitting the early modern Atlantic World together became unraveled and new polities and connections, formal and informal, emerged from the ruins. In its Luso-Atlantic variant, the principal thrust of scholarly research has concerned the processes – long-term preconditions, medium-term precipitants, and short-term triggers – which culminated in Brazil's formal, political independence in the early 1820s. Historians have noted and analyzed how the timing, nature, and extent of Brazil's separation from Portugal differed from the processes by which British North America, French Saint-Domingue, and Spanish America wrested sovereignty from their respective metropoles. Yet there have been surprisingly few attempts to de-center the process of imperial breakdown, challenge its inevitability and completeness, explore the repercussions of decolonization in Portugal, trace empire's lingering political impact in Brazil, or challenge the appropriateness of the "Age of Revolution(s)" as an interpretive framework. These gaps, and the historiographical silence concerning these absences, are curious and provocative. After all, Brazil's independence was a rather anti-climactic coda to a sixty-year, strenuous, Crown-directed effort to reform, revive, and reconfigure the Portuguese empire, a non sequitur after approximately three hundred years of unceasing interaction – bonds forged in the crucible of maritime discovery, conquest, settlement, slavery, war, and commerce – between Portugal and the continents bordering and archipelagos dotting the Atlantic Ocean. It would be astounding if a political edifice buttressed by culture, religion, coercive power, capital, and personnel collapsed vertiginously, its debris vanished without leaving a trace, and its centuries-old connections were eviscerated, all by the time formal declarations of independence were made, recognized, and enshrined in international law. But that impression is precisely the one that a reader might come away with after surveying the bulk of the historical writing on the subject.

Such an impression would be inaccurate and distorting. After all, "empires do not always plot themselves so neatly along curvaceous inclines and declines."[1] As the following chapters demonstrate, Brazil's independence was a highly contingent, generally unsought, and somewhat undesirable break from the previous half-century's trajectory. When it finally was achieved, the Portuguese empire was severely diminished, whether measured by territorial control, economic resources, or international prestige. Yet many of the connections linking the component parts of the Luso-Atlantic World – intellectual, political, commercial (including the slave trade) – remained unsevered, undisturbed, or impervious to the actions, plots, and schemes of the statesmen who inherited the polities emerging from the carcass of empire. In fact, as in the Spanish empire, many of the connections paradoxically intensified as the two shores of the Luso-Atlantic world veered toward a final reckoning.[2] Contemporaries rejected the prognosis that imperial contraction was irreversible or that the reconciliation and reunification of the former empire's parts in some mutually satisfactory arrangement was a fantasy. Nor was this sentiment confined to elites: throughout the Americas, popular appropriation of royalist symbols and other markers of Old Regime hierarchies was widespread.[3] Interestingly, nineteenth-century Brazilian historians were cognizant of the contingent, ambivalent, and incomplete nature of independence. But their conception of an "amicable divorce," or peaceful exchange of power between members of the Braganza dynasty, as well as the mid-twentieth-century scholarly conception of Brazil's independence as an "agreement among elites," became anathema to later generations of historians, who discarded these insights in what was otherwise a salutary exercise in revisionism.[4]

---

[1] Adelman 2006, p. 7.
[2] Fernández Sebastián 2009, pp. 28–31.
[3] For example, Méndez 2005; and Echeverri 2011; as Landers 2010 argued, "even as monarchical systems broke down, however, for many Atlantic creoles, they still seemed their best hope ... [they] pinned their hopes for freedom on a personal relationship with a distant monarch and on centuries-old legal, religious and social constructs," p. 233; Blanchard 2008 contended that "in the first years of the independence wars, the majority of slaves in Venezuela and New Granada had found the opportunities and rewards offered by the Crown more attractive than anything offered by the patriots," p. 36; on counter-revolutionary and royalist doctrines in general, see Hamnett 1978.
[4] Much of the first view was articulated by Varnhagen in the decades immediately following independence, particularly with regard to the agency he attributed to Dom Pedro. See Varnhagen 1957; the second view, and phrase, is from Prado 1963, pp. 49–50. As Kraay and Reis 2009 explained, these older views have been discredited:

Of course, such fantasies of re-integration went unrealized in the decades after 1825. By the late nineteenth century, besides cultural-linguistic-religious ties, Brazil and Portugal had undergone divergent historical evolution. There were few links between them, except for the thousands of impoverished Portuguese immigrants who flocked to Brazil.[5] This later paucity justified treating the earlier imperial crisis teleologically. Conflicts were depicted as leading inexorably to separation, economic structures were presumed to produce readily discernible political consequences, and the formal recognition of Brazil's status as an independent state in 1825 was assumed to have definitively brought down the curtain on the drama of the Atlantic World.[6] Such conclusions were fortified further by the priorities of nation-focused (and nationalist) historiography.[7] In Brazil, the histories of colony and nation were treated as separate entities, independence and the coalescence of post-colonial polity were celebrated, and endogenous historical evolution was emphasized.[8] In Portugal, the decades following the transfer of the Court to Brazil (1807–8) were studied almost without reference to Brazil and the surviving remnants of Portugal's empire until quite recently.[9]

Portuguese and Brazilian historians, however, are not uniquely culpable. The study of the breakdown of the Atlantic empires c. 1760–1830,

the new emphasis is on changes to political culture, popular mobilization, serious threats to the social order, and intense debates concerning the type of reform to be adopted, p. 400; this critique has been extended to regional bias, challenging the notion that exclusively *Carioca* and *Paulista* elites drew up plans for Brazil's future and imposed it on the rest of Portuguese America. See, for example, Machado 2010; recently, however, the study of political and economic elites, and their decisive influence on historical outcomes, has come back into vogue. See, among others, Malerba 2000; and Fragoso and Florentino 2001.

[5] On early nineteenth-century immigration, see Barbosa 2009; for the late nineteenth century, see E. Viotti da Costa 1985.

[6] Though Buarque de Holanda 1962, who stressed a prolonged transition between colony and nation, lasting until 1831, was an influential exception.

[7] What Chiaramonte 2010a said of Spanish America holds true for Brazil: "neither the present-day Latin American nations nor their relevant nationalities existed at the time of independence. Nations were not the foundation but the (frequently late) outcome of these movements," p. 25.

[8] Important exceptions must be noted. Many of these are discussed in the essays contained in Jancsó 2005.

[9] In nineteenth-century Portuguese historiography and popular culture, there was more of an erasure than an "invention" of decolonization, in the sense conveyed for twentieth-century France by Shepard 2006, pp. 4–5, 272; Interest in colonial Brazil (and its independence) was shown by Portuguese intellectuals, and the Salazar regime, in the mid twentieth century as Portugal intensified its imperial efforts in Southern Africa. On "Luso-tropicalismo" and related phenomena, see, most recently, Dávila 2010; this instrumental curiosity flowed from a wider, mutual Luso-Brazilian rediscovery in the early twentieth century, as analyzed by Muller 2011.

particularly in Anglophone scholarship, has been dominated by the paradigm of the "Age of Revolution(s)," most often associated with R. R. Palmer.[10] While salutary in many respects, particularly in facilitating comparative study and promoting awareness of global and transnational processes, it has compounded the distortions spawned by nation-centric historiography of the Luso-Atlantic World.[11] In place of a panoply of "exceptional" or "unique" national paths toward imperial breakdown and post-colonial state formation, a single route was proposed: that of the US and France during the pre-Napoleonic phase of the Revolution. It was a

single movement, revolutionary in character, for which the word "democratic" is appropriate and enlightening; a movement which, however different in different countries, was everywhere aimed against closed elites, self-selecting power groups, hereditary castes, and forms of special advantage or discrimination that no longer served any useful purpose. These were summed up in such terms as feudalism, aristocracy, and privilege.[12]

Palmer devoted only a few pages to the breakdown of the Iberian empires, but he left little doubt that these were largely derivative phenomena: "All revolutions since 1800 ... have learned from the 18th-century Revolution of Western Civilization. They have been inspired by its success, echoed its ideals, used its methods."[13] Undoubtedly, to a degree, this statement is accurate: connections between revolutions and revolutionaries in the Atlantic world abounded and deliberate emulation was rampant. But Palmer's claim, like the assumption underpinning "modernization" theory gaining adherents at the time of the

---

[10] Palmer 1954; Palmer 1959–1964; criticized and updated in Armitage and Subrahmanyan 2010, and in Paquette and Brown 2013, which provides a fuller summary and criticism of the historiographical tradition than is possible here. On the connection between Palmer (and Godechot) and other genealogies of Atlantic History, see O'Reilly 2004 and Tortarola 2008. Of course, there is a second "Age of Revolution(s)" tradition, associated with Hobsbawm 1962, whose emphasis on economic disruptions and transformations is beyond the scope of the present book.

[11] Compare to Elliott's critique of the misleading and anachronistic focus on "revolution" during the seventeenth-century "General Crisis." See Elliott 1969, esp. pp. 44, 55.

[12] Palmer 1964, vol. II, p. 572; Another progenitor of the concept of the "Age of Revolution(s)," Godechot, argued that, many local contexts and multiple causes notwithstanding, "these revolutions had a similar objective: to establish a new regime in which citizens would enjoy greater equality and liberty and participate more fully in central government and administration." See Godechot 1965, p. 27.

[13] Palmer 1964, vol. II, p. 574. Godechot was even more explicit about the French origins, and therefore derivative quality, of all subsequent revolutions: "The soldiers of the Consulate and Empire carried revolutionary doctrines to regions where they had as yet hardly penetrated ... From Iberia they were carried to Spanish and Portuguese America." See Godechot 1965, pp. 6–7.

publication of *The Age of Democratic Revolution*, is based upon various assumptions – of a single model of and pathway to political modernity, of the diffusion of "enlightenment" from core to periphery, of the imitative character of political thought in the non-European world – which have been challenged and debunked recently.[14] Indeed, the "Age of Revolutions" should be recast on the basis of these new insights and realizations.

For the study of the Luso-Brazilian World *c.* 1770–1850, the existing "Age of Revolution(s)" paradigm poses two special difficulties. The first problem with the paradigm is that it encourages scholars to downplay the largely successful efforts of late eighteenth-century reformers who preserved and transformed imperial structures and fortified connections between far-flung territories. If one of the most prominent contemporary interpreters of the late eighteenth century is to be believed, the efforts of such exponents of "moderate" enlightenment were "simply inadequate" and may be judged a "comprehensive failure" across Europe and the Americas.[15] But this verdict fits awkwardly when applied to the Luso-Brazilian case, where the end of empire proved to be a rude, unanticipated shock, an event which legions of Crown officials, nobles, clerics, and merchants tried to forestall, if not prevent entirely, as they watched the crumbling of imperial structures across the Atlantic World.[16] With the benefit of hindsight, they sought to divert the river of History and believed that they had engineered this feat, forcing it to flow away from revolution and toward regeneration and reform. A focus on circuits of revolutionary activity and long-term processes culminating in imperial dissolution, therefore, tends anachronistically to foreground agents of radical change at the expense of partisans of stasis, rejuvenated tradition, or moderate reshuffling. As an historian recently noted, "Revolution did not begin as secessionist episodes ... much more common in the complex breakdown was the exploration of models of re-accommodating colonies into imperial formations, a groping for an arrangement that would stabilize, not dissolve empires."[17] Monarchs, Crown officials, colonial administrators, "conservative" political writers, and Brazilian "collaborators" or "loyalists," among others, have been relegated to the periphery of a

---

[14] Eisenstadt 2005; Roninger and Waisman 2002; J. Robertson 2005; Roldán Vera and Caruso 2007; Fernández Sebastián 2009; and Paquette 2009b.

[15] Israel 2010, pp. 121–23 passim.

[16] Nor were the Portuguese alone in this endeavor: on the surprisingly flexible and collaborative aspects of Spanish imperial institutions in the same period, see Grafe and Irigoin 2008.

[17] Adelman 2008, pp. 320, 332; Adelman 2006, p. 8.

historiographical tradition oriented toward dramatic and irreversible change.[18] This book seeks to recover these historical actors and to demonstrate that they, too, played key roles in the "Age of Revolution(s)," an era which encompassed experiences and phenomena besides revolution and rupture. Many participants considered the uprisings, which scholars now understand to have ushered in a new historical epoch, as little more than ephemeral disturbances. They remained confident that the rebels would soon return to the fold.

Even where the new political experiments flourished, sovereignty did not preclude intensive interactions between new states and old metropoles. This observation suggests a second problem with the "Age of Revolution(s)" paradigm. Its trope of disjuncture and discontinuity precludes adequate appreciation of the connections persisting well after formal dominion was declared extinct. Declarations of independence, and the international recognition of the nascent states brought into existence by political speech acts and armed struggle, were as much normative aspirations as faithful descriptions of actual conditions.[19] International trade, diplomatic treaties, socio-economic and legal structures and institutions, dynastic arrangements, religion and culture, ideological solidarity, friendships, kinship ties, and much else survived the "Age of Revolution(s)" and complicated the coalescence and consolidation of national-states.[20] Particularly in Chapters 3, 4, and 5, this book emphasizes the way that ruptures did not always lead to disruption and discontinuity. Though independence and sovereignty, at the conceptual level, may appear incompatible with the persistence of connections, in practice they coexisted. It is this book's aim to revise the understanding of the "Age of Revolution(s)" to incorporate such phenomena, in the hope that the Luso-Brazilian case will come to be

---

[18] Though L. Souza 2006, which focuses primarily on the first half of eighteenth century, is a notable exception.

[19] On diplomatic recognition in international law in historical perspective, see Fabry 2010; on the significance of recognition in the US context, see Golove and Hulsebosch 2010. As Armitage 2007 explains, "declarations of independence were primarily assertions of sovereignty within an expanding universe of such sovereigns," p. 141. The definition provided in Swiss jurist Emmerich de Vattel's *Law of Nations* (1758), which became the standard guide to norms on the subject of independence, suggests why historians have tended to conflate independence with the evisceration of connections: "Every nation which governs itself, under any formula whatsoever, without dependency on any foreign country, is a sovereign state," quoted in Armitage 2007, pp. 38–39.

[20] In his global survey of this period, C. Bayly has described the uneven nature of change as "unstable pluralism," in which "a small industrial economy and limited representative government in Western Europe flourished alongside a patchwork of dynastic states, shored up imperial thrones, and dubiously legitimate European colonial provinces." See Bayly 2004, p. 127.

understood as "un-exceptional" and instead worthy of integration into a revamped paradigm.

Many historians, from a range of perspectives, studying Brazil and Spanish America in the nineteenth century have noted and analyzed the colonial "legacies," "heritage," and "detritus" with which former Ibero-American dominions were encumbered, and which they could not expunge, after independence.[21] Some of this new scholarship, especially on Spanish America, has prompted a reconsideration of "independence" and a shift away from viewing the post-colonial era as a clean break from the past.[22] In Brazil, throughout the late 1820s and 1830s, groups frustrated with the conservative political settlement hoped for a "second revolution of independence" to salvage the first.[23] While most of the heirlooms of the overthrown colonial regimes are maligned in Latin American historiography (e.g. fiscal apparatus, slavery, Indian policy, export-oriented economies, military orientation of civil administration),[24] a few receive tepid approbation (e.g. robust municipal institutions, constitutional culture, educational and scientific ethos, legal apparatus).[25] As the "black legend" of Iberian colonialism's monolithically malicious influence wanes, further rehabilitation may be anticipated. Moreover, many historians have shown, in nuanced ways, how post-colonial Latin America's independence was threatened (and its sovereignty compromised) by unequal relations with more powerful states and regions as well as its disadvantageous place in the networks, structures, and processes through which capital, credit (and debt), and forced labor flowed. Concepts and theories such as "informal empire," "dependency," "gunboat diplomacy," and "neo-colonialism," while heavily criticized, have illumined the severe geopolitical limits within which new polities stumbling out of empire's wreckage operated.[26]

---

[21] Buarque de Holanda 1962; Stein and Stein 1970; Silva Dias 1972; Adelman 1999; Lewin 2003; Paquette and Brown 2011 and 2013; interestingly, historians of North America have begun to recognize the persistence of connections with Europe. As Onuf observed, "American independence did not initiate an era of isolation ... to the contrary, commercial, cultural, and political connections multiplied and intensified, and independent Americans were increasingly drawn into an interdependent Atlantic system ... only in the narrowest political sense had provincial patriots escaped metropolitan domination." See Onuf 2010, pp. 3, 5.

[22] See, for example, Thurner 1997; and Larson 2004.

[23] Souza 1987, p. 177.

[24] J. H. Rodrigues 1975; Viotti da Costa 1985; Centeno 2002; and Larson 2004. As an historian noted recently, "viewed from the prism of nationalism, the vestiges of ecclesiastical and noble privilege embodying the Portuguese *ancien régime* underscored for liberals how Brazil's fragile identity amounted to little more than that of an imperfectly emancipated colony." See Lewin 2003, vol. II, p. 42.

[25] Dym 2006; Chiaramonte 2010b; and Zahler 2010.

[26] Robinson and Gallagher 1953; Stein and Stein 1970; and Brown 2008.

New scholarship on nineteenth-century slavery and the slave trade, and coerced migration in general, for example, which rightly emphasizes its scale and brutality, sheds further light on the non-linearity of historical change and the discrepancy between "liberal" doctrines, ideologies, and legislation, on the one hand, and barbarous practices on the other.[27] In a more positive light, recent historians have identified an array of less coercive (though sometimes still perniciously destructive) "exchanges" between Europe and Latin America during and after independence, from direct contact characterized by large-scale voluntary migration and adventurers who fought for (and settled in) the new states to more passive forms of solidarity with constitutionalism and federalism animating the post-Napoleonic "Liberal International," the transatlantic book trade, and the diffusion of political and social thought from Europe to Ibero-America.[28]

While operating outside of an imperial framework, historians of Europe have long recognized that the institutions, attitudes, structures, and intellectual horizons of the pre-revolutionary "Old Regime," or at least their vestiges, survived and flourished well into the nineteenth century.[29] More recently, scholars have become interested in the long aftermath and repercussions of colonial dismemberment on the ex-metropole. This interest has propelled research into its economic, political, and ideological impact: the fate of former royalists, loyalists, and imperial agents and soldiers; the transformation of administration in the remaining colonies; and the incorporation of the colonial past into debates concerning constitutionalism and national identity in the nineteenth and twentieth centuries.[30] There has been scarcely any research of this type for Portugal.[31] As two historians observed, "beginning in the 1830s, Brazil undoubtedly loses its importance to Portuguese history, but even to a greater extent in Portuguese historiography."[32] This

---

[27] Viotti da Costa 1985; Schmidt-Nowara 1999; Fradera 2005; Blackburn 1988 and 2011.

[28] Hale 1968; Brown 2006; Blaufarb 2007; Isabella 2009; Racine 2010; Paquette and Brown 2011 and 2013.

[29] Above all, Mayer 1981.

[30] Costeloe 1986; Gould 2000; Fradera 2005; Schmidt-Nowara 2006; Todd 2011; Jasanoff 2011; and Hamnett 2011; on intellectual continuities in British imperialism in the same period, see Bayly 1989; and Drayton 2000; on the economic impact (or purported lack thereof) on Spain, see Prados de la Escosura 1988.

[31] The notable exception is Alexandre 1993. One feature of Portuguese cultural history, however, has been discussed as, in part, a legacy of the political turmoil of the first decades of the nineteenth century: the musical genre of Fado. But the debate over the Brazilian contribution to its evolution remains fierce. See Sucena 2002, pp. 19–20.

[32] Cervo and Magalhães 2000, p. 128; the converse is equally true: as Bethencourt 2003 explained, "Brazilian independence brought with it, as is natural, the necessity of creating a new collective memory and a new historiography," p. 172.

absence, though, is curious. For example, many of the leading political figures in Portugal between 1825 and 1850 had significant experience in Brazil: António José Severim de Noronha, future Duque da Terceira, served as governor of Grão-Pará, while João Oliveira e Daun, future Duque de Saldanha, fought in the Banda Oriental and subsequently was governor of Rio Grande do Sul. The men, therefore, who shaped Portuguese politics "after Brazil" were full-fledged servants of empire, and their early experiences in Brazil marked their later trajectories in underappreciated ways.[33] More generally, recognition of the numerous continuities and persistent linkages with the imperial past not only permits the writing of national history in a broader context, salutary in itself, but also encourages a reframing of late colonial history in a way that de-emphasizes breakdown and crisis, thus drawing attention to the forces favoring and fostering the survival, not demise, of imperial institutions, mentalities, and relationships.

This book is indelibly informed by the insights of the scholarship referenced above, to say nothing of the enormous debt incurred by reading hundreds of excellent Portuguese-language books which the next five chapters attempt to synthesize. It is an analytically informed narrative of selected episodes of Portuguese imperial history which illustrate the argument that the rupture which reconfigured the Luso-Atlantic World in the early nineteenth century must be understood with reference to the countervailing, conciliatory, conservative forces which outnumbered and overwhelmed more radical forces seeking or tending toward imperial disaggregation. The break-up of the Portuguese empire occurred against the backdrop of a reform-oriented ultramarine administration, an increasingly integrated Luso-Atlantic economy (held together by commerce, personnel, and ideology) and, in its final moments, a shared, transatlantic constitutional process. Revolution, war, and independence shook and frayed, but did not completely shatter and tear, all of the bonds in the Luso-Atlantic World. The impact of Brazil's independence in Portugal was immense. Furthermore, the partial, incomplete nature of the break introduced ambiguities that would shape, and entwine, the histories of Portugal and Brazil for decades. The most obvious examples, discussed at length in Chapters 2, 4, and 5, are, respectively, the survival of the Braganza dynasty in each country, Portuguese liberals' dependence on the vagaries of Brazilian

---

[33] These Portuguese figures might be compared with the "Ayacuchos," defeated Spanish royalists who returned to the Peninsula after Spanish-American independence and deeply influenced Spanish politics in the 1830s and 1840s. See Sobrevilla Perea 2011.

politics, and Brazil's reliance on Portuguese Africa for its supply of slaves precisely at the moment in which the overhaul and development of those territories was contemplated in Lisbon.

Lesser-known episodes also produced underappreciated, long-term impact. The 1826 Portuguese Constitution, for example, examined in Chapter 3, better known as the *Carta Constitucional*, remained in force, except for brief periods (1828–34, 1836–42) and with only slight modification through revisions and "additional acts" (1852, 1865, 1896, 1907), until the fall of the monarchy in 1910.[34] The *Carta* was drawn up by Dom Pedro, Emperor of Brazil, in Rio de Janeiro in late April 1826, almost a year after the treaty by which Portugal recognized Brazil's independence was signed. The death of his father, Dom João VI, in March 1826 left Dom Pedro undisputed heir to the Portuguese throne. The *Carta* embodied the spirit of an anti-popular, revivified monarchy. It was designed largely to mollify the Holy Alliance and appease Brazilians wary of their emperor's continued connection to the ex-metropole Portugal.

In Europe, however, it came to be viewed both as a threat to royal legitimacy and the rallying cry of Portuguese liberals and their sympathizers abroad.[35] The 1826 *Carta* sits at the center of the story told in this book. Many of the themes running through this study intersect in the *Carta*'s composition, promulgation, and reception. In Portugal, the *Carta* emblemized the assumptions, aspirations, and fears of those who had not fully absorbed, or accepted, the break represented by Brazilian independence. In the 1820s and 1830s, Portuguese men and women did not operate in a world of political absolutes and static conditions. Instead, their turbulent age was marked by fluidity and interrupted continuities. Undoubtedly, older forms of government had been deprived of their timelessness and unquestioned legitimacy, but so too had the incarnate figments of feverish political imaginations which had spawned unprecedented horror, bloodshed, and economic dislocation. The likelihood of compromise, therefore, was great, even if, paradoxically, the men and women who entered politics were ardent, belligerent,

---

[34] These modifications did not significantly curtail crown authority: not only did the royal person remain inviolable and sacred, but the monarch could dismiss ministers without providing a justification, dissolve the assembly, and veto laws emanating from the legislative branch while retaining the leading role in public life. See Magalhães 1927, p. 23; Perhaps the only limitations on Crown authority as a result of 1852 amendments were the requirement that all foreign treaties would have to appear before the Cortes for ratification and the abolition of the death penalty for political crimes. See Miranda 2001, p. 37.

[35] Discussed in Paquette 2011b.

and uncompromising.[36] As extremist forces pummeled each other, compromise appeared more rather than less likely. Exhausted, many political participants groped toward a middle ground. Degrees of separation, perhaps in the form of a loose (con)federation, appeared a more likely outcome for the Luso-Atlantic world, as it did (briefly) in the Hispanic sphere.[37] Dom Pedro remained heir to the Portuguese throne and he had no intention of surrendering his right to it. With its strong resemblance to Brazil's 1824 Constitution, the *Carta* portended an eventual, if distant, reunion of the crowns. While Dom Pedro was motivated primarily by desire to ensure his dynasty's survival, his efforts were embraced by many in Portugal who believed that the ex-metropole's independence was imperiled without robust political and economic ties to Brazil. The *Carta* thus seemed to herald the dawning of a new post-revolutionary age, in which political options were circumscribed, extremes less tolerated, the range of possible outcomes narrowed considerably, and the political horizons foreshortened. It produced the opposite of its intended effect, however, a story recounted in Chapters 3 and 4.

There is no shortage of studies focusing on Spanish American and Brazilian independence in this present decade of relentless bicentenary celebrations and commemorations.[38] This book does not share their focus. On the contrary, it moves in the opposite direction. It aims to reconstruct a history of that epoch which downplays and decenters its supposedly defining event, out of neither caprice, nor a contrarian disposition, nor for revisionism's sake, but on the grounds that a focus on rupture and divergence is egregiously anachronistic, a view shared increasingly by historians of Latin American independence. Many of this book's themes inevitably intersect with, and profit from, this burgeoning literature, though this book's focus on international relations, global intellectual history, conservative elites, and trans-regional processes produces distinct inflections. Recently, new insights have challenged and transformed scholarly as well as popular conceptions of "independence." Broadly speaking, the freshest, most innovative work focuses on historical actors and populations previously excluded from, or at least

---

[36] As A. Herculano said of the second quarter of the nineteenth century, in his 1867 introduction to *A Voz do Profeta*, "the political fevers were ardent, indomitable, because they derived from conviction," reproduced in L. Neves *et al* 2007, p. 94.
[37] Portillo 2006.
[38] For an invaluable comparative study, see Hamnett 1997. The best recent synthesis of Spanish American independence is Lucena Giraldo 2010.

marginalized in, traditional, triumphalist narratives.[39] This scholarship has convincingly broadened social and subaltern historiography's engagement with topics previously considered the exclusive province of elite political-diplomatic history or a more rarified history of ideas. The Brazilian case follows the broader pattern, in motion for the past half century. In 1960, an eminent historian wrote old-fashioned political history's epitaph: "obviously, the recent historiography of Brazil in the first half of the nineteenth century has made inadequate the older preoccupation with politics and personalities."[40] In 2001, another historian confirmed this earlier pronouncement, noting that the "most dramatic shift [in the historiography] has been the move away from the ruling classes and elites."[41] Though there always has been a steady stream of biographies chronicling the flaws, foibles, and virtues of leading political figures, such older tendencies are fading away, replaced with new directions that stress the cultural and social aspects of Brazil's history.

Yet the scholarly shift away from the study of politics, political personalities, and statecraft, while salutary in so many respects – both scholarly and societal – was too abrupt, too extreme, and too complete.[42] Recently, an historian lamented that, in recent historiography, "there has been very little focus on policy-making and the legislative process."[43] While accurate, this observation is hardly original. As early as 1973, an unabashed partisan of the then-unfashionable "conventional and traditional" sources suggested that historians should "approach politics through ideas with the presupposition that the rationale or logic of central government policy and the assumptions of the governing elite are still so insufficiently understood as to warrant searching examination."[44] Fortunately, this insight is now taken seriously. In large part, rising historical interest in, and support for, intellectual history has nurtured a flock of new books and international collaborative projects concerning the history of political thought (and concepts) in the Ibero-Atlantic World.[45]

[39] For overviews, see Jancsó 2005 and Pimenta 2008.

[40] Stein 1960, p. 251.   [41] Russell-Wood 2001a, p. 82.

[42] Though it should be observed that attention has not debunked old myths completely: long-ignored peoples and their voices, individual and collective, while now seen and heard, are not yet fully integrated into the historiography. As Sweet 2011 argued, "the condescension of Atlantic History as enlightened, democratic triumphalism often obscures the African epistemologies and ways of being ... these epistemological strands are sewn deeply into the fabric of Atlantic History. Yet they remain mostly obscured in the broader tapestry of European–American exceptionalism," p. 231. Obviously, historians, and society at large, have a long way to go before a more accurate, balanced portrait of past epochs is reached.

[43] Beattie 2003, p. 37.   [44] Hale 1973, p. 61.

[45] Above all, Fernández Sebastián and Fuentes 2002 and Fernández Sebastián 2009; and Posada-Carbó and Jaksić 2011.

While heavily influenced by this new work, it is the present author's view that such insights can, and should, be pushed further. Elite political projects, dynastic considerations, and the intellectual imaginaries and agency (not to mention the jealousies, personal shortcomings, and deplorably poor judgment) of leading political actors have been relegated too far to the historiographical sidelines, with distorting effect. In part, this book is an extended exercise in calling back into existence suitably amended aspects of the old historiography to redress the imbalance of the new. To emphasize the role of individuals, such as Brazilian emperor Dom Pedro I, in the historical trajectories of two hemispheres is neither to rehearse elite-driven models of historical change nor to erase marginalized, subaltern groups from the historical record. Rather, it forms part of an effort to recover and reconstruct a major mechanism through which politics were made in a specific historical era, however laudatory or despicable its means, ends, prevailing practices, and systematic exclusion of the vast majority of the population. Similarly, to emphasize the transatlantic political context in which events in both Brazil and Portugal unfolded is not intended to diminish local, popular experiences and participation. Rather, the aim is to draw attention to the geopolitical exigencies and contingencies that shaped the milieu in which local actors – whether plebeians or patricians, emperors or slaves – operated.

This book's emphasis on high politics is justifiable, particularly in the Luso-Brazilian World. The Crown's place at the apex of the political pyramid in the Portuguese empire was well established and secure from the early modern period onward. As a contemporary historian of Colonial Brazil noted, "the weakness of the power of the viceroy, the existence of multiple institutional checks, the incorporation of Brazilian posts into the hierarchy of office and the channels of promotion, and the constant need to refer matters to Portugal" all served to reinforce the interdependence of the colonies and the metropolis, of the bureaucracy and the Crown.[46] The Crown benefited enormously from the unstable balance among local, regional, and central agencies. As another contemporary historian put it, one must recognize "the constant presence of the Crown in all spheres of organizational culture, distributing privileges, legitimizing nominations, ratifying decisions, and establishing judicial and financial control ... the 'nebula of power' that defined the Portuguese empire was kept together by the king."[47]

---

[46] Schwartz 1973, pp. 362, 365; see also Russell-Wood 2002, p. 114.
[47] F. Bethencourt, "Political Configurations and Local Powers," in Bethencourt and Curto 2007, pp. 199–200.

Accepting the validity of this insight does not imply that there existed a centralized state in Portugal during the early modern period. Legal historians have shown convincingly that nothing of the sort existed. Instead, both in Portugal and Brazil, authority was highly pluralistic. This heterogeneity impeded the imposition of regular government and thereby limited the Crown's field of action.[48] It is possible to conclude, provisionally, that the Crown was omnipresent even if it was far from omnipotent.

At the same time, however, it is paradoxical that a major obstacle to recognition of the connections which survived colonialism is that periodization continues to be linked closely to dynastic chronology and demarcations drawn from international law. As a scholar recently observed, historians grant "existential status" to periodization, ignoring (or sometimes erasing) the "historicity of fundamental political categories" and "retroactively reifying categories."[49] This assertion is especially valid for the histories of Portugal and Brazil, which continued to collide and intersect after formal recognition of Brazil's independence in 1825. "Preoccupation with the national epoch," an historian of the British empire has argued, "also has endorsed a degree of insularity that has tended to marginalize international influences."[50] The same holds true for Portugal and Brazil. Only by erasing the line separating colonial from national history, or at least blurring the boundary between them, will the subjects of this book be understood.[51]

The argument sketched here is developed in five chapters. Chapter 1 offers a synoptic and synthetic overview of reform efforts throughout the Portuguese empire in the late eighteenth century. Its main purpose is to highlight how policy (and governance) was pan-imperial in orientation and how symmetry, an intra-imperial "division of labor," and the interdependence among its component territories were pursued. It highlights efforts to integrate and develop rustic peripheries, and create a transatlantic cadre of administrators and intellectuals linked to the state (scientists, engineers, jurists, and political economists) through

---

[48] Hespanha 2010.
[49] K. Davis 2008, pp. 6, 20, 134. Along the same lines, Symes 2011 argued that "these acts of naming do not create historical reality; they create an appearance of it, a false ontology," p. 724; the perils of periodization for the 1820s are discussed more fully in Paquette and Brown 2013.
[50] Hopkins 1999, p. 202.
[51] Recently, Atlantic historians have shown themselves willing to amend traditional periodization, appreciating that "its terminus is ... fluid and contested," Games 2006, p. 747; also see Greene 2004 and 2007; and Greene and Morgan 2009. Nevertheless, the problem of delineating periods in global history is a broader one with which historians must grapple. For an attempt to do so, see Bayly 2004, especially p. 168.

educational reform. While it is largely based on secondary literature, there are archival research-driven sections related to Portugal's African strategy, trade policy, and negative assessments of the reform enterprise. Overall, Chapter 1 conveys the impression of a far-from-moribund, increasingly efficient and integrated empire, though plagued by structural problems and geopolitical deficits, prior to the political cataclysm of 1807–8.

Chapter 2 analyzes the metamorphosis the empire underwent as a result of the French Revolutionary Wars and their aftermath. Focusing on the period 1808–23, the first part of the chapter traces the transfer of the Court from Lisbon to Rio de Janeiro and the political-economic impact of the court's absence on peninsular Portugal. The second part of the chapter concentrates on the processes culminating in the disintegration of the empire, beginning with the Porto Revolution of 1820 and the efforts it incited to install a constitutional monarchy suitable for a transcontinental empire. This discussion is preceded by a historical treatment of constitutionalism in Portugal c. 1770–1820 and the foreign influences informing it, including the 1812 Spanish Constitution. The third and final part of Chapter 2 examines the Brazilian response to the Portuguese upheaval, which ultimately precipitated imperial collapse, concluding with an overview of the first Brazilian efforts at constitution-making in the 1823 Constituent Assembly, whose deliberations were cut short by Dom Pedro's dissolution of that body.

Chapter 3 picks up the story in 1823, with the overthrow of the constitutional regime in Portugal and the restoration of Dom João VI as absolute monarch, ruling without a written constitution and unrestrained by any representative body. In Brazil, at exactly the same moment, Dom Pedro's similar actions provoked major resistance, especially in the northeast. This 1823 moment was crucial: the fate of the Ibero-Atlantic world hung in the balance and the likelihood of reconciliation between Portugal and Brazil was great. The chapter explores the ultimately failed efforts to reach some mutually acceptable compromise. The chapter then turns to Portuguese and Brazilian constitutional history in 1824–26. While the effort to write new constitutions might appear to signal divergent historical trajectories, the unresolved nature of the Portugal–Brazil relationship infused the process of constitution-making and influenced its outcome. Portugal's 1825 recognition of Brazilian independence was a prelude to the episode that sits at the center of the book: Dom Pedro's promulgation of a *Carta Constitucional* for Portugal in 1826. The chapter concludes with a discussion of the initial reactions to this audacious gesture. An effort to situate it in broader geopolitical context is also made, focusing on the role of British diplomat Sir Charles Stuart in the fabrication of the *Carta* and its conveyance to Europe.

Chapter 4 explores why and how Dom Pedro's *Carta*, and his associated plan to install his daughter, Dona Maria, on the Portuguese throne, failed. The chapter focuses on the Portuguese Civil War (1828–34), particularly the political thought underpinning the reign of Dom Miguel and that animating the exiled "liberal" opposition, which coalesced around a Regency established on the Azorean island of Terceira and which, eventually, prevailed. The Civil War is presented as an outgrowth of Portugal's unstable post-imperial condition, with each faction espousing a distinct vision of Portugal's future. Accordingly, the emphasis is on political-legal thought as gleaned from the fierce pamphlet wars carried on by *emigrados* and *Miguelistas* across Western Europe. The conflict is situated in its international context, including Great Power rivalry, the advent of the July Monarchy in France, and the shifting terrain of Brazilian politics.

Chapter 5 explores a crucial, if neglected, aspect of post-Civil War Portugal's political landscape, focusing on spasmodic efforts to pursue the imperial career seemingly abandoned with the loss of Brazil. Beginning with post-1825 debates about commerce and Portugal's viability as an independent state shorn of its overseas empire, the chapter reconstructs efforts after 1834 to establish colonies of white settlement in African territories claimed by Portugal, particularly Angola and Mozambique. In this respect, Portuguese imperial schemes in the 1830s and 1840s occurred in the shadow of Brazilian decolonization. Though Brazil's relevance to Portuguese politics faded in these decades, the persistence of the slave trade – both Brazil's dependence on it and Portuguese Africa's economic orientation toward it – meant that the histories of Portugal and Brazil would remain entwined until nearly mid-century.

1   The reform of empire in the late eighteenth century

This chapter presents an overview of the Portuguese empire in the late eighteenth and early nineteenth centuries. It concentrates primarily on the reforms undertaken and the modes of governance prevailing in the period following the eclipse of Marquês de Pombal in 1777 and before the crisis precipitated by the French invasion and occupation of the Iberian Peninsula in 1807–8. It also studies two challenges – less regulated international commerce and a slave-dependent economy – which increasingly preoccupied statesmen and whose resolution, or lack thereof, proved decisive in the political outcomes of subsequent decades. The chapter's overarching argument is that the late eighteenth century was characterized by rigorous and sustained attempts to integrate the empire's various territorial components and a quickening of intellectual life in branches of knowledge with direct application to public affairs. These two trends account for the empire's relative flourishing in an epoch that witnessed the collapse of other transatlantic polities. Reformers may not have overhauled the basic contours of the empire, but they succeeded in improving the overall institutional framework and turning existing structures to the Crown's advantage. In addition, they introduced ancillary institutions, forms of "useful knowledge," and efficacious administrative and economic practices. A political culture of reformism to reverse geopolitical decline and avert imperial collapse permeated both ultramarine and peninsular administration, whose ranks were filled with homogeneous cadres of university-trained, polyglot, and bi-continental men. If they could not begin afresh, they could at least make what existed function better and foment a range of secondary institutions and novel practices to stave off the imperial crises which other European Atlantic empires were suffering.

Part I describes how the goal of imperial integration was pursued in the latter decades of the eighteenth century. It involved, first, the extirpation of agents and factors beyond the grasp of Crown government and, second, the multiplication of connections among the various parts through the unified training, and subsequent circulation, of public officials. The chapter then turns to the political thought, including political economy, percolating in the Portuguese world in the final decades of the eighteenth century, during the reign of Dona Maria I, demonstrating the permeability of Portuguese intellectual life to foreign currents and how these were adapted to serve policy needs. Bringing together these first two sections, the chapter then turns to the strategies pursued by the Crown to reorganize territory, incorporate rustic peripheries, and gain greater control over resources and subjects. Part II traces the results of these policies in the first decades of the nineteenth century, focusing on debates surrounding less regulated commerce and the slave trade, striving to suggest continuities between the pre-1808 and post-1808 periods. Overall, the aim of Chapter 1 is to present a panorama of the intersections of intellectual life and public affairs in the Portuguese empire, conceived of, and treated as, a potentially unified whole, which disputes the anachronistic view that imperial crisis was pre-ordained and inevitable. As they surveyed the waves of revolutions sweeping away the empires of the Atlantic World, particularly the North American and Haitian revolutions, Luso-Brazilian planners redoubled their efforts at reform and refused to accept the inevitability of such a crisis in the South Atlantic. Concentrating on the antecedents of later fissures detracts from full appreciation of how spectacular, and destabilizing, imperial crisis proved when it finally occurred in the first decades of the nineteenth century after a long, uninterrupted stretch of reform and renewal. And it undermines recognition of the strategies, ploys, and substantive reconceptualization of colonial administration which Crown officials undertook, with surprising success, before 1807.

PART I

Extirpation, circulation, and integration

In the second half of the eighteenth century, the territories under the aegis of the Portuguese Crown were conceived of, and often treated as, a unified, potentially fluidly functioning entity. As an historian recently observed, political reformers and writers "conceived of the [all possessions] as a single whole, a single 'political system'."[1] Policy was conceived not only in the context of the densely populated littorals and mining

---

[1] D. Curto, "Dom Rodrigo de Sousa Coutinho e a Casa Literaria do Arco do Cego," in F. M. G. de Campos 1999, pp. 26–27.

zones of Brazil, but also for Angola, Cape Verde, São Tomé, Guinea, Mozambique, Goa, Macau, and the eastern Atlantic archipelagos of the Azores and Madeira, as well as the frontier zones, hinterlands, backlands, and fluvial routes of Brazil's interior. Conceived as a single entity, each of the empire's parts would perform a particular function.[2] The integrationist goal, a more holistic approach, might be termed "developmental empire," in which the Crown "sought to activate latent and underutilized resources in a world that was becoming increasingly specialized."[3] This did not mean that "predatory" tactics and techniques, the crude extraction of resources and coercive practices, were absent. On the contrary. But such an approach favored long-term objectives over short-term gains and required a conception of the colonial economy's potential as more capacious than unsophisticated plunder and rapine. Late eighteenth-century reform thus was premised on the differential productivity, or a "division of labor," within the empire,[4] where each colony would contribute, through careful planning and harmonization, to the collective greatness and imperial self-sufficiency through the products which seemed to flow most naturally from it. There was disagreement concerning the optimal techniques to be employed and mechanisms favored, but the basic contours of the strategy remained fairly consistent for the latter part of the century.

Depicting the period c. 1770–1810 as the heyday of an "integrationist" vision of empire may seem to contradict the prevailing scholarly consensus. For most commentators, the period was a prelude to imperial disintegration, not integration, when fissures were exposed, fragmentation increased, proto-independence agitation and conspiracies multiplied, and profound economic re-orientation seemed to ensure that Portugal would follow the path trodden by other European empires toward dissolution. The transfer of the Court (1807–8) seemed to confirm this direction, as Portugal's centrality diminished and Brazil enjoyed unprecedented autonomy and became the new imperial center. Integration, however, implied neither equality nor equity. "Together and unequal" summed up the Crown's strategy. It was neither a rejection of hierarchical understandings nor an assertion of the underlying similitude of the

---

[2] The term "integrationist" is used somewhat anachronistically: in Portuguese historiography, "integracionista" was associated with the position relative to Brazil taken by the peninsular Cortes deputies associated with Fernandes Tomás (1821–22); see Alexandre 1993, p. 711. However, the concepts of "integrated development" and "harmonization of interests" are employed in contemporary Brazilian historiography. See Novais 2001, p. 299; and Lyra 1994, p. 44.

[3] Hopkins 1999, p. 206.

[4] J. L. Cardoso, "Nas Malhas do Império: A Economia Política e a Política Colonial de D. Rodrigo de Souza Coutinho," in Cardoso 2001, p. 81.

component parts. The Peninsula remained the intended primary beneficiary of all policies.

Dom Rodrigo de Souza Coutinho, Minister for Colonial Affairs from 1796, often depicted as a symbol of the new-fangled reform spirit, pursued fairly traditional imperial aims.[5] He and his coterie strove to maintain Brazil as a producer of agricultural commodities intended for export to Portugal as well as a captive market for peninsular manufacturers. As one of his correspondents noted, "Portugal's colonies should be happy without being opulent ... the government should strive to encourage the cultivation of the land in the colonies, while making the colonists dependent on the industry of the metropole."[6] The opposite policy, it was believed, spelled disaster. If Brazil developed manufactures to supplement its "fertile and abundant agriculture," Dom Rodrigo's predecessor, Martinho de Mello e Castro, had warned, its colonists would soon "become completely independent of Portugal."[7] Souza Coutinho spun a virtue out of a necessity, justifying the policy on the basis of liberal economic ideas then coming into vogue. He insisted to a skeptical Brazilian viceroy that "this exchange of goods between Portugal and Brazil will result in the greatest wealth and happiness of all of his Majesty's vassals."[8] Maintaining the status quo, however, required new methods. An economic ideology based on the extraction of natural resources, notably minerals, was substituted by a developmental, agrarian one, which called for the intensified interaction among the empire's component parts as well as a sharpening of the intra-imperial division of labor. The result, optimistic Crown officials believed, would not be the exploitation and beggaring of ultramarine territories, but increased overall, shared prosperity.[9]

---

[5] Souza Coutinho (1755–1812) held the post of Secretary for the Navy and Colonial Dominions until 1801. He later served as Secretary of State for War and Foreign Affairs following the Portuguese monarchy's forced relocation to Rio de Janeiro from 1808 until his death in 1812. On Dom Rodrigo, see Maxwell 1973; J. L. Cardoso 2001; Maxwell 2003; A. M. D. Silva 2006.

[6] João da Costa Cordeiro, "Memoria sobre a Prosperidade da Nação Portuguesa" (1797), quoted in J. L. Cardoso 2001, p. 83. On the Portuguese economy in general in this period, see Magalhães Godinho 1955 and Silbert 1966.

[7] ANRJ, Secretário de Estado, cod. 67, vol. 13, Mello e Castro to Luis de Vasconcelos, January 5, 1785, fo. 15. In 1785, an *alvará* prohibiting manufacturing in the colonies was issued. Martinho de Mello e Castro (1716–95) held many posts over a long career: Viceroy of Brazil, Portuguese envoy to the Hague and London, and Secretary of State for Navy and Overseas Colonies (1770–95).

[8] R. de Souza Coutinho, quoted in J. L. Cardoso 2001, p. 81.

[9] The unintended consequences of this strategy were not anticipated: "the new compromises of reform in imperial capitals and entrepôt dissolved older, more archaic compromises," Adelman 2006, pp. 48–49.

The model the late-eighteenth century reformers envisaged was premised on mutually advantageous cooperation through collaboration. Three constant preoccupations of metropolitan officials informed their actions: first, Portugal's economic decadence, a conviction that colonial prosperity could offset the Peninsula's seemingly insuperable disadvantages; second, the need to leverage the Atlantic colonies to secure Portugal's political independence, by extracting British diplomatic support and relying on its ally's naval supremacy; and, third, the maintenance of territorial integrity, especially as independence movements tore empires apart throughout the Atlantic World. Recently, historians of the Luso-Brazilian empire have shifted focus away from conflict to alliances, compromises, conciliatory tendencies, and symbiotic coexistence, practices which tended to buttress existing institutional arrangements and diminish the likelihood of conflict.[10]

Imperial integration was reinforced by two related personnel policies. The first was the blurring of the line between metropole and colony through university education. Brazilians (and later subjects from other colonies) had been incorporated into a transatlantic bureaucracy from the first stages of colonization. The principal mechanism for recruitment was the University of Coimbra. Unlike in Spanish America, where the presence of numerous universities made relocation for higher education unnecessary, no university was established in Brazil. Legal education, then, became the common experience linking civilian administrators to one another. Coimbra was the training ground for imperial service, where the "bureaucratic socialization which readied a man for the robe of office" occurred.[11] The sheer number of Brazilian students passing through Coimbra indicates the extent of this policy and suggests its impact. In 1766–70 alone, 196 Brazilians matriculated whereas in 1791–95, 80 matriculated.[12] Overall, 866 Brazilian-born subjects studied at Coimbra between 1772 and 1822.[13]

The expulsion of the Jesuits, the closure of the University of Évora, and the termination of the Jesuit colleges created an educational vacuum which Pombal sought to fill.[14] Fittingly, Pombal's overhaul of Coimbra's curriculum in 1772 was entrusted to a Brazilian, Francisco de Lemos. Lemos aimed to extirpate scholasticism, infuse the curriculum with new doctrines, and establish new faculties of mathematics and

---

[10] Falcon 1996.   [11] Schwartz 1973, p. 361.
[12] F. T. de Fonseca 1999, p. 530.
[13] C. G. Mota 2006, p. 68; J. M. de Carvalho 1982, p. 384.
[14] S. J. Miller 1978, p. 247.

the sciences.[15] As anticipated, the Coimbra reform strengthened the connection between higher education and state service, symbolized by the preference for natural and civil law over Roman and canon law. The number of graduates in medicine, mathematics, and natural science likewise increased at the expense of canon lawyers and theologians.[16] The advancement of "useful knowledge" was prized above all else. Well after the implementation of the reform, Souza Coutinho warned of the "danger" of education sponsored by religious institutions. He believed that such institutions inculcated "prejudices contrary to the enthusiasm which should be inspired in youth for the active life, for the love of the sovereign and the *patria*, and for [a career in] administration, upon which depends the future greatness of the nation."[17] Almost thirty years later, Principal Souza, then head of the *Governadores do Reino* administering Portugal during the Court's absence, advised Dom João that the reduction of the number of chairs in Roman Law would aid the kingdom's prosperity. He argued for their replacement with chairs in Portuguese maritime, military, and mercantile law as well as economics and public administration. Principal Souza contended that "it is a shame to study the laws which are no longer in effect while ignoring national law [*leis patrias*] and those branches of the natural sciences which can influence the wealth of nations, and increase the power, and force, of the sovereign."[18] By the early nineteenth century, an instrumental approach to education helped to conjure a vision of a genuinely Luso-Brazilian empire, one which brought individuals from across the empire together for common training. Intentionally or not, such a tendency favored a pan-territorial approach to reform which somewhat defused metropolitan-colonial tensions.[19] For all of the resentment caused by the Pombaline reforms, colonial office-holders largely escaped unscathed and the bonds tying the Brazilian-born administrative

---

[15] On Lemos's reforms in general, see Braga 1898, vol. III, pp. 193–300 passim; and Araújo 2000. Compare to the reform of the University of Seville's curriculum by Pablo de Olavide undertaken in 1768 as well as the comparatively bleak situation of the Castilian universities in the late eighteenth century. See Kagan 1974, pp. 227–36 passim.

[16] Often the study of these subjects was combined and students could pursue "joint degrees." Of the 568 Brazilians studying law at Coimbra between 1772 and 1822, for example, 281 concurrently studied mathematics or the natural sciences, and some students undertook study in three separate subjects. See C. G. Mota 2006, p. 68.

[17] R. de Souza Coutinho to Mello e Castro, January 3, 1787, in Souza Coutinho 1993, vol. I, p. 44.

[18] Principal Souza to Dom João, February 22, 1815, reproduced in A. Pereira 1953, vol. III, p. 178.

[19] K. Maxwell, "The Idea of a Luso-Brazilian Empire," in Maxwell 2003, p. 142.

elite to metropolitan institutions were strengthened.[20] Yet integration through education did not imply equality. The Peninsula remained the empire's undisputed center. In 1768, the Overseas Council (*Conselho Ultramarino*) rejected a petition from Minas Gerais to build a medical school. Only theological seminaries were approved, of which the Seminário de Olinda (Pernambuco), founded in 1798, was the most renowned. With the Court's arrival in 1808, medical and military academies were established.[21] Yet even after Brazil's elevation to the status of a kingdom coequal with Portugal in 1815, the Crown rejected proposals to found a New World university.[22]

The second, closely related policy that encouraged imperial integration and a trans-territorial approach to policy in the late eighteenth century was the practice of rotating government officials throughout the empire. This was a long-standing practice. In the sixteenth and seventeenth centuries, there was a "multi-continental quality" of service to the crown: viceroys, governors, judges and magistrates, senior civil servants, and soldiers were "constantly on the move."[23] In the eighteenth century, Portuguese-born and Brazilian-born graduates continued to cross the globe in the service of the state. It was not unusual for a single individual to serve on three continents over the course of an administrative career, making him attuned to the differences between the empire's component parts.[24]

The Souza Coutinho family furnished a clear, if extreme, example of this phenomenon: Dom Francisco, father of the previously mentioned Dom Rodrigo and Principal Souza, served as a colonial governor in Angola and an ambassador to the courts of Madrid and London, while his sons served in various capacities from Turin to Belem (Pará) to London. The Souza Coutinho family's itineraries, while remarkable, were hardly unique. Dom António Álvares da Cunha, born in Portugal,

---

[20] Even Brazilians who did not attend Coimbra found ample scope for advancement, as they occupied many of the non-political offices of Justice and Treasury, to say nothing of the clerks, notaries, and tax collectors ubiquitous in colonial Brazil. See S. Schwartz, "Elite Politics and the Growth of a Peasantry in Late Colonial Brazil," in Russell-Wood 1975, pp. 141–42.

[21] J. M. de Carvalho 1982, p. 382. It should be noted that students studied science, mathematics, and modern languages at the Olinda Seminary, not strictly theological subjects.

[22] See Chapter 2, p. 102.

[23] Russell-Wood 1992, pp. 64–65; Barman interpreted this system of rotations and short-term appointments in a negative light, as a means of preempting threats to "the weakness of [the Crown's] administrative machinery," a sign that it was "jealous of its prerogatives." See Barman 1988, p. 23.

[24] It must be conceded that their long, often dismal tenures abroad sometimes served to make them suspicious of "universalizing" tendencies, of policies applicable everywhere.

spent years in Brazil, where he mapped the region between Vila Rica and the Paraguay River, before he was sent by Pombal to Angola (1753–58) for a similar purpose.[25] João da Costa Xavier, born in Rio de Janeiro, served as Secretary General of Mozambique in 1767–68 and later was governor of Sofala from 1777. One of the *Inconfidentes* of Minas, who was exiled to Angola, José Alvares Maciel, wrote a *memoria* on iron production in Angola in 1799, thus making a curious transition from exiled conspirator to agent in the service of the Crown. Francisco José de Lacerda Almeida, born in Brazil, educated at Coimbra, led two scientific expeditions to Mato Grosso, then became a professor at the Royal Naval Academy in Lisbon, before assuming the governorship of the Rios de Sena in the late 1790s, where his remit was to traverse Africa, from Mozambique to Angola. He died en route.[26] The Brazilian-born medic José Pinto de Azevedo traveled to Angola to study dysentery and tetanus before returning to Rio to study the principal diseases there.[27] The Coimbra-trained *Carioca* naturalist João da Silva Feijó served as an administrator in Cape Verde before embarking on a "philosophical voyage" to Ceará, where he wrote numerous tracts, and brought plant cuttings to the Royal Botanical Garden in Lisbon. Dom Diogo de Sousa, Conde do Rio Pardo, served as a governor and captain-general of Mozambique (1793–98), before moving to Brazil to hold the same post in Maranhão (1798), then moved south to become the first captain-general of Rio Grande de São Pedro (1807–14), before ending his career as viceroy and captain-general of India (from 1816).[28] Many further examples could of course be cited in support of the same argument. The Crown sought to harness the firsthand knowledge, personal connections, and networks of patronage accumulated by these former governors and magistrates, sometimes appointing them to the Overseas Council, which continued to shape imperial policy even after the rise of ministerial government under Pombal. In fact, experience as a Crown servant overseas became a virtual prerequisite for appointment to the Council. Of the sixty-two men called to serve as Councilors between 1750 and 1807, forty-eight had overseas administrative experience: forty in Brazil, fifteen in *Estado da Índia*, and six in West Africa.[29]

---

[25] C. M. Santos 2010, p. 544.

[26] Pereira 1999, pp. 153, 156–57.

[27] Silva Dias 1968, p. 151.

[28] Russell-Wood 2001b, p. 15. These connections survived the breakdown of empire: Goan Brahmin liberal Bernardo Peres da Silva, for example, participated in revolutionary activity and constitution-making in India, Brazil, and Portugal between 1820 and 1836. See Bayly 2012, p. 46.

[29] Myrup 2010, pp. 204, 216–17.

The pursuit of an integrated empire was hampered and constrained by various obstacles. In order to understand them, the Portuguese empire's earlier trajectory must be appreciated and recapitulated. At the turn of the eighteenth century, gold and diamond strikes in Brazil, combined with the recovery of the sugar industry there, revived the Crown's previously flagging fortunes.[30] The influx of gold made possible the import of many products from the northern European ports of Hamburg, Amsterdam, and London, which soon drained Portugal of the specie pouring into its treasury from Brazil's mines. The seemingly limitless flow of mineral wealth, therefore, masked an otherwise undesirable and unsustainable arrangement. The Brazilian windfall produced some lasting effects: it underwrote a great system of public works under Dom João V (1706–50), including a massive aqueduct that carried potable water to Lisbon, financed the construction of royal palaces at Mafra, Queluz, and Ajuda, and permitted the sumptuous adornment of churches, convents, and monasteries. Nevertheless, the gold drain caused great anxiety, even if it ensured British naval support, particularly as mineral yields began to decline toward mid-century.[31]

Pombal, firmly ensconced as Dom José's principal minister after the 1755 Lisbon earthquake, inherited an unsustainable system in need of tweaking, if not overhaul. His response to the earthquake afforded a crucial opening, but Portugal's dismal performance in the Seven Years War, which revealed a largely incompetent army, inadequate fortifications, and unreliable diplomatic alliances, provided a significant impetus as well.[32] In the 1760s and 1770s, Pombal presided over a re-orientation of the empire, even though many of his specific policies were abandoned or reversed after the fall of his ministry upon Dom José's death in 1777. Among Pombal's most astute insights was the recognition that the Crown's incomplete control over its own territory, resources, and subjects needed to be addressed urgently. There were diverse manifestations of this deplorable phenomenon, and obstacles were internal and external, both intrinsic to the development of royal authority and colonial expansion and extrinsic to Portugal, for a shifting balance of economic power in Europe was transforming the geopolitical arena in which Portugal competed. Internal obstacles included the Crown's weakness relative to the nobility, which prejudiced the uniform administration of justice and hampered fiscal innovation;

---

[30] These themes are covered comprehensively in Boxer 1962; Bethell 1984; and Disney 2009.
[31] Bethell 1984; Russell-Wood 1992; and Disney 2009.
[32] Maxwell 1995; Monteiro 2006; and A. S. Pereira 2009.

the morass of accumulated legislation without codification; the political power of the Church, stemming from its vast economic resources beyond the grasp of the royal fisc and its near monopoly on education, as well as the extensive autonomy and wealth of the Jesuits in the New World; and a dilatory colonial administration, with limited capacity to impose its will on a society accustomed to scant interference.[33] The external obstacles included overweening British economic and political influence, enshrined infamously in the 1703 Methuen Treaty (itself pre-dated by earlier entangling treaties), in metropolitan Portugal and its overseas possessions; rampant contraband trade; and a still rapacious Spain, whose penchant for territorial aggrandizement was confirmed by its 1762 invasion. Furthermore, depleted resource endowments, such as declining mineral yields from the Americas, which had buoyed state finances earlier in the century, threatened to exacerbate these problems while the small size and relatively uncompetitive nature of Portuguese industry, combined with the country's agricultural underdevelopment, provided a firm basis for pessimism.[34]

Pombal, his acolytes, and their successors were convinced that Portugal and its overseas possessions suffered from "backwardness" – material, cultural, and intellectual – which had to be confronted and overcome in order to stave off decadence and terminal decline.[35] They sought to extirpate, overcome, or sidestep these obstacles, empowering the Crown by diminishing the privileges of the nobility, inserting the state's tentacles into the economy, especially in the aftermath of the Lisbon earthquake, and orchestrating the international campaign which resulted in the expulsion of the Jesuits from Portuguese territory, the confiscation of their property, and the reorganization of elite education away from scholastic learning to "useful knowledge" embodied by natural science and political economy.[36] Pombal also cut down on ecclesiastical amortization. Legislation of 1766, 1769, and 1775 made it almost impossible to donate, bequeath, or otherwise transfer land to the Church.[37] In some senses, the intensity, rapidity, and scope of Pombal's reforms represented a decisive break from the past. Yet his efforts were informed by the insights, aims, and experience of forerunner reformers, particularly Conde de Ericeira, who had sought to foster industry using protectionist policies along Colbertian lines in the late seventeenth century, and Dom Luís da Cunha, a prominent diplomat whose interest in British

---

[33] Maxwell 1973 and 1995.   [34] J. L. Cardoso 2003.
[35] A. R. C. da Silva 2006, pp. 39–40.
[36] S. J. Miller 1978, pp. 240–50; Monteiro 2006; Maxwell 1995.
[37] N. G. Monteiro, "A Occupação da Terra," in Lains and Silva 2005, vol. I, p. 87.

political economy was inherited by Pombal.[38] Pombal thus accentuated certain pre-existing aspects of Portuguese political culture by erasing those which distracted from it. The extreme reactions his reforms provoked should not distract attention from recognition that Pombal was a pragmatic and subtle adapter. His government moved hesitantly and was marked by a compromise between old and new.[39]

Pombal believed that Portugal's fortunes could be improved through comprehensive colonial reform. He revamped the Luso-Brazilian commercial system: sugar, tobacco, and gold were protected by new legislation, more effective revenue-collection mechanisms were implemented, and long-delayed administrative reforms were undertaken.[40] Pombal blamed the aforementioned Methuen Treaty for the "notorious decline in our marine and in our foreign and domestic commerce," adding that even this disadvantageous treaty was further "abused and violated" by English merchants in Portugal.[41] The Treaty sanctioned British penetration of the Portuguese market, permitting the duty-free entry of woolen goods into Lisbon and Porto and offering Portuguese merchants reciprocal advantages on the British market. From the early eighteenth century, the massive influx of Brazilian gold was used by Portugal to reduce deficits and purchase foreign (mainly British) goods, which effectively smothered Portugal's domestic manufactures.[42] Pombal was thus faced with the delicate task of balancing Portugal's dependence on its military-diplomatic alliance with Britain while simultaneously circumventing the advantages enjoyed by Britain in Portuguese markets in the Old World and the New.[43]

Though Pombal recognized as early as the 1740s that "all business conducted in foreign countries was insecure and contingent" because of the "ambition and greed it inspired in other countries," he excluded colonial trade from this analysis. On the contrary, it was potentially "secure and perpetual," so long as "foreigners were excluded" and adequate care was taken to "watch over colonial commerce."[44] The formula Pombal favored involved the formation of monopoly companies and the vigorous crackdown on contraband. Pombal's preference for monopoly companies is foreshadowed in his London journals, written while he served as Portugal's ambassador there from 1739 to 1743. He first praised the usefulness of companies to "fertilize" and "sprout"

---

[38] Boxer 1962; Hanson 1981; Maxwell 1995, pp. 16, 43.
[39] Maxwell 1995; Falcon 1982, p. 445.
[40] These policies are described in exquisite detail in Maxwell 1973.
[41] Pombal 1986, p. 76.   [42] Maxwell 1995, pp. 42–43.
[43] Maxwell 1973, pp. 31–35.   [44] Pombal 1986, p. 42.

colonial commerce.[45] "The utility of a company," he explained, "is proven by the experience of all European states which have established them, collecting great revenues as a result."[46] Following his ascent to power, trading companies became an essential component of his broader design, particularly the Companies of Grão Pará and Maranhão, and Pernambuco and Paraíba, by which Pombal sought to develop new export commodities, including cotton, rice, cacao, and coffee, all of which were unaffected by existing commercial treaties.[47] He also hoped to improve outdated methods of production and gain control over economic activity to the extent that he could guarantee the quality of products and regulate prices.[48] In 1755, Pombal described companies as the "only way to reclaim the commerce of all Portuguese America from the hands of foreigners."[49] With foreign influence extirpated, economic development, premised on slave labor, commenced in earnest. As Pombal's half-brother, an administrator in Amazonia, explained, the Grão-Pará Company's importation of slaves could turn the "excellent and infinite land," now "deserted farms and wild forests," into "lucrative *engenhos* and huge plantations."[50] The Company, which was granted a monopoly on the shipment of African slaves from Bissau and Cacheu, brought nine thousand enslaved Africans to Amazonia between 1757 and 1772.[51]

The overseas companies formed part of a broader strategy to break the chain of credit established by British merchants, depriving them

---

[45] On this fertile period in Pombal's intellectual development, see Maxwell 1995, pp. 4–10. It has been suggested that Pombal's inspiration was the Company of Ostende, the inner workings of which he became familiar while in Vienna, not English or French companies. See Correia 1965, p. 90. It is entirely possible that both were major influences; Furthermore, it is conceivable that Portuguese precedents were just as important: in 1669 and 1692, chartered companies for Cape Verde, Guinea, Grão Pará and Maranhão, and India had been established. See Maxwell 1995, p. 43.

[46] Pombal 1986, p. 136. For a positive appraisal of the impact of the Pombaline companies, see Shaw 1998; for a critical view, see Francisco Ribeiro da Silva, "Pombal e os Ingleses (Incidências Económicas e Relacões Internacionais)," in *Actas do Congresso* 2001.

[47] It must be conceded that not all of these developments can be attributed directly to commercial rivalry with Britain; some were a direct response to new exigencies provoked by declining mineral yields in Brazil, plunging gold prices on the world market, and the escalating costs associated with securing the southern frontier with Spanish America. See Alden 1969, p. 353.

[48] A. Mansuy-Diniz Silva, "Portugal and Brazil: Imperial Re-Organization, 1750–1808," in Bethell 1984, p. 490.

[49] Pombal, quoted in Maxwell 1973, p. 19.

[50] Francisco Xavier de Mendonça to Diogo de Mendonça, January 18, 1754, in *Amazônia Pombalina* 1963, pp. 456–57.

[51] Carreira 1983, p. 50. By 1815, seventy thousand Africans had been sold as slaves in Amazonia. See Hawthorne 2010, pp. 2–3.

of the sums due to them from the long-term credit they had extended to Portuguese merchants and intermediaries. They had a peninsular analogue in the privileged company for Port Wine established in the Douro.[52] Pombal managed to halve the number of foreign merchants operating in Portugal, replacing them with national merchants.[53] But the companies, and similar initiatives launched in the same spirit, failed to match the great expectations, at least in the short term. By 1776–77, less than one-quarter of shipments to the colonies were composed of national manufactures whereas Portuguese-made textiles amounted to a mere 30 percent of the total dispatched to the colonies.[54] These trading companies remained in existence until Pombal's fall from power in 1778, after which they were dismantled and a less regulated trade regime was established.[55] An astute and influential observer, Francisco de Souza Coutinho, noted that both Pombaline colonial companies "did not generate the results which their exclusive privileges promised, leaving those populations suffering from the same lack of products from Portugal [as they did before]." They remained "miserable skeletons."[56] After the dismantlement of the companies, however, some products encouraged by Pombal produced a huge, beneficent economic impact, including cotton. *Maranhense* planters exploited the unmet demand caused by the American Revolution (1775–83) and used windfall profits to finance their purchase of African slaves. By 1790, Brazilian cotton comprised 30 percent of British imports of that product.[57] Yet such belated success came too late to save Pombal's companies. Their short-term practical failure, not more abstract, theoretical arguments drawn from emergent doctrines of political economy, sealed their fate. But due to their later success, privileged companies re-emerged as a viable policy alternative in the nineteenth century, as shall be discussed in Chapter 5. Even in the eighteenth century, the Grão-Pará company's great detractor, Souza Coutinho, for example, remained an advocate for privileged companies to develop Indian Ocean commerce, for otherwise the "*Estado da Índia* would fall forever into English hands."[58] Under his son, Dom Rodrigo, in the late 1790s, there was revived interest in privileged trade companies, though none were ultimately established. A company for the north

---

[52] Maxwell 1995.   [53] Shaw 1998, pp. 547–49.
[54] Pedreira 2000, p. 844.
[55] On the Pombaline companies in Brazil, see Carreira 1983.
[56] [F. de Souza Coutinho], "Breve e Util Ideia, de Commercio, Navegação e Conquistas d'Azia, e da África" (1779), in *Arquivos de Angola*, vol. I, no. 3 (1933).
[57] MacLachlan 1997, p. 110; S. Schwartz, "De Ouro a Algodão: A Economia Brasileira no Século XVIII," in Bethencourt 1998, p. 95.
[58] [F. de Souza Coutinho], "Breve e Util Ideia."

of Brazil, including Pará, intended to foment population growth and bolster economic activity, was proposed.[59] There were numerous proponents of a privileged trade company for Mozambique throughout the late eighteenth century.[60] Nevertheless, lingering distaste for Pombal, and the mixed results achieved by his companies, probably account for the failure of these efforts to come to fruition.[61]

The debate concerning trading companies persisted because the problem it was designed to solve – contraband trade – refused to disappear. Pombal and his successors instructed officials to repress contraband and tighten up the avenues of legal trade. Pombal's attitude toward clandestine commerce is revealed in a letter to the Brazilian Viceroy Lavradio: "underlying [Britain's] pacific system of commerce is an insufferable perfidy."[62] But it was clear that elimination of contraband would be impossible so long as Portuguese shipping, and the products it carried, remained inferior to its competitors. With the exception of Angola's ports, Pombal made no effort to interrupt trade between Portugal's African footholds and international merchants. Between 1759 and 1779, for example, 294 Portuguese ships stopped at São Tomé whereas 581 English ships, 234 French ships, and 44 Dutch ships dropped anchor in same period. Many of these ships, of course, were involved in the slave trade. Between 1765 and 1779, thirty-two French vessels transported 9,150 African slaves from Mozambique to Mauritius.[63]

But Pombal sought to exclude foreign traders from Portuguese Africa's trade with Brazil. Among Pombal's chief priorities was to boost (and guarantee) the supply of slaves for Brazil. Without regular slave shipments, Pombal warned, Brazil's "agriculture would disappear, and the production of sugar and tobacco, to say nothing of

---

[59] For example, see BNRJ, M.S. I-28, 28, 32, Antônio de Abreu Guimarães, "Methodo Facil, Proprio e Util para se Animar e Promover a Importante Povoação do Grão Pará, suas Lavouras, Fabricas, Navegação e Comércio com Utilidade Geral, e do Proprio Estado" (1799).

[60] See the *relação* of Pedro Saldanha de Albuquerque, December 19, 1758, in *Relações de Moçambique Setecentista* 1955, p. 118; and J. Capela 2002, p. 74, for a description of a proposed 1779 East African company.

[61] For example, see ANRJ, cod. 807, vol. I, Fernando Delgado Freire de Castilho to R. de Souza Coutinho (c. 1797–1801) on the Capitania da Paraíba do Norte, in which he blamed the Pombal's Pernambuco company for having "extinguished the fortunes of Paraíba, destroying by means of monopoly the most productive plantations." A similar condemnation came from his brother, then Governor of Pará, who informed Dom Rodrigo that "even nineteen years after its extinction, the vices and effects the company produced still torment the inhabitants of this province." APEP, cod. 549, Francisco de Souza Coutinho to R. de Souza Coutinho, August 21, 1797.

[62] Conde de Oeiras [Pombal] to Marquês do Lavradio, April 14, 1769, in Mendonça 1960, p. 36.

[63] C. Neves 1989, pp. 114–17.

livestock agriculture and the cutting of precious wood, would cease to exist."[64] He was keen to prevent foreign interlopers from interfering with this trade and was alarmed by reports that British contraband slave traders were transporting slaves to Spanish ships, lurking just off the coast, which then slipped away across the Atlantic toward Buenos Aires carrying this human cargo.[65] The privileged trade companies were designed to wrest control for the metropole over this Africa-Brazil nexus, but the challenge was inherited by future generations of administrators. An "unacceptable breach in the commerce of [Angola]" was lamented by administrators throughout the 1760s and 1770s.[66] In 1769, Portugal constructed the fortress of Novo Redondo, situated between Luanda and Benguela, to protect against the internationalization of the slave trade.[67] But a single fort proved inadequate. In correspondence concerning the Cabinda enclave, Bahia's governor reported in 1783 that "foreign ships bring the same products as ours, but of higher quality, as well as gold and silver or other precious metals. All the Princes who govern in that region speak English and French fluently, and also understand Dutch, but very few speak Portuguese, for very few of our ships travel there."[68] As a result of such intelligence, the Portuguese constructed a fortress at Cabinda to exclude traders from these nations. But this fortress was captured by French forces in 1784. By 1790, Angola's governor complained that the level of contraband led to huge losses in the Crown's share.[69] In the early nineteenth century, officials continued to lament contraband. One letter complained of foreign traders on the Costa da Mina, who, in addition to violating the "law of nations, disobey the law established in Europe among all nations by which colonial commerce takes place solely with the metropole ... for colonial commerce should benefit the nation which established and developed the colony, and not other [nations]."[70] In Brazil, contraband trade was out of control. In 1805,

---

[64] AHU, Angola, cx. 43, doc. 111 "Conde de Oeiras sobre o Modo de Recuperação da Agricultura, Navegação e Comércio de Angola," November 20, 1760; on the Angola-Brazil connection, see J. Miller 1988; and Ferreira 2003.

[65] AHU, Angola, cx. 43, doc. 39, "Carta do Governador António de Vasconcelos," June 20, 1760.

[66] AHU, Angola, cx. 51, doc. 15, F. de Souza Coutinho to Mendonça Furtado, March 17, 1767.

[67] Candido 2006, p. 27.

[68] ANRJ, Secretário de Estado do Brasil, cod. 67, vol. 11, Vasconcellos to Mello e Castro, June 30, 1783.

[69] Barão de Mossamedes, quoted in Candido 2006, p. 28.

[70] ANRJ, Vice-Reinado, cx. 748, pacote 1, "Carta dada pelo Rodrigo Coelho Machado Torres sobre o comercio de Costa da Mina" (n.d.).

one official lamented, "the contraband trade in which foreign ships engage in Brazilian harbors is manifest and scandalous."[71]

As may be inferred from these citations, foreigners were not the sole obstacle to metropolitan control over the waterways and ocean routes connecting its colonial possessions. Portugal's own subjects were equally culpable, eager and willing collaborators with foreigners in illicit trade. Part of Pombal's campaign against smuggling concerned the exclusion of Brazilians from certain professions (e.g. travelling merchants, goldsmiths) whose members could engage easily in illicit trade, hence reserving the Brazilian market for peninsular merchants.[72] After Pombal's fall, Mello e Castro pursued an aggressive regulatory policy in Minas Gerais, seeking to tighten control over and prevent the leaking of gold and diamonds through the imposition of a wildly unpopular per capita tax, the *derrama*, to guarantee an annual quota.[73]

Legislation, however, could achieve only so much. Broader structural forces were at play. Brazil's trade with other parts of the empire further shunted metropolitan Portugal to the fringes of the Southern Atlantic system. Brazil's development – both agriculture and mining – was reliant on bilateral trade between the littorals of Southern Africa and South America. From the mid seventeenth century, Brazilian products – especially *cachaça* and tobacco, but also horses, manioc, and dried fish – accounted for half of the value of purchases of African slaves, creating a Southern Atlantic economy largely independent of the metropole. Between 1736 and 1770, only 15 percent of ships arriving in Luanda departed from Lisbon, with 41 percent from Rio de Janeiro, 22.5 percent from Pernambuco, and 22 percent from Bahia.[74] Nor was this trade confined to the Atlantic. Indian textiles from Goa formed a large part (perhaps one third of the total) of cargoes of Brazilian ships bound for Angola in the eighteenth century. Between 1741 and 1762, for example, twelve of the twenty-six ships returning from Goa and Macau to Lisbon called at Bahia.[75] One remedy Pombal sought to apply to turn this South Atlantic–South Asian commercial web to the Crown's advantage was to require, from 1761, that all ships departing the *Estado da Índia* would call at Luanda en route to Lisbon. In Luanda, the merchants would pay duties of 10 percent

[71] Visconde de Anadia to António de Araújo de Azeredo [Conde da Barca], July 11, 1805, quoted in Pijning 2007, p. 349.
[72] Alden 1969, p. 394.
[73] Maxwell 1973 persuasively links the imposition of the *derrama* to the conspiracies culminating in the *Inconfidência Mineira* in the late 1780s.
[74] Alencastro 2000, pp. 250, 324–25, 354.
[75] Ferreira 2003, pp. 57–66 passim.

on the goods they offloaded, an attractive proposition given normal rates. Pombal wanted all intra-imperial commerce to have Portugal as its principal hub, with the crucial exception of the slave trade, which would be conducted directly, and efficiently, between the littorals of West Africa and Brazil through company intermediaries.[76] He therefore sought to prevent ships leaving Goa from bypassing Lisbon and heading straight for Brazilian ports after a brief stop in Luanda. In 1772, the Crown realized that its strategy was failing to produce the intended result. It therefore declared illegal direct commerce between India and Brazil, and further sought to discourage direct non-slave trade commercial intercourse between African ports and Brazil.[77] Moreover, Portuguese and Brazilian ships from Goa which called at Angola were forbidden from offloading their merchandise in Luanda and were permitted only to take aboard products destined for sale in Portugal.[78]

Since the slave trade dominated all commercial activity in Luanda, the attempt to disaggregate the slave trade component of the economy from other sectors was difficult, if not impossible. Nevertheless, the Portuguese government clung to the notion that it was attainable within a well-designed regulatory framework. "It is a generally accepted and followed maxim," Mello e Castro declared in 1772, that

it is the metropole that should conduct commerce between the colonies, instead of the colonies conducting this commerce amongst themselves ... [Luanda] has become an entrepôt for a general commerce between Asia, Africa, and America, to the total exclusion of this kingdom ... the colonies take all of the benefit and utility of this trade.[79]

Yet it is clear that such diagnoses and a flurry of decrees failed to produce substantive alterations. In 1779, seven years after the Crown resolved to act, Mello e Castro noted in his instructions to the incoming governor of Angola that "it is impossible to observe without great pain that our Brazilian dominions have absorbed all of the commerce and

---

[76] In order to ensure that this traffic went between Brazil and Africa, Pombal outlawed slavery in Portugal itself, thus discouraging ships from making their way north of the equator and diverting slave shipments from Brazil's booming agricultural sector. For an analysis of Pombal's slave trade policy, see Maxwell 1995.

[77] C. Neves 1989, p. 38. There were several intermediate steps as well: in 1769, liberty of commerce for Brazilian ships in East Africa was granted, though this was suppressed two years later because Asian goods were flowing into Brazil, which were then traded to Angola, thus preventing the Pernambuco Company from obtaining in Lisbon the products it needed for its Angola–Brazil trade. See J. Capela 2002, p. 73.

[78] Couto 1971, p. 29.

[79] AHU, Angola, cx. 56, doc. 49, Mello e Castro to the King, June 19, 1772.

navigation of the African coast, to the total exclusion of Portugal."[80] In 1783, Mello e Castro sought to shut down the contraband trade which Bahian merchants conducted directly with South and East Asia, particularly the "very pernicious clandestine smuggling of tobacco," without paying duties.[81] In 1785, he warned that if Brazil's control over these trades continued then the "utility and wealth of these important colonies would become the sole patrimony of the inhabitants of Brazil and the foreign nations with which they trade; whereas Portugal would enjoy nothing more than superficial, sterile, and useless dominion over them."[82] In spite of these efforts, Brazilians remained masters of the commerce conducted between the ports of Luanda and Benguela while peninsular merchants remained both scarce and uncompetitive.[83] As in Spanish America, trade increasingly was conducted exclusively between the West African coast and Southern Brazil's littoral. It evolved out of the orbit of metropolitan interests and controls. The irony was, in a contemporary historian's phrase, that the South Atlantic world was a "world made by empire but autonomous from imperial authority."[84]

Part of the difficulty with eliminating contraband (and extra-legal trade of all kinds) was the Atlantic economy's dependence on it. The Crown, while vigorously seeking to keep interlopers out of its own territories, sanctioned the flagrant violation of the 1751 prohibition on exporting slaves to non-Portuguese controlled ports. Up to 60 percent of the slaves disembarked in the Rio de la Plata came from Brazil and Mozambique in the last decades of the eighteenth century, an illicit trade which, in turn, provided the Portuguese Atlantic economy with a steady infusion of silver, offsetting in part declining mineral yields in Brazil itself.[85] By 1808, contraband was so prevalent that it had ceased to be considered illicit. It had, in Viceroy Conde de Arcos's phrase, "rapidly gained acceptance as an innocent and legal enterprise" among Brazilians.[86] Reform, and broader structural forces, had unleashed dynamics uneasily suppressed even by avid officials. The slave trade, in particular, "had evolved outside of the orbit of metropolitan interest and control."[87]

---

[80] "Instruções de Martinho de Mello e Castro ao Governador de Angola, José Gonçalo de Camara" (1779), quoted in Dias 1936, p. 6.
[81] ANRJ, Secretário de Estado do Brasil, cod. 67, vol. 11, Mello e Castro to L. de Vasconcellos e Souza, February 14, 1783.
[82] ANRJ, Secretário de Estado do Brasil, cod. 67, vol. 13, Mello e Castro to L. de Vasconcellos e Souza, January 5, 1785, fo. 14 v.
[83] Couto 1971, p. 29.   [84] Adelman 2006, p. 83.
[85] Borucki 2011, pp. 81, 90.   [86] Quoted in Pijning 2007, p. 365.
[87] Adelman 2006, pp. 73–77.

But the forces generating tensions, and contradictions, within the system did not go entirely unchecked. There were many countervailing forces, particularly at the level of policy and personnel, which enabled the Crown to gain greater control over the empire's resources, subjects, and revenue streams even as subterranean forces eroded metropolitan primacy. Through a host of measures, they managed to extirpate threats, integrate territory, and enhance the circulation of products and people throughout the empire in the late eighteenth century, staving off the full effects of the forces undermining cohesion. The next section, then, explores the intellectual underpinnings of the policies put in place in the decades after Pombal's fall from power in 1777.

After Pombal: agrarianism and ideologies of development

The fall of Pombal and the accession of Dona Maria I was long considered by historians a major disjuncture resulting in the reversal, abandonment, or slow dismantlement of many key features of his reform program.[88] Yet the much-vaunted *Viradeira* was less comprehensive than both contemporaries alleged and the older historiography corroborated.[89] In many respects, in the judgment of a recent historian, "there was a desire to remedy problematic situations and maintain an equilibrium among different, opposed groups in society."[90] Undoubtedly, the transition to Dona Maria's reign ushered in change. Privileged companies were dismantled and some tax duties, including that on salt, were reduced, while price fixing on wool was eliminated.[91] Pombal's enemies were rehabilitated (and, in some cases, released from prison) and material aid was extended to the exiled Jesuits in Italy (though they were not invited to return; nor was compensation for their confiscated property offered). But the disgraced Marquis's son, Conde de Oeiras, retained his post as President of the *Câmara de Lisboa*, many figures indubitably loyal to Pombal kept their jobs and titles, and the Pombaline spirit permeated the administrative ranks.[92] In this modified, more modest, appraisal of the *Viradeira*, the most distinctive change ushered in by Dona Maria's accession was the restoration of the aristocracy's

---

[88] Maxwell 1973 is an important exception.
[89] On the discontinuities between the Pombaline and Marian periods, see Beirão 1944; M. Domingues 1972; and Borrêcho 1993.
[90] Z. O. de Castro 1992, p. 12.
[91] Beirão 1944, pp. 130–32.
[92] Z. O. de Castro 1992, p. 13. A good example of administrative continuity is Mello e Castro, colonial minister since 1770, who retained his post into the 1790s.

rights, privileges, and immunities, which Pombaline regalism had undermined both in practice and through legislation. In the first years of Dona Maria's reign, the renewal of noble titles and *merces* increased with great velocity, even if the Crown's supremacy over the aristocracy and the shift from a form of governance based on diffuse, decentralized *conselhos* to more hierarchical Crown-appointed secretaries of state proved an irreversible aspect of the Pombaline legacy.[93]

The *Viradeira*'s impact thus has proven difficult to assess in part because post-1779 initiatives often built on Pombal's policy.[94] Efforts to collect and analyze data pertaining to colonies had been pursued by the *Junta do Comércio, Agricultura e Navegação*, founded in 1755, which was the body responsible for fomenting all branches of the economy.[95] After wresting control over education from the Jesuits, he founded the *Colégio dos Nobres* in 1760–61. Political economy was introduced and disseminated with the establishment of the *Aula de Comércio* in 1770.[96] Above all, the general impact of the secularizing reforms of the Coimbra curriculum, which produced a cadre of administrators-in-waiting trained in the natural sciences, cartography, and other methods of quantifying, systematizing, and codifying data, must be acknowledged. The Coimbra reforms were linked to a broader encouragement of the study of natural history, botany, and applied sciences. A Natural History Museum and Royal Botanical Garden were founded in Ajuda (Lisbon) under the direction of the Paduan polymath Domenico Vandelli, originally recruited to Portugal by Pombal as the first professor of chemistry at Coimbra. From 1777, Coimbra graduates soon descended upon Ajuda for further training, forming the cadre of the men who directed the scientific expeditions throughout the empire in the last quarter of the eighteenth century.[97]

While such continuities merit attention, the flowering of the academies and societies, though inconceivable without Pombal's earlier initiatives, undeniably occurred after 1779. The pace, frequency, intensity,

---

[93] Monteiro 2006, pp. 198–99. Monteiro noted that, excepting the noble titles/houses suppressed in 1759, the rest of those attacked by Pombal were restored to their former status under Dona Maria, a situation that would remain unchanged until 1832; the number of titled houses increased most substantially in the 1790s, and by 1820 their number had almost doubled, to 103 from 54, according to Disney 2009, vol. I, p. 313.

[94] A. R. C. da Silva 2006, pp. 48–52.

[95] Falcon 1982, p. 450.

[96] A. Almodovar and J. L. Cardoso, "From Learned Societies to Professional Associations: The Establishment of the Economist Profession in Portugal," in Augello and Guidi 2001, p. 127.

[97] Brigola 2003, pp. 100–40, 335.

and scope of these efforts represented a break from the Pombaline past. Broadly speaking, the Crown endeavored to tap civil society's resources to realize its ambitions. Statesmen believed, in Brazilian bishop and intellectual Azeredo Coutinho's phrase, that "education, customs, commerce, laws, discipline, vices, errors, opinions, and other factors decide the fate of empires."[98] Officials therefore encouraged scientists, ethnographers, travelers, and philosophically inclined administrators to submit reports which offered descriptive, and sometimes analytical, accounts of various natural, economic, and agricultural phenomena. These state-supported efforts – the maps drawn, the collections of flora and fauna assembled, and the reports penned – made the empire less abstract and made viable plans to extract natural resources and enhance the interdependence of the various ultramarine provinces.[99] The close affiliation of natural scientists, mathematicians, engineers, and men of letters was not without its perils. These men became dependent on state patronage. The production and dissemination of knowledge was thus converted into a means of social and professional advancement. Such dependence turned men of learning into the collaborators of a state intent on expanding the sphere of its authority.[100] There were numerous opportunities for such collaboration in the final quarter of the eighteenth century. Various new institutions were founded and patronized by the Crown during Dona Maria's reign: a Royal Naval Academy (1779); the *Casa Pia* (1782); a Royal Academy of Fortification, Artillery and Design (1790); a Royal Public library (1796); Royal Maritime, Military, and Geographic Society (1798); and a Royal Coast Guard Academy (1796).[101] The Royal Maritime Society, for example, attempted to improve cartography, develop new navigational techniques and charts, study ocean currents, compile detailed tidal charts, and draw topographical maps for the military's use.[102] All of these institutions were highly cosmopolitan and represented spaces in which books and ideas, regardless of provenance or language, were exchanged with few restrictions.

[98] Azeredo Coutinho 1966, p. 59.
[99] Raminelli 2008, p. 13. For the Spanish counterpart, see De Vos 2007 and Bleichmar 2012.
[100] Raminelli 2008, p. 137; Safier 2008, pp. 114–15. On the neglected connection between the enlightenment and "traditional centers of learning and official cultural institutions," see Hesse 2006, p. 502.
[101] On these latter of these societies, see P. F. de Matos 1981, pp. 251–79 passim; R. Cunha 1967. Additional information concerning the activities of the *Sociedade Marítima* may be found in the SGL, "Reservados" 146-maço 5–29.
[102] These activities are enumerated in Pereira 1832, pp. 62–63.

Perhaps the most influential of these new institutions was the Academy of Sciences (*Academia das Ciências de Lisboa*), founded in 1779. Its chief patron was an inveterate enemy of the disgraced Marquês, Duque de Lafões, Dona Maria I's uncle. The Academy was entrusted with the herculean task of amassing, analyzing, and diffusing knowledge concerning Portuguese colonial products, commodities, minerals, and geography in order to harness them more effectively. Among the Academy's chief duties was the dissemination of manuals and *memórias* on best practices in agriculture and the encouragement of modern techniques and practices. The Academy became a bastion of what its leading historian has termed *"agrarismo,"* or agrarianism, a term more suitable than physiocracy given the scarcity of explicit references to Quesnay or other French political economists associated with him in Portugal. Furthermore, an emphasis on agriculture and agrarian development was coupled with a distaste for mercantilism and special economic privileges, including monopoly. Such attitudes may be attributed to the anti-Pombaline sentiment, pervasive during the *Viradeira*, not a more sophisticated, physiocrat-inspired embrace of free trade ideas.[103]

Agrarianism represented an intellectual effort to conciliate between the forces of tradition and currents of modernization and to inscribe innovation within a conservative framework, as well as a direct response to declining mineral yields in Brazil. The prevailing spirit of accommodation and coexistence was symbolized by the Palace of Queluz – pink, rococo, set in the countryside, a far cry from the reserved neoclassicism of Pombaline urbanism – which became the main place from which new initiatives were directed and monitored. Agrarianism also intersected with, and served to fortify, other projects, specifically plans for an integrated empire, with the circulation of natural products and commodities acting as the glue connecting far-flung territories as well as the means to develop each part.[104] Agrarianism thus remained a flexible,

---

[103] J. L. Cardoso 1989, pp. 56, 67–74, 100, 122. Recently, some historians have challenged the sharp dichotomy between Pombaline mercantilism and Marian agrarian-free trade ideology, stressing the "eclecticism" of Portuguese political economy from 1750 on, including the influence of European cameralism. See A. M. Cunha 2010, p. 2; one might also point out that Marian agrarianism emerged directly from the institutions – university reform, botanical gardens, etc. – founded by Pombal. On these themes, see also Z. O. de Castro 1992; A. R. C. da Silva 2006; Kirschner 2009. There are clear connections between agrarianism and the contemporary British discourse of "improvement." See Drayton 2000.

[104] There were, of course, great limitations to the integrated vision. As A. R. C. da Silva 2006 argued, "though they shared mental schemes with a scientific basis in a transatlantic perspective, [Luso-Brazilian] bureaucrats and intellectuals demonstrated a much more fragmented and geographically specific awareness than that of metropolitan policy-makers," p. 167.

mobile rhetoric, one that could be utilized to support a range of ostensibly contradictory positions. On the one hand, it served the interests of Brazilians in search of greater prominence or an enhanced role within the transatlantic economy. On the other, it was employed by those who desired a concentration of resources on metropolitan Portugal, with less attention paid to its ultramarine appendages. The first position is represented by Azeredo Coutinho, who argued that "the metropole and the colonies, mainly with respect to agriculture and the products of the land, should be considered as a single building of a farmer, whose aim is to keep his house in the enjoyment of abundance and to have an overflow which he may sell to others."[105] Azeredo Coutinho argued that the cultivation and export of tropical commodities was beneficial to all parts of the Portuguese empire, providing "innumerable sailors and carpenters with employment, without which they would slip into laziness and poverty, the chief enemies of the state."[106] The notion that the prosperity of both hemispheres depended on agricultural growth could be manipulated by Brazilian merchants clamoring for assistance, including the defense of the slave trade. In the 1790s, Bahian merchants petitioned the Crown, claiming that "the happiness of the colonies consists in the expansion of their agriculture which has always depended on the number of workers devoted to it. Slave workers (for lack of others) are those who cultivate the immense lands of Brazil ... Any objections to the slave trade are attacks on the population, commerce, and income of Your Majesty."[107]

The second, pro-metropolitan position is represented by Diogo Inacio Pina Manique (1733–1805), who was suspicious of overreliance on colonial trade. He praised the Romans for having realized that "all of the precious goods of the East were useless without agriculture, from which are drawn the things that sustain life (*generos da primeira necessidade*) and by which population, and therefore the number of vassals, grows."[108] Five years later, in a private letter, he blamed Portugal's agricultural and population decline on overseas expansion. "The ambition of men to obtain riches," he indicated, prompted a veritable exodus from Portugal, leaving it with a smaller population and untilled fields.[109] If not exactly an anti-colonial discourse, Pina Manique seems to have imbibed Montesquieu's diagnosis of the ills facing the Iberian empires. His agrarianism suggests that new-fangled doctrines could be applied

---

[105] Azeredo Coutinho 1992, p. 153.
[106] Ibid., p. 196.
[107] Quoted in Postma and Schwartz 1995, p. 436.
[108] "Oficio de Pina Manique" (1785), in Tavares and Santos Pinto 1990, p. 140.
[109] "Carta de Pina Manique" (1785), in ibid., p. 148.

just as easily to the metropole as to the colonies, flexible enough to be used to argue for and against a range of mutually exclusive policies.

In its pursuit of agricultural improvement, the Academy of Sciences patronized and disseminated numerous tracts which advocated the transport of plants from one part of the empire to another, particularly Asian plants in Brazil. Dom Rodrigo described the "naturalization," or adaptation, of all economically valuable plants from other nations and their colonies as "a great object of the legislator."[110] This policy was pursued for the purposes of import substitution (lessening imports from abroad through self-sufficiency), the cultivation of additional commodities for export, and the creation of new linkages between component territories of the empire. Such efforts built on earlier initiatives: tobacco from Virginia was introduced in Bahia in 1757 whereas Carolina rice was grown in Pará and Maranhão by 1765.[111] One prescient Academy writer in the late 1780s, describing the means by which the Dutch "had taken coffee from Arabia to Suriname, where it was then smuggled to French Guiana," argued that the Portuguese authorities should obtain coffee plants since Brazil's climate and terrain differed little from the neighboring South American footholds of the Dutch and French.[112] Other advocates preferred the collection of Asian spices and their cultivation in Brazil, envisioning the capture of the European market.[113] In the 1780s and 1790s, there were frequent attempts to send pepper and cinnamon from India for cultivation in Bahia.[114]

An institutional manifestation of this obsession with such exchanges were botanical gardens. Following the success of the Lisbon botanical garden, the final decade of the eighteenth century saw their extension to Brazil. The first, founded in Belém (Pará) in 1796, was intended to serve as a model for others, though imitative efforts appeared slowly. Dom Rodrigo's plans for new gardens in Mozambique and Goa, for example, never came to fruition.[115] In 1808, the Court ordered the establishment of botanical gardens in São Paulo, Bahia, Pernambuco, Mato Grosso, and Goias. A botanical garden in Rio de Janeiro was opened in 1810, while Olinda's was operating by 1811.[116]

---

[110] R. de Souza Coutinho, "Memoria sobre o Melhoramento do Domínios de sua Majestade na América" (1797), in Souza Coutinho 1993, vol. II, p. 53. On the Academy's tracts, see Lyra 1994, p. 43.

[111] Silva Dias 1968, p. 112.

[112] João de Loureiro, "Da Transplantação das Árvores Mais Úteis de Países Remotos" (1789), in Memórias Económicas 1990, p. 126.

[113] See letters of Felix de Avellar Brotero to R. de Souza Coutinho, December 2, 1799, and November 4, 1799, reproduced in Jobim 1986, pp. 69–70, 76.

[114] Russell-Wood 1992, p. 155.   [115] Almeida 1975, p. 403.

[116] Jobim 1986, p. 91; M. B. N. da Silva 1999, pp. 27, 30, 60–62.

The integration of the natural sciences into the Coimbra curriculum, botanical exchange, new currents of political economy, and the interest in mapping, cataloguing, and describing empire converged in the scientific expeditions sent by the Crown to various ultramarine dominions from 1777. There were precedents for such expeditions: scientific-military expeditions were carried out prior to the 1750 Luso-Spanish treaty which definitively defined Ibero-America's borders, themselves modeled on earlier Franco-Spanish philosophical voyages.[117] Pre-Pombaline expeditions had a scientific component – the collection of empirical data, cartography, the taking of measurements – which would be inherited by later explorers.[118] Vandelli was the driving force behind the expeditions and he guided a generation of scientist-administrators, instructing them how to "collect, preserve, and remit" to Portugal the plants, minerals, and other objects they encountered during their peregrinations.[119] The best known of the expeditions undertaken was led by Alexandre Rodrigues Ferreira (1756–1815) between 1782 and 1792 to remote regions of Brazil.[120] Far from being a dispassionate search for knowledge, the military-administrative dimension of these expeditions was clear. Joaquim José da Silva and Manuel Galvão da Silva, for example, who led the expeditions sent in the late 1780s to Angola and Mozambique, respectively, played the dual roles of chief naturalist and administrator for those colonies.[121]

Apart from Crown efforts in the principal cities of the empire, there were further efforts in the provinces to debate and disseminate doctrines of political economy, which formed part of a broader effort to foment agricultural production and local craft industries. Among other foreign works, Spanish reformer Campomanes's tract on popular industry was translated into Portuguese and published in 1778.[122] There were various efforts to form economic societies, inspired by earlier precedents in Dublin (1731), Florence (1753), London (1754), and elsewhere, but chiefly by contemporary Spanish examples.[123] These forerunners had numerous goals, including the reform of public finance, the dissemination of agronomical knowledge and commercial skills, the training of peasants and craftsmen,

[117] Brigola 2003; Safier 2008.
[118] A. Domingues 1991, p. 17.
[119] Vandelli (1779), cited in Brigola 2003.
[120] On these expeditions, see Simon 1983.
[121] Mello Pereira 2010, p. 153; Russell-Wood 1992, p. 176.
[122] Pedro Rodríguez de Campomanes, *Discurso Acerca do Modo de Fomentar a Industria do Povo* (Lisbon, 1778).
[123] On contemporary Spanish economic societies, see Paquette 2008, ch. 4.

the promotion of technical innovations, and the economic education of the upper classes.[124] In Portugal, the first economic society was founded in Ponte de Lima (Minho) (1779); it was followed by societies in Elvas (1781), the Douro (1783), Évora (1784), Valença (1789), and Funchal (1790).[125] In a speech opening the Ponte de Lima society, called the *Sociedade Económica dos Amigos do Bem Público*, one of its members claimed that its remit was broad, encompassing not only agriculture and cottage industries, but also the mechanical arts and manufactures. He christened the society "a school of politics, where the nobility is taught how to conduct itself when placed in positions of responsibility, the sublime science of understanding the true interests of the state."[126] Few of these societies, in contrast to their Spanish counterparts, survived beyond infancy and their long-term influence is difficult to assess. They were never extended to Brazil, unlike in Spanish America, where they multiplied and flourished.

The publication and translation projects which the economic societies might otherwise have undertaken were subsumed into the extensive publication program undertaken by the *Casa Literaria do Arco do Cego*, based in Lisbon, which operated between 1799 and 1801. The brainchild of Souza Coutinho in the 1790s, it was directed by the *Mineiro* Franciscan and botanist, José Mariano da Conceição Veloso (1742–1811).[127] Its purpose was to publish and disseminate the most important works of agronomy for a Luso-Atlantic readership. Already as ambassador in Turin in the 1780s, Souza Coutinho noted that "given the present state of learning in Europe, with the *luzes* diffused generally throughout the continent, those states and nations which have played the most important role in politics are those which have protected and encouraged the *luzes*."[128] Souza Coutinho commissioned a list of foreign-language books concerning agriculture to be drawn up which would "provide the best ideas which we can take advantage

[124] M. Augello and M. Guidi, "Nineteenth-century Economic Societies in a Comparative Approach," in Augello and Guidi 2001, pp. 6–7; J. Livesey's stimulating thesis concerning the counterintuitive relationship between the rise of civil society and the British empire's disempowerment of local, provincial elites resonates in the seeming contradiction between the existence of a robust local civic life in an age of state centralization in Portugal. See Livesey 2009, pp. 7, 23.

[125] J. L. Cardoso 1989, pp. 110–11.

[126] Manuel da Silva Baptista Vasconcelos, quoted ibid., p. 111. On this society, see Ramos 2007, p. 109.

[127] F. M. G. de Campos 1999, pp. 26–45; Safier 2009a.

[128] Souza Coutinho, "Discurso em que se Prova a Necessidade e Utilidade dos Estudos e Conhecimentos Hidrodinâmicas em Portugal" (1787), in R. de Souza Coutinho 1993, vol. I, p. 174.

of."[129] Dom Rodrigo (and many others) believed that the dissemination of knowledge would result in greater productivity. As Dom Rodrigo described the initiative, these tracts would be printed "at the expense of the *Real Fazenda*" and sent to the governors in Brazil in order to "spread [new] knowledge which could produce considerable advantages" or to "perfect old methods of cultivation." The tracts included titles such as *Memoria sobre a Reforma dos Alambiques* and *Methodo para Preparar a Cochinilha*, as well as an untitled description of sugar-processing methods in the English and French Antilles. He encouraged the local *câmaras* to award prizes to those who first successfully introduced these new or improved methods, and promised that he would hire someone to "translate many useful works to expand as *culturas* of Brazil."[130] Veloso ultimately undertook this enormous task, collecting agricultural tracts, mainly in French and English and related chiefly to the Antillean sugar industry, translating them, and publishing them together under the title *O Fazendeiro do Brasil*, eleven volumes of which had appeared by 1806.[131] Veloso envisioned an encore second series, chiefly translations of works concerned with ranching and livestock production, but he only succeeded in publishing a first volume on cheese, milk, and butter.[132]

Few of these initiatives and new institutions had counterparts in the colonies prior to the transfer of the Court, when Coast Guard and Military academies were established in Rio de Janeiro (1810). In the eighteenth century, Viceroy Lavradio sanctioned the creation of an *Academia Científica* in 1772. It was renamed the *Sociedade Literaria* in 1786 and survived until 1794. It produced *memórias* on indigo, cochineal, and other products while disseminating European treatises on chemistry, natural history, and astronomy. The obvious limitations on colonial intellectual life were the absences of a printing press—this

---

[129] BNRJ, Coleção Linhares, I-29, 16, 35, "Lista de Livros de Agricultura Ingleses nos quais se encontrão as melhores idéias para se aproveitar" (n.d.); It should be noted that Souza Coutinho was highly regarded by the British political writers he encountered while in Turin, including Arthur Young, who praised him in the 1791 *Annals of Agriculture*; Dom Rodrigo's schemes were not viewed favorably by others whose enlightened credentials were equally impeccable. F. S. Constâncio declared that Dom Rodrigo accomplished little because "his imagination was too wild, and his temper too violent, even to put into practice the confused and superficial ideas which agitated his mind ... his numerous projects were either defective in principle or perverted in their execution"; see Constâncio, "The State of Portugal during the Last 30 Years," in the *Monthly Repository of English Literature* (Paris, 1808), reproduced in Constâncio 1995, p. 15.

[130] ANRJ, Secretário de Estado do Brasil, cod. 67, vol. 23, R. de Souza Coutinho to Rezende, January 3 and 4, 1798 and March 2, 1798, fos. 2, 6, 28.

[131] R. Marquese 1999, pp. 104–5.

[132] Galloway 1979, p. 775.

arrived with the royal family in 1808—and a university, both of which conspired to diminish the number of venues where polite, literate exchanges occurred and the number of Brazilians equipped to participate in them. But the Court's presence from 1808 offered fresh opportunities. At least one government official advocated the establishment of economic societies in every captaincy, province, and *conquista* of the empire, devoted to "discovering effective means of promoting the prosperity of various branches of industry and agriculture."[133] José Bonifácio pressed for the creation of schools offering instruction in modern chemistry applicable to agriculture.[134] Reformist tracts, heirs of the *Arco do Cego* initiative, continued to be published, including Bahian planter Manuel Jacinto de Sampaio e Melo's 1816 *Novo Método de Fazer o Açucar*.[135] As late as 1819, the Crown still received, though with lesser frequency, proposals for new initiatives in the north of Brazil. "With more exotic plants," one such tract argued, "Pará could become a new Ceylon."[136]

The impact of foreign ideas: emulation and its discontents

Like their Spanish counterparts, Portuguese reformers had a deeply ambivalent attitude toward foreign ideas, concepts, and models. Economic nationalism and geopolitical competition generated the resentment and envy of rivals. But extensive experience abroad, an intellectual cosmopolitanism characteristic of the late enlightenment, and a pragmatism engendered by long apprenticeships in the rough-and-tumble world of politics fueled robust engagement with non-Portuguese ideas and practices. Such experiences often led to the conclusion that cautious, critical emulation was the sole path to national renewal. Emulation, then, would enable policy-makers to harness the ideas they believed had permitted rivals to surpass them,

---

[133] Ambrosio Joaquim dos Reis, "Sobre a Situação da Monarquia Portuguesa depois da Paz de Paris de 1814, indicando algumas providências para a melhorar" (1815), reproduced in J. V. Capela 1993, doc. 7, p. 116.

[134] José Bonifácio de Andrada e Silva, "Necessidade de uma Academia de Agricultura no Brasil" (n.d.), in Bonifácio 1973, p. 45.

[135] R. Marquese 1999, p. 112.

[136] IHGB, lata 289, pasta 6, "Memória que contém breves e vagas reflexões sobre a Capitanía do Pará" (1819). It is evident that this idea was attractive, for the former Intendant-General for Guiana in 1809–10, J. Severiano Maciel da Costa, later the influential politician Marquês de Queluz, boasted in 1821 that he had been responsible for bringing higher-grade sugar to Brazil from French Guiana during the occupation, "which is far superior to what we had and its introduction has tripled the profits of the *engenhos*," quoted in Macedo 1983, pp. 59–60.

self-consciously adapt them to local circumstances, and outstrip their rivals.[137]

Many of the prominent figures of the Luso-Atlantic enlightenment spent significant periods abroad, or maintained extensive networks of foreign contacts: Martinho de Mendonça de Pina e Proença (1693–1743), an important exponent of Lockean ideas, met Christian Wolf in Saxony, wrote tracts on the education of the nobility, and served as a governor in Brazil on several occasions.[138] Dom Francisco Xavier de Meneses (1674–1743) was a member of the Royal Society of London and director of Portugal's Royal Academy of History. Luís Antonio Vernei's *O Verdadeiro Methodo de Estudar*, published in Naples in 1746, exerted tremendous influence. Pombal's pedigree, boasting ambassadorial stints in London and Vienna, is emblematic of a broader phenomenon. Pombal's enemy, Duque de Lafões, wiled away his exile in London, where he became a member of the Royal Society, and later served Frederick the Great during the Seven Years War, before returning to Portugal in the late 1770s.[139] Portugal also was remarkably receptive to foreign intellectuals and several of the pivotal figures and texts in Portuguese enlightened reform hailed from abroad. The aforementioned Paduan Vandelli directed the botanical garden at Ajuda and galvanized the scientific expeditions sent to far-flung portions of the Portuguese empire in the 1770s and 1780s. Major palaces and public buildings drew inspiration from the designs of foreign architects. The Palace-Monastery of Mafra, for example, was built by the German architect J. F. Ludwig between 1717 and 1730 while Coimbra's astronomical observatory was designed according to the principles of English military engineering.[140]

The existing historiography's emphasis on *estrangeirados* – both Portuguese enamored of, and reliant upon, ideas derived from abroad and foreigners who influenced Portuguese intellectual life – suggests the absence of a "native" enlightenment in Portugal, or at least its derivative nature and shallow roots.[141] It may be argued, however, that the attempt

---

[137] Self-conscious emulation in Portugal is discussed in Maxwell 1973; and Maxwell 1995. More generally, see Drayton 2000; Paquette 2008; and Reinert 2011.

[138] Maxwell 1995, p. 10.

[139] Monteiro and Costa 2006. Not that his cosmopolitan pedigree impressed everyone: William Beckford complained that "he is so like an old lady of the bedchamber, so fiddle faddle, and so coquettish and so gossiping." See Beckford 2006, p. 117.

[140] Beales 2003, p. 123; and Delaforce 2002, p. 265.

[141] On the problem of core-periphery diffusionist models in the enlightenment, see J. Robertson 2005; and Hesse 2006. For a general critique of their pernicious influence in understanding Ibero-Atlantic intellectual life *c.* 1750–1850, see Fernández Sebastián 2009.

to uncover the foreign origins of, say, Pombal's urban renewal of Lisbon is a misconceived enterprise, for foreign influences intermingled with Portuguese precedent in peculiar circumstances to create an original style.[142] Recognition of foreign influence, then, should not serve to disparage the limits and provincialism of Portuguese intellectual life, thus discrediting it. Instead, Portuguese cultural life's foreign accent may be interpreted more charitably, as suggestive of the unusual intellectual openness that prevailed. It was accepted widely, often without comment, by contemporaries. Two examples from very different spheres illustrate this point. First, at the inaugural performance at the Real Teatro de São Carlos (June 30, 1793), itself named in honor of the Dona Carlota Joaquina, the Spanish princess recently married to the future Dom João VI, the opera *La Ballerina Amante*, by Italian Domenico Cimarosa, was performed. The entire cast came from Italy, including the *castrato* Caporalini; Russian candles illuminated the hall, drawing attention to the beams constructed with wood from Brazil.[143] Second, the intellectual underpinnings of Portuguese regalism were an amalgam of ideas drawn from non-Portuguese writers and home-grown talent. To provide intellectual ballast to his sweeping efforts to expel the Jesuits from Portuguese territory and reduce the Inquisition to a tribunal dependent on the Portuguese state, Pombal ordered the translation of Nicolaus von Hontheim's 1763 treatise opposing the monarchical conception of the papacy. Yet Pombaline regalism also was nurtured by Portuguese texts, including Antonio Ribeiro dos Santos's *De Sacerdotio et Imperio* (1770), which called for the Church to be considered autonomous and separate from the state, limited to doctrines and sacraments.[144] These two examples suggest the inadequacy of center-periphery models of cultural diffusion in attempting to understand Portuguese intellectual life. The compatibility of cultural forms of different provenance permitted a rich hybrid culture to flourish.

Beyond libretti and canon law tracts, international influence seeped into Portugal from the experience of travel. Some Luso-Brazilian students spurned Coimbra and pursued degrees from Montpellier, Edinburgh, and several Central European universities. Extended periods of diplomatic service also encouraged a receptiveness to foreign

[142] França 1983, pp. 160, 304–5. As Hesse 2006 noted, "in most places, the European enlightenment emerged and operated in a series of self-constituting, polycentric, transnational, and multilingual moments at local, regional and even continental levels," p. 505.
[143] Boléo 2009, p. 241; Brito 1989, p. 110.
[144] Maxwell 1995, pp. 91–94; compare with Spanish regalism, as analyzed in Paquette 2008, ch. 2.

ideas. In a dispatch from Turin, Dom Rodrigo remarked, "among the duties of a diplomat who resides at a foreign court perhaps there is none more interesting and useful than that of recording and transmitting the current state of affairs in the country, the causes which have secured its prosperity or hastened its decline."[145] In another document, he suggested that "it is a just ambition of all governments to bring to their vassals the *luzes* enjoyed by more enlightened nations, recognizing that a nation's future greatness depends on the use of such principles."[146] "Agriculture is not something learned by chance," another political writer noted; "it is an art, even a science":

When the king of Naples wanted to improve the agriculture of his kingdom, he sent an intelligent man to apprentice himself to one of the most successful farmers in England, in order to learn the best techniques. Upon his return [to Naples], the king ordered that this man set up a school, and gave him land upon which he could practice, for the benefit of all, what he had learned abroad.[147]

The translation program undertaken by the *Arco do Cego* was but one response to this challenge. Another was the policy of dispatching university-educated men to foreign countries to observe techniques and practices pertinent to Portugal in all areas of commerce and agriculture. The *Arco do Cego*'s mastermind, Veloso, for example, relied on agents stationed abroad to collect relevant publications. In September 1798, he instructed the twenty-four-year-old Brazilian Hipólito da Costa, in Philadelphia, to send to Lisbon "all the works that are printed related to political, economic, physical or geographical subjects."[148] Hipólito was further commissioned to acquire as much information as possible in the nascent USA concerning tobacco, linen, and fruit-bearing trees in addition to the mercantile regulations (e.g. customs and tariffs) then in effect.[149] Other Coimbra men, such as the *Paulista* José Bonifácio, were sent to Central and Eastern Europe to imbibe new advances in chemistry, metallurgy, and mineralogy.[150]

As Souza Coutinho and others hinted, Portuguese political writers and reformers of the late eighteenth century were intensely aware, and

---

[145] R. de Souza Coutinho, "Reflexões Políticas sobre os Motivos da Prosperidade da Agricultura deste País, que Servem a Fazer Praticamente as Vantajosas Consequências dos Sábios Princípios Adotados" (1789), in Souza Coutinho 1993, vol. I, p. 141.

[146] Souza Coutinho, "Recopilação dos Ofícios Expedidos de Turim no Ano de 1786," January 3, 1787, in R. de Souza Coutinho 1993, vol. I, p. 79.

[147] ANRJ, Diversos Códices 807, vol. 21, Agostinho Ignácio da Costa Quintela, "Verdadeiro Projeto ou Breve Discurso para se Aumentar a Agricultura em Portugal" (n.d.), fo. 7.

[148] Quoted in Safier 2009a, p. 263.

[149] E. F. dos Santos 1999, p. 114.   [150] Lyra 1994, p. 48.

often ashamed, that their nation had fallen behind the rest of Europe (though they surely exaggerated the gap). They therefore sought to expedite the process of "catching up" through the eclectic consumption of foreign ideas and texts. William Beckford described an impassioned speech given to him in 1787 by Prince Dom José (1761–88), heir to the throne before he succumbed to smallpox, in which he revealed a plan to "clear away the rubbish of ages" by adopting the policies of Joseph II of Austria, confessing he hoped that he possessed "sufficient manliness to imitate them."[151] But importation from abroad was not "artificial" grafting or imposition on to an inert or unresponsive Portuguese reality. There was nothing meretricious about it. Creative borrowing was a response to circumstances where tradition held sway.[152]

The argument, however, should not be overstated. Suspicion toward foreign ideas, often deemed hostile to religion, was pervasive. The Inquisition, enfeebled by Pombal, pursued an active campaign against the readers of purportedly atheistic and impious texts, forcing distribution and discussion of them underground. Before the outbreak of the French Revolution, there was significant resistance to "novelties." Not all administrators were enamored by their potential for edification, believing that they generated more trouble than enlightenment. "Novelties," Viceroy Lavradio observed in 1770, "do not offer this country anything that could be of interest to anyone, and only serve to increase unrest, thus multiplying the cares of he who governs it."[153] After 1789, advocacy of emulation by government officials declined dramatically. The methods of enlightened absolutist regimes, for example, were defended as equally as meritorious as those employed by constitutional monarchies.[154] The underlying tension between the state as a sponsor of enlightenment, as an incubator of ideas in the public interest, and as a repressive force surfaced. This tension is embodied in the figure of Pina Manique, who served as intendant-general of police from 1780 until 1803, combining the assiduous care of police functions – the vigilant surveillance of all places of assembly, especially taverns and cafes, for signs of subversive activity – with the ambitions of a farsighted social reformer. He founded new institutions aimed at

---

[151] Beckford 1834, vol. II, pp. 222–26 passim.
[152] A. R. C. da Silva 2006, pp. 39, 79.
[153] Lavradio to Conde de Vilaverde, September 11, 1770, in Lavradio 1978, p. 46.
[154] In a 1791 dispatch, Souza Coutinho remarked that "absolutist governments can produce a level of public prosperity not merely to the absurd and unstable government of France, but also to those governments in which the principles of liberty are perfectly understood and where limited monarchy exists, as in England." Souza Coutinho (1791), quoted in Alves da Silva 1997, p. 86.

poor relief; galvanized the study of science, medicine, and the arts; and oversaw road-building.[155] But thwarting the spread of revolutionary doctrines took priority over all else. As he wrote in 1799, "my responsibility is to extinguish any seditious spark, blown into Portugal by the spirit of the century, which might result in revolutionary upheaval and compromise the security of the state."[156] Fears of revolutionary plots in Portugal's colonies were equally pervasive. Mello e Castro granted a passport to the French naturalist La Peyrouse in 1792, but alerted Portuguese officials in Brazil to the "pernicious and perverse intent of the Clubs in Europe to propagate their destructive principles of liberty and equality," ideas with which they "destroyed" France, "converting the best of governments into a horrid anarchy, reducing in three years a nation which was once so opulent to a decadent, or ruined, state." He wrote that such ideas already had reached the "French colonies, causing the slaves to rise up against their *senhores* and igniting a civil war, in which the most horrendous cruelties have been committed, exceeding even those of the most barbaric and ferocious nations."[157]

Such anxieties were pervasive, forcing even Souza Coutinho to recoil from his enthusiasm for the translation and dissemination of texts from other languages. During the heyday of translation projects, which reached its apogee in the *Arco do Cego* project, Souza Coutinho reconsidered his older notions concerning public instruction with a view toward preventing revolutionary ideas from infecting the populace. He instructed the officials in Bahia to encourage the study of ancient Greek, arguing that

given the latest and disgraceful convulsions which have agitated Europe, the study of ancient languages, and their immortal authors, helps to preserve respect for, and veneration of, things established long ago and serves as a corrective to, and defense against, the [ideas] of innovators.[158]

In the first decades of the nineteenth century, frustrated political writers lamented that reformers who "dared decry the evils [Portugal's empire] endured" would be branded as "impious, atheistic, incendiary, revolutionary Jacobins, worthy of hatred and persecution."[159]

---

[155] Disney 2009, vol. I, 319.
[156] Pina Manique to Marquez Majordomo Mor, August 8, 1799, quoted in Biléu, "Pina Manique," vol. II, p. 80.
[157] ANRJ, Secretário de Estado do Brasil, cod. 67, vol. 18, Mello e Castro to Conde de Rezende [José Luiz de Castro], February 21, 1792, fo. 149v; Philippe Picot, Baron de la Peyrouse (1744–1818).
[158] ANRJ, Vice-Reinado, cx. 748, pacote 1, R. de Souza Coutinho to Fernando José de Portugal, August 5, 1799.
[159] JCBL, Codex Portugal 7, "Ensaio Económico e Político sobre o Pará" (1816), fo. 30.

Politically induced fear of foreign influences was joined to a concern that the uncritical adulation of foreign ideas would not yield the results Portuguese policy-makers desired. Borrowing alone would not meet Portugal's goals. Vandelli displayed his cognizance of this fact when he argued that "we have an almost exorbitant abundance of economic books, written in many languages, but not everything contained in these books is applicable to the climate of this country."[160] It was the spirit, and not the exact policy, which should be imitated. Vandelli held up England, France, Denmark, Sweden, and Switzerland as examples where "good laws and prizes encourage the agriculture of those countries."[161] It was these factors, not a surfeit of translated texts, which would determine Portugal's fortunes.

Controlling territory, re-shaping subjects

Though the Crown's first priority was the extirpation of obstacles blocking growth, a close second was the reorganization of territory and concomitant establishment of new institutions, all in the pursuit of improvement of subjects and lands for the benefit of the sovereign and polity, in accordance with the ideas sketched in the previous section. The Crown's active incorporation of rustic peripheries in the Old World and New is one of the defining features of the period. The term "periphery" should be understood in the broadest, least disparaging, and most capacious sense. Generally speaking, peripheries were a heterogeneous collection of under- or unpopulated zones, not yet contributing fully to the colonial or metropolitan economy, but endowed with resources or a strategic geographic position making them worthy targets of government attention and largesse. They were located near Lisbon – the Alentejo was a common target – as well as on distant frontiers far from even second-tier colonial outposts. The aims and strategy in all cases was remarkably similar: the establishment of effective political control and the economic integration of the territory in question into pre-existing commercial dynamics.

---

[160] Domingos Vandelli, "Memoria sobre a pública instrução agrária" (1788), in J. V. Serrão 1994, p. 131; earlier debates on this topic may be found in Maxwell 1973, pp. 1–2.
[161] D. Vandelli, "Memoria sobre a Agricultura deste Reino e das Suas Conquistas" (1789), in *Memórias Económicas* 1990, p. 127; prizes for agricultural improvement in Brazil were proposed by Souza Coutinho in 1798. See ANRJ, Secretário de Estado do Brasil, cod. 67, vol. 23, R. de Souza Coutinho to Rezende, January 4, 1798, fo. 6.

As previously outlined, Pombal sought to govern the empire as a whole, striving to integrate its far-flung components into a more cohesive and complementary unit centered at Lisbon. To be sure, he prioritized already prosperous "core" areas. As he told Lavradio in the early 1760s, "the greatest and most important interest of the Portuguese crown today is the security and conservation of Rio de Janeiro in its current respectable state."[162] Colonial policy from 1760 until 1808 reflected this assessment, and Pombal ignored numerous pleas from peripheries during his ascendancy. In 1758, the Viceroy of India, Conde da Ega, reported that Goa was "in the saddest state imaginable, without a navy, without troops, its commerce extinct, and its manufactures collapsed, and a people in dire poverty." Yet, as late as 1764, Pombal apologetically informed him that no assistance was forthcoming, for the costs incurred in the pursuit of reforms in Portugal itself – including the reorganization of the army and the construction of better fortifications – "do not permit SM to provide relief for the *conquistas*, at least those that are not for the moment vulnerable to attack."[163]

These caveats and exceptions notwithstanding, metropolitan administrators sought to enhance the interaction, cooperation, and interdependence of the different territories, which entailed lavishing attention on the periphery. Officials strove to increase their control over territory. Policy implementation was impossible without significant modification to the territories targeted for change. Territorial organization was defective insofar as it impeded the exercise of metropolitan power and the uniform administration of justice.[164] There were many manifestations of this re-imagining and re-shaping of imperial space: the definition and preservation of Brazil's outer limits, including its borders with Spanish America and French Guiana; the creation of new administrative divisions; the conquest and colonization of lands beyond the pale of settlement, one which deprived Amerindians of self-government or, as in Amazonia, sought to make them docile vassals, fashioning them into a compliant workforce; the founding of new towns to foment commerce and consumption; European settlement schemes through induced emigration; and the clearing of forests, the extension of roads, and the improvement of the navigability of fluvial routes.

---

[162] Quoted in Hoppe 1970, p. 307.

[163] Conde da Ega to Joaquim da Costa Corte-Real, December 10, 1758; and Conde de Oeiras [Pombal] to Conde da Ega, April 10, 1764, both reproduced in Saldanha 1984, pp. 106, 283; in 1763, Pombal explicitly had ordered the end of the *Estado da Índia*'s further territorial expansion; thereafter, its policy was to be "defensive and non-expansionary"; see Disney 2009, vol. II, p. 322.

[164] A. C. N. da Silva 1998, p. 373.

Such an undertaking required the extirpation of groups whose activities and autonomy interfered with Crown objectives, whether the *commissarios volantes*, contraband traders, or economically powerful Jesuits. Closely linked to this pursuit, and often simultaneous with it, was the quest for local, empirical knowledge which could inform policy. Using geographical maps, population charts, historical texts, and political treatises, an historian has observed recently, the Portuguese state "began to impose grids and graphs onto rivers, forests, and Amerindian settlements."[165] Pombal's tenure in office coincided with administrative innovations tending toward bureaucratic rationalization, including the standardization of the information contained in administrative reports sent from the colonies. As an historian of Pombaline Angola explained recently, "by means of a uniform reading grid, that distant world, seemingly different and plural, became simultaneously perceptible and manipulable, thanks to methods of normalized description and assessment."[166] There were numerous obstacles to the realization of this objective, not least the personnel. A pervasive sense developed that administration in Brazil, as elsewhere, had been poor and that the selection of administrators according to different criteria was urgent. "One of the chief causes of America's decadence," Vasconcelos told Mello e Castro, was the "lack of zeal and diligence of its governors," who brought with them "laziness and indolence" and therefore left the *povos* under their government "without law, order, discipline, industry, or commerce."[167]

The root problem, however, was the absence of information that could inform policy, define its objectives, and set its limits. "[We] need better information concerning the physical and political state of the Ultramarine dominions," Dom Rodrigo bluntly stated in 1796.[168] In a letter to Bahia's governor, he stressed that such knowledge was necessary to "determine the necessary measures to promote the good of [the king's] vassals." To that end, he solicited geographical descriptions and topographical maps, together with accounts of the population, divided by race ("*brancos, negros, e pardos*"). Above all, Dom Rodrigo requested "a most detailed *relação*, which gives the precise quantity and quality of this *estado*'s products and their final destination, together with a specific description of which goods are imported from [Portugal]

[165] Safier 2008, p. 113.
[166] C. M. Santos 2010, p. 546.
[167] ANRJ, Secretário de Estado do Brasil, cod. 67, vol. 12, Vasconcelos to Mello e Castro, October 2, 1784, fos. 232v.–233.
[168] ANRJ, cod. 67, vol. 21, R. de Souza Coutinho to Rezende, September 1, 1796, fo. 72.

to Bahia, indicating which ones are actually of Portuguese origin."[169]
The quest for more precise information of the sort solicited by Dom
Rodrigo soon dovetailed with an infatuation with data and statistics
(however primitive) which would inform colonial administration until
the eve of Brazil's independence. In 1803, a political economist contended that training in economics should be mandatory for any person
seeking admission to higher education or seeking government employment.[170] "Without statistics," an administrator noted in his 1819 report
on Maranhão, "public administration will commit fresh errors every
day ... the legislator, the economist, the diplomat, and the general can
neither plan or improve," and policy will be nothing but "the offspring
of caprice and despotism."[171]

Territory, too, demanded reorganization and reconfiguration. Direct
communication between Lisbon and Mozambique, whose officials formerly had reported to their superiors in Goa, was established from
1752.[172] The seat of the Brazilian viceroyalty was transferred from Bahia
to Rio de Janeiro in 1763. New captaincies were carved from territories
too large to administer directly. Between 1752 and 1754, the Crown
subsumed the remaining donatory captaincies, indemnifying former
holders with pensions and titles. The quasi-independent territory of
Amazonia, comprising Grão-Pará and Maranhão, was dissolved but
remained dependent on Lisbon, not Rio de Janeiro. Efforts were made
to integrate far-flung regions into an imperial communication network.[173] One step toward this goal was the abolition of the *frota* (fleet)
system in 1765: thereafter licensed vessels were free to sail between
ports where privileged companies did not enjoy exclusive rights.[174] A
second important innovation was the creation of a uniform, state-run
postal service, which linked the coastal ports to the interior of Brazil,
a major step toward the strategic integration of Brazil.[175] Within territories, new urban planning techniques and theories, which came into
vogue during the reconstruction of Lisbon after the 1755 earthquake,
with neatly drawn grids and symmetrical squares to replace the disor-
ganized medieval topography, were exported to Porto, the Algarve, and
then to Brazil. A network of towns was founded on southern coastal and

---

[169] BNRJ, 33, 29, 50, R. de Souza Coutinho to Fernando José de Portugal, September
14, 1796.
[170] Brito 1803, vol. I, p. 66.
[171] Lago 1822, p. 9; the report was written in 1819, and published three years later.
[172] *Relações de Moçambique Setecentista* 1955, p. 6.
[173] On these and other changes, see Falcon 2001, p. 194; and Barman 1988, p. 21.
[174] Mansuy-Diniz Silva, "Portugal and Brazil," in Bethell 1984, p. 491.
[175] Davidson 1970, p. 84.

highland routes, resembling those urbanization projects undertaken previously in the north of Brazil.[176]

To territorial reorganization was joined the refashioning of the populations contained within their boundaries. In Amazonia, under the direction of Pombal's half-brother, Francisco Xavier de Mendonça Furtado, the Crown broke decisively with its traditional policy of leaving Indian communities isolated in Church-run *aldeias* by encouraging intermarriage with Portuguese settlers, acculturation, and what one historian aptly termed the "occidentalization" of Amazonian space.[177] Portuguese soldiers who intermarried were eligible for various rewards, including freedom from certain types of service and deployment.[178] The 1757 Indian Directorate was an almost revolutionary initiative, seeking not merely to transform economic production and the *aldeias* into peninsular-style towns, but also to acculturate indigenous inhabitants through the promotion of Portuguese cultural norms of dress, language, and religion. Nudity, for example, was banned.[179] Indians were expected to interact and compete with *mestiços*, freed blacks, and poor whites. Non-elite Indians were compelled to devote themselves to agriculture, or expeditions to collect natural products, or to toil away in state service.[180] Indian policy was complemented by fresh attempts to wrest control of territory from absentee or derelict owners. The Crown then made pacified territories attractive to settlement, the nuclei of which were newly established towns. The state recruited European settlers, with three hundred Azorean families arriving in the decade of the 1760s.[181] Portuguese residents of the moribund fortress-town of Mazagão, in modern Morocco, too, were transplanted to Amazonia in 1769–70. More than two thousand Mazangistas eventually settled in Macapá, Vila Nova de Mazagão, and other new urban nuclei.[182] Various inducements were offered to entice settlers and to encourage intermarriage with indigenous women, but settlers seeking to leave Pará were stymied by various regulations, including the need to obtain the governor's permission before leaving and the general prohibition forbidding ships from disembarking with illicit passengers on board.[183] Analogous efforts were made throughout Brazil. In the Eastern *Sertão*, for example,

[176] Delson 1976, pp. 41, 46.
[177] A. Domingues 2000, p. 66.
[178] Ibid., p. 105.
[179] Sommer 2000, p. 69.
[180] Harris 2010, pp. 115, 141; Roller 2010, p. 436.
[181] Sommer 2000, pp. 70–71, 75, 95.
[182] Vidal 2007, pp. 18, 38.
[183] A. Domingues 2000, pp. 100–101.

eighty or more *bandeiras* set out in the second half of the eighteenth century.[184] In 1803, the transplanted monarchy declared war on the Botocudo Indians and offered various inducements for Europeans to settle the newly conquered territory. These included: a ten-year exemption from payment of the tithe collected by the government on behalf of the Church; and excused payment of debts owed to the Crown for six years; no taxes imposed on goods imported to, or exported from, the region for a decade; and the stipulation that military commanders could divide up among them *sesmarias* on lands seized from the Botocudo.[185]

The acquisition of, or at least securing recognition of control over, territory also resulted from arrangements and compromises with rival European powers. The fuzzily demarcated borders separating Spanish and Portuguese America spawned disputes between Madrid and Lisbon, sometimes pushing them to the brink of war. The 1750 Treaty of Madrid (the so-called "Treaty of the Limits") guaranteed Spanish control of the Colonia de Sacramento, and exclusive jurisdiction over the Río de la Plata, in exchange for recognition of Portuguese supremacy in the Amazon, a great swathe of territory on the eastern bank of the Uruguay river, and a mutual guarantee of support should either of their American colonies suffer attack from a third power. By 1761, however, Pombal's misgivings about the forfeiture of both Colonia and navigation rights on the Río de la Plata, combined with Charles III's dissatisfaction with the extent of the ceded territory, again put the Iberian neighbors on the brink of war. Throughout the 1760s and 1770s, proxy skirmishes in the Banda Oriental ensued, as the terms of the 1750 Treaty were honored rarely if at all. Spanish administrators in Buenos Aires disparaged the "bad faith and sophistries of the Portuguese, who try to persuade Europe that we have usurped that which is rightfully theirs."[186] The 1777 Treaty of San Ildefonso effectively ended the dispute, certifying Portugal's loss of Colônia de Sacramento, but its retention of coastal Rio Grande do Sul and its recovery of Santa Catarina. Spain, for its part, maintained control of the Seven Missions territory.[187] The 1778 Treaty of El Pardo significantly enhanced the "*amizade e garantia*" between the two Iberian neighbors, further buttressed in 1785 by the fateful marriage of the Prince Dom João to the Princess Dona Carlota Joaquina. By the terms of the 1778 treaty, Portugal ceded the islands of Ano Bom and Fernando Po' to Spain, providing it with the long-desired

---

[184] Langfur 2006, p. 164.   [185] Ibid., pp. 273–74.
[186] Archivo General de la Nación [Buenos Aires], IX-4-3-6, Molina to Bucareli, October 28, 1766.
[187] Alden 1961, pp. 60, 72–73; Alden 1969, pp. 154–65.

foothold on the African coast for the slave trade it had relinquished in the 1479 Treaty of Alcaçovas. The Portuguese Crown, which had paid scant attention to these islands, ceded them in exchange for a freer hand in the Banda Oriental.[188] In this way, territorial consolidation was contingent upon, and sometimes occurred as a result of, geopolitical settlements. It relied on the swapping of territories in order to pursue imperial priorities.

These arrangements had practical consequences. The 1777 and 1778 treaties, for example, enabled Portugal to encourage wheat-growing. Cereals had been among Portugal's major imports throughout the eighteenth century – from Morocco, Italy, and the Germanic States – with an adverse impact on its balance of payments.[189] Portugal reduced its foreign dependence by importing wheat from Rio Grande do Sul. Furthermore, the newly productive region supplied the drought-ravaged northeast of Brazil with dried meat, hides, and wheat during its famine years of 1791–93 and 1809–10.[190] Secure control over territory, then, made possible concerted economic development, served the cause of a self-contained, integrated empire, and set the stage for further territorial gains. With the outbreak of revolution in Spanish America in 1808–9, the Crown expanded its machinations in the Banda Oriental, which it occupied in 1811–12. After a forced retreat, Portugal reoccupied the contested territory in 1816, with the aim of creating a natural, more easily defended border, gaining access to the Uruguay and Paraná rivers, and forming a buffer zone blocking the revolutionary contagion from infecting Brazil.[191]

Overlapping chronologically, though animated by different aims, was the invasion of French Guiana in 1809, a relatively modest reprisal for

---

[188] Not everyone agreed that Fernando Po' and Ano Bom were disposable. The *Ouvidor Geral* of São Tomé argued that "the people of Ano Bom have a talent for commerce ... for this island to be a useful colony, it would need but a little encouragement." See AHU, S. Tomé, cx. 13, docs. 13 and 27, Caetano Bernardo Pimente Castro de Mesquita to Mello e Castro, February 10 and 24, 1771; Mello e Castro, too, evidently agreed, for he had warned "should [Fernando Po' and Ano Bom] fall into the hands of another industrious nation, all of the advantages currently gained by S. Tomé would be lost ... we would have to give up our commerce with the kingdom of Benin." See AHU, S. Tomé, cx. 12, Mello e Castro, "Quarta Instrucção para Vicente Gomes Ferreira sobre a Ilha de Fernão do Pó," July 16, 1770; on Spain's problems gaining control over its new colonial possession, see Paquette 2008, ch. 3.

[189] Before 1778, Naples and Genoa accounted for 50 percent of imported wheat, but thereafter Holland, Russia, Britain, and France become the largest importers. See J. V. Serrao, "A Agricultura," in Lains and Silva 2005, vol. I, p. 167.

[190] Bauss 1983, pp. 519–27 passim; though there was opposition to such a policy. See ANRJ, Secretário de Estado do Brasil, cod. 67, vol. 16, Vasconcelos e Sousa to Mello e Castro, May 12, 1788, fo. 68.

[191] Seckinger 1984, p. 59.

the havoc wrought by Napoleon's armies in Portugal. Between its occupation in 1809 and its return to France as part of the postwar peace
settlement, signed belatedly in 1817, a bounty of proposals to harness the
economic potential of the colony proliferated.[192] Apart from appropri-
ating valuable spices and economically useful plants from Guiana, few
plans came to fruition and the colony proved a useful bargaining chip
in diplomatic negotiations, earning Portugal a seat at the diplomatic
table in Paris in 1814 and in Vienna the following year.[193] Nevertheless,
these proposals for Guiana bear the mark of the economic development ideology that frequently insinuated itself in official correspondence. According to Portuguese commentators, the French had failed
in Guiana because, apart from "not knowing how to form and follow a
fixed plan for its prosperity," they had "ignored the lessons of experience, freely adopting seductive and grandiose plans founded in illusory
theories."[194] Although the Crown had noted in its initial instructions
after the conquest that it intended to establish a "free system of exports
and imports,"[195] it remains unclear whether its commitment produced
practical results. The governor was given scant opportunity to act on
his plans, as customs taxes on imports were raised, though the regulation of slaves and livestock remained unchanged.[196]

The drive for territorial expansion was tempered by fear of rivals'
designs on Luso-Atlantic peripheries. In spite of their status as but-
tresses to Brazilian growth as providers of slaves, officials realized that
the non-slave sectors of the economies of Portugal's African possessions
required attention and encouragement. Pombaline-era correspondence routinely bemoaned the "decadence" of Portuguese Africa.[197] In
his *Memórias*, written in the mid 1770s, Francisco de Souza Coutinho
noted that Angola, "this most important *conquista*, was, until my tenure
[as governor], subject to the greatest level of neglect imaginable."[198] The

---

[192] For perhaps the most intriguing of these, see BNRJ, 7, 2, 37, Manuel Marquez,
"Descripção Abreviada das Vantagens e Recursos que offerecem a posição de
Goyana, antigamente Francesa, e suas Producções relativamente aos Estados do Pará
e do Brazil," (March 24, 1810). The author was, for a time, governor of Cayenne and
Guiana.

[193] Goycochêa 1963, pp. 166, 191.

[194] BNRJ, 5, 3, 12, Manuel Marquez, "Memoria sobre a Goyanna Franceza" (November
26, 1810).

[195] Dom João VI, "Instruções ao Intendente-Geral da Polícia" (June 10, 1809), quoted
in Macedo 1983, p. 58.

[196] C. F. S. Cardoso 1984, p. 160.

[197] For a sophisticated example of this lamentation, see Ignacio Caetano Xavier,
"Noticias dos Dominios Portuguezes na Costa de África Oriental," December 26,
1758, reproduced in Andrade 1955.

[198] "Memórias do Reino de Angola e suas Conquistas, escritos em Lisboa nos anos de
1773 e 1775," reproduced in *Arquivos de Angola* 1939, vol. IV, p. 173.

schemes proposed to remedy this condition focused on both commerce and agriculture. Pombal, infatuated with privileged trade companies since his stint as ambassador in London in the early 1740s, resisted the temptation to establish such companies in Africa, in stark contrast to his policy for the north of Brazil.[199] He rejected pleas from administrators who argued that privileged companies were a foolproof way to increase economic activity.[200]

Pombal was animated by another vision for Portugal's African *conquistas*.[201] He favorably compared Angola's prospects to other European establishments in West Africa. Dismissing the footholds of Portugal's rivals as merely "simple trading stations [*feitorias*]," "several miserable forts, without population, and in some cases without soldiers, which do not resemble a colony at all," Pombal contended that it would be "inconvenient to adopt" such foreign examples as a model. The sole object of other European states, Pombal noted, "was the slave trade, of transporting slaves to their colonies in America." Angola, on the contrary, was not a mere "trading post," for Portugal had a "populous city," São Paulo da Assumpção de Luanda, and many "colonies of Portuguese [subjects] far from the coast" in the interior.[202] Seeking to reduce Portugal's dependence on iron imports from Russia and Spain, Pombal encouraged the establishment of an iron foundry in Angola. Several buildings were erected, but the Basque iron masters recruited for the project died shortly after their arrival.[203] Regardless of its ultimate success, Pombal's plan for the urbanization of the hinterlands of Luanda and Benguela, the creation of a permanent colony of European settlement, and experiments with small-scale industrialization represented a decisive break with past policy.[204]

Schemes for African agricultural improvement and colonies of settlement assumed somewhat greater priority after 1770, as the Crown sought to diversify the economy. Members of Lisbon's Academy of Sciences offered ebullient assessments of Portuguese Africa's prospects. While lamenting that they remained sparsely cultivated, Vandelli praised Cape Verde as "fertile," the islands of the gulf of Guinea as "very fertile," and

---

[199] Pombal's favorable attitude toward colonial trade may be found in Pombal 1986. His views are discussed in Maxwell 1973.

[200] "Carta de Pedro de Saldanha de Albuquerque," December 19, 1758, reproduced in Andrade 1955, p. 118.

[201] On Pombaline policy in eighteenth-century Angola in general, see C. M. Santos 2010.

[202] Report attributed to Pombal, found in AHU, Angola, cx. 43, doc. 111, dated November 20, 1760.

[203] Birmingham 2003, p. 95.

[204] C. M. Santos 2010, p. 541.

Angola as "potentially a rich kingdom."[205] In 1770, the Crown instructed colonial administrators in São Tomé to create an inventory of the island's various agricultural products and to rank their potential for improvement. In 1789, the *capitão-mor*, João Baptista e Silva, reported that "no European power possessed an island which could so easily produce cinnamon, pepper, and coffee," claims which aroused the curiosity of the Crown.[206] The cultivation of coffee, in particular, would enable inhabitants of São Tomé to "recover what had been lost, to free themselves from poverty, and to return to the former flourishing state, when sugar was grown [there], before its cultivation was transferred to Brazil."[207]

Visions of promoting European emigration and settlement percolated. A 1762 *memoria* on East Africa called attracting European settlers a "great necessity."[208] Such schemes required a transformation of the imperial mindset. Angola had been viewed largely as a penal colony (a "colony of bandits and thieves," of "vagabonds and army deserters ... who brought with them only vices and few virtues") and it was believed that little could be achieved until the influence of these "corrupt men and customs" was curbed.[209] Government would be adapted to the unfavorable circumstances, to men who lacked "knowledge of any form of government that would be worthy of the name, who have no notion of industry, culture, commerce or work ethic."[210] Souza Coutinho and his successors urged Lisbon to end its policy of sending convicts (*degredados*) to Angola. For the colony to have any chance of improvement, it was necessary to introduce "good and capable people," ideally "married couples and other industrious people of all professions." Only then could

---

[205] D. Vandelli, "Memoria," in *Memórias Económicas* 1990, p. 130. In another unpublished manuscript, however, Vandelli argued that "India and the coasts of Africa have no purpose other than commerce," a situation he compared unfavourably to that of Brazil, which was suitable for both commerce and agriculture. See BAj., MS 54-V-14, Vandelli, "Memórias sobre o Commercio de Portugal e suas Colonias," fos. 29–39v passim.

[206] AHU, S. Tomé, cx. 12, doc. 36, July 13, 1770; ibid., cx. 22, doc. 59, "Descrição da Ilha de S. Tomé," April 13, 1789.

[207] AHU, S. Tomé, cx. 21, doc. 69, "Carta do Capitão-Mor de S. Tomé, João Baptista e Silva, propondo soluções para se pôr fim á decadencia das ilhas" (1782); in subsequent correspondence, Silva would invoke the success of Portugal's rival empires to push for coffee's cultivation in S. Tomé: "the Dutch have planted it in Java and Ceylon; the French in Martinique, Saint Domingue and Cayenne; these two nations have profited much from this product"; see AHU, S. Tomé, cx. 22, doc. 59

[208] [Anon], "Memórias da Costa d'Africa Oriental e Algumas Reflexões Uteis para Establecer Melhor, e Fazer Mais Florente o seu Comercio" (1762), reproduced in *Relações* 1955, p. 222.

[209] AHU, Angola, cx. 50, doc. 63, Souza Coutinho to Mendonça Furtado, March 4, 1766; ibid., cx. 51, doc. 62, December 16, 1767; ibid., cx. 53, doc. 71, October 18, 1769.

[210] AHU, Angola, cx. 56, doc. 52, Mello e Castro "Instrucção para D. António de Lencastre, Governador e Capitão-Geral do Reino de Angola [*sic*]" (n.d. [1772]).

the colony be considered as "good and profitable as Brazil."[211] Souza
Coutinho advised Pombal to encourage the immigration of women to
Angola. Their presence, he argued, "would be the best instrument to
establish order and tranquility in men corrupted by natural liberty."[212]
There also were calls for dispatching skilled Europeans to African colonies on either a temporary or a permanent basis. In one case, a correspondent in Bissau requested that the government send individuals who
could "serve as models for the natives of this country in their farming
methods, in their harvesting, in their cutting of wood ... the *nacionaes*
are capable of imitating perfectly that which they observe."[213]

Pombal's aspiration to establish agricultural settlements in Portuguese
Africa, however, was a far-fetched fantasy. Besides the barrier of disease, the paltry size of the European population there foreclosed anything but long-range plans. In 1777, for example, the official population
of Luanda was a meager 1,519 persons, of whom 938 were slaves.[214]
Mozambique, too, failed to develop into a settler colony in the eighteenth century: there were few urban centers or Portuguese *moradores*,
while much of the territory continued to be held by *prazo* holders, not
Crown agents.[215] Expectations for the rapid and full-scale transformation of Portuguese Africa into something other than a slave emporium were low. Beyond the perceived sub-standard quality of available
prospective colonists, other conditions impeded Angola's (and, by
extension, Portuguese Africa's) rapid development. Francisco de Souza
Coutinho summarized these obstacles in a 1770 dispatch:

it is certain that in order to conserve and improve our colonies in Africa, it will
be necessary for your excellency to employ all of your energies in that direction.
To conserve America, one needs but a light touch for the salubrious climate,
the fame of its riches, and the security of its commerce will continue to attract
the appropriate measures to itself.[216]

---

[211] AHU, Angola, cx. 52, doc. 36, F. de Souza Coutinho to Mendonça Furtado, October
30, 1768; there was clearly a racial dimension to his derisive characterization of
Angola's present inhabitants: "the uselessness of the caste of individuals, which the
mixture of different [types of] blood has produced." AHU, Angola, cx. 53, doc. 71,
October 18, 1769.

[212] Souza Coutinho to Pombal (October 18, 1769), quoted in Dias 1936, p. 54.

[213] BPMP, cod. 190, [attrib. Bernardo António Alves d'Andrade], "Planta da Praça
de Bissão, e suas adjacentes ... offerecidas ao Illo. Exo. S. Luiz Pinto de Souza
Coutinho" [1796]. For an earlier, similar argument, see "Memoria da Costa d'Africa
Oriental," p. 222.

[214] C. M. Santos 2008, p. 271. NB: This figure excludes the 612 soldiers stationed in
Luanda.

[215] Disney 2009, vol. II, p. 358.

[216] F. de Souza Coutinho (June 8, 1770), quoted in Amaral Nogueira 1960, p. 108.
Concerning Dom Francisco's tenure in Luanda, Birmingham concluded "all his
endeavors came to nothing," in Birmingham 1966, p. 155.

There were several spasmodic efforts to improve the living conditions of subjects in Portuguese Africa through the establishment of hospitals and schools. In 1766, for example, Souza Coutinho wrote to his subordinate in Benguela, lamenting the "irremediable hardships that the inhabitants of Benguela have suffered for centuries" and promising the construction of a hospital there.[217] Yet many of these projects were never pursued, and in 1784 the *Ouvidor Geral*, in recommending the creation of primary schools and a chair of Latin, lamented the paucity of institutions for the colony's improvement: "Angola does not have the appearance of an older, well-established colony, but rather resembles a recently conquered land."[218] Seventeen years later, in 1801, an Angolan governor received a rebuke from the Minister for Colonial Affairs, Rodrigo de Souza Coutinho, Dom Francisco's son, for having failed to establish schools in spite of a 1799 royal order requiring him to do so. The governor acknowledged having received the order, but explained his failure to execute it. "Where," he asked the minister incredulously, "would one find teachers for such a school?"[219]

The attempt to re-imagine and re-shape African and American spaces and subjects had its counterpart in peninsular Portugal. Like their physiocratic contemporaries in France, Portuguese reformers strove to overcome the uneconomic division of territory, removing obstacles to the circulation of goods, simplifying taxes and imposts, and attacking corporate privilege.[220] The never-implemented *Lei da Reforma das Comarcas* (1790) represented the culmination of a long series of initiatives which intended to implement a unified judicial system and guarantee the more prompt, efficacious administration of justice throughout the kingdom. In part inspired by the Spanish Marquis of Ensenada's great *Catastro*, peninsular officials gathered more precise data concerning territory, endowing decision-making with a rational, quantitative basis. Under Pombal, new bishoprics were created (Penafiel 1769; Pinhel 1770; and Castelo Branco 1771) and the number of intendants and superintendents multiplied.[221] The 1790 legislation, which sought to reduce distances and size of jurisdictions within each *comarca*, to

[217] AHU, Angola, cx. 50, doc. 12, F. de Souza Coutinho, "Instrucoens Gerais," May 28, 1766.

[218] AHU, Angola, cx. 68, doc. 46, "Oficio do Ouvidor Geral Francisco Xavier de Machado," March 20, 1784.

[219] AHU, Angola, cx. 101, doc. 101, Miguel António de Mello to R. de Souza Coutinho, August 17, 1801.

[220] For France, most recently, see Cheney 2010, p. 164.

[221] A. C. N. da Silva 1998, pp. 33, 72–73.

eliminate territorial enclaves, and to create jurisdictional districts sufficiently populated to cover the cost of the salaries of officials, was never
implemented, mainly due to the vested interests it threatened.[222] In the
late 1790s, as the French revolutionary wars raged and neighboring
Spain's finances collapsed, more radical measures to assert Crown control over peninsular territory and resources were contemplated. Souza
Coutinho broached the possibility of the abolition of *morgados* and *cape-
las*, the disamortization of the wealth of religious orders, the extinction
of the *dizimos*, and the curtailment of seigneurial rights. The demands
of war, which required the Portuguese Crown to raise revenue quickly,
led to the raising of taxes and imposts, in violation of the ancient privileges, thus further alienating much of the nobility from the cause of
reform.[223]

Beyond such radical measures, many less controversial improvements were pursued, though with mixed results. Infrastructural development, for example, was prioritized in the 1780s and 1790s, as land
transport remained primitive. Transporting crops from the agrarian
interior to coastal cities remained beset by obstacles. Italian traveler
(and political writer) Giuseppe Gorani, who visited Portugal in the
mid 1760s, remarked that the Portuguese "go frequently to their colonies, seldom venture abroad, and rarely travel around their own country: it would be easier to arrange a ship to sail to Goa or Brazil than it
would to encounter a carriage [from Lisbon] to take one to Coimbra or
Braga."[224] Two *alvarás*, issued in 1791 and 1796, respectively, sought
to redress this nagging issue, calling for the creation of new roads from
Lisbon to Santarém, from Porto to Coimbra, and from Porto to various
points in the Alto-Douro.[225] As in Spain, there were vigorous efforts
to redistribute population more evenly throughout Portugal. Fear of
the Alentejo's sparse population prompted an effort to repopulate it
through emigration inducements and royal edict. In 1787, four hundred Azorean families were transplanted to the Alentejo, supplement-
ing the five hundred *casais* brought to Évora from Vila Viçosa earlier
in the decade.[226] Reform, regardless of its success, was pursued in the
context of the empire as a whole, with the aim of turning far-flung colonies and metropolitan peripheries into an integrated and malleable
space.

---

[222] Ibid., pp. 351, 353, 371.   [223] Kirschner 2009, pp. 181–83.
[224] Gorani 1945, p. 99.
[225] Tavares and Santos Pinto 1990, p. 51.
[226] Ibid., p. 63; in the 1820s, such efforts would be ridiculed by *Vintistas* such as Soares
Franco.

Negative appraisals of reform before 1808

The level and intensity of reform activity in the late eighteenth-century Luso-Brazilian empire failed to produce many of the effects its advocates desired. Amidst myriad efforts to encourage the cultivation of new crops and other exportable products, for example, there were notable failures. Forest policy (timber) was one such disappointment. Production levels remained low and prices high, despite the fact that Brazil possessed the best timber, for which European demand was steady.[227] For all the commitment to methodical planning, hair-brained schemes and quixotic pet projects abounded. Many pipe dreams were pursued in Amazonia, where officials and merchants fantasized about an export boom based on indigenous products such as cacao, sarsaparilla, nuts, turtle lard, and manatees.[228] Even well-conceived projects often produced fateful side effects: besides failing to reach anticipated yields owing to the paucity of quality mills and the dearth of seed, rice production in Pará and Maranhão resulted in an ecological disaster, destroying vast swathes of forest and reducing much of Maranhão to scrub plain.[229]

False starts and missteps aside, it is necessary to recall that the two decades preceding the Court's transfer from Lisbon to Rio de Janeiro witnessed remarkable growth and change. Yet much of this expansion proved merely opportunistic, resulting from the dislocations caused by the disintegration of other Atlantic empires, and reliant on heightened demand for products from largely unreformed sectors of colonial economy, notably sugar. For all of the new initiatives and energy, the basic characteristics of the Luso-Atlantic system remained untouched by reform. Lisbon and Porto continued as entrepôt for Brazilian products, most of which were re-exported to northern European ports while Brazil was, legally at least, an exclusive market for Portuguese goods.[230] This stasis offended some reformers' sensibilities. Political writers were shocked by the intractable backwardness of metropolitan Portugal's agriculture, horrified in particular by the amount of uncultivated yet arable, habitable yet underpopulated, land.[231] The situation in Brazil was similar. In Bahia, the political writer Vilhena marveled with chagrin: "How can it be that a country so blessed by nature, so rich in all that is essential, [and] so vast in the size of its territory, is inhabited by such a small number of people, the majority

---

[227] S. W. Miller 2000, p. 212.   [228] Roller 2010, p. 437.
[229] Hawthorne 2010, p. 155.   [230] Alexandre 1993, p. 85.
[231] ANTT, MR, mç. 356 (cx. 477), [Anon.], "Sobre o Modo de Aproveitar os Baldios" (n.d.).

of whom are poor, and many of whom are starving [*esfaimado*]."[232] In Pará, an anonymous commentator complained that the province's "wealth, abundance, fertility, and resources were unknown, forsaken, disparaged and wasted."[233] In distant Timor, the state of affairs was simply "deplorable."[234] Similar grim appraisals proliferated elsewhere on the eve of the nineteenth century.

The political economist Brito offered several hypotheses to explain this lamentable state of affairs. He argued that Portugal's plight was attributable to its ministers' failure to "follow one system with constancy."[235] He also blamed Pombal's obsession with mercantilist-inspired policy, which meant that "new scientific discoveries arrived very late, making the reform of the system very difficult."[236] Whether or not Pombal and his successors were culpable, Brito correctly signaled the problem of disseminating new insights and implementing reform. The impact of reform efforts proved uneven partly due to poor distribution. Copies of the *Arco do Cego*'s masterpiece, *O Fazendeiro do Brasil*, for example, were shipped to Brazil, but failed to reach landowners, the intended audience. *O Fazendeiro* rotted away in government warehouses until the 1820s, when the surviving copies were used as raw material for the manufacture of fireworks.[237] Bureaucratic error, however, may have been less consequential than planters' lack of interest in the new-fangled agronomy. As the traveler Henry Koster observed of the Northeastern planters in 1815:

it is quite hopeless to expect a rapid change of system among men who had not even heard that there existed other agriculturists besides themselves; who were astonished to learn that Brazil was not the only country in which sugar was made ... they continue year after year the system which was followed by their fathers, without any wish to improve, and without the knowledge that any improvement could be made.[238]

Koster's disparaging account smacks of exaggeration and cultural chauvinism, but the rudimentary knowledge of the planters he encountered in his travels is plausible. Even committed and active reformers expressed doubts concerning the utility of their efforts. In a 1781 letter

[232] Vilhena, Carta XXIV "Pensamentos Políticos" (*c.* 1798–1800), in Vilhena 1969, vol. III, p. 914.
[233] JCBL, Codex Portugal 7, "Ensaio Económico e Político sobre o Pará" [1816], fo. 14.
[234] Newberry, Vault Folio Greenlee, MS 422, Conde de Sarzedas [Viceroy of the *Estado da Índia*], "Instruções," given to Vitorino Freire Cunha Gusmão [Governor of Timor], April 30, 1811, fo. 1.
[235] Brito 1803, vol. I, pp. 74–75.
[236] Ibid., p. 73.   [237] Galloway 1979, p. 776, fn. 39.
[238] Koster 1816, p. 376.

to Vandelli, written from Bahia, José da Silva Lisboa, subsequently a major political economist and crown propagandist, expressed grave doubt concerning the practical impact of printing and disseminating tracts on agricultural themes. "Our century is the century of agriculture," he noted, "everybody writes about this subject from the comfort of his study, perhaps without having ever worked the earth. Agriculture is easier and more attractive, therefore, to write about than to actually engage in."[239] Firsthand understanding of local circumstances thus conditioned the reception of new works of political economy and agricultural science, producing skepticism concerning their usefulness and applicability in non-European circumstances.

The clear limits of reform and the intransigent obstacles to comprehensive change frustrated even the most indefatigable reformers. José Bonifácio de Andrada e Silva (1763–1838), later a towering figure of Brazil's transition to independence, remained in Portugal as an administrator following his Coimbra education and scientific travels in Central Europe. In 1804, he denounced the forces of inertia that stymied his reforming efforts. "All of the orders and recommendations I gave in years past," he reported with ill-disguised disgust, "have been forgotten, ignored, or rejected. And what good can come from orders issued to careless officials and lazy *câmaras*, comprised of ignorant people without any sense of public spirit? The only thing I have gained from my efforts is calumny and disdain [directed at me]."[240] For other officials, particularly on the imperial periphery, the enormity of their task in the face of innumerable obstacles proved daunting and the absence of state support dispiriting. A Coimbra-educated official was overwhelmed by the variety and extent of the problems that thwarted "progress" in Maranhão. These included climate, the "absence of civilization and industry," the proximity of "wild" Indians, the absence of state support for agriculture, and a "fatal" public administration.[241] And, indeed, even where reformers' efforts met with "success," the unintended consequences were undesirable, as they upset the delicate equipoise of the realm.[242] Integration was only partially achieved before the political crisis of 1807–8 blocked such schemes.[243] While remaining cognizant of the great efforts made, the slowness, irregularity, and

---

[239] Quoted in D. Carvalho 1985, p. 44.
[240] ANTT, MR, mç. 356 (cx. 477), J. B. de Andrada e Silva [from Coimbra] to Conde de Vila Verde, December 5, 1804.
[241] Lago 1822, p. 25.   [242] Adelman 1999, p. 21.
[243] Even in *c.* 1800, Brazil's economy remained a "series of systems, some of which were mutually connected whereas others remained nearly isolated." See Furtado 1971, p. 6.

unevenness of change, which the Coimbra-trained generation found so disconcerting and confusing, must always be borne in mind.

PART II

The second part of this chapter addresses two of the major issues – less regulated ("free") trade and the slave trade – with which the politicians and political writers of the Luso-Atlantic world grappled from the 1790s. The issues were linked and they represented threats to the vision of an interconnected and integrated empire pursued by Pombal and his successors. The extent to which foreign merchants and agents should be permitted to insinuate themselves in Luso-Brazilian economic spaces was addressed in Part I. But the advent of the French Revolution complicated efforts to exclude foreign traders. Portugal was forced to rely even more heavily on its British ally, which made access to markets the precondition of its naval protection. This external political-military dependence deepened precisely at the moment when the Brazilian economy's reliance on imports of African slaves deepened, due in part to the unprecedented opportunities afforded by the dislocations in the global commodities market. Britain's abolition of the slave trade in 1807 was followed by its efforts to coerce its client states to follow suit. Its support for the Braganza dynasty after 1807, including its famous transfer of the Court from Lisbon to Rio de Janeiro at the end of that year, was contingent on Portugal's pledge to end the slave trade and to open Luso-Brazilian markets to British merchants and merchandise, arrangements enshrined in the decisive, controversial treaties of 1808 and 1810. Thus, debates about less regulated trade (i.e. the foreign penetration of colonial markets), the slave trade, and the prospects for empire in a post-monopoly, post-slave trade era grew increasingly fierce after 1790.

The perils and opportunities of free trade

The Luso-Atlantic economy's development intensified in the early 1790s. Planters and merchants rushed to exploit the collapse of Saint-Domingue's economy and to meet the global demand for sugar. Between 1791 and 1804, Saint-Domingue sugar exports slumped from 80,000 tons per year to 24,000.[244] Sugar exports from Bahia alone doubled between 1789 and 1795 and the number of mills in Rio de Janeiro

---

[244] Andrews 2004, p. 19.

increased by 20 percent.[245] Rising production helped to fuel a concomitant rise in the demand for slaves: between 1790 and 1810, approximately 23,500 Africans were sold into slavery each year, 9,200 into Rio
de Janeiro alone.[246] Elsewhere in the empire, new commodities – rice,
cotton, coffee, and cacao – which had been introduced during Pombal's
ascendancy now produced a noticeable impact on colonial economic
growth and also a favorable effect on Portugal's balance of trade. In
Goa, for example, rice production increased by 136 percent between
1786 and 1791.[247] The export of northern Brazilian cotton also sharply
increased in the same period, as the early phase of British industrialization boosted demand.[248] Between 1796 and 1811, cotton composed
one quarter of the value of Portugal's colonial exports, a huge increase
over earlier levels.[249] Overall, exports from Portugal and its possessions quadrupled between 1789 and 1807. By the mid 1790s, Portugal
enjoyed a balance of payments surplus, a situation unthinkable just a
decade earlier.[250]

While a favorable balance of trade meant the diminished influence
of rival states, like Britain, its price was Portugal's deepening dependence on Brazil and the increasing autonomy of the South Atlantic economy.[251] Brazilian products accounted for 60 percent of Portugal's (re-)
exports to other European markets between 1796 and 1811.[252] As in
the early eighteenth century, metropolitan Portugal's fate was tied to
Brazil's, making the impact of the Court's transfer in 1808 more dramatic. The transfer also abruptly ended efforts to legislate for the empire
as a whole. Portugal's legal monopoly was shattered by the opening of
Brazil's ports to foreign ships in 1808, permanently sanctioned by the
1810 commercial treaty with Britain.[253] The 1808 *Carta Régia* opening the ports allowed for direct commerce between Brazil and nations
friendly to Portugal subject to import duties of 24 percent *ad valorem*
on dry goods. The 1810 Treaty, by requiring Portugal to eliminate all
prohibitions on British manufactures and to reduce import duties to

[245] J. J. Reis and F. dos Santos Gomes, "Repercussions of the Haitian Revolution in
Brazil, 1791–1850," in Geggus and Fiering 2009, p. 284.
[246] M. Florentino, "Slave Trading and Slave Traders in Rio de Janeiro, 1790–1830,"
in Curto and Lovejoy 2004, p. 62. More generally, see Florentino 1995; see also
Schultz 2005, pp. 273–74.
[247] Lopes 1999, p. 55.   [248] Manchester 1972 [1933], p. 52.
[249] J. J. de Andrade Arruda, "A Produção Económica," in Oliveira Marques and Serrão
1986, p. 100.
[250] Barman 1988, p. 9.   [251] Adelman 2006.
[252] Barickman 1998, p. 19.
[253] For a discussion of the background and impact of the opening of Brazil's ports, see
J. L. Cardoso 2008.

15 percent *ad valorem* – essentially preferential rights or "most-friendly nation" status – opened the flood gates to foreign products. Unlike the 1703 Methuen Treaty, which retained the trappings of reciprocity, the 1810 Treaty denied entrance to British markets of Brazilian products, including sugar and coffee, similar to those produced by Britain's own colonies.[254] To a degree, these legislative acts recognized de jure what was happening already de facto: Britain's competitive superiority and Portugal's inability to maintain a closed system of colonial trade. Colonial monopoly ceased to be effective and though Portuguese ministers implored administrators in Brazil to crack down on contraband, situations in which to exert their authority were limited.

Well before the fateful agreements of 1808 and 1810, many Portuguese political writers argued that efforts to enforce colonial monopoly were misguided. They held that only less regulated commerce, foreign and domestic, would improve agriculture. In an anonymous late eighteenth-century tract, one writer endorsed the "abolition of all prohibitive legislation, especially concerning grain ... the general law [should be] that liberty is the basis for commerce."[255] Such ideas, of course, together with anti-Pombaline sentiments, informed the abolition of the two privileged trade companies in 1778–79. Monopolies of all sorts came under attack later in the century. Pombal's Port Wine trade monopoly[256] was fiercely criticized by Souza Coutinho, who urged the Crown to "destroy such a ruinous system, so absurd in every way." As a result, he predicted, "our sovereign would double or even triple the state's revenue and also bolster the progress of agriculture, alleviate poverty and cause the nation's wealth to increase."[257] As colonial minister in the late 1790s, Dom Rodrigo oversaw the abolition of royal monopolies over whaling and salt.[258] His opposition to monopolies (and the contracting out of revenue collection) stemmed from his conviction that intelligent reform was indispensable if Portugal were to avoid France's collapse.[259] He perceived the advantages of an international division of labor, with the Luso-Brazilian empire accepting its place in the Atlantic economy as a producer of agricultural products for export to more industrialized, wealthier nations which dominated global commerce.[260]

---

[254] Manchester 1972, pp. 69, 72, 89.
[255] ANTT, MR, mç. 356/ cx. 476, [Anon.], "Prenoções para formar hum plano economico de melhoramento da agricultura d'entre Douro e Minho" (n.d.).
[256] On Pombal's *Companhia Geral da Agricultura das Vinhas do Alto Douro*, established in 1756, see Maxwell 1995, pp. 63, 70–71.
[257] Souza Coutinho, "Reflexões Políticas," p. 148.
[258] Andrade Arruda, "A Produção Económica," p. 146.
[259] On this point, see Maxwell 2003, p. 133.
[260] Pedreira 1994, p. 473.

The 1808–10 commercial legislation stemming from the diplomatic arrangements of the same years, overwhelmingly favorable to Britain, was criticized in many quarters. The distaste built on years of animosity. "Many of the Portuguese," Robert Southey observed in the late 1790s, "dislike the English influence and reprobate the Methuen Treaty as the ruin of their commerce."[261] By 1798, Portuguese economic writers lambasted Britain and the Methuen Treaty as the "greatest, undisguised enemy of our industry."[262] In 1807–8, the Secretary for Foreign Affairs and War, Conde da Barca, predicted that opening Luso-Brazilian ports to British products would "cause great ruin." He was incredulous that Portugal would contemplate such measures. "What nation," he asked, "has adopted in practice the principles of free trade expressed by the author of *The Wealth of Nations*? Why have they not been adopted yet by England, for whom Smith explicitly wrote?" The danger for Portugal, Conde da Barca argued, was that its lower level of economic development compared with Britain ("in capital, mercantile knowledge, industry, the size of its merchant marine, the size of its economy, in the progress of its natural and exact sciences") meant that in practice there could be "no reciprocity," regardless of the Treaty's language.[263]

Many free trade skeptics were likewise unconvinced that an export-led economy was sustainable in the long run. Between 1796 and 1811, sugar accounted for more than a third of the value of exports.[264] As an economic historian concluded, "without Brazilian products, it would be difficult for Portugal to maintain a favorable balance of trade with foreign nations."[265] Before the advent of coffee cultivation, Brazilian agriculture was plugging production gaps created by extraordinary, and anomalous, market conditions.[266] What would happen when the British, Dutch, French, and Spanish colonies resumed their pre-war levels of production? Various answers were suggested. In 1815,

---

[261] Southey 1799, p. 402.
[262] ANTT, MR, mç. 356 (cx. 476), [Felisberto Ignacio Januario Cordero], "Dissertação sobre a Origem da Decadencia das Fabricas ..." (1798); modern economic historians have disputed this view. As J. L. Cardoso contended, "Portuguese historiography has demonstrated that the [Methuen] Treaty was not, nor could have been, an insuperable stigma, or original sin of Portuguese industrial development." See Cardoso, "Leitura e Interpretação do Tratado de Methuen," in Cardoso 2003, p. 27.
[263] ADB, ACB, SIFAA 37, 122, "Parecer [do Conde da Barca]" (1808); António Araújo e Azevedo (1754–1817), Conde da Barca, served in many key posts between 1804 and 1817, including Secretary for Foreign Affairs and War, Secretary of the *Reino*, and Secretary of Navy and Colonies.
[264] Andrade Arruda, "A Produção Económica," p. 101.
[265] Andrade Arruda 1980, p. 293.
[266] Furtado 1971, p. 99; Flory 1981, p. 10.

one political writer argued for the need to produce mainly for the local, domestic market. He predicted a scenario in which competition from the colonies of other nations drove down sugar and cotton prices, obliging Brazil to produce less. This "inconvenient" situation would leave a "great pool of labor without employment, which could become lazy and driftless with the diminishment of the cultivation of colonial products." His proposed response to this anticipated predicament was twofold: first, to develop industry in Brazil and manufacture products for the consumption of the internal market as well as for export; second, to shift the focus of agriculture from tropical commodities to "subsistence crops and livestock," enumerating wheat, corn, rice, vegetables, dairy products, and salted beef.[267] This fear remained ubiquitous in the 1820s, after Brazil's independence. Crown advisor João Severiano Maciel da Costa (1769–1833), later Marquês de Queluz, lamented that he could not "predict what will become of our agricultural industry, which is the only one we have. Who will consume our exports and return us a profit now that the entire world is cultivating our products with a blind fury?"[268]

The suspected architect, and certainly the most overt champion, of the 1808–10 commercial decrees was Silva Lisboa. The Bahia-born, Coimbra-educated political economist and crown servant assailed the "ruinous" mercantile system premised on "false principles" which not only turned "commercial statutes into labyrinths of restrictions" and rendered impossible the economy's efflorescence, but also provoked "rancorous political animosities and bloody wars."[269] For inspiration, he turned to Adam Smith, whom he christened the "second father of *gente civilisada.*"[270] *The Wealth of Nations,* Silva Lisboa contended, "established the chief principles which statesmen should

---

[267] ADB, ACB, SIFAA 43, 30, [Anon.], "Memórias sobre o Nosso Comércio com Inglaterra" [n.d., early nineteenth century].

[268] Maciel da Costa, May 6, 1826, quoted in Flory 1981, p. 10. Of course, large-scale, export-oriented monoculture did not dominate everywhere: plantation and non-plantation forms of agriculture produced for a robust local market in Bahia throughout the colonial period. See Barickman 1998, p. 2.

[269] Silva Lisboa 1820, pp. 116–17. On Silva Lisboa's political thought, see Paim 1968; Adelman 2006; and Paquette 2009b.

[270] Silva Lisboa 1818, Pt. II, p. 67; the moniker given to Smith is intelligible in light of Silva Lisboa's 1804 pronouncement that political economy "might be called the art of civilizing." See his *Princípios de Econômia Política* (Lisbon, 1804), reprinted in Silva Lisboa 1993, p. 11. By the 1820s, however, Silva Lisboa's readings of Say and Malthus would lead him to conclude that even in Smith's work there were "imperfections and errors, even notable incoherent passages"; see his Silva Lisboa 1820, p. 120. On Silva Lisboa's understanding of Smith, particularly his conception of political economy as a moral science, see Almodovar and Cardoso 1999, p. 62.

follow ... who desire to promote the prosperity of their country."[271] He therefore praised deregulation of Brazil's international commerce as the action of an "enlightened prince" who comprehended that the "unrestricted extension of the market is the true motor of all *trabalho util.*"[272] Though he remained convinced that Brazil's short-term (and even medium-term) future would be as an agrarian, export-orientated economy, Silva Lisboa castigated those who balked at the abolition of colonial monopoly. He argued that "freedom of commerce will not subordinate the metropole to its ultramarine dominions; instead, it will stimulate the growth of all parts of the monarchy according to their natural mode, and not at the expense of the rest."[273] If the ports were opened, Brazilian exports would not be "destined to follow false channels, forced into predetermined circuits, and compelled to seek recourse in clandestine trade which has produced the lamentable stagnation of the colonies."[274] He pointed to the nascent USA, blazing the path which he hoped that Brazil would follow: "without exclusive companies, monopolies, conquests or factories [on the west coast of Africa], without disturbing the inhabitants of any country, it enjoys commerce as far as Asia. England knows that it faces a fearful rival."[275] Silva Lisboa viewed international trade as a mechanism to prevent not only the sort of domestic social upheaval which had engulfed other colonies whose economies were reliant on slave labor, notably Saint-Domingue, but also the political chaos which had succeeded commercial stagnation in Spanish America. He argued that Napoleon's Continental system prefigured Europe's descent into barbarism:

France is sliding down the ladder of civilization. It will soon be deprived of innumerable sciences, ideas, industries, and sources of wealth which maritime

---

[271] Silva Lisboa 1811b, p. 16; it was Silva Lisboa's son, Bento, who translated extended excerpts of the *Wealth of Nations* into Portuguese in these same years.

[272] Silva Lisboa 1811a, p. 22.

[273] Ibid., p. 155; also see Winch 1965.

[274] Silva Lisboa 1818, p. 70; here Silva Lisboa's understanding of political economy and reform reflects broader European eighteenth-century trends. As J. Robertson has suggested, political economy was "no longer concerned with the aggrandizement of governments at each other's expense"; moreover, the "purpose of reform should be the removal of obstacles to the optimal course of development." See Robertson 2005, pp. 29, 37.

[275] Silva Lisboa, *Observações sobre o Comércio Franco*, in Silva Lisboa 2001, p. 179. Silva Lisboa's praise of the USA should not be altogether surprising. As Maxwell pointed out, "those who saw the North American model as relevant tended to see it as the conservative option, a solution to the colonial dilemma that preserved the basic social organization, especially the system of slavery, but brought political emancipation from Europe." See his "Hegemonies Old and New," in Maxwell 2003, pp. 86–87.

commerce and the celestial art of navigation sustain. It is astonishing that Europe, after reaching the apex of civilization, will consent to becoming little more than a second sub-Saharan Africa.[276]

For Silva Lisboa, then, as for many of his contemporaries, there existed a strong correlation between economic growth, social harmony, and cultural flourishing. For this reason, he repudiated the English Navigation Acts, hailed by Pombal and his successors as venerable models, describing the formation of such companies as a "great error."[277] He warned that "imitation would result in a sad parody of English policy, which is not a model of *liberalidade* in every respect." The Navigation Acts, he contended, only made sense given Britain's geographic position, whereas their implementation would prove ruinous in other countries operating under different constraints. Such misapplication, he warned, "has caused many injustices, political animosities, and wars."[278]

The immediate and dramatic impact of the 1808–10 treaties is notorious. In 1814, Viscount Strangford, chief negotiator of those treaties, boasted that "the entire annihilation of the Old Colonial System of Brazil has been effected by the late treaty, and all attempts at reviving it have been forever precluded by the 32nd article of that instrument."[279] By 1812, Portuguese America took half as much British merchandise as either the USA or the British West Indies, and 25 percent more than Asia. For Portugal, the metropole, this policy shift produced much-lamented consequences. By 1818, for example, the value of English exports to Brazil exceeded that of Portuguese; of these British exports, almost 90 percent were wool and cotton manufactures. If Portuguese merchants suffered the most from the new trade legislation, Brazilian producers benefited: eight ninths of Bahia's and three quarters of Pernambuco's cotton exports were destined for Britain.[280]

In addition to dismantling the mercantile exclusions which characterized the "Old Colonial System," the 1810 treaty also undercut the enlightened reform emphasis on imperial unity, integration, and

---

[276] Silva Lisboa 1810, p. 107
[277] Silva Lisboa 1815, p. 86.
[278] Silva Lisboa 1811b, p. 53.
[279] Percy Smythe, 6th Viscount Strangford (1780–1855) [from Rio] to Castlereagh, February 20, 1814, in Webster 1938, vol. I, p. 173.
[280] Manchester 1972, p. 97. The British presence in Brazil's markets, however, must not be overstated. J. Pedreira has shown that between 1812 and 1821 Brazilian imports from Britain remained fairly stagnant; only in 1818 did they match the value of imports from Portugal. See Pedreira 2000, pp. 858–59. Similarly, the benefits for Brazil must not be overstated: currency devaluation and the doubling of the value of the pound between 1810 and 1820 was behind a rise in prices of imported articles, with a particularly harsh impact on the urban population. See Furtado 1971, p. 105.

interdependence, subjecting a previously self-contained system to the logic of the international division of labor, and increasing the relative importance of export agriculture.[281] While these shifts were accepted as unavoidable expedients during the French occupation, the restoration of the peace led neither to the resumption of Portugal's previous share of Brazil's commerce nor to the return of the seat of empire to the Old World.[282] The normalization after 1814 of what had been justified as wartime exigencies had major repercussions in the next decade, culminating in vociferous debates in the Lisbon Cortes in 1821–22 amidst Brazilian protests against Portugal's "recolonization" ambitions.[283] Nor was this merely a matter of Peninsular–Brazilian conflict. Crown officials resented the disproportionate, long-term advantages gained by Britain at the moment in which Portugal was enveloped by crisis. At the 1815 Congress of Vienna, one of the Portuguese negotiators, Pedro de Souza Holstein, Conde de Palmela, proposed the abrogation of the 1810 Treaty in exchange for the complete abolition of the slave trade, including that which flourished south of the equator. This proposal was shot down by Castlereagh, but the very suggestion indicated the ubiquitous perception that the commercial concessions were deemed extremely, if not fatally, deleterious.[284]

The slave trade, slavery, and European settlement schemes at the turn of the nineteenth century

Had Palmela's proposed swap of the abolition of the slave trade for the abrogation of the 1808 and 1810 treaties become widely known, it certainly would have touched off a political firestorm throughout the Luso-Brazilian world. This is not to suggest, of course, that the evils of slavery from moral-religious, economic, and political perspectives were unknown (though they were seldom articulated publicly). The desirability of replacing slave-dependent societies with colonies of white settlement was routinely discussed, without controversy. In Part I of this chapter, it was shown how the Portuguese Crown actively encouraged European settlement of sparsely populated strategic points in its empire, whether to protect the vulnerable coasts of São Paulo, Santa

---

[281] On the 1810 treaty in general, see Pedreira 1994, p. 473.

[282] For an excellent analysis, see J. Pedreira, "O Fim do Império Luso-Brasileiro," in Bethencourt and Chaudhuri 1998, vol. IV, p. 217.

[283] Alexandre 1993. For an analysis of the 1810 treaty, see pp. 261–338 passim; on Portuguese debates after 1814, see pp. 399–401; on Brazilian complaints, see M. R. Berbel, "A Retórica da Recolonização," in Jancsó 2005, pp. 791–808.

[284] V. Alexandre, "O Processo de Independência do Brasil," in Bethencourt and Chaudhuri 1998, vol. IV, p. 21.

Catarina, and Rio Grande do Sul from interlopers, "Europeanize" Grão-Pará through intermarriage, or promote settlement on land seized violently from Amerindians in Minas Gerais (and elsewhere). Throughout the eighteenth century, impoverished Azoreans, evacuated residents of Mazagão, and other "surplus" populations were encouraged to transplant themselves to Brazil. The inducements included land grants, provision of tools, and exemption from military service for up to ten years.[285] But the Crown adamantly opposed emigration from metropolitan Portugal, an opposition that stemmed from a broader fear of depopulation.[286]

There was also a great backlash, as noted previously, against reliance on convict colonists, particularly in Southern Africa, stemming from the belief that this type of individual produced a malicious, corrupting influence. Instead, married families of impeccable morals and unsullied obedience, always difficult to find, were desired. Though enthusiasm for settlement schemes in general waned and actual initiatives petered out in the middle of the eighteenth century, they did not vanish entirely. A decade after his return to Europe from Angola, Francisco de Souza Coutinho remained convinced that Portugal should accelerate the number of prisoners sent to Angola. In Brazil and Portugal, he explained, "many miserable men die in prison, from which the State could derive a great benefit, for while their vices decrease their [moral] worth, they can be useful in pursuing this work. As a result, many may change their ways and become good members of the community." But he noted that Portugal must commit fully to this change, not merely sending a single cohort of *degredados*, but "repeating this action many times, for the task is great and demands constant attention."[287] This notion of rehabilitating of deviants through settler colonialism also appealed to the Bahian political writer Vilhena, who floated the idea of sending "lazy people" in Brazil to Angola (and the island of Fernando Noronha, off Pernambuco) to work while taking their children, tutoring them, and turning them into "productive and useful subjects."[288]

For the foreseeable future, however, the Luso-Atlantic economy would depend on slaves, not voluntary settlers. This is not to suggest, as indicated previously, that slavery's existence was accepted uncritically. The

[285] Delson 1976, p. 46.
[286] Various laws (1709, 1711, 1720, and 1732) sought to limit, if not prohibit, the depopulation of Portugal. See G. S. Ribeiro 2002, pp. 152–53.
[287] BPMP, cod. 437, "Memórias do Reyno de Angola e suas Conquistas, Escritas em Lisboa nos Annos de 1773 & 1775 por Francisco Innocencio de Souza Coutinho," 2 documents: 1. September 17, 1773; and 2. February 3, 1775, fos. 58, 58v.
[288] Vilhena, Carta XXIV (late eighteenth century), in Vilhena 1987, p. 61.

Pombaline period witnessed the issuance of numerous slave decrees. In 1761, the Crown decreed that all African slaves landing in the kingdom would be declared free if they were disembarked on Portuguese soil. In 1773, a second decree freed all remaining slaves in Portugal.[289] The motives underlying these decrees were complex, but they were clearly designed to discourage the diversion of captive Africans bound for the mines and plantations of Brazil to Europe, thus re-enforcing the Pombaline vision of an imperial division of labor. The survival of slavery was not attributable solely to the absence of free European labor, of course. Slaves were much more than a source of labor. The entire South Atlantic economy was premised on the trade. As an historian argued, "African slaves became the medium through which merchants peripheral to the main commercial flows of their time were able, at high risk, to convert goods that were of relatively low currency value in Europe into currency credits and ultimately into specie."[290]

The outbreak of the revolution in Saint-Domingue and the rising tide of European abolitionism led to an upsurge of anxiety among Brazil's white population. By the late 1790s, fear of the "Haitianization" of Brazil was widespread, and political discourses emerged linking the corruption of customs with slaveholding and slavery.[291] One of Dom João's principal advisors, Tomas Antônio de Vilanova Portugal, decried slavery as Brazil's "intrinsic weakness," arguing that slaves were less productive than free laborers. "No master," he contended, "gets from his slaves the amount of work an entrepreneur obtains from an equal number of workers, because the slave works with repugnance ... Therefore, it is useless to expect increases in industry, crafts, agriculture etc as long as these occupations are mainly the work of slaves."[292] Fear, anxiety, and economic principles, however, did not translate into political action. In Brazil, none of the meliorist legislation concerning slavery in other European empires, such as the French *Code Noir* (1685) or the Spanish *Código Negro* (1785 and 1789), was devised or implemented.[293]

Nevertheless, support for slavery was no longer expressed with unreserved enthusiasm after the Haitian Revolution. When Azeredo Coutinho composed an extended, general apology for slavery in 1798, Lisbon's Academy of Sciences refused to endorse his ideas or publish

---

[289] Russell-Wood 1978, p. 41.
[290] J. Miller 1988, p. 685.
[291] J. Rodrigues 2000, pp. 91, 209–11; Blackburn 1988, pp. 384–85; and Blackburn 2011, p. 233.
[292] Vilanova Portugal, "Parecer sobre a Questão da Escravatura" (October 1814), quoted in Clayton 1977, p. 101.
[293] Russell-Wood 1978, p. 41.

his tract in Portugal.[294] Until the early nineteenth century, however, there was scant mention of abolition – immediate, short-term, or partial – of the slave trade, let alone slavery itself.[295] An anti-slavery discourse eventually crept into the reform proposals of various Brazilian *letrados*, but it was driven less by humanitarian sentiment than by the conviction that Brazil's racial imbalance endangered its stability and order.[296] The specter of slave rebellion haunted Brazil's elite. In 1798, in the so-called Bahian "Tailors' Conspiracy," *mulato* soldiers and artisans rose up, their demands informed by French and Haitian revolutionary principles. In 1817, free blacks and *mulatos* joined white planters and merchants in the Pernambucan Revolution. A frightened and indignant Portuguese observer in Recife observed that "the half-castes, *mulatos*, and blacks went about in such an insolent manner, saying 'we are all equal.'"[297]

These events, and Britain's legal abolition of the transatlantic slave trade in 1807, forced the Luso-Brazilian elite to grapple with slavery's uncertain future. In signing the 1808 and 1810 treaties with Britain, the Portuguese Crown committed itself to abolition. In the 1810s, a new consensus emerged: a defense of gradualism.[298] The negotiations at Vienna (1815) made explicit abolitionism's momentum and this awareness triggered further debate on the future of Brazil's economy and the function of Portugal's African possessions.[299] Most government officials were enraged by Britain's high-handed tactics, its "illegal and scandalous methods," but recognized that "Britain knows that it can act with impunity toward us without fearing any sort of retaliation."[300] Indeed, metropolitan Portugal was effectively occupied by British troops and

---

[294] *Analise sobre a Justiça do Comércio do Resgate dos Escravos da Costa da África* was eventually published in London. On the Academy of Science's negative attitude toward the ideas expressed, see Alexandre, "As Periferias," in Bethencourt and Chaudhuri 1998, vol. IV, pp. 48–52.

[295] Marques 2006, p. 54; Alexandre, "O Processo de Independência," p. 19.

[296] Rocha 2000, p. 64; Maxwell 1984, p. 598.

[297] Jancsó 1996; Kraay 2001, p. 105; Andrews 2004, pp. 75, 90 (quotation).

[298] Marques 2006, p. 61; NB: language concerning the gradual abolition of the slave trade is found in the February 1810 Treaty of Alliance and Friendship, not the separate Treaty of Commerce and Navigation.

[299] In his letter to Conde da Barca from Vienna, Saldanha da Gama (later Conde do Porto Santo) reported that "you cannot imagine how this issue [abolition of slave trade] is discussed here," indicating that Bissau and Cacheu would "be seized by England" if Portugal were to refuse to cooperate. See his letter of January 26, 1815, reproduced in J. V. Capela 1993, doc. 6, p. 99.

[300] Ambrosio Joaquim dos Reis, "Sobre a Situação da Monarquia Portuguesa depois da Paz de Paris de 1814, indicando algumas providências para a melhorar" (1815), reproduced in J. V. Capela 1993, doc. 7, p. 107.

the royal family showed no signs of returning to the Old World, as shall be discussed in Chapter 2.

The apparent imminent end of the slave pipeline provoked renewed calls for a transition from forced, African to free, European labor. This "substitution must begin now," one of Portugal's delegates to the Congress of Vienna warned. The conditions for facilitating the immigration of European labor to Brazil were propitious, in his view, for peace coincided with dismal economic conditions throughout Europe, "swelling the ranks of the discontent." Pointing to the large numbers of Irish and Germans forsaking their homelands for Canada and the USA, he recommended sending agents to Dublin and Hamburg to recruit potential colonists.[301] Silva Lisboa endorsed the "substitution" of European colonists (*povoadores*) for Africans, something which he had advocated previously as a potential antidote to the purported contagion of slave rebellion. While noting that French and English colonists were the most desirable, he thought Belgium, Holland, Germany, Switzerland, and German states more likely sources. He even suggested lifting religious barriers, noting that Jews, Muslims, and Protestants would be just as good colonists as Catholics. However, there were numerous obstacles, chief among which was mandatory military service, which "impedes marriage, decreases reproduction, and diminishes agricultural activity." Freed from such a requirement, Silva Lisboa contended, the population would increase, new towns would be formed, and the state would gain men to defend it against the "disorder and insurrection of slaves."[302]

Silva Lisboa recognised, however, the paradox that such trade depended on commodities produced by forced labor, necessitating in turn the accelerated importation of slaves. This phenomenon altered the racial composition of society which, in turn, he argued, undermined the process of "civilization" and raised the spectre of catastrophic instability. Silva Lisboa therefore urged the "whitening" (*embranquiçamento*) of Brazil's population through European immigration. Such voluntary European immigration could mitigate the impact of forced migration from Africa. The state would have to intervene before market forces created a society whose racial composition augured calamity. Brazil would only "advance with free people (*gente livre*), of European extraction, because they are more intelligent, moral and industrious, and

[301] ADB, ACB, SIFAA 13, 19, 3, Manoel Rodrigues Gameiro Pessoa [from Vienna] to Conde da Barca, January 3, 1815.
[302] José da Silva Lisboa, "Parecer dado por ordem superior sobre os expedientes necessarios ao progresso e melhoramento da população do Brasil" (1816), reproduced in J. V. Capela 1993, doc. 19, pp. 319–28 passim.

productive."[303] Silva Lisboa believed that immigrants would flock to Brazil when it furnished conditions which resembled those of Europe, only more salutary, with improved prospects for land tenure. This conjuncture, however, could only result from rising levels of wealth, itself contingent on slavery's expansion. Brazil, Silva Lisboa asserted, "can be a place for immigrants whose overcrowding in cities is the cause of their poverty, wrongdoing, and wars that afflict Europe."[304] Like Silva Lisboa, Vilanova Portugal envisaged Brazil's transformation from a society of slave-dependent *fazendas* to one of prosperous agricultural communities of small farms, owned and worked by rooted freeholders of European descent.[305] Such a transition was predicated on a new *Lei Agraria*, the division of privately held property not in productive use. He found it "strange that [existing policy makes it] easier to bring blacks than whites [*negros do que brancos*] to Brazil."[306] He therefore endorsed the immigration proposals then percolating, recommending subsidies to entice Europeans. He warned Dom João that "the venture will be costly," but he was convinced that

farmers will love the soil they can call their own and the sovereign whose benevolence provided them with it ... they will bring with them knowledge of the latest agricultural techniques which will make the interior flourish and serve as an example to others. Their willingness to work the land themselves, without slaves, will serve as an example.[307]

Crown servants believed that there were plenty of precedents for their proposed policies and they actively searched for appropriate models in foreign lands. Portugal's envoy to St Petersburg, for example, enthusiastically wrote to Vilanova Portugal concerning the Russian government's tactics and strategy for establishing internal colonies and encouraging emigration from abroad to settle sparsely populated frontier zones. Starting from the premise that Brazil and Russia "found themselves in analogous circumstances," he urged the government to subsidize emigration as Russia had done. He gushed that almost eighteen thousand settlers, "of different nations and faiths, but mainly Germans," had arrived in Russia between 1803 and 1812 alone.[308] Other models

[303] Silva Lisboa 1822b, p. 36.   [304] Silva Lisboa 1822a, p. 21.
[305] Clayton 1977, p. 173. Vilanova hoped to achieve this goal by ending the *sesmarias* and instead dividing the land, which would then be distributed by the local *câmaras*. See Vilanova Portugal, "Parecer sobre a Questão da Escravatura" (October 1814), quoted in Clayton 1977, p. 334.
[306] Ibid., p. 335.
[307] Vilanova Portugal to Dom João, December 19, 1817, quoted in Clayton 1977, pp. 176–77.
[308] "Ofício (no. 140) de Luís António de Abreu e Lima [in St. Petersburg] ... para Tomás António de Vila Nova Portugal, remetendo-lhe um memorial intitulado 'Conditions

were equally influential as Luso-Brazilian officials searched for a magic formula, including the late eighteenth-century Spanish population schemes in the Sierra Morena and General van der Bosch's schemes for the Low Countries (particularly Holland) in 1818–20. In the 1820s and 1830s, books such as L. F. Huerne de Pommeuse's *Des Colonies Agricoles et leurs avantages* (1832) and E. G. Wakefield's tracts, including *Letter from Sydney* (1829) and *England and America* (1833), would prove enormously influential.[309] "Whitening" and long-term prosperity, therefore, were inextricably linked in Vilanova Portugal's and Silva Lisboa's thoughts. Nor were they alone. Leading Brazilian political writers and actors of all political stripes, including Hipólito da Costa, José Bonifácio de Andrada, and José Carneiro de Campos, entertained similar ideas.[310] José Bonifácio called slavery the "gangrene of our prosperity" and repeatedly claimed that "the population we want is a white one."[311]

Such views resonated with recently launched initiatives. In 1808, fifteen hundred Azorean families were ordered to resettle in Rio Grande do Sul. In 1811, the Crown approved measures to found colonies on lands expropriated from Amerindians in the captaincies of Bahia, Minas Gerais, and Espírito Santo.[312] In 1811, the Crown founded a settlement intended for Irish immigrants in Rio Grande do Sul. In 1818, Dom João levied an import tax on slaves and earmarked half of the receipts to subsidize European immigration.[313] In the same year, under the sponsorship of Dona Leopoldina (Prince Dom Pedro's first, Austrian-born wife), extensive land grants were made to establish a

pour la Réception des Colons en Russie,'" May 12, 1819; document found in ANTT, APASG, cx. 2, mç. 4. Certainly, this interest was neither isolated not unreciprocated: Georges Henri von Lagsdorff, a German traveler who served as Russian consul in Rio de Janeiro from 1813, published a pamphlet (in French) in Paris in 1820 which was effectively a guide for prospective immigrants to Brazil. This pamphlet was translated into Portuguese and published in Rio de Janeiro in 1822. See Jean Glenisson, "Um Emigrante Francês no Brasil: Jean Etienne Seraine (1827–1854)," in Vidal and Luca 2009, p. 123.

[309] Many of these schemes and books are discussed in Ferreira 1834, pp. 3–38 passim; for insight into how, in British contexts, support for white colonial emigration and settlement was, in part, linked to the romantic critique of the conception of poverty (and its alleviation) espoused in liberal political economy, see O'Brien 2009, pp. 161–79.

[310] On Bonifácio's views, see Maxwell 1984, p. 547; and A. R. C. da Silva 1999. For Carneiro de Campos, see *Documentos ... Independência* 1923, vol. I, p. 364. On the link between *comércio livre* and European immigration in early nineteenth-century Brazilian thought, see K. Maxwell and M. B. N. da Silva, "A Política," in Serrão and Marques 1986, vol. VIII, pp. 370–72.

[311] Quoted in Maxwell 1984, p. 542.

[312] Iotti 2001, p. 347.   [313] Cavaliero 1993, p. 67.

Swiss colony in Southern Bahia and an eponymous German settlement, São Leopoldo, in Rio Grande do Sul.[314] But plans for a community of freehold, yeoman farmers foundered when the majority of these settlers acquired slaves. The Crown regarded this unanticipated preference as an unwelcome example to other prospective immigrants as it sought to wean Brazil, unsuccessfully, from its addiction to African slave labor. In May 1818 Crown agents recruited and transported a hundred Swiss Catholic families to found a new settlement in Rio de Janeiro province, called Vila de Nova Friburgo. In 1820, an *alvará* officially established the new settlement, with the expressed aim of "populating and making productive unpopulated land and producing food crops for the city of Rio de Janeiro, which is growing in size and suffers from periodic crises of subsistence."[315] Independence provided a further impulse. An 1823 law authorized provincial presidents to promote the settlement of foreigners in territories under their control. The Brazilian state contracted with physician and adventurer Georg Anton Schäffer to recruit German-speaking colonists, luring them with the promise of land, tax exemption for eight years, allotments of food and seed, and religious freedom. The only condition was the inalienability of land for ten years. At least 5,350 German immigrants arrived in Rio Grande do Sul between 1824 and 1830.[316] In addition to settlement schemes, Dom Pedro recruited large numbers of Irish and German mercenaries to Brazil in the mid 1820s, for the purpose of waging war in the Platine area, and also pacifying Brazil's cities, an ultimately misguided scheme that backfired badly, as discussed in Chapters 3 and 4.

The notion of replacing African slaves with European laborers was not endorsed universally. One objection stemmed from slavery's ubiquitous influence. How could the slave trade be suppressed when it had insinuated itself into every aspect of the economy and social life? British traveler Luccock concluded that the slave trade "must long be of vast importance," noting not only its indispensability to shipping, agriculture, and treasury receipts, but its role in every aspect of private and public life, down to the candle wax burned in church ceremonies and used to light private homes.[317] Unsurprisingly, given this reality and the slow trickle of European settlers, the 1820s became the decade during which more slaves were sold into bondage in Brazil than in any previous decade.[318] Other commentators, including Carneiro de Campos, were

---

[314] Baum 1965, p. 175; G. S. Ribeiro 2002, pp. 152–59.
[315] *Alvará* of January 3, 1820, quoted in Iotti 2001, p. 21.
[316] Browne 1972 passim; Iotti 2001, pp. 22, 347.
[317] Luccock 1820, pp. 593–94.
[318] Andrews 2004, p. 77.

more circumspect, wondering aloud whether Brazil's fragile political system could absorb new immigrants.[319]

British abolitionist pressures, however, forced such reservations to be shelved temporarily. Dom Pedro told Brazil's General Assembly in 1830 that he was prepared to "take all measures demanded by good faith and humanity" to eliminate the slave trade "in any form it is found, regardless of pretext" and to "facilitate the immigration of free labor (*braços uteis*), giving them uncultivated lands."[320] Even after his abdication, this policy remained in effect. In his report to the General Assembly in 1833, Foreign Minister Bento da Silva Lisboa, son of the aforementioned Bahian political economist, called for easing the naturalization regulations to encourage "foreigners of good *costumes*," ideally German, French, or English-speaking, to come to Brazil. He urged the advertisement of Brazil's generous policies in Europe in order to "generate excitement and the immigration of industrious people."[321] By 1837, active *Sociedades de Colonização* existed in Rio de Janeiro and Salvador.[322]

While these initiatives continued apace, there was a growing sentiment that immigration inducement schemes were misguided. According to a document entitled "Swiss Colonists in the Brazils," an account of a meeting of Swiss residents in London on 1821, the situation was rather grave:

though every attention has been directed by the Portuguese government towards preparations that might ensure the comfort of the settlers on their arrival, many unforeseen difficulties intervened ... owing to the thick woods, the very un-level face of the country ... but few of the subdivisions of the lands appear yet to have been made.[323]

Subsequently, deputies in independent Brazil's Assembly became skeptical of such schemes.[324] In 1828, Senator Nicolau de Campos Vergueiro dismissed the recent settlements of German immigrants as misguided, a profligate undertaking producing uneven results.[325] By 1829, a pamphlet published in Portugal claimed that

instead of dedicating themselves to agriculture, the Irish and Swiss colonists fled the countryside and can be found begging for alms in the cities [of Brazil].

---

[319] Carneiro de Campos, in *APBAC*, October 3, 1823, t. 6, p. 26.
[320] Dom Pedro, "Fallas do Throno," May 3, 1830, in *Fallas do Throno* 1977, p. 179.
[321] Bento da Silva Lisboa, April 26, 1833, reproduced in *Relatório Apresentado* 1833, pp. 20–21.
[322] António Paulino Limpo de Abreu, May 1837, reproduced in *Relatório Apresentado* 1837, p. 6.
[323] Document found in ANTT, MNE, cx. 745.
[324] J. H. Rodrigues 1965, p. 148.   [325] Iotti 2001, p. 22.

Do not fool yourself: the only type of agriculture possible in Brazil is that done on sugar plantations, and this cannot flourish without slave labor. Anything else is doomed to fail and is an utter waste of time.[326]

The riots incited by Irish and German mercenaries' behavior, combined with the arrival of Portuguese political *Emigrados*, turned the tide of both popular and elite opinion against immigration schemes. Foreigners were sometimes accused of undermining the unity of Brazil during the Regency period. Sometimes, of course, such accusations were accurate: Giuseppe Garibaldi, later the great champion of Italian unification, arrived in Rio de Janeiro in 1835 with a view toward a career as a merchant seaman. By 1837, he had become a corsair for the rebels of Rio Grande do Sul during the *Farroupilha*, using his ship, *The Mazzini*, to launch attacks on Brazilian shipping.[327] By 1838, the Minister of Foreign Affairs conceded that "colonization can only be truly useful to a country when the direction, development, and method is not subject to the whims" of entrepreneurs who seek to profit from the enterprise.[328] Yet, by 1843, a new scheme for the recruitment of foreign colonists was presented to the Assembly and, in 1850, colonization once again became an official goal of Brazil's government.[329] In the 1870s and 1880s, as the abolition of slavery loomed, immigration schemes again became fashionable. Between 1872 and 1887, São Paulo alone received 166,000 European immigrants, mostly Portuguese and Italians. In the decade following abolition in 1888, more than 800,000 European immigrants arrived in Brazil.[330] These later developments would have been inconceivable without the debates, processes, and schemes recounted and analyzed in this chapter.

Reform efforts met with failure as well as success. Sometimes reform initiatives were informed by cutting-edge political economy while at other moments they were animated by nothing more than the venality of officials. Yet the dominant impression of the forty years preceding the Napoleonic occupation of the Iberian Peninsula is one of renewal and ever-closer imperial coordination, or at least a ubiquitous optimism that both of these ends were within reach and that Crown agents were working doggedly toward them. To be sure, without a highly

---

[326] See [Anon.], *Golpe de Vista sobre o Império do Brasil* 1829, pp. 14–15.
[327] Riall 2007, pp. 37–38.
[328] António Peregrino Maciel Monteiro, May 1838, reproduced in *Relatório Apresentado* 1838, p. 16.
[329] Mattos 1987, pp. 239–40; on British and Irish immigrants to Brazil in the late nineteenth century, see Marshall 2005.
[330] Viotti da Costa 1985, p. 124.

improbable, favorable conjuncture of geopolitical events and trends –
from Saint-Domingue's collapse to Britain's ascendancy – in which
Portuguese statesmen played no direct role, Portugal's position would
have been distinctly weaker than it ultimately was on the cusp of the
nineteenth century. Yet the spirit of reform and a political culture that
favored policy experimentation were at least partially responsible for
the anticipation of such crises and the nimble, opportunistic reaction
to them once they occurred.

In the nineteenth century, however, this favorable conjuncture would
be overwhelmed by less propitious events and trends – from republican
revolutions in neighboring Spanish America to Britain's insistence on
the slave trade's abolition and its rejection of colonial monopoly – to
which Portugal would struggle to adjust. Furthermore, the preponderance of economic power within the empire shifted decisively to Brazil,
turning peninsular Portugal into a periphery of the empire of which
it remained the legal, administrative, and historical center. As shall
be analyzed in Chapter 2, it was the political turmoil wrought by the
French occupation from late 1807 which converted this situation into
a crisis. War, together with the transfer of the seat of government, set
off a chain reaction of constitutional debates and political unrest, and
brought about a final reckoning.

2 From foreign invasion to imperial disintegration

This chapter describes and analyzes the crisis into which the Portuguese empire entered from the 1807 Napoleonic invasion until Brazil's declaration of independence in 1822. Several aspects of this period, particularly the transfer of the Court from Lisbon to Rio de Janeiro, have benefited from exhaustive scholarly attention and thus receive mere summary treatment in this chapter. The purpose of the analysis offered here is to demonstrate how the various parts of the Portuguese empire came to be reconfigured as a result of Portugal's involuntary involvement in the French Revolutionary Wars. On the one hand, this chapter demonstrates how, for Portugal, the experience of occupation, first by a belligerent (France) and then by an ally (Britain), not only deprived it of the advantages and status of being the seat of a global empire, but also paved the way for the overthrow of royal absolutism and the installation of a constitutionalist regime. On the other hand, this chapter argues that Brazil's experience of becoming the seat of government, surrounded by revolutionary Spanish American republics, favored the emergence of a conception of empire incompatible with the one dominant before 1807–8. These propositions are defended and elaborated upon in the following three parts. In Part I, Portugal's precarious place in the European state system is introduced, the impact of the French occupation is explained, and the consequences of the transfer of the Court to the New World are discussed. The analysis then turns to the growing discontent with the configuration of the empire after 1815, which resulted in conspiracies and revolts in both Portugal and Brazil. Part I concludes with the processes culminating in the 1820 Porto Revolution which sought to establish, at a minimum, a mixed monarchy with a written constitution and robust representative institutions.

Part II switches gears, focusing on the long pre-history of the 1820–21 crisis, specifically the shifting meaning of constitutionalism in the Luso-Atlantic world in the late eighteenth century. It explores the influence exerted by foreign constitutionalism – Spanish, French, and British – on the Portuguese legal imagination between 1808 and 1823

84

and recounts the struggle of the revolutionary assembly, or Cortes, to frame a new constitution. Part II also integrates conservative political thought, with its distinct understandings of constitutionalism, monarchy, and revolution, into the broader panorama. Part III investigates the schism that opened up between Portugal and Brazil during the 1820–23 revolutionary period, which ultimately resulted in imperial disintegration. Though consideration of popular manifestations of political attitudes would be valuable, Part III narrows the scope to the intellectual rifts and irreconcilable conceptions of empire at the elite level. It pays careful attention to the Lisbon Cortes debates, featuring both Peninsular and Brazilian deputies, in an effort to emphasize the contingent and far from inevitable nature of the conflict that developed. Part III, and Chapter 2 as a whole, concludes with an analysis of the debates of Brazil's first Constituent Assembly, convened in 1823, suggesting how conflicts over the nature and scope of executive authority, as well as disputes between partisans of centralism and federalism, were extensions of the disputes animating the Lisbon Cortes, thus hoping to underscore the often neglected link between colonial and early national political history.

PART I

Occupation, liberation, and desperation: Portugal and the French revolutionary wars

Imperial Portugal was swept up involuntarily in the maelstrom of the Age of Revolutions.[1] It is customary, and sensible, to record November 1807 as the watershed moment, when French soldiers, led by General Jean-Andoche Junot, occupied Lisbon, prompting the transfer of the Braganza family and its Court to the New World. But the decade preceding 1808 deserves attention, for it witnessed the slow fraying of the Luso-Brazilian empire's bonds and the obsolescence of some of its integrationist schemes. From 1793, Portugal was embroiled in the turmoil engulfing the rest of Europe, signing anti-French agreements with Spain and Britain, and even participating in a Spanish-led invasion of Southern France in September of that year. Following Spain's withdrawal from the First Coalition in 1795, France demanded that Portugal sever its British

---

[1] For a recent overview of the historiography, see the essays in Cardoso, Monteiro, and Serrão 2010. On European international relations in this period more generally, see Scott 2006, chs. 10 and 11.

alliance, declare itself neutral, pay France an indemnity, and grant its former adversary privileged commercial concessions. Portugal refused to yield, without repercussions, but the ultimatum permanently divided the cabinet, as some members soured on the British Alliance and gravitated toward conciliation with France. The cabinet deadlock culminated in a declaration of neutrality in 1797, a move bound to satisfy neither suitor. The consequences of straying from Albion's bosom became manifest in the 1801 Spanish invasion of Portugal, the so-called "War of the Oranges," which resulted from a Franco-Spanish accord to conquer and partition Portugal in the event that it adhered to the British alliance. Though Spain's forces merely overran a few border fortresses, the exposure of Lusitanian weakness compelled its acquiescence to harsh terms, including the payment of an indemnity and commercial concessions to Spain's ally France.[2] Crucially, Portugal pledged to close its harbors to British vessels. In 1803, Dom João again declared Portugal's neutrality and closed his kingdom's ports to both French and British ships. As in 1797, such a position proved untenable: Bonaparte rejected it outright and demanded that Portuguese authorities pay a penalty of one million *livres* by mid 1804 for their insouciance. Portugal refused to comply, but nevertheless clung to a neutral position throughout 1804, when Spain and France issued an invitation to join an anti-British alliance.[3]

Portugal's involvement in this first phase of the Napoleonic Wars proved detrimental to public finance. Dom João was compelled to issue two public loans (1796 and 1801). By 1798, public debt amounted to almost 80 percent of government revenue, a dramatic change from the halcyon years of 1762–76, when there was no public debt.[4] Technically, Britain's long-standing alliance with Portugal remained in effect, but Portugal's vacillation and bad faith irked British representatives. A 1793 treaty reaffirmed all of Britain's obligations toward Portugal and, between 1796 and 1801, Britain furnished its Iberian ally with massive quantities of arms and other materiel to bolster its flagging war effort: at least 31,000 muskets, 11,300 carbines, 3,300 pistols, 14,300 swords, 10,000 barrels of powder, 20 canon, and over £200,000 in credit. Furthermore, in 1797, Pitt persuaded the House of Commons to vote an additional £500,000 to Portugal.[5] Yet the Portuguese government's perceived comportment – irresolute, unreliable, and unpredictable – angered British critics, who foresaw no option but the evacuation

[2] Schroeder 1994, p. 223.
[3] Grab 2003, pp. 145–46.
[4] Cardoso and Lains 2010, p. 254.
[5] Sherwig 1969, pp. 136–38.

Figure 1 James Godby, engraving, after a painting by Domenico Pellegrini. "[Dom João] His Royal Highness, the Prince of the Brazils and Prince Regent of Portugal" (London: Edward Orme, 1808).

of the Braganzas from the Peninsula and their transfer to Brazil. Lord Hawkesbury, then foreign secretary, made two unsuccessful overtures for a preemptive, peacetime transfer in 1801 and 1803. In his view, "this proposition would have the double effect not only of securing Portuguese settlements but, under possible circumstances, the Portuguese Navy against the designs of France."[6] Hawkesbury was prescient: the situation unfolded as he had predicted. In the interim, the Spanish prime minister Manuel de Godoy, after unceasing machinations, reached a further agreement with France for the partition of Portugal, by which the former would receive a newly carved principality. But Napoleon either lost interest or became preoccupied with other matters, including a proposed general peace from which Spain would be excluded.[7] In 1807, however, he resolved to seal the leaky Lusitanian breach in his Continental System. He demanded the closure of Portugal's ports to British ships, the confiscation of British merchandise, and the arrest of British subjects. Portugal complied with the first demand, on October 20, but balked at the second and third demands. France then raised the stakes, insisting on garrisoning and commanding Portugal's coastal fortresses.[8] Meanwhile, the Franco-Spanish Treaty of Fontainebleau revived the forsaken plan for the partition of Portugal, also promising Charles IV all of Portuguese America. But, infamously, Napoleon's negotiations proved a ploy to distract attention from his genuine plot: the occupation of Spain and, at the very least, the annexation of the north and northeast of that country.[9]

Before Portugal could comply with or reject French demands, Britain issued Dom João's cabinet with an ultimatum to either renew its treaty obligations and evacuate Lisbon for Rio de Janeiro, with British support, or else be abandoned and witness its fleet burned by the British navy, an encore of Britain's performance just months earlier in Copenhagen's harbor, to prevent the seizure and use of its warships by the French.[10] As part of the convention, signed in London by Domingos de Souza Coutinho and then foreign secretary George Canning in late October 1807, Britain promised not to recognize any prince from a dynasty other than the Braganzas on the Portuguese throne. But Canning wrested huge concessions in exchange: Portugal would accede to the occupation of Madeira, and Santa Catarina, in southern Brazil, would

---

[6] Hawkesbury to Lord R. S. Fitzgerald (October 1803), quoted in Sherwig 1969, p. 141, fn. 79.
[7] Schroeder 1994, p. 338.   [8] Broers 1996, p. 156.
[9] Schroeder 1994, p. 338.
[10] Bethell 1970b, p. 6; Robson 2011.

become a free port. But Conde da Barca, then Minister of Foreign Affairs and War, repudiated this last concession and refused to ratify it.[11] The long-standing Cabinet feuds between pro-French (led by Conde da Barca) and pro-British (led by Rodrigo de Souza Coutinho, now Conde de Linhares) factions came to a head. In different ways, each set of demands, British and French, was onerous and hostile, raising a frightening array of problems.[12] Finally, the Portuguese cabinet accepted the British offer, the economic price of which was, as discussed in Chapter 1, the effective surrender of its colonial monopoly, along with the occupation of Madeira and Goa.[13] Defenders of the British alliance claimed their opponents operated in a fantasy world. Without Britain's support, everything was imperiled: "neither the state of the nation, nor the condition of the state of the army and navy, will permit Portugal to flourish without the English Alliance."[14] These arguments emerged victorious and the Court – and courtiers, belongings, records, libraries – embarked for the New World under British protection.

The other principal result of the mass exodus from Lisbon was the chaotic, but easily accomplished, occupation of Lisbon by Junot's twenty-five-thousand-strong army. From December 1807 to June 1808, Junot ruled over a stunned if unpacified Portugal.[15] Aspiring to become, like Murat in Naples, the king of a new French satellite state, Junot trod carefully and avoided conflict with his collaborators. He left untouched most administrative, judicial, and fiscal structures and enjoyed a corresponding level of collaboration, from both *afrancesados* and others who hoped to maintain the status quo in perpetuity.[16] But such a posture soon became untenable. Junot dissolved the Regency Council in February 1808 and declared Dom João (and the Braganza dynasty) officially deposed. Furthermore, the militia was disbanded,

---

[11] M. B. N. da Silva 2008b, p. 41. On the convention from a British perspective, see Robson 2011, pp. 129–30.

[12] These are treated in exquisite detail in Alexandre 1993, pp. 207–30.

[13] Goa had been occupied already by the "uninvited and unwelcome" British in 1799 as a preemptive measure. See Disney 2009, vol. II, p. 330.

[14] BAj. 54-XI-23, doc. 157, "Memoria sobre os Motivos Politicos da Amizade de Portugal com a Inglaterra" (1808), fos. 11–12. As Schultz 2001 explained, there was a great deal of opposition to the transfer of the Court to the New World: "while the idea alienated members of the nobility without interests in Brazil, it also was perceived as catering to British concerns and, hence, jeopardizing whatever possibility of neutrality remained," p. 28.

[15] Nicknamed "the Tempest," Junot was a close associate of Napoleon from the siege of Toulon onward. He participated in campaigns in Italy, Egypt, and Palestine, in addition to having served as French ambassador to Lisbon. In Portugal, after 1808, Junot assumed the title Duque de Abrantes. See Esdaile 2003, p. 18.

[16] Ana Cristina Bartolomeu de Araújo, "As Invasões Francesas e a Afirmação das Ideias Liberais," in Torgal and Roque 1993, p. 27.

and, crucially, several units of Portugal's regular army, totaling six thousand men, were incorporated into the French army. The so-called "Portuguese Legion," or "*Legiao d'Alorna*," fought under French colors in Spain, Austria, and Russia.[17]

The flaws in Junot's strategy became visible as Portugal recovered from the traumatic shock of occupation. Junot was forced to govern over an increasingly restless populace. Various aspirations, as well as fears and anxieties, jostled for primacy among Portuguese opposed to French rule: the desire to restore a member of the Braganza dynasty to the throne; a fear of Portugal's imminent annexation into Spain; and the trepidation felt by the clergy and nobility concerning their privileges should Junot impose the civil code. In addition, the brutality of the French occupation, and the intensity and pace of Junot's reforms, insti-gated a chauvinistic backlash. Various uprisings against the French – first in Porto, later in Minho and the Algarve – sparked the proliferation of local juntas resistant to French rule. These coalesced, quickly and seamlessly compared with the contemporaneous situation in Spain, to recognize the supreme authority of the Porto Junta, led by Bishop Dom António José de Castro.[18]

The Porto *Junta Suprema*'s effort to resist the French occupation was bolstered by the arrival of a British expeditionary force in August 1808, under the command of Sir Arthur Wellesley, the future Duke of Wellington. After a joint Anglo-Portuguese force defeated Junot's troops at Vimiero, France sued for peace and, by the terms of the Convention of Sintra, French armies evacuated Portugal, with their weapons and the booty accumulated during the occupation – exceedingly lenient terms which triggered indignant uproar in Portugal and Britain.[19] The transformation of the Portuguese army was entrusted to William Carr, later Viscount Beresford (1768–1854),[20] who purged old officers, intro-duced conscription, commissioned new officers, raised pay, revamped

---

[17] Grab 2003, p. 147; Broers 1996, p. 156; F. O. Cetre estimates that nine thousand Portuguese comprised the legion, in six infantry and three cavalry regiments, claim-ing that only five hundred survived. See Cetre, "Beresford and the Portuguese Army," in Berkeley 1991, p. 150. See also Roger Kann, "Les Portugais de la Grande Armée de Napoleon" in the same volume.

[18] Broers 1996, pp. 156–58.

[19] Esdaile 2003, pp. 101–2. William Wordsworth was among those outraged, penning a tract on the subject. On his (and Coleridge's and Southey's) indignation, see Coleman 1989.

[20] Beresford's experience included participation in the expedition to the Cape of Good Hope in 1806, resulting in the capture of the Dutch colony there, and in Home Popham's seizure of Buenos Aires later that year. In Buenos Aires, Beresford was promoted to major general and acted as de facto governor there for two months. See Newitt and Robson 2004, p. 17

training methods, and imposed unprecedented discipline, eventually increasing the number of active troops to thirty thousand.[21] The financial outlay entailed was enormous.

Though mobilization of the country's resources for total war ultimately turned Beresford into a de facto viceroy, political authority officially resided in a regency council, reconstituted in September 1808. The question of how Portugal and its Atlantic archipelagos should be governed in the wake of the Court's transfer was vexing. The *Governadores do Reino* lacked ample power to determine and execute policy. The absence of a representative of the royal family among the *Governadores* further marginalized and undermined their status. In late 1808, Conde da Barca endorsed advice proffered by other counselors to establish a full-fledged regency with Dona Maria Benedita at its head, whose "virtues and good qualities could make [Dom João] confident that the tranquility and security" of Portugal were handled properly. There was nothing to fear from a regency, for "delegated power would have clear limits"; it would not make foreign policy or exercise "rights that are truly royal [*magistatico*]."[22] The British ambassador, Villiers, believed that any regency, regardless of form and composition, would struggle without a Cortes, or some equivalent body representing the various estates of the kingdom. He advocated a "small, efficient regency, secured, improved and extended by the Cortes," to be convoked in the name of the king to execute its "old, established objects, the furnishing of extraordinary aids, the levying of extraordinary taxes and making fundamental ordinances."[23] Dom João remained unmoved by these suggestions. He insisted on ruling from Rio de Janeiro, with the *Governadores* serving as mere conduits of his will. The *Governadores* increasingly were deprived of their already meager authority. For example, the Overseas Council, its relevance obviated by the Court's transfer, ceased to function altogether. Thereafter all correspondence pertaining to African or Asian affairs bypassed Lisbon and was sent directly to Rio de Janeiro, where the secretaries of state resided.[24]

Though stripped of authority, the *Governadores* retained responsibility for the unpopular, thankless task of devising new taxes, disposing of Crown land, collecting unpaid rents, and implementing new revenue-generating mechanisms designed to meet wartime exigencies. Imposed on a populace and economy already ravaged by foreign

---

[21] Among others, see F. D. Costa 2008.
[22] ADB, ACB, SIFAA 37, 107, Conde da Barca to Dom João (then Prince-Regent), December 26, 1808.
[23] Villiers, May 14, 1809, quoted in Martins 2008, pp. 69–70.
[24] Myrup 2010, p. 217.

occupation, these fiscal innovations failed to generate the anticipated yield. Further British subsidies flowed into Portugal and, by 1809, the Regency's deficit reached almost £1 million, in spite of £270,000 received from Britain. In 1810, the British subsidy rose to £1 million, though much of this sum arrived in the form of food aid, shipped from Britain. The price of staples doubled in 1810 owing to poor harvests and overall economic dislocation. In addition to aid distributed to the *Governadores*, Dom João sought emergency, discretionary funds to keep his new fledgling (and spendthrift) bureaucracy in Rio de Janeiro afloat. In 1809, he raised a £600,000 loan in London, guaranteed by the British government, a mere third of which was earmarked for the Peninsula. British subsidies and military presence, predictably, translated into direct political influence. There was a British representative on the *Governadores* from 1809, with a right to vote on military and financial matters.[25]

Beresford transformed Portugal into a veritable "barrack-state" for good reason. There were two further French invasions, under generals Soult and Masséna, respectively. Masséna's August 1810 invasion, with sixty-five thousand soldiers, the largest French force sent to Portugal, was defeated in large part as a result of Wellington's skillful tactics. He withdrew behind the lines at Torres Vedras, an impregnable system of defense works near Lisbon, and waited out the French army's siege. By March 1811, Masséna's army had succumbed to combat casualties, hunger, and disease, retreating to the Spanish border.[26] This achievement was impressive. As a contemporary historian has observed, "the dictatorship of Beresford produced the only army of the period to achieve sustained, consistent victories over the French."[27]

The price of victory, however, was outrageously steep. Portugal's population declined by more than three hundred thousand between 1807 and 1811 and its economic infrastructure was severely damaged. The kingdom's roads, always poor, now became veritable obstacles to commercial activity.[28] Even cultural institutions had been laid waste. By 1811, the Museum and Botanical Garden at Ajuda, for example, were in total disrepair, pilfered, ravaged, and then abandoned by the

---

[25] Grab 2003, p. 149; Sherwig 1969, pp. 201, 218–29, 231, 241; Fernando Marques 1990, p. 26. The British representatives were first John Charles Villiers and then Sir Charles Stuart.

[26] Esdaile 2003, pp. 311–13; Grab 2003, p. 150. On Portuguese opposition to Napoleon's tactics, see Horward 1989, pp. 48–49.

[27] Broers 1996, p. 217.

[28] See the 1813 *memoria* quoted in Serrão 1989, vol. I, p. 86; Esdaile 2003 estimated that eighty thousand civilians perished during Masséna's invasion, p. 333.

French (Napoleon had authorized Etienne Geoffrey de Sainte-Hilaire in 1808 to transport plant samples back to the *Jardin des Plantes* and the *Musée d'Histoire Naturelle* in Paris). They were deprived, too, of the dynamic presence of Vandelli, Rodrigues Ferreira, and other naturalist-scientists, who had fled Portugal.[29] The years 1808 to 1813 also were a period of acute commercial crisis, as Portuguese exports to Brazil plummeted to a quarter of their 1796–1806 level. Though the cessation of hostilities permitted the partial recuperation of the Brazil trade, which reached 95 percent of its earlier level between 1816 and 1822, the transit trade of re-exports, whether of European products sent on to Brazil via Portugal or Brazilian products re-exported to other European states via Lusitanian ports, was never regained.[30] The militarization of social-economic resources, the successive, destructive occupations by both allied and enemy forces, and the economic impact of the Court's protracted stay in Brazil produced effects from which Portugal struggled to recover for decades. By 1812, public debt stood at 4.3 years-worth of government revenue.[31] With the productive sectors of the economy devastated, the size of the British subsidy ballooned, reaching almost £4 million in 1813–14.[32] In such a forlorn state, the expansion of British influence was inevitable. Beresford was the unrivaled master of Portugal by late 1811, eventually elevated to Portuguese marquisate, though a vice-regal title might have reflected his stature more accurately.[33]

Many Portuguese, at both elite and popular level, blamed Britain for the economic calamity afflicting Portugal, pointing to the 1808 and 1810 agreements. One commentator christened them a "Pandora's Box" and a "death blow" for commerce, industry, and navigation.[34] While bemoaning the ill effects of the treaties, however, many commentators also looked deeper and offered an altogether less favorable diagnosis and long-term prognosis. Portugal's crisis required the "complete overhaul of its administration and a shift in the political economy underpinning its policies," the inadequacy of which was revealed by the 1808–14 debacle.[35] The Court's presence in the New World was

---

[29] ANTT, MR, cx. 318, mc. 236, Aguiar to Patriarcha Eleita de Lisboa, April 27, 1811; Mello Pereira 2010, p. 166; Russell-Wood 1992; p. 177.

[30] J. Pedreira, "O Fim do Império Luso-Brasileiro," in Bethencourt and Chaudhuri 2000, vol. IV, p. 224; Alexandre 1993.

[31] Cardoso and Lains 2010, p. 255.

[32] Sherwig 1969, p. 264.

[33] Beresford was first elevated to the title of Conde de Trancoso and subsequently Marquês do Campo Maior.

[34] *O Portuguez*, no. 37 (May 1817), p. 132.

[35] *Espelho Politico e Moral* (London), no. 16 (August 17, 1813), p. 121; on economic discourse in Portugal *c.* 1808–12, see Alexandre 1993, p. 223.

Figure 2 Charles Turner, engraving/aquatint, after a painting by Thomas Staunton St. Clair. "City of Coimbra" (London: C. Turner and Colnaghi, 1812–15).

lamented. Lisbon merchants petitioned the Crown, begging Dom
João to devise measures to rehabilitate national shipping and to free
Portugal from the British military yoke.[36] Aware of their vulnerability, they resented Crown policy, which favored Brazilian over peninsular merchants. They imagined alternative institutional solutions to
provide them with greater security.[37] The *Governadores* bombarded
Dom João with dire prognostications, unsubtle warnings, and scarcely
concealed admonishments. If the navy and merchant marine declined
further, Principal Souza predicted in 1814, Portugal would drop to
the rank of a "small duchy in Germany or Italy." And if its population
dwindled and its agriculture stagnated further, he warned, Portugal
would be reduced to "insignificance, without the means to sustain its
independence."[38]

The road to a *Reino Unido*: the court in Rio de Janeiro and the reconfiguration of the Portuguese empire

The Crown's reliance on Britain deepened and the Braganzas displayed few signs of budging from their "Tropical Versailles."[39] Already
in March 1810, a *Carta Régia* justified the sudden embrace of economic
liberalism, stressing the priority of agriculture and offering a savage
critique of the customs system prevailing before 1808.[40] But ideology
played only a slight role in the Court's calculations and posture. The
inverse fortunes of the New World and the Old weighed most heavily. Portugal's presumably irreversible degradation contrasted starkly
with the Court's efflorescence in a Brazil of bountiful resources and
boundless potential prosperity. The choice of Rio de Janeiro as the new
(if still unofficial) seat of the monarchy was far from random or arbitrary. As indicated in Chapter 1, from the mid eighteenth century, it
had become a crossroads where various supply lines converged: minerals from Minas Gerais, wheat and hides from Rio Grande do Sul,
and tobacco from Bahia. Furthermore, it was a chief entrepôt of the
transatlantic slave trade by 1800. The relocation of the viceregal capital from Bahia in 1763 reflected these shifts, as well as presaging the
southward reorientation of Brazil's economy.[41] The November 1807

---

[36] Pedreira and Costa 2008, p. 335.
[37] Alexandre 1993, p. 399.
[38] Principal Souza to Dom João, January 22, 1814, quoted in A. Pereira 1953–58, vol.
III, pp. 168, 170.
[39] The phrase belongs to Oliveira Lima 1996; revived and redeployed by Schultz
2001.
[40] Alexandre 1993, p. 232.   [41] Slemian 2004.

fleet carried fourteen members of the royal family, the Council of State, Justices of Court of Appeals and the High Court, many members of the nobility and the high clergy, not to mention diamonds, silver, jewels, the contents of the royal library, a printing press, and many government records.[42] The Crown also subsidized the relocation, along with subsistence and pay, of many state employees with particular expertise, including physicians, architects, librarians, musicians, and a riding master.[43] The Court's presence transformed the viceregal capital. The Crown embarked on a massive public building and works program, recreating in Rio de Janeiro the administrative apparatuses previously functioning in Lisbon. Much of this construction, and the maintenance of the Court, was paid for, in cash and in kind, by the *Carioca* elite: palaces were lent to the displaced nobility; public subscriptions raised significant funds; and capital for public edifices was supplied.[44] Besides the proliferation of new posts and offices, Dom João further rewarded the generosity and manifest loyalty of Brazil's elite, ingratiating himself by lavishly doling out titles of nobility (254 of all ranks by 1821) and granting at least 4,500 of his Brazilian subjects membership in one of the four coveted knightly orders.[45]

Historians have offered many competing interpretations of what transpired in Rio de Janeiro between 1808 and 1821. The older historiography was divided: some scholars depicted the new institutions as mere replicas of Portuguese models whereas others drew attention to the administrative innovation that occurred in a previously colonial space. In the past forty years, historians have emphasized the transfer of the monarchy as a "Brazilian inversion," when Brazil's relation to Portugal and other dominions was radically repositioned, or else have portrayed the period as a crucible in which a new conception of empire was forged. Certainly, the migration of the court transformed Brazil from a "conglomeration of captaincies subordinated to a single prince" into a political entity inscribed in a single territory with a center of gravity in Rio de Janeiro.[46] There are, of course, many hybrid forms and gradations of the interpretations summarized here.[47]

Amidst the scholarly disagreement, several phenomena should be borne in mind. First, the size of the political administration expanded enormously. The bureaucratic ranks swelled: the number of treasury

---

[42] Manchester 1972, p. 77; more generally, see Schwarcz 2002.
[43] Manchester 1972, pp. 78–79
[44] Kirschner 2009, p. 151.   [45] Schwarcz 2002, p. 255.
[46] Jancsó and Pimenta 2000, p. 154.
[47] For the most recent summary of the existing historiography, see Wehling 2007, pp. 75–92; for recent, nuanced treatments, see Malerba 2000 and Schultz 2001.

employees more than trebled while the number of customs officials doubled.[48] Second, there was a proliferation of new judicial institutions and posts. New *comarcas* were created, along with thirty-eight new *juizados de fora*, while a *relação* for Maranhão was established in 1812, with another for Pernambuco in place nine years later.[49] The burgeoning state payroll, and the lavish maintenance of the Court, led to the introduction of new taxes, including those on tobacco and newly arrived slaves, in addition to a stamp duty.[50] Third, the centralization of power in Rio de Janeiro was established de jure, clarifying and consolidating the preponderance of economic clout it enjoyed from the last decades of the eighteenth century. The population jumped from 50,000 in 1808 to 110,000 a decade later. Fourth, 1808–21 was a period of territorial aggrandizement, with the military occupation of border territories claimed by France and Spain, as discussed in Chapter 1, as well as the seizure of Amerindian lands in Minas Gerais. It was also a period in which plots were hatched to send Dona Carlota Joaquina, wife of the Prince Regent, the only member of the Spanish royal family outside of Napoleon's custody, to Buenos Aires and declare herself regent of the acephalous Spanish Atlantic Monarchy.[51] Fifth, the presence of the court buoyed public life: new theaters, promenades, and public parks were constructed, thanks to new sources of patronage, while (censorship notwithstanding) a nascent print culture gave fresh impetus to colonial intellectual life. The fine and design arts were nurtured through the establishment of an Academy of Beaux-Artes, advanced significantly by the arrival of the French artistic mission in 1816, whose members – painters Jean-Baptiste Debret and Nicolas Antoine Taunay, architect Grandjean de Montigny, and sculptor Auguste Taunay – exerted tremendous influence on Brazilian taste and style.[52]

The Branganzas' "Tropical Versailles" met with criticism as well as praise. Many travelers were unimpressed, including Luccock, who dismissed the new public buildings as "wretchedly defective copies of the [European] originals, which they pretend to imitate."[53] The editor of the London-based *O Portuguez* argued that the institutions erected in Brazil should have been abolished in Portugal instead of being

---

[48] Manchester 1972, p. 80.   [49] Wehling 2007, pp. 82, 89.
[50] M. B. N. da Silva 2008b, p. 109.
[51] S. M. Pereira 2008, pp. 83–84.
[52] Schwarcz 2008; G. S. Ribeiro 2008, pp. 251.
[53] Luccock 1820, p. 52. However, some travelers were impressed: Maria Graham, resident there in 1821–23, noted that "some solid works have been executed since I last saw Rio; new fountains opened, aqueducts repaired, all the forts and public works visibly improved. There is everywhere an air of business." Graham 1824, p. 219.

transferred across the ocean.[54] Modern historians described the new government administration as plagued by "corruption and peculation."[55] But these assessments should not distract from the underlying purpose of the Crown's fervent activity upon disembarking in the New World. If enlightenment was tolerated, the arts nurtured, and public instruction encouraged within bounds, the principal aim was the aggrandizement and security of the burgeoning state. In his 1818 apotheosis of the Court's beneficent impact on Brazil, Silva Lisboa intimated that "the *luzes* are not only a sign of splendor, but also serve to support the Crown. Experience has shown that *povos rudes* are more difficult to rule over and more likely to be deluded by cabals of ambitious and turbulent men." "Polished" subjects, Silva Lisboa and his like-minded peers maintained, knew "their rights and duties," "obey promptly," and were "more constant in accepting their subordinate position" and "more respectful of the authorities."[56]

The seat of the monarchy was expected to revert back to Lisbon at the conclusion of a general peace, a return Dom João had promised explicitly. Undoubtedly, fear was expressed as early as 1809 that the Court's transfer would be made permanent. This concern echoed mid-eighteenth-century deliberations. In 1732, an Overseas Councilor argued that "it is obvious that if Brazil is placed in one scale of the balance and Portugal in the other, the former will weigh far more heavily than the latter; and consequently the larger and richer will not consent to being ruled by the smaller and poorer." In 1738 Dom Luís da Cunha pushed this insight further, urging Dom João to transfer the seat of the monarchy to Brazil and assume the title of "Emperor of the West," an idea revisited by Souza Coutinho in his famous 1797 *memoria*.[57] In 1814–15, then, such a permanent political reconfiguration to reflect the empire's economic proportions was a familiar proposition. Yet the general certainty of the Court's return was such that George Canning was sent to Lisbon as British ambassador in 1814. The *Governadores* sought to demobilize rapidly, slashing military expenditure, and replacing British officers with Portuguese. Dom João appeared increasingly receptive to confronting the kingdom's long-festering problems. In early 1815, Dom João acknowledged Portugal's deteriorated condition.

---

[54] Rocha Loureiro's *O Portuguez* (1816), quoted in M. B. N. da Silva 2008b, p. 108.
[55] Oliveira Lima 1996, p. 84.
[56] Silva Lisboa 1818, vol. I, p. 21. He also argued that "the annals of empire demonstrate the inferiority and weakness of nations not instructed in the sciences and arts," vol. I, p. 125.
[57] Costa and Cunha quotations cited in Boxer 1962, p. 323. On Souza Coutinho's *memoria*, see Maxwell 1973.

An 1815 *alvará* expressed a commitment to "promote and animate" Portugal's agriculture and to pursue "all possible measures to alleviate my loyal vassals of the evils caused by war."[58] But these preparations and preliminaries came to nothing and the Court failed to relocate. Instead, Brazil was raised to the status of a kingdom, coequal with Portugal. Writing from Vienna in January 1815, the Portuguese diplomats who formed Portugal's delegation to the Congress jointly informed Marquês de Aguiar that Talleyrand, then chief French negotiator, had made such a suggestion in order to "flatter (*lisonjear*) its people and destroy the unfavorable idea that it is a mere colony." The Portuguese delegation concluded that "Your Excellency may well imagine the impression that such a comment from Monsieur de Talleyrand made on us."[59] In a private letter to Conde da Barca, António de Saldanha da Gama added that Talleyrand encouraged Dom João to remain in Brazil while sending his firstborn son (Dom Pedro) to Portugal to act as "viceroy [*vice-rei*]."[60] Whether or not these suggestions truly were attributable to Talleyrand,[61] clarifying the postwar seat of government was increasingly urgent. Hipólito da Costa had referred to the creation of a "*Reino Unido*" from April 1815, well before this status was decreed.[62] The complexion of the debate over the Court's presence in the New World continued after Brazil's elevation to a *reino*. Conde da Barca and Vilanova Portugal advocated for the Court to remain in Brazil; Palmela argued for a return to Portugal; and Silvestre Pinheiro Ferreira pronounced that each option was fraught with distinct dangers and drawbacks.[63] If the eighteenth-century trio of Costa, Cunha, and Souza Coutinho had exhibited rare foresight in prophesying an eventual recalibration of the European and American parts of the empire, nineteenth-century Crown advisors enjoyed the comparatively straightforward task of conceding that a return to the status quo ante was impossible. Various alternative scenarios were

---

[58] *Alvará*, April 11, 1815, quoted in Azevedo 1944, p. 120.

[59] "Officio de Conde de Palmella, de António de Saldanha da Gama e Joaquim Lobo da Silveira a Marquêz de Aguiar," January 26, 1815, in Biker 1879, vol. 18 (10 of *Supplemento*), p. 318.

[60] Saldanha da Gama [from Vienna] to Conde da Barca, January 26, 1815, reproduced in J. V. Capela 1993, doc. 6, p. 100. Previously a colonial official in Maranhão (1802) and Angola (1807–10), António de Saldanha da Gama (1778–1839), later elevated to the title Conde de Porto Santo, was a peer of the realm from 1826 and the first president of Lisbon's *Câmara Municipal* in the late 1830s.

[61] Oliveira Lima suspected that the *Reino Unido* was actually Palmela's suggestion, but that it was dressed up as Talleyrand's idea in case it were ill received at Court. See Oliveira Lima 1996, pp. 335–36.

[62] M. B. N. da Silva 2008b, p. 74.

[63] Kirschner 2009, pp. 185, 195, 198.

envisaged by policy-makers as they grappled with the optimal institutional arrangement to reflect Brazil's economic and political preponderance. Saldanha da Gama believed a branch (*"ramo"*) of the royal family should remain in Brazil.[64] Others contended that the seat of the monarchy was less important than the quality of its governance: only enlightened, sure-handed government could forestall Brazil's imitation of its Spanish American neighbors. The Crown, one of Barca's correspondents advised, must make "a wise choice in the governors who administer the principal ports, experienced and energetic men, whose patriotism is above suspicion."[65] After 1815, new titles and statuses notwithstanding, the late eighteenth-century ideal of an integrated Luso-Brazilian empire became increasingly remote. Now polycentric, separated by vast distances, observers realized that "only unity and perfect harmony of action can form [these parts] into a body capable of resisting threats which come at it from all directions."[66]

The elevation of Brazil to the rank of a kingdom coequal with Portugal generated great excitement and prompted a proliferation of proposals for its territorial and administrative reorganization. The influential (and prolific) official Reis argued that providing both Portugal and Brazil with "equal prerogatives and privileges" would "destroy any jealousy concerning the primacy of one over the other."[67] From Philadelphia, José Correia da Serra wrote to Conde da Barca, praising the "unification of all parts of the monarchy into a single entity" as "singularly sublime and happy."[68] Among the proposals was one for the creation of a new capital city deep in the interior (far from the coast), justified on the basis of drawing population from the littorals, opening up new commercial routes, improving communication, consolidating control over claimed but lightly populated territory, and upgrading the defense of Brazil. It was further argued that a capital city in the interior, with a more temperate climate, would be superior to Rio de Janeiro, where "the heat makes impossible sustained activity and saps one's energy."[69]

---

[64] ADB, ACB, SIFAA/ 9, 7, 2, Saldanha da Gama to Conde da Barca, January 1, 1815.
[65] ADB, ACB, SIFAA/ 15, 1, 8, Ambrosio Joaquim dos Reis [from London] to Conde da Barca, December 22, 1813.
[66] ADB, ACB, SIFAA/ 15, 1, 12, Reis [from Vienna] to Conde da Barca, November 22, 1814.
[67] Reis, "Sobre a Situação da Monarquia Portuguesa depois da Paz de Paris de 1814, indicando algumas providências para a melhorar" (1815), reproduced in J. V. Capela 1993, doc. 7, pp. 122–23.
[68] ADB, ACB, SIFAA/ 16, 22, 10, José Correia da Serra [from Philadelphia] to Conde da Barca, July 18, 1816.
[69] ADB, ACB, SIFAA/ 15, 1, 31, Reis to Conde da Barca, August 24, 1816.

Other commentators were less ebullient about the prospects for the *Reino Unido*. From London, Hipólito da Costa argued that the name change meant little. A wholesale administrative change was required, in his view, for the persistence of "military government" stood opposed to the "happiness of the people and the improvement of the country, appropriate only for the government of a conquered province, which is no longer Brazil's position."[70] As shall be clarified in the next section, proponents of republican government in Brazil construed the creation of the *Reino Unido* as a setback while in the provinces, such as Pernambuco, Rio de Janeiro's emergent hegemony appeared ratified as the *Carioca* capital stepped into the breach formerly occupied by Lisbon. Among other problems, the creation of a "united kingdom" bore no relation to reality. It implied a primordial or inherent unity of Brazil which was contested bitterly. In Europe, the decree came as a shock, a surprising reaction given that its elevation to the status of a kingdom merely "consecrated an established fact, legitimated a situation that could not be denied," in one historian's phrase.[71] The Portuguese *emigrado* press angrily contended that the measure was excessive and lamented the "humiliating, injurious, and awkward status of a colony" to which "the cradle of the monarchy" was reduced. It was henceforth necessary to travel to Rio de Janeiro to handle any matter of importance, they complained, which they deemed an "intolerable disgrace." "Ah, *Senhor*," *O Portuguez* cried, "Your Majesty has but two arms yet you seek to embrace two worlds with them!"[72] By 1817, the situation had deteriorated further. *O Portuguez* declared that "Portugal is ruined," struggling under a "weak, clumsy, contradictory, ignorant, corrupt, and irresolute government."[73] After the 1820 Porto Revolution, Vilanova Portugal confirmed that elevating Brazil to the status of a kingdom had instigated the revolt, for the decision was taken "without being accompanied by laws to usher into existence the heralded union" or to dispel fears that the court would remain in Brazil, "thus leaving the cradle of the monarchy abandoned, in the position of a mere colony."[74] This is precisely what the revolutionary intellectual Manuel Borges Carneiro argued in an 1821 pamphlet: the title *"Reino Unido"* was undermined by "nature and an ocean of two million leagues; it was invented to further the aim of colonizing and exploiting [Portugal]."[75]

---

[70] [Hipólito da Costa], *Correio Braziliense*, vol. XVII, September 1816, p. 372.
[71] Oliveira Lima 1996, p. 343.
[72] *O Portuguez*, vol. 5 (August 1, 1816), p. 347; vol. 4 (February 10, 1816), p. 365.
[73] *O Portuguez*, vol. 6 (1817), p. 618.
[74] ANTT, MNE, livro 467, Vilanova Portugal to "J.M.," January 7, 1821, fo. 73.
[75] [Borges Carneiro] 1821a, pp. 86–87.

Opinions, however, were not polarized irremediably between 1815 and 1820. A solution to placate and conciliate both sides of the Atlantic was thought eminently possible. Many observers realized that Brazil's complete dependence on Lisbon was impractical. But some feared that a genuinely bipolar empire portended its dissolution, not rejuvenation. Peninsular advocates of Brazil's administrative reorganization and the economic development refrained from endorsing changes that would make the former colony self-sufficient through some form of "home rule" and attenuate its already frayed bonds with the beleaguered metropole. In 1816, for example, Reis warned Conde da Barca that establishing a university in Brazil would be dangerous, "promoted by those who always confuse Brazil's prospects in the distant future with its present state." A Brazilian university would be "pernicious," he argued, for the "production of *bachareis* and *letrados*" would "multiply the number of idle talkers (*falladores*), sweet-mouthed poets (*poetas de agoa doce*), and propagators of liberal ideas and the rights of man. This sort of man is noxious to every country, but infinitely more dangerous in one where the majority of the population is composed of slaves and people of color." Reis identified a second disadvantage associated with a university in Brazil: it would "cut the sole thread of dependence of Brazil on Portugal which promotes the perpetual union of the two principal members of the monarchy."[76] The idea of maintaining a single center (*"uma só cabeça"*) in the context of a *Reino Unido* remained a priority for most peninsular policy-makers and advisors before the outbreak of the 1820 Porto Revolution.[77]

In practical terms, the elevation of Brazil to the status of a kingdom exacerbated Portugal's grim reality. It effectively acknowledged the permanent shift of the empire's center. Selection of the "American option" also required the British military presence in the Peninsula after the 1815 general peace. Only a large, disciplined foreign army could guarantee order, suffocate dissent, and deter Spanish machinations to exploit Portugal's undisguisable weakness.[78] Accordingly, Beresford was named Marshal General of all of Portugal's forces, in Europe and America, in 1816. Furthermore, Portugal's military resources were put at Brazil's disposal, not the other way around, in a perversion of the colony–metropole relationship. Dom João ordered the best soldiers and officers in the Portuguese army, numbering more than five thousand, transferred to Brazil in order to participate in the campaign to capture

---

[76] ADB, ACB, SIFAA/ 15, 1, 31, Reis to Conde da Barca, August 24, 1816.

[77] See, for example, the letter of José Anselmo Correa Henriques [representative to the Hanseatic States] to Dom João, October 6, 1820, reproduced in Mendonça 1984, p. 432.

[78] Alexandre 1993, pp. 392, 339.

Montevideo. The impact of this decision was twofold. First, it further inflamed peninsular resentment of the Court and its unresponsive attitude to Portugal's plight. As Beresford informed Conde da Barca in 1817:

you must have foreseen the ruinous consequences of the occupation of Montevideo, the enormous expense to which it has put this kingdom and the Brazilian treasury ... if you wish the Crown of Portugal to remain in the Royal Family of Bragança, His Majesty must return here ... we have at present here no government at all.[79]

Second, the occupation of territory claimed by Spain put the Iberian powers on a collision course toward war, a conflict in which Portugal would fight without its best soldiers. As external invasion loomed, Saldanha da Gama warned that Spain "desires nothing more than some pretext to invade Portugal, and re-unite it to the Spanish Monarchy," which might have transpired had General Riego's 1820 revolt, and the subsequent installation of the *Trienio Liberal*, not intervened.[80]

Revolt in an age of restoration, 1815–1823

In 1815, it appeared that Portugal and its empire had escaped, narrowly, from the chaos unleashed by the French Revolution. However, 1817 proved a tumultuous year, a prelude to the full-fledged discord which previously destroyed the corroded foundations of the French, British, and Spanish empires. Significant threats from within had always been present. An array of local conspiracies, revolts, and acts of resistance from the 1780s presaged and, to some extent, inspired later revolutionary activity. In 1787, Goan priests and laymen were implicated in plots to instigate local military regiments to rise up against Portuguese rule in the Estado da Índia and to declare a republic under the protection of military rulers.[81] In the late 1780s, the republican-infused

---

[79] Beresford to Conde da Barca, August 11, 1817, quoted in M. Newitt, "Lord Beresford and the *Governadores* of Portugal," in Newitt and Robson 2004, pp. 105–8.

[80] ANTT, APASG, cx. 1, mç. 1, Saldanha da Gama to Vilanova Portugal, May (?), 1819. It should be noted that Dom João's 1816 Montevideo campaign (and occupation) gave a further justification for the British presence as a bulwark against a retaliatory Spanish invasion. With regard to the likelihood of a Spanish invasion of Portugal, T. Anna argued that Ferdinand VII's planned expedition to Buenos Aires in 1819–20 was part of a broader plot to conquer Portugal. The king's *camarilla* hoped that an attack on the Portuguese army in the Banda Oriental would provoke a declaration of war by the Portuguese court in Brazil, which would then permit the pursuit of Spain's expansionist ambitions in the Peninsula. See Anna 1978, pp. 358–67.

[81] Bayly 2009, p. 24. Disney doubted whether this Goan plot, the "Pinto Conspiracy," "amounted to much more than loose talk from a few disgruntled individuals," Disney 2009, vol. II, p. 328.

Inconfidência Mineira unfolded in the heart of Minas Gerais.[82] The 1798 Bahian "Tailors' Revolt" (or *Inconfidência Bahiana*), led by *mulato* soldiers and artisans, sought to establish independence from Portugal, create a republic based in electoral democracy, abolish slavery, and bring about full equality between blacks and whites.[83] Another conspiracy with similarly far-reaching objectives was hatched in Pernambuco in 1801.[84]

Throughout Brazil, the "Haitian example" was exploited and manipulated by fear-mongering champions of slavery, though not without basis. In 1805, for example, the image of General Jean-Jacques Desallines appeared on the medallions of several members of the Rio de Janeiro black militia.[85] The ubiquity and extent of slave rebellion anxiety is suggested by the fact that a whopping 80 percent of registered crimes in Rio de Janeiro between 1808 and 1821 were attributed to slaves, who were subjected to intense surveillance and remained under constant suspicion.[86] The presence of *quilombos* across Brazil frightened Brazil's white population, who feared that the maroons aspired to turn Brazil into a "second Haiti."[87] Numerous small-scale slave rebellions and conspiracies (1809, 1814, and 1816) heightened such anxieties (or hopes). The white Brazilian elite found that republicanism and democracy were dangerous concepts and were scared off from experimenting with them in a society with such a high proportion of enslaved Africans and free people of color. Such fears pushed the white Brazilian elite back into the arms of more progressive elements of metropolitan government and away from flirtation with republican and separatist doctrines. The impact of North American revolutionary republicanism and federalism, so influential in Minas Gerais and elsewhere in Brazil during the 1780s, was rejected by the 1790s.[88] For this reason, such turbulence notwithstanding, scholars must avoid synecdoche. While important and long-ignored (and suppressed) by earlier generations of historians, uprisings against colonial rule and the existing socio-economic-political

---

[82] Above all, see Maxwell 1973, esp. 132–135 for the aims of the conspirators.

[83] Andrews 2004, p. 90.

[84] C. G. Mota 2008, p. 53.

[85] Schultz 2005, p. 271. On the impact of the Haitian revolution in the Atlantic World more generally, see Geggus 2001; and Geggus and Fiering 2009.

[86] Slemian 2004, p. 74. However, it should be noted that two thirds of the victims of crimes in Rio de Janeiro during the same period were slaves. See Klein and Vinson 2007, p. 189.

[87] M. J. M. de Carvalho 2006, pp. 1–27; on the contemporary Hispanic Caribbean situation, see Gibson 2010.

[88] K. Maxwell, "The Impact of the American Revolution in Spain and Portugal and their Empires," in Greene and Pole 2000, pp. 542–43.

order occurred sporadically, were of limited duration, and never blossomed into trans-local movements. In many key nodes of empire, there were no outward signs of discontent at all. In Rio de Janeiro, for example, there was a notable paucity of avowed threats, let alone an open insurrection, against colonial rule from 1794–1808, precisely the years when fear of the French and Haitian Revolutionary "contagion" reached its height.[89]

In Portugal, the large number of *afrancesados* who flocked to Junot in 1807–8 confirmed the existence of a robust, subversive, if subterranean, Masonic presence. Freemasonry was alternately tolerated and persecuted in the Luso-Brazilian world. Hounded by the Inquisition in the 1740s and 1750s, Freemasons enjoyed benign neglect under Pombal, when at least three lodges operated openly in Lisbon. Conde Lippe's military reforms further exposed Portuguese troops to Masonic rites and practices. The *Viradeira*, however, was punctuated by a fresh series of prosecutions. *Pedreiros-Livres* were accused of heresy, atheism, unbelief, and libertinage. Freemasons were subjected to additional surveillance after the outbreak of the French Revolution, becoming victims of harsh interrogation techniques and arbitrary imprisonment. Yet even at the height of paranoia and persecution, at least one lodge composed entirely of Portuguese operated in Lisbon. Furthermore, ranking political and cultural figures, including Mello e Castro, Souza Coutinho, and the poet Bocage, were members of lodges or openly sympathetic to Masonic tenets.[90] At the turn of the nineteenth century, Portuguese Freemasons received assurances that they would no longer be persecuted if they banded together to form their own national grand lodge, the result being the founding of the *Grande Oriente Lusitano* between 1801 and 1806.[91] Nevertheless, these assurances appear not to have been fully justified: for example, Hipólito da Costa was incarcerated for his masonic activity for three years (1802–5) before he escaped to London to found the influential *Correio Braziliense*.[92]

An 1817 revolt in the northeastern Brazilian province of Pernambuco posed a genuine threat both to monarchy and to the empire's territorial unity. Surrounded by nascent Spanish American revolutionary republics, it is unsurprising that the Pernambucan revolutionaries were

---

[89] Higgs 1984, p. 27.
[90] Oliveira Marques 1988, pp. 29–35 passim.
[91] Disney 2009, vol. I, p. 322.
[92] Safier 2009b, p. 285. Hipólito was held at the prison of Limoeiro, which was visited in 1824 by John Bowring, who described it as a "horrible place of confinement. It is a representation, on a grander scale, of all the filth and misery of which I have given some details in speaking of the Spanish gaols"; see Bowring 1824, p. 307.

imbued with similar ideas. Some modern historians have described it as a potential "center of attraction for an independent Brazil, or the first independent part of a disaggregated kingdom."[93] Unlike previous civil disturbances in Brazil, which had rarely moved beyond the conspiracy phase, the rebels seized the capital (Recife), and attacked what they considered monarchical despotism, particularly onerous tax levies. They tore royal symbols from military uniforms and Church façades, prohibiting forms of address smacking of privilege and hierarchy. Curiously, the revolution was not anti-clerical, but actually benefited from the local clergy's explicit blessing.[94] Since it was defeated before its leaders managed to establish an independent government throughout the entire province, the Pernambucan Revolution's significance remained largely symbolic. It demonstrated that political separation from Portugal was an aspiration harbored by at least a small cadre of Brazilians. It also raised the prospect of territorial fragmentation fueled by regional patriotism and drew attention to the anti-monarchical ideologies percolating in Brazil.

In Portugal, official fears concerning revolutionary conspiracies largely went unrealized until 1808, due in part to Pina Manique's effective police and espionage networks. Junot's native collaborators demonstrated, however, that discontent bubbled just beneath the surface, especially at the elite level. The Court's failure to return to Portugal after 1815, the persistence (and extent) of the British occupation, and unabated economic malaise dissipated whatever national solidarity was forged in the collective expulsion of the French armies. In 1817, a fledgling conspiracy, organized by a secret society called the "Supremo Conselho Regenerador" was detected, investigated, and suppressed. The "Gomes Freire Conspiracy" was named for the popular general, presumably a Freemason, previously one of the commanders of the Portuguese legion that fought in Napoleon's armies, and who probably played a passive, secondary role in the eponymous affair. Those who used his name plotted to arrest Beresford, expel other foreigners, and orchestrate the acclamation of Gomes Freire at the head of a newly established provisional government. The conspirators plotted to convoke a Cortes, with a view toward declaring a constitutional monarchy. As it turned out, the conspirators' designs were uncovered prematurely

---

[93] Oliveira Lima 1996, p. 552; Mello 2004 made the point that viewing the 1817 Pernambucan Revolution as "separatist" movement is inaccurate for it implies the existence of a unitary and unified Brazil that, in 1817, did not exist, pp. 39, 44; also see C. G. Mota 1972a.

[94] Mosher 2008, pp. 23–38.

and many of them, including Gomes Freire, were executed.[95] The suppression of the 1817 Pernambucan and Lisbon uprisings, however, failed to decapitate radicalism, instead pushing it further underground. In Porto, a new secret society, the *Sinedrio*, met from 1818, under the leadership of Manuel Fernandes Tomás, deeply inspired by the example and doctrines of the Spanish American revolutions.

Even after the suppression of the Gomes Freire Conspiracy, Dom João displayed little inclination to return to the Old World. The *Governoradores* sent him strongly worded letters imploring him to do so, describing the "delicate" situation that demanded "great attention" and "prompt remedies." Two urgent matters cropped up routinely in this correspondence: first, that revenues had declined drastically since 1808 and that the ordinary expenses of even a skeletal administration went unmet, resulting in mounting public debt; second, that the "prolonged absence" of the king had generated widespread "disgust and mistrust," diminishing the "spirit of the nation." They requested a "clarification of [his] true intentions" with regard to future relations between Brazil and Portugal. They wondered aloud whether the seat of the monarchy would shift permanently to Rio de Janeiro, expressing the hope that Dom João would "waste no time in taking steps to unite" Portugal and Brazil, betraying their suspicions.[96] The 1818 acclamation of Dom João, celebrated in Rio de Janeiro, was received as a rude blow in Portugal. While a celebration of royal authority as well as the unity of the *Reino Unido*, it left the matter of the permanent seat of the monarchy undetermined and confirmed the worst fears of Portuguese observers.[97]

Between 1817 and 1820, the London-based *emigrado* press, discussed in the next section of this chapter, was especially vociferous, calling for a reunion of the Cortes, for a written constitution, and for the prompt return of the Court to the Old World. In Portugal itself, the brutal suppression of the Gomes Freire conspirators led to a muted (or perhaps sublimated) outpouring of proposals calling for the improvement of the kingdom's agriculture. Routinely lamented were the size of Portugal's population, which most writers held was below its optimal level, unequal land distribution, which squeezed small proprietors, and the administrative organization of Portuguese territory, which thwarted the implementation of a coherent, Crown-directed strategy. All of these "had

---

[95] Pedreira and Costa 2008, p. 339; Isabel Nobre Vargues, "O Processo de Formação do Primeiro Movimento Liberal: A Revolução de 1820," in Torgal and Roque 1993, p. 51.
[96] ANTT, MNE, Governadores do Reino to Dom João, January 15, 1818.
[97] On the 1818 acclamation, see Schultz 2007, pp. 372–75.

been developed in an age when the principles of political economy were entirely unknown" and thus were in need of overhaul in accordance with such new-fangled principles.[98] But the Crown took little heed of such advice and prescriptions. In March 1820, Beresford informed a confidant that

> the state of affairs here is indeed very critical, and no one sees that better than I do ... there is here no attempt to rectify abuses, that are really weighing down the state itself, and which must in the end destroy it, and that end is not far off. Only at Rio is there any chance of getting any reform and that I fear is very slight.[99]

Beresford wrote tirelessly to Dom João, urging him to change various policies to ameliorate Portugal's plight. On the brink of crisis in 1820, he informed the monarch that foreign grain was flooding the country, causing rapid fluctuation in prices, but received no instructions.[100] He eventually sailed to Rio de Janeiro to express these views directly when his written entreaties met with indifference.[101]

Simmering discontent, an unresponsive government, and carefully plotted conspiracies helped to ensure that Portugal was swept up in the Southern European revolutions which blazed in 1820. Revolution in Spain, sparked by Riego's *pronunciamiento*, led to the reinstallation of a liberal constitutional regime in Spain, known as the *Trienio Liberal*, in March. Naples followed suit in July, and the revolution's leaders adopted the 1812 Cádiz Constitution as their standard.[102] With constitutional-ist governments ensconced in Spain and Naples, the August barracks uprisings in Porto quickly spread throughout Portugal and its empire, reverberating in Goa, where a mutiny against the viceroy occurred in September 1821.[103] In Portugal, a Junta was formed in Porto. It pro-claimed the "regeneration" of Portugal's institutions by convoking the

---

[98] BPMP, MSS. 1743, [Manoel Portugal], "Reflexoens sobre of Augmento d'Agricultura em Portugal," August 1817.

[99] Beresford to Sir David Pack, March 11, 1820, quoted in M. Newitt, "Lord Beresford," in Newitt and Robson 2004, p. 103.

[100] "Memorial dirigido pelo Marechal-General [Beresford], Marquês de Campo Maior, a D. João VI, sobre a forma de remediar a decadencia da agricultura em Portugal," June 19, 1820, document found in ANTT, APASG, cx. 2, mç. 4.

[101] Barman 1988, p. 68.

[102] On the reception of the 1812 Spanish Constitution in Naples, see J. A. Davis 2006. Davis made clear that local knowledge of it often was incomplete and "hazy" (p. 296), its positive reception attributable to local circumstances instead of a more abstract, universal appeal. For Neapolitans, it was the counterpart of, and counterpoint to, an 1812 constitution adopted in Sicily, which was favored by separatists. As Davis concluded, "although democratic in its electoral processes, the Spanish constitution did not threaten the unity of the [Neapolitan] monarchy," p. 304.

[103] On the Goa mutiny, see Bayly 2012, p. 44.

Cortes, a long-defunct representative institution described in Part II of this chapter, bringing together the Three Estates, or *Trés Estados*, of the realm, comprising the Clergy, Nobility, and People, or *Povo*, for the task of writing a new constitution for the empire. The Porto Junta also demanded Dom João's immediate return to the Peninsula. In November, the absence of any discernible progress led the Lisbon garrison to declare the 1812 Spanish Constitution in effect until the Cortes, called for January 1821, could frame a new constitution specifically for Portugal.[104]

Portugal's economic degradation would become a major justification for the 1820 Porto Revolution, as the avalanche of declarations and pamphlets testify. A leading *Vintista* argued that Portugal's plight resulted from "centuries of errors," arguing that all laws required "the most circumspect and serious reform."[105] The revolutionaries blamed the twelve-year separation from their sovereign, depriving them of the resources of *ultramar*, and the depredations by enemy and allied occupations. The "disastrous" 1808 and 1810 treaties with Britain were denounced for causing the "decadence" of Portuguese industry and reducing the Peninsula "to the status of a colony," a fatal insult to "national dignity."[106] Other pamphlets lamented the Peninsula's "boatless navy, unpaid army with foreign generals, immense poverty, rising rates of prostitution," and other social ills which combined to produce "confusion and disorder."[107] Commerce, industry, and agriculture had been suffocated by a superabundance of taxes, imposts, and restrictions. Should outdated, misconceived, and pernicious restrictions suddenly be recognized as an engine of prosperity, Borges Carneiro joked, no people could boast better legislation than the Portuguese.[108] Soares Franco attacked all forms of economic privilege ("a great barbarism") and outdated legislation (denounced as "confused, onerous, and arbitrary"), assailing seigneurial jurisdiction, ecclesiastical imposts, and aristocratic exemptions in particular.[109] They searched for inspiration everywhere. *O Portuguez Constitucional Regenerado* argued that Joseph II's reforms in Austria were worthy of careful consideration, particularly with regard to public revenues, law codes, and ecclesiastical matters.[110] Another writer argued that it was his brother Leopold's system

---

[104] Barman 1988, p. 63.
[105] Manuel Fernandes Tomás, "Relatório sobre o Estado e Administração do Reino" (February 1821), in Tomás 1820, pp. 52, 73.
[106] *Manifesto da Nação Portuguesa* 1820, p. 2.
[107] [Anon.], *O Constitucional Justificado* 1820, p. 13.
[108] Borges Carneiro 1820, p. 126.
[109] Franco 1820–21, Ensaio 2, pp. 9, 11, 26. 29; Ensaio 4, p. 30.
[110] *O Portuguez Constitucional Regenerado*, no. 22 (August 27, 1821), p. 75.

of regulating agricultural imposts that was the "most just, straightforward, economical, productive" and applicable to Portugal.[111] Inspiration
came not only from abroad, but also from Portugal's recent history.
Long-maligned, Pombal was rehabilitated by the *Vintistas* (and their
Brazilian counterparts), who lamented that his best initiatives had
been undone, or severely undermined, by his Marian successors.[112]
Nothing survived of his system except "ministerial despotism," which
in Pombal's "beneficent hands produced great things, but in those of
his successors proved a scourge."[113]

Yet the *Vintistas* were aware of the limits of legal change to transform
Portugal's political, economic, and social reality. How much economic
good would result from modification of the feudal law as long as the
clergy possessed the majority of the nation's wealth, when real property
was concentrated in the hands of a few individuals or families, and while
the general system of taxation remained unreformed? New laws might
remove certain obstacles to economic development, but the structural
problems and accumulated insidious effects of long-standing practices
would not be reversed easily. Some believed that even ambitious legislative tinkering would do less than the enforcement of already existing laws
and the improved administration of justice.[114] These reservations notwithstanding, the Cortes's aspirations were ambitious and far-reaching.
Fernandes Tomás's *Relatório* was perhaps the best-known compendium
of proposed reforms, but myriad other projects were approved by the
Cortes as worthy objectives, many of which went unrealized: freedom of
the press; new criminal and civil codes; the extinction of feudal, baron-
ial rights; the abolition of the tribunals of the Inquisition; a reduction in
the number of regular clergy and nuns; concession of amnesty for political prisoners; the abolition of exclusive privileges; and the creation of
a Bank of Lisbon.[115] Yet the conditions for their realization were not as
propitious in Portugal as they were elsewhere. In 1822, Royer-Collard
remarked that France had witnessed "the old society perish, and with
it that crowd of domestic institutions and magistracies which it carried within it, strong bundles of private rights, two republics within

---

[111] *Vozes dos Leaes Portugueses* 1820, vol. I, p. 28.
[112] Franco 1820–21, Ensaio 1, p. 37.
[113] Maciel da Costa 1821, pp. 16–17.
[114] ANTT, MR, mç. 356 (cx. 476), João Cardoso da Cunha Araújo, "Propor as providencias que julgar convenientes para se facilitar a execução das leyes actualmente em
vigor a bom da agricultura e economia política," October 29, 1821.
[115] Vargues, "O Processo," p. 62; on the process that culminated in the abolition of
the Inquisition's tribunals in 1821 (though subsequently undone), see Bethencourt
2009, pp. 416–20.

the monarchy."[116] But no revolution had swept away the institutions of the Old Regime in Portugal. Unlike Spain, where Napoleon's brother, José I, partially implemented the overhaul of Spanish society before his power ebbed, Portugal escaped largely unscathed. The aristocracy remained unchastened, the ecclesiastical establishment recalcitrant. Only in the latter phase of the Civil War, as discussed in Chapter 4, under Mouzinho da Silveira's direction, would legislation aim to transform Portuguese society and economy fundamentally.[117]

The forces of tradition would not surrender easily. News of the Porto Revolution's outbreak reached Rio de Janeiro in mid October. The reaction of Dom João's coterie was indignant yet not intransigent. His chief advisor, Vilanova Portugal, bluntly stated that "the Cortes is illegal ... it cannot tell the People that it possesses the authority to impose its laws on the King. Nevertheless, it has been summoned and it would be more harmful to dissolve it ... it is necessary to duly authorize it so that its acts which are not in violation of the customs and laws of the kingdom can be sanctioned."[118] Months later, Vilanova Portugal again urged a measured response to the Porto Revolution, for "it cannot be ignored that liberal ideas have been diffused widely throughout Europe, inculcating the idea that only representative governments can secure the happiness of the people. The Portuguese have swallowed these ideas." However, it would be unwise to concede the legitimacy of the revolutionaries' action and voluntarily divest the crown of authority. Passions could be tamed and threats diminished through the "judicious reform of various branches of administration."[119] After the initial enthusiasm dissipated, the Crown could restore the older order of things. For Vilanova Portugal and others, concessions, compromise, and occasional cooperation were necessary to stave off a radicalization of the Porto Revolution, whose ricochet impact in Brazil was dreaded. For Dom João's counselors, republicanism was indistinguishable from the violent involvement of the lower orders of society in the domain of politics. Vilanova Portugal predicted that, "like in Buenos Aires, it

---

[116] Quoted in Craiutu 2003, p. 165. This state of affairs was not altogether cause for celebration and actually led many liberals to share the royalist belief that the "creation of intermediary powers between the government and the population was the only way to preserve a stable liberal regime in a leveled society such as France." See de Dijn 2008, p. 128.

[117] Above all, see Monteiro 2003.

[118] Vilanova Portugal to Dom João, October 29, 1820, quoted in Clayton 1977, p. 247.

[119] ANTT, MNE, livro 467, Vilanova Portugal to Dom João, February 4, 1821, fos. 92–93, 95; in a slightly earlier letter, he put the matter more bluntly: "retain the ancient customs of the kingdom ...the country will not be pacified by giving up authority, but rather by declaring that you want to correct abuses." Vilanova Portugal to Dom João, January 14, 1821, quoted in Clayton 1977, p. 259.

will be impossible to prevent the blacks (*pretos*) from taking part in the revolution" in Brazil unless the revolutionary embers were snuffed out in Portugal.[120] Ultimately, Dom João acquiesced, departed for Lisbon, promised to rule as a constitutional monarch, and left his son, Dom Pedro, behind in Rio de Janeiro, in possession of full regency powers. Dom João was persuaded to follow this course of action by the mobilization of the Portuguese army units stationed in Brazil, some of which verged on mutiny in favor of the Porto Revolution.[121]

There was great international enthusiasm for the Iberian and Neapolitan Revolutions of 1820. "It is almost impossible," a British observer gushed, "not to be of the opinion that the revolutions now effected in Spain and Portugal will be followed sooner or later, by similar and more eventful changes upon the rest of the continent – I might perhaps say, of the *world!*"[122] Of Portugal's revolution in particular, François Guizot declared that "no revolution had been made with more unanimity and less effort," guided by the need for national independence and the desire for free institutions.[123] The Portuguese Revolution was therefore embraced by the "Liberal International," in one historian's felicitous phrase, a Europe-wide and transatlantic civil society.[124] But where it counted most, in the throne rooms and foreign ministries of Metternich-dominated Europe, the reaction was hostile. Trepidation concerning abrupt constitutional changes was widespread and the Holy Alliance unequivocally condemned the adoption of the 1812 Cádiz Constitution in Naples, Piedmont, Spain, and Portugal, a theme treated later in this chapter.[125] The Alliance's *Protocol Préliminaire*, issued at the Congress of Troppau in November 1820, asserted the right to force states "which have undergone a change of government due to revolution … back into the bosom of the Great Alliance." For Metternich and his supporters, the Alliance could not stand aside and permit sovereigns to oversee political experiments, for these endangered neighboring states and would neither "arrest the progress of the evil that we are fighting, nor … guarantee the social order against the most pernicious shocks."[126] As Metternich later put it:

the only sense of the word "constitution" that is admissible in the monarchical system is that of an organization of public powers under the supreme, indivisible, and inalienable authority of the monarch … in every other sense,

---

[120] ANTT, MNE, livro 467, Vilanova Portugal to "J.M.," January 7, 1821, fo. 76.
[121] Barman 1988.
[122] Baillie 1825, vol. I, pp. 33–34.
[123] Guizot 1821, p. 325.   [124] Isabella 2009, p. 23.
[125] On European diplomacy in this period, see the essays in Sked 1979.
[126] Metternich, quoted in Schroeder 1962, pp. 89–90.

constitution is the equivalent of anarchy and the supposed division of powers the death of monarchical government.[127]

In 1821, at the Congress of Laibach, Metternich elaborated on the doctrine that the Great Powers, in the name of the independence of all states and peace among them, had the duty to supervise smaller states and prevent them from taking ill-advised steps in the conduct of their internal affairs.[128] Essentially, this policy was aggressively interventionist and condoned robust interference to achieve the desired political result. Metternich acted on this threat when the Austrian army overwhelmed Neapolitan forces in Spring 1821, effectively crushing the revolution there.[129]

But Portugal was a separate case. Saldanha da Gama attended the Laibach Congress and lamented that the Alliance refused to intervene in Portugal unless France and Britain took the lead. In a subsequent dispatch, he elaborated that while Austria, Russia, and Prussia were disgusted by the Iberian revolutions, no action with regard to Portugal would be taken without British involvement, for "Portugal is considered a mere satellite in the orbit of the planet Great Britain."[130] For its part, Britain would not countenance interference and continued to assert that political events in Portugal, Naples, and Spain were, in Castlereagh's phrase, "strictly speaking, only reforms, or domestic upsets, and do not attack materially any other state."[131] While disturbed by events in Portugal, which he described glumly as part of a "revolutionary torrent" flowing "in an almost uninterrupted and continuous stream from the other side of the Atlantic," Castlereagh opposed Britain's direct involvement as well as interference from the other Great Powers. His efforts to convey this attitude to Dom João were ineffective. In February 1821, Castlereagh lamented that "His Most Faithful Majesty is laying on his oats in the delusive hope that the Holy Alliance will undertake a crusade for the re-establishment of the old system in Portugal." He expressed his displeasure at the diplomatic

---

[127] Quoted in Schroeder 1962, p. 201, fn. 22.
[128] Ibid., pp. 126–27.   [129] J. A. Davis 2006.
[130] ANTT, APASG, cx. 1, mç. 2, Saldanha da Gama [from Laibach] to Palmela, February 3, 1821; and Saldanha da Gama [from Paris] to Palmela, March 10, 1821.
[131] Castlereagh, quoted in Webster 1925, p. 283. Of course, Castlereagh's point was a technical one and left his reactionary credentials impeccable. In a letter to Metternich (May 6, 1821), he noted that "although we have made an immense progress against radicalism, the monster still lives, and shows himself in new shapes; but we do not despair of crushing him by time and perseverance," in Castlereagh 1853, p. 259. Metternich was clearly uneasy with all of the options for the settlement of peninsular affairs, viewing the imposition by the French of something resembling the 1814 *Chartre* as the worst of all the possible scenarios, for it would be an unequivocal endorsement by the Powers of constitutional government and thus represent a horrendous precedent, with potential repercussions for Austria's Italian sphere. See Schroeder 1962, p. 200.

machinations by which the ailing king endeavored to make the British "not auxiliaries, as our treaties have made us, but principals in the defence of Portugal, not in resistance to ordinary invasion but in combating even revolutionary movements to which our engagements were never intended to apply."[132] Dom João, then, was left to his own devices, at least temporarily. While operating under the constant threat of foreign intermeddling, Luso-Brazilian politics was permitted to evolve between 1821 and 1823 without heavy-handed foreign intervention.

Political journalism, exile, and the emergence of critics of the Old Regime

The political upheaval that gripped the Portuguese empire between 1817 and 1823, conservative critics remarked, was the result of unscrupulous "Jacobins" who employed print to inflame public passions. While this characterization was specious, they correctly diagnosed the disruptive impact of political journalism. The French invasions irrevocably changed the public culture of politics (the term "public sphere," while convenient and common, is misleading in Portugal's case). The Peninsular War witnessed an outpouring of pamphlets and other ephemera, unprecedented (and never to be repeated) in Portuguese history. Over two thousand pamphlets, caricatures, proclamations, and broadsides were published, most of them anti-French, patriotic exhortations to resist the invader, and professions of loyalty to royalty and the Catholic religion. About half of this deluge secured the approval of the *Imprensa Régia*, which remained active and published many of them.[133] In addition to pamphlets and other ephemera, the French invasions were accompanied by the advent of a periodical press in Portugal. There was some semblance of a press in the eighteenth-century. Fifty-four new periodicals were launched between 1750 and 1800, though few of these survived for long. Furthermore, Pombal's creation of the *Real Mesa Censória* in 1768 produced a sharp drop in new publications (only fifteen new publications appeared during Pombal's ascendancy), while the creation of the *Imprensa Régia* in 1769 brought the control of print firmly into state hands.[134] The result was the conspicuous absence of political journalism in the late eighteenth century.

---

[132] Castlereagh 1853, pp. 244, 251–52.

[133] Araújo, "Invasões Francesas," in Torgal and Roque 1993 pp. 42–43.

[134] Araújo 2003, p. 68; Tengarrinha 1989, p. 46. It should be noted that the creation of the *Real Mesa Censória* was part of the enlargement of the Pombaline state's surveillance apparatus: in 1768, the Inquisition was turned into a state institution and the following year all property of the *Santo Ofício* passed to the national treasury; see Schwarcz 2002, pp. 107–8.

Still, the strict limits notwithstanding, the periodical press was championed by those who argued that newspapers and journals were the "best means to diffuse to the general public the knowledge of the *sabios*" and put their "discoveries" in a form in which it could be consumed, "stimulating in the *povo* the desire to learn."[135] Such views were embraced by Portuguese political writers after 1815. In the interim, the French Revolutionary Wars shaped the development of the press. The first Portuguese daily, the *Diário Lisbonense*, published with the government's imprimatur, appeared in 1809 and survived until 1813. Weekly periodicals surfaced as well, though most of these were translations of news items concerning the Peninsular War culled from Spanish or English papers. Political journalism, however, was suppressed by the authorities. Rocha Loureiro founded *O Correio da Peninsula*, which unabashedly lobbied for the establishment of a constitutional monarchy in Portugal. It was suppressed and Rocha Loureiro and his collaborators sought refuge abroad. For this reason, the Portuguese periodical press was devoted largely to literature, the arts, and recreation, in addition to anti-French propaganda. The only periodical carrying political news was the government-controlled *Gazeta de Lisboa*.[136]

Brazil, of course, lacked a printing press until the Court's arrival in 1808. Nevertheless, an active intellectual culture, often subterranean, flourished, composed of readers who nourished their interests on books brought legally, and illegally, into Brazil.[137] There was a massive importation of anti-Napoleonic literature into Brazil in the early nineteenth century. The proliferation of pro-monarchy and anti-French propaganda was complemented by a censorship regime that strove to block the entry of potentially seditious texts into Portugal and Brazil.[138] The *Real Mesa Censória* operated in overdrive throughout the Portuguese Atlantic. Freemasons were thought to have "embraced the French system in order to perturb public tranquility and introduce anarchy everywhere."[139] The vigilance of the *Governadores do Reino* in the 1810s earned the approbation of the Rio-based ministers who noted that they had "done well in prohibiting and taking measures to suppress all newspapers and pamphlets [*papeis*] which in any way could be dangerous to the security of the realm."[140]

---

[135] *Prospecto d'um Jornal Enciclopedico* (Lisbon 1778), quoted in Santos Alves 2005, p. 317.
[136] Tengarrinha 1989, pp. 57–62, 73.
[137] Villalta 1999.   [138] M. B. N. da Silva 2008a, p. 153.
[139] ANTT, MR [Rio de Janeiro], cx. 317, mç. 236, Conde de Aguiar to Sr. Patriarcha Eleita de Lisboa, March 17, 1810.
[140] Ibid., May 26, 1810.

In Brazil, a new institution, the *Mesa do Desembargo do Paço*, was created in 1808. In addition to works by the dastardly French trinity of Rousseau-Voltaire-Condorcet (to say nothing of lesser French writers), those of Beccaria, Gibbon, Hume, Montesquieu, Locke, Pufendorf, and William Robertson were denied entry by energetic censors, whose ranks included Frei António d'Arrabida (who later played a significant role in framing the 1824 Brazilian Constitution, discussed in Chapter 3) and José da Silva Lisboa. Predictably, the French booksellers of Rio de Janeiro were denied the licenses they requested to import forbidden books until 1822. Not only were booksellers rebuffed, but the petitions of teachers, lawyers, and other professionals for dispensation to read unlicensed material also were rejected.[141] Vigilance extended beyond Rio de Janeiro. In distant São Luis (Maranhão), administrators received strict orders to contain the revolutionary contagion. US ships were turned away from the harbors because of America's trade and connections with France, which allegedly dispatched "revolutionaries to spread their message in Spanish and Portuguese dominions."[142]

The censorship and persecution faced by journalists in both Brazil and Portugal prompted many of them to flee abroad, particularly to England, where freedom of press was more ample. The previously mentioned Rocha Loureiro regrouped and published *O Espelho*, and then *O Portuguez*, in London. Hipólito da Costa published *O Correio Brasiliense* there from 1808. Solano Constâncio, in his Paris-based *O Observador Lusitano em Paris*, captured the spirit animating the exiled journalists: "Politics, which for centuries was the exclusive preserve of government officials, has become the object of curiosity of all in our time."[143] At first, these periodicals were considered a nuisance, not a threat. The 1817 conspiracies and uprisings in both Lisbon and Pernambuco, however, changed the government's approach. In the wake of the Gomes Freire Conspiracy, the *Governadores* explicitly blamed the *Correio Brasiliense* and *O Portuguez* for divulging "revolutionary and incendiary maxims" on both shores of the Atlantic. By 1820, various royal orders had been issued prohibiting, and ordering the seizure of, those two periodicals, as well as *O Campeão*.[144]

But the influence of such publications should not be exaggerated. As a leading historian has argued, Old Regime reading practices, which viewed texts as "reserved for a few initiates or else men notable for

[141] L. Neves 1999a, pp. 665–97 passim.
[142] APEM, Registros Gerais, livro 15 (1796–1818), February 28, 1811.
[143] F. S. Constâncio [January 1, 1815], quoted in Tengarrinha 1989, p. 73.
[144] Tengarrinha 1989, p. 98.

their dignity, training, and *luzes*," persisted until at least 1820 in Brazil, and to a significant extent throughout the Lusophone world. Books circulated, but often were confined to elite circles, which enjoyed tacit permission within recognizable boundaries.[145] Nevertheless, the revolutionary moment sparked by the 1820 Porto uprising produced, and was nurtured by, the expansion of a reading public on both shores of the Atlantic. In Lisbon, in February 1821 alone, seventeen new political periodicals were founded. Between 1821 and 1823, 107 new periodicals appeared, the most important of which was Manuel Fernandes Tomás's *O Independente*. The absolutist reaction in 1823 forced many of the journalists and publishers into exile, if they were fortunate enough to escape imprisonment. With the exception of the year of the *Carta's* arrival (1826), during which forty-eight new periodicals were founded, the remainder of the 1820s witnessed the precipitous decline of the press. The connection between political journalism and political upheaval was, therefore, far from coincidental or accidental. Borges Carneiro and Mouzinho da Silveira, among many others, were convinced that the press was the most powerful tool in the liberal arsenal, necessary to spread new doctrines, justify new institutions, and combat the propaganda of constitutionalism's opponents.[146]

PART II

Constitutionalism in Portugal: enlightenment jurisprudence, the "ancient constitution," and the making of the 1822 Constitution

There is a scholarly consensus that early modern Portugal was a corporate society, in which the Crown enjoyed uneasy preeminence over other bodies. The king was qualitatively different from the nobility: he was the ultimate arbiter of justice and responsible for the enforcement of law, empowered to hear appeals and dispense grace. If the Crown's symbolic superiority over other powers was clear, its compromised legislative authority, institutional weakness, and fiscal limitations undercut its position. In the seventeenth century, the Church enjoyed freedom from monarchical interference. According to some measures, the Crown's dominion extended to a mere third of the country: 30–35 percent of land was under its direct control and only 42 percent of all

---

[145] L. Neves 1999a, p. 697.
[146] Tengarrinha 1989, pp. 125, 140–41.

vassals under its jurisdiction; more than a quarter of Portugal's land was not subject to *correição régia*. Outside of the large urban centers (with the notable exceptions of Aveiro, Vila Real, and Bragança), where the Crown was ascendant, the military orders and lay nobility enjoyed significant control over Portugal's land, wealth, and the exercise of legal jurisdiction. There was, then, a constant tension between the unity and autonomy of the various parts of the polity, which was simultaneously monarchical and pluralist: the concentration of power in the Crown's hands, and its concomitant capacity to supersede competing seigneurial and ecclesiastical jurisdictions, would not occur until the eighteenth century.[147] Until then, Portugal's political culture was characterized by the special rights and prerogatives of multiple semi-autonomous bodies, corporations, and social units, which together conspired to thwart any attempts at consolidation by the Crown.

Instead, the Crown was embedded in a complex, interdependent system, of which the Cortes was one of many bodies.[148] In general, it was an assembly of the Three Estates, or *Três Estados*, of the realm (clergy, nobles, and commoners). There is scholarly debate concerning the function and composition of the Cortes before the fourteenth century. The first assembly that was more than a royal council met in 1211 while popular participation, which was probably merely a royal expedient to secure extra taxation, was registered for the first time at the Cortes of Leiria in 1254.[149] After a brief golden age in the fourteenth and fifteenth centuries, it re-emerged following the restoration of Portugal's independence after 1640, for the purpose of handling issues surrounding royal succession and taxation.[150] The problem was that the supposed precedent for the Cortes as it emerged in the late seventeenth century, the so-called Cortes of Lamego, which supposedly convened in 1143, was revealed later to have been a forgery, though this was not confirmed until the nineteenth century.[151] Recently, historians have shown that the medieval Cortes never enjoyed anything resembling popular sovereignty, as nineteenth- and twentieth-century liberal historiography, in search of precedents for mixed monarchy, asserted.[152]

---

[147] Hespanha 1994, pp. 343, 422, 427, 431, 436–38, 527–28; Cardim 1998, p. 185.

[148] Cardim 1998, p. 186.

[149] Wheeler and Opello 2010, pp. 93–94; Oliveira Marques 1972, vol. I, p. 99.

[150] On the nature and function of the Cortes in the early modern period, see A. Bareto Xavier, A. M. Hespanha, and P. Cardim, "A Representação da Sociedade e do Poder," in Hespanha 1993, pp. 121–55.

[151] The circumstances surrounding the forgery of documents related to the Cortes of Lamego, primarily to justify Dom João IV's revolt against Spain in 1640, are described in depth in Oliveira Marques 1972, vol. I, pp. 325–27.

[152] Cardim 1998, p. 185.

Still, the long-standing existence of a Cortes, conceived narrowly as a representative body and counterweight to royal power, regardless of its actual authority, served as a reminder that Portugal's ancient constitution possessed at least some representative features. In this sense, the Portuguese situation resembled the Spanish one, where the Crown was dependent on the Cortes for at least some of its revenue, as much as 60 percent between 1640 and 1650.[153]

In Portugal, colonial wealth tipped the scales in the Crown's favor, providing new sources of revenue, fresh opportunities for military and political action, and new administrative units, appointments to which the Crown controlled.[154] The influx of gold and diamonds after the Brazilian mineral strikes of the late 1690s permitted the Crown to dispense with the nuisance of convening the Cortes, which met for the last time in 1697–98. But the Crown's control of patronage, and its generally freer hand, should not disguise the fact that Portugal, peninsula and overseas dominions alike, were also pluralistic, with competing and cooperating corporate bodies sharing juridical and political authority.[155] In general, then, throughout the territories composing the Portuguese empire, the Crown was ascendant, but its centralizing pretensions were constrained by a morass of legislation, accumulated over several centuries, which served to preserve the positions of privileged groups even as the Crown's authority itself was strengthened as a result of colonial ventures and the booty they yielded.

Efforts to draw up a new legal code in the eighteenth century revived dormant debates concerning the nature of Portugal's "constitution." The term "constitution" in early modern Europe, of course, did not refer merely to a written document, or charter, or solely to the form of government, but also encompassed factors relating to the functioning of the body politic, including social structure, institutions, and customs. All were subsumed in the term "constitution." By the mid eighteenth century, though, the definition had been narrowed considerably. In 1758, Emmerich de Vattel stated that "the fundamental regulation that determines the manner in which public authority should be regulated is the constitution of a state."[156] This mid-eighteenth-century conception jostled for primacy with other, older meanings of "constitution," often grouped under the heading "fundamental law," or *lei fundamental*. As in France, many usages and understandings coexisted, making its

---

[153] I. A. A. Thompson 1982, p. 39.
[154] Hespanha 1994, pp. 473, 496.
[155] Hespanha 2010, p. 75.
[156] Quoted in Stourzh 1988, p. 35.

deployment in political argument immensely attractive to every political persuasion. As an historian has demonstrated, "by the early seventeenth century, it had become the standard term for any laws, rights,
privileges or customs that writers thought of special importance for the
well-being of a community."[157] In Portugal, both terms, "*constituição*"
and "*lei fundamental*," circulated widely by the middle of the eighteenth
century.

Building on a 1778 decree, Dona Maria established a *Junta de Revisão
e Censura do Novo Código*, directed by an old Pombaline hand, José de
Seabra da Silva, in 1784. The Junta's purpose was to compile the dispersed, fragmented laws which had accumulated since the restoration
of Portugal's independence from Spain in 1640, endow them with some
semblance of order, remove redundancies and resolve contradictions,
and fashion them into a systematized legal code.[158] One of the Junta's
members was António Ribeiro dos Santos, a regalist canon lawyer, who
advocated the need for robust royal authority, particularly relative to the
Church.[159] But Ribeiro dos Santos simultaneously held that the Cortes,
a stalwart feature of Portugal's juridical past, should be convened to
recalibrate the relative power of the various corporations and orders
within the monarchy. He thus proposed to revitalize tradition in order
to prop up beleaguered absolutism. Though aware of the perils posed
by the revival of the Cortes almost a century after it had last been convened, he believed that circumstances required it.[160] In a widely circulated manuscript, "On the Origin of Princely Power," he argued that

the convocation of the Cortes can bring with it, due to the bad disposition
of its vassals, terrible consequences for a prince: but this will not necessarily
occur. If a prince is good, if he governs well, if he demonstrates a willingness
to improve his government, the convocation of the Cortes will benefit him and,
far from threatening his throne, will provide a new, firm foundation for his
government.[161]

The timing of the appearance of Ribeiro dos Santos's manuscript was
awful. In 1789, his views on the Cortes were attacked by jurist Pascoal
de Melo Freire (1738–98), a colleague on the Junta as well as a Coimbra
professor. Melo Freire contended that his colleague's theories threatened the throne. Ribeiro dos Santos did nothing to endear himself to

---

[157] Thompson 1986, p. 1110.
[158] Beirão 1944, p. 226.
[159] Ribeiro dos Santos's *De Sacerdotio et Imperio* (1770) offered a clear-eyed regalist
statement that the Church should be autonomous and separate from the state, with
concern limited to doctrine and sacraments. See Maxwell 1995, pp. 94–95.
[160] J. E. Pereira 1983, pp. 165, 166, 263.
[161] Ribeiro dos Santos, quoted in J. E. Pereira 1983, p. 264.

Melo Freire when he penned a commentary on Melo Freire's draft of a public and criminal code, intended to replace the outdated *Ordenações Filipinas*. He accused Melo Freire of confusing the order of operations. A *lei fundamental* was necessary before any such code could be drawn up or reformed, for the latter served as the basis for the former, not the other way round. In Ribeiro dos Santos's view, a prince's first duty was to uphold the fundamental laws of the kingdom, which emanated from the original foundation of society.[162] Interestingly, though probably not as a result of Ribeiro dos Santos's criticism, Melo Freire never submitted his drafts for royal approval. Had he done so, Portugal might have preceded Austria and France as the first country with a uniform civil code.[163] As things turned out, the task of codifying dispersed legislation would fall to the *Vintistas* two decades later.

But Melo Freire did not remain silent altogether. He refused to permit his colleague's assertions to stand unchallenged. He denounced Ribeiro dos Santos's allegedly anti-monarchical tendencies, and clarified his own position on fundamental laws and constitutions. Melo Freire maintained that the monarch was encumbered by few restrictions and that he was, undoubtedly, unrestrained by the terms of Portugal's *lei fundamental*, which determined nothing except the order of royal succession. Royal authority emanated from the right of succession, itself based on earlier conquest, not some social pact or contract enshrined in a written constitution, which he ridiculed as something existing "only in the minds and convoluted imaginations of some philosophers." Melo Freire went further still, rejecting the notion of supposedly sacrosanct privileges and special rights, particularly the *foros*, claiming that they were not inviolable. While he stopped short of championing a "tyrannical or despotic king," and stressed the importance of secure property rights and a well-administered judicial system, Melo Freire wanted few limits on the king's pursuit of the "public good" as he deemed fit. Furthermore, the entire political system should produce "vassals who love and respect their prince; not those who [falsely] claim possession of chimerical and seditious privileges and rights."[164]

In many regards, Melo Freire and Ribeiro dos Santos were unlikely adversaries. Staunch regalists who sought to curb the authority of the papacy, ecclesiastical privilege, and canon law, both Crown servants were unmistakable products of Pombal's overhaul of the Coimbra

---

[162] Ribeiro dos Santos's manuscript "Notas ao Plano," quoted in J. E. Pereira 1983, p. 269.

[163] Lewin 2003, vol. I, p. 133.

[164] Melo Freire, quoted in J. E. Pereira 1983, pp. 293, 301; on other understandings of the "constitution" in the Luso-Atlantic world in this period, see Neves 2003, p. 67.

curriculum. Like other late eighteenth-century jurists, they shared an abiding interest in the Iberian legal heritage, emphasizing the primacy of existing national law, including customary law, to the exclusion of Roman civil law and canon law. As in Spain, this prompted interest in the historical evolution of Portuguese institutions, the post-Roman, pre-Islamic Visigothic past. It had been the Visigoths, for example, who enshrined in law the calling of assemblies, a precedent from which Portugal's medieval Cortes descended.[165] The rediscovery of this proto-national legislation, which renewed debates on the nature of Portugal's ancient constitution, coincided with the vogue for written constitutions, popular sovereignty, and legislative assemblies, forcing them into dialogue.

Shared interests, background, and regalist predisposition notwithstanding, Melo Freire and Ribeiro dos Santos reached divergent conclusions regarding the nature of the Cortes in particular and the character of Portugal's ancient constitution in general. Ribeiro dos Santos's vision of a monarch whose authority was derived from, and limited by, a fundamental law, coexisting with the Cortes, ran contrary to Melo Freire's understanding of the king as superior to the Cortes (and all other institutions). In Melo Freire's interpretation of Portugal's legal past, the Cortes was a consultative, not legislative, body, which convened at the king's pleasure and could not frame legislation constraining him.[166] In 1789, Melo Freire bested his adversary. After their intellectual feud, the faintest suggestion of convening a Cortes became incendiary, even a punishable offense. In 1799, when Seabra da Silva gently suggested the convocation of the Cortes in order to confirm Dom João as regent, he was sacked.[167]

But the debate was far from settled and the ideas of both Melo Freire and Ribeiro Santos were employed eclectically by later proponents of constitutionalism. In the 1820s, for example, Ribeiro dos Santos was rehabilitated by the revolutionary liberals as a proto-*Vintista*, a controversial and selective appropriation.[168] Melo Freire's ideas, too, were integrated into the emerging canon of liberal jurisprudence by way of an extensive commentary written by one of his students, published

---

[165] See Lewin 2003, vol. I, pp. 123–47 passim. On the late eighteenth-century Spanish infatuation with the Visigothic legal inheritance, see Paquette 2008, chapters 1 and 2.

[166] Cardim 1998, p. 178.

[167] Vargues 1997, p. 112. In the second half of the seventeenth century, the Cortes had been convened on several occasions to ratify or otherwise confirm the succession to the throne or a royal marriage that would impact succession. See Oliveira Marques 1972, vol. I, p. 393.

[168] J. E. Pereira 1983, p. 261.

between 1818 and 1824.[169] Borges Carneiro would draw on both figures as he sought to raze the legal foundations of the Old Regime, adapting Pombaline jurisprudence to meet the requirements of liberal constitutional government.[170]

In the intervening period 1790–1820, a superabundance of factors influenced the development of Portuguese constitutionalism. The term "constitutionalism," defined as a theory and practice of mixed monarchy operating within the boundaries established by a written constitution based on modern principles limiting the authority of the executive, is preferred to "liberalism" in this context (and for the remainder of the book). The terms "liberal" and "liberalism" appear in these pages. Recourse to them is unavoidable, all the more so because many of the historical actors studied here used the term to describe themselves and their political projects or were described as such by their enemies who hurled "liberal" as an epithet. However, the meanings of "liberal" and "liberalism" were multiple and in constant flux during the period under examination, throughout Europe and the Americas. A careful exegesis of each usage, while valuable, is impossible given the scope and chronological span of this study. For contemporaries, the significance of the term was varied, changing, and often ambiguous.[171] It has been a frustratingly fissiparous concept. Historians of other European countries in the same period face an analogous challenge. In France, liberalism was "used to describe a disparate section of the Restoration political elite, which was loosely united in criticism of most Bourbon governments ... [it was] a flag of negotiation, compromise, and convenience."[172] In Italian exile circles it was similarly vague, coming to embody constitutionalism, a revised international order, civil-political freedoms, gradual progress, and social reform.[173] In Spain, at least before 1830, there were great internal divisions among those who called themselves "liberal," which led to significant changes of meaning.[174] The same was true in Spanish America. These shifting and mutually contradictory aspects of "liberalism" (as well as other terms equally fraught with ambiguity, like "absolutism") has encouraged some historians to adopt alternative frameworks, polarities, dyads, and antonyms such as "reform" versus "traditionalism."[175]

---

[169] Lewin 2003, vol. I, p. 152.   [170] Ibid., p. 155.

[171] As Posada-Carbó and Jaksić 2011 judiciously pointed out, "it would be a mistake to speak of a liberal tradition in the singular, or to refer to 'liberals' in a generic way, as if they were adherents of a uniform and well-defined school of thought," p. 41.

[172] Pilbeam 1991, pp. 80, 98.

[173] Isabella 2009, p. 25.

[174] Fernández Sebastián and Fuentes 2002, p. 420.

[175] Breña 2006, pp. 46–56.

There was a similar multiplicity in the Portuguese Atlantic World. Before the Cortes of Cádiz (1810–12), there only existed an idea of economic, not political, liberalism. Liberalism acquired a more precise meaning during the Civil War,[176] but even then, as Alexandre Herculano noted in 1867, "liberals were eclectic … they were not unified by a common set of principles."[177] In Brazil, the situation was even more complicated. For some, liberalism before 1825 meant "the liquidation of colonial ties without the fundamental reform of institutions."[178] For other Brazilians in this same period it signified the elimination of state regulation and interference in the economy, but not political independence. In Brazil, and throughout the Ibero-Atlantic world, the paradoxical rise of "liberal" economic ideologies with the persistence (and expansion) of chattel slavery produced further complications and contradictions.[179] By the 1820s, then, the term "liberal" in the Luso-Brazilian world could refer to many different and sometimes mutually inconsistent goals, beliefs, and political projects: political independence from Portugal; less regulated trade; decentralized government; anti-clericalism; and abolitionism.[180] Throughout the Ibero-Atlantic world, it was only from the 1830s that those who used the term "liberal" or "liberalism" had in mind a relatively coherent set of ideas, institutions, and political practices, which explains the reluctance to utilize this terminology in discussing the 1810–30 period.[181]

In addition to the Portuguese legal traditions discussed previously, constitutional stimuli wafted in from abroad, first from France and then from Spain. Junot convened the *Junta dos Trés Estados* in May 1808. This was not a Cortes, to be sure, but a nominally representative body, revived by Junot for the self-serving purpose of petitioning Napoleon to place a new king on Portugal's vacant throne. The origins of this Junta may be located in the seventeenth-century War of Independence, when

---

[176] Monteiro 2008, pp. 101–6.
[177] Quoted in França 1974, vol. I, p. 174.
[178] Andrade Arruda, "A Produção Económica," in Marques and Serrão 1986.
[179] Schultz 2001, p. 4. Viotti da Costa 1985 concludes that "the intellectual elite created an ideology that hid the contradictions inherent in the system," pp. 7–8. As a political scientist has framed it: "the new [Brazilian] regime's legitimacy rested on liberal claims, but the social order was founded on features utterly inimical to such claims: slavery, hierarchy, authority, patronage and favor," see Chrisholm 2002, p. 109. For recent debates in Brazilian liberalism, see Peixoto 2001; more generally, Losurdo 2011, pp. 37, 71.
[180] Malerba 1994, p. 102.
[181] J. Fernández Sebastián, "Liberalismos Nacientes en el Atlántico Iberoamericano: 'Liberal' como Concepto y como Identidad Política, 1750–1850," in Fernández Sebastián 2009, p. 719.

Dom João IV governed with the assistance of a rump legislature, whose remit was confined to the fiscal aspects of war-making against Spain: soldiers' pay, equipment, fortifications, and finance, especially the creation and collection of extraordinary, new, and temporary taxes.[182] This Junta, however, had not been convened for over a century, an unsurprising non-occurrence given that the Cortes itself had ceased to meet in 1698. The revived Junta, hand-picked by Junot, begged Napoleon to bestow a constitution upon Portugal similar to that given previously to the Grand Duchy of Warsaw. The Warsaw Constitution was unequivocally a constitutional monarchy, boasting a bicameral legislature, whose representatives would be elected by municipal *câmaras*. Equality before the law, the establishment of the Napoleonic Code, and the sale of mortmain were also broached.[183]

The second external influence on Portuguese constitutional thought came from Spain. In many regards, Francisco Martínez Marina's historicist account of the Cortes, particularly his *Teória de las Cortes* (1813), resonated and dovetailed with the Melo Freire–Ribeiro dos Santos debate in Portugal. Martínez located the origins of modern liberalism – chiefly representative institutions – in Spain's medieval past, suggesting that the people's representatives had participated in political decision-making alongside the king.[184] This conception of constitutionalism sought to synthesize laws available in old statutes, with a special emphasis on the rights historically acquired by the distinct groups (estates, regions, and municipalities) composing the Spanish Monarchy.[185] Martínez's historical constitutionalism proved influential in Portugal, including in José António de Sá's *Defeza dos Direitos Nacionaes e Reaes da Monarquia Portuguesa* (1816), which identified (falsely) the Cortes of Lamego of 1143 as the founding moment of Portugal's authentic ancient constitution. Such ideas were fleshed out and made explicit in Cypriano Rodrigues das Chagas's *As Cortes, ou Direitos do Povo Português* (1820), which claimed that the medieval Cortes moderated the absolute power of kings and expressed the interests of the people.[186] This position, of course, was highly controversial, and was rejected by many jurists and

---

[182] Vargues 1997, p. 112. On the *Junta dos Três Estados* during the seventeenth-century war against Spain, see F. D. Costa 2004, pp. 27–33.

[183] Vargues 1997, pp. 113–14; Hespanha 2008. Interestingly, Seabra da Silva reappeared during this episode: though he recused himself from service in Junot's administration, he suggested to Junot the need to convene the *Junta dos Três Estados*. See Beirão 1944, p. 341.

[184] On Spanish and Spanish-American constitutionalism and liberalism, see Breña 2006; on the idea of historical constitutionalism in Spain, see Herr 1958.

[185] Portillo Valdés 2002, p. 189.

[186] Cardim 1998, pp. 179–80, 181.

political writers, as shall be shown in a subsequent section of the present chapter. But it is crucial to recall that these traditions of legal-historical scholarship and polemic conditioned the reception and use of foreign constitutional models, including the 1812 Spanish Constitution, which exerted tremendous influence in the Luso-Atlantic World.[187] In addition to the influence of the 1812 Cádiz Constitution, the flurry of republican constitutions that proliferated during the 1810s in Spanish America resonated throughout the Luso-Atlantic sphere, including in the 1817 Pernambucan Revolution.[188] While many of these constitutions also bore the deep imprint of successive French Constitutions of the 1790s, they had been suitably amended and updated, and thus drew attention from Portuguese commentators. There was a great interconnection and interchange between European and Latin American liberal and revolutionary ideologies.[189]

The third general influence after 1814 on Portuguese constitutionalism was the French *Chartre*, the first in the wave of self-fashioned "moderate" constitutions which sought to mediate between the extremes of unbridled reaction and revolutionary republicanism. *O Portuguez*, based in London, published many articles on a range of constitutional models. Besides the French *Chartre* and British constitution, its editor, Rocha Loureiro, often commented upon excerpts drawn from the constitutions of the Low Countries (1815) and the Grand Duchy of Baden (1818). Other constitutions and legal codes debated in émigré newspapers included Tuscany's criminal code, three of the French Constitutions (1791, 1793, 1795), the constitution of the Grand Duchy of Hesse-Darmstad of the Germanic Confederation, and the US 1787 Constitution. After the 1820 Porto Revolution, unsurprisingly, more constitutions were brought forward for public scrutiny and were incorporated into debates, both periodical and parliamentary. Perhaps the most important compendium was the *Collecção de Constituicoes Antigas e Modernas*, published in 1820, which contained not only all of the "Fundamental Laws" of Portugal (including the Cortes of Lamego), but also an array of French Constitutions (and the Declaration of the Rights of Man), Louis XVIII's *Chartre*, and the proceedings of the Cortes of Cádiz. Another important, widely circulated collection was the *Obras Constitucionaes de Hespanha e Napoles*, published in Lisbon in 1820–21.[190] These weighty tomes were joined by a slew of slimmer

[187] Quijada 2008; Berbel 2008. For a comparative study of Spanish and Portuguese constitutionalism in this period, see Varela Suanzes-Carpegna 2010.
[188] The literature is enormous. In English, see Barman 1988 and Mosher 2008.
[189] Isabella 2009, p. 47.
[190] Vargues 1997, pp. 115, 131, 134.

pamphlets and booklets which reprinted translations of the Cádiz Constitution.

It is accurate, then, to observe that constitutionalism was "in the air," though such a vague pronouncement would insinuate that Portuguese constitutionalism's origins were exogenous, that the spark was received from abroad. It is more precise, however, to assert that the Portuguese empire, in the throes of a protracted political and economic transformation, was compelled to reconsider its legal infrastructure. Its legal inheritance was now viewed afresh in the light cast by the constitutional explosions in neighboring states. Given the multiplicity of influences, it is unsurprising that the meaning of "constitution" was contested fiercely. By 1815, however, to advocate constitutionalism meant to champion a written constitution that clearly defined the scope and nature of the authority of each component of the political community and, consequently, was anti-absolutist to some extent. O Campeão captured the prevailing attitude in 1820 when it defined the "political constitution of a state as nothing more than the fundamental law that creates, divides, and authorizes the various powers."[191] Proponents of constitutional monarchy hoped to carve out a role for an elected assembly wielding some degree of legislative authority (or check on executive power). As early as 1816, the editors of O Portuguez called on Dom João to convene a "general assembly," arguing that "national representation, as practiced in England or the United States, was the sole remedy to heal the desperate infirmity" afflicting Portugal and Brazil. O Portuguez promised that "fear of a constitution" was unjustified, for far from "diminishing royal authority, it augmented the power and dignity of the throne, raising it to an almost divine stature."[192]

In fact, as O Portuguez contended, Portugal's former prosperity and grandeza was attributable to its Cortes and the ancient constitution of which that body formed an indispensable part, while its "decadence" was due to the destruction and ruin of that constitution. O Campeão Portuguez contended that the convocation of a Cortes would not "foment revolution, but rather suffocate the revolutionary spirit."[193] This was because the Cortes was an essential component, even the "most sacred and important" part, of Portugal's "ancient political edifice." This was why, in O Campeão's view, the Cortes of Cádiz should be interpreted properly as a "counter-revolution," a "return to the earliest

---

[191] O Campeão Portuguez, vol. II (May 16, 1820), p. 341.
[192] O Portuguez, vol. V (1816), pp. 361–62.
[193] O Campeão Portuguez, vol. I (August 16, 1819), p. 128.

institutions."[194] The convocation of the Portuguese Cortes, then, was portrayed as a restoration of long-forsaken institutions, not an overthrow of existing ones or the introduction of new-fangled innovations alien to its political and juridical heritage.

The champions of written constitutionalism, however, imbued the refashioned Cortes with the tenets of modern constitutional theory. Such innovations were explained away or justified as consonant with the function and purpose of its extinct predecessor. The Portuguese revolutionaries of the early 1820s presented their project as a return to the values of the now-degraded past, a protest against an administration which had "violated our *foros* and rights, and destroyed our liberties, thus profaning our laudable customs, which characterized the Portuguese since the founding of the monarchy."[195] The establishment of the Cortes was not an "innovation," but the "restitution of the ancient and beneficent institutions, corrected and applied in accordance with the *luzes do século*."[196] The restoration, or regeneration, was necessary because Portugal's public institutions had been degraded. For Borges Carneiro, Portugal's "happiness had ended with [the last meeting of] its Cortes," as a "cadre of egoists, enemies of the public good," including "self-interested favorites (*validos*)," "triumphed" and assumed the reins of power.[197] In Almeida Garrett's formulation, the Portuguese, "declared free at the Cortes of Lamego, became the slaves of vile, ambitious, and insatiable men."[198] Absolutism, in other words, was a pernicious innovation, and Portugal's plight could be attributed to the perversion of its traditional constitutional heritage. Revolutionaries thus fashioned themselves as part of a proud lineage, stretching back to the English Magna Carta, the "first offspring of European liberty." After passing to France, and then Spain, Ferdandes Tomás's newspaper, *O Independente*, explained in 1822, the "sacred tree of liberty" was brought to, and planted in, Portugal. There it grew so strong that "it was as if it was a plant truly indigenous to the country" and the Portuguese were seeking to show the world that "we are worthy of possessing and cultivating it."[199]

In spite of the enthusiasm for written constitutions, revolutionary ardor masked numerous discrepancies of opinion and unresolved

[194] *O Campeão Portuguez*, vol. II (May 16, 1820), p. 345.
[195] A Junta Provisional do Governo Supremo do Reino, "Aos Portugueses," August 24, 1820, in *Collecção Geral e Curiosa* 1820, n.p.
[196] *Manifesto da Nação Portuguesa* (December 15, 1820), p. 6.
[197] Borges Carneiro 1820, pp. 22–23, 26–27.
[198] Almeida Garrett, "O Dia 24 de Agosto," reproduced in Serrão 1979, p. 57.
[199] *O Independente*, vol. II, no. 1 (January 2, 1822), pp. 185–86.

debates which dated back to Melo Freire and Ribeiro dos Santos. The first debate concerned whether Portugal's ancient, unwritten constitution was, in fact, a constitutional monarchy; that is, whether legislative authority was shared between the monarch and a body of representatives (whether defined as the traditional estates or as an undifferentiated mass of the population). On one extreme stood those who argued that legislative authority resided entirely in the Cortes, and on the other those who insisted that it was possessed solely by the monarch. The second debate concerned the origin of sovereignty. Was it possessed by the monarch or by some authority preceding the foundation of society? Did the monarch possess it by virtue of conquest or by "divine" right, or, alternatively, did it originate with the "people" or "nation," however conceptualized and delimited? This second dispute flowed into a third large debate concerning which power – legislative or executive – was preeminent and thus empowered to block, or veto, the actions of the other.

If the bedrock of the liberal arguments was historical precedent, their interpretation of that constitutional past, of the origins and scope of representative government, was plainly revolutionary. The *Vintistas* argued that the role of the Cortes was legislative, not merely consultative. In fact, they argued, the entire legislative power resided in the Cortes. The laws that the Cortes might pass, in Fernandes Tomás's words, "depended on the King's sanction." The king, however, did not possess a veto. To give the king the authority to veto legislation, he claimed, would "harm the nation, because it would block our reform."[200] This view contradicted that held by absolutism's champions, who argued that legislative authority resided solely in the person of the monarch, with the Cortes serving in a mere consultative capacity. Self-proclaimed moderate, though still royalist, figures argued that sovereignty, defined as the authority to make law, was shared between the monarch and representatives chosen by various groups of people, and did not reside solely in any one of the institutions that made up the government.[201] This moderate stance was rejected by partisans of both extremes. The *Vintistas* insisted that the Cortes stood at the apex of the hierarchy of legislative, executive, and judicial power. Otherwise, Borges Carneiro warned, "constitutional government will become a three-headed monster."[202]

The debates of 1820–23, then, never rested solely on historical interpretation and legal precedent. To re-make the Portuguese monarchy,

---

[200] M. F. Tomás, February 26, 1821, in Tomás 1974, pp. 81, 84.
[201] Pinheiro Ferreira, *DC*, July 14, 1821, pp. 1551–52.
[202] Borges Carneiro, *DC*, February 9, 1822, pp. 133–34.

to re-conceptualize its constituent parts, and to re-calibrate the relations among them involved innovation and a break from the past. It was impossible to adhere faithfully to older forms of organization. "Men today do not think like those who lived in the time of Dom Afonso Henriques or Dom Pedro II. Today there are different sorts of men, different customs, and ways of thinking."[203] It was for this reason that the themes broached and projects pursued would be different from those of the past. Silva Lisboa made a similar argument in a Rio-based newspaper: "the most sacred constitutions, those most useful in the first days of a monarchy, over the course of time become impractical, like all things made by men, who cannot make things for perpetuity by their very nature."[204] One of the chief innovations proposed by the *Vintistas* involved the form of the Cortes. The model proposed in 1820 did not adhere to the older model, the convocation of the *Três Estados*. Borges Carneiro conceded that his co-revolutionists were discarding the older form, but he contended that the *Três Estados* was no longer useful for it "divided the nation into parties and each estate seeks to aggrandize its own; and divides discussion of affairs which should be considered together."[205] Other critics of the *Três Estados* called it "prejudicial to the nation," preventing legal equality and inspiring mutual antagonism.[206] In place of estates, the *Vintistas* sought a single *câmara*, or chamber, which was an embrace of the Spanish model and a rejection of the bicameralism enshrined in the French *Chartre*, the US Constitution, and the British parliamentary system.[207] Another innovation was legally protected freedom of expression. As the revolutionaries put it: "the Inquisition, the *Inconfidência*, true monsters of the social order, horrible invention of despots and tyrants, no longer exist. Humanity, and Reason, have recovered their *foros*."[208] The liberals of 1822, as well as the 1826 *Carta*'s champions, needed the power of the state, as much to destroy the old order as to establish a new one.[209]

In the event, geopolitical pressures, expediency, and the suitability of the Cádiz Constitution led to its immediate adoption in Portugal and Brazil as an interim constitution while the Cortes framed a new Fundamental Law. The 1812 Cádiz Constitution married legal tradition

---

[203] Miranda n.d., p. 51.
[204] *O Conciliador do Reino Unido*, no. 3 (March 24, 1821), p. 22.
[205] Borges Carneiro 1820, 78–79.
[206] Chagas 1821, pp. 12–13.
[207] On broader European debates concerning bicameralism, see de Dijn 2005.
[208] *As Cortes Geraes … aos Brasileiros* 1821, p. 1.
[209] Hespanha 2004, pp. 7–8.

with new-fangled political doctrines.[210] One *Vintista* declared that "Spain is an example to all of the world and it is our model."[211] Another pamphleteer declared that the Cádiz Constitution would be an "excellent base," which "with a few obvious modifications, is perfectly suited to Portugal."[212] One newspaper argued that the Spanish Constitution "should govern the great European family"[213] whereas another gushed that it was "the greatest wonder of the world" because of its perfection: "Nothing could be added to it without making it defective while nothing could be taken away without diminishing its greatness."[214] From abroad, Jeremy Bentham urged the Portuguese to adopt the 1812 Spanish Constitution without revision: "adopt it as a mass: time admits not of picking and choosing ... to find ready-made a work already so suitable, is a blessing too great for expectation."[215]

Not everyone shared Bentham's enthusiasm. In the Cortes itself, Moura contended that the Spanish example could not be followed by the Portuguese as their "situation was very different [for] we are in great union with our overseas provinces."[216] Monteiro concurred, claiming that it was unnecessary to imitate the "errors" of the Spaniards with regard to the representation of *ultramar* in the Cortes's ranks: "We should not imitate blindly, but only following mature examination and reflection."[217] Other Portuguese liberals were less enamored of foreign models altogether, even if they held the Cádiz Constitution in high regard. The provenance of the constitution was less important than its content and efficacy: "the best constitution for Portugal is neither that of Spain, nor France, nor England, nor one more or less liberal

---

[210] In his famous assessment of the Cádiz Constitution in the 1850s, K. Marx argued that it was a "reproduction of the ancient *fueros*, but read in light of the French Revolution, and adapted to the wants of modern society ... [yet] far from being a servile copy of the French constitution of 1791, it was a genuine and original offspring of Spanish intellectual life, regenerating the ancient and national institutions, introducing the measures of reform loudly demanded by the most celebrated authors and statesmen of the eighteenth century, making inevitable concessions to popular prejudice"; see Marx, "Revolution in Spain [VI]," November 24, 1854, in Marx and Engels 1939, pp. 63, 68. For modern assessments, see Chust and Frasquet 2004.

[211] Lavradio 1820, p. 37.

[212] [Anon.], *Reflexões ... Pacto Social* 1821, p. 80.

[213] *O Portuguez Constitucional Regenerado*, no. 26 (August 31, 1821), p. 113.

[214] *O Escudo*, no. 5 (1823), pp. 95–96.

[215] Bentham 1821, "Letter to the Portuguese Nation," p. 47.

[216] Moura, November 14, 1821, in *PBDP*, p. 306.

[217] Ibid., p. 309. This reference may be to the policy during the Trienio after 1820, not the Cortes of Cádiz. As Anna 1983 noted, even in 1820, the Spanish liberal regime did little to conciliate with America: overseas representation remained disproportionate; no commercial equality was contemplated; royalist viceroys and captains-general exercised power in an autocratic fashion even if their titles were changed to reflect the political principles of the new regime, p. 226.

Pl. 45.

ACCEPTATION PROVISOIRE DE LA CONSTITUTION DE LISBONNE,

à Rio de Janeiro, en 1821.

Figure 3 Jean-Baptiste Debret. "Acceptation Provisoire de la Constitution de Lisbonne, à Rio de Janeiro en 1821" (Paris, 1839).

than any of those, but rather [whichever] one assures the happiness of the Portuguese."[218] Fernandes Tomás made a similar point: "we are not making laws for Englishmen, but rather for the Portuguese, and the great task is to make [these laws] appropriate to their customs."[219] Pereira do Carmo went further, arguing that "to the extent possible, our constitution should appear in Portuguese dress, devoid as much as possible of foreign fashions."[220] A nation, Sarmento added in a speech to the Cortes, might "admire the institutions of another, but to suddenly adopt them is no more possible than borrowing the arms and legs of a neighbor whose beauty we envy."[221] In spite of "rivalry" born from "old injuries" and a "spirit of independence," Almeida Garrett conceded that the Portuguese and Spanish constitutions were "almost identical, distinguished only by turns of phrase, words or emphasis." Both constitutions, he believed, could be grouped together under the designation "sistema de liberdade meridional."[222]

There were, however, several key differences between the 1812 Spanish Constitution and the 1822 Portuguese Constitution framed by the Cortes. First, the Portuguese document made explicit the king's status as a "constitutional" monarch whereas the Spanish predecessor indicated only that the kingdom was a "moderate" monarchy; second, in the Portuguese Constitution executive power was shared between the king and the secretaries of state, whereas in the Spanish Constitution it resided in king alone; third, the Portuguese Constitution allowed for direct suffrage with significant limits, whereas the Spanish Constitution enshrined universal but indirect suffrage; fourth, the Portuguese Constitution did not impose term limits on deputies, whereas in the Spanish Constitution they were limited to a single term; fifth, the Cádiz Constitution offered more guarantees for freedom of the press than its Portuguese counterpart; and sixth, the 1822 Portuguese Constitution was a compact document, in stark contrast to the sprawling Spanish Constitution.[223] But the question of similarities and differences was, to a large extent, moot. The 1822

---

[218] *Reflexões sobre a Necessidade de Promover* 1822, p. 65.
[219] *DC*, January 2, 1822, p. 3564.
[220] *DC*, January 4, 1822, p. 3588.
[221] *DC*, January 24, 1822, p. 3835.
[222] Almeida Garrett, "Da Europa e da America...," in Almeida Garrett 1985, p. 90; Almeida Garrett 2005, p. 41. This is not to say that praise for the Cádiz Constitution was unmixed with criticism: for example, one 1821 critic noted that it was "long-winded, repetitive, [containing] mistakes and [needless] details" which needed improvement before it could be adopted in Portugal. See translator's preface to [Anon.], *Considerações Políticas sobre as Mudanças* 1821, p. 4.
[223] Miranda 2001, pp. 14–15.

Constitution would never be implemented fully. As described at length in Chapter 3, anti-constitutional forces, in league with foreign governments, managed to snuff out the Southern European revolutions. As mentioned previously, Metternich crushed the Neapolitan Revolution. In Spain, the French army, led by the Duke of Angoulême, crossed the Pyrenees, toppled the *Trienio Liberal* government, and restored Ferdinand VII, again, to absolute power in 1823. Ferdinand promptly unleashed a wave of white terror and reprisals, much to the consternation of his liberators.[224] For a brief moment, Portugal stood alone. But the Cortes's popularity waned precipitously and the forces of reaction soon put an end to the first *Regeneração*.

Portuguese conservative thought in the age of revolutions

The constitutional ideas of the *Vintistas* were bitterly contested by politicians, theorists, and pamphleteers steeped in the conservative intellectual tradition. The influences on Portuguese conservative thought were heterogeneous. Burke, de Bonald, Haller, de Maistre, and Savigny informed ideas and attitudes across the spectrum, from flexible conservatives, such as Palmela, to unrepentant absolutists. An anti-Jacobin, rabidly counter-revolutionary tradition, inspired in part by the Abbé Barruel (1741–1820), also exerted great influence.[225]

Portugal's major conservative publicist of the pre-1808 era was Marquês de Penalva.[226] He outlined the case against anti-monarchical revolutionary change in his widely disseminated *Dissertação a Favor da Monarquia* (1799). Penalva argued that monarchy was not only the best political system, but also the only form of government worthy of the appellation "system." Other types of government inevitably tended toward "disorder." Constitutional monarchy, for example, suffered from divided sovereignty, which generated "contradictory" policies prejudiced by either "old friendships or animosities." It was often guided by "personal interests" alone, divorced from those of the nation. Only by ceding all rights to the king could the benefits derived from society

---

[224] On Ferdinand VII's restoration, see Fontana 1979; Fontana 2006; and Anna 1983.

[225] See Godechot 1972 for an overview of "counter-revolutionary" thought in France, much of which is applicable to Portugal. For an overview of German neo-absolutism, see Droz 1967. As D. McMahon noted, "Catholic enemies of the Enlightenment in Europe and the New World borrowed from French authors, translated French books, and repeated arguments that circulated freely through the world-wide network of the Church." See McMahon 2001, p. 11.

[226] Fernando Teles da Silva Caminha e Menezes, third Marquês de Penalva (1754–1818).

be enjoyed. Not only did monarchy preserve order ("the only institution capable of handling the rudder during a political shipwreck"), but Penalva regarded it as the sole source of "concord, the union of [social] forces, equal subordination [to a single power], common customs, and reciprocal interest; all of the things which contribute to the birth of patriotism."[227] For Penalva, it was a fundamental error to locate monarchy's origins either in conquest by martial force or in general acclamation by the populace. Instead, it was necessary to recognize the "divine will" responsible for the establishment of kingship. Such a doctrine had consequences for Penalva's understanding of political liberty, which he believed could be restricted according to the king's judgment, for it did not exist in any meaningful sense prior to the advent of monarchy.[228]

But while exalting the monarchy and rejecting popular, representative institutions, and written constitutionalism, Penalva's brand of monarchism was not "regalist," in the capacious Pombaline sense of the term. All authority, at its origin, might emanate from the king, but the preservation of political order and social cohesion hinged on its delegation to, and exercise by, the nobility. The extensive privileges enjoyed by this latter body were justified by its function as a buttress to monarchy. In Penalva's conception of Portugal's ancient constitution, the nobility's place at the center of public life was affirmed. The alliance between the monarchy and the nobility was reinvigorated and strengthened, understood as a defense against the occult forces conspiring to foment revolution and disseminating doctrines of popular sovereignty. This "mutual dependence" between the king and his "first subjects [*subditos*]," Penalva explained in an 1805 letter to the Prince Regent, Dom João, must be maintained, for otherwise a "dangerous schism" would permit "evil-doers" to "rise suddenly and enjoy honors without deserving them, striving to ascend in the hierarchy without paying the ancient and honorable price paid by our esteemed ancestors."[229] In his celebration of nobility's role in preventing revolution, Penalva was an exponent of ideas belonging to what a distinguished historian classified as "historical conservatism": anti-regalist, anti-absolutist, and pro-aristocratic.[230]

Penalva's ideas, while influential, competed for primacy against other conservative doctrines that percolated, specifically those which might be termed "enlightened absolutist" or "integral absolutist."[231]

---

[227] Penalva 1799, pp. 18–19.   [228] Ibid., pp. 39, 48.
[229] "Carta que o Marquês de Penalva Escreveu ao Principe Regente em 1805," quoted in Pintassilgo 1987, pp. 172–73.
[230] Godechot 1972, p. 4.   [231] Ibid., p. 13.

Ultramontanism, too, exerted great influence. Yet another important strain of Portuguese conservative thought *c.* 1790–1830, especially in its popular manifestations, was virulent anti-Masonism. As elsewhere in Europe, Freemasons were suspected of scheming to topple thrones, accused of subverting religion, and blamed when revolutionary outbreaks occurred.[232] The aforementioned Abbé Barruel, who popularized the notion that revolution, and the destruction it wrought, was providential punishment for intellectual and moral decline, was published in Portuguese translation.[233] The alleged association of Freemasonry/anti-clericalism and revolution strengthened and made explicit the mutual reliance of the Church and monarchy. In Portugal and Brazil, the various *inconfidências* and subterranean conspiracies, many of which did have verifiable Masonic links, if not direct inspiration, fueled animosity toward Freemasons from those political writers who defended the indissoluble alliance between the throne and the altar. "The only remedy for *pedreiros-livres*, the heroic remedy," Macedo contended, "is force, because a mason alive, a strong throne, and secure religion are incompatible things."[234] Later the anti-masonic discourse became tinged furthered with anti-Semitism: masons were considered "masked Jews ... who seek the re-establishment of their nation under the Law of Moses."[235] Anti-masonic, anti-scientific, and anti-enlightenment language provided a means, as one historian has phrased it, "to radically simplify complex phenomena, providing a master narrative through which orthodox Catholics could understand the changes overtaking their society."[236]

The 1820 Porto Revolution, and the Cortes's effort to frame a written constitution, furnished conservative writers with fresh confirmation of their prejudices. The "French Revolution," used routinely as shorthand for political and social apocalypse, had finally reached Portugal.[237] The

[232] On the links between Freemasonry and constitutionalism, see Jacob 1991, pp. 15, 213, 216.
[233] Godechot 1972, p. 41; McMahon 2001, p. 59. Various translations of Barruel's work circulated in Portugal, including his *História Abbreviada da Perseguição, Assasinato e do Desterro do Clero Francez durante a Revolução* (1795–96).
[234] [J. A. de Macedo], *O Espectador Portuguez* 1816, vol. III, no. 12, p. 93.
[235] *Periódico para o Bons Realistas*, no. 13 (July 12, 1828), p. 13; on this affiliation of anti-masonry and anti-semitism, see Malheiro da Silva 1993, p. 171.
[236] McMahon 2001, pp. 27–28.
[237] The conservative writers are not entirely consistent on this point. They often lumped the French Constitution of 1791 and the Spanish Constitution of 1812 together, just as they often elided differences between revolutionary movements across space and time. As Madre de Deos 1823b noted, "these absurd subversives ... have few differences between them," p. 9. Their analysis of the 1812 Spanish Constitution was

alleged continuity and parallels between the late eighteenth-century French Revolution and the Portuguese upheaval of 1820–23 was commented upon endlessly: "today's revolutionaries have the same principles as those followed by previous revolutionaries; they even use the same language [*linguagem*]."[238] The chief fears expressed were the subversion of the political-social order, the trampling of the Church's temporal authority, and the impious attack on Catholicism. *Vintista* religious toleration and advocacy of freedom of expression were pilloried by conservative writers. The Bishop of Viseu's 1822 sermons warned that the French Revolution, by destroying the "best institutions," had resulted only in "perversity, disorder, and general annihilation."[239] A year later, he railed against "corrupting books" and "innovators" whose "false promises" should be feared.[240] The culmination of their anxieties was the 1822 Constitution, against which conservative writers turned their ire. One of the most prolific of these writers, Faustino José da Madre de Deos, accused these "wicked men of distorting even the meaning of words." In the mouth of a liberal, the words "regeneration," "liberty," and "virtue" were inverted to "disorder," "deception," and "depravity," respectively.[241] The liberal revolution (1820–23) had taken advantage of the "crass ignorance of the people" to convince them that "Portugal had never possessed a constitution."[242] Here the anti-*philosophe* discourse was grafted on to the modern opposition to liberalism, mirroring what happened in Restoration France.[243]

Madre de Deos's screed formed part of a broader discourse embraced by conservative writers in the early 1820s. They championed two linked, if sometimes contradictory, causes: the preservation of the rights and privileges of the nobility and clergy – the estates from which many of them hailed – and the traditional aspects of the monarchy, by which they generally meant the royal prerogatives and government institutions pre-dating Portugal's 1580 absorption into Spain. Taken together, these features constituted Portugal's unwritten "ancient constitution."

heavily influenced by Haller 1823, which had previously had been translated into French.

[238] [Anon.], *Monarchia Portugueza Restituida* 1823, p. 51.

[239] "Cauzas da Revolução Franceza" (1822), in Lobo 1848, vol. I, p. 367.

[240] Sermon of December 9, 1823, in Lobo 1853, vol. III, pp. 86–88 passim. It may be assumed that Lobo referred not only to the avalanche of books, newspapers, and pamphlets published by Portuguese writers, but also to the cheap editions of Voltaire, Rousseau, and other *philosophes* that flooded the European book market after 1815; see McMahon 2001, p. 158.

[241] Madre de Deos 1823c, p. 64.

[242] Madre de Deos 1823b, p. 9.

[243] McMahon 2001, p. 167.

They downplayed the internal tensions and contradictions of this arrangement, as each estate or component had sought to establish its preeminence over the rest. But regardless of these tensions, defenders of the monarch, the nobility, and the clergy shared an embrace of custom, preferring the unwritten, "ancient" constitution over positive law. For Penalva, the nobility was "the defender of both monarchy and of the people, to whom it furnishes protection, government, and a good example to emulate."[244] Visconde de Santarém, perhaps the most sophisticated of the Miguelist writers, who are presented in Chapter 4, argued that when the nobility was deprived of its long-established participation in government, replaced by a representative assembly drawn from commoners, the division of the country into "factions" inevitably followed, destroying the "connections and harmony within the kingdom" and leading to the "violent death of central authority."[245]

Conservative thinkers embraced the notion that Portugal possessed an unwritten, "ancient" constitution, or *lei fundamental*. They scorned the burgeoning fad for written constitutions. This position led them to celebrate the centuries-long existence of the Cortes while unequivocally rejecting the notion that it had functioned as a legislative body and a check on monarchical power. Penalva made this point clearly at the turn of the nineteenth century, when he argued that "the authority of the Cortes was purely consultative, and never deliberative ... the king sought to listen to his vassals, who never dared to believe that they had ceased to be subjects [*subditos*]."[246] An anonymous 1817 *Discurso* asserted that royal authority derived directly and exclusively from God. The Portuguese monarchy, therefore, "never depended on the *Povos* or any other person whatsoever." This same tract offered a regalist analysis of the Cortes de Lamego: "It was not by the authority or the counsel of the People, nor did the people confer the power or authority to [Dom Afonso Henriques], for he already possessed it from the time of his father's death. The Cortes of Lamego was convoked for the sole purpose of determining the line of succession to the throne, and the regulation of it [in the future] by means of a *lei fundamental*."[247] In this view, the Cortes's authority was radically limited, the pact confined solely to the manner of determining the royal succession, not the nature of monarchy. Such ideas were diffused more widely following

---

[244] Penalva 1799, pp. 63–64.
[245] Quoted in Lousada 1987.
[246] Penalva 1799, pp. 130–31.
[247] BAj., 54-XI-16, no. 117, [Anon.], "Discurso em que se Demonstra que o Poder dos Reis não Depende dos Povos, e Mormente a dos Senhores Reis de Portugal" [1817], fos. 1v., 9.

the publication of António Caetano do Amaral's 1819 *Para a História da Legislação e Costumes de Portugal*, which conceded the historical existence of the Cortes of Lamego, but insisted that it, like every subsequent Cortes, had been merely consultative, not legislative.[248] The Cortes was an advisory board, a council of state at most.

This conception of the Cortes's limited function prevailed among conservative writers at the outset of the 1820 Revolution. Madre de Deos accused the upstart liberals of misunderstanding that institution's history. Its origins supposedly lay in the twelfth-century Cortes held at Lamego, though there was already widespread suspicion that knowledge concerning this alleged Cortes was based on a seventeenth-century forgery (which ultimately it turned out to be).[249] At Lamego, it was claimed, the *Três Estados* had agreed that Portugal would be an "absolute monarchy; that is, a government with a single prince independent of all other human powers."[250] This *lei fundamental*, conservative publicists argued, was unalterable. The Cortes at Lamego declared nothing concerning amendment. "The Cortes of Lamego is the true *Carta*," Daun wrote, "the Magna Carta of Portugal; a *Carta* which neither kings nor the nation can, should, or ever have a right to alter without reciprocal consent, for the fundamental laws cannot be revoked."[251] Madre de Deos ridiculed the 1821 Cortes for having "dispensed with the formality" of convocation by the king and inclusion of the clergy and nobility in its ranks, "assuming a name to which it was not entitled," and arrogating to itself the right to "legislate or discard legislation on any and every subject based on its will alone."[252]

In effect, these conservative writers argued, the 1822 Constitution replaced the traditional "constitution, which had enabled Portugal to achieve greatness over seven centuries."[253] "The Republicans of Holland," yet another publicist argued, "were never as free as the Portuguese were before the era of the *Regeneração*," for "our ancient Cortes is the best example of a political constitution in an independent and hereditary monarchy."[254] Following Dom João's 1823 restoration, discussed extensively in Chapter 3, efforts to diffuse this

---

[248] Cardim 1998, p. 181. Innumerable tracts make this argument: for one of the most coherent, see Pinto 1824.
[249] Oliveira Marques 1972, vol. I, pp. 325–27.
[250] Madre de Deos 1823c, pp. 155–56; a formulation reintroduced in Madre de Deos 1825, p. 62.
[251] Daun 1829, p. 11.
[252] Madre de Deos 1823c, pp. 151, 156.
[253] Madre de Deos 1823b, p. 49.
[254] [Anon.], *Refutação Methodica* 1824, pp. 12–14 passim.

concept of the Cortes gathered force. A flurry of publications and manuscripts, asserting that Portugal historically had been an absolute monarchy, denounced the *Vintistas* as fools: "their government lacked legitimacy and could not sustain itself; it may be compared to a bronze statue whose head and legs are made of mud, something that can never remain upright for long."[255] Lisbon's Academy of Sciences published various documents purportedly produced by the late seventeenth-century Cortes, presenting an image of a docile Cortes, uncritically obeying the wishes of the king, in 1824. In that same year, Joaquim José Pedro Lopes's tract on the origins, structure, and authority of the Cortes was published, though the staggering erudition contained therein can be reduced to the assertion that the Cortes historically was merely consultative, not legislative.[256] Taken as a whole, conservative political discourse in the early 1820s condemned modern constitutionalism and offered a historicist rebuttal, asserting the adequacy and relevance of Portugal's early modern institutions. They disagreed, of course, about how that heritage should be interpreted, but they were united in their opposition to *Vintista* constitutional theory and practice. Though they ultimately prevailed in 1823–26, the genie had escaped from the bottle. *Vintista* doctrines drifted across the ocean, where they mingled with Brazilian political ideas, themselves informed by Spanish American republicanism. By the time conservative forces gained the upper hand in the Peninsula, Brazil was independent of Portugal. How a revolutionary constitutional process intended to "regenerate" all parts of the Portuguese empire (albeit unequally) resulted in its abrupt dismemberment is the subject of Part III of this chapter.

PART III

Judicious reform, empire redux, new-fangled federation, or permanent separation? The dissolution of the Portuguese empire, 1821–1823

The causes underpinning and the processes resulting in Brazil's political independence, narrowly conceived, have been studied, almost

---

[255] JCBL, Codex Portugal 8, "Narração abreviada da Rebellião de Portugal perpetrada na Cidade do Porto em 24 d'Agosto de 1820 por Inimigos do Altar, e do Throno" (1823), fos. 16v.–17.
[256] Cardim 1998, p. 182.

exhaustively, by historians.[257] The scholarly consensus is that a confluence of factors, and the collaboration of strange bedfellows, produced the break with Portugal. Brazilian independence was anything but a calm, relatively conflict-free affair. This view represents a major revision of the nineteenth-century historical "myth," in the judgment of a leading historian of the 1970s, of "an independence without blood, the separation of a son from his father, an amicable [familial] disagreement." Independence is now recognized as "the product of a war, not a gift from Portugal, nor an internal agreement" of the House of Braganza.[258] Nor was it, as some twentieth-century historians would have it, an "agreement between elites," who decided upon the course of Brazil's historical trajectory among themselves and imposed it upon the rest of Portuguese America.[259] The subsequent avalanche of books and articles produced in the past forty years has pushed this conclusion even further, revealing the key roles played by slaves, free people of color, poor whites, mercenaries, journalists, incendiary street orators, and elites from far-flung regions in Brazil (e.g. Pará), as well as state-affiliated intellectuals.[260]

The causes might be broken down usefully into long-term preconditions, intermediate-term precipitants, and short-term triggers.[261] Among the most important preconditions was the slow "autonomization" of the South Atlantic world, in motion from the seventeenth century, whose main dynamics marginalized metropolitan Portugal. The slave trade was the principal driver of this process.[262] While Lisbon continued to be a significant entrepôt, the Brazilian economy increasingly produced for a broader European market while simultaneously developing a larger internal/domestic market.[263] The precipitants of independence are legion. The transfer of the Court, which made Brazil's administration autonomous, inspired a collective self-confidence, culminating in, and symbolized by, the raising of the former colony to the position of

---

[257] The relevant bibliography is too immense to summarize here. For a sampling with copious references, see Jancsó 2005. For older (still valuable) perspectives in English, see Bethell 1989 and Maxwell 2003; in Portuguese, Oliveira Lima 1989, T. Monteiro 1981; and C. G. Mota 1972b.

[258] J. H. Rodrigues 1975, vol. V, p. 228.

[259] Prado Júnior 1963.

[260] This new literature is bulging in size, as well as brimming with insights. Among others, see Lustosa 2000; G. S. Ribeiro 2002; Neves 2003; Jancsó 2005; and Machado 2010.

[261] Borrowed from Stone 1972, which he applied to the seventeenth-century English Civil War. For an application of this typology to the dissolution of the Spanish empire, see Paquette 2009a.

[262] Alencastro 2000; Adelman 2006.

[263] Maxwell 1973; Alexandre 1993; and Adelman 2006.

a kingdom coequal with Portugal in 1815.[264] The broad influence of political and economic liberalism, itself the offspring of Enlightenment currents, deserves mention. So, too, does the revaluation of the political model upon which the ancién regime was based during the revolutionary upheaval gripping neighboring Spanish America. The Portuguese state, with its centralizing aspirations, was challenged as empires from Boston to Buenos Aires imploded, revealing the Luso-Brazilian status quo to be both untenable and anachronistic, the conscientious efforts of reformers notwithstanding. The devastation of Portugal wrought by the Napoleonic occupation made apparent the difficulty of maintaining an integrated empire with Lisbon at its center.[265] Another precipitant was the fear – racial, political, and economic – gripping Brazil's elite. Political instability would prod Brazil down the road traveled by Saint-Domingue and Spanish America while fragmentation and republicanism threatened to reverse the newfound economic prosperity.[266] Brazil's elite was naturally predisposed against the Cortes's projects which sought to shift decision-making and the economic center back to Lisbon. With Portugal unable to offer protection against "revolution from below," Brazilian elites protected themselves through a "conservative revolution of independence."[267]

The short-term triggers resulting in Brazilian political independence were myriad. Undoubtedly, the Cortes's hostile posturing and actions fueled separatist passions. Palace intrigues, the individual idiosyncrasies of major political actors, the role of incendiary journalists, professional ambition, ardor for constitutionalism, the thousands of small actions performed by local autonomists, soldiers, republicans, and slaves all pushed the Luso-Brazilian empire toward a final reckoning. The existence of a multiplicity of causes, most of which had nothing to do with one another except insofar as they destabilized the political situation, is a chief reason why it is more accurate to frame this demise of empire as "disaggregation" than as independence.[268] Focus on that series of events, and their subsequent enshrinement in international law, emphasizes too strongly the territorial unity and proto-national solidarity present in Brazil, the coherent direction and intentions of its leading political actors, the control exercised by a single center, and the extent to which the colonial order was, in fact, dismantled after colonialism. On the contrary, it is the survival, and even reconstitution, of

[264] See this discussion in this chapter, pp. 99–103.
[265] Above all, Alexandre 1993.
[266] Andrews 2004.   [267] Morton 1974.
[268] Holanda 1962.

certain facets of the overthrown ancién regime that accounts for the trajectories of Brazil and Portugal, and the frequent recrossings of their respective paths, in the decades after independence.

Part III focuses on only one understudied aspect of this enormous and complex process, with no pretensions whatsoever of comprehensive treatment. The Cortes debates, it is argued, link the processes of imperial reform and conflict, discussed in Chapters 1 and 2, with the long aftermath of incomplete, partial imperial breakdown in both Portugal and Brazil after 1822, discussed in Chapters 3, 4, and 5. Self-aggrandizing and inspired, the peninsular *Vintistas* conceived of themselves as engaged in an epic and global struggle to throw off the dead weight of the feudal past and endow the empire with new institutions. They neither harbored an intention of dismembering the empire nor wished to preside over its disintegration. On the contrary, the maintenance of imperial unity was a major assumption of the *Vintistas* as well as of their detractors.[269] Brazil's independence would imperil Portugal's political survival, a fact well known to both *Vintistas* and Portuguese-born government ministers. As Vilanova Portugal noted, "if Brazil separates and cuts off its intercourse with Portugal, this kingdom must collapse. She would have to be considered like Hanover with respect to Great Britain."[270] Portugal without Brazil, a publicist predicted, "must become a secondary power, similar to a pygmy among giants ... it risks becoming a province of Spain, and, if this happens, the name Portuguese will become extinct in Europe, more obscure than it was [from 1580–1640], and without the least hope of recovering [its independence]."[271] With Brazil, however, Portugal possessed the material resources and manpower to resist predatory nations harboring annexationist designs, such as Spain, not to mention colonial markets with which to entice potential allies, chiefly Britain.[272]

The peninsular deputies to the Cortes were pulled in two mutually exclusive directions. On the one hand, they sought the extension of liberal institutions and legal equality across the empire. On the other, they envisaged the "regeneration" of the peninsular economy and the restoration of the metropole's place at the center of an intercontinental entity which had become increasingly integrated during the age of enlightened

---

[269] For example, see January 30, 1821, speech by Pereira do Carmo, quoted in Proença 1987, p. 42.

[270] "Parecer de Thomaz António de Vilanova Portugal," January 7, 1821, in *Documentos ... Independência* 1923, p. 216.

[271] [Anon.], "Reflexões sobre a Necessidade de Promover a União dos Estados ..." (1822), reproduced in Faoro 1973, pp. 10, 35.

[272] Sousa Sequeira 1821, p. 8.

reform.[273] *Vintistas* thus wedded the destruction of Old Regime institutions to a selective return to the status quo ante, stripping Brazil of the de facto and de jure autonomy it had acquired since 1808. "Revolutionary ideas were widespread," Marquês de Fronteira recalled in his memoirs, "everyone wanted the Court to return to Lisbon, and they loathed the idea of becoming a colony of a colony."[274] Almeida Garrett signaled the shift to which the revolutionaries aspired: "yesterday slaves, today free; yesterday subjects of tyranny, today men; yesterday miserable colonists, today citizens."[275] Besides the British army of occupation, the Court's continued residence in Rio de Janeiro (though not the king himself) was blamed for this litany of evils. The "perfidious" *Carioca* Court, he moaned, had "oppressed, bled, and robbed" Portugal.[276] Another pamphleteer argued that the Court's presence in Rio de Janeiro had reduced peninsular Portugal to a state of the "second or even third order," its place in Europe "akin to that of Saxony, or perhaps Naples and Sardinia."[277]

The *Vintista* approach to Brazil was denounced loudly by Brazilians after 1821 as a "recolonization" effort, a view echoed by generations of Brazilian historians. But this appraisal deserves closer scrutiny. Above all, it is crucial to recall that thirty-nine of the forty-six Brazilian deputies who took their seats in the Cortes signed the "*Bazes*" subsequently elaborated into the 1822 Constitution. In other words, the vast majority of the Brazilian representatives endorsed a political arrangement designed to strengthen and formalize the union between the two sides of the Atlantic. Only later would the direction of the Cortes's deliberations alienate the Brazilian deputies and spur them to forsake the transatlantic constitutional process.[278] It is also crucial to recall that the word "independence" in 1821–22 was not associated exclusively with the call for Brazil's definitive and irrevocable separation from Portugal; often it referred solely to administrative autonomy, a modest form of devolution or "home rule."[279] The Cortes's policy has been misunderstood

[273] As Lewin explained, when Luso-Brazilian liberals referred to "equality before the law," they had in mind the "destruction of what they deemed legal distinctions. Their emphasis on juridical equality emanated from their opposition to Braganzan absolutism rather than being inspired by either French or American revolutionary notions of political equality." See Lewin 2003, vol. II, p. 22.

[274] Fronteira 1928, pt. II, p. 194.

[275] Almeida Garrett, "O Dia 24 de Agosto," in Serrão 1979, p. 49.

[276] Ibid., p. 50.

[277] [Anon.], *Reflexões sobre a Necessidade de Promover* 1822, pp. 6, 40.

[278] A. T. da Mota 1972, pp. 80, 98; on Brazilian deputies, see Boehrer 1960; and Berbel 1999.

[279] E. Viotti da Costa, "The Political Emancipation of Brazil," in Russell-Wood 1975, p. 72. For overviews of the political thought of independence, see Barretto 1973; and E. F. dos Santos 1999.

because it was not appreciated against the broader backdrop of its members' peculiar jurisprudential and linguistic context. What animated the Cortes deputies was a commitment to universal jurisdiction, the consistent application of law throughout Portuguese territory, without exception. They sought to create "institutions which unite, as much as possible, the parts of our monarchy." They explicitly rejected laws "appropriate to ultramarine provinces," as Britain had done in North America,[280] as well as the exclusionary, "illiberal," and "despotic" policy adopted by the Cortes of Cádiz toward Spanish America a decade earlier.[281] Brazilians would enjoy "the same constitution, the same civil liberty, the same political liberty, [and] the same guarantees" as the Portuguese.[282] Since "the nation is singular, all [local] differences should disappear."[283] For this reason, several of the deputies sought to delay major constitutional discussions until the arrival of the Brazilian deputies.

Conciliatory rhetoric and legal universalism aside, the *Vintistas* insisted that there must exist "a single point at which supreme authority resides."[284] Dom João's decision to leave Dom Pedro in Brazil as Prince Regent was, therefore, unacceptable. Moura summarized the prevailing sentiments when he argued that "the Portuguese throne was born at Ourique and Portugal must always remain the seat of the monarchy."[285] The *Vintistas* also refused to accept the economic arrangements enshrined in the 1808–10 decrees and treaties. For them, economic policy must be consistent with political union. They called for the abolition of "all odious barriers" which prevented full economic integration and a "real and genuine" union.[286] Borges Carneiro insisted that there must be "commercial restrictions which favor Portugal as much as they favor Brazil," for "liberty without rules is always pernicious."[287]

To create this new system, the bastions of reaction would be neutralized and the Lisbon Cortes converted into the mitochondria of revolutionary transformation. The ancient constitution would be suspended, "Tropical Versailles" dismantled, and supreme authority invested in the Cortes. The Cortes's high-handed tactics and rhetoric should not shroud awareness of these fairly constant goals. Following Dom João's recall to Lisbon, the Cortes commenced an assault on the institutions

[280] Moura, February 9, 1822, in *PBDP*, p. 53.
[281] Sarmento, April 25, 1821, in *PBDP*, p. 97.
[282] Moura, May 21, 1822, in *PBDP*, p. 238.
[283] Bettencourt, November 12, 1821, in *PBDP*, p. 300.
[284] Freire, February 9, 1822, in *PBDP*, p. 52.
[285] Moura, July 3, 1822, in *PBDP*, p. 454.
[286] Pereira do Carmo, March 15, 1822, in *PBDP*, p. 117.
[287] Borges Carneiro, April 9, 1822, in *PBDP*, p. 126.

created in Brazil after 1808. An October 1821 *Carta de Lei* indirectly deprived Rio de Janeiro of its status as the capital by establishing a new political, military, and financial administrative apparatus for Brazil. *Juntas Provisorias de Governo* in each province, subject directly to the king, now resident in Lisbon, were decreed, which made Prince Regent Dom Pedro's government superfluous.[288] A new *Junta da Fazenda*, too, was made directly responsible to the Cortes and the king. A January 1822 *Carta de Lei* issued by the Cortes further abolished all tribunals and related institutions established in Brazil since 1808, dampening all expectations that Rio might remain a center of a bipolar empire. The impact of the Cortes's legislation, which passed against the vociferous objections of the Brazilian deputies then in Lisbon, was to shift the center of political gravity decisively back to Portugal, thus making the continued presence of the Court in Brazil redundant. With Rio de Janeiro stripped of its institutions, authority, and preeminence, now that new quasi-governmental structures loyal to Lisbon were installed in the provinces, the recall of Dom Pedro to Lisbon was inevitable. Dom Pedro's recall, however, was mishandled. It backfired and instead instigated acts of defiance culminating in his declaration of Brazil's independence, which proved to be a preemptive "counter-revolution" as much as an assertion of national sovereignty.[289]

The actions and proclamations of the Portuguese deputies riled their Brazilian counterparts. António Carlos de Andrada Machado e Silva (1773–1845) and his cohort contested the Peninsula-centered economic vision of the Luso-Brazilian empire's future, insinuating strongly that Portugal strove to reimpose the colonial yoke. "There cannot exist harmony between two parts of a nation when the interests of one are sacrificed to the other," he argued in the Lisbon Cortes; "monopoly, like despotism, moves unceasingly to halt liberty."[290] Instead, to safeguard liberty, Brazil must exercise autonomy over its own affairs. Brazilian deputies called for authority to be delegated to Brazilian political entities. They pointed to Scotland, and especially Ireland, as pertinent European examples.[291] While admitting that there must be a single seat of government, António Carlos argued that there could exist "as many administrative apparatuses as necessary."[292] Portuguese deputies attacked his logic as spurious. They contended that there was a major difference between independent countries "forming a new pact for the

[288] Proença 1987, p. 47; Barman 1988, p. 81.
[289] Maxwell 2003.
[290] A. C. de Andrada Machado, April 15, 1822, in *PBDP*, p. 139.
[291] A. C. de Andrada Machado, February 11, 1822, in *PBDP*, p. 59.
[292] A. C. de Andrada Machado, August 7, 1822, in *PBDP*, p. 494.

purposes of joining together" for the first time and the situation in which they found themselves. Brazil "had been united to Portugal since its discovery."[293] Portuguese deputies were baffled and incensed by the accusations of António Carlos and the Brazilians. Moura stated that

the Cortes never sought to govern Brazil according to a system different than that of Portugal; it has sought equal rights, and equality of representation ... it never adopted the language of the English and Spanish with regard to their colonies.[294]

On the contrary, the Cortes's aims were diametrically opposed to those of rival empires. As Pereira do Carmo observed, "[the British and Spanish] sent despotism to *ultramar* whereas we send constitutional liberty; they brought arbitrary government whereas we brought law; they imposed slavery whereas we impose the equality of rights of the Portuguese of both hemispheres."[295] As the situation grew more desperate, and secession became a plausible scenario, further concessions were extended to mollify the Brazilians, the most important of which was approval for the convocation of a Constituent and Legislative Assembly for Brazil in June 1822, to be "invested with that portion of sovereignty that essentially belongs to the people of that great and rich continent." The Cortes made clear that this decision was designed to "maintain the integrity of the empire and the *justo decoro*" of Brazil, ensuring it "independence" of action to handle its own affairs while deepening its union with the broader "*grande família Portuguesa*."[296] Yet it was clear that this Brazilian Assembly would enjoy but limited jurisdiction. Unlike the Cortes, it would not possess executive power; its remit was purely administrative. The new fundamental law, or constitution, would be framed by the Lisbon Cortes alone, to which the Brazilians would send deputies, and it would be enforced on both sides of the Atlantic.

Such a concession did not go far enough in the judgment of some of the Brazilian deputies and other observers. "There cannot be permanent union between Portugal and Brazil without the establishment of a special *Câmara* of the Cortes in Brazil in addition to that of Portugal," in the appraisal of one pamphleteer.[297] This arrangement, another publicist argued, was "the only way to save the integrity of the monarchy."[298]

[293] Trigoso, February 11, 1822, in *PBDP*, p. 59.
[294] Moura, May 22, 1822, in *PBDP*, p. 263.
[295] Pereira do Carmo, November 14, 1821, in *PBDP*, pp. 302–3.
[296] "Decreto mandando convocar uma Assembléia Constituinte e Legislativa no Reino do Brazil," June 3, 1822, reproduced in Biker 1879, vol. 21 (13), p. 113.
[297] Reis 1822, p. 12. On the general intellectual context, see Berbel 1999.
[298] [Anon.], *Considerações sobre as Cortes do Brasil* 1822, p. 19.

Others went further, declaring that Brazil "should be independent, connected to Portugal only by links of friendship, treaties, and reciprocal commerce," an arrangement believed to be "equally advantageous" to both states.[299] By mid June 1822, a Cortes commission to assess Brazil's place in the empire produced a report. It noted that "a complete union of Brazil and Portugal was impossible, for certain matters must be subject to different legislation," which meant that Brazil must possess a "permanent, and ample, delegation of executive power." The report proposed the creation of two separate congresses, composed of elected representatives, one in Lisbon and the other in Rio, to devise ordinary legislation. The "provinces" of Africa and Asia would choose into which kingdom they wished to "incorporate" for the purposes of representation. In addition to these two Congresses, there would be a Cortes Geraes, with fifty deputies, divided equally between Brazil and Portugal, to handle matters related to defense, foreign affairs, and other such affairs of state.[300]

This proposal, however, was anathema to the majority of the *Vintistas*. For them, Brazil was, in juridical terms, nothing greater than a province, which should be subordinate to a single, central authority. As Fernandes Tomás rhetorically enquired, with ill-concealed incredulity, "we can legislate for Beira, Minho, Trás-os-Montes, [but] we are forbidden from legislating for Brazil." He considered America to be a "continuation of Portugal." Far from being "heterogeneous nations," requiring multiple legislative bodies, Portugal and Brazil were "a single *povo*, with the same laws, customs, and history."[301] The creation of two congresses, one on each side of the Atlantic, Borges Carneiro reasoned, would be "a two-headed monster," a notion as outrageous as the suggestion that "the tree of liberty had two trunks."[302] Though he eventually conceded the potential benefits of "delegating a certain amount of authority" to Brazil, mainly for the purposes of administrative expediency,[303] most Portuguese deputies adamantly refused to countenance the possibility. Guerreiro, for example, argued that the Cortes's task was

---

[299] [Anon.], *Reflexões sobre o Pacto Social*, p. 80.

[300] "Parecer da Commissão Encarregada da Redacção dos Artigos Addicionaes á Constituição Portugueza, referentes ao Brasil," June 15, 1822 (in *DC*, July 26, 1822), reprinted in A. Vianna 1922, vol. II, pp. 495–500 passim.

[301] Fernandes Tomás, July 1, 1822, in *PBDP*, p. 441.

[302] Borges Carneiro, June 26, 1822, in *PBDP*, p. 410.

[303] "There should be in East Africa, in India, and in China a certain delegation of authority (which could be entrusted to the *Senados* of Goa and Macao) which could expedite greatly affairs in which Portugal enjoys the executive power." See Borges Carneiro, August 7, 1822, in *PBDP*, p. 496.

the "destruction of the provincial spirit," which multiple delegations of executive authority promised to foster.[304]

The acrimonious quality of these disputes should not preclude awareness that many other participants in these debates, both inside and outside of the Cortes, staked out more conciliatory positions, though their moderate voices were often drowned out by the revolutionary din. Some deputies argued that they would not allow disagreements over constitutional niceties to blossom into a full-fledged independence movement. Britain had unwisely permitted "a few tea leaves" to escalate into permanent separation from its North American colonies. Unlike France in Saint-Domingue, Portugal would not allow "inappropriate legislation" to spur descent into bloody warfare. Mediation and reconciliation were possible.[305] To ensure that the "contagion of revolution" did not extend to Brazil, it would be necessary to use something beyond "coercive measures" more likely to "inflame than to extinguish the revolutionary spirit." Instead, reform would dissipate the "pernicious idea that [either Portugal or Brazil] must be a colony of the other, instead of mutually assisting each other in every branch of industry and commerce."[306] Soares Franco, for example, advocated the construction of roads between the major cities of Pernambuco, Bahia, and Rio de Janeiro, whereas others urged infrastructural improvements and legal changes conducive to economic development.[307]

In order to understand how these disagreements served to erode the bonds tying Portugal to Brazil, it is necessary to survey briefly the situation in Brazil at the time of these disputes. News of the Porto Revolution contributed to the great agitation in Rio de Janeiro and subsequent upheaval there, but it was not the sole catalyst. The Spanish American Wars of Independence continued to rage and the probability of the victory of republican over royalist forces increased markedly following the defeat of General Pablo Morillo's reconquest expedition; the aftertaste of the 1817 Pernambuco Revolution remained bitter; and social upheaval inched ever closer. Less apocalyptically, Brazil's new status as a kingdom, coequal with Portugal, raised the still unresolved matter of which institutional framework would best encompass the legal and economic changes within the empire. Could, and should, Brazil remain the seat of empire? Would peninsular Portugal accept this dramatic change without recompense?

---

[304] Guerreiro, August 7, 1822, in *PBDP*, pp. 496–97.
[305] Pereira do Carmo, March 23, 1822, in *PBDP*, p. 351.
[306] ANTT MNE (Legação de Portugal em Inglaterra), cx. 744, José Luiz de Souza to Vilanova Portugal, January 7, 1821.
[307] Soares Franco 1820–21, Ensaio 4, p. 38.

The arrival of news concerning the Porto Revolution came precisely at the moment when these issues were being discussed. The Brazilian reaction was extremely mixed, varying widely by geography and ideology. At least at its initial stages, the upheaval in Portugal symbolized three things: first, the (re-)tilting of the political axis toward Portugal; second, the increased likelihood of a constitutional monarchy, based on the Constitution of Cádiz; and, third, the opportunity for a recalibration of the connections among different parts of the empire. In short, the Porto Revolution was not greeted with uncompromising cries of separatism. On the contrary, the commitment to the *Reino Unido* (and the Portuguese nation) was intense and ubiquitous.[308] Bahia, along with the northern and northeastern provinces, adhered to the constitutional system immediately, in February 1821.[309] They accepted the Lisbon Cortes as the legitimate political unit to which they would send representatives, empowered to make decisions by which they would be bound. In Pará, the provisional Junta assured the Lisbon Cortes that "the inhabitants incessantly praise the constitutional system and claim that it has produced their happiness." Pará was linked by "indissoluble bonds" to Portugal, and the Junta promised to deal swiftly with manifestations of "subversive ideas" which threatened that "firm union."[310] In Ceará, the provincial government declared, "we embrace the same cause as our brothers in Portugal to whom we are linked by the sacred bonds of kinship, friendship, and reciprocal, common interests."[311] In Maranhão, the *Conciliador do Maranhão* argued that imperial unity was the sole option for Brazil, which was unprepared for independence. Instead of imagining a future resembling that of the USA, the editor claimed that Buenos Aires's fate was the more probable scenario, were independence declared, where "dissension and civil war between the various provinces" produced "horrendous anarchy."[312]

In general, then, the Porto Revolution's promise of a new constitution establishing liberal institutions, drafted by representatives drawn from across the empire, was an exhilarating prospect to all but inveterate monarchists and nativists, of whom there remained many. Initially, at least, Brazilian constitutionalists had great expectations for the Lisbon

---

[308] Slemian 2004, p. 125.
[309] For Pernambuco, see Bernardes 2006, p. 368.
[310] APEP, cod. 742, Junta Provisoria do Governo Civil da Provincia do Grão Pará to the Cortes, June 22, August 1, and November 12, 1822 passim. On liberalism in Pará in this period, see Coelho 1993, p. 311.
[311] APEC, Fondo Governo da Capitania do Ceará, 02–03–13–07–25 (antigo 26), *bando* of May 7, 1821, fo. 201v.
[312] *O Conciliador do Maranhão*, no. 38 (November 17, 1821), n.p.

Cortes: "Aren't we all Portuguese? Do we not speak the same language? Pertain to the same state, with the same King, the same [political] maxims, the same customs, and even the same religion? Why, then, don't we place our trust in the deliberations of the most vigilant and enlightened government that we possess?"[313] Certainly, there was talk of "emancipation" and "independence" in 1821. Yet, as previously indicated, it referred to Brazilian administrative autonomy and legal equality with Portugal. Similarly, the term *"Brasileiro"* (and its cognates *"Brasiliense"* and *"Brasilico"*) existed, but its usage was not an alternative, in this crucial moment, to *"Português."*[314] *"O Brasil"* was neither the focus of identity nor capable of attracting loyalty.[315] On the contrary, there were multiple overlapping and mutually reinforcing identities in the period 1815–22: Bahia or São Paulo might be considered one's *"patria,"* Brazil one's *"pais,"* and Portugal one's "nation" without any sense that such identities were mutually exclusive, or that these challenged the common and broader loyalty to the king.[316] Furthermore, to be a "constitutionalist" in Brazil before 1822 indicated a preference for a union with Portugal along the lines to be drawn up by the Cortes, whereas to be a *"corcunda,"* or anti-constitutionalist, was the equivalent of championing "disorder, factionalism, rebellion, [and] anarchy."[317]

Three groups emerged in Brazil around 1821–22, which historians have designated "parties": a European party which favored Luso-Brazilian unity according to the Constitution to be drawn up in Lisbon; a "democratic" or "republican" faction, which wanted independence and highly autonomous provincial governments; and an "aristocratic" party, composed mainly of landowners and public officials, major beneficiaries of the transfer of the Court, who sought outright independence, with a unitary government centered at Rio de Janeiro.[318] It was this latter party which claimed that the Cortes wanted to "recolonize" Brazil, a propaganda campaign conducted by those who wanted Dom Pedro to reject the Cortes's demand that he return and, furthermore, sought to vilify the Cortes's efforts to strip Rio de Janeiro of the institutions, and prestigious posts, which had transformed it from a relative backwater into the capital of a global empire.[319] The divisions among these three groups, however, were not particularly sharp, and there was increasing overlap as the political situation unfolded.

---

[313] Falcão 1821, p. 4.   [314] Slemian 2004, pp. 125, 167.
[315] Barman 1988, p. 28.
[316] Jancsó and Pimenta 2000, p. 131.
[317] Falcão 1821, p. 3.   [318] Proença 1987, p. 48.
[319] Slemian 2004, p. 127.

These were the conditions, then, amidst which the Lisbon Cortes debates proceeded. The intention of Portuguese deputies to conserve the empire at any price was revealed, however, in its decision to dispatch troops to Brazil. Such an act was interpreted, obviously, as hostile and confirmed Brazilian suspicions. From this point, the Lisbon Cortes's approach to Brazil operated on two parallel tracks. The first track was more conciliatory, seeking to coax, cajole, and soothe. The second was outright belligerent and foresaw a final, military reckoning. "Rio de Janeiro," Borges Carneiro observed, "has become the spiritual center of insurrection and of partisanship; this must be stopped."[320] The Cortes ordered Dom Pedro to return to Lisbon in late September 1821. The condescending tone in its order served only to escalate tensions. Upon his return to Europe, the Cortes insisted, Dom Pedro would travel to England, France, and Spain, "accompanied by enlightened and vir-tuous men committed to constitutional government," with the aim of fashioning the errant prince into a constitutional monarch.[321] In January 1822, even before news of the Cortes's *Carta da Lei*, which abolished most institutions set up in Brazil since 1808, crossed the Atlantic, Dom Pedro, in his famous *"Fico"* declaration, refused to comply with the Cortes's demand that he return to Europe. His recalcitrance caused the Portuguese army divisions stationed in Rio de Janeiro to rebel, in an effort to force Dom Pedro's obedience and compliance. He retaliated by expelling them from Brazil, aligning himself closely with the Brazilian "nativists" seeking outright independence. By May, he declared himself Brazil's "Perpetual Defender."[322]

Underpinning Dom Pedro's actions was the rising antipathy of the Brazilian elite for the Lisbon Cortes. A January 1822 letter co-signed by many Brazilians, including José Bonifácio de Andrada e Silva, argued that compliance with the Cortes's decree to disband Brazil's administrative institutions was unreasonable. "How can [the Cortes] strip Brazil of the institutions which are guarantors of its future prosperity?" they enquired. After twelve years of relative autonomy, how could the Brazilians "suffer again as vile colonists"? The Cortes demands were nothing more than "unprecedented despotism" and "political perjury."[323] In a letter to Dom Pedro, José Bonifácio expressed that the *Paulistas* "could no longer hide their just resentment ... of unconstitutional acts [practiced by the Lisbon Cortes], by which they seek to delude and enslave a free people ... reducing

---

[320] Borges Carneiro, August 23, 1821, in *PBDP*, p. 195.
[321] Document dated September 29, 1821, reproduced in Biker 1879, vol. 21 (13), p. 27.
[322] Manchester 1932; Barman 1988.
[323] *Collecção da Correspondência Official* 1822, letter no. 15, addressed to Dom João, January 2, 1822, p. 22.

[Brazil] to a mere colony."[324] The early months of 1822 also witnessed the rapid proliferation of a pamphlet culture and periodical press, much of which expressed indignation with the Cortes and urged Brazil's secession from the *Reino Unido*.[325] The Cortes had deprived Brazil of legislative authority, eliminated its executive power, extinguished its judiciary, and legally reimposed pre-1808 commercial restrictions, all of which "degraded" the notion that it was a kingdom coequal with Portugal.[326] The Cortes's economic policy, in particular, generated great dissatisfaction. The *Carioca* newspaper *Reverbero Constitucional* argued that "if the industry of that kingdom were more advanced, its manufactures could compete in the [Brazilian] market with those brought by foreigners, and surely they would be preferred."[327]

For the Lisbon Cortes, Dom Pedro's refusal to comply with its demands amounted to a declaration of war. One deputy argued that "factionalists who seek to perturb established order and pervert the sentiments of sincere union" must be stopped.[328] Yet many deputies still clung to the belief that good government, constructed upon the foundation of a sound constitution, would vanquish all antagonism. "The true army we should send is our constitution ... applying equally to all, it will destroy the despotism [bad government] that previously existed."[329] Castello Branco argued that sending troops could have "no other purpose than to enslave and colonize."[330] As late as August 1822, the Cortes issued a proclamation forswearing the use of force against Brazil: "our union must depend only on the affections and interests that produce reciprocal advantages, the family names and ancestors we share, friendship, the same laws, and equal protection before them.[331] As the likelihood of Brazilian independence increased, however, Portuguese politicians and publicists vocalized resentment of the demands made by their New World counterparts and the rhetoric concerning "recolonization" ambitions or the "enslavement" of Brazil by Portugal. As *O Conciliador Lusitano* put it, "how many such Brazilian slaves have we seen occupying the highest positions of this kingdom, and employed in the law courts! Surely everyone would want to be a

---

[324] "Representação ao Príncipe," January 3, 1822, in *Andrada e Silva* 2002, p. 135. On José Bonifácio's political thought, see A. R. C. da Silva 1999.

[325] On radical politics in Rio de Janeiro in these years, see Leite 2000.

[326] On these and other complaints, see Gama 1822, p. 5.

[327] *Reverbero Constitucional Fluminense*, no. 8 (January 1, 1822), p. 94.

[328] Moura, May 21, 1822, in *PBDP*, p. 240.

[329] Abbade de Medrões, August 25, 1821, in *PBDP*, pp. 202–3.

[330] Castello Branco, May 21, 1822, in *PBDP*, p. 240.

[331] "Proclamação das Cortes Geraes, Extraordinarias e Constituintes da Nação Portugueza," August 17, 1822, in Biker 1879, vol. 21 (13), p. 159.

PEDRO PRIMEIRO,

Imperador Constitucional do Brazil.

Figure 4 P. Langlumé, lithograph, after a painting by David Pradier. "Pedro Primeiro, Imperador Constitucional do Brasil" (1822).

slave of this sort: honors, *dignidades*, wealth, and pre-eminence are not the usual experience of slaves."[332] In July 1822, the Cortes issued three decrees: the first demanded that the signatories of the São Paulo letter sent to Dom Pedro be brought to trial; the second annulled the previously called meeting of the Council of *Procuradores* (which set the stage for the convocation of the Brazilian Assembly); and the third commanded Dom Pedro to obey the Cortes and return to Portugal.[333]

Even before news of Dom Pedro's September 7, 1822, "*Grito de Ipiranga*" reached Portugal, the Cortes had grown weary of his refusals. On September 24, 1822, the Cortes decreed that if Dom Pedro did not return to Portugal shortly, he would forfeit his right to succession. The Cortes further annulled its June decree convoking a constituent assembly for Brazil. At this September 1822 juncture, conciliation gave way to belligerence. The sole mediation would be the force of arms. As Rio de Janeiro's intransigence hardened, a different vision gained adherents among the *Vintistas*, that of "retaining certain provinces in the North [of Brazil], from which we enjoy a profitable commerce with the others."[334] Ultimately, the designs of the Cortes would be cut short by the restoration of Dom João in Spring 1823. But even before the Cortes was toppled and its deputies either imprisoned or exiled, the naval force it had sent to the north of Brazil, the richest and most populous region deemed amenable to reunification, lost a decisive battle off Salvador (Bahia) on May 4, 1823, and Portuguese garrisons evacuated the city early July.[335] Thereafter, while saber-rattling continued, the prospect of military reconquest became remote. The last Portuguese troops left Brazil for Portugal, via Montevideo, in March 1824.[336]

Between colony and independent polity: the interstitial character of the *Assembléia Constituinte*

Brazil's first assembly, which convened as Portuguese naval forces menaced the northeast's coastlines and two years before Brazil's independence was recognized officially, boasted predictably heterogeneous origins. On the one hand, it resulted directly from the Cortes's belated conciliation effort, a response to Brazilian demands for political and administrative autonomy. The Cortes reluctantly endorsed the creation

---

[332] *O Conciliador Lusitano*, July 1, 1822, pp. 58–59.
[333] Manchester 1932.
[334] Soares Franco, September 21, 1822, in *PBDP*, p. 557.
[335] Vale 1996, p. 46; Bethell 1989, p. 35.
[336] Bethell 1989, p. 35.

of a Brazilian assembly, within narrow limits. On the other hand, Dom Pedro managed to turn the Cortes's concession to his own advantage, convoking an assembly and thus undermining the Cortes's authority by asserting the royal origins of political authority, and, at a stroke, publicly demonstrating his sympathy for representative (and constitutional) government. Though both the Lisbon Cortes and Dom Pedro conceded the practical need for a Brazilian Assembly, or *Assembléia Constituinte*, it became transformed into the revolutionary, proto-national institution when the Cortes revoked its earlier decree. The deputies returned in elections for a Cortes-sanctioned body became revolutionaries overnight as the political terrain shifted. But the Assembly did not emerge solely from the crucible of conflict. The notion of a legislative assembly for Brazil had a long pedigree, dating to the period after 1815 especially, but with earlier roots in the Luso-Brazilian reaction to the Spanish American independence movements. As underlined previously, it gathered force owing to the Cortes's effort to placate Brazilians and undercut separatism, offering an appealing halfway house for those desirous of independence but wary of reckless schemes for achieving it, and in the sincere attempts by many on both sides of the Atlantic to strike upon a mutually acceptable compromise alternative to imperial fragmentation.

For reasons which will become clear, the history of the Assembly has been deeply contested. Historian and politician Homem de Mello summed up the debate in 1863: "According to some, it was a Jacobin club; for others, a body composed of mediocre men; and many people speak of its dissolution as if it were the most beneficial act of the *Primeiro Reinado*, without knowing so much as one work, or even one act, of that Assembly."[337] The Assembly's deputies were born in the New World, but many were members of the "Generation of the 1790s,"[338] trained in law, both canon and civil, as well as the natural sciences and mathematics, at Coimbra. The laws governing the Portuguese monarchy, therefore, were those with which they were most familiar and, as they groped toward independence, the framework within which they operated. Yet they were keen to demonstrate their break with that shared tradition. As a result, their debates relied as much on North American, European, and Spanish American experience and jurisprudence as on Portuguese legal precedent. It also deserves notice that few of these men were inveterate, radical revolutionaries. Several of the Brazilian

---

[337] Homem de Mello, *Correio Mercantil*, October 30, 1863, reproduced in Senado Federal 1973, p. 127. There are several good modern histories of the Assembly, including C. Rodrigues 2002.
[338] Maxwell 2003.

deputies sent to the Lisbon Cortes later served in the Assembly, including leading figures such Andrada Machado, Araújo Lima, Vergueiro, Alencar, Aguiar de Andrada, Muniz Tavares, and Pinheiro.[339] Their constitutional thought, therefore, was embedded inextricably in what they considered to be the failed effort to keep the empire together.

As they sought to frame a constitution for Brazil, Portuguese legal tradition and foreign constitutional models informed their deliberations. Some insisted that the English parliamentary system offered "the sole practical solution to the problem of liberty without *licença*."[340] The overriding tenor of their comments was an endorsement of what they styled "moderate" constitutionalism and an avoidance of unbridled liberty: "the celebrated Burke shows definitively that liberty detests exaggerated chimeras as much as base servilism."[341] This formula was repeated in various ways: "not licentious liberty, but liberty correctly understood [*bem-entendida*]"[342] or "a constitution without demagogues and anarchy."[343] The Assembly's deputies stressed that they were embarked on a new enterprise, not beholden to Portuguese or European tradition. Montesuma stressed that "we are not the Cortes of Lamego," arguing that the Assembly's function went beyond being a mere consultative body. It "must legislate on those matters entrusted to it by the nation (*nação*)." Anything that impeded the exercise of that right was "null, illegitimate, despotic, and tyrannical."[344] Similarly, other European precedents were belittled as inappropriate models: "the American system has nothing in common with that of Europe; this New World is separated from the Old not only by the ocean, but by its interests."[345] Another deputy disputed that the British constitutional system was an applicable model, for it "arose out of the ancient feudal system, the abuses of which could not be removed [from its constitution]" whereas Brazil's very different circumstances ("there was never a feudal system in Brazil") made the comparison a faulty one.[346] Arguing against trial by jury, for example, Silva Lisboa asserted that "the imitation of foreign institutions, even when they are good in themselves, does not always produce a salutary effect in other countries."[347] Along similar lines, Costa Aguiar argued, "the best institutions cannot be adopted

---

[339] Bonavides 1996, p. 22.
[340] Andrada Machado, May 2, 1823, in *APBAC*, t. 1, p. 35.
[341] Andrada Machado, May 6, 1823, in *APBAC*, t. 1, p. 51.
[342] Dias, May 6, 1823, in *APBAC*, t. 1, p. 52.
[343] José Bonifácio Andrada e Silva, May 6, 1823, in *APBAC*, t. 1, p. 53.
[344] Montesuma, September 16, 1823, in *APBAC*, t. 5, p. 139.
[345] Vergueiro, August 30, 1823, in *APBAC*, t. 4, p. 204.
[346] Henriques de Rezende, July 5, 1823, in *APBAC*, t. 3, p. 37.
[347] Silva Lisboa, October 21, 1823, in *APBAC*, t. 6, pp. 156–57.

at once; nations do not become free as a result of suddenly and violently being deprived of their old usages and practices."[348] Nor was the United States a desirable model. The former thirteen colonies lacked a common center and each colony possessed its own representative chamber to handle its affairs, whereas Brazil was graced by "a person with whom no one can compare, a person elevated by birth, whose primacy [among us] is uncontestable." Dom Pedro was the "common center," ensconced in Rio, which permitted the unification of Brazil's far-flung provinces. A federal system, some deputies argued, was unsuited to Brazil, because it was composed of provinces, not self-sufficient states.[349]

Yet in spite of their protests and assertions of inapplicability, the constitutional thought of the Assembly's deputies bore the heavy imprint of European debates. Several deputies were unwilling to discard the relevance and utility of the 1822 Portuguese Constitution, and thus its 1812 Cádiz Constitution forerunner, simply because the hostile Lisbon Cortes framed that document. One orator claimed that Spain's current (1823) troubles resulted not from its constitution, but rather from the behavior of its king, Ferdinand VIII, "the sole author of the disorders and disgraces" plaguing Spain.[350] Another prominent legislator, Carneiro de Campos, argued that new-found chauvinism toward the Portuguese Constitution was self-defeating. "The germ of disunion and the difference of interests and rights led to [Brazil's] separation" from Portugal, he noted, not any "defects" of that constitution.[351] Maciel da Costa, too, criticized the Cortes's actions, not the Constitution itself, citing that body's "furor for legislating ... its abolition of some institutions and alteration of others, without improving public administration," which produced only popular discontent.[352] This evidence is not presented to suggest that the 1822 Portuguese Constitution was uncritically embraced. Andrada Machado, for example, labeled both the Spanish and Portuguese Constitutions as "defective" because each failed to produce "harmony" between branches of government and lacked an institutional mechanism to "conciliate the interests."[353] Nevertheless, European precedent, particularly the Iberian constitutional experiments in which many of the Assembly's deputies had participated, was the point of departure for most debates.

---

[348] Costa Aguiar, October 25, 1823, in *APBAC*, t. 6, pp. 186–87.
[349] Vergueiro, September 18, 1823, in *APBAC*, t. 5, p. 166.
[350] Carneiro da Cunha, May 6, 1823, in *APBAC*, t. 1, p. 53.
[351] Carneiro de Campos, May 6, 1823, in *APBAC*, t. 1, p. 54.
[352] Maciel da Costa, August 8, 1823, in *APBAC*, t. 4, p. 54.
[353] Andada Machado, May 16, 1823, in *APBAC*, t. 1, p. 91.

More than the provenance of the constitutional models, the chief concern of most deputies was the balance of the respective powers, "clear distinctions between different powers and the achievement of harmony amongst powers."[354] Dom Pedro's insistence that it was his prerogative to convoke or dissolve the Assembly worried not only deputies with republican sympathies, but also those of a more moderate cast. Unsurprisingly, the allowance made for additional intermediary bodies separating the monarch and the Assembly concerned them. Here the continued existence of a Council of State loomed large. Andrada Machado claimed that it undermined representative government, for "the nation has no other *procuradores* except its [elected] deputies."[355] The deputies were neither democrats nor avowed republicans. Democracy and republicanism were considered wildly out of place in Brazil. Democratic principles, for example, were compared to "coins found beneath old ruins, which are unusable and fit only for a museum."[356] Liberty often proved to be a "false goddess," the "mother of disorder and anarchy; only order and public security enable the individual to prosper and ensure the stability of empires."[357] In spite of these political leanings, many feared that legislative authority was too loosely defined and too easily impinged upon by the monarch. The system of government could easily give way to an "absolute monarchy in which the [members of the] legislature become little more than counselors to the monarch."[358] For this reason, the monarch's ability to initiate as well as decree legislation, and the scope of his veto power, were among the most fiercely debated subjects. To ensure that the "natural tendency for despotism" was avoided, powers were to be delineated clearly. One deputy argued that "by no means should the decrees of the Assembly depend upon the sanction of the monarch."[359] Another argued that the Assembly, not the emperor, was sovereign: "it exercises the right of sovereignty of the nation."[360]

---

[354] President's Response to Emperor's speech, May 3, 1823, in *APBAC*, t. 1, pp. 23, 42–43.
[355] Andrada Machado, June 10, 1823, in *APBAC*, t. 2, p. 43.
[356] Henriques de Rezende, May 22, 1823, in *APBAC*, t. 1, p. 139.
[357] Carvalho e Mello, September 18, 1823, in *APBAC*, t. 5, p. 165.
[358] Carneiro de Campos, June 26, 1823, in *APBAC*, t. 2, pp. 164–65.
[359] Henriques de Rezende, June 26, 1823, in *APBAC*, t. 2, p. 168.
[360] França, July 29, 1823, in *APBAC*, t. 3, p. 168. Recapitulation of these arguments should not distract attention from the fact that there were advocates of enhanced royal authority in the Assembly. While in the minority, Silva Lisboa argued that "the legislative power should not substitute itself for that of the executive, which enjoys the trust of the nation to ensure public security"; see Silva Lisboa, November 11, 1823, in *APBAC*, t. 6, p. 306.

If the first major dispute involved the relationship of legislative to executive power, of the Assembly to the emperor, the second division concerned the relationship of the new polity's center (Rio de Janeiro and, generally, the southeast) with the rest of Brazil. The key context in which this debate transpired was the Lisbon Cortes's cunning, divisive strategy of exploiting regional rivalry by offering the northern and northeastern Brazilian provinces significant oversight of their affairs in exchange for remaining part of a unified Luso-Brazilian empire. The Assembly sought to claw power back for the central government and to avoid the fragmentation of Brazil heralded by the Cortes's actions. As the deputy Rodrigues de Carvalho observed, "when the provinces embraced the constitutional system, they began to consider themselves in isolation, separated entirely from the supreme power ... without connection to other provinces [as] the people of each province judged itself to be sovereign."[361] Not only had this state of affairs proved damaging, it also opened the possibility of several of these provinces rejoining Portugal, to the exclusion of the southern part of Brazil. Other deputies depicted provincial distrust of Rio's intentions as arising from a gigantic misunderstanding. One deputy claimed that, in the north of the country, "the absence of political ideas" was joined by fear that the "flattering name of independence" would really mask "new thick chains [of bondage]."[362] This combination accounted for the disorder. Another deputy blamed the "disquiet" of the provinces on the "rapid transition from [political] slavery to liberty" and a "misunderstanding of the term 'popular sovereignty' [soberania do povo]."[363]

Yet not all deputies subscribed to this polite explanation. Some unequivocally, and unapologetically, endorsed a centralized, unitary government. António Carlos decried the "monstrous form of government in the provinces, this hydra with many heads which mutually destroy one another; it is necessary to decapitate them."[364] The palpable sense that Brazil's survival as a unitary state was imperiled elevated tempers and tensions which, under ordinary circumstances, might have abated. José Bonifácio exclaimed that "we are surrounded by carbonari and a thousand other enemies [perturbadores] of public order."[365] Other deputies were more precise. Railing against "parties," or factions, Nogueira da Gama identified four "enemies of our sacred cause": the "party" of the Portuguese Cortes [who sought to return Portugal

[361] Rodrigues de Carvalho, May 27, 1823, in APBAC, t. 1, p. 176.
[362] Xavier de Carvalho, June 16, 1823, in APBAC, t. 2, pp. 70–71.
[363] Carneiro de Campos, June 16, 1823, in APBAC, t. 2, p. 77.
[364] Andrada Machado, July 3, 1823, in APBAC, t. 3, p. 18.
[365] José Bonifácio, May 17, 1823, in APBAC, t. 1, p. 103.

to the status of a colony]; the "party" of republicanism who sought to "splinter the provinces into independent republics"; the "party" containing "admirers of the constitution of Portugal" who seek to be "linked to Portugal in a federation"; and finally, the "anarchist party."[366] Increasingly, the enemy of Brazil's independence was perceived within Brazil's borders, not from Portugal or any other European state. In July 1823, José Bonifácio vilified those who envisioned a federal system. He pilloried these "bishops without a pope" who dreamed of a "monstrous system, with a nominal center of power, with each province functioning as its own republic, in which they can be absolute chiefs, *corcundas* and *despóticos*."[367] Other arguments against federalism were expressed by Silva Lisboa, who called it the system of "ambitious men who aspire to run their own provinces and monopolize the great honors of government." These "ill-intentioned" individuals had fomented a "mania for confederations."[368]

These views, of course, were hotly contested. Some deputies disagreed that a single system of law could be designed to encompass the heterogeneity contained in Brazilian territory. Andrade e Lima argued that "laws must be adapted to [specific] circumstances ... legislation that suits [those living on] the banks of the River Plate can never be fully appropriate in the Amazon."[369] Furthermore, deputies from Brazil's northeast warned the Assembly against imposing its will on the restless north and northeast. Such extreme action would discredit the Assembly, "tainting its inaugural labors with bloodshed, despotism, and arbitrariness."[370] As shall be shown in the next chapter, such prognostications proved frightfully accurate.

The Assembly's debates touched on a range of subjects, many of which are beyond the scope of the present study. Some of these discussions, however, deserve brief mention, as they foreshadow themes appearing in later chapters. The vexing question of how Portuguese living in Brazil after independence should be treated is one such theme. While several deputies, including Muniz Tavares, called for Portuguese remaining in Brazil to be expelled en masse, more moderate deputies believed that they should be considered "citizens" as soon as they were naturalized. As a result of the "new social compact," Portuguese could become members of "the new [political] family," as citizens.[371] The

[366] Nogueira da Gama, May 26, 1823, in *APBAC*, t. 1, p. 169.
[367] José Bonifácio, July 15, 1823, in *APBAC*, t. 3, p. 84.
[368] Silva Lisboa, September 17, 1823, in *APBAC*, t. 5, pp. 156–57.
[369] Andrade e Lima, June 19, 1823, in *APBAC*, t. 2, p. 100.
[370] Mariano Cavalcanti, July 10, 1823, in *APBAC*, t. 3, pp. 66–67.
[371] Araújo Lima, June 25, 1823, in *APBAC*, t. 2, p. 153.

Ceará deputy Alencar argued that hostility toward Portuguese would subside as soon as Portugal recognized Brazil's independence: "we will be friends, our ports will be open to them, our commerce, and our wealth will be shared with them ... for [the similarity of] habits, religion, language, kinship, affection guarantee our mutual communication."[372]

Such conciliatory rhetoric aside, citizenship remained a fiercely contested category in the nascent polity. It became less capacious. Exclusions multiplied. One deputy summarized the way that citizenship should be limited: "all individuals are members of society; yet not all enjoy the same prerogatives; nor are all of them citizens." In particular, former slaves, and their children, had neither "acquired our customs nor reached a certain degree of civilisation" necessary in order to be considered a "Brazilian citizen."[373] Those of African descent were systematically excluded, and the arguments of Silva Lisboa and Maciel da Costa proved crucial in justifying this policy. The latter argued that "security, not philanthropy, must guide our decisions in this matter. Philanthropy caused the collapse of the flourishing French colonies. As soon as the 'Rights of Man' were declared there, the Africans became the instruments of the greatest horrors imaginable."[374] Silva Lisboa argued that education would slowly make those of African ancestry capable of full social participation, but he stressed that this day lay in the distant future.[375]

The Assembly's *Projecto* of the Constitution, framed primarily by António Carlos de Andrada Machado and dated August 30, 1823, resembled in many respects the 1822 Portuguese Constitution, particularly in its establishment of norms concerning individual rights (including trial by jury, religious liberty, and the inviolability of property), its enumeration of the duties of the citizen, and its articulation of norms concerning public instruction and public assistance. These similarities should not be that surprising, perhaps, since some of its framers had served as deputies at the Lisbon Cortes.[376] There were salient differences, however, between the documents. These included: first, a much more restricted suffrage in Brazil; second, the establishment of a bicameral legislature in Brazil, which included a senate with a life

---

[372] Alencar, September 16, 1823, in *APBAC*, t. 5, pp. 142–43.
[373] Almeida e Albuquerque, September 24, 1823, in *APBAC*, t. 5, pp. 233–34.
[374] Maciel da Costa, September 30, 1823, in *APBAC*, t. 5, p. 264.
[375] Silva Lisboa, September 30, 1823, in *APBAC*, t. 5, pp. 260–61 and 267.
[376] On the issue of the *Projecto*'s authorship, see J. H. Rodrigues, "O Segundo Conselho de Estado 1823–24," in Senado Federal 1973, vol. II, p. xx; P. Bonavides, "Constitucionalismo Luso-Brasileiro: Influxos Recíprocos," in Miranda 1996, p. 22.

term; and third, the allowance for a robust executive in the Brazilian 1823 document, manifested in the fact that there was a provision for a Council of State nominated personally by the emperor, and not, as in the Portuguese 1822 Constitution, selected by the Cortes.[377] Nevertheless, the *Projecto* denied the emperor an absolute veto over legislation emanating from the General Assembly (articles 112–16), though it did allow him to "give laws in his own name" (article 142). None of these provisions satisfied Dom Pedro, as will be made clear in Chapter 3. In November 1823, he dissolved the Assembly, promising to promulgate a constitution "more liberal than that which the extinct Assembly has written."[378]

At the end of the year 1823, it would appear that the forces of political reaction had triumphed in both the Old World and the New. The Braganza dynasty (and the authority it wielded) was, legally at least, as strong as it had been in 1807. Of course, much had changed, above all the separation of Brazil from Portugal. But the process resulting in separation necessitated, as this chapter has demonstrated, a paradoxically intensified interaction between the two shores of the Atlantic, which had deepened their shared constitutional-intellectual culture and blurred the lines between Portuguese and Brazilian, even if it also sharpened those differences which were indelible. In late 1823, then, with unalloyed monarchism resurgent in both Portugal and Brazil, the stage was set for either a grand reconciliation or a definitive, formal separation. While the latter option ultimately prevailed, the 1823–26 period, the subject of the next chapter, witnessed political actors in Lisbon and Rio de Janeiro groping toward new political arrangements amidst circumstances which they scarcely had anticipated, much less planned.

---

[377] Miranda 2001, pp. 26–27.
[378] Dom Pedro, "Manifesto de sua Magestade o Imperador aos Brasileiros," November 16, 1823, in *Fallas do Throno* 1977, p. 1–13.

3 Decolonization's progeny: restoration, disaggregation, and recalibration

> The present station of Portugal is so anomalous, and the recent years of her history are crowded with events so unusual, that the House will perhaps not think that I am unprofitably wasting its time.
>
> George Canning, December 12, 1826

The dissolution of the Brazilian Assembly and the defeat of the Portuguese navy in 1823 were not the final moments in the transatlantic saga. The years between 1823 and 1826 were marked by the failure to separate the two sides of the Atlantic in a definitive manner, even if Portugal extended formal recognition of Brazil's independence in August 1825. Dom Pedro, now Emperor of Brazil, remained at the center of the political storm, seeking to consolidate his fledgling regime amidst adverse circumstances while keeping ajar an escape hatch from New World revolutions in the form of the Portuguese throne, to which he remained the legally sanctioned heir. As a result, the political histories of Portugal and Brazil remained entwined in the years after 1823.

This chapter reconstructs and analyzes several of the political connections which survived, or were created during, imperial disaggregation, focusing on the genesis of the 1826 *Carta Constitucional* and its reception in Portugal, where it was presented as the new *lei fundamental*. Written by Dom Pedro in consultation with a coterie of advisors, the *Carta* was a superficial retouching of the constitution Pedro had promulgated and imposed on Brazil in 1824.[1] This 1824 Brazilian Constitution was itself the culmination of a political process in which he rejected a draft constitution modeled on the 1822 Portuguese Constitution, which was, in turn, an adaptation of the Spanish Constitution of 1812. As will be described in greater detail, the 1824 Brazilian and 1826 Portuguese Constitutions established a hereditary constitutional monarchy, with

---

[1] On the relationship between these two documents, see Torres 1972; and Afonso Arinos de Melo Franco, "Introdução," to *O Constitucionalismo de D. Pedro I* 1972.

two chambers, but featured a robust executive power. Dom Pedro's *Carta*, then, was an explicit repudiation of representative institutions endowed with significant legislative power and an attempt to re-outfit absolutism with the political language of purportedly "moderate" constitutionalism.[2]

The chapter is divided into two parts. Part I examines the reaction in Brazil to Dom Pedro's dissolution of the Assembly and promulgation of the 1824 Constitution. It focuses on the armed insurrection it provoked in the northeast of Brazil, the Confederation of the Equator. The scene then shifts to Portugal, where the Lisbon Cortes was overthrown and Dom João was restored as an unencumbered monarch in 1823. Part I concludes with an analysis of the negotiations between Portugal and Brazil resulting in diplomatic recognition. The aim is to demonstrate that plans for the reunification of Portugal and Brazil continued to percolate until 1825 and that Dom João's death in early 1826 once again brought this possibility to the fore.

Part II explores the immediate impact of Dom João's death in Brazil, which resulted in Dom Pedro being offered the Portuguese Crown. It focuses on the process by which Dom Pedro resolved to grant Portugal a charter on the model of his 1824 Brazilian Constitution and then abdicate immediately in favor of his young, Brazilian-born daughter, Dona Maria da Gloria. Part II provides little-known details of the *Carta*'s composition, situating this crucial episode in its Latin American as well as European context. The reception of the *Carta* in Portugal is explored, particularly the negative reaction it provoked. The chapter concludes with a "micro-international" history of the *Carta*, focusing on the extraordinary embassy of the British diplomat Sir Charles Stuart, the eventual courier of the *Carta* from Rio de Janeiro to Lisbon. An effort is made to explain the international dynamics into which Luso-Brazilian contestation over the *Carta* was inserted. In sum, Chapter 3 makes the case for revising traditional periodization, which privileges the recognition of Brazil, and focusing on the unresolved aspects of empire's demise. In doing so, it encourages understanding Portuguese politics in the late 1820s and early 1830s as an outgrowth of the unsettled circumstances precipitated, and the political turmoil unleashed, by imperial disaggregation.

---

[2] Dom Pedro's constitutionalism might be considered as a case study of what A. Mayer identified as a broader nineteenth-century phenomenon: "The old elites excelled at selectively ingesting, adapting, and assimilating new ideas and practices without seriously endangering their traditional status, temperament, and outlook." See Mayer 1981, p. 13

PART I

In the shadow of the Cortes: Dom Pedro, the Confederation of the Equator, and the Brazilian Constitution of 1824

A great deal of ink has been spilled on Dom Pedro's political thought. For some historians, he was "liberal in ideas but often despotic in conduct"[3] or "torn between advanced ideas and traditional sentiments."[4] Others have been less charitable. A contemporary remembered him as "a despot by inclination and habit, brought up among miserable slaves, tyrannical *senhores*, and vile courtesans; his first inclination was always to violence."[5] Another historian doubted the sincerity of his "liberal" convictions, claiming that he followed the fashion of the moment to win adulation.[6] Examining the evidence in the early twentieth century, a North American historian conceded that "to evaluate a man of such contrasts is extremely difficult."[7] Not only was Dom Pedro mercurial by temperament, but he was in different states of mind, levels of maturation, and distinct political circumstances between 1821 and 1834, the apex of his political career. It is therefore more prudent to trace his attitudes at particular moments in order to gain a sense of his rationale for a particular action.

Insight into Dom Pedro's early political views during the turbulent 1820–23 period may be gleaned from the correspondence of his first wife, Dona Leopoldina, with her father, Francis I of Austria. In June 1821, she wrote that "it is truly miserable [in Rio de Janeiro], and each day offers new scenes of revolt. My husband, unfortunately, adores the new principles and fails to act firmly, [unaware that] terror is the only way of ending a rebellion; and I fear that he will become aware of this [truth] too late, at his own expense. I can only foresee a dark future."[8] When the Assembly was convoked in June 1822, Dona Leopoldina was apoplectic: "my *esposo*, who lamentably loves all novelties, is starry-eyed and, unfortunately, it appears, will pay for it."[9] From this and other accounts, Dom Pedro emerges as genuinely enamored of new

---

[3] Sousa 1957, vol. II, p. 672.
[4] Oliveira Lima 1925, p. 41.
[5] Constâncio 1839, vol. II, p. 414.
[6] Pereira da Silva 1875, p. 272.
[7] Manchester 1932, p. 176.
[8] Dona Leopoldina to Francis I [of Austria], June 9, 1821, in Leopoldina 2006, p. 381.
[9] Dona Leopoldina to Francis I [of Austria], June 23, 1822, in Leopoldina 2006, p. 400.

constitutional doctrines and determined to demonstrate this posture publicly, regardless of the countervailing views and overt disapproval of his intimates and counselors.

But while his position bordered on political apostasy for those of counter-revolutionary dispositions, Dom Pedro did not countenance all new-fangled views. In particular, he rejected outright the notion of a representative body, whether Portugal's Cortes or Brazil's Assembly, empowered to frame a constitution. Certainly, he had favored the con- vocation of a Brazilian Assembly ("without a Cortes, Brazil cannot be happy") in mid 1822, but this attitude was adopted mainly to defy the Lisbon Cortes.[10] He evidently conceived of such representative institu- tions as consultative bodies, subordinate to the monarch. He recoiled at the prospect of governing within the limits determined by a repre- sentative body. The earliest glimmerings of such ideas may be gleaned from his letters to his father in the months preceding the declaration of "Independence or Death!"—the so-called *Grito do Ipiranga*"—in September 1822. The main idea conveyed in his letters is a strong repudiation of the Cortes's alleged right to compose a constitution: "the Brazilians and I are in favor of a constitution, but we seek to honor the sovereign by having the subjects obey him."[11] By July 1822, he informed Dom João that "circumstances oblige me to convoke an Assembly," but reassured him that such a move was "merely a formality, for I am the one who executes your decrees and none that emanate from there [i.e. the Assembly]."[12] In August, he openly disparaged the Cortes for hav- ing "betrayed the hopes and interests of Brazil in so vile a manner ... seeking to lay new chains upon it and humiliate it as if it were Portugal's slave."[13] And by September 1822, his disaffection complete, he railed against the "Machiavellian, factious, chaos-causing, and pest-like Cortes."[14]

This attitude would soon be redirected at the Brazilian Assembly that "circumstances" had compelled Dom Pedro to convene before independence had been declared. But he neither appears to have repu- diated his constitutional principles entirely nor to have made public his conviction that constitutions were "gifts from the throne." Dom Pedro, who moonlighted as a journalist, though he rarely signed his name, implored the Assembly in a newspaper article to "frame a constitution

[10] Dom Pedro to Dom João, May 21, 1822, quoted in E. F. dos Santos 1999, p. 281.
[11] Dom Pedro to Dom João, March 14, 1822, quoted in Pedro I 1941, pp. 58–59.
[12] Dom Pedro to Dom João, July 26, 1822, in Pedro I 1941, p. 69.
[13] "Manifesto do Principe-Regent do Brasil aos Governos e Nações Amigas," August 6, 1822, reproduced in Biker 1879, vol. 21 (13), pp. 143, 145.
[14] Dom Pedro to Dom João, September 22, 1822, in Pedro I 1941, p. 74.

free of the errors plaguing the Portuguese Constitution, which is not only theoretical, and therefore impractical, but is not based on experience."[15] In opening the Assembly in May 1823, Dom Pedro offered perhaps the clearest public statement of his constitutional thought. Demanding a "wise, just, appropriate and executable constitution" which "harmonized" legislative, executive, and judicial power, he warned the Assembly not to frame a constitution that resembled those of "France of 1791 and 1792, whose foundation was utterly theoretical and metaphysical, as the experiences of France, Spain and, lately, Portugal have proven." These constitutions, he asserted, did not promote "general happiness," but rather "licentious liberty," exposing its people to the "horrors of anarchy."[16]

Even before a *Projecto* of the Brazilian Constitution was drafted by the Assembly, Dom Pedro had clashed with some of the deputies. When the debates in the Assembly appeared unlikely to produce a constitution that differed significantly from that produced by the 1822 Lisbon Cortes, Dom Pedro abruptly dissolved it. When he did so, on November 12, 1823, he acted from a position of bolstered strength. Just three days earlier, on November 9, Lord Cochrane's fleet had entered Rio de Janeiro, having vanquished opposition to Brazilian independence in the northern provinces.[17] Furthermore, news of the *Vilafrancada* uprising in Portugal, discussed in the next section, which had overthrown the Cortes and restored Dom João as absolute monarch, undoubtedly influenced this decision. There was no longer a strategic need to outflank the Lisbon Cortes by setting up a rival representative body in Brazil.[18] In dissolving the Assembly, Dom Pedro claimed that it had threatened Brazil's independence, its territorial integrity, and the constitutional system. As noted in Chapter 2, he promised to issue a constitution "twice as liberal as that which the Assembly had written," attributing his sudden action to the rising "spirit of disunion" purveyed by the "chaos-causing faction."[19] According to one of the emperor's stalwart apologists, Silva Lisboa, the *Projecto* for a constitution drafted by the Assembly was imbued with the spirit of "Spanish American republicanism." The principles followed by this "revolutionary hydra" were

---

[15] [Dom Pedro], "O Anglo-Maníaco e, por isso, o Constitucional Puro," February 1823, originally published in the *Diário do Governo* [Rio de Janeiro], reprinted in H. Vianna 1967, p. 58.

[16] Dom Pedro, "Falla do Throno" (to the Assembly), May 3, 1823, in *Fallas do Throno* 1977, p. 37.

[17] Vale 2004, pp. 151–54.

[18] On the impact of the *Vilafrancada* in Brazil, see Kirschner 2009, p. 241.

[19] Dom Pedro, "Manifesto de sua Majestade o Imperador aos Brasileiros," November 16, 1823, in *Fallas do Throno* 1977, pp. 81–83

"opposed to those adopted by the Great Powers of Europe, which had elevated humanity to its present level of civilization."[20] Putting this vitriol and hyperbole aside, it is crucial to recall Pedro's promise to rule as a constitutional monarch, only not in a system in which the constitution was imposed upon, instead of "freely given" (*outorgada*) by, the monarch. Dom Pedro's undimmed enthusiasm for constitutions meeting such criteria must not be shrouded. As late as February 1824, he declared in private correspondence: "if I were obliged to govern without a constitution, I would sooner give up my throne, for I want to govern hearts filled with *brio* and honour, marked by freedom and not slavery."[21] At this stage, then, the question for Dom Pedro became what sort of constitution was appropriate for Brazil.[22]

In the Luso-Brazilian world, as suggested in Chapter 2, the influence of the political thought of the French Restoration was ascendant, particularly the model of the 1814 French *Chartre*. For those critical of radical constitutions based on the 1791 French Constitution, including the 1812 Spanish Constitution, the *Chartre* offered a plausible alternative.[23] Royer-Collard remarked that the *Chartre* was "nothing else than the indissoluble alliance of the legitimate power from whence it emanates with the natural liberties it recognizes and consecrates."[24] Guizot called it a "victory of the partisans of the English constitution ... over the republicans as well as the supporters of the ancient monarchy."[25] Although some scholars might dismiss Guizot's claim as dubious,[26] it was at least superficially accurate and suggested how the "English" constitution could be adapted to circumstances found on the

---

[20] Silva Lisboa 1825, pp. 7–8.
[21] AMI, II-POB.00.02.1824.P1.B.C.1–3, Dom Pedro to António Telles da Silva, February 2, 1824.
[22] There was great interest in Dom Pedro's constitutional tendencies among Portuguese in both Portugal and abroad. F. Solano Constâncio remarked in an 1823 letter that "it will be interesting to see the type of constitution Dom Pedro will give to the Brazilians. It will be undoubtedly based on Iturbide's [Mexican constitution], and probably executed in the same manner. Perhaps Dom Pedro will have the same luck." Solano Constâncio [in London] to Silvestre Pinheiro Ferreira, August 26, 1823, quoted in Sousa 1988, p. 335.
[23] Though Rosanvallon 1994 linked the 1791, 1814, and 1830 constitutions: "La France a cherché à conjuger le principe monarchique avec les libertés modernes," p. 19. On moderate constitutionalism in the Luso-Brazilian world, see Canaveira 1988.
[24] Royer-Collard, quoted in Starzinger 1991, p. 27.
[25] Guizot, quoted in Neely 1991, p. 185. On Guizot, see Rosanvallon 1985; and Craiutu 2003. On Guizot's influence in Brazil, see Needell 2006, pp. 76–79.
[26] As Alexander pointed out, "the Restoration preserved much of the legacy of the Revolution of 1789, but it did so through the filter of reforms instituted under Bonaparte. Retention of the Napoleonic Code meant that legal equality would be maintained, and there would be no return to the ancien régime fiscal or office-holding privileges." See Alexander 2003, pp. 2–3.

continent. It was, then, perhaps the *Chartre*'s much-vaunted moderation that appealed, offering an alternative to radical, even democratic projects and those which aimed to reinstate an unfettered, absolutist monarch modeled after Ferdinand VII's restoration in Spain between 1814 and 1820. Both extremes had brought destabilization in their wake. Admiration and emulation of the *Chartre* boasted the further advantage of being consonant with the political principles of Restoration Europe, something of which Brazilians eager to secure the recognition of those Old World states were keenly aware. Luso-Brazilian moderates would have agreed with Guizot, who stated in 1817 that "what we need is internal peace, the union of all citizens around the throne, the stable functioning of institutions, the free development of public and civil virtues." It was the search for the *juste milieu*, of "liberty united with order," the political space between "despotism and anarchy."[27]

As early as 1820, the notion of a Crown-issued *Carta* on the 1814 French model had been floated by Palmela to Dom João.[28] Dom Pedro was undoubtedly well versed in the French constitutional theory then in vogue, and aware of Palmela's proposal, as well as cognizant of the recent constitutional experiments in Portugal. Furthermore, he received corroborating advice from various quarters, including from a small rump of the now-dissolved Constituent Assembly that he trusted, and which now formed his *Conselho de Estado*. He also sought the counsel of Lord Cochrane, who advised him that it was exigent to "declare the type of government he planned to adopt" in order to allay suspicion in Brazil's provinces as well as to quell the anxiety of the Holy Alliance. Cochrane suggested that it would be strategically prudent to declare the British Constitution as the model after which Brazil's constitution would be fashioned. It would be difficult, Cochrane reasoned, for critics to find fault with a "limited monarchy, surrounded by a free people, enriched by industry which the security of property, by means of just laws, never fails to produce."[29] Nevertheless, Dom Pedro and his advisors were aware that it would be impossible to imitate other constitutional models slavishly; the task was to adapt them to Brazil's circumstances.[30]

[27] Guizot, quoted in Craiutu 2003, p. 81.
[28] Palmela to Dom João, November 18, 1820, in Palmela 1851, vol. I, pp. 144–45.
[29] AMI, I-POB.14.11.1823.Coc.c, Lord Cochrane to Dom Pedro, November 14, 1823.
[30] More conservative voices, such as Silva Lisboa, warned that "the imitation of foreign institutions, though they are themselves good, does not always produce beneficent results in all countries"; see the speech given by Silva Lisboa, October 21, 1823, in *APBAC*, vol. VI, pp. 156–57. A similar sentiment was subsequently expressed by Ferreira 1835, p. 176.

The 1824 Constitution was based on a new *Projecto* framed by Dom Pedro's Council of State and published in December 1823. It was drafted primarily by José Joaquim Carneiro de Campos (1768–1836), ennobled as the Marquês de Caravelas from 1826.[31] Carneiro de Campos had relied heavily on António Carlos de Andrada Machado's earlier *Projecto*, which meant that the substantive difference between the Assembly's proposal and the one that eventually served as the basis for Brazil's constitution was slight.[32] The larger issue at stake was the person, or institution, authorized to frame and promulgate a *lei fundamental*. Still, the similarity between the two documents generated confusion in subsequent decades, even among those who had been involved intimately in the process. In 1840, António Carlos boasted to Brazil's Chamber of Deputies:

And what did I do? After having established the fundamental bases, I took the best from all the other existing constitutions, picking and modifying that which seemed to me the most applicable to our present state ... the present constitution is an exact copy of that which I wrote then.[33]

But this boast has only partial merit for archival sources reveal that the emperor and his Council of State were influenced more decisively by two further *Projectos*, sources whose imprint on the 1824 Brazilian Constitution are just as pronounced as António Carlos's and Carneiro de Campos's *Projectos*. The authors of these documents are Frei Francisco de Santa Teresa de Jesus Sampaio, a close advisor and also the editor of the *Diário do Governo*, and Francisco Gomes da Silva, better known to posterity by his moniker *O Chalaça*, his crony and confidant.

Frei Sampaio's "Projecto de uma Constituição Monárquica" (1823) is notable for its insistence on the constitution as a document designed to ensure "internal security" and protect the state from "formidable convulsions." Its preamble celebrated "true mixed monarchy," and the "harmony" achieved through the division of powers.[34] This harmony is described as the "fundamental key" to the system, one capable of

---

[31] On Carneiro de Campos's political thought, see C. E. C. Lynch, "A Vocação Sociológica do Legislador: O Pensamento Político do Marquês de Caravelas (1768–1836)," in G. S. Ribeiro 2008, pp. 149–73.

[32] J. H. Rodrigues, "O Segundo Conselho de Estado, 1823–24," in Senado Federal 1973, pp. xx–xxi. J. Armitage contended that Carneiro de Campos's *Projecto* was influenced heavily by the constitution of the Netherlands, the Fundamental Code of Norway, and the 1791 French Constitution. See Armitage 1836, vol. I, pp. 154–55. Armitage had a low opinion of the *Conselho*'s constitutional instincts: "as a body, they were but ill-qualified for the task to which they were intrusted," vol. I, p. 360.

[33] António Carlos de Andrada Machado, April 24, 1840 to Câmara de Deputados, quoted in Menezes 1974, p. 25.

[34] Sampaio's *Projecto*, reproduced in Menezes 1974, p. 63.

"tranquilizing the spirit of the people, so commonly deluded by false promises of its leadership." Besides providing the monarch with a role in initiating legislation, it praised the virtues of bicameralism, particularly the function of a senate, which he described as an "asylum for the aristocracy." It also called for the monarch's absolute veto power over legislation. Without it, Frei Sampaio argued, the emperor would be "denied the capacity to conserve the mixed monarchy and it would become a monarchy in name only."[35]

Gomes da Silva's "Bases para um Projeto de Constituição" (1823) is notable for having made the first reference to the "*Poder Moderador*," though incompletely articulated, an institution that would figure prominently in both the 1824 Constitution and the *Carta*. As in Frei Sampaio's "Projecto," harmonious balance was key to the "conservation of political liberty," though this time with four instead of three powers. A senate with life-term appointments was advocated, with the selection of senators remaining the exclusive prerogative of the monarch. The guarantees of the constitution were clearly enumerated and relatively expansive, including property rights, limited freedom of the press, the right to petition, and "free public instruction for all classes of citizens."[36]

This attempt to learn from, and avert, the excesses of revolution encouraged an engagement with Benjamin Constant's constitutional thought, particularly as expressed in his 1814 *Cours de Politique Consitutionnelle*. Constant was convinced that legislative and executive powers were bound to encroach upon one another unless they were kept apart by a third power which Constant called the *pouvoir préservateur* or *pouvoir neutre*. This third power would not so much limit the scope of political authority (a condition which Constant assumed), but, by "protecting the different branches of government from mutual interference, it contributes to the happiness and improvement of the governed."[37] Later, Constant argued that hobbling the executive with constitutional obstructions could be harmful and destabilizing.[38] Though Constant's argument was extremely nuanced, his concept of the *pouvoir neutre* and the need for a less encumbered executive in some spheres was embraced and manipulated by proponents of enhanced executive power, including in Brazil.[39]

[35] Menezes 1974, pp. 64–66 passim.
[36] Gomes da Silva's *Bazes*, in Menezes 1974, pp. 76–79 passim.
[37] Constant, quoted in B. Fontana 1991, p. 64.
[38] Holmes 1984, p. 137.
[39] On the reception of Constant in Brazil, see C. E. C. Lynch 2005. A good example of Dom Pedro's selective reading of Constant was the neglect of his endorsement of ample freedom for municipalities from extensive executive power, which Constant

The 1824 Constitution differed from its forerunners in its emphasis on the emperor's function as guarantor of harmonious interaction among the different branches of government. It was this goal that justified the creation of a robust executive and also the insinuation of the emperor into almost all branches of government. Legislation emanating from the General Assembly required the emperor's "sanction" (article 13). But the most obvious break was the creation of the Moderating Power which was described as "the key (*chave*) of the entire political system, and is the private attribute of the Emperor, as the Supreme chief of the Nation, its First Representative, so that he can work tirelessly for the maintenance of independence, and equilibrium and harmony between the other political powers" (article 98). The Moderating Power did not overlap with the executive powers also exercised by the emperor, but rather made them more expansive, thus encroaching on the powers that the Assembly's *Projecto* attributed to the legislative branch. Among the attributes of the Moderating Power were the dissolution of the Chamber of Deputies in cases where the "nation's salvation depended on it"; the power to nominate and dismiss ministers; and the nomination of senators (article 101).[40]

The dissolution of the Assembly (November) and the publication of the Council's *Projecto* (December), followed closely by the promulgation of the 1824 Constitution (February), provoked active, armed resistance in the northeast and north of Brazil. Dissent coalesced into a broader federalist movement, which eventually baptized itself the Confederation of the Equator, centered in Recife.[41] The leaders of the Confederation rejected Dom Pedro's actions, claiming that they threatened to destroy popular sovereignty and provincial autonomy, substituted a centralized government in Rio de Janeiro for the old metropolitan capital of Lisbon, and endowed the executive (that is, the emperor) with the preponderance of political power. Often depicted as a secessionist movement seeking to establish an independent republic, the Confederation, which was overthrown by September 1824, aimed to establish a political system at once more moderate and more radical than generally supposed. Its president, Manuel de Carvalho Paes de Andrade, a veteran of the 1817 Pernambucan Revolution, called for the obliteration of the oligarchical institutions inherited from Europe

believed helped to guarantee individual liberty. By contrast, this aspect of Constant's thought generated great debate in Mexico. See Hale 1968, pp. 60–71.

[40] A copy of the 1824 Constitution is reprinted in Campanhole and Campanhole 1971.

[41] For an overview of the Confederation, see Mello 2004; in the broader context of Pernambucan history, see Ferraz 1996 and Mosher 2008.

and for the creation of a federal Brazil, one in which the provinces retained some control over their own affairs. The Confederation wanted local control over taxation, education, and public works. They sought devolution in the context of a genuine Brazil-wide revolution. De-centralized constitutional government, based on a renegotiated social compact, was their goal. There were several radical streaks, including Carvalho Paes de Andrade's expressed desire to stop the importation of slaves into Pernambuco, though he neither acted to abolish slavery nor encouraged the manumission of slaves.[42] At its core, whatever its limitations and internal contradictions, the Confederation offered a different model of Brazilian unity than that envisaged by Dom Pedro and enshrined in his 1824 Constitution.

The intellectual motor propelling the Confederation was Frei Joaquim do Amor Divino Caneca, editor of the influential rebel newspaper *Typhis Pernambucano*.[43] Frei Caneca argued that Dom Pedro had usurped Brazil's independence, implanting tyranny where freedom should have prevailed. He tirelessly denounced arbitrary government, arguing that each province of Brazil retained sovereignty until it voluntarily submitted to a mutually beneficial, limited union with the other provinces. The centralizing ambitions of Rio de Janeiro conflicted with the mutually advantageous federal arrangement to be agreed upon with representatives of other provinces, which independence briefly seemed to augur. Frei Caneca disputed the notion that Rio de Janeiro was the obvious center of this federation, regarding it as merely one among many independent states, none of which possessed the right to dictate to any other. "One province does not have the right to oblige another province to do anything," Caneca argued:

each can follow the path that suits it best: it can choose the form of government that it judges to be best suited to its situation and can therefore conduct itself in the manner most conducive to its happiness ... the promised, but not consummated, union of the provinces has been dissolved [by Dom Pedro] and, for this reason, each province has regained its independence and sovereignty.[44]

---

[42] Bernardes 2006, p. 629; Mosher 2008, pp. 71–77.
[43] Frei Caneca was not the sole voice: Bahian Cipriano Barata was active in Pernambuco, publishing the *Sentinela da Liberdade* until his arrest in November 1823. He made it easy for the authorities, stating bluntly and repeatedly that "the constitution should be the will of the people[s], not the Emperor ... [if not,] it should not be accepted because the provinces are free and independent," in *Sentinela da Liberdade na Guarita de Pernambuco Alerta!*, October 8, 1823, in Barata 2008, p. 485.
[44] [Caneca], *O Typhis Pernambucano*, no. 21 (June 10, 1824), reproduced in Caneca 1984, pp. 186–87.

Under the 1824 Constitution, Frei Caneca concluded, the "provincial councils are mere phantasms with which to delude the people."[45] To his advocacy of provincial autonomy, Frei Caneca added a republican critique of political developments of 1823–24. He protested against oligarchical institutions, particularly the life-term of the senate which stood in stark contrast with the short tenure of the deputies. Caneca argued that this disparity served to "augment the interests of the Emperor and to create as a result a new nobility to oppress the people."[46] Equally onerous was the Moderating Power inserted into Dom Pedro's 1824 Constitution: "The *Poder Moderador* is a Machiavellian invention and is the key to the oppression now felt by the Brazilian nation."[47] Making the executive power the attribute solely of the monarch, Caneca contended, might appear the best way to defend the empire, but its more likely result was the "despotism of the crown, [giving it] the means to oppress the nation, the means by which, history tells us, despots enslaved Asia and Europe."[48]

Caneca's *Typhis* articulated broader currents of discontent. The 1824 Pernambucan Revolution was considered by imperial authorities a far greater threat than its 1817 forerunner. In military official Lima e Silva's estimation, the 1817 Revolution had not been a popular revolution, as a reactionary populace helped capture the "*malvados*." In 1824, by contrast, "the majority of the people are involved," animated by words and ideas such as "constitution, liberty, popular sovereignty, and other such doctrines with which people are deluded."[49] The political leaders of the Confederation echoed both Frei Caneca's political thought and popular sentiments. As President Carvalho Paes de Andrade pithily put the matter: "constitutions, laws, and human institutions are made for the people, and not the people for them."[50] The Confederation's secretary declared, "we want our right to an Assembly, even taking into account the difficulties and vicissitudes which are inevitably part of the establishment of liberty and always accompany the first steps taken by a

---

[45] "Processo de Frei Joaquim do Amor Divino Caneca em 1824," reproduced in Caneca 1984, p. 271.
[46] Speech of Frei Caneca, June 6, 1824, reproduced in Brandão 1924, p. 191.
[47] Ibid., p. 190.
[48] "Processo de Frei Joaquim do Amor Divino Caneca em 1824," reproduced in Caneca 1984, p. 271.
[49] Brig. General Francisco de Lima e Silva to João Vieira de Carvalho [Secretario de Estado da Guerra], September 1, 1824, published in *Publicações do Archivo Público Nacional* 1924, vol. XXII, p. 377.
[50] [Carvalho Paes de Andrade], "Manifesto da Confederação do Equador," July 2, 1824, reproduced in Brandão 1924, p. 206.

new nation."[51] Nor were such sentiments confined to Recife. Copycat and loosely allied rebel governments sprang up in six of the northern and northeastern provinces, most notably in Ceará and Rio Grande do Norte, giving the Confederation greater claim to a regional mantle. In Fortaleza, the revolutionary leadership was convinced that Dom Pedro's 1824 Constitution would be rejected by the populace: "I believe the *Projecto da Constituição* will not be sworn to here, for the free man does not consent to his enslavement without fighting to the death."[52]

While chiefly animated by the drive for provincial autonomy and republican principles, the popular phase of the movement also was fueled by anti-Portuguese animus and nativist chauvinism. In the northeast, many interpreted Dom Pedro's actions as presaging an assault on independence and a reunion with Portugal. Carvalho Paes de Andrade stated this fear explicitly in a July 1824 proclamation in which he alleged that the emperor's dissolution of the Assembly was part of a broader strategy of "dividing us, and encouraging the king of Portugal to attack us in our homes! ... we shall soon be under attack from Portuguese bayonets and canons. Brazilians must unite for our salvation, establishing a supreme government which is truly constitutional, entrusted with our mutual defense and salvation."[53] Given this inflammatory rhetoric, it is unsurprising that the first act of Ceará's revolutionary government was to sack all Portuguese holding public employment, replacing them with Brazilians, allegedly because the Portuguese acted in "bad faith" and sought to "subject [Brazil] to slavery." The revolutionary government claimed that its action was necessary for the "people are almost mutinied with news of an invasion from Europe" and that this anger would be directed against Portuguese inhabitants of the province.[54]

It is clear, too, that material want and poor governance helped to wrest popular support for the Confederation. Lord Cochrane described well the situation prevailing in the northeast in 1823–24:

there had been no amelioration whatsoever in the condition of the people ... All the old colonial imports and duties remained without alteration; the manifold hindrances to commerce and agriculture still existed; and arbitrary power everywhere exercised uncontrolled: so that in place of being benefited

---

[51] Speech of José Natividade Saldanha, Secretary of the Confederation, June 17, 1824, reproduced in Brandão 1924, p. 194.
[52] Tristão Glaz de Alencar Araripe to Governor of Piauhi, May 14, 1824, in *A Confederação do Equador no Ceará* 2005, vol. I, p. 84.
[53] Carvalho Paes de Andrade, "Proclamação," July 2, 1824.
[54] "Officios dirigidos aos Ouvidores da Comarca do Ceará" [by Tristão Araripe], May 28 and 29, 1824, in *A Confederação do Equador no Ceará* 2005, vol. I, p. 178.

by emancipation from the Portuguese yoke, the condition of the great mass of the population was literally worse than before.[55]

Ultimately, it was the superior force of the imperial army dispatched from Rio de Janeiro that crushed the Confederation, supported by wealthier, well-connected Pernambucan elites who felt their position was endangered as the revolution took an increasingly radical turn. Bahia's failure to join the Confederation, in spite of pervasive sympathy in that province for Pernambuco's revolutionaries, greatly limited the movement's geographical scope.[56] But support for the Confederation undoubtedly ebbed, too, as a result of the effective imperial propaganda campaign unleashed, which depicted the struggle between Pernambucan federalists and the emperor as one pitting chaos against order, fragmentation against unity, unbridled anarchy against Brazil's survival as an independent state. The irrepressible Silva Lisboa spearheaded this effort, calling for a merciless destruction of the "hydra of Jacobinism and the specter of federalism," prophesying that the Confederation was imitating the "futility and instability of constitutions from Mexico to Chile, none of which was either able to form stable and regular government or able to secure the confidence of foreign governments."[57] Other commentators argued that only Dom Pedro could guarantee "public tranquility and individual security."[58] A naval blockade isolated Recife from late July 1824 and the city fell in mid September, though a sizeable contingent loyal to the Confederation fled to the interior of Ceará, where they continued a fitful resistance until late November. After imperial control was re-established, most of the local elite were pardoned, though the triumphant army of pacification displayed little clemency toward less connected, more pugnacious, unapologetically outspoken men like Frei Caneca, who was executed along with fifteen of his comrades.[59]

Though the Confederation was suppressed without mercy, it affected Dom Pedro, making him suspicious of written constitutions, and exasperated with the impotence of paper to produce political reality. In an 1825 letter, he complained: "what arguments can win over these

---

[55] Cochrane 1869, vol. I, pp. 271–72.
[56] There were civil and military conspiracies to align Bahia with Pernambuco in 1824; imperial authorities mounted a concerted campaign to appease Bahia, winning the support of local elites, and the province rejected the Confederation's overtures to join in the common cause. One may interpret the barracks uprising of the Periquitos in late 1824 as a belated effort to follow such a Confederation-style revolutionary path. See Kraay and Reis 2009, pp. 409–10, 432; also see Mosher 2008.
[57] Silva Lisboa 1824a, pp. 1, 7; see also the memorable invective in Silva Lisboa 1824b.
[58] *Analyse do "Projecto de Governo"* 1824, pp. 1, 8.
[59] Mosher 2008, p. 76.

malcontents? What arguments can there possibly be? Gunpowder and bullets, it appears, and nothing else."[60] These sentiments would shape Dom Pedro's understanding of constitutional government when he framed Portugal's 1826 *Carta*, prompting him to empower the nobility and executive to an even greater extent than he had in the 1824 Constitution. But constitutional alterations could only accomplish so much. In the aftermath of the Confederation's suppression, parts of the northeast, particulary Ceará, were afflicted by terrible drought. Hardship, however, did not eviscerate the revolutionary spirit. Even after the Confederation's repression, government officials noted that great distrust of, and hostility toward, the central government remained. This was in part the result of the "Machiavellianism introduced by the collaborators of the detestable democratic faction." Under such circumstances, harsh repression of discontent was counterproductive. Far from firming up the integrity of the empire and consolidating domestic tranquility, "such action produces only hatred, re-inflaming latent discord."[61] Another ex-official and keen commentator endorsed this "containment" approach, though on different grounds. He agreed that separatist and secessionist sentiments were ubiquitous, but argued that this fact was irrelevant so long as there existed few potential leaders: "men capable of leading the people require a degree of enlightenment and capabilities: Brazilians are naturally lazy and the knowledge required [to lead a revolution] exists in very few minds."[62] In the late 1820s, the central government's control over the provinces remained tenuous at best. As one observer noted as late as 1829, "the empire is extremely divided and the authority of the central government is slight: one might compare Brazil to a spider whose legs are very long, but whose body is very small."[63]

The 1823 restoration in Portugal and the making of neo-absolutism

Though the histories of the two countries were increasingly divergent, the trajectory of Portuguese politics resembled that of Brazil in 1823. Indeed, the US consul believed that the dissolution of the Brazilian

---

[60] AMI, II-POB.27.01.1825.PI.B.c.1–11, Dom Pedro to Felisberto Caldeira Brant (Barbacena), January 27, 1825.

[61] ANRJ, IJJ⁹ 248 (Pernambuco), Francisco de Lima e Silva to Clemente Ferreira França, February 13, 1825.

[62] Lill.L., Stuart MSS, Governador Rego, "Breve Lance d'olhos sobre o Brasil" (n.d.).

[63] José Inacio de Abreu e Lima, as reported in diary entry of February 4, 1829, in Sá da Bandeira 1975, vol. I, pp. 148–49.

Assembly presaged a new Portuguese effort to reunite with its former
colony: it "can hardly be considered otherwise than as the abandonment of independence. There are more natives of Portugal in [Rio de
Janeiro] than Brazilians, and it is possible that the King will be invited
to return."[64] Portuguese and Brazilian politics seemed to converge
again. The Lisbon Cortes Dom Pedro loathed and blamed for having
precipitated his declaration of Brazil's independence was disbanded in
June 1823. This act occurred in the aftermath of the anti-constitutional
uprising which took Dom Miguel, Dom Pedro's younger brother, as its
symbol and figurehead, the so-called *Vilafrancada*, in late May.

Dom João's termination of the 1820–23 constitutional experiment
began propitiously. There was widespread support for the action,
attributable both to mounting disaffection with the tenor and action
of the Cortes and to the anti-revolutionary tide rising across Europe.
In February 1823, in the northern Portuguese cities of Vila Real and
Chaves, Conde de Amarante led an armed uprising against the constitutional government.[65] Anti-constitutionalists were further emboldened when French armies, led by the Duke of Angoulême,[66] flooded
across the Pyrenees in 1823, crushing the reinvigorated constitutional
regime in Spain. As in revolution, so in counter-revolution: events in
Spain inspired *Vintismo*'s enemies in Portugal to end the constitutional
experiment. The *Vilafrancada*, then, was merely the final blow. Sensing
the macabre direction of events and sentiments, constitutionalists fled
the country or else faced imprisonment. Many commentators began to
query the necessity of a new *lei fundamental* altogether. Portugal's abys-
mal state, both under the Old Regime and under the Revolutionary
Cortes, buoyed moderate reformers. Domingos de Souza Coutinho, for
example, conceded the desire to "abolish arbitrary despotism," but he
rejected the argument that the Cortes had an "obligation to create a
new and a priori constitution." Instead, it would be better to "revise
what has existed, to note what has [fallen into abeyance] and recover
it, to amplify and innovate, but not to touch that which deserves to be
conserved." In particular, he argued that the effective exclusion of the
nobility from the Cortes and the existence of a single chamber had given
rise to a "scene of confusion, a monstrous power without limits, and
thus despotic and arbitrary."[67] The victory of the neo-absolutists was so

---

[64] Condy Raguet, US Consul, to J. Q. Adams, Secretary of State, November 12, 1823,
   in Manning 1925, vol. II, p. 768.
[65] Lousada and Ferreira 2006, p. 36; Vargues 1985, p. 532.
[66] Louis Antoine of France (1775–1844), eldest son of Charles X and hence Dauphin
   (1824–30).
[67] D. de Souza Coutinho 1823, pp. xvii, xxvi, xlvi.

complete that Almeida Garrett confessed that the prospect of a lasting and secure constitutional regime was an "absurd proposition" given the "circumstances of the people and the existing [ruling] classes."[68]

Yet the question of how far Dom João would push matters remained unanswered. If he followed Ferdinand VII's lead, he risked appearing as a puppet of Spain, which itself was a French satellite. Portugal enjoyed and sought to maintain some autonomy, itself contingent on British support. Britain was loath to lose its precious continental foothold after having expended blood, treasure, and a decade-long effort. Furthermore, Portugal's gravitation toward the Franco-Spanish axis would upset Europe's fragile balance of power. As a modern historian explained, France could not extend its influence too far and aggrandize itself, for "beneath the roiled surface of European politics lay a deep, calm sea of restraints, recognized limits and cooperative purposes."[69] Portugal was left, therefore, with some room for maneuver. On June 18, 1823, in the immediate aftermath of his restoration, Dom João promised to promulgate a constitution, or *lei fundamental*, and established a junta for this specific purpose. The following day, a second decree was issued, establishing another, separate junta to review all existing legislation, particularly that passed by the defunct Cortes. These moves were, undoubtedly, self-consciously moderate, conciliatory gestures, since they did not abolish *Vintismo* legislation outright.[70] Dom João's decree entrusted the seven members of the junta to determine, after "mature reflection," which laws "conform to the true principles of universal public law, to the principles of the monarchy, to the rights and just liberties of citizens, and to the uses, customs and opinions of the Portuguese people (*povo*)," indicating that he would "confirm those that [met this requirement] while revoking the rest."[71]

The Constitutional Junta was composed of an array of ultra-royalists and also more moderate constitutionalists. It met for the first time in early July at the Palace of Rocio. Palmela served as the Junta's president and delivered a speech blasting the 1822 Constitution for having introduced "innovations contrary to the customs and will of the

[68] Almeida Garrett, "Apontamentos," November 24, 1823, in Almeida Garrett 1985.
[69] Schroeder 1994, pp. 627–28.
[70] Hespanha 2004, p. 35. Far from a break with tradition, the creation of these juntas could be justified further as an effort, stretching back to the final decades of the eighteenth century, at legal reform. In 1778–79, Dona Maria had created a junta to frame a new legal code (*Novo Código*), an attempt to consolidate existing statutes and systematize the law. A similar junta was created in Spain, which was itself based directly on Russian precedent.
[71] J. Martins, R. Rangel, and A. Santiago, "Projecto Institucional do Tradicionalismo Reformista: a Crítica da Legislação Vintista pela Junta de Revisão das Leis," in M. H. Pereira 1982, vol. I, p. 155.

nation." He argued that the Junta's task was to "produce a document whose intent was not the development of vague and abstract theses, but rather one that provided practical guarantees for the most essential rights (*direitos*) and secured the most solid basis for public prosperity."[72] As noted previously, Palmela had proposed a *Carta Constitucional* on the French model on several occasions. He had advocated the issue of a "limited" *Carta* in 1820, pointing to France where the *Chartre* engendered "tranquility, placating all parties, conciliating their respective ambitions, satisfying the revolutionaries and the nobility ... difficulties that seemed almost insuperable in 1814."[73] Echoing Burke, he argued that Portugal should attempt to "amend and perfect the existing edifice instead of trying to raise a new one from the foundation."[74] In the wake of Dom João's restoration in 1823, Palmela took up the idea again, viewing the *Chartre* as a mechanism to prop up royal authority. In a letter to Chateaubriand, he praised Ferdinand VII's restoration in Spain, certifying that the demise of the Trienio would "facilitate and greatly accelerate the Portuguese counter-revolution." He further added that "the *Carta* Dom João planned to give (*outorgar*)" would "heal the wounds the revolution inflicted, and bolster the prospects for a period of durable calm."[75] Palmela was aware that the French had encouraged Ferdinand VII to issue a new constitution, on the model of the *Chartre*, a plan which had been "abandoned for the greater part of the provinces petitioned the King against such a [political] system."[76] Palmela, then, understood that he had to tread carefully.

From what legal historians have pieced together from dispersed, fragmented evidence, Palmela envisioned a *Carta* that enshrined a legislative power shared between the king and the Cortes (made up of the *Três Estados*, now divided into two chambers, with the Clergy and the Nobility in an upper chamber, and the *Procuradores do Povo* in the second, lower chamber). The king alone would decide when to convoke the Cortes (and also when to prolong its sessions or dissolve it). The legislation it passed would lack the force of law until sanctioned by the king. Royal sanction and the authority to convoke the chambers, then, would serve to bypass the thorny issue of legislative sovereignty while leaving no doubt where it lay. Executive power and unfettered control

---

[72] Dias 1988, appendix, doc. 2, p. 302.
[73] Palmela to Dom João, November 18, 1820, in Palmela 1851, vol. I, pp. 144–45.
[74] Palmela to Pinheiro Ferreira, June 14, 1821, in Palmela 1851, vol. I, p. 201.
[75] Palmela to Chateaubriand, June 1823, in Biker 1879, vol. 20 (12 of supplement), pp. 281–83 passim.
[76] ANTT, MNE (Legação de Portugal em Espanha), cx. 665, António de Saldanha da Gama to Palmela, October 22, 1823.

over foreign policy would be reserved to the king alone, whose person remained "sacred and inviolable."[77]

A commission, presided over by Palmela, was entrusted with the task of drafting the *Projecto*.[78] They met over several days at the Convento da Graça and submitted their *Projecto* to Palmela, but the full Junta was not convened to discuss it for several months.[79] The 1823 *Projecto*, which essentially reflected Palmela's constitutional ideas, has been judged by modern historians as a forward-looking effort to frame a moderate constitution in the face of ever more belligerent neo-absolutism, enshrining some unequivocally liberal elements, including the acceptance of a separation of powers; an enlarged sphere for parliamentary intervention and checks on executive power; a modern conception of representation; and a recognition of individual rights and the equality of all citizens before the law.[80] When the full Junta finally was convened, in late September 1823, Palmela asked its members whether the *Projecto* left the traditional form of government unaltered, promised to revive Portugal's public law, and would be harmonious with the new political institutions then fashionable throughout Europe.[81] One of the members argued that Portugal always had been a "moderate," or "mixed," monarchy in which the king shared authority, especially concerning fiscal matters, with the Cortes. In this way, convoking a Cortes was not necessarily a violation of the existing *lei fundamental*.[82]

But such moderate voices were drowned out by those whose skepticism toward representative government remained unshaken. One Junta member, for example, contended that royal power was not merely executive, but also legislative, arguing that "legislative power should be exercised collectively by the king and the two chambers."[83] Other Junta members thought even this view was too moderate, maintaining that the monarch alone exercised both executive and legislative power; in short, that sovereignty was undivided. Here the late eighteenth-century debates between Ribeiro Santos and Melo Freire were resolved in the latter's favor. The intransigence of the Junta's ultras foreclosed the

---

[77] Dias 1988, pp. 222–23.
[78] Curiously, Nogueira had been one of the supplicants of the *Junta dos Três Estados* which had petitioned Napoleon (via Junot) for a written constitution in 1808. See Mesquita 2006, p. 69.
[79] Process described by Trigoso 1933, pp. 184–85.
[80] A. M. Hespanha, "O Projecto Institucional do Tradicionalismo Reformista: Um Projecto de Constituição de Francisco Manuel Trigoso de Aragão Morato," in M. H. Pereira 1982, vol. I, p. 74; Mesquita 2006, p. 118.
[81] Palmela's speech of September 29, 1823, as reported in Trigoso 1933, p. 187.
[82] Hespanha 2004, p. 145.
[83] Dias 1988, appendix, doc. 2, p. 310.

possibility of compromise. Another member, for example, refused "to concede to the Cortes anything more than consultative authority." Anything more would "divide sovereignty ... overthrow the most essential principal of our ancient institutions, and trample underfoot the greatness and status of the throne."[84] In spite of several conciliatory voices urging moderate or mixed government, the Junta failed to produce a *lei fundamental*. In fact, a January 1824 *parecer* of the Junta urged the retention of the ancient constitution: "as Portugal was great, respected, and prosperous under its ancient political constitution, the Junta could never hope to devise, nor discover, a *projecto* of a new *Carta de Lei Fundamental* more worthy of proposing to VM than the complete restoration, and preservation, of the Ancient Constitution."[85] The Junta was not, however, unanimous in this assessment. As late as February 1824, Palmela proposed new *Bazes* for a *Carta*, not dissimilar to those he had entertained in June–July 1823, to "stop the fermentation of spirits," which included "indivisible" executive power exercised by the "inviolable person of *El-Rei*," with legislative power "exercised collectively by a bicameral Cortes." Further aspects of Palmela's *Bazes* included some allowance for individual liberties and "moderate" freedom of the press.[86]

Before the Junta resolved its differences, however, a second absolutist reaction, the so-called *Abrilada*, again with Dom Miguel as its figurehead, occurred in April 1824. The *Abrilada* was the latest manifestation of the ultra-absolutist faction's displeasure with Dom João's conciliatory posture, first toward the Cortes and then toward modern constitutionalism in general. Before the 1807 transfer of the Court to Brazil, there had been various conspiracies to depose him, the most elaborate of which was the 1805–6 "Conspiracy of the Fidalgos," at Mafra, whose leaders sought to install Dona Carlota Joaquina at the head of a regency.[87] In April 1822, there had been a plot, the "Conspiracy of Rua Formosa," which aimed to dissolve the Cortes, convoke a new one on the older, seventeenth-century model (with two chambers), depose Dom João, and put Dona Carlota Joaquina in charge, with Dom Miguel as commander-in-chief of the army. Furthermore, the

[84] Dias 1988, appendix, doc. 7, pp. 322–23.
[85] BPMP, MSS. 1915, "Parecer da Junta para preparer o Projecto para hua Nova Carta de Ley Fundamental," January 2, 1824.
[86] Palmela's *Bazes* (February 1824), in Palmela 1851, vol. I, p. 172.
[87] S. M. Pereira 2008, pp. 56–57. Pereira quoted from an August 1806 letter from Dona Carlota to her father, Don Carlos IV of Spain, which makes her complicity in the plot against her husband certain. She justified her actions "to prevent much blood from flowing." Letter of August 13, 1806, p. 61.

queen was admired widely for her uncompromising hostility toward the Cortes, symbolized by her public refusal to swear to uphold the 1822 Constitution, a position considered more dignified than her husband's meek acquiescence. The Cortes punished this defiance with the threat of banishment, but she clung steadfastly to her position.[88] From 1822 to 1826, Dona Carlota was celebrated for her defiance and figured prominently in various ultra-royalist plots, in both the Old World and the New. This was not a new role for her. Being the only significant member of the Spanish royal family not in Napoleon's clutches, various conspiracies were hatched involving her. Between 1811 and 1813, for example, there was a plan to place her at the head of a regency during her brother Ferdinand VII's "captivity," with a view toward succeeding him in case of his premature death. Dona Carlota's rights were debated in the Cortes of Cádiz. Spanish and Spanish American conservatives and royalists construed her "cause" as useful to them, providing them with a figure around whom to rally, a viable alternative to the sovereignty claimed by the Cortes.[89] She continued to play a similar function in the Southern European conservative political imagination in the 1820s and her shadow hung heavily over the *Abrilada*.

The *Abrilada* foreclosed a constitutional solution, however tentative or moderate, to Portugal's political limbo. The rising counter-revolutionary tide across Europe strengthened the conspirators' hand. The French elections of March 1824 produced a landslide victory for the Ultras, which seemed to augur a broader rejection of liberalism in Western Europe.[90] Unlike the *Vilafrancada*, which was welcomed by Dom João, Dom Miguel's latest actions did not earn similar approbation. Beginning with the suspicious murder of the uncooperative Marqués de Loulé in February 1824, the *Abrilada*'s architects did not disguise their political intentions. Hundreds of civilians and military officials suspected either of loyalty to Dom João or sympathetic to liberalism were imprisoned. The king himself was sequestered at the Palácio da Bemposta, Palmela was incarcerated in the Torre de Belém, while Subserra was protected by the French ambassador Hyde de Neuville.[91] In a proclamation issued from aboard the English ship *Windsor Castle*, stationed in the Tagus,

[88] Lousada and Ferreira 2006, pp. 32, 35; Vargues 1985, p. 531.
[89] Dona Carlota was legally eligible to succeed to the Spanish throne owing to the revocation of the Salic Law by Carlos IV in the Cortes in 1789. On the various plans to place Dona Carlota either on the Spanish throne or at the head of a regency, see S. M. Pereira 2008, pp. 93–110.
[90] Tombs 1996, p. 341; Lyons 2006, p. 29.
[91] Fernando Pereira Marques, "Do Vintismo ao Cabralismo," in A. Reis 1990, pp. 41–43; and I. N. Vargues and L. R. Torgal, "Da Revolução à Contra-Revolução: Vintismo, Cartismo, Absolutismo," in Torgal and Roque 1993, p. 71.

to which he had fled, Dom João castigated the "sinister inspiration" and "treacherous counselors" who incited Dom Miguel to take actions which were neither "just nor necessary" and which "attacked [Dom João's] indivisible royal authority."[92]

The consequences of the *Abrilada* were immense. Dom João was restored to the throne, but behaved tentatively, seemingly aware of the fragility of his authority and the insecurity of his person. Dom João effectively banned his wife from Court while Dom Miguel was ordered to leave the Peninsula, going first to England and then to Vienna, where he frittered away his days hunting and in other frivolous pursuits. As Dom João pondered his options, he received unsolicited advice, including from his Madrid-based daughter Dona Maria Thereza, widow of the late Spanish Prince Pedro Carlos. The Infanta begged her father to recall the "terrible memory" of the seventeenth-century Cortes, which had "diminished royal authority." The present situation, she warned, was even less propitious, with "too many heads filled with radical ideas" and the prospect of being "subjugated under the yoke of the Cortes" highly probable.[93] On June 4, 1824, though, Dom João acted precisely as the Junta had counseled in January and his daughter now advised, declaring the "ancient foundation of the monarchy intact," claiming that it contained all of the elements necessary to "protect religion, defend the throne, secure individual rights, and guarantee effective public administration."[94] An *alvará* issued the following day, June 5, annulled all of the Cortes's decrees, laws, and "innovations," declaring them "void of all authority."[95] These measures were not entirely reactionary, for in a message circulated to representatives of foreign powers Dom João indicated that the *Antigas Cortes* would be called in due course and stated that a new *lei fundamental* would be issued, "founded, to the extent possible, on the basis of the ancient laws of the kingdom, perfected as demanded by the century in which we live, with a view

[92] Houghton MS *90–300F, untitled document, dated May 9, 1824 and published in the Impressão Regia, located in "Collection of Portuguese Broadsides and Other Documents relating to Miguelismo (1799–1835)."

[93] AMI, I-POB.03.06.1824.MT.P.c.1–3, Maria Thereza to Dom João VI, letters of June 3 and June 24, 1824 passim. Infanta Maria Teresa was an influential figure behind the scenes, and surely more needs to be learned about her role in these affairs. After Don Pedro Carlos's death in 1810, she joined the rest of the Braganzas in Brazil until 1821, when she returned to Lisbon, before moving back to Madrid at the invitation of her uncle and brother-in-law Ferdinand VII. See A. Pereira 1938, pp. 49–54 passim.

[94] "Carta de Lei pela qual El-Rei Dom João VI declarava a antiga, verdadeira e unica constituição da Monarchia Portugueza, mandando chamar a Cortes os Trés Estados do Reino," June 4, 1824, in Biker 1879, vol. 20 (12), p. 366.

[95] "Alvará Annulando os Decretos e Leis das Cortes," June 5, 1824, in Biker 1879, vol. 20 (12), p. 369.

toward the institutions existing in other constitutional monarchies."[96] Of course, he had made an equivalent promise just a year earlier, one which he broke in flagrant fashion. Furthermore, it remains unclear which factions Dom João's promises were intended to console. Foreign courts reviled the notion of the convocation of the Cortes. Genuine constitutionalists (the few who had not sought refuge abroad after either the *Vilafrancada* or the *Abrilada*) expected little from the duplicitous (or at least chronically vacillating) Dom João. Arch-absolutists were dissatisfied, plotting in October 1824 to assassinate the king's ministers, force Dom João to abdicate, and install Dona Carlota at the head of a regency to await the triumphant return of Dom Miguel from Vienna.[97] In January 1825, amidst these intrigues, the Palmela–Subserra ministry fell, depriving the government of its moderate leadership.

Concerning Dom João's constitutional intentions, an eminent early twentieth-century historian argued that "he probably did not know [whether or not he intended to promulgate a *Carta*], entertaining different opinions, attracted to opposed and confused ideas, torn by competing motives."[98] There is some validity in this analysis, but it ignores his consistent sympathy for some form of written constitutionalism in the final two years of his life. Dom João's attitudes toward constitutionalism are clarified somewhat in an 1824 letter sent by Palmela to Porto Santo, then ambassador at Madrid. In July 1824, Palmela described his involvement in the Junta. He indicated that little headway had been made toward drafting a constitution before the re-establishment of the traditional laws of the kingdom, "in such a way that SM fulfilled his royal promise but did so with the least possible sacrifice, and without surrendering a single prerogative belonging to the Crown." Palmela confided to Porto Santo that he now planned to arrange for the convocation of the *Trés Estados*, but that its role would be perfunctory ("We are taking all imaginable precautions to ensure that this meeting does not degenerate into an Assembly of Demagogues"). The mechanism to guarantee this result was to have each *braço* represented by a small number of vetted individuals and permitted to convene for a fixed, short period of time. It would be, Palmela promised, "nothing more than a *grande Conselho de Estado*." As for international objections to the convocation of the *Trés Estados*, particularly from Spain, Palmela conjectured that there would not be any protest: "I believe that *Senhor Don Fernando VII* is not unaware that the acclamations of Carlos V

---

[96] Quoted in Hespanha, "O Projecto," p. 74.
[97] Vargues and Torgal, "Da Revolução à Contra-Revolução," p. 71.
[98] Oliveira Lima 1997, pp. 660–61.

are not any less seditious than the cries of 'Viva Riego.'"[99] There were many reasons, therefore, to fear the ultra-conservatives in 1824. The *Vilafrancada* and *Abrilada* had made clear that they were unafraid of plotting and executing a *coup d'état*.

The subject of Brazil was not absent from these deliberations. During the cabinet debate concerning recognition, Subserra, who adamantly opposed it, conceded that the decision belonged exclusively to Dom João, but reminded him that "renouncing his rights to Brazil would make the convocation of the Cortes indispensable," an unsubtle warning about the negative reaction such an action would provoke.[100] Moderate royalists, including Palmela and Porto Santo, accepted this logic, especially when Dom João indicated that he was leaning toward recognizing Brazil's independence and confirming Dom Pedro as heir to the Portuguese throne in a single stroke. Dom João, Palmela noted, would probably be forced to convoke the *Três Estados* in this case, "a promise he repeatedly and spontaneously gave, never lost sight of, and which he anxiously wishes to fulfill." It had been postponed owing to the reservations of continental allies and the lack of a "calm moment, free of revolutionary intrigue" in which to "operate unimpeded, and without risk of being misinterpreted or curtailed." The main concern was Spain's reaction, for Ferdinand VII adamantly refused to countenance recognition of his "rebellious subjects" in the Americas.[101] But Palmela believed, as previously indicated, that the calming effect of this action produced in Portugal would placate Spain for "the example of paternal and moderate administration in this kingdom cannot by people of good sense be considered a danger for Spain."[102] The stage was therefore set for negotiations to recognize Brazil.

Reconciliation, reconquest, or recognition? Portugal and Brazil, 1823–1826

Brazil's independence, declared by Dom Pedro in 1822, was contested by Portugal and would not be recognized officially until 1825. The Cortes resorted to military action in response to Dom Pedro's declaration, though the forces it possessed were inadequate for the enormous

---

[99] ANTT, APASG, cx. 1, mç. 2, Palmela to Porto Santo, "Oficio Reservado no. 13," July 10, 1824.
[100] BNL, MSS 149, doc. 107, [Subserra], "Parecer que deo S. Exmo. no Conselho d'Estado que se fez em 11 de Outubro de 1824, sobre os negocios do Brasil," fo. 3.
[101] Costeloe 1986.
[102] ANTT, APASG, cx. 1, mç. 2, Palmela to Porto Santo, "Oficio Reservado no. 26," January 10, 1825.

task. João Oliveira e Daun, subsequently Conde de Saldanha, refused to lead an expedition to the northeast of Brazil in February 1823, claiming that the Cortes's ambition to seize and occupy Recife and Bahia simultaneously was ludicrous given Portugal's scant resources.[103] The paltry armada that eventually embarked accomplished little beyond harassing the new regime and kindling nativist resentment. The decisive naval battle, the result of which confirmed Saldanha's misgivings, occurred at the exact moment of Dom João's restoration in Portugal. Following the *Vilafrancada*, there were numerous efforts to conciliate the two sides, forestall complete independence, and retain some link between them. After all, Dom Pedro's declaration of independence was made against the Cortes and its "recolonizing" ambitions. Surely, the restoration of absolutism in Portugal would alter his calculus, to say nothing of sentiments arising from filial piety.

In mid 1823, just after the restoration of Dom João, Subserra was in a conciliatory mood, dispatching instructions to Portuguese agents in Rio de Janeiro to offer Dom Pedro a compromise. He proposed that Dom João would be recognized as sovereign of Brazil and Portugal; Brazil would receive a *"Carta* accommodated to the peculiarities of its location and other such circumstances"; and legislation pertaining to Brazil would have to receive Dom Pedro's sanction before its enforcement. Furthermore, Brazilian and Portuguese subjects could "promiscuously serve in both kingdoms; and the costs of maintaining the navy, the diplomatic corps, and [servicing the] public debt would be shared between Portugal and Brazil."[104] Such aspirations were not as far-fetched as they might appear in hindsight. Similar proposals percolated in Brazil. In July 1823, several *Carioca* pamphlets urged reconciliation with Portugal and the cessation of "fratricidal hostilities." One pamphlet even called for the complete reintegration of the entire Luso-Atlantic world, suggesting that Angola and Mozambique should enjoy the option of aligning more closely with Brazil, with a similar offer held out to the Azores, Madeira, and Cape Verde. The same pamphlet called for complete free movement within the empire and, consonant with Subserra's proposal, reciprocal "rights, privileges, and advantages" for subjects of both Brazil and Portugal.[105]

---

[103] Saldanha 1823, p. 7.
[104] "Instrucções Secretas do Conde de Subserra," July 22, 1823, reproduced in *Documentos para a História das Cortes* 1883, vol. I, pp. 812–13; There also exists a letter from Dom João to Dom Pedro, dated July 23, 1823, in which the elder Braganza expressed hope that his son would restore "the previous relations between Portuguese of both hemispheres." See *Relatório dos Commissarios* 1824, p. 28.
[105] *O Conselho da Boa Amizade* (1823), pp. 5–7 passim.

Though a prominent diplomatic historian has asserted that continental Europe posed no threat to Latin America after 1823, and that Anglo-American hegemony was accepted within certain bounds, contemporaries in the Luso-Brazilian world viewed matters differently.[106] Recognition of a full, unfettered recognition was far from a *fait accompli*. Portugal's military hand was weak, but its goals were bolstered considerably by the Holy Alliance's strong if passive opposition. Britain, too, could not recognize Brazil before Portugal did so. Such a step would represent a blatant violation of its treaties with Portugal and the principles of legitimacy it purportedly espoused.[107] Just across the border, the Trienio Liberal's collapse and the vengeful restoration of Ferdinand VII to unfettered power suggested that Spain would redouble its efforts to reconquer at least some slice of Spanish America. As a consequence, Portugal's bargaining position appeared strengthened. Various forces, then, converged to urge a degree of reconciliation. Any recognition Dom Pedro might win from Europe would be limited and begrudging. For example, Austria made clear to Dom Pedro's agents that it would never recognize him as "Emperor of Brazil," but perhaps instead "Defender, or Protector, or whichever title is compatible with the sovereignty of his father ... [for] recognizing the title of 'Emperor' would be tantamount to sanctioning rebellion against his father."[108] In mid 1823, then, some species of transatlantic confederation, a compromise solution, was a plausible and desirable outcome after tempers had subsided and reason-of-state calculations prevailed.

Nevertheless, Portugal's entreaties were rebuffed. The emissary proposing such terms was refused an audience with Dom Pedro and a letter sent from Dom João to his son went undelivered. Portuguese resentment rose precipitously. A significant, well-placed cadre of politicians and Crown advisors refused to accede to recognition of Brazil's independence. The formerly conciliatory Subserra detected a "demagogic faction" behind the independence movement, hell-bent on establishing a "bloody" and "order-subverting democracy." In his view, Dom Pedro was being "manipulated" like an "instrument" while the empire, as a monarchical system of government, was a chimera, a "fantastical idea to delude the people." As soon as independence was recognized, Subserra predicted, a cabal of malevolent democrats would "dismantle the new monarchy piece by piece" and the spirit of rebellion in Rio

---

[106] Schroeder 1994, p. 635.
[107] Though Canning was prepared to offer recognition in exchange for the complete abolition of the slave trade in 1822. See Bethell 1970a.
[108] Felisberto Brant [in London] to J. Bonifácio de Andrada, April 3, 1823, published in *Publicações do Archivo Público Nacional* 1907, vol. VII, doc. 22, p. 321.

de Janeiro would emanate outward to the provinces until all of Brazil was embroiled in revolution from which would emerge, after bloodshed, separate republics.[109] By 1824, Subserra was a vocal proponent of invading Brazil. He believed that there was a significant pro-Portuguese faction ("*um grande partido europeio*") in Pernambuco, Maranhão, and Pará, which controlled the "preponderance of the industry and wealth of Brazil," still desirous of reconstituting the *Reino Unido*. He interpreted the Brazilian government's expulsion of the Portuguese regiments in Bahia and Pernambuco as proof of its "fear" of this prospect. Pro-Portuguese sympathizers needed but Dom João's explicit support to rise up in favor of the old order. Brazil's independence, full or partial, could still be averted.[110] Other influential commentators maintained that the disunity of Brazil, specifically Rio de Janeiro's weak hold over the distant provinces, afforded an opportunity. After all, several provinces had adhered to the Lisbon Cortes and rejected Rio de Janeiro's hegemony in 1821–22. Vilanova Portugal argued that the northern provinces remained "separate bodies" eager to toss off Rio's yoke and join with Portugal, perhaps extending as far south as the Rio de São Francisco.[111]

The irrepressible Subserra contended that a military expedition to the north of Brazil might yield a worthwhile result. Control over Pará, he argued, would permit further conquest of the immense *sertão*, enabling Portugal to "slowly take advantage of the riches of its territory."[112] Subserra also favored fighting against Brazil's independence on the grounds that it was a fatal affront to national pride:

England did not resign itself to failure in its struggle with its American colonies, nor did France with Saint-Domingue. They may have not succeeded in their objectives, but at least they enjoyed the honor derived from such a struggle, and honor is one of the means by which nations sustain themselves.[113]

[109] BNL, MSS 149, doc. 106, [Conde de Subserra], "Relatório do Ministro de Estado, encarregado dos Negocios da Marinha, e do Ultramar," January 9, 1824, fo. 5; and doc. 107, [Subserra], "Parecer que deo S. Exmo. no Conselho d'Estado que se fez em 11 de Outubro de 1824, sobre os negocios do Brasil," fo. 3.

[110] BNL, MSS 149, doc. 106, [Subserra], "Relatório do Ministro de Estado, encarregado dos Negocios da Marinha, e do Ultramar," January 9, 1824, fo. 11.

[111] "Notas e Esclarecimentos de Thomaz António de Vilanova Portugal sobre o seu Parecer," February–March 1824, reproduced in *Documentos ... Independência* 1923, vol. I, p. 110. Interestingly, Vilanova Portugal's argument was that Portugal must try to reconquer or otherwise rejoin itself to some of the Brazilian provinces because "Portugal's own territory is so small that it cannot constitute a kingdom on its own."

[112] BNL, MSS 149, no. 106, [Subserra], "Relatório do Ministro do Estado, encarregado do Negocios da Marinha, e do Ultramar," January 9, 1824, fo. 12.

[113] BNL, MSS 149, doc. 107, [Subserra], "Parecer que deo S. Exmo. no Conselho d'Estado que se fez em 11 de Outubro de 1824, sobre os negocios do Brasil," fo. 2v.

Besides the influential party that believed Brazil could, and should, be recolonized, there was another group of counselors who were persuaded that, judging from the still-simmering revolutionary currents throughout Brazil, Dom Pedro's position was "critical and precarious." They contended that recognition of Brazil would prop up his throne, mollify the considerable number of Portuguese residents in Brazil, and provide him with a reliable ally upon which to depend should his political fortunes fade further. By supporting a beleaguered Dom Pedro, Portugal could secure favorable terms for recognition. They envisioned a strict alliance between Portugal and Brazil, stopping well short of a revivified *Reino Unido*, but optimistically imagining the eventual reintegration of the realms. In the short term, Palmela reminded Dom João's cabinet, "the transfer of the monarchy [in 1807–8] completely destroyed the colonial system," and expending effort, blood, and treasure to re-establish the status quo ante was doomed.[114] He later elaborated to another correspondent that "emancipation" was a "natural stirring in any colony that has attained a certain level of power and population."[115]

However, the advantages of mutual accommodation were legion, especially because Dom Pedro was assailed relentlessly by a revolutionary, republican, and increasingly nativist faction. Portugal might countenance Brazil's independence, but certainly not as a republican state, which would destroy forever any chance of reconciliation under the Braganza dynasty. In January 1824 Porto Santo wrote to Palmela concerning "a revolution in Rio de Janeiro in support of the Royal Prince," his spin on the dissolution of the Assembly, arguing that Portugal should send, "as quickly as possible, reinforcements of troops to assist the Royal Prince, as well as to Bahia and Pernambuco so that those important and rich captaincies do not establish republics or governments independent of Rio de Janeiro."[116] Palmela clearly agreed. Dom Pedro's misguided convocation of the Assembly, for example, had won him "fleeting popularity at the cost of his decorum, his authority, and the integrity of Brazil." He was convinced that "only a true union with his august father could save Brazil." By February 1824, Palmela noted that Dom João had "ordered all maritime resources in Portugal mobilized and offered in support of the [Brazilian] royalists, of which there undoubtedly remain some, and

[114] "Relatório do Ministro dos Negocios Estrangeiros do Reino de Portugal, Marquêz de Palmella, sobre as Relações entre Portugal e Brasil," January 9, 1824, reproduced in *Documentos ... Independência* 1923, vol. I, p. 85.
[115] Palmela to Barão de Binder [Austrian Representative], May 11, 1824, in Palmela 1851, vol. I, pp. 396–97.
[116] ANTT, MNE, cx. 665, Porto Santo to Palmela, January 27, 1824.

to aid *Sua Alteza Real* so that he might preserve the delegated authority which he exercises."[117] Support, therefore, would be offered to ameliorate Dom Pedro's plight and bring Brazil back into the European fold to some degree through an alliance with its royalist faction. At the very least, a successful operation would firm up the monarchy's foundations in the New World and secure it for the Braganza dynasty, a consideration which factored heavily in the deliberations. Palmela presented Portugal's unwillingness to accept Brazil's complete, unfettered independence to Baron Binder, the Austrian envoy, as Portugal's contribution to the wider struggle that pitted "revolution and royalty, order and anarchy," an effort to block "the frightful spread of the republican and federal system in South America."[118]

Altruism and ideology, however, were not the only factors in play. The support offered to Dom Pedro was contingent on re-attaching the two sides of the Atlantic to each other. At least in public, Dom Pedro showed scant interest in such approaches. In June 1824, he expressed his displeasure with the "chimerical plans of a new reunion and subjection" percolating in Lisbon, castigating "some Portuguese ministers, either willfully blind or else blinded by ambition, who sought war, useless war" instead of "well-calculated and mutually advantageous commerce and solid guarantees of peace and a durable friendship."[119] Palmela requested British intervention to buttress the two-pronged operation of preserving monarchy and healing the rift between Brazil and Portugal, an overture Britain rejected.[120] As late as October 1824, during the protracted negotiations resulting in Portugal's recognition of Brazil's independence, Palmela furnished the negotiators with an amended version of Subserra's 1823 reconciliation proposal. Its most important clauses included: first, "a reciprocally independent administration, yet still preserving perpetual union"; second, a rotating residence of the sovereign "as the circumstances require"; third, the adherence of both Portugal and Brazil to the same political treaties, but the ability to negotiate separate commercial treaties; and fourth, "the creation and maintenance of a single navy," with implied mutual defense treaties.[121] When

---

[117] ANTT, APASG, cx. 1, mç. 2, Palmela to Porto Santo, "Ofício Reservado no. 9," February 29, 1824.
[118] Palmela to Binder, October 18, 1823, in *Publicações do Archivo Público Nacional*, vol. IV, p. 195.
[119] Dom Pedro, Proclamação, June 10, 1824, reproduced in *Documentos ... Cortes* 1883, vol. I, p. 893.
[120] Proença 1987, p. 71.
[121] Palmela's "Esboço de um acto de reconciliação entre Portugal e o Brasil," included in Palmela to Conde de Villa Real, October 12, 1824, in Biker 1879, vol. 22 (14), p. 270.

hopes for a "*união sincera*" subsided, but as Dom Pedro's dissolution of the Assembly triggered further upheaval, notably the Confederation of the Equator, this group remained convinced that Dom Pedro would be forced eventually to the bargaining table. They expected to obtain an advantageous financial settlement from Brazil as well as a favorable commercial treaty. Such arrangements would relieve some of the financial distress felt acutely in Portugal, which undermined its political stability. As Palmela admitted to Porto Santo, "in truth, the situation of our Treasury is desperate, and we must hope for some relief from our reconciliation with Brazil ... the separation of Brazil has cut Portugal's revenue in half."[122] Portugal's government dangled a further inducement: the guarantee that Dom Pedro's succession to the Portuguese throne was unclouded by the events of 1820–24. Palmela believed that Portugal would benefit as well from "reconciliation" with Dom Pedro, "by which we may not only avoid the sad prospect of future trouble, but also secure the succession to the throne of the legitimate heir."[123]

Intrigues at the Portuguese court, and personal relationships, factored significantly in the political settlement of the 1823–26 period. As previously noted, Dom João rightly feared for his life: his wife, his son, and members of their enthusiastic entourage unceasingly plotted against him, and there exists abundant official correspondence attesting to conspiracies and other symptoms of disloyalty.[124] In the *Abrilada*'s aftermath, Palmela informed Vila Real that the king was threatened by those who either sought to implement a democratic constitution or else install "a usurping prince and, under the name of royalism and religion, vengeance, fanaticism, and the ugliest of passions."[125] In September 1824, Palmela appealed desperately to Subserra to "save the ship of state" and to defend Dom João against the machinations of "the entire royal family, supported by the self-interested and impassioned men found in such abundance amongst the privileged classes." He implored him that "Reason, Portugal's welfare, and a virtuous and enlightened

---

[122] ANTT, APASG, cx. 1, mç. 2, Palmela to Porto Santo, "Ofício Reservado no. 25," January 10, 1825.

[123] ANTT, APASG, cx. 1, mç. 2, Palmela to Porto Santo, "Ofício Reservado no. 26," January 10, 1825.

[124] Though many went out of their way to deny or else conceal that any plot was afoot: Subserra told Dom João that "from what I have observed, I have not seen any threat against the precious life of SAR, and if there were such a plot, I would be the first to sacrifice mine ... in everything I have heard, in all of the speeches given, nothing was said against your royal authority." See ANTT, APASG, cx. 2, mç. 4, Manuel Ignâcio Martins Pamplona Corte Real (Conde de Subserra) to Dom João VI, May 27, 1823.

[125] Palmela to Conde de Villa Real, June 13, 1824, reproduced in Biker 1879, vol. 20 (12), p. 373.

(if indecisive and timid) King cannot become victims of hatred and intrigue."[126]

In Rio de Janeiro, Dom Pedro was livid as details of the various plots against his increasingly infirm father trickled in. In July 1824, he informed Dom João that, "if these rumors prove true, that [Dom Miguel] betrayed VM, then from today forward he is no longer my brother, for a good son can never love those who betray [his father]." But Dom Pedro's letter conveyed more than sympathy and belated solidarity. It contained the advice that Dom João's recognition of Brazil's independence was more urgent than ever, and in Dom João's "personal interest." Brazil's "stability" was steadily increasing as it "indubitably acquired more physical and moral force each day, and could never be conquered by old, wretched Portugal. The greater effort Portugal sank into such an enterprise, the more it destroyed itself. For Portugal without friendly relations with Brazil was without commerce and, without commerce, it amounted to nothing." He lambasted the counselors who encouraged Dom João to reconquer Brazil, advice which augured "a plague of misfortune." Furthermore, Dom Pedro told Dom João that "his life was in danger" and that the support he received from other nations "would not save his life." The recognition of Brazil, though, could bring the ailing king major benefits. By reviving Portugal's maritime commerce, new life would be breathed into its domestic economy ("the day laborer will have money with which to satisfy his family's hunger; the idle artisan will work again"). Furthermore, Dom João's personal position would be bolstered and he would be empowered to "crush the Portuguese aristocracy, which since 1806 has worked to topple the throne and to put into effect their infernal plans." Recognition of Brazil would "free [Dom João] from the daggers of the assassins who surround [him]." Professing his filial devotion, Dom Pedro reminded his father that "I, your son, never sought to become Emperor, but the love of the Brazilians made me one ... [in accordance with circumstances] predicted by VM, and consistent with the recommendation VM made in your letter of March 31, 1821." He concluded by exhorting his father to "win to your side the discontented elements of Portuguese society. By granting them a constitution, you will rule Portugal forever, for all of your subjects will love you."[127] In stark contrast to the Portuguese ministers urging support for Dom Pedro to save him from impending republican-inspired social revolution, in this letter the emperor indicates that Brazil could rescue Portugal from political cataclysm. Among

---

[126] BNL., Reservados, MSS 149, doc. 210, Palmela to Subserra, September 1824.
[127] BAj. 54-X-7, no. 161/175, Dom Pedro to Dom João, July 15, 1824.

the many fascinating themes to be teased from this correspondence, the overriding importance of dynastic considerations leaps to the fore. If they did not trump geopolitical concerns, they seriously jostled with such concerns for primacy.

The negotiations resulting in Portuguese recognition of Brazil's independence and the resumption of commercial and political relations between the two countries were, at this late stage, long after hostilities had halted, surprisingly complex and murky. Many factors remained in play besides dynastic ones. There was pressure to conclude a treaty ending hostilities with Brazil before the expiry of the 1810 Anglo-Portuguese treaty later that year. Otherwise, it was feared that Britain would negotiate a treaty recognizing Brazil's independence and gain trade advantages as a result, all to the detriment of Portugal's merchants.[128] Furthermore, an Anglo-Brazilian treaty would diminish Portugal's leverage in its quest to wrest an indemnity from Brazil. In March–April 1825, the negotiations continued apace and the possibility that the foreign and commercial policies of Portugal and Brazil would remain aligned by some formal convention, however limited, was plausible. The chief disputes preventing an agreement of this type concerned the line of succession to the Portuguese throne, the mutual defense treaty, and the size (amount) of the indemnity.[129] Furthermore, there was the seemingly minor issue, though a major preoccupation of the negotiators, concerning the titles Dom João and Dom Pedro would hold after independence. The Portuguese king demanded to be regarded as the "Emperor" (with his son as "Emperor-Regent" of Brazil), assuming that the two states continued to share a single navy, foreign policy (including a joint consular service), and other institutions of mutual support.[130]

Eventually, the two sides agreed on terms, enshrined in the Treaty of August 29, 1825. Brazil and Portugal were separated definitively according to international law. The reality, however, was much murkier. Dom João informed his son, "I have ratified the treaty; you are not unaware

---

[128] "Officio do Conde de Villa Real to Dom Miguel António de Mello," March 2, 1825, in Biker 1879, vol. 23 (15), p. 9.

[129] It had already been agreed that the scope of the indemnity would be limited to an agreement between sovereign states, for loss of property, and not personal recompense for royal property forfeited or left behind in Brazil, which would be dealt with separately at a later date. The claims of private individuals were supposed to be adjudicated by a mixed commission, which was never convened.

[130] "Exposição do Conde de Porto Santo a El-Rei," March 30, 1825; and "Circular do Conde de Porto Santo aos Representantes de Portugal nas Côrtes Estrangeiras," June 22, 1825, both reproduced in Biker 1879, vol. 23 (15), pp. 28–35 passim. On the controversy over the title of "emperor," see Manchester 1951, p. 95.

how many sacrifices I have made for you. If you are grateful, you must work to cement the mutual happiness of these [two] peoples which Divine Providence entrusted to my care."[131] Familial loyalty partially accounted for the persistence of connections. The £2 million indemnity that Brazil secretly agreed to pay Portugal and the still-undetermined matter of royal succession also factored heavily. The indemnity, a secret "pecuniary convention" clause of the 1825 Treaty, loomed large given the decimated state of Portuguese finances. The indemnity was meant to cover the loan Portugal had assumed in London in 1823, some of which was spent mounting its ill-fated reconquest effort, with the rest earmarked to offset somewhat the declining revenues anticipated from diminished bilateral trade. The sum of £600,000 was to be paid within one year of the Treaty, with the rest paid as soon as Brazil's new London loan was disbursed.[132] For Brazil, secrecy was necessitated not only by national honor (the French navy had extracted a similar indemnity from Haiti earlier that year; more importantly, the notion of compensating Portugal for its invasion was anathema to Brazilian patriots), but also because of its own precarious finances. A £3.7 million Rothschild loan of 1824 was exhausted by 1826 and further debt obligations threatened to capsize the ship of state.[133] The indemnity would remain an issue in Portuguese–Brazilian relations throughout the 1820s, as recounted in Chapter 4.

PART II

The empire strikes back: the Atlantic origins and repercussions of the 1826 Portuguese *Carta Constitucional*

Formal recognition in 1825 did not signify that the affairs of Portugal and Brazil would be entirely disentangled. Viewed from outside of the corridors of power, there was nothing definitive about the separation for some observers. The break seemed illogical, well after the 1825 Treaty. One pamphleteer enquired "is not this moment propitious to cement in everlasting fashion the reciprocal happiness of both nations? What is a Brazilian but a son, grandson or great grandson of a Portuguese?"[134] As

---

[131] Quoted in Sousa 1957, vol. III, t. 2, p. 643.
[132] Cervo and Magalhães 2000, p. 188.
[133] Macaulay 1988, p. 194.
[134] *O Correio Interceptado* (1825), Carta 1, pp. 10–11.

noted previously, Dom João begged Dom Pedro to care for the welfare of Portugal. Though somewhat veiled, his meaning was clear: Brazil's "independence" should not be regarded as permanent. Dom Pedro should interfere unhesitatingly in the Peninsula's affairs. Since the Juntas of 1823–24 failed to produce a new constitution and the "ancient constitution" was restored by Dom João, the rules governing royal succession remained unmodified. Due to inaction, therefore, Dom Pedro's status as heir to the Portuguese throne was uncontested, though his claim was muddied by his 1824 Brazilian Constitution's stipulation that the two states were never to unite again under a single crown. In addition, there was the non-juridical, but perhaps more important, fact that Dom Pedro was the figurehead, if not the chief architect, of the dismemberment of the Portuguese empire just three years earlier, a fact that made him anathema to peninsular liberals and ultras alike.

The failure of the 1825 Treaty to clarify the matter of succession was noticed widely. It was a profoundly unsettling silence. As one newspaper noted with alarm and chagrin, "how could a treaty be ratified without a clear declaration on a matter of such importance? Who fails to realize that the death of a king always causes a crisis of state?"[135] The unresolved matter of succession irked many, for it favored Dom Pedro and promised a sustained connection between Portugal and Brazil. As British ambassador William A'Court reported in December 1825, "the *fidalgos* are dissatisfied to a man. They are intriguing in every possible way ... the watchword among them is, 'no *dose of agoa de colonia*' – no dependence upon Brazil."[136] His health in terminal decline, Dom João nominated a regency to rule in his stead, headed by Princess Dona Isabel Maria.[137] Dom Miguel, still in Vienna, was excluded. Such an arrangement fostered further disquiet, as Dom Pedro's succession, though unmentioned, was effectively confirmed by the creation of a regency and the exclusion of Dom Miguel.

Dom João died on March 10, 1826.[138] News of his death reached Rio de Janeiro six weeks later, on April 25. There is some evidence that Dom Pedro had planned for this contingency, even entertaining the idea of granting a constitutional charter to Portugal as early as October 1825.[139]

---

[135] Ibid., p. 12.
[136] Lill.L., Stuart MSS, William A'Court [in Lisbon] to H. Chamberlain (Private), December 17, 1825.
[137] On the composition of this regency, see Fernando Pereira Marques, "Do Vintismo ao Cabralismo," in A. Reis 1990, p. 44.
[138] A recent analysis of Dom João's body found high concentrations of arsenic, possible evidence that he was poisoned. See Pedreira and Costa 2008, p. 423.
[139] See TNA, FO 13/5, Stuart to Canning, October 20, 1825, fos. 22–23, for these ruminations.

On the day news of his father's death arrived, Dom Pedro sent a circular to his closest advisors, informing them that a regency had been formed in Portugal until he "decided what is permitted to him as heir to the kingdom." He acknowledged the "delicate" state of opinion in Brazil, "jealous (*zeloso*) of its independence" and whether its sovereignty would be deemed threatened were its emperor to become king of Portugal, so long as "the two nations remain completely separate." He further queried whether such a situation would violate Brazil's constitution and, crucially, whether it would be possible for a European nation to be governed from the New World. He also questioned how, were such a state of affairs impossible to sustain, the abdication of the Portuguese Crown should proceed and to whom should the scepter pass.[140]

The emperor received a number of responses between April 26 and 28.[141] Visconde de Barbacena reminded the emperor that the 1824 Constitution forbade him from leaving Brazilian territory without the Assembly's consent and further prohibited the union of the crowns.[142] But Barbacena saw no obstacles to the acceptance and simultaneous wearing of the two separate crowns which "belonged to Pedro by the right of birth." Frei António de Arrábida informed the emperor that he had three mutually exclusive choices: first, to reign in Portugal; second, "to give them a *Carta* extracted from the English and French Constitutions"; and third, to make his Brazilian-born daughter, Dona Maria da Gloria, the Queen of Portugal. Ultimately, Dom Pedro pursued all three options simultaneously, even though Frei Arrábida considered them mutually exclusive. Visconde de Vilareal cautioned the emperor against abdication, which he believed would prove "eminently disagreeable" to Brazilians who would "become fearful that future events would be hostile to their independence." Barão de Alcântara likewise maintained that union was unfeasible, noting that the difficulties accompanying the separation of Brazil from Portugal portended even greater obstacles to their reunification. He warned of potential popular disturbances by Brazilians unable to appreciate the nuanced differences between the former colonial condition and the new form of union entertained by Dom Pedro in his circular. Much more desirable would be to reserve the right of succession for his heirs, and, in a single stroke, incorporate Portugal's colonies in Africa, particularly Angola,

---

[140] AMI, I-POB.25.04.1826.PI.B.do/MFN 10841.
[141] All of the documents related to this topic are found in the unbound, unfolioed folder AMI, I-POB.25.04.1826.PI.B.do/MFN 10841, in which the material in the next paragraphs is to be found unless otherwise noted.
[142] Felisberto Caldeira Brant Pontes (1772–1842), Visconde de Barbacena.

into Brazil.[143] A separate conversation on the same day, with Crown official João da Rocha Pinto, provided a further glimpse into the emperor's state of mind. According to Rocha Pinto, Dom Pedro was unable to decide whether he would abdicate or retain the Portuguese Crown, cursing the Lusitanian inheritance as a "crown of thorns." Rocha Pinto replied, "place this crown of thorns, then, on top of another crown, so the thorns do not prick you."[144]

The swiftness of these deliberations was not conducive to cautious contemplation. Portugal's situation demanded immediate action, but an equally important context was the impending reopening of the Brazilian General Assembly on May 3, 1826. It would be the first meeting of an elected, representative body since Dom Pedro dissolved the Constituent Assembly in November 1823. It thus marked the end of almost thirty months of "quasi-autocratic rule," in one historian's apt phrase.[145] The 1824 Constitution, of course, was still in effect, but it had been suspended various times, including when the Confederation of the Equator's participants were tried before special tribunals and executed in flagrant violation of the legal protections guaranteed by the Constitution. Dom Pedro's foreign policy offered little solace, as his government had flirted in 1825 with arming the bands of royalists in Upper Peru after their military defeat at Ayacucho, an arrangement never consummated.[146] Dom Pedro's apparent hostility toward constitutional government was particularly dangerous in 1824–26 when the tide seemed to turn irreversibly against monarchism throughout the Americas. Spanish aspirations in Peru sputtered to a halt, and no armies of reconquest were amassed on the Iberian Peninsula.[147] Iturbide's demise in Mexico was interpreted by Bolívar as the "third volume of the history of American princes. Dessalines, Christophe and [Iturbide] have all ended the same.

---

[143] Though this last suggestion was a non-starter. In an 1826 letter to Palmela, George Canning declared that he had "no hesitation in saying that any attempt by the Brazilian government to make itself master of the remaining colonial possessions of Portugal would entitle his Most Faithful Majesty to call upon his ally the King of Britain for prompt and effectual interposition," Canning to Palmela, February 3, 1826, in Canning 1887, vol. I, p. 11. Wellington made the same point three years later: "We do not intend to allow the Portuguese monarchy in Europe to be further weakened by the seizure of its remaining colonies by the Emperor of Brazil, or by their being revolutionized," Wellington to Aberdeen, August 17, 1828, in Wellington 1973, vol. IV, p. 623.

[144] Conversation between João da Rocha Pinto and Sá da Bandeira, reported in diary entry of December 31, 1828, in Sá da Bandeira 1975, vol. I, p. 121.

[145] Macaulay 1988, p. 192.

[146] Seckinger 1984, p. 35.

[147] Though, in 1829, Fernando VII launched an ill-planned, ill-fated invasion of Mexico via Cuba.

The emperor of Brazil may follow them and devotees of monarchy should take heed."[148] Dom Pedro further rankled Spanish American republicans by embroiling Brazil in a profligate and bloody quagmire in the Banda Oriental. By the cessation of hostilities in August 1828, it had cost Brazil the equivalent of US $30 million and eight thousand lives.[149] In 1826, then, Dom Pedro was aware of the inauspicious historical moment in which he was operating. Dom João's death provided him with a fresh opportunity to consolidate his connection to Europe, assert his independence from the Holy Alliance, burnish his liberal credentials at home and abroad, secure a European throne for his children (if not for himself), and gain an ally (Portugal) in the struggle over the Banda Oriental.[150] But time was of the essence.

After receiving counsel from various quarters, Dom Pedro resolved to grant Portugal the charter long promised by his deceased father and incubated in the aborted Juntas. This document would ultimately take the form of the *Carta Constitucional*, largely a replica of the 1824 Brazilian Constitution. They were, in an eminent historian's phrase, "twin statutes, originating from the same source."[151] As Portuguese legal historians have demonstrated, several of the defunct Juntas' constitutional projects appear to be forerunners of the *Carta*, a resemblance that undermines the "*Cartista* myth of rupture." There are unmistakable similarities, if not continuities, between the proposals discussed by the peninsular Juntas of 1823–24 and the institutions called forth by the *Carta*,[152] including the king's veto, his power to dissolve the Cortes, and bicameralism with a life senate/upper chamber. But documentary evidence has not come to light suggesting that Dom Pedro or his advisors had perused copies of these constitutional projects, either before the promulgation of the 1824 Brazilian Constitution (very unlikely) or during the revision of that document to fashion the 1826 *Carta*. Whatever similarities existed were accidental or coincidental, a convergence resulting from the same constitutional and jurisprudential milieu.[153] Furthermore, there was a gulf between the ideas entertained by the 1823–24 Portuguese Junta and those entertained by Dom Pedro. These differences may be ascertained from Palmela's open disdain for Brazil's 1824 Constitution, an attitude at odds with his later role as standard-bearer of the *Carta*. In May 1824, he predicted that, "like

---

[148] Bolívar to Santander, January 6, 1825, quoted in Seckinger 1984, p. 33.
[149] Macaulay 1988, p. 211; on British mediation, see Winn 1976.
[150] Oliveira Lima 1925, pp. 62, 112.
[151] Sousa 1957, vol. III, p. 661.
[152] Hespanha 2004, pp. 19, 150.
[153] Mesquita 2006, p. 119.

other ephemeral documents of the same type, which we repeatedly have seen fail, it does not contain anything that suggests its durability. The different elements that comprise the white population [of Brazil], diffused over the great territory of that land, make any *projecto* for a uniform constitution chimerical."[154] So, while modern historians have identified continuities between the Junta's *Projecto* and the *Carta*, contemporaries did not link them. A more likely scenario, though somewhat unsatisfying in its imprecision, is that a consensus emerged spontaneously among royalists, nurtured by the triple stimuli of French Restoration political thought, a revulsion toward the extremes of *Vintismo* and republicanism, and a wariness toward the backward-gazing hyperbole of hard-line ultra conservatives. But it is crucial to remember, amidst recognition of continuities and convergences, that the ultimate sources of the *Carta* were the forerunner Brazilian *Projectos* culminating in the 1824 Constitution. The possibility that this Brazilian creation would be imposed on Portugal was predicted by Porto Santo as early as 1824. Terrified by this prospect, he fought, unsuccessfully, during the negotiations resulting in the recognition of Brazilian independence to have the 1824 Constitution abolished as a precondition for recognition.

With the advice of his counselors in mind, Dom Pedro and Gomes da Silva commenced the revisions of the 1824 Brazilian Constitution to accommodate it to Portugal's circumstances.[155] They took published copies of the December 1823 Brazilian *Projecto* (written in large part by Carneiro de Campos) as their point of departure. In less than three days, they rearranged the order of articles, eliminated references specific to Brazil, modified language, and made obvious substitutions. Using multiple copies of the 1823 *Projecto*, they swapped annotated texts and attached short explanatory notes to justify the amendments each had made. Dom Pedro objected to Gomes da Silva's crossing out of the word "constitutional [*constitucional*]" to describe the government of Portugal. As he explained, "if a king gives a constitution, the government is constitutional, and it does not seem advisable to remove a word to which at the present time the people have taken such a fancy."[156] At the conclusion of three days, the foundation of the 1824 Brazilian Constitution was fashioned into the Portuguese *Carta*. The most salient differences between these documents were: first, that the religious basis was muted, as the invocation of the Holy Trinity was excised;

[154] Palmela to Barão de Binder, May 11, 1824, in Palmela 1851, vol. I, pp. 396–97.
[155] This process is well known. Besides the documents cited below, also reproduced in *Constitucionalismo de D Pedro I* 1972, it is described at length in Gomes da Silva 1831, esp. 88–91.
[156] AMI, II-POB.29.04.1826.P1.B.do.1–6.

second, that religious freedom in Portugal was confined to foreigners, whereas in Brazil it was more extensive; third, that the 1826 *Carta*
guaranteed the existence of a hereditary nobility, whereas the Brazilian
Constitution substituted a non-hereditary nobility composed of peers
chosen by the emperor, usually in exchange for services rendered to the
state; and, fourth, that the Portuguese *Carta* gave the king an absolute
veto over legislation, whereas in Brazil the emperor could merely suspend the taking effect of this legislation.[157] But the most striking feature
was the retention, even amplification, of the "Moderating Power" in the
Carta, particularly because Dom Pedro attributed to the monarch an
absolute veto over legislation emanating from parliament.[158]

Though keen to assert his right to the Portuguese throne, Dom
Pedro realized that the short-term restoration of a union between the
two sides of the Atlantic was unrealistic. He therefore pursued a course
of action to secure the Crown for his daughter, Dona Maria, which
entailed promulgating the *Carta*, and forcing Dom Miguel to swear
allegiance to it, while also arranging for his brother's eventual marriage
to his daughter. After these arrangements had been made, Dom Pedro
would abdicate the Portuguese throne. The prospect of Dom Miguel
as regent during Maria's minority was imperfect, but palatable, certainly better than the unsavory alternatives. Yet to be certain that this
state of affairs would transpire, he declared that the regency headed by
his sister, Dona Isabel Maria, would continue to administer the kingdom until Dom Miguel swore his allegiance to the *Carta* and agreed to
marry his niece. But all of these dynastic considerations were subsidiary
to, and contingent upon, the acceptance of the *Carta*. The similarity of
the two constitutions speaks not only to the *Carta*'s hasty composition,
but also to Dom Pedro's ultimate aspiration to unify the two kingdoms
in the future. It may be presumed that constitutional uniformity would
facilitate the realization of the goal of reunification.

Various draft articles omitted from the final version of the *Carta* suggest Dom Pedro's desire to retain a firm grip on Portuguese affairs
after his abdication. Notes exchanged between Dom Pedro and Gomes
da Silva indicate that they were preoccupied with the question of what
should happen were the young queen, like her great-grandmother and
namesake, Dona Maria I, to become incapacitated or to die without an
heir. In a draft article excised at the last moment from the final version
of the *Carta*, there existed a provision stating that if the Portuguese
Assembly confirmed the queen's physical inability to rule, and this status were acknowledged by the Brazilian Assembly, then a royal prince

[157] Miranda 2001, p. 33.   [158] Hespanha 2004, p. 259.

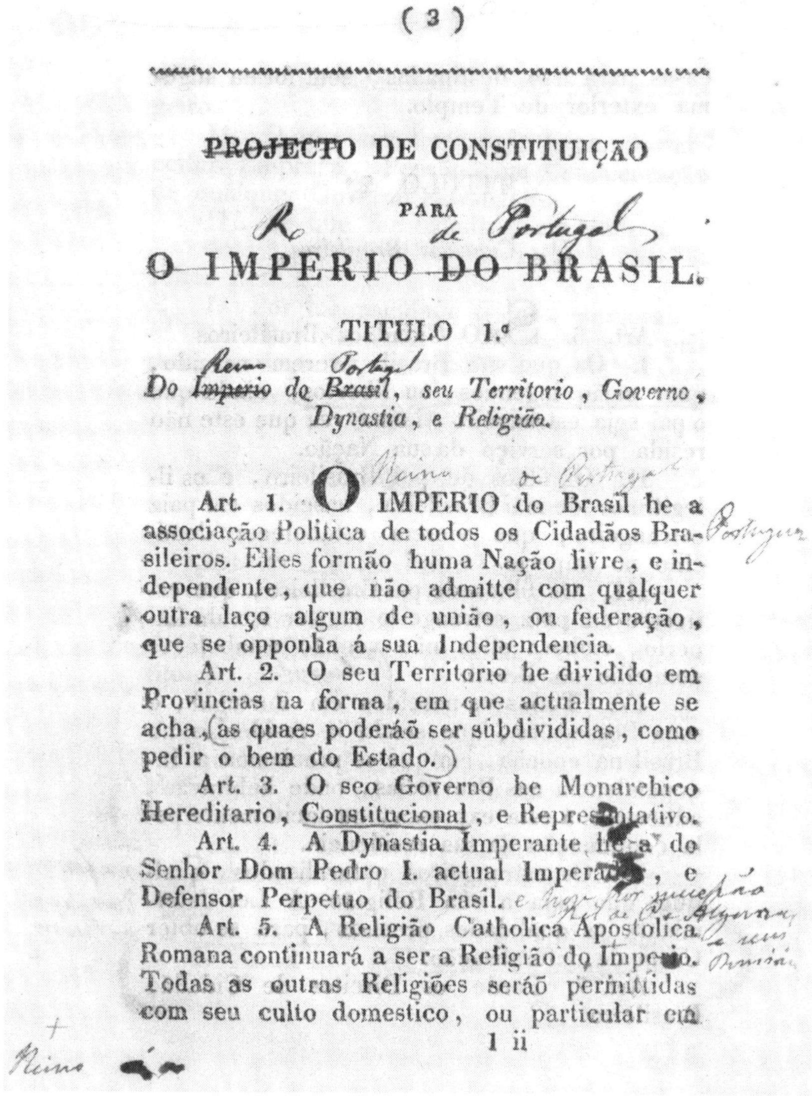

(3)

~~~~~~

~~PROJECTO~~ DE CONSTITUIÇÃO

PARA de Portugal

O ~~IMPERIO DO BRASIL.~~

TITULO 1.º

Do ~~Imperio~~ *Reino* d~~o~~ *Portugal* ~~Brasil~~, seu Territorio , Governo , Dynastia , e Religião.

Art. 1.   O IMPERIO do Brasil *Reino de Portugal* he a associação Politica de todos os Cidadãos Bra- *Portugues* sileiros. Elles formão huma Nação livre , e independente , que não admitte com qualquer outra laço algum de união , ou federação , que se opponha á sua Independencia.

Art. 2.   O seu Territorio he dividido em Provincias na forma , em que actualmente se acha ,(as quaes poderáõ ser subdivididas , como pedir o bem do Estado.)

Art. 3.   O seo Governo he Monarchico Hereditario , Constitucional , e Representativo.

Art. 4.   A Dynastia Imperante he-a do Senhor Dom Pedro I. actual Imperador , e Defensor Perpetuo do Brasil.

Art. 5.   A Religião Catholica Apostolica Romana continuará a ser a Religião do Imperio. Todas as outras Religiões serão permittidas com seu culto domestico , ou particular em

1 ii

Figure 5 April 1826 revision, by Dom Pedro I and Francisco Gomes da Silva, of the 1823 Brazilian Constitutional *Projecto*.

could rule, whether as regent or perhaps in his own right. In this draft article, the language was vague, but it is clear that Dom Pedro could serve as regent (which ultimately happened in the latter phase of the Civil War) if his daughter predeceased him. Of course, such active intervention in the affairs of another state was forbidden explicitly by the 1824 Brazilian Constitution, which Pedro himself had framed and promulgated, making recourse to ambiguous language necessary.[159] As mentioned previously, Dom Pedro also issued three ancillary decrees to accompany the *Carta* and to ease its reception: first, he abdicated in favor of Dona Maria, stipulating her eventual marriage to Dom Miguel; second, he confirmed the already established Regency to rule until then and named its members; and third, he granted a general political amnesty, a rather quixotic attempt to wipe the slate clean after the mutual recriminations of 1817–26, paving the way for the repatriation of political refugees (and the release of those who had been imprisoned before they could flee).

The initial reception of the *Carta* in Portugal

After considerable delay, the *Carta* arrived in Lisbon on July 1, transported by Sir Charles Stuart, whose curious role is discussed in a later section of this chapter.[160] News of Dom Pedro's actions, however, had already arrived. Notice of them had been published in France, in the journal *L'Étoile*, on June 19.[161] Although the text of the *Carta* was not published immediately, a description of the *Carta* (and Dom Pedro's accompanying decrees) was published in the *Gazeta de Lisboa* on July 3. The *Carta* was greeted with public celebrations. Poems were composed and recited in public, praising the "Liberal Constitution" as a "gift from God" that promised to usher in an era of "peace," "union," and "stability." This "divine" constitution, widely understood to have been written solely by Dom Pedro's hand, was lauded as a "model for other nations" covetous of similar liberties. Very quickly, however, the initial euphoria subsided and the Portuguese political class splintered into groups in favor and opposed to the *Carta*. Infanta Isabel Maria sought to rally support for it. She declared that it should not be interpreted as

---

[159] AMI, II-POB.29.04.1826.P1.B.do.1–6.
[160] There is some discrepancy in the records about how and when it was intended to be presented to the Portuguese public. Certain documentation indicates that it was supposed to be endorsed/ratified by the *Três Estados do Reino* that was to be convened before being presented to the public.
[161] Sá 1969, p. 86, fn. 36.

a "concession to the revolutionary spirit, but rather as a spontaneously given gift from His Majesty's legitimate power, an emanation of his deep wisdom (*profunda sabedoria*)."[162]

But discontent proved difficult to dissipate. As a later section explains, Stuart's ubiquitous role in Luso-Brazilian affairs in 1824–26 had become an irritant to many, even those favorably disposed to the *Carta*. The symbolism of his role as courier exceeded the ample boundaries of tolerable British interference in Portugal's internal affairs. From exile in France, Subserra characterized Stuart's involvement as "humiliating" and "proof that England, if it has not been the architect, is certainly disposed to support this innovation."[163] According to Porto Santo, Stuart's hand in the matter was "bound to increase the suspicions of the other Powers, attributing to England the decisions made in Brazil." Porto Santo was convinced that the *Carta* was a dead letter and that the European governments were "ready to use all at the very least indirect means in their power to block its implementation."[164] These prescient observations aside, the initial reports from Dom Pedro's trusted sources painted a more encouraging picture of the *Carta*'s reception. Writing from Lisbon in the immediate aftermath of its publication, Stuart informed the emperor that his *Carta* "already [had] produced many beneficial effects, greeted with enthusiasm by the liberals while enjoying the good will of the moderate royalists." Stuart guaranteed that when "public opinion" was influenced the "principal opponents of the new system will soon take their place alongside the supporters."[165] The emperor continued to receive reassuring reports in subsequent correspondence. One correspondent indicated that the unrest since the *Carta*'s appearance was little more than the aftershocks of the clashes between "movements informed by the spirit of 1820 against those of 1823," insisting that the *Carta*'s "institutions [were] destined to neutralize both."[166] Several leading political figures saw the *Carta* as a savior, a document which would put an end to increasingly rancorous partisan conflict. Soon after its arrival, Palmela wrote that

[162] Dona Isabel Maria, "Proclamação," July 12, 1826, reproduced in *Documentos ... Cortes* 1883, vol. II, p. 59.
[163] BNL, Reservados, MSS 149, doc. 127, Conde de Subserra [in Auteuil, France], June 24, 1826.
[164] ANTT, MNE, livro 468, Porto Santo to Palmela, July 13, 1826, fo. 213.
[165] C. Stuart to Dom Pedro, July 16, 1826, in *Archivo Diplomático da Independencia* 1925, vol. VI, pp. 188–89.
[166] AMI, II-POB.22.01.1827.Por.do.1–23, "Golpe de vista político sobre Portugal, na sua posição, assim interna, como externa, nas ultimas seis meses do anno 1826."

if well-intentioned men of different parties join together to prefer moderate liberty, legitimately acquired, instead of the abstract theories of democrats and the stagnation caused by absolute power, the *Carta* will usher in an era of alliance [between different parties] and will come to be seen as a gift from heaven.[167]

When the *Carta* arrived in Portugal, Palmela urged the skeptical Porto Santo to endorse it, whatever its problems. It was necessary to give European courts the impression that the *Carta* "preserved the authority and dignity that is proper to a monarchy [and that] it does not furnish the ill-intentioned revolutionaries of 1820 with a pretext to renew their struggle."[168] This stance seems to have been a common strategy among moderate royalists. In a revealing 1826 letter addressed to Marquês de Pombal, his correspondent stated that "in France, all *homens de bem* speak of the *Chartre*. We therefore should speak of the *Carta* or *Lei Fundamental*, but never of the *Constituição*, leaving [this term] for the friends of Manuel Fernandes [Tómas]."[169]

But not all key political figures assumed such a conciliatory posture. Already in July, there were uprisings against the *Carta*, and liberalism in general, in Trás-os-Montes. Everything hinged on Dom Miguel, who was still at the Court of Vienna. Concerning the Infante, Palmela noted that "all reports indicate that his conduct is consistent with his high birth; and it is to be hoped that the practical education he received during his travels modifies somewhat the fire of his character and age." Yet, by all means, Palmela believed, Dom Miguel must remain abroad, for his return would "bring with it the worst misfortunes for this kingdom."[170] It is interesting, however, that far from setting off a succession crisis in Portugal, Dom Pedro was accepted as heir to the throne upon his father's death.[171] In fact, from his Vienna asylum, Dom Miguel wrote to Dom Pedro, presenting himself as "the most humble vassal, recognizing VM Imperial as my legitimate sovereign and heir and successor to the Crown of our glorious ancestors."[172] This pledge,

---

[167] Palmela (August 11, 1826), quoted in A. Vianna 1958, vol. III, pp. 38–39.
[168] Palmela to Porto Santo, August 5, 1826, in Palmela 1851, vol. II, p. 415.
[169] BNL, Colecção Pombalina 716, [illegible] to Pombal, July 19, 1826, fo. 264.
[170] ANTT, APASG, cx. 1, mç. 2, Palmela to Porto Santo, "Ofício Reservado no. 26," January 10, 1825. In an earlier letter to Porto Santo (July 10, 1824), Palmela had described Dom Miguel's champions (as well as Don Carlos's across the border in Spain) as "royalists more dangerous to legitimate kings than demagogic revolutionaries," in Biker 1879, vol. 20 (12), p. 392.
[171] This fact appears to have been uncontroversial: as S. C. da Costa 1995 showed, the deputation sent to Rio de Janeiro to convey news of Dom João's death was composed of future Miguelists, suggesting that they understood Dom Pedro to be heir to the throne, p. 212.
[172] Dom Miguel to Dom Pedro, April 6, 1826, in *Documentos ... Cortes* 1883, vol. II, p. 24. As Lousada and Ferreira pointed out, there is a great deal of controversy concerning

however, was sworn before the *Carta*'s arrival. In Vienna, Dom Miguel
was bombarded with pleas to return to Portugal to head off revolutionary conspiracies. One letter from early 1826 informed Dom Miguel
("the tutelary angel of Portugal is Miguel the Angel, the only one who
can defend us") that "the infamous party, which seemed to have been
defeated in 1823, never disappeared: the theater set may have changed,
but the play remains the same, and the actors are the same comedians
as before. But now the revolutionary party has gained control of the
upper echelons of the state!"[173] Another correspondent lamented that
since the Infante's departure from the kingdom, his supporters were
subject to frightful reprisals for "the *Perversos*, finding themselves at
liberty and restored to the highest positions of state, unleashed every
malignant plan imaginable, persecuting with impunity your Majesty's
honorable and loyal vassals and reducing them to penury."[174]

After the *Carta*'s arrival in Portugal, the Braganza family became
deeply divided. Dom Miguel's sister, Infanta Dona Maria Francisca de
Assis, advised her brother not to swear allegiance to the *Carta* and, at all
costs, to avoid a marriage to their niece Dona Maria. "Remember," she
instructed, "that you are a Christian, that you are a son of the House of
Braganza, and that you are Portuguese: do nothing that could possibly
harm any of these three attributes."[175] By October 1826, the Regent
Dona Isabel Maria informed Dom Pedro that their uncooperative
brother had failed to swear allegiance, noting that this noncompliance
jeopardized his status as regent-in-waiting. After praising the "wise
constitution" that her brother had "generously" issued and declaring
that "without it, Portugal was lost and would remain lost," she prophesied that "when Miguel enters the country, Portugal will be swimming
in blood and all shall be lost. For the love of God, dear brother, do not
delude yourself on this point."[176] Dona Isabel Maria's fears proved justified and Dom Pedro was compelled to plead his case directly to Dom
Miguel. After imploring his brother to "sustain the *Carta* with all his

whether Dom Miguel actually swore allegiance to the *Carta* and acquiesced to his
brother's arrangements. A ceremony definitely took place, but in Miguelist political
mythology, Dom Miguel either did not swear on a Bible or moved his lips without
speaking, both of which would have invalidated his oath. See Lousada and Ferreira
2006, p. 106.

[173] BAj., 54-X-33, no. 44, [Anon.], "Ao Serenissimo Principe" [before March 1826],
fos. 2, 12.

[174] BAj., 54-XI-44, no. 20, Francisco Henriques Teixeira [Divisão Realista da Provincia
do Além-Tejo] to Dom Miguel [in Vienna], August 1826, fo. 1v.

[175] Dona Maria Francisca de Assis to Dom Miguel, November 5, 1826, reproduced in
Pereira 1938, Carta XIX, p. 100.

[176] AMI, II-POB.14.10.1826.IM.P.c., Dona Isabel Maria to Dom Pedro, October 14,
1826.

strength," Pedro described it an "anchor, which can save the ship of state from the great political tempest that threatened [Portugal] with total ruin." The constitution, Pedro continued, was merely a means to a greater end:

Constitutional liberty, properly conceived, is a safeguard that should be defended by all men of religion and good sense. Extremes should be avoided, for in politics it is the middle course (meio termo) that should be followed.[177]

As Dom Miguel weighed his next move, unrest spread throughout Portugal. Revolts in favor of Dom Miguel broke out in the Algarve and Alentejo in October–November.[178] In October, Lavradio informed Palmela that "it seems that a civil war has begun," a generally held view. It would be small consolation to "agree upon a remedy when the sick man has lost most of his vital force."[179] By mid November 1826, the Portuguese government appealed to Great Britain for military assistance, claiming that a Spanish invasion was imminent. This was not an exaggeration. Though Spain was officially friendly and neutral toward Portugal, Ferdinand VII was actively helping to organize, arm, and fund a Miguelist military intervention. The withdrawal of Russian and French support, combined with the arrival of four thousand British troops in December 1826, served to quell unrest in Portugal temporarily and forced the Spanish government to abandon its planned invasion, under General Francisco de Longa, of its Iberian neighbor.[180]

By early 1827, however, the situation worsened again. Lavradio told Palmela that even if the Carta were implemented in its entirety, its ultra-royalist and aristocratic detractors would continue to seek "its destruction and the substitution of the most abominable despotism" while ultra-liberals would unceasingly work to "re-establish an illegitimate constitution."[181] In July 1827, popular rebellion against the government instigated Saldanha's resignation as Minister of War.[182] Military conspiracies, mutinies, and revolts were the norm by early 1828, particularly in northern and rural Portugal. Marquês de Chaves pronounced against the Carta. The Regency sent Bernardo de Sá da Nogueira and the rehabilitated Saldanha to suppress it, which they

[177] AMI, II-POB.1828.P1.B.doc.1–152 (pasta 1).
[178] Vargues 1985, p. 536.
[179] ANTT, MNE, cx. 153, Lavradio to Palmela, October 13, 1826.
[180] R. Bullen, "The Great Powers and the Iberian Peninsula 1815–1848," in Sked 1979, p. 67; J. Fontana 2006, pp. 214–15.
[181] ANTT, MNE, cx. 153, Lavradio to Palmela, January 27, 1827; in an earlier letter to Palmela, Lavradio had exclaimed that he was "unsure which of the two parties [was] more frightening," ANTT, MNE, cx. 153, September 9, 1826.
[182] Vargues 1985, p. 538.

failed to achieve conclusively. It became unclear how long the Regency could sustain itself and fend off its enemies. By 1828, the deficit represented 35 percent of total revenue, and the treasury remained reliant on customs receipts, which amounted to 40 percent of total revenue.[183]

These grim economic conditions and the ferocity of political discord made the establishment of the *Carta* almost impossible. Dom Miguel's coup would face scant resistance. The *Carta* had promised order and failed to fulfill that promise. As Santarém, a leading Miguelist, noted, the *Carta* was misused by the "enemies of order" to "overthrow legitimate government." The *Carta*, then, was prone to disorder and other more extreme measures were necessary.[184] Santarém informed Palmela in Spring 1828 that Portugal's independence was imperiled, for its current political circumstances perturbed the Concert of Europe: "Your Excellency can well anticipate the evil consequences for the independence of this country, and for the consolidation of its institutions, if the men who made the Revolution of 1820 appear as the defenders of the present government."[185] Amidst these conditions, Dom Miguel re-entered Portugal. The Queen Dowager's birthday (April 25) was chosen as the occasion for his acclamation in Coimbra. Parliament was dissolved and the ministry overhauled. King Miguel I, as he was acclaimed, enjoyed not only popular support, but also the preponderance of the clergy and nobility, for reasons discussed in Chapter 4.[186] Nevertheless, he was keen to avoid giving the impression that his accession was a usurpation. As he pleaded to Ferdinand VII, "I did not seek the throne; but I desire to sustain it, along with the laws and glory of the Portuguese people."[187]

Fearing the worst, individuals with known constitutionalist sympathies fled abroad en masse. Clashes between *Cartistas* and Miguelists occurred throughout the country. Liberal resistance in the north culminated in the creation of the *Junta Provisoria* in Porto in May, which survived relentless assaults for almost seven weeks. Liberal exiles in Britain chartered a ship, *The Belfast*, to aid the Junta, but it was repulsed as it attempted to land and returned ignominiously to London. Overwhelmed, and without prospects of succor, the besieged liberal forces retreated across the border into Galicia. Palmela wrote poignantly to Dom Pedro, informing him that "the Portuguese nation,

---

[183] Cardoso and Lains 2010, pp. 256–57.
[184] ANTT, MNE, cx. 154, Santarém to Palmela, March 22, 1828.
[185] ANTT, MNE, cx. 153, Santarém to Palmela, April 5, 1828.
[186] Of the 143 members of the titular nobility, 83 flocked to his standard, and more than half of the clergy sided with his regime, too. See Lousada andFerreira 2006, p. 139.
[187] Boe.C., MS 409.1, Dom Miguel to Ferdinand VII, July 26, 1828.

after twenty years of disgraceful hardship, has now slipped into the final abyss of degradation and misery."[188] Palmela was not exaggerating. The reprisals were fierce and brutal. Miguelist ad hoc tribunals tried over eight thousand men in Porto alone for their collaboration with the Junta, with most of these hasty processes concluding in convictions and harsh sentences.[189] Santarém, by then Foreign Minister, justified the severity of the regime's persecution of its opponents. He insisted that the great political crises in the histories of all nations were marked by the "rigorous" and "extreme application of the law ... In applying the primitive laws of the monarchy to save the ship of state, it is not the sovereign who punishes [violators of the law], but rather the laws as they are applied which punish."[190] Besides hounding dissidents into exile (estimates vary widely from ten thousand to fifty thousand),[191] and the extensive recourse to dank prisons and judicial torture, various other types of repression were employed. Press freedom was radically curtailed. There were only thirteen political newspapers in 1829, down from fifty-three in 1826 and below the forty-two which would circulate in 1836. There were major purges of school teachers. In 1828–29, at least 127 teachers were fired, and a further 90 dismissed in 1830, presumably for their suspected political beliefs.[192] Institutions of higher education were denounced as a burden to the state. At least one commentator urged the number of students attending Coimbra be slashed for "too many doctors are prejudicial to the state."[193] This advice notwithstanding, when Dom Miguel invited the Jesuits to return to Portugal in 1829, he granted them permission to teach at Coimbra, though very few Jesuits returned in spite of these inducements.[194] Miguelist pamphleteer Frei Fortunato de São Boaventura (1777–1844), put in charge of reforming the Coimbra curriculum in 1831, sought to reverse the 1772 curriculum reform, reverting to its mid-eighteenth-century predecessor, ultimately a failed effort.[195] Though facing constraints similar to those of its predecessor

[188] Palmela to Emperor of Brazil, August 9, 1828, in Palmela 1869, vol. IV, pp. 94–95.
[189] Lousada and Ferreira 2006, p. 119.
[190] ANTT, MNE, livro 580, Santarém to Visconde d'Asseca, Reservado no. 173, June 18, 1829.
[191] Sá 1964 puts the figure at thirteen thousand *emigrados* by 1831, p. 98.
[192] Marques and Serrão 2002, pp. 443, 355.
[193] BNL, Colecção Pombalina 471, António Joaquim de Barros e Aguiar, "Ensaios Económicos, e Politicos sobre o Governo, e Administracão da Fazenda, dedicados ao Serenissima Senhor D. Miguel" (1828), fo. 37.
[194] S. J. Miller 1978, p. 378.
[195] Ibid., p. 392. Frei Fortunato did not stay long in Coimbra because he was soon named Archbishop of Évora. On Frei Fortunato and the Miguelist critique of liberalism and enlightenment, see the essays in Universidade Católica Portuguesa 2009.

government, Dom Miguel's regime sought to remake Portuguese society in its own image, extirpating allegedly pernicious institutions bequeathed by the eighteenth-century reformers, and seeking a return to an imagined, primeval past, a quest analyzed in Chapter 4.

Sir Charles Stuart, British recognition of Brazil, and the international history of the 1826 *Carta*

Brazil's political independence was considered a *fait accompli* by most European powers almost immediately following Dom Pedro's declaration on the banks of the Ipiranga in 1822. Two outstanding, closely entwined questions remained unanswered: what sort of relationship, if any, would develop between Portugal and Brazil? And what kind of political regimes would prevail in each state, given the internal pressures making monarchy's survival improbable in the New World? More than any other Great Power, Britain was keenly interested in the answers to these questions.[196] The fall of the Portuguese liberal-revolutionary regime in 1823 was satisfactory to most onlookers, though the French army's role in overthrowing Spain's *Trienio Liberal*, which produced a ricochet effect in Portugal, reminded British officials of the fragility of their influence in peninsular affairs. Still, Canning remarked privately that "the counter-revolution there is just what one could wish," disparaging "those revolutionists [as] the scum of the earth, and the Portuguese earth, fierce, rascally, thieving, ignorant ragamuffins, hating England and laboring with all their might to entrap us into war."[197] Nor would adherence to the much vaunted principles of non-interference thwart the expansion of British influence in Portugal. Wellington maintained that propping up Dom João's throne following the 1823 *Vilafrancada* was prudent politics: "indeed it must tend to give [Britain] all the weight it would desire to have in the settlement of the affairs of the Peninsula, and of those between Portugal and the Brazils."[198] Disdain for revolution, exasperation with the Portuguese Crown's inept conduct, and a desire to expand influence, then, informed British policy in the years prior to the issue of the *Carta*.

Although there was great suspicion toward Britain's motivation and reliability as an ally, along with some outright Anglophobia, as detailed in Chapters 1 and 2, the importance of maintaining intact the British

---

[196] On British involvement in the processes resulting in the dissolution of the Iberian empires, see Temperley 1925; Kaufmann 1951; J. Lynch 1969; Waddell 1987; Schroeder 1994; Paquette 2004; and Brown 2006.

[197] Canning to Bagot July 14, 1823, in Canning 1909, vol. II, 183.

[198] Wellington to Canning, August 3, 1823, in Wellington 1973, vol. II, pp. 113–14.

Alliance was a position shared by many of the leading figures of the eighteenth- and nineteenth-century Luso-Brazilian world. Azeredo Coutinho described Britain as the country with which Portugal "should preserve the greatest friendship," particularly for the "prompt and efficacious relief" it could expect from its more powerful ally.[199] Rodrigo de Souza Coutinho, another staunch Anglophile, firmly defended the alliance, including the economic concessions it entailed, against its increasingly vocal detractors. Not only was Britain the "largest consumer of our products due to differences in climate," but it was the "fault" of the Portuguese that their domestic manufactures did not rival those of Britain.[200] Even in 1823, Portugal's alliance with Britain remained an unalterable pillar of its foreign policy, as much to guarantee its independence as to protect the remnants of its overseas possessions. Palmela described the British treaties as serving Portugal's "permanent interest," warning that her remaining overseas territories would be "lost or severely compromised should those treaties be ruptured."[201] The reasons for these sentiments, described fully in Chapters 1 and 2, can only be recapitulated briefly here: the experience of the Peninsular War; the ubiquitous threat of Spanish invasion, occupation, and annexation; the belief that Britain's commitment to Portuguese sovereignty served as a bulwark against the machinations of the Holy Alliance; and the positive appraisal, in some sectors of elite opinion, of the British army's presence as an inhibitor of domestic discord in Portugal.

Fissures developed after 1822, however, as Britain's amicable conduct toward Brazil irked Portuguese nationalists already suspicious of Albion's motives. As early as 1822, Canning entertained recognition of Brazil, though he believed that the abolition of the slave trade should precede it.[202] The restoration of absolutism in Portugal was not accompanied by British backing for Portugal's ill-starred reconquest efforts. By late 1824, Subserra complained that Canning's policy aimed to "sever all of the bonds between Portugal and Brazil, converting the latter into a country entirely dependent on Britain, and [Britain] seems already to have reached an agreement to this effect with the Brazilians."[203] Britain had,

[199] Azeredo Coutinho, *Ensaio Económico* (1794), reprinted in Azeredo Coutinho 1992, p. 113.
[200] R. de Souza Coutinho to Dom João VI, December 30, 1796, quoted in A. M. D. Silva 2006, vol. II, p. 340.
[201] ANTT, APASG, cx. 1, mç. 2, Palmela to Porto Santo, "Ofício Reservado no. 3," November 1, 1823; the phrase *"interesse permanente"* is repeated in Palmela to Porto Santo, "Ofício Reservado no. 4," November 7, 1823.
[202] Bethell 1970b, p. 31.
[203] BNL, MSS 149, doc. 107, [Subserra], "Parecer que deo S. Exmo. no Conselho d'Estado que se fez em 11 de Outubro de 1824, sobre os negocios do Brasil," fos. 2–2v.

in fact, grown weary of propping up Dom João, especially as his agents dithered after the reconquest efforts fizzled. The fall of the Subserra ministry, ardently opposed to recognition of Brazil, was welcomed by Canning, but changes at the top failed to usher in a more conciliatory policy. Wellington informed Canning in early 1825 that the delay could provoke Brazil's blockade of Lisbon or Porto and its seizure of Portugal's African possessions. "Our guarantee," Wellington wrote, "would not oblige us to go to war in such a case ... All we shall be bound to do is to see that Portugal is entire at the termination of the hostilities."[204]

A review of the extant British government correspondence suggests that a definitive settlement that did not jeopardize British economic interests, or portend further political cataclysms, was the foremost objective, not the paranoid neo-colonial scenario sketched by Subserra. The preservation of monarchy, guided by an administration amenable to foreign trade and favorable to the slave trade's suppression, was the priority. In late 1823, Canning argued that "the conservation of monarchy in one part at least of the great continent of America is an object of vital importance to the Old World."[205] This "object" remained unchanged in 1825–26, in part because Canning conceived of political independence as a precursor to the recalibration of relations between Europe and America. As Canning informed A'Court, "We have uniformly, anxiously, and avowedly laboured for the preservation of monarchy in Brazil." But there was little indication, at least in January 1825, of how this goal affected the eventual settlement between Portugal and Brazil. Canning wanted Brazil "not dissevered" from the monarchy of Portugal, though he recognized a full-fledged union to be impossible and undesirable.[206]

Britain's active role in the transaction of Brazil's independence appears natural and unsurprising given its previous involvement in the transfer of the Braganzas to the New World, the burgeoning trade it enjoyed with Brazil (enshrined in the 1808 and 1810 Treaties negotiated by Strangford), and the sphere of military and political influence it had carved for itself in the Luso-Atlantic World. Besides the unsatisfactory economic consequences of a prolonged stalemate, the impending expiration in 1825 of the 1810 Commercial Treaty, including the slave trade clauses by which the signatories were bound to abolish the abominable traffic, made resolution of the differences between Portugal and Brazil urgent.

---

[204] Wellington to Canning, n.d., in Wellington 1973, vol. II, pp. 420–21.
[205] Canning to Sir Edward Thornton, December 23, 1823, in Webster 1938, vol. II, p. 243.
[206] TNA, FO 63/294, Canning to A'Court, January 1, 1825, fo. 20v.

Canning turned to an experienced diplomat, and old Portuguese hand, Sir Charles Stuart, to mediate and also to negotiate an Anglo-Brazilian commercial treaty, which would represent de facto recognition. The grandson of former prime minister Lord Bute (1762–63), he served for four years as British minister to Lisbon, during which time he sat on the Regency Council (1810–14), possessing a right to vote on military and financial matters. He evidently executed his assignment satisfactorily, earning a KB in 1812, forging a wide set of contacts, and (from a distance) earning the trust of Dom João, who bestowed upon him the title of Conde de Machico, on the island of Madeira, an honor carrying an annual pension of four *contos* payable from the *Fazenda Real* of Madeira.[207] Besides Beresford, commander-and-chief of the Portuguese army from 1809, Stuart was the most influential Briton in Portugal during the last phase of the French Revolutionary Wars.[208] While in Portugal, he evidently read widely on Portuguese history (or at least expended great energy in the acquisition of rare books and manuscripts). At his death, after which his library was auctioned (1855), his collection boasted an impressive array of manuscripts belonging formerly to Pombal, including all of his London correspondence (1738–40); the lion's share of his dispatches from his Vienna embassy of the mid 1740s; an anonymous "Discurso sobre o Commercio da Azia," dated 1747; and a smattering of documents related to the Portuguese Cortes's history before its final 1698 meeting.[209] It may be inferred that his grasp of Portuguese commercial, diplomatic, and constitutional history was unparalleled in the British foreign service. His post-Portugal career had been equally illustrious. Present at the Congress of Vienna, Stuart served as ambassador to Paris in the early years of the Restoration. Nor had he lost interest in the Ibero-Atlantic world, snatching up a considerable number of shares of the British-owned and operated Real del Monte Company, engaged in mining ventures in Mexico from 1824.[210]

---

[207] Though his acceptance of this title and pension did not pass through the proper channels, further enflaming Stuart's dispute with Canning in 1826. According to Canning, "no trace is to be found of any permission for YE of any honor or emolument." See TNA, FO 13/17, Canning to Stuart (draft), July 19, 1826, fo. 111.

[208] J. H. Rodrigues claimed that Stuart spoke Portuguese very well and published, in 1823, *Fragmentos de um Cancioneiro Inédito*. See J. H. Rodrigues 1975, vol. V, p. 147; J. B. de Sousa 2011 claimed that these *Fragmentos* were published in Paris.

[209] *Catalogue of a Valuable Library* 1855, pp. 59, 208–9, 213.

[210] For references to Stuart's interest in Real del Monte, which troubled Canning on conflict-of-interest grounds, see Bonnabeau 1974; for the history of the company, see Randall 1972. Perhaps more alarming, though probably unknown at the time, was Stuart's alleged involvement with unidentified British mining agents with claims in Minas Gerais. Bonnabeau 1974 indicated that "before Stuart left London, he gave them 'assurances of protection,' though at what price is not clear," p. 22.

In March 1825, Stuart was authorized to travel to both Lisbon and Rio de Janeiro for the purposes previously outlined. He was instructed to persuade Portugal to recognize Brazil and to travel to Rio de Janeiro, regardless of the result of his exhortation, to negotiate a commercial treaty.[211] This latter objective, of course, could be pursued more easily were Portugal's recognition of Brazil's independence accomplished. Otherwise, a dangerous precedent would be set – Britain's abrogation of its treaty obligations to Portugal – and Portuguese fealty to Britain jeopardized. Nor could Britain impose its will unilaterally, for this would violate the principle of non-interference and excite the jealousy of other European states. In this way, Brazil was considered entirely distinct from the Spanish American republics, with whom Canning signed treaties of "amity and commerce." As Canning (in)famously explained to the House of Commons in 1826 (in a speech advocating military support for the beleaguered Portuguese regency, as shall be explained), the New World was brought into legal existence to redress the imbalance of the Old, specifically to counter French ambitions, in league with its Bourbon ally Spain, to extend its influence across the Atlantic. Nevertheless, Portugal's stubborn conduct harmed British interests and, it was feared, threatened the survival of monarchy in Brazil. Stuart, then, while remaining an active-duty British diplomat leading a delegation empowered to negotiate a commercial treaty with (and recognition of) Brazil, simultaneously was named Portugal's minister plenipotentiary to Brazil for the purposes of concluding a treaty of recognition, an extraordinary dual role later lamented by Canning as "unexampled." The Portuguese government's decision to entrust such a mission to a foreign agent, it has been noted recently, was an "alarming sign of the deterioration of Portugal's international position."[212]

The arrival of the British mission caused more consternation than delight. Barbacena warned Dom Pedro about the Stuart mission in March 1825:

The British legation is composed entirely of Portuguese speakers. I have good reason to believe that this choice is to promote the frequent and direct communication between the legation and VM, something which should be avoided at all costs, because it will lead to an uncomfortable familiarity, such as Strangford enjoyed with your august father, and which Stuart will strive to replicate on his mission.[213]

---

[211] On the Stuart mission from a Brazilian nationalist viewpoint, see Freitas 1958, part 5; for a splendid account of its non-political dimensions, particularly the stunning watercolors produced by the artistic attaché Charles Landseer, see Bethell 2010.

[212] Alexandre 1993, p. 764.

[213] AMI, Barbacena to Dom Pedro, March 4, 1825.

It is clear that Brazilian officials were anxious to avoid a repeat of the 1808–10 agreements into which the Braganzas had entered under duress. Later in 1825, after Portuguese recognition had been won, yet while the Anglo-Brazilian treaties hung in the balance, Brazil's representative in London cautioned Dom Pedro against "putting Brazil under the influence [of Britain], as it would be difficult to extricate itself later, as the example of Portugal demonstrates ... Brazil should be the friend of Great Britain, but not its pupil."[214] Brazil's relations with Britain needed to be cordial without being intimate.

Britain, however, was operating under separate, unrelated constraints. Canning clearly was concerned about how British involvement, however limited, would be construed by other European courts:

Our position between the two countries is purely mediatorial. But should our mediation prove fruitless, there are questions arising out of the Treaty of 1810 to be settled with each party ... Portugal has from the beginning been apprised that such was the case, and has been repeatedly warned of the near approach of that period at which the revisal of the Treaty of 1810 would be pressed upon us as strongly at Rio de Janeiro as at Lisbon.

He reiterated and reaffirmed Wellington's position concerning Britain's stance should there be a renewed outbreak of hostilities between Portugal and Brazil. "In that war, our duty would be impartial neutrality," Canning stressed in his instructions to Stuart,

so long as Portugal, by continuing to claim Brazil as a colony, continued to give to that war the character of a civil contest ... [but should Portugal recognize Brazil's independence,] by placing Brazil in the situation of a foreign state towards Portugal, [this act] would give to Portugal a claim upon [Britain] in honour, and in good faith, for assistance in case of any attack from Brazil. Portugal has no right to call upon us for our aid in reducing a revolted colony, but she has a right to call for it against the aggression of a foreign power.[215]

Such instructions left little ambiguity. Portugal must abandon all "contre-projets" aimed at the retention of some connection (e.g. defensive alliance, loose federation, common foreign policy) with its former colony and recognize Brazil's absolute independence. Yet Brazil, too, must consider carefully its conduct, particularly with regard to any scheme to annex beleaguered Portugal's African colonies or else disturb the fragile equipoise of the former metropole's domestic politics. With that matter settled, the revision and extension of Britain's commercial

[214] AMI, II POB-25.11.1825-PES.C.1–2, Manuel Rodrigues Gameiro Pessoa [from London] to Dom Pedro I, November 27, 1825.
[215] Lill.L., Stuart MSS, Canning to Stuart, May 10, 1825.

treaties with each country, as well as Britain's recognition of Brazil's independence, could proceed.

Yet matters were not so clear-cut from Portugal's perspective, as reconstructed in a previous section, for a complete rupture with Brazil was never envisaged. A partial connection was the desired settlement. Due to the Braganza dynasty's survival on both continents, many Portuguese statesmen foresaw the eventual reunion of the two countries. But this anticipated occurrence made the terms of recognition crucial. It was precisely Brazil's potential to foment political disturbances in Portugal that prompted Porto Santo, then foreign secretary, to bring this possibility to Stuart's attention. Portugal would relinquish its reconquest ambitions, he conceded, assuming Brazil's payment of a £3 million (later reduced to £2 million) indemnity for royal and public property. But these considerations were subsidiary, from Porto Santo's perspective, to the stumbling block of the 1824 Brazilian Constitution. It was ill-suited either to "secure the integrity of the empire or to sustain monarchical government." Its continued existence, he prophesied, undermined the "tranquility and happiness" of Portugal: Brazil would "export subversive doctrines," leaving the former metropole "contaminated." The Braganza dynasty would therefore be imperiled in the Old World and the New, and the likelihood of interference by the Congress System increased.[216] Porto Santo was particularly troubled, presciently, as it turned out, by the prospect of the imposition of Brazil's Constitution on Portugal after Dom Pedro's eventual succession. Porto Santo's own political preferences aside, he foresaw the problems inherent in a plan to place both Crowns on the head of an emperor whose refusal to forsake certain incendiary political principles made him anathema to Portugal's homegrown anti-constitutionalists as well as to the leading states of Europe. The delicate plans to secure the reunion of Portugal with Brazil, to exclude Dom Miguel and his reactionary cabal from power, and to install a self-consciously moderate, reformist (yet unmistakably monarchical) regime were jeopardized by Dom Pedro's obstinate infatuation with constitutionalism. The reunion of the Crowns would be complicated by the incompatibility of the systems of government prevailing in each state. Porto Santo therefore insisted on the 1824 Constitution's abolition as a precondition of Portuguese recognition.[217]

---

[216] Lill.L., Stuart MSS, Porto Santo to Stuart, May 23, 1825.

[217] Bonnabeau 1974, pp. 42–44. The suggestion was not as outlandish as it sounds: Dom Pedro had supposedly offered abolition of the 1824 Constitution in exchange for Austrian recognition of his regime earlier that year. See Bonnabeau 1974, p. 47.

Whatever Stuart's personal views (he probably sympathized with Porto Santo), any effort to sidetrack the negotiations, aimed solely to secure the recognition of Brazil's independence, in order to revise the Brazilian Constitution was thwarted by Canning. The foreign secretary warned Stuart that "it is not upon a preference for this or that form of government, with which (whatever may be our speculative opinions) we have practically no concern; but it is upon the broad general principle of non-interference with the internal institutions of other states, which has so often, within these last few years, been proclaimed in His Majesty's name."[218] But it was not only the European Powers' reactions that Canning feared. He foresaw fierce reaction in Brazil itself to the fortification of the monarchy or the removal of recently granted constitutional guarantees: "if there were to be any suspicion excited of an intention to do away [with] the checks by which the monarch is restrained (in theory rather than in practice), a conclusion would probably be to sweep away both the monarchy and the monarch."[219] Stuart was thus forbidden from confronting such matters directly during the negotiation.

Stuart's position, however, soon became more complicated. In August, Dom Pedro made Stuart his plenipotentiary and mediator for potential disputes arising with Portugal after recognition of independence, a signal to the Portuguese authorities, particularly his father, who highly esteemed Stuart, that Brazil was negotiating in good faith. Stuart subsequently was named, in 1825, Dom João's plenipotentiary to Brazil for the purpose of concluding a commercial treaty, thus further intermingling his roles and competing commitments. But multiple, sometimes conflicting roles did not imply protracted negotiation. Dom Pedro and his advisors were desperate to secure recognition. The Cisplatine War over the Banda Oriental, which threatened to erupt into an international conflict pitting a coalition of Spanish-American Republics against monarchical Brazil, to say nothing of the republican threat simmering within the empire's own borders, forced the hand of Brazilian negotiators.[220] Portugal's recognition of Brazil, though it deferred many weighty issues for subsequent negotiations, was regarded as Stuart's diplomatic triumph. Even A'Court, no great friend of Stuart's, wrote

---

[218] Lill.L., Stuart MSS, Canning to Stuart, December 8, 1825; though this stance departed from British policy of 1823, when Canning sought (in vain) to persuade Spain to change its constitution in order to avert a French invasion. See Schroeder 1994, p. 626.

[219] Lill L., Stuart MSS, Canning to Stuart, June 25, 1825.

[220] Bonnabeau 1974, p. 223; on the South American diplomatic context in general, see Seckinger 1984.

ebulliently to Canning that "a great deal is due to the ability displayed throughout the whole business by Sir Charles Stuart. In the hands of one less gifted with talent, firmness, perseverance and unalterable temper, it is more than probable that the mediation might still have failed … the Treaty of Rio may be considered as setting the final seal on the total emancipation of America."[221]

Hyperbole aside, the independence of Ibero-America, and the preservation of monarchy there, may indeed have received a boost from the Treaty. But the problem of royal succession remained unresolved and the Treaty's silence ensured that the separation augured by recognition would be incomplete. To the matter of succession should be added the failure to reach a trade agreement between Portugal and Brazil, the economic consequences of which for both countries were immense. Ambiguity would characterize their connection for at least nine years. Given the muddle, it is unsurprising that British policy was inconsistent. Canning's shifting, and often ill-defined, position regarding the Portuguese succession is indicative of indecision, if not vacillation. A'Court made clear that succession was the most pressing issue and that Portuguese domestic politics would be stalled until it was clarified. The possibility of Dom Pedro's succession, A'Court warned, was anathema to extreme partisans of all political convictions: "the Ultras, both royalist and liberal, would have had Dom Pedro's right formally annulled … and accuse him of having prepared a *dose de agoa de colonia* (Eau de Cologne) which the nation ought not to swallow. To understand this pleasantry, it must be recollected that *colonia* means colony, as well as cologne."[222] Having failed to receive a reply to his repeated enquiries, he asked Canning directly, with some exasperation: "Again, what is the real wish of the British government with respect to the separation of the Brazils? Is it desired to make that separation absolute and entire, or is it an object of our policy to reunite the two crowns on the head of Dom Pedro? Is Sir Charles Stuart's treaty the whole of what we wish, or the first step toward what we wish?"[223] In late 1825, Canning unequivocally replied to A'Court, stating that "Don Pedro remains undoubted heir to the Crown of Portugal, according to the fundamental laws of that kingdom."[224]

When approached by Portuguese diplomats, however, Canning refused to guarantee the Brazilian emperor's succession. Nevertheless,

[221] A'Court to Canning, November 13, 1825, in Webster 1938, vol. II, p. 269.
[222] TNA, FO 63/299, A'Court to Canning, November 24, 1825, fos. 200, 200v.
[223] TNA, FO 63/299, A'Court to Canning, December 9, 1825, fo. 246v.
[224] Canning to A'Court, November 23, 1825, in Webster 1938, vol. II, p. 272.

in a letter to Palmela, whom he knew intimately and esteemed highly, he stated that "the British government is far from unwilling to see the Crowns of Portugal and Brazil united on the same head."[225] But Canning noted that Britain was unable "to guarantee beforehand an unknown settlement which is to be established by any authority, the nature of which is not yet known."[226] It is unclear what, if any, were the practical consequences, or envisioned configurations, of these excruciatingly vague verbal gymnastics. The official correspondence is deafeningly silent on the matter of how, for example, Dom Pedro might govern both states in his own lifetime, the practical arrangements it would entail and constitutional mechanisms (or modifications) such a move would necessitate. Canning's subsequent frenzied effort to prevent the reunion of Portugal and Brazil after 1826 raises the possibility that his vagueness formed part of a bargaining strategy to lure Brazil into signing a new commercial treaty with Britain. For it is only after that treaty was signed that the Foreign Office's position shifted away from the possibility of uniting the two Crowns. However, Canning's shifting position could also be explained by the unexpected outrage in Portugal occasioned by the *Carta*'s arrival, which augured a fresh spate of radical revolutions or more virulent strains of reaction.

In late 1825 to early 1826, however, Britain could not extricate itself from Luso-Brazilian affairs. Independence appeared, in fact, to have complicated and deepened that involvement. Brazilian and Portuguese officials continued to look to London for guidance as they navigated the equally treacherous shoals of anti-monarchical revolution and arch-absolutist reaction. It is in this context that Stuart reappeared to assume a leading role. In addition to serving as chief negotiator for Britain as it sought to extend the expiring 1810 Treaty, Stuart remained embroiled in the negotiations for a post-independence commercial treaty between Portugal and Brazil, shuttling between Lisbon and Rio. As previously noted, he had been empowered by Dom João to represent his interests, a position he added to the equivalent service he rendered to Dom Pedro, who bestowed upon him the title of Marquês de Angra (Azores). In short, he was representing three courts simultaneously in two separate negotiations, in addition to serving as de facto mediator between Brazil and Portugal. Canning was undoubtedly impressed by Stuart's dexterity and ability to ingratiate himself to two monarchs, insinuating himself so intimately in their affairs. Yet the diverse roles he had assumed, none of which conflicted explicitly with British policy

---

[225] Canning to Palmela, February 3, 1826, in Canning 1887, vol. I, p. 7.
[226] Ibid., p. 10.

except insofar as they threatened to drag Britain into conflicts far beyond the scope of its immediate interests, made Stuart's position dangerously ambiguous and highly irregular.

Stuart's behavior during mediation between Portugal and Brazil caused Canning great consternation. His monarchist sympathies were well known and infuriated Canning, who detected in his dispatches "the highest strain of ultraism" while his conduct betrayed commitment to the "highest principles of legitimacy."[227] Stuart had strenuously denied similar allegations on earlier occasions, and rebuked Canning in a strongly worded, snide letter, saying that he "was assured that his health, coupled with a wish for a constitutional government, was drunk at several of the public meetings that took place in Lisbon yesterday."[228] Canning's fury with Stuart's brash conduct and undisguised irreverence, however justified, could have little effect. Besides his successful mediation of the August 1825 Luso-Brazilian Treaty, Stuart remained too deeply embroiled in too many delicate affairs to be unceremoniously sacked. His unexampled, privileged position – representing, in varying capacities, three governments – also meant that he was perfectly placed to observe, and participate in, affairs well beyond the scope of the formal instructions he received from London. As he shuttled between Rio and Lisbon, his involvement in the impending Portuguese succession crisis was almost inevitable.

Dom João's failing health in the first months of 1826, which obliged him to nominate a Regency council to govern temporarily in his stead, made the 1825 Treaty's failure to clarify the succession glaringly obvious, and its remedy urgent. In a private dispatch, A'Court implored Stuart, then in Rio de Janeiro, to act decisively, for Portugal's political future hung in the balance: "you will see how important it is, in every point of view, that the successor's pleasure should be expressed immediately, without an instant's loss of time ... I can only repeat, lose no time!"[229] Stuart needed little encouragement to spring into action.

---

[227] Canning to Viscount Granville, March 6, 1826, in Canning 1887, vol. I, p. 19. However, the ideological dimensions of their conflict should not be overstated, as clashing personalities and professional rivalry were a more likely source of their dispute. Canning noted that "a greater, at least a fresher cause, of grievance was my steady, repeated refusal to give him a roving commission to all the New States of South America"; see the previously cited letter to Granville of March 6. This great personal animosity did not prevent Stuart's daughter, Charlotte, from marrying Canning's son (and future first Viceroy of India), Charles ("Carlo"), in 1835. See Franklin 2008, p. 245.

[228] Stuart to Canning, May 14, 1825, quoted in Franklin 2008, p. 172.

[229] Lill.L., Stuart MSS, A'Court [in Lisbon] to Stuart [in Rio de Janeiro], March 7, 1826.

While not matching Strangford's intimacy with, and influence on, the emperor's father, he managed to convert himself into a routinely consulted authority and genial companion to Dom Pedro. But the resolution of such a vexing matter tested the capacity of even such an experienced diplomat. The ink on the 1825 Luso-Brazilian Treaty had barely dried, and a further, clarifying convention concerning royal succession would both excite nativist outrage in Brazil and confirm Portuguese reactionaries' fears of an impending deluge of "*agoa da colonia*," perhaps toppling an infirm Dom João and his all-too-brazen son in a single stroke. Options were restricted still further by Dom João's frequently expressed, but never publicly proclaimed, desire to have his son succeed him.[230] The eventuality of Dom Pedro's succession, however, became a focus of exchanges between A'Court and Canning. All of the potential arrangements – Dom Pedro's abdication of the throne, the marriage of Dom Miguel to Dona Maria, the promulgation of a *Carta* – were broached by mid March 1826.[231] Dom João's death, and the immediate dispatch of a courier from Lisbon to Rio de Janeiro, meant that the crisis came to a head sooner than anticipated by British officials. These circumstances left Stuart without clear instructions from the Foreign Office.

In truth, however, Stuart probably relished the extemporaneous conduct afforded by such a dramatic, pivotal event. He was not caught unaware, as the subject of the succession had cropped up repeatedly in the negotiations resulting in the August 1825 Treaty he mediated, though no determination had been made. In the final months of 1825 and the first months of 1826, the topic had been raised afresh in Stuart's audiences with the emperor. In October 1825, he reported that "HRH's views with respect to Portugal have undergone a considerable change, and that he is tenacious of every right which contributes to secure his succession to the throne of that kingdom ... among the projects he entertains for the future regeneration of the government, [one is] the establishment of a charter, and other schemes of which it is not easy to trace the source."[232] In his dispatch from Bahia, six months later, Stuart noted again that the emperor broached the possibility of Dona Maria's marriage to her uncle, but later recoiled at the suggestion: "the possible contingency of further male issue, and the desire to retain the moveable part of his inheritance (jewels, gold etc.), have, for the present,

[230] "You may be assured, Sir, that the guarantee of the succession in the direct line, should the direct heir be willing to accept it, is the thing which is nearest to the heart of [Dom João]." See TNA, FO 63/307, A'Court to Canning, February 4, 1826.
[231] TNA, FO 63/307, A'Court and Canning, March 14 and 16, 1826.
[232] TNA, FO 13/5, Stuart to Canning, October 20, 1825, fos. 22v–23.

banished the idea from His IM's mind."[233] The most salient aspects of
these dispatches are Dom Pedro's plan, foreseen by Porto Santo, and
presaged by his correspondence with Dom João following the *Abrilada*,
to issue a *Carta* for Portugal and to maintain as firm a link as politically
feasible to Europe, for reasons of material support, and to secure the
succession of his direct male heir to the Brazilian throne.

Into this cauldron of considerations, Stuart's personal views must
be introduced. It was widely believed at the Foreign Office that his
assessment of the nascent Ibero-American states' prospects was cyn-
ically bleak, that independence was a doomed, ephemeral experiment,
and that even monarchical regimes, like Brazil's, were endangered
without a firm connection to Europe.[234] One contemporary historian labeled him a "persistent Cassandra, predicting the formation of
an anti-Brazilian coalition and conjuring up apocalyptic visions of
the destruction of the monarchy and the fragmentation of Brazil into
a number of republics."[235] This assessment is largely accurate, but it
should be tempered by the fact that Stuart's views were informed by
empirical observation, not guided by mere ideology. Any preconceived
notions he may have harbored were confirmed as he traveled widely in
Brazil during 1825–26. In early 1825, as recognition hung in the balance, he remarked that "the true limits of the Prince Royal's authority
do not extend beyond the two provinces of Rio de Janeiro and Minas
Geraes." The other provinces, too, were "gradually giving way to local
habits better suited to a federal government than to the maintenance of
the monarchical system of which they are supposed to form a part."[236]
Writing from Bahia less than a year later, he said: "I am assured that,
from Pernambuco to the frontier of Cayenne, [Dom Pedro] has not a
man in arms."[237] The emperor's comportment, erratic and impulsive,
moreover, foreshadowed trouble. Stuart was repelled by his desperately
arbitrary conduct, including the

publication of numerous decrees, and introducing material changes in each
department of the provincial administration ... it is a fortunate circumstance
that the imperial visit did not extend to Pernambuco, for I am assured that
a similar course in that presidency would not only have compromised the

---

[233] TNA, FO 13/18, Stuart to Canning, March 11, 1826, fos. 123v–24.
[234] As Canning made clear to Stuart after he recalled him to London following the
promulgation of the *Carta*, "I was not unaware how much [Stuart] disapproved those
views of Lord Liverpool and mine (for I have no right to call them mine exclusively)
respecting the recognition of the new states, which had been adopted by the British
government." See Lill.L., Stuart MSS, Canning to Stuart, August 28, 1826.
[235] Seckinger 1984, p. 146.
[236] TNA, FO 13/4, Stuart to Canning, July 16, 1825, fo. 98.
[237] TNA, FO 13/18, Stuart to Canning, March 15, 1826, fo. 146v.

tranquility of the northern provinces of Brazil, but have endangered the existence of their present connection with the central government.[238]

Stuart's impressions of Brazil, and his conception of strategies best suited to preserve New World monarchies, undoubtedly infused the advice he offered to Dom Pedro, who increasingly solicited his counsel and shared his more intimate thoughts immediately preceding the arrival of the news of Dom João's death in Rio. They also provide a glimpse into Dom Pedro's interior world before the succession crisis, particularly his attitude toward the inviolability of law, the tenuous nature of his authority, and his dynastic preoccupations on the eve of his hemisphere-rattling decisions.

Stuart's dispatches not only clarify his role in the elaboration of the *Carta*, but also Dom Pedro's intentions with regard to Portugal. Upon learning of his father's death, on April 26, Dom Pedro admitted to Stuart that "impossible as it was that the two countries should ever be reunited, the two Crowns might ... be placed on the same head, provided he should find it possible to govern Portugal from thence." The following day, April 27, Dom Pedro "declared his intention to accept the Crown of Portugal ... he then talked of conciliating the affections of the Portuguese by giving them a constitutional charter and, if the war should turn out unsuccessful in the South, of obtaining military succour from Portugal with a view to diminish the burthen which is already severely felt in this country." Stuart claimed that he pointed out the difficulties of convening a Cortes: even in its "ancient and legitimate" form, it would be "viewed with jealousy in Spain and France." Stuart reported that the emperor's advisors, particularly Marquês de Paranaguá, "entered fully into the spirit of this objection," to the extent that "for several days, no other constitutional system, but such as should be founded upon the ancient institutions of Portugal, was thought of."[239] Stuart's dispatch confirms other previously cited accounts of Dom Pedro's reaction, particularly regarding his vacillation, but adds two new, important elements: first, Dom Pedro viewed the grant of a constitution in the context of his strategy for the Cisplatine War, using the enticement of a *Carta* to gain a military alliance or else recourse to funds; and, second, Dom Pedro's enthrallment with written constitutions informed by new-fangled political ideas had waned, to the extent that he gladly dispensed with a Cortes to appease "jealous" European powers, something he earlier had held to be consonant with Portugal's "ancient constitution."

[238] TNA, FO 13/18, Stuart to Canning, April 15, 1826, fos. 152–54v.
[239] TNA, FO 13/18, Stuart to Canning, April 30, 1826, fos. 245–49 passim.

Yet Stuart's claim that, from April 27, "no other constitutional system ... was thought of," is suspect. The *Carta* was promulgated on April 29. Stuart knew of its existence on April 28, at the latest. This inaccuracy notwithstanding, Dom Pedro appears to have announced his intention with regard to the Portuguese succession on either the evening of April 27 or the following morning. Even an apparently unequivocal pronouncement, dated by Stuart as April 28, however, that he would assume the government of Portugal "for his children, until such time as the Cortes should decide which child is to wear the Crown and thereby complete the separation of the two countries, and that he should convoke the Ancient Cortes for that purpose immediately," was retracted soon after it was uttered. After a further bout of ambivalence, he determined to grant a *Carta*, marry his daughter to Dom Miguel, and abdicate the throne after this last event had been consummated. Revealingly, it was only at this advanced stage that Sir Charles deemed it proper to intervene ("I thought the consequences of this change too important to be passed over without comment"). At an audience with Dom Pedro, he informed the emperor that "it was absolutely necessary that the constitutional changes which he meditated [were announced] in such a manner that they should not appear to emanate from his Brazilian advisors," but rather from the emperor himself, in his capacity as Dom Pedro IV of Portugal. This advice may explain why all references to the Council of State, whose 1823 *Projecto* formed the template for the *Carta*, were expunged when it was published. Dom Pedro, according to Stuart, was loath to abide by Portugal's "ancient institutions," which were not, "in every respect, suited to the present day." Furthermore, Stuart reported, Dom Pedro held that the "Cortes was a constituent body subject to a thousand inconveniences which a charter alone could remove." Dom Pedro then "produced his project of the constitution already completed, to the compilation of which he had devoted the greater part of the week and the joy with which he spoke of its contents shows that the promulgation of this act is the principal inducement held out to him by his advisors for the abdication of the crown of Portugal." Dom Pedro told Stuart that "[the *Carta*] upheld the prerogatives of the sovereign, and the power of the nobility, [and] he could not coincide in the fears I seemed to entertain respecting its possible effect in other [European] countries."[240]

---

[240] Ibid., fos. 253–62v passim. Gomes da Silva's recollection of Dom Pedro's attitude toward Portuguese institutions was rather different: Dom Pedro gave Portugal a constitution "the beauty of which was that it only changed the manner of dress [of old institutions], for the passage of time had forced a change in old wardrobes." See Gomes da Silva 1831, p. 91.

If Stuart's recounting is accurate (and there is some cause to doubt its veracity and completeness on certain points), the *Carta* reflected Dom Pedro's deepening misgivings concerning representative institutions, but his desire to appear eminently pro-constitutional. It also is evident that he conceived of the *Carta*, particularly his control over appointments to the Regency, as a vehicle to maintain a firm and free hand in Portuguese affairs for the foreseeable future, while simultaneously appearing to have voluntarily abdicated and divested himself of further involvement, a move designed to placate Portuguese ultras wary of another splash of *"agoa da colonia"* as well as Brazilian nativists fearful of their new nation's continued connection to the Old World.[241] Dona Maria, age seven, could hardly be expected to marry her uncle for some time, during which period Dom Miguel would remain subordinate to a regency council named by Dom Pedro. On its surface, and from the perspective of its fabricators, then, the *Carta*, and its attendant decrees, was an ingenious solution to multiple problems: it would mollify hostile parties in Portugal, heal the familial rift plaguing the Braganzas since the *Abrilada*, and cleverly postpone, in a politically palatable manner, Dom Pedro's relinquishment of influence in Portuguese affairs.

Two of the most controversial questions after the *Carta*'s delivery were, first, Stuart's role in its elaboration and, second, the rationale behind his selection as courier. These were hardly mundane or trivial matters: fervent Anglophobes saw Britain's nefarious hand in the entire affair whereas Stuart's involvement implied Britain's endorsement of a political solution bound to rankle Europe's leading powers. Stuart does appear to have been consulted regularly between April 26 and 29, 1826, and he certainly was present throughout most of the crucial deliberation, with the notable exception of the *Carta*'s redaction. But the extent and nature of his influence is difficult to ascertain. It is known that Dom Pedro consulted Stuart on which nobles to nominate for the *Pares* created by the *Carta*. In Stuart's presence, according to Stuart's testimony, Dom Pedro "read through the names of the Peers, commenting at the same time upon the conduct and character of every individual," expressing special vitriol for Subserra and Vilareal, judgments concerning which Stuart must have acquiesced, as their

---

[241] Dom Pedro's intentions were understood immediately upon the arrival of the *Carta* in Europe. The exiled Subserra was incredulous that during the minority of Maria II Dom Pedro reserved right to nominate members of the regency, exclaiming "he is de facto king of Portugal!" See BNL, Reservados, MSS 149, doc. 127, Notes of Conde de Subserra [in Auteuil, France], June 24, 1826.

names were omitted.[242] Lord Howard de Walden, then a junior diplomat accompanying Stuart on his mission, downplayed Stuart's role in the manufacture of the *Carta*.[243] He also confirmed that Stuart was a reluctant messenger. As de Walden recalled, "the Emperor again urged C.S. to become the bearer of these instruments [i.e. the *Carta*], and in consenting at length to be so, his Excellency protested against all responsibility for the contents thereof."[244]

Stuart's connection to the *Carta* forms part of a broader pattern of Anglo-Latin American relations in this period, evident in negotiations over the slave trade and later over the Banda Oriental. Britain's capacity for "direct manipulation" remained "limited," and its influence often proved "less awesome than it might appear."[245] But perception mattered, and Britain's influence was often overestimated, with a combination of envy and disgust, by contemporary observers. For this reason, whatever his actual role, Stuart expected a great backlash for his actions from the Foreign Office. In his April 30 dispatch to Canning, sent just prior to his departure from Rio for Lisbon, he blamed his superior for having failed to furnish him with instructions "sufficiently decisive" on the Portuguese succession to inform his conversations with Dom Pedro. He claimed that he had been compelled to "maintain a reserve upon many points, where a more active interference might perhaps have been conformable to the intentions of my Court."[246] Stuart was exhausted by juggling multiple diplomatic roles for more than a year. In a July 14 letter, he advised a friend, "whatever misfortunate occurs to you through life, never go to the Brazils."[247] Yet a week later, evidently rejuvenated, he expressed pride in his handiwork, boasting that his "operations have been attended with all the success I could wish. I do not know if you and your friends approve of the course that has been followed, but, depend on it, it will be the salvation of [Portugal], and ... places us on higher

---

[242] TNA, FO 13/10, Stuart to Canning, May 4, 1826.

[243] As de Walden wrote, "The Emperor of Brazil, in conversing with Charles Stuart upon His Majesty's views with respect to Portugal, talked of giving that kingdom a constitutional charter. This communication induced C.S. to point out the necessity of acting with caution in the affair, whose efforts in that respect had a temporary effect." See his "Memorandum: The Conveyance of the Portuguese Charter to Europe by Sir Charles Stuart," in TNA, FO 360/1, Howard de Walden Papers, n.d.; Charles Augustus Ellis, 6th Baron Howard de Walden, would serve as British envoy to Lisbon 1834–46.

[244] "Memorandum: The Conveyance of the Portuguese Charter to Europe by Sir Charles Stuart," in TNA, FO 360/1, Howard de Walden Papers, n.d.

[245] Seckinger 1984, pp. 163–64; though British influence was significant in certain ways. See, for example, Brown 2008.

[246] TNA, FO 13/18, Stuart to Canning, April 30, 1826, fos. 253–53v.

[247] TNA, FO 360/4, Stuart to Lord Lowther, July 14, 1826.

ground than ever."[248] His self-aggrandizement reached its apogee with his wife, to whom he bragged: "[I do not] believe a more successful or remarkable embassy than mine ever went out of England."[249] Even in official correspondence, he believed that the *Carta* would prove a panacea for Portugal's ills. He was certain that it would meet with popular approval: "the opponents of the system, which the Emperor of Brazil has thought it expedient to adopt for the government of this country, being unable to struggle against the divided will of the great majority of the nation, their numbers have gradually diminished."[250] To Dom Pedro, he wrote that "[the *Carta*] has already produced very beneficial results, by restraining the exaltation of the liberals and conciliating the good will of the royalists."[251]

The reaction in British circles to the *Carta*'s arrival was varied, but they were uniformly at variance with Stuart's self-congratulatory mood. One of the reasons for displeasure was that Stuart's ship, conveying the courier and the *Carta*, arrived in Lisbon well after another ship carrying the news had arrived in France. Thus, by the time Stuart crossed the Atlantic, the *Carta* (or news of its contents) was in political play. Its reception could not be managed. The most pressing concerns for A'Court and Canning were, first, the perception of Britain's implied endorsement due to Stuart's service as courier; and, second, dispelling the fear that the *Carta* was a stalking horse for either the eventual reunion of Portugal with Brazil or Dom Pedro's indefinite direction of Portuguese affairs. With regard to the first matter, very little could be done in the short term to redress the damage. Anglophobia had been roused; British denials seemed implausible. British mediation in the August 1825 Luso-Brazilian Treaty had caused outrage in Lisbon.[252] The arrival of the *Carta* only exacerbated those sentiments. As A'Court reported, "The appearance of Sir Charles Stuart's (an Englishman) name in the business has excited a very great jealousy, though it is evident that he can act in other character than that of Portuguese

---

[248] Stuart to Lord Lowther, July 22, 1826, quoted in Franklin 2008, p. 188. Yet Stuart may have protested too much. During Dom Miguel's reign, Santarém, then serving as Foreign Minister, would inform the Portuguese representative in Berlin that Stuart had told him that he had been "against the concession of the *Carta*, even though the entire world thinks he was behind this missive. He rejects this accusation and is therefore ready to do everything in his power to help consolidate the current system." Santarém, quoted in A. Vianna 1922, p. 35.

[249] TNA, FO 360/4, Stuart to Lady Stuart, July 15, 1826.

[250] Lill.L., Stuart MSS, Stuart to ?, July 29, 1826, memorandum entitled "Favourable Aspect of the Affairs in this Country."

[251] Stuart to Dom Pedro I, July 16, 1826, in Franklin 2008.

[252] "The angry feeling toward us on account of the Brazilian treaty has not yet subsided." See TNA, FO 63/299, A'Court to Canning, November 24, 1825, fo. 200.

plenipotentiary."[253] Canning did the obvious thing to save face, and recalled Stuart from Lisbon.[254] The public justification for Stuart's recall was not the conveyance of the *Carta*, but a second offense, no less important: that of bungling the Anglo-Brazilian commercial treaty. The treaty negotiated by Stuart was rejected by the British government and renegotiated later in 1826 by Robert Gordon. Gordon also concluded an Anglo-Brazilian slave trade accord in November, by which Brazil promised to end the trade by 1830. In August 1827, an Anglo-Brazilian commercial treaty was signed, which imposed a maximum tariff of 15 percent on British goods.[255]

Removing Stuart was accomplished without delay, but the second, more explosive issue of the realignment of Portugal with Brazil was more complex. There is some indication that Stuart realized that he had been duped, or at least misled, concerning Dom Pedro's deep-seated aspirations. Soon after arriving in Lisbon, in a "secret & confidential" dispatch, he claimed to have uncovered, in the form of a memorandum, plans for a clandestine alliance between Dom Pedro and unnamed Portuguese officials. "This memorandum fell into my hands on the day I left Rio," he claimed, entitled "O Pacto de Familia" between Brazil and Portugal.[256] Canning reached the same conclusion, without the discovery of additional documents. He interpreted the *Carta*'s arrival as inaugurating a new era of Brazilian-Portuguese cooperation. His

---

[253] TNA, FO 63/308, A'Court to Canning, July 5, 1826. But, in private correspondence, Canning notified Stuart that "it is the desire and determination of HM government to avoid, as far as possible, the appearance of any direct influence of British agency in the establishment of the new order of things in Portugal." See TNA, FO 13/17, Canning to Stuart (draft), July 22, 1826, fo. 121v.

[254] Stuart believed himself to be disgraced permanently, his future prospects bleak: "I have no chance of employment or promotion and shall only be maltreated and abused for measures which are perfectly correct or for errors in which I bore no part." See TNA, FO 360/4, Stuart to Lady Elizabeth Stuart, July 23, 1826. His friends, including Charles Vaughan, the British Ambassador to the USA, wrote "I cannot but regret the strange treatment which your useful services upon your last mission has brought down upon you. To me, it is inexplicable ... my nerves have been upon the tremble ever since [I heard], and as I happen to be employed in a country which at this moment occupies a good deal of the attention of our government, & with a bargaining, tenacious people, like the Americans, ever since what has happened in your case, I dream of nothing but wiggings, & disavowals & recalls." Still Vaughan discouraged Stuart from leaving the diplomatic service, suggesting that Stuart seek a return to the embassy in France. See Lill.L., Stuart MSS, Vaughan to Stuart, December 5, 1826; Stuart was later rehabilitated by Wellington, who secured for him the title Baron Stuart de Rothesay (Rothesay being on the Isle of Bute), and sent back to France for further diplomatic service during the July Monarchy.

[255] Bethell 1970b, pp. 57–60.

[256] Lill.L., Stuart MSS, Stuart [from Lisbon] to ?, July 14, 1826, marked "Secret & Confidential."

dispatch to A'Court was unambiguous: "The sooner the separation of Portugal from Brazil is definitively settled, the better ... [you should] discourage all such [arrangements] as tend to prolong the period of an ambiguous and undefined connection between them ... above all things, Y.E. is to discourage any engagement between Portugal and Brazil in the nature of an offensive or even defensive alliance."[257] The specter of a loose, or defensive, alliance – alluded to so often in 1824–25, whether in Dom Pedro's correspondence with his father or in Palmela's failed *"contre-projet"* – appeared to Canning, and other European statesmen, to have been resuscitated surreptitiously, after having been blocked explicitly by the terms of the August 1825 Treaty. Porto Santo's dire warning of the dangers of diplomatic recognition without the abolition of the 1824 Constitution now appeared justified. Canning wrote again to A'Court in October, observing that

it is impossible not to infer (as is inferred at Rio de Janeiro) from these circumstances that the Emperor Dom Pedro looks to keep the management of Portugal as long as possible in his own hands, not without a secret notion of falling back upon that kingdom if anything untoward should occur to him in Brazil ... Full credit must always be given to him for the sacrifice [i.e. abdication], but once made it cannot be recalled.[258]

Canning's presentiment – the planned reunion of Portugal with Brazil – was confirmed by A'Court. In his November 1 dispatch, for example, he reported that, "for some days past, decrees of the Emperor of Brazil have been in circulation here, giving titles, honors and commands to Portuguese subjects, and in the kingdom of Portugal ... such an interference in domestic affairs – with the internal administration of this country –, is considered to be at variance with the Emperor's engagements."[259] A'Court, aware of the resentment toward Dom Pedro harbored by both liberals and royalists, assured Canning that the political arrangements stipulated by the *Carta* were a dead letter. "You may be quite sure, Sir," he told Canning, that "anti-Brazilian feeling here is too strong and too general to allow of Portugal's being governed for any definite period from the other side of the Atlantic."[260] To Stuart, whom A'Court blamed for this political hurricane, he was frankly insulting, deprecating his grasp of Portuguese politics. "It appears to me," he told Stuart, "that you do not yet thoroughly know these people ... things

[257] TNA, FO 63/306, Canning to A'Court, August 30, 1826.
[258] TNA, FO 63/306, Canning to A'Court, October 11, 1826.
[259] TNA, FO 63/310, A'Court to Canning, November 1, 1826.
[260] A'Court to Canning, October 26, 1826, in Webster 1938, vol. II, p. 275.

here are not going on very prosperously here – your ___ from Rio has proved a sort of Pandora's Box."[261]

A'Court cannot be accused of hyperbole. The *Carta*'s arrival shattered the relative, perhaps false, calm prevailing among European states in mid 1826. While the *Carta* would be praised by Benjamin Constant, it was hardly consonant with the prevailing political mood. The period 1825–26 was the high point of political reaction, in France and elsewhere, symbolized by Charles X's lavish, backward-gazing coronation and the ultra-royalist attacks on the 1814 *Chartre* in the second half of the 1820s.[262] Canning operated under no illusions: the calamitous scale of the European reaction was incalculable. "I cannot reason," he sighed, "from probabilities in respect to the proceedings of a diplomatic agent placed in a position, so far as I know, unexampled."[263] He was correct. Metternich lamented that "nothing is more problematical than the application of the deplorable work of Dom Pedro. It would be difficult to know how Portugal is governed now, for each day presents singular anomalies."[264] In Spain, Dom Pedro's actions reportedly caused "great and widespread disgust," while the Spanish emissary to Russia recorded that Tsar Nicholas was alarmed by the "maniacal and unexpected" events transpiring in Portugal.[265] By August, as indicated in the previous section, anti-*Cartista* uprisings had spread throughout Portugal, and Spanish officials were aiding rebels, who openly proclaimed their support for Dom Miguel's acclamation.

Britain was placed in an unenviable position. The bickering between Stuart and Canning notwithstanding, Canning was privately convinced that not even Stuart's outsized ego could have induced him to midwife the *Carta*'s birth. Canning knew that Stuart always had advised Dom Pedro against abdication of the Portuguese throne, in spite of the emperor's repeated efforts "in moments of difficulty or pique … to cut matters short by abdication."[266] Such a view was not necessarily at variance with British policy. Canning always had hoped that Dom Pedro's reliance on dynastic connections in Europe to prop up

---

[261] Lill.L., A'Court to Stuart, October 27, 1826.

[262] Lyons 2006, pp. 34–36.

[263] TNA, FO 63/306, Canning to A'Court, August 19, 1826.

[264] Metternich to Count Bombelles, September 7, 1826, in Metternich 1970, vol. IV, p. 330.

[265] First quotation, Duque de Villahermosa to Duque de Infantado, June 23, 1826; second quotation from a report written by D. Juan Paez de la Cadena, Spanish emissary to Moscow, September 26, 1826. Both quoted in Brancato 1988, pp. 470–71; J. Fontana 2006 observed that Ferdinand VII was "obsessed with the problem of Portugal," p. 217.

[266] Canning to Granville, July 3, 1826, in Canning 1887, p. 68.

his throne would make him more malleable. He concluded that Stuart would neither champion a *Carta* so inconsistent with his own political principles nor advocate a dynastic arrangement destined to perturb the post-1815 European geopolitical edifice of which he was a (minor) architect. Though Canning insisted that Stuart had possessed "no authority to act in any matter of this kind," he recognized the opportunity that Stuart's conduct afforded him. He conceded that he could not "justly disapprove of what [Stuart] had done."[267]

Canning's personal views aside, the *Carta*'s arrival upset the Peninsula's fragile equipoise. Miguelists had fled to Spain while Spanish liberals (including those in exile) converged on Lisbon. Fernando VII was prepared to authorize General Francisco de Longa's invasion, which would have endangered Europe's balance of power, if not precipitated a larger conflagration. The British prime minister, Lord Liverpool, was anxious to avoid a military clash with Spain and indefinite involvement in Portuguese politics, a position he shared with the Cabinet. The mobilization and dispatch of an expeditionary force amounted to a policy of deterrence, meant to avert conflict, which played well with sectors of domestic opinion demanding solidarity with liberal movements abroad and also with isolationists nervous about continental entanglements.[268] In a December speech in the House of Commons, delivered chiefly in order to rally support for sending four thousand troops to the Tagus, at the request of the Portuguese government, Canning daintily denied that Britain was the "contriver and imposer of the Portuguese Constitution." He affirmed that "it is not [Britain's] duty or her practice to offer suggestions for the internal regulation of foreign states." This disavowal notwithstanding, Canning noted that it was "impossible for an Englishman not to wish [the *Carta*] well," since it was "founded on principles in a great degree similar to those of our own, though differently modified."[269] Canning justified military intervention to prevent Portugal from being "trampled down." British involvement was necessary "not to rule, not to dictate, not to prescribe constitutions, but to defend and preserve the independence of an ally" and to prevent full-blown "national degradation."[270] This high-blown rhetoric aside, the expeditionary force's remit was limited, forbidden from serving as an army of observation along the Spanish frontier or skirmishing with Spanish regular troops. For Liverpool, as his biographer pointed out,

---

[267] Canning to Granville, July 2, 1826, in Canning 1887, p. 117.
[268] Gash 1984, pp. 240–43 passim.
[269] Canning 1826, pp. 28–29.   [270] Ibid., pp. 61, 39.

"the Portuguese episode was a limited operation, under specific treaty obligations, with a specific object."[271] Wellington, his successor as prime minister from 1828 but at the time a member of the Cabinet, concurred. In sending Beresford back to Portugal in late 1826, Wellington reiterated the policy of non-interference in Portuguese politics apart from "[restoring] order, regularity, and discipline to this mass of confusion and mutiny." In a subsequent letter, he elaborated that "Portugal will continue to be a thorn in the side of [England], and a burthen of great risk and danger, till the military establishments of that country can be reformed and put into a state of efficiency."[272]

Canning's florid speech to the Commons, then, merely masked the pervasive distaste for the *Carta*, and for Britain's guardianship of it, that percolated in official circles. The "principles of policy" in Canning's speech were denounced by Lord Grey as "unsound, its boastings unfounded, its threats foolish and imprudent in the highest degree." The *Carta* itself was viewed as a nuisance. Writing from Buenos Aires, British diplomat John Lord Ponsonby, who in May 1826 had stumbled in his effort to broker a settlement with the emperor over the Banda Oriental, remarked caustically that "Dom Pedro hates liberty as much as Sir Toby Belch did water." He noted that the *Carta*'s genesis lay in the emperor's collaboration with

> his pimp [Gomes da Silva] and Benjamin Constant (I mean his book, not the great philosopher in his proper person). And so one morning after breakfast they sat down and, by dinner, out came the Constitution, now the palladium of Lusitania, the despair of Spain, the envy of the Turk, and care and nursling of great statesmen, governments, and kings.[273]

Formal recognition of Brazil's independence failed to sever the political connections between Portugal and its former colony, a fact much lamented on both shores of the Atlantic. Even if Dom Pedro had considered the promulgation and imposition of his 1826 *Carta* to be a benevolent act of farewell, Brazilian nativists undoubtedly were dismayed by the tendency of this document to further embroil Brazil in, instead of extricate it from, European affairs. In Portugal, as Chapter 4 will demonstrate, the *Carta* instigated a fresh round of upheaval, bringing

---

[271] Gash 1984, pp. 245–46.
[272] Wellington to Beresford, October 9, 1826, Wellington 1973, vol. III, p. 413; and see December 5, 1826, pp. 476–77.
[273] Ponsonby to Bagot, October 17, 1826, in Canning 1909, p. 310; The offer of British mediation would be taken up (or imposed) in 1828, when the independent buffer state of Uruguay was established, thus ending the profligate stalemate in the Rio de la Plata. See Winn 1976.

into stark relief the political disputes which had been percolating in the Peninsula for at least thirty years. Though often referred to as the "Civil War," the pronounced international dimensions of the conflict proved that it was anything but an insular matter. Brazil's decolonization cast a long shadow over ostensibly post-imperial Portugal and over the outcome of its internal political convulsions.

4   The last Atlantic revolution: *emigrados*, Miguelists, and the Portuguese Civil War

This chapter narrates and analyzes key episodes of the Portuguese Civil War (1828–34), focusing on its intellectual and international dimensions. It is divided into three parts. Part I examines the political thought animating Dom Miguel's regime, particularly the Miguelist depiction of constitutionalism, its conception of monarchy, and its understanding of Portugal's historical trajectory since 1808. The chapter then turns to the fate of the *Carta*'s supporters, particularly those who escaped to exile abroad. It traces the movements of these heterogeneous and geographically dispersed *emigrados*, often described collectively (and misleadingly) as "Liberals" in the existing historiography, particularly their faltering efforts to build a united front against the Miguelist regime. The difficulties they experienced, and the hardships they endured, as they sought to do so is studied. Emphasis is placed on the ideological cleavages dividing them, most of which remained unresolved well into the 1830s and 1840s. Nevertheless, a unified *emigrado* cohort managed, improbably, to establish a Regency in Dona Maria II's name on the Azorean island of Terceira, which defiantly rejected Dom Miguel's legitimacy and never succumbed to the forces sent to subdue it.

Part II focuses on the Azorean Regency, functioning from mid 1829, particularly its administration, goals, and long-term strategy. Two major, related events transformed the beleaguered Regency's fortunes: first, the 1830 July Revolution in France, which turned back the neo-absolutist tide which had swept over Western Europe from 1823; and second, Dom Pedro's abdication of the Brazilian Crown in 1831, which left the ex-emperor casting about Paris and London in search of a new vocation. The political thaw after 1830, linked to Dom Pedro's renewed interest in his daughter's resurgent cause, greatly enhanced the *emigrados'* chances of success, though they remained stranded, and surrounded, on a small island in the middle of the Atlantic Ocean, unrecognized by any European power. Though Dom Pedro's return to prominence generated anxiety, the Regency's military forces, a significant portion of which comprised foreign mercenaries and fellow

235

travelers, successfully invaded Portugal, overthrew Dom Miguel, nominally restored the *Carta*, and placed Dona Maria on the throne.

The shorter Part III concentrates on the international dimensions of the Portuguese Civil War, focusing on British involvement, Spanish skullduggery, and the role of foreign troops and finance in the conflict's outcome. Overall, Chapter 4 argues that Portuguese politics between 1825 and 1834 cannot be understood without reference to broader European trends and Brazilian politics. The geographic location of the Azorean island of Terceira symbolizes the confluence of forces from both shores of the Atlantic shaping the Portugal Civil War's trajectory while the pivotal role played by the (ex-)Brazilian emperor Dom Pedro in the conflict's outcome suggests the lingering effects of imperial dismemberment in Portuguese "domestic" politics after Brazil formally gained political independence in 1825. The Civil War is thus recast not only as an episode in the history of European cycles of revolution and reaction, but also as part of the long aftermath of early nineteenth-century decolonization.

PART I

Dom Miguel, conservative political thought, foreign constitutional models, and the reaction to the 1826 *Carta*

> What motive can there possibly be for favoring the doctrines of Voltaire, Rousseau, Benjamin Constant, and Jeremy Bentham [over] those of Moses, Plato, Joseph, David, and Isaiah [?][1]

The 1828 coup that brought Dom Miguel to the throne was buttressed by political ideas which his followers claimed were the genuine offspring of the Portuguese tradition.[2] Miguelism also bore the imprint of political doctrines imported from abroad and thus reflected recent disputes over the scope and nature of royal power throughout Europe.[3] While the heterogeneous nature of Miguelism should be noted, several common threads linked its partisans. These included an anti-revolutionary bias; a suspicion of foreigners' malevolent influence; a tendency to praise

---

[1] Madre de Deos 1823a, pp. 58–59.
[2] For changing perceptions of Dom Miguel's reign in the nineteenth and twentieth centuries, see Pina 2003.
[3] For general works on Miguelism's origins and international connections, see Campos 1931 and Lousada 1987.

Figure 6 J. Sjober, engraving, after a painting by Gonsalva. "Dom Miguel, Tyrann von Portugal" (Vienna, 1830).

(lavishly) Portugal's supposedly glorious national past; the value placed on the "lessons of history" over "reason"; a pessimistic view of human nature; an explicitly providentialist conception of history; an organic conception of society; and a defense of long-standing privileges enjoyed by various corporate bodies (i.e. the clergy and nobility).[4]

Miguelism was not, however, a unitary doctrine, comprising a fixed set of immutable principles. It sheltered several inconsistent ideas under a single standard. Political pragmatism induced its proponents to de-emphasize differences and foreground shared convictions. The first variety of Miguelism was imbued by a desire to "restore" the Crown to its supposedly "ancient" grandeur and unencumbered state, before its authority had been eroded by the inconvenient limitations imposed by representative institutions. The origins of this aspect were heterogeneous, intermingling eighteenth-century regalism with the revamped discourses of "legitimacy" in vogue in a post-revolutionary Europe that relied on purportedly historicist celebrations of pre-modern institutions.[5] A second type of Miguelism was inconsistent with the first variant. It was a pro-aristocratic ideology maintaining that the monarch and the aristocracy should mutually enforce each other's power. It considered both early modern absolutism and doctrines of popular sovereignty equally pernicious, reserving special disgust for the modernizing, anti-corporatist discourses associated with Crown-directed enlightened reform. The third ideological stream that flowed into Miguelism was its exultation of the clergy – its historical importance in Portugal's development, the extent of its wealth, and its continued relevance as a bulwark against the destructive impiety of contemporary life – and a defensive loathing for the anti-clericalism of the previous half-century. This third type was consistent with the second, pro-aristocratic element of Miguelism, but was in tension with the first. After all, regalists conceived of the power, property, and privileges of the Church as an obstacle to the Crown's aggrandizement, as the Pombaline expulsion of the Jesuits evinced. To these three competing types of Miguelism, a fourth might be added, though its internal inconsistency and superficiality often saw the intermingling of all three. This was what has been termed "popular" Miguelism, combining a

---

[4] M. A. Lousada, "O Miguelismo, um Discurso Contrarevolucionario," in Monteiro, Costa, and Domingues 1989, p. 121; on the pessimism of Miguelism, see Mesquita 2006, p. 331.

[5] Yet as G. Ruggiero pointed out long ago, the historical imagination of politically conservative romanticism was riddled with contradictions: "their love of history ... turned into anti-historical fetishism" or "medieval utopianism." See Ruggiero 1959, pp. 227–28.

combustible mixture of fervent nationalism (often manifested as xenophobia) and ultra-Catholicism, expressed with an anti-intellectual (and
sometimes anti-modern) tenor, which converted Dom Miguel into a
figurehead for many distinct, often local, causes and grievances.

Miguelism was thus both the culmination and the last gasp of the
earlier tradition of counter-revolutionary political thought discussed in
Chapter 2.[6] Miguelists were heirs to the mantle of Portuguese conservative writers who, like their counterparts throughout Europe, sought to
justify the monarchy's existence and to reassert its preeminence during
the French Revolutionary and Restoration periods.[7] It was necessarily
heterogeneous, not merely an indignant reaction against enlightenment
radicalism and the intellectual streams that fed into nineteenth-century
liberalism. Some of its exponents espoused rationalist doctrines and
offered arguments steeped in legal precedent.[8] In Portugal, the French
occupation and the subsequent restoration of the Braganza dynasty
was accompanied by an eruption of pamphlets and other ephemera.
Miguelists also were descendants of the political writers who, supported by the Crown, excoriated the *Vintistas*, and liberals everywhere,
for hastily discarding Portugal's "ancient constitution" and starting
afresh. This inheritance informed the indignant response to the 1826
Carta and provided the architects of Dom Miguel's short, contested
reign with their political vocabulary and frame of reference.

A major continuity in conservative thought between 1820 and 1834
was the notion that the clamoring for constitutional change resulted
from nefarious cabals of foreign agents. Foreigners were suspect because
they brought other religions (chiefly Protestantism) to the awareness of
the "incautious and insipid" Portuguese, who were tempted to convert to them, thus further undermining Catholicism.[9] The epithets

---

[6] See Chapter 2, pp. 134–40; With the notable exception of the figure of Visconde de
Santarém, Miguelist intellectuals shared very little of the royalism in vogue in Paris
during the 1820s. As Mansel 2001 explained, "instead of being seduced by liberal cer-
tainties and defying Napoleon, many of the younger generation modeled themselves
on Chateaubriand and preferred the emotionalism, cosmopolitanism, and Catholicism
associated with royalism," p. 184. There was, for example, no counterpart in Portugal
to the Parisian *Société Royale des Bonnes Lettres* founded in 1821.

[7] The scholarly literature on this topic is vast: one writer who exerted great influence
on Iberian neo-absolutism was the Swiss political writer Karl Ludwig von Haller, best
known for his *Restauration der Staatswissenschaften* (1816), but also author of a widely
circulated tract lambasting the 1812 Spanish Constitution, translated into Spanish
(see Haller 1823). For Haller, the sovereign reigned not as a result of the delegation of
authority, but by the right conferred by his own strength. See Droz 1967, pp. 10–11.

[8] For parallels with France, see Popkin 1980, p. 170.

[9] BNL, Reservados, Colecção Pombalina 471, António Joaquim de Barros e Aguiar,
"Ensaios Económicos, e Políticos sobre o Governo, e Administração da Fazenda,
dedicados ao Serenissima Senhor D. Miguel" (1828), fos. 30–31.

"liberalism" and "foreign" were used synonymously. While this suspicion was, in part, a hysterical fear of an international Masonic plot,
it also stemmed from two further convictions. The first was the belief
that new-fangled "foreign" constitutionalism was incompatible with
Portuguese institutions. The second notion was that all constitutional
forms introduced into Portugal from abroad were animated by revolutionary doctrines. Conservative writers traced a direct line of descent
from the 1791 French Constitution to the 1812 Spanish Constitution
to the political aspirations of *Vintismo*. Pamphleteer Madre de Deos
argued that if the intention of the 1820 revolutionaries had been truly
to "diminish the misfortunes which afflicted Portugal," their choice of
constitutional models was inappropriate. Conflating the 1791 French
and the 1812 Spanish Constitutions, he declared that these documents
had combined to "flood Europe with tears, blood, mourning, thiev-
ery, treason, vengeance, and assassins." He chastised the framers of
Portugal's 1822 Constitution for having ignored other models, notably
the British Constitution "under which Britain had prospered" or, less
enthusiastically, the *Chartre* of Louis XVIII, "under which France had
been restored to its ancient and respectable splendor in a mere eight
years."[10] Macedo linked Spanish decadence with its 1812 Constitution.
The former "arbiter of two worlds" had been "reduced" to a "skeleton,"
deprived of its "majesty, greatness, opulence, colonies, treasure, shipping, army, commerce, and arts; and what's more, its customs, religion,
unity, fraternal and social bonds, divided into factions."[11] Portuguese
liberals' adoption of this document, without alteration, and then foolish
framing of another resembling it closely, was inexcusable. "There could
be nothing more ridiculous, illegal, shameful, or despotic," another
pamphleteer claimed.[12]

Yet even what was described as "moderate" constitutionalism was
attacked and described as anathema to Portuguese institutions. The
French 1814 *Chartre* was subject to conservative criticism. Macedo
depicted it as a thinly veiled revolutionary plot to "trick monarchs" by
reducing them to a "shadow" of their former authority, restricting or
diminishing their action at every turn. The promise to "rid [the nation]

---

[10] Madre de Deos 1823c, pp. 158–59. Daun claimed that the 1812 Spanish
Constitution's "foundation, institutions, language, and conduct were the same as the
French Revolution when it began," in Daun 1823, pp. 141–42. Frei Fortunato de São
Boaventura echoed this judgment, calling the Constitution of Cádiz a "mere transla-
tion" of the 1791 French Constitution, and was incredulous that such an "offspring of
dark forces" was "received in Cádiz and Lisbon as a masterpiece of human wisdom."
See São Boaventura 1828, p. 7; Much of this critique of Cádiz constitutionalism may
be traced back to Haller 1823.

[11] Macedo 1827, no. 6, p. 3.   [12] Daun 1823, p. 14.

of tyranny" served merely as a pretext to "multiply the number of tyrants."[13] The rampant Anglophobia among Miguelists meant that even the comparatively moderate English constitutionalism was attacked. Prior to the upheavals of the early 1820s, Macedo mocked the fashionable mania for British political life, noting that he was "impressed" by Portuguese who, "after taking a stroll around Falmouth or visiting the dunes, suddenly consider themselves very wise, literate, gifted, instructed, and capable of governing the world."[14] In the 1820s, satire gave way to bitter denunciation. The Magna Carta had been "extorted by force" from its kings. Furthermore, Britain's prosperity and maritime greatness were attributed not to its "political institutions," as often claimed, but rather to "ingenious and good" laws in those two areas alone. In domestic politics, however, Britain was afflicted by "disastrous anarchy," in which there existed a veritable and widespread "mania" for statecraft that produced "disgraceful consequences."[15]

The hostility toward Britain stemmed from its interference in Portuguese affairs. The three chief episodes were the British role in the transfer of the Court to Brazil in 1807 and in dismantling of colonial trade restrictions in 1808–10; the stationing of British troops, under Beresford's command, in Portugal to safeguard the Regency following the expulsion of the Napoleonic army; and the role of British agents in the fabrication and imposition of the 1826 *Carta*. One Miguelist observed in 1828 that it was to the English involvement in Portuguese affairs from 1807 that "we can date the beginning of Portugal's humiliation, the beginning of an era in which more was lost than during the sixty years that Portugal was under Spanish rule."[16] Another of Dom Miguel's correspondents noted that "Your Majesty must look at England as the most ambitious and most arrogant nation in the world, and the one that has most wronged Portugal."[17] Britain's diplomatic chicanery was blamed for Brazil's independence, with the continuing consequences of the 1810 Treaty held in contempt. "We discovered Africa, we conquered India, we had immense settlements in Brazil," the political writer Gama e Castro recalled, "but after we had spilled our blood and invested our capital, the English arrived and, with a single commercial treaty, took away everything."[18] Another anti-British theme was the

---

[13] Macedo 1830, no. 3 (September 26), p. 7.
[14] *O Espectador Portuguez. Jornal de Litteratura, e Critico* (1816), vol. II, no. 3, p. 12.
[15] [Anon.], *Cathecismo Politico* 1828, p. 10.
[16] BAj., 54-VI-52, doc. 38, "A Conspiração contra o Principe D. Miguel" (1828), fos. 49–52 passim.
[17] BAj. 54-x-33, no. 9, [Um Trás-Montano] to Dom Miguel, May 22, 1828, fo. 14.
[18] Gama e Castro 1841, p. 403.

corruption of pure-minded Portuguese by Britons: Britain was blamed for the anti-Miguelist tracts that trickled into Portugal from abroad while British agents were accused of disseminating them.[19] British practices and ideologies were so pernicious that the slightest exposure to them proved corrosive. As evidence, Miguelist writers cited the fate of utilitarian doctrines in Spanish America. "Even the arch-republican Bolívar prohibited the use of Bentham's writings in Colombian universities," Madre de Deos railed, "what kind of pest have the *corifeos* of liberalism introduced into Portuguese society that not even [Spanish American] republicans want it in their own house!"[20]

Of the various injuries inflicted by Britain on Portugal, Sir Charles Stuart's role as the courier of the *Carta*, and Britain's subsequent protection of it, was the least pardonable. As one of Dom Miguel's correspondents put it, "when Charles Stuart arrived in Lisbon, bringing from Rio the *Carta*, this fatal document was approved by the masons and the rumor spread through the country that the British government would guarantee it, a rumor that greatly dispirited the honorable, true Portuguese."[21] The Bishop of Viseu lamented that Stuart brought, "in his bag, or perhaps in his pocket, a fateful, insidious and treacherous gift."[22] Another commentator derided the *Carta* as the work of an "Anglo-maniac sect," convinced that, by importing British institutions, such as trial by jury, "Portugal would be raised suddenly to a power of the first rank."[23] The vague resemblance of the *Carta* to Britain's constitutional arrangements became suspect in an intellectual milieu averse to foreign innovation. "Britain does not have the right to impose its laws on us ... everything that applies to England does not apply to Portugal."[24] To do so was merely fashionable, lacking substance, for the champions of the *Carta* failed to transfer to Portugal "what is called the 'public spirit of England' along with these institutions."[25] "Imitators"

[19] ANTT, MNE, Santarém to d'Asseca, Reservado no. 187, August 8, 1829.
[20] Madre de Deos 1828b, p. 17.
[21] BAj., 54-XI-44, no. 20, Francisco Henriques Teixeira [Divisão Realista da Provincia do Além-Tejo] to Dom Miguel [in Vienna], August ?, 1826, fo. 3.
[22] Lobo, "Rezumida Noticia da Vida de D. Nuno Caetano Alvares Pereira de Mello," in Lobo 1849, vol. II, p. 387.
[23] [Anon.], *Exposição Genuina* 1828, pp. 29–32; on the history and suspected authorship of this pamphlet, see Hespanha 2004, p. 155, fn. 368.
[24] [Anon./Realistas Portuguezes], *Analyse e Refutação* 1829, pp. 13–14; various Miguelist writers believed the *Carta* was not only brought by an English agent, but also was largely a copy of the "British constitution." For a clear statement of this belief, see BAj. 54-VI-52, "A Conspiração" (1828), no. 38, fo. 34.
[25] Lobo, "Rezumida Noticia," in Lobo 1849, vol. II, pp. 386–87.

of the British constitution were subject to extreme criticism from the opponents of the *Carta*. Such efforts could never "produce anything useful, if only its exterior is copied." It would much more advisable to explore alternative "arrangements" which reconciled non-traditional forms of representation with hereditary monarchy.[26]

Yet while conservative writers denounced the demerits of specific constitutions, their overarching argument was that foreign models, simply because of their provenance, should never be imposed in Portugal, whether through revolutionary means or royal acquiescence. In his influential 1825 tract *Os Povos, e os Reis*, Madre de Deos argued that "it would be very dangerous for humanity if the United States' Constitution were introduced in Russia, just as it would be dangerous to introduce absolute monarchy in the United States."[27] For all of their superficially attractive elements, the institutions enshrined in liberal constitutions established abroad were impracticable in Portugal. "The fascinating theories concerning [multiple legislative] chambers, juries, habeas corpus, and all else which constitutes liberalism," a pamphleteer wrote, are "exotic plants, which die among us, and cannot flower in a soil to which they do not belong."[28] The *Carta* was similarly tainted, another writer argued, for it was "perfectly antipathetic to our customs, our opinions, our sensibility, and our character." It reflected the "system followed by all of the architects of new political edifices since 1789, to accommodate the land to the constitution and not the constitution to the land."[29] By tarnishing the *Carta* as a foreign import – the brainchild of Anglo-French-Brazilian plotters – Miguelist pamphleteers, journalists, and political writers sought to discredit it and demonstrate its utter incompatibility with Portuguese institutions.

The "cause of Dom Miguel" and the turbulent politics of the late 1820s

The distinct causes of the counter-revolution, "legitimacy," and Dom Miguel became indistinguishable from 1823. There was scant indication that this would happen even a year earlier. In 1823, after all, Dom Miguel was twenty-one years old and had spent his formative years (from age five to age eighteen) in Rio de Janeiro. But his role, aided

---

[26] [Anon.], *Sobre a Constituição da Inglaterra* 1827, p. 69.
[27] Madre de Deos 1825, p. 98.
[28] Daun 1829, p. 20.
[29] Lobo, "Rezumida Noticia," in Lobo 1849, vol. II, p. 386.

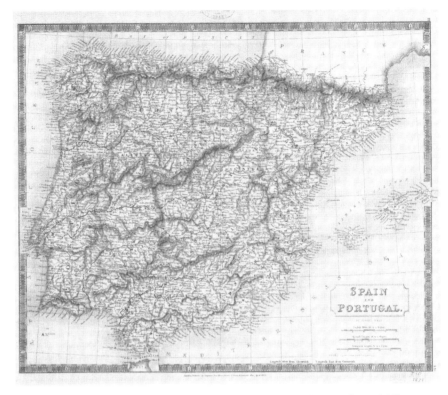

Figure 7 S. Hall. "[Map of] Spain and Portugal" (London, 1828).

and abetted by his mother, in the overthrow of the Cortes in 1823, Dom João's increasingly conciliatory stance toward modern constitutionalism, and Dom Pedro's defection to Brazil prompted conservatives to hail him as a savior. His exile after the *Abrilada* only heightened his appeal among the troops, titular nobility, and populace. The dissolution of the Cortes and the suspension of the constitution in 1823 emboldened conservative writers to disseminate their views on constitutional change more widely, in the hope of preventing another revolutionary outbreak. Madre de Deos defended the thesis that "the people do not have the right (*direito*) to change their legitimate form of government."[30] Instead, they were "obligated to not disobey legitimately constituted authority."[31] Other pamphleteers and journalists highlighted

[30] Madre de Deos 1825, pp. 13, 85.
[31] Madre de Deos 1825, p. 118.

the ill effects of revolutions, which had left the monarchy with "a shadow of its former power, but without dignity, majesty, or authority … the King was no longer a King, but rather [equivalent to] the Doge [of Venice]."[32] Such political arrangements, conservative scribblers argued, not only departed from precedent, but resulted from a misunderstanding of sovereignty. Revisiting its supposedly unimpeachable divine origins, re-popularized in Portugal at the turn of the century, one publicist contended that "no constitution can result from deliberation" for "the rights of sovereignty neither have defined origins nor known authors." He argued that religion was the foundation of the "science of legislation": "You read too many Benthams and Constants," he scolded, "when you should have read Bossuet."[33] As evidence for such claims, conservative writers blamed the Cortes for "the loss of Brazil, the enormous public debt, and the draining of national wealth." The 1820–23 Revolution was a "crocodile which swallowed peoples and nations whole."[34] The *Vintistas* had "interrupted the peaceful, useful, and glorious epoch in Brazil."[35]

Yet the recognition of Brazil's independence by Portugal in 1825, which dashed dreams of their reconciliation and reunion in the short term, posed new problems for neo-absolutist writers. Madre de Deos was alarmed that the vague terms of Brazil's independence would precipitate a succession crisis. Stating unambiguously that "everyone recognizes that Dom Pedro is the legitimate successor to the Portuguese Crown," he argued that Portugal and Brazil might once again form a "united kingdom" under his rule. But this possibility was fraught with danger, for Portugal then would face the quandary of either fighting for the preservation of "pure monarchy" or embracing Dom Pedro's heterodox 1824 Constitution. Such a dilemma was unavoidable, Madre de Deos contended, because "no state can be governed by different and opposed forms of government, a monstrous anomaly, which could only produce divisions." Moreover, he argued that should Dom Pedro's 1824 Brazilian Constitution be imposed on Portugal, "the door would be open for the subversion of all legitimate monarchies," warning that foreign intervention, led by the Holy Alliance, would then be inevitable.[36]

[32] Daun 1823, p. 70–71.
[33] [Anon.], *Bazes Eternas* 1824, pp. 38, 47.
[34] *O Punhal dos Corcundas*, no. 10 (1823), p. 93; no. 25 (1823), p. 350.
[35] Daun 1823, pp. 77–78.
[36] Madre de Deos 1825, p. 119.

As discussed in the previous section, the imposition of the *Carta* in 1826 triggered the next development in conservative thought, pushing it further toward extreme absolutism, and culminating in Dom Miguel's coup in 1828. The nineteenth-century historian Oliveira Martins described the *Carta*'s incomplete quality, to which he attributed the range of reactions it provoked: "it was a statement of principles, a catechism, a skeleton still missing musculature. It was a sketch or, perhaps, a map on which the names of the rivers and cities were still to be marked."[37] The first objection was that the *Carta* resembled the 1822 constitution too closely, itself modeled on French and Spanish precedent. It repeated the "errors" of *Vintismo*, but "with honey on its lips."[38] The *Vintistas* had sought to "reform the nation according to abstract theories, without heeding the instructive lessons of experience."[39] The *Carta*, too, was deemed "perfectly antipathetic to our customs, our opinions, our sensibility and our character." It reflected the "system followed by all of the architects of new political edifices since 1789, to accommodate the land to the constitution and not the constitution to the land."[40] The embrace of the *Carta* by those who previously had favored the 1822 Constitution was therefore suspect. "The only enthusiasts [for the *Carta*] are driven by a chaos-causing instinct, without character, morals or sense of custom, who, in theaters and cafés, speak of nothing except liberty."[41] The government-published *Gazeta de Lisboa* denounced this "prestige of an illusory liberty" and the men who strove to "substitute the benign and tranquil government of kings with the ferocious dominion of congresses, patriotic societies, and clubs."[42] Other Miguelist arguments against the *Carta* used the precarious political situation in newly independent Latin American states as evidence for the wisdom of "ancient laws" and an excuse for eschewing "adventurers, so-called political regenerators, obsessed with innovative theories." They cited Mexico as an example of where "dangerous doctrines and false principles have been the sole origin of all of the calamities and horrors afflicting that country." As further evidence for the wisdom of adhering to "ancient laws" and obeying long-established authorities, Miguelists compared independent Mexico's plight with

[37] Oliveira Martins 1883, vol. I, p. 74.
[38] Macedo 1828–29a, no. 2 (September 21, 1828), p. 13.
[39] *O Amigo do Bem Público, ou o Realista Constitucional* (1826), no. 1, n.p.
[40] Lobo, "Rezumida Noticia," in Lobo 1849, vol. II, p. 386.
[41] *O Realista: Amigo da Observacia da Lei*, no. 1 (September 26, 1826), n.p.
[42] *Gazeta de Lisboa*, no. 142 (June 17, 1828), p. 802.

Cuba's prosperity. Cuba had "flourished" and "avoided revolutionary upheaval," remaining "loyal to its legitimate sovereign." It had been "rewarded" with the "great increase of its prosperity."[43]

As the "liberal" (anti-Miguelist) opposition, discussed in later sections of this chapter, coalesced on the island of Terceira and its allies became more vocal elsewhere in Europe, and as Dom Miguel's regime failed to obtain the recognition it coveted from key European states, his supporters engaged in a propaganda campaign to justify his actions. For Dom Miguel's coup to be considered even remotely legitimate, Dom Pedro's right to the succession had to be refuted. This raised an uncomfortable problem: the entire nation, including conservative jurists and Dom Miguel himself, had acknowledged the elder brother's rights to the throne after Dom João's death. It was necessary, therefore, to argue that Dom Pedro had forfeited his rights or that the dynastic reshuffling accompanying the *Carta* had violated Dom Miguel's rights. Dom Miguel's publicists concocted four reasons for denying Dom Pedro's right to succeed. First, he had become the sovereign of another country. Second, he not only had approved of Brazil's rebellion, but had led the revolt. Third, he had declared war on Portugal in order to "dismember" the empire. Fourth, by imposing his *Carta*, he had violated Portugal's fundamental law. Some critics conceded that Dom Pedro's decision to craft Brazil's 1824 Constitution had been perfectly reasonable. "A new nation, a new monarchy, a new government," a Miguelist pamphleteer claimed, "requires a new act, convention, constitution, charter or fundamental law." But such a law was inapplicable to Portugal, where it could only undergo "dangerous mutation."[44]

Dom Pedro's interference in Portugal's internal affairs, too, was unacceptable because his two constitutional documents purportedly contradicted each other. "By the treaty of August 29, 1825, Brazilians are to be considered foreigners before the King of Portugal; but the King of Portugal is the Emperor of Brazil: therefore it follows that Brazilians are foreigners before the Emperor of Brazil."[45] Dom Pedro's rights through primogeniture had been clouded by his conduct. Not only had he become the sovereign of another country, but he had "declared war on Portugal, his country, and dismembered one of its

---

[43] *Gazeta de Lisboa*, no. 199 (August 24, 1829), p. 823. The image of a disordered, chaotic state of Ibero-America after independence cropped up frequently in Miguelist pamphlets. See for example, [Anon.], *Golpe de Vista ... Brasil* 1829, pp. 17–18.
[44] Castel-Branco 1831, p. 31.   [45] Madre de Deos 1828d, p. 9.

most considerable dominions."[46] This charge was deemed sufficient for Dom Miguel to rise up and reassert his alleged rights. As one of his apologists contended:

the fundamental laws are immutable, and the sovereign must respect them, as they are attached to his Crown. He cannot consent to his rights being diminished or degraded ... Should new circumstances, a revolution in the state of affairs, make these laws inappropriate, then he can devise new ones and eliminate others. But it is necessary to bring them to the attention of the nation ... These fundamental laws precede the greatness of the prince, and they should survive him.[47]

Macedo baldly pilloried the imprudence, and impudence, of issuing a new constitution. Moving beyond the question of Dom Pedro's right to issue the *Carta*, he declared that "to issue a new constitution, it must be demonstrated that [reform] cannot occur without it ... it must be shown, through an examination of history, that the monarchy's present constitution is inadequate."[48]

Though Miguelists shared these views, different factions drew divergent conclusions from them. In the erudite *Memórias para a História e Theoria das Cortes Geraes* (1827), written by Visconde de Santarém, subsequently Dom Miguel's foreign minister, the author claimed that Portugal's system of representation was "much older than any other such system in Europe" and that it even had established "guarantees of individual [rights] so acclaimed by modern publicists." Not only was the "ancient" Cortes legitimate, but its former structure and function remained efficacious.[49] In his view, the king was the unifying force, coordinating the activities of the various estates and groups. Santarém's views were not anti-monarchical in any obvious sense, for he believed that legitimate action required royal approval.[50] But his views were quite distinct from the neo-absolutism advocated by most of Dom Miguel's supporters. For them, there was no need for a new

---

[46] [Anon.], *Golpe de Vista ... Dom Miguel* 1829, pp. 5–6.

[47] Avelar 1828, pp. 22–23. Others disputed Dom Pedro's right to change the Fundamental Law(s) of Portugal. There were certain "primordial laws (*leis primordiaes*)," Gama e Castro argued, "that not even the monarch himself can destroy, because it is by those very laws that he is king [in the first place]." See Gama e Castro 1933, p. 31.

[48] Macedo 1828, no. 4 (December 3, 1828), p. 10.

[49] Santarém 1827, pp. iii–v passim; Calling him "one of the ablest statesman of the age," one anonymous publicist in 1830 suggested that Santarém's *Memórias* was an "illumined publication [that] greatly facilitated the convocation of the Three Estates, assembled in Cortes, in July 1828." See [Anon./Hum Amigo de Verdade], *Scraps and Stubborn Facts* 1830, p. 25.

[50] Cardim 1998, p. 182.

lei fundamental, nor any need to amend the existing one, even if to adapt institutions to contemporary demands. Santarém's treatment of the Cortes reflected his pro-aristocratic leanings and his suspicion of ministerial government in a centralized monarchy, a goal which was shared by both advocates of the Pombaline style of government and liberal institutions.

Santarém's celebration of the Cortes, though, was overshadowed by ultra-absolutist Miguelists, who rejected the purported immutability of laws and defended certain innovations as salutary and efficient. Madre de Deos bluntly stated that "the legislator is not a slave to the laws."[51] Macedo explicitly rejected Santarém's position that the Cortes, ancient or modern, wielded much power. Whatever recommendations it made "drew their force from the authority of the sovereign, who had to approve them, and ensure that they were obeyed."[52] With characteristic clarity and pith, Macedo summarized the goals of the ultra-absolutist Miguelists:

an independent, free, and absolute king, who can enforce laws without restrictions, and not merely enforce them, but also author them without competition from any other authority, for the law is the will of the superior to his subjects in accordance with the eternal principles of justice.[53]

While the words "constitution" and "fundamental law" had been mostly interchangeable between 1821 and 1828, the hostility toward constitutionalists led to a decoupling of these terms. For some absolutists, "constitution" became a byword for "revolution, the usurpation of legitimate sovereignty, and license to engage in depraved actions."[54] The 1822 Portuguese Constitution was blamed for the ills which had befallen Portugal, notably the loss of Brazil.[55] According to Macedo, its vaunted reforms amounted to "public rapine" while the "liberal system" was tantamount to "oriental depotism."[56] "All of these so-called chambers, moderating powers and such," Macedo argued, are merely "the acts of rebellion of children against their parents, of vassals against their monarchs."[57] "Mixed government," Madre de Deos wrote, "by a sophistic twisting of language, has been given the name of 'constitutional monarchy,' but it is not a monarchy

---

51 Madre de Deos 1828b, p. 4.
52 Macedo 1820, p. 10.
53 Macedo 1830, no. 1 (September 6), p. 11.
54 São José 1830, p. 2.
55 São Boaventura 1828, p. 8.
56 Macedo 1830, no. 3 (September 26), p. 5.
57 Macedo 1829a, no. 22, (August 2), p. 14

in any recognizable form."[58] Denouncing constitutionalism was shorthand for a whole variety of practices the Miguelists found execrable. One of the most loathsome was freedom of the press and the contaminating flow of information received from abroad. Freedom of the press was denounced as "nothing more than the freedom to insult Christianity."[59] Writing to Dom Miguel, Santarém argued, striking an unprecedentedly neo-absolutist vein, that "in an absolute monarchy (*monarquia pura*), the public spirit does not need to be informed by periodicals which inspire animosities and engage in diatribes … in an absolute monarchy, vassals should be satisfied with passive obedience."[60]

The *Carta*, its supporters, and the first phase of the Civil War

The *Carta*'s supporters were attacked, Lavradio informed Palmela in 1827, from "two groups that sought its destruction: the first who want to replace it with a pure and abominable despotism; the second who want to re-establish a constitution of illegitimate origin, which but a short time ago led Portugal to disgrace."[61] In this sense, the *Carta*'s champions were defined by what they opposed, by their distaste for extremes, by their cosmopolitan outlook, and by their acquiescence to monarchy in some form. The first generation of men who came to be known as "*Cartistas*" thus formed a heterogeneous group, though of a pronounced moderate cast. To chastened *Vintistas*, the allowance for a representative chamber, elections, and a reasonable guarantee of (limited) individual rights was an improvement over the status quo. To self-styled moderate royalists, the retention of the royal prerogative, the creation of a hereditary, life-term, Crown-nominated upper chamber (*Pares*), limited elections, robust protection of property rights, and the confirmation of Catholicism as the religion of the state were reassuring features of Dom Pedro's *Carta*.[62] To these modernizing monarchists, then, who thought Dom Miguel and his circle retrograde, the *Carta* was imperfect but palatable, and they sought common ground with those cautious liberals not enraptured by visions of the 1822 Constitution's restoration.

---

[58] Madre de Deos 1828c, p. 6.
[59] *A Contra-Mina*, no. 20 (1830), p. 7.
[60] Santarém to Dom Miguel (1828), Santarém 1918, vol. I, pp. 585–86. It is clear that Santarém's views drifted toward neo-absolutism during his period as a Miguelist minister, at least in his public pronouncements.
[61] ANTT, MNE, cx. 153, Lavradio to Palmela, January 27, 1827.
[62] Hespanha 2004, p. 365.

Yet dyed-in-the-wool liberals, the *Vintistas* and their intellectual comrades, greeted the *Carta*'s arrival with distrust. As in Brazil, the Cortes's role in the redaction of the constitution was obviated by the promulgation of a royal charter, a "gift" from the throne. However, even radical liberals perceived a partial victory in the grant of a constitution, endowing constitutionalism with a royal imprimatur, something which Dom João's vacillation and undelivered promises, not to mention Dom Miguel's reactionary tendencies, had precluded between 1823 and 1826.[63] Still, the same men who had favored the Cortes in its struggle with Dom Pedro in 1822–23 to rescue the *Reino Unido*, and had witnessed the emperor's subsequent erratic, high-handed treatment of representative institutions in Brazil, were inevitably uneasy. But the rising tide of ultra-royalism across Europe and the rabid anti-constitutionalism of the Miguelists encouraged their grudging acquiescence or tepid support.

In voicing support for the *Carta*, some of its adherents repudiated the 1822 Constitution and strove to highlight its distinct origin from that controversial document. The *Velho Liberal* described the 1822 Constitution as "eminently democratic in its organization, for not having been issued by the governors for the governed, but rather by the latter for the former, attacking monarchical principles, and exposing the Portuguese to the disasters that harmed Naples and Spain."[64] The disavowal of the 1822 Constitution, now dismissed by self-described "moderates" as "the offspring more of desperation and suffering than ingenuity in the service of patriotism," was coupled with the assumption that the "old system" was untenable. The *Carta*'s "middle way" (*meio termo*) was embraced as a viable alternative.[65] Interestingly, its origins in, and similarity to, the political thought of the French Restoration and the 1814 *Chartre* notwithstanding, the *Carta* was more frequently compared to the "British Constitution" than to its more immediate, and eponymous, forerunner. One enthusiast gushed at "the similarity of our constitutional charter with that of Great Britain, the origin of its greatness and splendor."[66] There were practical as well as ideological reasons for the assertion of such an institutional affinity. In the wake of Ferdinand VII's restoration in Spain (1823), constitutional government

---

[63] As the British ambassador to Portugal noted, "the Liberals would certainly rather submit to D. Pedro's continued rule than run even the slightest chance of the alternative put forward by the Ultras, of Dom Miguel as absolute King." See A'Court to Canning, October 28, 1826, in Webster 1938, vol. II, p. 275.

[64] *Considerações do Velho Liberal* (1826), p. 3.

[65] *A Funda de David Defonte do Clarim Portugues* (1826), no. 3, n.p.

[66] *Resumo Histórico do Parlamento de Inglaterra* (1826).

in Portugal depended on Britain's guarantee, and not that of France, whose hostility to liberal government across the Pyrenees had been made plain.

As might be expected of a persecuted, exiled group, the *Carta*'s defenders spent much of their intellectual energy reacting to Miguelist vituperative propaganda. The result was a brand of political thought forged in the crucible of acute conflict and characterized by its self-described consistency with traditional institutions. They contended that the *Carta* not only conserved but also restored the ancient constitution. The *Carta* incorporated all of its elements, they argued, which had been "dispersed in separate laws, in customs, and traditional uses," endowing them with the "regularity and harmony" which that venerable legal hodgepodge lacked.[67] The two *Câmaras* established by the *Carta*, for example, served the same function as the *Três Estados* of the traditional Cortes, with the *Pares* reserved for the nobility and clergy and the *Deputados* for the remainder of the population.[68] The provision for a representative chamber was sufficient proof of the *Carta*'s legitimacy, its basis in tradition. Such "ancient privileges and liberties," which Braganzan absolutism had "demolished," were now being "reconstructed."[69] *Paquete de Portugal* argued that the *Carta* was the "true restoration of our long-lost, ancient *foros* and rights."[70] The *Carta*'s defenders asserted its "perfect consistency" with "monarchical principles and [existing] national legislation." They highlighted its preservation of a "hereditary, unencumbered, and independent" sovereign and its affirmation of Roman Catholicism as the state religion. Furthermore, the *Carta* conformed to Portugal's "uses and customs." Ultra-royalists were thus attacked on their own ground. How could the *Três Estados*, convoked by Dom Miguel, "arrogate to itself the authority to choose the King? Have they forgotten, perhaps, that the Crown of Portugal is hereditary and not elective?"[71] It was this argument that Dom Pedro would pick up when he placed himself at the head of the *emigrado* cause in Portugal and presented his *Carta* as consistent with the *lei fundamental*. His February 1832 *Manifesto* declared, "This *Carta* is truly an affirmation and extension of the *Lei Fundamental* of the Monarchy."[72]

Yet the defense of tradition was complemented by an uncompromising demand for reform. Absolutism's legacy was deemed pernicious

---

[67] Almeida Garrett 2005 [1830], p. 125.
[68] [Anon.], *Reflexões … Partido Apostolico* 1828, pp. 21–23.
[69] C. Carvalho 1832a, p. 8.
[70] *Paquete de Portugal*, vol. II, no. 24 (February 2, 1830), pp. 344–45.
[71] [Anon.], *Reflexões … Partido Apostolico* 1828, pp. 21–23.
[72] Dom Pedro, quoted in Hespanha 2004, p. 201.

and Portugal's recent misfortunes – military occupation, civil strife, and imperial collapse – made radical overhaul unavoidable. Decadence had precipitated the decline of traditional institutions, which the *Carta* sought to "revive, though fitted to the spirit of the age." Furthermore, royal authority was asserted, and enlarged, by constitutional reform: "every monarch has the right to change or alter the political constitution of his state, if it seems to him appropriate to advance the interest or happiness of the people."[73] An older enlightenment-era language of "public happiness"[74] thus fused with a new emphasis on written constitutionalism, leavened with justifications borrowed from the expanding corpus of neo-absolutist writings.

Defenders of the *Carta* also rejected the Miguelist argument that Dom Pedro had forfeited his right to succeed to the throne either for having resided outside of the kingdom or else for having worn concurrently the Crown of another state. This argument demanded a rebuttal because if he had been stripped of his status as heir, then he could neither issue a *Carta* nor abdicate in favor of his daughter. Dom Pedro's defenders dismissed the argument that he was a "foreigner" and thus had forfeited his right to the throne.[75] The *Carta*'s defenders further rejected the Miguelist contention that the failure to bring together the *Três Estados* to ratify the change in the line of succession and the *Carta* itself invalidated both of those acts. Dom Pedro's succession did not require ratification, his allies argued, as it was consistent with the Fundamental Law. They remained silent, however, on the second matter, preferring to show how the *Carta* was consistent with, or at least did not violate, the *lei fundamental*. But at least one writer argued that the *Três Estado*'s approval of major changes to the structure of the monarchy was superfluous in some instances, citing the separation of Brazil from Portugal as an example.[76] This argument went unnoticed until the tide of the Civil War turned. After 1832, though, Dom Pedro's failure to have convoked a representative body, either to assent to his *Carta* or to approve the actions of the Regency he had named, engendered fierce disputes among the *emigrados* fighting for Dona Maria's cause concerning the limits to, and nature of, the monarchy enshrined in it.

[73] *O Imparcial*, no. 8 (August 12, 1826), pp. 30–31.
[74] On this theme, see Paquette 2008, ch. 2.
[75] Rocha 1828, p. 7. Miguelist arguments of this type were circulating as early as 1826. In an unpublished manuscript from 1826, one political writer noted that "the *Carta* is illegal, derives from an illegitimate authority and thus can be considered a mere irritant, of no legal standing." See Boe.C. MS 50:266.3, "Protesto d'hum Portuguez fiel aos deveres de bom Catholica, e d'honorado cidadão, para ser apresentado no Acto do Juramento que por Obrigado a prestar a Carta Constitucional de 1826," fo. 7.
[76] Rocha 1828, p. 58.

These lofty (and arcane) discussions, however, must be appreciated against the backdrop of the desperate situation of those who opposed Dom Miguel's newly installed regime. After a last stand in the north of Portugal in 1828, defenders of the *Carta* and Dona Maria's rights either fled across the Spanish border into Galicia or else embarked hastily for an uncertain future abroad, dispersed throughout the western fringe of Europe. Exile was a plight to which Portugal's constitutionalists were accustomed: some had resided abroad to exercise more ample freedom of expression from the turn of the nineteenth century whereas those who either had collaborated with the Napoleonic occupation, or were suspected of radical political sympathies, found themselves unwelcome after the recovery of Portuguese sovereignty in 1812. The 1812–20 period witnessed the efflorescence of a broadly liberal opposition in exile. As discussed in Chapter 2, three *emigrado* publications, *O Investigador Portuguez* (1811–19), *O Portuguez* (1814–22), and *O Campeão Portuguez* (1819–22), flourished in London, joining other established organs of dissent, most prominently the *Correio Brasiliense*, and a smattering of ephemeral journals and newspapers. The pages of these Portuguese-language periodicals were populated with reform proposals, piercing barbs, revelations of government scandals or misconduct, as well as synopses of foreign books deemed pertinent to Portugal's situation.[77] Their editorial boards and avid readers articulated many of the ideas animating the 1820 Porto Revolution. In 1823, following Dom João's restoration, many of the self-proclaimed *Regeneradores* voluntarily sought refuge abroad, fearing reprisals from ascendant absolutists. Almeida Garrett, José Ferreira Borges, Francisco Xavier Monteiro, and Simão Margiochi were among those who fled to England, while others, including Bernardo de Sá da Nogueira, later Marquês de Sá da Bandeira, sought refuge in Paris.[78]

Yet many of these exiles returned in 1826 upon the promulgation of the *Carta*, which was twinned with a general political amnesty, circumstances which augured the establishment of a moderate monarchy. Press freedom, though ephemeral, encouraged a fresh wave of periodicals. Almeida Garrett, for example, co-founded two newspapers – *O Português* and *O Cronista* – in 1826–27 alone.[79] Of course, many aspects of the *Carta* were anathema to these men. The upper legislative chamber (*Pares*), hand-picked by Dom Pedro from the ranks of the nobility, was

---

[77] A. H. de Oliveira Marques, "A Conjuntura," in Marques and Serrão 2002, pp. 546–47.
[78] Vargues and Torgal, "Da Revolução à Contra-Revolução," in Torgal and Roque 1993, p. 79.
[79] França 1974, vol. I, p. 110.

one distasteful measure. So, too, was the reversal of even tepid *Vintismo* legislation concerning religious toleration, including the suppression of the Inquisition (*Tribunal do Santo-Officio*), and, especially, the abolition of the immunities and judicial privileges of the clergy. Furthermore, to the shock of secular-leaning liberals, the newly installed Regency's effort to placate the clergy, including a decree to permit all *prelados* to sit in the *Câmara dos Pares*, strengthened the bond between Church and State.[80] The two years (1826–28) between the *Carta*'s arrival and the Miguelist coup, therefore, were tumultuous. The *Carta* was attacked, forcing constitutionalists of all shades to become the apologists for a document of which they were wary, a charter imposed from above, a "gift from the throne," not the long-desired mutual compact between the monarch and the representatives of the *Povo*. But the rising tide of popular royalism in Portugal, combined with an international environment hostile to anything smacking of radicalism, compelled them to put aside temporarily certain intramural differences.

Rightly fearing retribution for their political convictions in Miguelist Portugal, they dispersed throughout Europe – to London via Plymouth, Falmouth, and Portsmouth; to Paris via Rennes and Brest; to Bruges, and Brussels – but also to Rio de Janeiro, where they sought relief from Dom Pedro. In Paris, they encountered sympathizers, notably Marquis de Lafayette,[81] secured subsidies from the French government (after 1830), mixed in literary circles, and attended the lectures of Victor Cousin and Guizot. They were a tiny community, numbering thirteen hundred at their height in 1831, a small group amidst the more than fifty thousand resident foreigners in Paris in the early 1830s.[82] In London, they intersected with the contingent of Spanish liberals, banished after the French-backed restoration of Ferdinand VII, and were swept up in transnational plots, including that hatched by exiled General Espoz y Mina for an Iberian Federal project, the *Junta Hispano-Lusitana*, which had clandestine agents spread throughout the Peninsula, the "Amigos de Mina," and enjoyed prominent sympathizers, including Saldanha.[83]

Though they mixed with other political exiles associated with the fragmented "Liberal International,"[84] the Portuguese *emigrados'*

---

[80] Ferreira 2002, p. 70.
[81] For the broader context of Lafayette's political activities *c.* 1830, see Kramer 1996.
[82] Kramer 1988, pp. 25–26.
[83] On Spanish liberal exiles more generally, see Llorens 1979; also Alonso and Muñoz 2011; Vargues and Torgal, "Da Revolução à Contra-Revolução," p. 85. Castells argued that Saldanha's interest had less to do with ideology and more to do with his fears for the weakness of any non-absolutist political regime that might be established in Portugal. See Castells 1989, p. 131.
[84] Isabella 2009.

conundrum was unlike that facing other dissident communities eking out a precarious existence abroad. Their rallying cry was a constitution written and imposed by a now-abdicated monarch, the present Emperor of Brazil, whose defiant attitude and unrepentant recalcitrance toward the European state system, more than his rebellion against his doddering father, irked many European statesmen, his commitment to monarchical principles notwithstanding. Yet Francis I of Austria was Dona Maria's maternal grandfather. She was a motherless victim of palace intrigue, betrothed to, and then deposed by, an uncle whose reputation for erratic behavior and proclivity to violence, however exaggerated, perturbed the architects of the Holy Alliance, who had inspected him at first hand during his Vienna exile. Combined with other pressures, uneasiness with Dom Miguel's comportment delayed official recognition of his regime, a delay that furnished Portuguese liberal exiles with hope.

The *emigrados*, their ideological divisions, and the formation of a united opposition to Dom Miguel

There were schisms and divisions among the *emigrados*, cleavages cutting across ideology, personality, and tactics. Stripped of the rhetoric of comradeship, they were united only in their opposition to Dom Miguel, or, more often, joined only by the usurper's vengeful hatred of them. For instance, Sá da Bandeira and Saldanha earned Miguelist enmity by commanding the forces sent to repress the anti-*Carta* revolts in 1827–28 whereas Palmela fell afoul for his uncooperative stance during the 1824 *Abrilada*. The various factions never ceased to view one another with mistrust, foreshadowing the hyper-fragmentation of Portuguese political life between 1834 and 1851. There were substantive causes behind their conflict, not just petty, personality-driven squabbles. The *Vintistas*, and their heirs, struggled to make common cause with the conservative patricians and the chameleon-like technocrats who served Dom João after 1823. For example, Palmela's career trajectory – experienced diplomat, vocal foe of the 1822 Constitution, and one of the architects of Dom João's 1823 restoration – made him an unlikely ally. In fact, Palmela's elevation from the title of "count" to that of "marquis" was attributable directly to his role in the *Vilafrancada*! Politically, he was a Portuguese Talleyrand, canny, cunning, and adaptable; personally, he was a Lusophone Metternich, handsome, eloquent, elegant, and urbane, boasting numerous sexual conquests, including a youthful Italian fling with Madame de Staël.[85]

---

[85] A characterization shared by Oliveira Martins 1883, vol. I, p. 110; for the de Staël-Palmela correspondence, see de Staël 1979.

In the existing historiography, the *emigrados* are bifurcated into two competing factions: the more radical followers of Saldanha and the politically conservative men who followed Palmela. But such a division is misleading. Both men had been key figures propping up Dom João's beleaguered regime from 1823. Saldanha, the grandson of Pombal, had escorted Dom João to Lisbon after the *Vilafrancada*, briefly served as a member of the 1826 Regency, and then occupied the post of Minister of War before he was forced to resign. Numerous other *emigrados* had collaborated in Dom João's restoration. The arch-reformer Mouzinho da Silveira served as a government minister in 1823 and a counselor to the 1826–28 Regency, in addition to his role as a conservative parliamentarian. Similar trajectories for many other figures could be traced. The *emigrado* leaders, on the whole, were a conservative bunch, composed of ardent monarchists boasting dubious and flimsy constitutionalist credentials.

But a common plight muted the natural rivalry between absolutism's former servants and those who, perpetually in opposition, had suffered as its victims. Only, perhaps, in the Age of Romanticism could such a diverse group be brought into tense equilibrium.[86] Though romantics, the *emigrados* were pragmatists, too. Seeking to dispel any suspicion of their motives, Almeida Garrett emphasized that their commitment to monarchy was unequivocal: "Portugal is situated in Europe, surrounded by monarchies; it has been a monarchy from the beginning … it cannot be anything other than a monarchy."[87] The change in government they sought to effect was not the "destructive" or "abrasive" variety of revolution that had ravaged Europe in the late eighteenth century, but a new species of political transformation, akin to a "magnetic force," at once "powerful yet serene."[88]

If the *emigrados*' stated goal was unambiguous from the outset – the restoration of the *Carta* under the rule of Dona Maria II – then the tactics they employed to achieve their aims generated unceasing dispute. There was a degree of consensus that Dom Pedro's involvement was indispensable. But in what capacity? His 1826 abdication, deemed irrevocable, made him legally irrelevant while his role as figurehead of Brazil's independence made him anathema to *emigrados*. Across the ocean, the 1824 Brazilian Constitution barred his absence from Brazil without the Assembly's explicit permission, an unlikely prospect. Furthermore, even staunch supporters of the *Carta* were unimpressed

---

[86] As J. Barzun observed, "the perfection of Romanticism is to bring into tense equilibrium many radical diversities." See Barzun 1950, vol. I, p. 383.
[87] Almeida Garrett 2005, pp. 123–24.
[88] Ibid., p. 40.

by Dom Pedro's farewell maneuvers in 1826, particularly his nomination of a Regency whose acts were not ratified by the Cortes, an omission undermining the *Carta* itself. Nevertheless, in the hostile political climate of 1828–29, many *emigrados* conceded that the formation of a regency was a logical first step, both to dissipate fears concerning the supposedly radical political aspirations they harbored and to serve as a standard around which to rally resistance to Dom Miguel. To more avid monarchists, it boasted the further advantage of consistency with the terms of Dom Pedro's 1826 abdication. Aligning their strategy with the *Carta* permitted them to drape themselves in the cloak of legitimacy. But the fragile unanimity in support of the Regency broke down as the mechanics of its functioning were debated. How were appointments to the Regency to be made and could the Emperor of Brazil make the nominations? Who would serve as regent to Dona Maria during her minority? Could the Regency long sustain itself, morally and financially, in foreign exile or was it necessary to establish a foothold in Portuguese territory, such as on one of the islands of the eastern Atlantic archipelagos or perhaps Cape Verde or São Tomé? In any case, what could the Regency, once installed and ensconced, bereft of funds and far from the Iberian Peninsula, actually accomplish? Would it wait passively for the political equivalent of a miracle, the implosion of the Miguelist regime?

The plight and exploits of the liberal *emigrados* between 1828 and 1834 are steeped in romantic myth, but a myth with genuine human misery at its core. As António de Oliveira Silva Gaio summarized in his mid-century historical novel *Mário* (1867), during the reign of Dom Miguel "the liberal party in Portugal was represented by women in mourning, children either orphaned or separated from their parents, and houses destroyed by force or else impoverished. Those [men] who were not behind bars, were either in exile or else hidden away."[89] For the *emigrados* themselves, Dom Miguel was an "oriental despot," indistinguishable from the "Barbary powers of Tripoli, Tunis, and Algiers."[90] Nor were such calumnies entirely baseless or simply rhetorical. Added to executions of leading *Vintistas*, such as Melo Breynor and Borges Carneiro, Dom Miguel's police stuffed the prisons of Limoeiro, São Jorge Castle, and the Torre de São Julião with political dissidents. The execrable state of the prisons meant that they were merely containers in which detainees rotted away. Furthermore, Dom Miguel developed an elaborate espionage network to track down suspected liberals in hiding, hounding them into exile.[91]

[89] Silva Gaio 1981, p. 96.   [90] Silva Maia 1841, p. 260.
[91] Vargues and Torgal, "Da Revolução à Contra-Revolução," p. 76.

In Silva Gaio's *Mário*, the eponymous protagonist follows an extreme, fantastical, and composite version of the experience shared by many of the liberal *emigrados*: he is sent as a prisoner from Lisbon to Luanda via Cape Verde. He escapes from a *presidio* near Mossamedes, and purchases passage aboard a slave ship to Rio de Janeiro where he convinces fellow *emigrados* floundering there to return to Europe with him in order to depose the "Usurper." He selflessly sells all of his jewels (which he somehow had retained during his African captivity and Atlantic odyssey) in order to recross the Atlantic, arriving in London where he joins Saldanha's rag-tag army, landing in Porto just in time to fend off the fateful Miguelist siege.[92] Though many elements in *Mário* mark it as a work of fiction, the Atlantic itineraries toward which it gestures are not exaggerated, and all of the interactions have some precedent, a composite sketch of the experiences of the *emigrados*.

Though the divisions among the *emigrados* were stark and often unbridgeable, exile proved both a leveling and a diversionary experience. It was marked, above all, by hardship. Pereira do Lago noted that "poverty affected all of us, but it did not bring dishonor. Hunger obliged some to seek charity whereas others were forced into debt, for which some were imprisoned later for unpaid debts to their creditors."[93] Even aristocrats were forced to pawn jewels to subsist, and they implored relatives to follow suit.[94] Condessa de Lumiares, residing with her three children in Paris, reportedly lacked the funds to purchase firewood in winter.[95] The correspondence of the Regency, established in 1829 and discussed in the next section, contains a substantial number of letters from groups of dispersed *emigrados*, reminding the political leadership of their loyalty and desperate circumstances, and sometimes chastising its failure to maintain regular payments.[96] It appears that these promised payments were more than fifteen months behind schedule in some cases. Accusations of graft, corruption, and inept mishandling were rife.[97] To penury was added pestilence: 1829–32 witnessed the first outbreak of the pan-European cholera epidemic, which claimed eighteen

---

[92] Silva Gaio 1981, pp. 316, 486.
[93] Lago 1834, vol. II, p. 516.
[94] Marquês de Sta. Iria to Condessa de Vila Real, January 7, 1830, in Ventura 2000, p. 57.
[95] Janke 1974, p. 67.
[96] For an example of such a letter, see ANTT, MNE, cx. 160, a petition from a group of *emigrados* based in Bruges, Belgium, November 6, 1830.
[97] A letter from an English supporter, who had helped to organize relief for Portuguese *emigrados* in Plymouth, lamented that the *emigrados* had been "15 months without receiving means from their own government." See ANTT, MNE, cx. 162, Jessep to Palmela, May 11, 1831.

thousand lives in Paris in 1832 alone, mainly among those enduring overcrowding, undernourishment, and poor sanitation, precisely the demographic cohort to which the *emigrados* belonged.[98] Hardship was not only material and corporal. It was emotional, too: the utter absence of personal news concerning family members remaining in Miguelist Portugal was a common experience, as the poignant letters of the Marquês de Sta. Iria suggest.[99]

Enduring the humiliation of abrupt impoverishment, they were confined by economy to the ports in which they landed or the downtrodden districts of the capitals in which they settled. The initial squalid conditions of the *emigrados* upon their arrival in Plymouth made their cause bleaker, with those of lesser means forced to huddle together in a "shed," christened the *Barração*. As a group of *emigrados* described it:

The *Barração* was a warehouse meant to store wood for construction, almost right on the water in Plymouth. Candido-José Xavier had rented it for 200 pounds per month (480$000) to house the Portuguese *emigrados* who lacked the means to pay for their own accommodation. In this bare warehouse, which lacked even glass windows, the unfortunate *emigrados* slept on the floor, on top of some hay, if any could be found. The *Barração* was extremely humid, with only earth for its floor, so that when it rained, it felt as if we were really living on a dock.[100]

There are few indications concerning how the *emigrados* passed the initial phase of exile. But as early as November 1828, a petition was signed by approximately twenty of them to found a "literary society [*sociedade litteraria*]" as a means to "take advantage of the time spent outside of the *patria* by bringing together the greatest amount of knowledge in all branches of learning, which in the future might allow its members to raise their nation to the greatest levels of prosperity and glory."[101] Luz Soriano recalled that they constructed an improvised theater and the younger *emigrados* from Coimbra (the *Academicos*) staged plays and published pamphlets criticizing the administration, which sought to curtail these extracurricular diversions.[102] These initial efforts eventually

[98] Lyons 2006, p. 171. On the connections (and lack thereof) between riots, civil disturbances, and political upheaval and disease in European countries affected by cholera, see Evans 1988, p. 131.
[99] See, for example, his letter of November 22, 1830, in Ventura 2000, p. 67.
[100] BPMP, MSS. 1783, "As Trez Noites do Barração, e outras Poesia, com Nottas Biograficas e Instrutivas, que formão hum resumo historico-critico da Administração, encarregada de soccerer os refugiados Portugueses em Plymouth, por Alguns Voluntarios Academicos," November 1828; it was later published by Joaquim Pinheiro das Chagas in Paris in 1834 under a shortened title.
[101] BPMP, M-AV-105, "Prospecto," signed in Plymouth, November 1828.
[102] Luz Soriano 1891, pp. 297–98.

expanded into *emigrado* newspapers, published in London, of which the most influential were *O Chaveco Liberal* (1829) and *O Precursor* (1831), both co-edited by Almeida Garrett.[103]

The poor quality and limited extent of the hospitality extended to the Portuguese *emigrados* who flocked to Rio de Janeiro after 1828 emerges from the historical record. Generosity, of course, is hard to measure except quantitatively. One sanguine contemporary commentator, for example, claimed that the *emigrados* were offered ample aid by means of public subscriptions and from the proceeds of government-sponsored lotteries. Additional support took the form of free lodging in private homes while some managed to marry well, thus "acquiring a fortune that they perhaps never would have acquired had they remained in Portugal."[104] But *emigrado* diaries and memoirs suggest a different story. While confirming the subscription and lottery to raise funds, Luz Soriano recounted how recourse to these methods occurred only because of the initial parsimony of Dom Pedro and the Brazilian government. When the subscription was finally collected, Dom Pedro's lover, Marquesa de Santos,[105] donated twice the amount contributed by the emperor. With those funds, Luz Soriano lamented, "a dilapidated convent was leased to house the *emigrados*, which appeared to be an exact copy of the *Barração* of Plymouth."[106] Modern historians confirm the great controversy that aid to *emigrados* provoked in Brazil, not least because the more desperate among them resorted to extra-legal means to subsist, something that fanned the flames of the Lusophobia (and xenophobia more generally) that prevailed in the aftermath of the foreign mercenary riots of 1828.[107]

Luz Soriano's memoir may be supplemented with anecdotes culled from Sá da Bandeira's diary. He was among the first *emigrados* to reach Brazil, via Plymouth, in November 1828, weary from the military retreat into Galicia after the demise of the Porto Junta. In Rio, he stayed with future members of the Regency, Mouzinho Albuquerque and José Antonio Guerreiro. It appears that he moved easily in the highest echelons of *Carioca* society, dining regularly with Gomes da Silva ("O Chalaça"),

---

[103] On Almeida Garrett's London experiences in those years, see J. B. de Sousa 2011. Such literary-political pursuits were not unique to the Portuguese; in fact, they followed in the path blazed by their Spanish predecessors. See, above all, Llorens 1979.

[104] Cunha Mattos 1833, vol. I, p. 99.

[105] Domitila de Castro Canto e Melo (1797–1867).

[106] Luz Soriano 1887, vol. I, p. 230. In his memoirs, Luz Soriano condemned Dom Pedro for "forsaking" and demonstrating "cruel indifference" to the *emigrados* who had journeyed to Rio de Janeiro.

[107] G. S. Ribeiro and V. Pereira, "O Primeiro Reinado em Revisão," in Grinberg and Salles 2009, pp. 163–64; more generally, see G. S. Ribeiro 2002.

enjoying frequent audiences with Dom Pedro, and exchanging confidential information with one of the principal imperial counselors, Marquês de Paranaguá.[108] But Sá da Bandeira soon became disillusioned with Brazilian officialdom's nonchalance toward Portugal's plight, particularly when he perceived that no material support was forthcoming. His late 1828 memorandum to Dom Pedro, in which he warned that Brazil's tranquility depended on the triumph of Portuguese liberalism, sketching a doomsday scenario of a joint Luso-Spanish reconquest venture of all of Ibero-America, went unheeded.[109] He was irritated by suggestions, made by Visconde de Itabayana (in London) and Marquês de Inhambupe (in Rio),[110] that the *emigrados* should congregate in Brazil, not in order to regroup and then launch an invasion of Miguelist Portugal, but "for the purpose of being integrated into the foreign [military] corps of this country, in service of the Empire." This plan, he recorded in his diary, would "accomplish nothing." As a result, he noted, "I am increasingly annoyed by this country, in spite of the warm hospitality offered by the people whom I know."[111] Nor were such observations condemned to the oblivion of Sá da Bandeira's diary. Rodrigo Pinto Pizarro, who clashed repeatedly with Dom Pedro from 1831, publicly denounced the emperor not only for mistreating the *emigrados* in Brazil, but for placing them under the auspices of the inspector in charge of foreign colonists, as if they were "Neapolitan boot-makers or rioters recently released from German prisons."[112]

In fact, the *emigrados*' arrival in Brazil could not have occurred at a less auspicious moment. Brazilian nativists, already alarmed by Dom Pedro's heavy recruitment of German and Irish mercenaries, interpreted the *emigrados*' arrival as further proof of the emperor's meddling in Portuguese affairs and his clandestine plan to unite the thrones, citing the threat to Brazil's independence posed by a "fifth column" of Portuguese resident in Brazil.[113] Certainly, there were dissonant

---

[108] Francisco Vilela Barbosa (1769–1846), Marquês de Paranaguá.

[109] On the invasion of Mexico Spain launched in 1829, which sent four thousand soldiers from Cuba, see Costeloe 1986, p. 99; on Iberian and Latin American liberals' understanding of their common cause in the late 1820s, see Ricketts 2011.

[110] António Luis Pereira da Cunha (1760–1837), Marquês de Inhambupe de Lima.

[111] Diary entries of November 19, 1828, and February 3–4, 1829, in Sá da Bandeira 1975, vol. I, pp. 113, 146–47.

[112] Rodrigo Pinto Pizarro, quoted in Braga 1903, p. 457. A British resident in Brazil during this period, Reverend Robert Walsh, confirmed the claims of Sá da Bandeira and Pizarro. He reported that the Portuguese *emigrados* were "placed under the care of the superintendent of colonies, and located in the interior." See Walsh 1830, vol. II, p. 446.

[113] Wisser 2006, p. 15. The similarity between rising Lusophobia in Brazil *c.* 1830 and the attempts in Spanish America to prevent the entry of Spaniards and the restriction

voices which ridiculed Lusophobia, demanding "how can one hate the Portuguese (today Brazilian citizens) if they compose a great part of this Brazilian nation? Is it possible that all of them are *corcundas* and malevolent absolutists?"[114] But the fear of a subterranean, foreign faction plotting against Brazil's independence was pervasive. As a Recife newspaper noted, "the recolonizing party, better known as the 'Column of the Throne and Altar,' is a secret cabal, composed of enemies of our independence and the representative system," mainly comprised of Portuguese.[115] A São Luis paper concurred: "Portugal still deludes itself by supposing that it will be re-joined to Brazil, with the latter as its colony. They do not heed the sad events of Mexico."[116] The *emigrados* appreciated the impact of Lusophobia on the Brazilian government's inaction, aware that public opinion was terribly suspicious of anything smacking of renewed Portuguese influence. The editors of the Lisbon-based *Paquete de Portugal* claimed that such an attitude was based on mistaken premise, for "Portugal harbors no grudge and has no jealousy of Brazil, whose recolonization nobody here desires. We do not lack overseas territories which are as well-endowed as those of the Brazilian Empire. We lack nothing but enough people [to populate the territories] and liberty."[117]

The *emigrados* were not immune to self-pity under such dire conditions. In the early months of exile, an *emigrado* publication enquired "what crimes have we Portuguese committed – we, the liberators of slaves – ... that we find ourselves today slaves, vagabonds, and banished fugitives?"[118] Material hardship aside, exile proved an intellectually stimulating period for some *emigrados*, who later heaped praise on the countries that offered them sanctuary. Paris, especially after the advent of the July Monarchy, was, as a modern historian has written,

---

in their participation in political life is remarkable. On Central America, see Dym 2008; on the expulsion of Spaniards from Mexico after 1830, see Sims 1990.

[114] *A Cigarra*, no. 4 (November 10, 1829), n.p.
[115] *O Constitucional*, no. 157 (December 30, 1830), pp. 2–3.
[116] *A Cigarra*, no. 17 (February 10, 1830), p. 75.
[117] *Paquete de Portugal*, vol. VII, no. 8 (April 5, 1831), p. 246; though perhaps such enlightened sentiments did not trickle down the social ladder. A Brazilian participant in the Portuguese Civil War was shocked by the attitudes toward Brazil harbored by the common folk of Porto with whom he conversed: "they cling to rather extravagant, prejudiced ideas about Brazil, including the impression that there are no white people or public education of any sort, that Brazil in 1832 remains as it was in the time of Pombal. They cannot quite comprehend that the Empire is a sovereign state, independent of Portugal. They dream of a voluntary reunion with Brazil or else a forced recolonization. Many people in the villages, and not a few in Porto itself, still refer to Brazilians as *os nossos Brazis*." See Cunha Mattos 1833, vol. I, p. 133.
[118] *O Portuguez Emigrado, ou Realista Constitucional*, no. 1 (October 7, 1828), p. 2.

"a cosmopolitan and relatively free environment for expatriates and a network for disseminating new creeds and theories ... there was a salon for almost any foreigner who wanted social contacts and who arrived with money, intellectual ambitions or political plans."[119] One of the most effusive, Pereira do Lago, was down and out in both Paris and London, as well as various cities in Belgium. He later confessed that he left Paris with great reluctance, "the asylum of the belles-arts, the temple of science, the home of good taste, the source of all pleasures, and the center of civilization." He praised London for its scientific, charitable, and philanthropic institutions, as well as its parks, monuments, security, and liberty.[120] Optimism pervades *emigrado* memoirs, specifically their shared belief that the progress of science and art would eviscerate rivalry between nations as "customs slowly begin to imitate and hence resemble one another."[121] For this reason, the snuffing out of liberty in one distant corner of Europe produced the most malicious effects elsewhere and many of the *emigrados* portrayed themselves as engaged in a common struggle with other exiles across Europe.[122] In his posthumously published memoirs, Silva Maia argued that the toppling of constitutional regimes in Spain and Portugal in 1823 harmed countries not directly under a tyrannical yoke, for their governments, in turn, drifted toward absolutism and, "in this way, human knowledge regressed."[123]

The experience of exile left these sentiments undimmed and the *emigrados* were further convinced that the liberal cause in Portugal formed part of a broader European and Atlantic story of inexorable progress and the diffusion of civilization. Many of the *emigrados* conceived of themselves as part of a broader process now encompassed by the term "The Age of Revolutions."[124] For Silva Maia, the 1776–83 North American Revolution "illuminated and clarified certain important questions for the peoples of Europe," prodding discussion

---

[119] Kramer 1988, pp. 6, 53.
[120] Lago 1834, vol. I, p. 244; vol. II, p. 540.
[121] Lago 1834, vol. II, p. 350–51.
[122] See Isabella 2009; on this sense of solidarity in the Shelley-Byron circle in England, see Stock 2010.
[123] Silva Maia 1841, pp. 246–47.
[124] In previous publications, the present author has questioned the distorting impact of a homogeneous, monolithic conception of an "Age of Revolutions," instead siding with those scholars, like Fernández Sebastián, who argue for multiple, winding paths which converged unpredictably in the road to political modernity. But it does not escape the present author's attention that the *emigrados*, like the *Vintistas* before them, were convinced that there was, in fact, a single path to modern politics, already trodden by other nations, onto which they sought to guide Portugal.

of "vital questions concerning the rights of man; the nature and origin of government; and the rights and mutual duties between rulers and subjects."[125] Almeida Garrett took melancholy pride in Brazil's independence, claiming that it was inspired by the 1820 Porto Revolution: "as Europe had received example and impulse of liberty from [North] America, it was just that it repaid its debt."[126] While rejecting the insinuation that they were "admirers and imitators of novelty" for its own sake, they argued that it was "desirable to adapt and imitate" the institutions and practices of other nations which were of "obvious utility" and "have been made almost sacred by their long existence."[127] Other *emigrados* defended a break with tradition, claiming that "modern civilization is producing uniformity among the nations of Europe and History shows us that different states, as they pass through the same revolutions, and experience similar vicissitudes, come to be governed by the same mechanisms and [political] systems."[128] Sebastião Xavier Botelho, formerly a governor of Mozambique, argued that "Europe views Portugal as an orphan of civilization, but now striving to be free, to extirpate its old errors, and to conform to the ideas of the present century ... [Portugal will achieve this result with] new laws, new institutions, and useful reforms drawn from the best law codes that the wisdom and experience of the more enlightened nations imparts."[129] Sá da Bandeira, too, believed that nothing more was required than the dissemination of ideas to dissipate ignorance. He fantasized about forming a society in Portugal devoted to the publication and distribution of small-format "useful" books.[130] In the struggle between the forces of ignorance – superstition and vestigial tradition – and enlightenment, public instruction was a vital vehicle for the diffusion of new doctrines. The creation of new public institutions, too, was the focus of efforts as early as the Civil War. In 1833 alone, Dom Pedro founded an art museum, a society for medical science and scientific literature, and a public library in Porto. These institutions were complemented with a new spate founded after 1834, chiefly in Lisbon. An academy of fine arts and a music conservatory were founded in 1835 and 1836, respectively. After the Civil War, there was a wave of new *sociedades promotoras*, distant yet recognizable progeny of the

[125] Silva Maia 1841, p. 253.
[126] Almeida Garrett, "Da Europa e da America e de sua Mutua Influencia na Causa da Civilisação e da Liberdade," in Almeida Garrett 1991, p. 85.
[127] Andrade 1831, pp. 42–43.
[128] [Anon.], *Investigações Políticas* 1833, pp. 16–17, 20–21.
[129] Botelho 1834a, p. 5.
[130] Diary entry of January 24, 1829, in Sá da Bandeira 1975, vol. I, p. 134.

eighteenth-century economic societies and more immediate heirs of *Vintismo*'s civic-minded intellectual efforts.[131]

But all of these successful ventures lay far in the future in 1828–29. The *emigrados'* survival hinged on the charity of strangers and the forbearance of foreign governments.[132] In England, authorities viewed the aggregation of political dissidents plotting a revolutionary return to their homeland as unacceptable, demanding that they seek refuge elsewhere. As Wellington told Aberdeen, "I beg the Marquis of Palmela to observe that we cannot allow His Majesty's dominions to be made the seat of the cabinet, the arsenal, and the harbor, by which war is being carried out in the name, but without the knowledge or consent, of Dom Pedro against Portugal."[133] Some *emigrados* denied that they were plotting a military expedition: "we defy the eyes of an Argus, aided by the best telescopes and microscopes in the world, to discover the least symptoms of conspiracy in a peaceable association of 3,000 unarmed men."[134] But this assertion rang hollow in light of their ill-disguised, furious preparations to invade Portugal.

After much lamentation, the *emigrados* readied themselves to leave Albion's shores. But where should they seek refuge? Palmela and others, including Silva Carvalho, maintained that the most viable option was to relocate to Rio de Janeiro, regroup, and plot from there.[135] Saldanha and his followers opposed leaving Europe, contending that such a move would be tantamount to capitulation. While in principle a defensible proposition, few options were available within Europe in 1829. Nevertheless, Saldanha and his followers rejected the "Brazilian option," a stance deemed insubordinate by the other *emigrado* factions. Along with Sá da Bandeira, Saldanha was persuaded that the next best option, besides Continental Europe, was the seizure of some part of Portuguese territory

---

[131] França 1974, vol. I, pp. 140–54 passim. The *Vintista* forerunners were the *Sociedade Promotora da Industria Nacional* (1821–22) and the *Sociedade Literaria Patriotica* (1822). As França 1974 observes, "the Romanticism of 1820 was not dead in 1834," p. 170.

[132] Though it appears that British charity was actually quite generous in many cases. It was only in May 1831, almost three years after their arrival en masse, that a Mr. Jessep, the "Treasurer for the Relief of Portuguese Emigrants in Plymouth," wrote apologetically to Palmela that "it appears impossible to arrange a new subscription" to "mitigate the hardships suffered by those victims of their good principles and misfortune." See ANTT, MNE, cx. 162, Jessep to Palmela, May 11, 1831.

[133] Wellington to Aberdeen, August 23, 1828, in Wellington 1973, vol. III, p. 655.

[134] *O Portuguez Emigrado, ou Realista Constitucional*, no. 7 (November 18, 1828), p. 53.

[135] In Silva Carvalho's phrase, only in Brazil "can we find secure means with which to return to Europe and vindicate the rights of Dona Maria." See Silva Carvalho [in Plymouth] to Palmela, December 6, 1828, reproduced in *Documentos para a História Contemporanea* 1891, vol. I, doc. 14 (p. 21).

and the establishment of a foothold there. They floated the possibility of the island of Mozambique, with a view toward funding the Regency through customs receipts derived from the Indian Ocean trade.[136]

The debate on destination raised the issue of authority among the *emigrados*: should there be an ultimate arbiter of disputes among them and, if so, who should exercise this function? The speed of events, and Dom Pedro's obtuseness, prodded them to organize themselves in a manner consonant with the *Carta*. The general consensus was that Palmela, who had been ambassador to London before he resigned in protest of Dom Miguel's usurpation, was the natural, as well as legal, leader.[137] But his past conduct perturbed many *emigrados*, a situation compounded by recriminations arising from the evacuation of Portugal. The debacle of the *Belfastada* was deemed cowardly by those who continued to fight and later endured the perils of a narrow, treacherous escape into Galicia. The other figures vying for leadership were equally divisive. Candido-José Xavier, nominally the director of the *Deposito Geral* at Plymouth, was a suspected *afrancesado* in 1809 and, subsequently, a deputy to the Cortes, before a brief, undistinguished tenure as Minister of War in 1827, which many considered marked by "anti-liberal" conduct. Paulo Midosi, secretary of the *Deposito*, had not fought in Galicia, and was thus an unknown entity, outside of a narrow coterie of *literati*.[138]

Those who sided with Saldanha on the issue of relocation strategy scattered to the ports of France (chiefly Brest) and Belgium. They were accused of avoiding the perilous voyage to Rio de Janeiro and instead seeking to "remain in Europe, enjoying a languorous existence, without risk or bother, eating the bread of Her Majesty."[139] Such scurrilous remarks may have contained some truth, but the Rio de Janeiro plan was hampered by serious logistical obstacles. It would be necessary to stop for provisions and fresh water, for it was nearly impossible to sail directly from an English port to Brazil. Normally, refreshments would have been obtained in Cape Verde, Madeira, or the Azores, but all of these were under the control of the Miguelists. The Canaries were mentioned as an option, but Ferdinand VII was vociferously supportive of his nephew, brother-in-law, and kindred spirit Dom Miguel.

---

[136] Diary entries of February 11 and 12, 1829, in Sá da Bandeira 1975, vol. I, pp. 152–53.

[137] Luz Soriano recalled that "the legality of [Palmela's] position could not be denied," though he hastened to denounce the "errors and vices" of his leadership. See Luz Soriano 1891, pp. 288–89.

[138] Luz Soriano 1891, p. 290.

[139] ANTT, MNE, cx. 160, Paulo Midosi (in Plymouth) to Palmela, April 9, 1829.

Any landing in Spanish territory, therefore, was certain to result in the arrest and imprisonment of the *emigrados*.

There was one island in the Azores, Terceira, however, which refused to swear allegiance to Dom Miguel and was, nominally and momentarily, independent. As early as September 1828, some *emigrados* clamored for its selection as a base for their operations. The pretext of stopping at Terceira for fresh water and victualing was feasible, but the British government remained intransigent, rightly fearing that the *emigrados* might disembark, abscond, and convert Terceira into a territorial foothold from which to invade continental Portugal, however outlandish, and hopeless, this prospect might appear. Were the Royal Navy to permit the *emigrados* to land at Terceira, it could be interpreted as aiding and abetting them, an act hostile to the Miguelist government. The Royal Navy therefore blockaded the island, repulsing a Saldanha-led band of six hundred *emigrados* from landing in January 1829, and forcing a retreat to Europe, where they regrouped in Paris. In February–March 1829, then, the *emigrados'* options appeared limited. But Terceira remained the best option, though some *emigrados* believed it to be far-fetched. As Midosi informed Palmela in April 1829, "Some here desire to head to Terceira, but I do not believe that there are many such men and those who do profess such a desire are persons whose actions are in perpetual opposition to explicit order of the established authority."[140]

After further wrangling, a brief stop in the Canaries en route to Brazil was arranged, but further opposition arose from the British owners of the ships contracted to transport the *emigrados*. According to Thomas Stubbs, the owners of the two ships in question (the *Bolívar* and the *Hayden*, respectively) were wary of leasing their ships for a transatlantic voyage, which they considered "ruinous." Similarly, even if they acquiesced to embarking for Brazil, they refused to permit a stop in Tenerife, which they claimed was unsafe for nautical and navigational reasons. The owners therefore insisted on stopping at Terceira, which appealed to the political imaginations of the *emigrados*. If disembarking proved impossible, however, owing to renewed British or Miguelist resistance, Stubbs suggested that the ships would re-route to Rio, a voyage posing a serious "risk to the lives of so many of the subjects of SMF, for it is very long without fresh supplies and water."[141]

---

[140] Ibid.
[141] ANTT, MNE, cx. 161, Thomas Stubbs to Palmela, February 12, 1829. Saldanha confirmed these problems – the British blockade of Terceira and impossibility of proceeding directly to Rio de Janeiro – noting also that there would be "an excessive number of men in each ship," making such a transatlantic passage hazardous. See ANTT, MNE, cx. 162, Saldanha to Palmela, June 30, 1829.

While a foothold in Portuguese territory was a desirable base for the beleaguered *emigrados*, other options existed. Initially, the exiles preferred to set up the Regency in Dona Maria's presence. Saldanha, however, believed that remaining in England was no longer an option for Dona Maria, mainly because of the British government's failure to condemn Dom Miguel's actions and its reluctance to throw its support behind the *emigrados*. As Saldanha remarked in a letter to Palmela,

Her Majesty may lack both an army and a navy, so she cannot redress [our] difficulties by recourse to arms, but she can protest her treatment in a dignified way, which, in my opinion, is to leave that perfidious land [i.e. Britain] ... this decorous action would embarrass the British government, for the persecution of an innocent sovereign never could be justified in the eyes of the English people.[142]

Saldanha's sentiments soon became widespread and resentment toward the British government mounted. *Emigrados* claimed that Britain furnished no support other than "the hospitality of the laws of the land."[143] Other *emigrados* angrily denounced British "machinations against our institutions," which they dated from the promulgation of the *Carta* in 1826.[144] Britain's failure to act on behalf of the *emigrados* perplexed them. One pamphleteer enquired "have those feelings of sympathy that moved [Britain] to liberate Greece, and to free the African Blacks, slackened toward the Portuguese, their oldest friends and allies, groaning now under the heaviest and worst of yokes, imposed by the most barbarous of tyrants?"[145] Other *emigrados* expressed confusion that their defense of legitimacy, of Dona Maria's right to the throne, was ignored by other European nations. In 1823, "popular insurrections" in Italy, Spain, and Portugal had been "disapproved of and defeated by Europe's cabinets. But now no Congress has been formed to vindicate legitimacy in Portugal nor avenge the insults hurled at the sovereignty of its queen."[146] A "nation ravaged for defending its legitimate monarch," *O Chaveco Liberal* lamented, "abandoned by all the Kings of the

---

142 ANTT, MNE, cx. 162, Saldanha [from Paris] to Palmela, March 9, 1829; yet all realized that British support, or at least acquiescence, was crucial to the liberal cause. As late as June 1831, a leading liberal official remarked that "the arrival of D. Maria II to England at the present moment seems to me to be both urgent and important." ANTT, MNE, cx. 165, Luiz António de Abreu e Lima to Thomas Mascarenhas, June 15, 1831.

143 Pizarro 1829, p. 5; though not all *emigrados* agreed on the merits of private British generosity. Silva Maia, for example, thought that the English masons hardly raised a finger to assist the *emigrados* and that more substantial support was found elsewhere, including Ostende. See Silva Maia 1841, p. 151.

144 *O Padre Malagrida, ou a Tezoira*, no. 3 (1828), p. 55.

145 [Anon.], *Neutrality* 1829, p. 27.   146 Dias 1829, p. 8.

world, delivered up to the Usurper's cleaver, is an unprecedented and terrible event."[147]

PART II

The Regency of Terceira

A confluence of geopolitical circumstances led eventually to a consensus to quit continental Europe, regroup on Terceira, use it as a base, and send Dona Maria II temporarily back to Brazil. Palmela came to accept the soundness of this plan and, by March 1829, sought to convince Barbacena, then Dom Pedro's chief envoy to Europe, of its wisdom. He ridiculed the notion that the Queen's return to Brazil would be regarded as a concession of defeat and acquiescence to Dom Miguel, arguing that the funds required to support a Court in adequate splendor were better allocated to sustain the Regency on Terceira.[148] In June 1829, Dom Pedro nominated a Regency, appointing those whom he most trusted and alienating many of those who believed his actions contravened the *Carta*, as will be analyzed in greater detail. The Regency was comprised of Palmela (as President), Conde de Vila Flor,[149] and José António Guerreiro. In the same month, Vila Flor managed to disembark on Terceira, installing himself as Governor and Captain-General of the Azores. By March 1830, the entire Regency was assembled on Terceira.

With a beachhead established in Portuguese territory, Dona Maria returned to Brazil in August 1829. The occupation of Terceira notwithstanding, the decision was interpreted as a massive defeat, moral as well as political, the tactical and fiscal necessity of it aside. Dom Pedro's advisor, Barbacena, escorted Dona Maria back to the New World and insisted on the temporary nature of the move. In a statement circulated to the Portuguese *emigrados*, Barbacena asserted that "far from abandoning the cause of his most precious daughter, SMI [Dom Pedro] remains firm in his resolution to never accept the usurpation." He added that all *emigrados* who wished to come to Brazil would be assured of "generous hospitality" as a reward for their brazen loyalty to the rightful Queen.[150] But Barbacena was putting a brave face on a

---

[147] *O Chaveco Liberal*, vol. I, no. 1 (September 9, 1829), p. 16.
[148] AMI, Palmela, "Nota sobre a Questão Portugueza em Março de 1829" [note enclosed in a letter from Barbacena to Gomes da Silva, cited below].
[149] António Jose Severim de Noronha (1792–1860), 7th Conde and first Marquês de Vila Flor, later (from 1832) 1st Duque da Terceira.
[150] ANTT, MNE, cx. 163, "Declaração feito pelo Marquêz de Barbacena aos Subditos Fieis de S. M. a Rainha de Portugal D. Maria II," August 27, 1829.

grave situation. He entertained no illusions concerning the symbolism of Dona Maria's return to Rio de Janeiro. In a private letter to Gomes da Silva, Barbacena made clear that should Dona Maria "return to her room at [the Palace of] S. Christovão, she would be considered again like any other of the Princesses, the memory of her usurped Crown would soon fade, and the Portuguese [*emigrados*] would consider themselves as humiliated and abandoned, their cause hopeless." Instead, he believed, she must be treated with the "same formality as the Queen of England or France would receive" were one of them to make a state visit.[151]

Emigrado disappointment with Brazil's parsimony was counteracted by the optimism unleashed by the July Revolution in France in 1830. Mouzinho de Albuquerque articulated the common hope entertained by the *emigrados*: "If the new public spirit of France succeeds in establishing and consolidating a representative government, built on the firm foundation of legally guaranteed liberty, this example will undoubtedly excite the same desire in many other European peoples."[152] Writing from Brussels, Abreu e Lima remarked that "the current state of Europe is not unfavorable for us, and, if Dom Pedro's declarations are those we anticipate, the triumph of legitimacy and justice in Portugal is at hand."[153] The debate now turned to tactics. At first, the Regency intended to gather the scattered *emigrados* together on Terceira, enticing them with an expenses-paid journey and the prospect of a respite from continental poverty. But this plan was soon abandoned, not least because the repercussions of the July Revolution did not radiate as far as Terceira, which remained hopelessly blockaded. Brazil's recognition – and the material resources this event would imply – remained outstanding, leading the Regency to conclude that gathering the *emigrados* on Terceira, "isolated in the middle of the ocean," where they could only be "passive observers" of the drama unfolding in Europe, was counterproductive. Much more promising under the propitious circumstances produced by the July Revolution was the prospect of encouraging the "compatriot refugees" in France and England to attempt to "instigate an insurrection" in Portugal itself.[154]

---

[151] AMI, Barbacena to Gomes da Silva, March 31, 1829.

[152] ANTT, MNE, livro 357, Luiz de Silva Mouzinho de Albuquerque to Conde do Sabugal, August 31, 1830.

[153] Luiz António de Abreu e Lima to Regency on Terceira, July 17, 1830, reproduced in Abreu e Lima 1874, p. 288. However, even Abreu e Lima's enthusiasm for the anticipated impact of the July Revolution had dimmed less than a year later: he lamented the "uncertainty and general agitation produced by the on-going combat between the old and new systems of government." See Abreu e Lima to Regency, April 11, 1831, reproduced in ibid., p. 424.

[154] ANTT, MNE, livro 357, Mouzinho de Albuquerque to Abreu e Lima, September 18, 1830; these citations, however, should not lead the reader to infer a close connection

By occupying a fragment of Portuguese territory, the *emigrados* hoped to stave off the recognition of the Miguelist regime by other European powers. One of the chief aims of Miguelist foreign policy was Britain's cooperation against the *emigrados* conspiring to launch an invasion of Portugal. Formal recognition of Dom Miguel's government would achieve this goal. In lieu of recognition, Dom Miguel's foreign minister, Santarém, sought an "Act of Guarantee," a pledge that Britain would come to Portugal's aid should an invasion force land on Portugal's shores, that British territory should not be used to plan such an invasion, and that Britain declare that Terceira was illegally occupied by rebels, which would mean that the Royal Navy would continue its blockade of that Azorean island.[155] This plan foundered after the July Revolution, which transformed the landscape of international politics. Fearing the repercussions in Portugal, Miguelist publicists shifted into high gear. "The goals of the revolutionaries are unchanging," Madre de Deos argued, "they aim to subvert the established order in all states in order to prepare the way for the empire of Masonry."[156] "What is this new [French] revolution," another Miguelist cried, "but a repetition or recapitulation of all of the iniquity and horror of the previous one, which caused great damage to every part of the known world?"[157]

For their part, the *emigrados* portrayed their occupation of Terceira not as an insolent revolt against a legitimate government, but rather as a legitimate government's struggle against a usurpation. As an *emigrado* pamphlet described the situation, "Portugal and Terceira are not two belligerent powers; nor can Terceira be called a rebellious island. They are both one and the same nation, there are no mutual treaties between them; nor are there treaties betwixt either of these parties with England or any other power."[158] After July 1830, the Regency believed that it could win formal recognition as the legitimate government of Portugal. At first, Palmela sought a form of indirect recognition from Britain or France, "some sort of act" that would enable the Regency to borrow funds to fund its military operations. Though he did not invoke explicitly the precedent of the treaties of "amity and commerce" Britain had

between the July Revolution and the direction of events in Portugal. As C. Church argued, "the connections between the July Days and the other outbursts was not organic but symbolic ... the symbolic trigger of the July Days interacted with existing stresses and strains ... for all their family resemblances, the events of 1830 were ultimately based on local problems." See Church 1983, pp. 38, 56.

[155] ANTT, MNE, livro 580, Visconde de Santarém to Visconde d'Asseca, Reservado no. 244, January 2, 1830.

[156] Madre de Deos 1832, pp. 6–7.

[157] [Anon.], *Resposta á Carta* 1830, p. 8.

[158] [Anon.], *Neutrality* 1829, p. 7.

concluded with the Latin American republics in the mid 1820s prior to full diplomatic recognition, he sought an equivalent arrangement. Palmela instructed Conde de Funchal in London to arrange for the "nomination of an [British] agent, even if possessing the mere title of 'consul,' sent out on an extraordinary mission. Even that gesture would produce a favorable effect for our cause."[159] In subsequent correspondence, after Dom Pedro placed himself at the head of the Regency, as will be explored in a subsequent section, Palmela implored Funchal to convey to the European powers that "Dom Pedro will not revolutionize Portugal." On the contrary, Dom Pedro "would do everything to prove (except for altering the *Carta*) that he shared the ideas of the Powers of Europe."[160]

The experience on Terceira, like many aspects of the experience of exile and the Civil War, was enveloped in myth, distorted by self-aggrandizement, and clouded by sentimentalism by the middle decades of the nineteenth century, as some of the participants wrote memoirs of their youthful heroics as they advanced in years. Nevertheless, while accounting for this tendency, Terceira was steeped in symbolism at the time, appealing greatly to the Romantic imagination, an island thrust in the middle of the Atlantic, the last stand of a desperate band of political exiles. As Marquês de Fronteira recorded, "though I had left the center of European civilization, having passed the better part of winter in the beautiful capital of France, I experienced great pleasure as I landed on this fragment of Portugal, after a long absence, having lost on many occasions the hope of ever returning to the patria. Wandering through the streets of Angra, I felt myself once again to be in Portugal."[161] Exile, with its opportunity for observing the customs of other nations, and the Azorean experience, with the vacant hours it afforded to reflection, was crucial in the generation of *emigrado* plans for Portugal's renewal after the Civil War. For example, Sá da Bandeira's private papers are littered with notes of which the following is typical: "By putting into practice the necessary reforms, with our nation governed by a liberal and enlightened government, we can entertain the happy prospect of rising to the level of the happiest nations of the world in a few short years." These reforms included the construction of modern roads and canals, the development of manufactures, and public instruction that concentrated on the industrial arts.[162] There were government-sponsored efforts to create some semblance of

---

[159] ANTT, MNE, livro 295, Palmela to Funchal, March 8, 1832.
[160] ANTT, MNE, livro 295, Palmela to Funchal, April 15, 1832.
[161] Fronteira 1928, pt. IV, p. 214.
[162] AHM, DIV/3/18/02/09/05, untitled note, dated 1830.

an intellectual life on Terceira. Voltaire's plays came back into vogue and were performed. A printing press was brought from London to Angra in February 1829 and the *Chronica da Terceira* was published from April 1830. Edited initially by Luz Soriano, it was both a digest of political news culled from various European and North American newspapers and a vehicle for disseminating more abstract ideas related to public administration, science, and art. It later became the official organ of the Regency. Luz Soriano also collaborated with Sá da Bandeira to publish the *Folhinha da Terceira* between 1830 and 1832, a hybrid almanac, historical compendium, and political manifesto which devoted attention to Portugal's African colonies and plans for their economic improvement.[163]

The Regency conceived of Terceira as a laboratory of reform and a foil to what they considered to be Dom Miguel's misgovernment. In this "small theater," the Regency planned to "experiment with all of the measures which they hoped, in a short time, would be applied throughout the monarchy." The success of the reforms on Terceira would offer yet further proof of the intentions and righteousness of the "liberal cause," they held. "Theoretical questions," the *Chronica* noted, "are beyond the grasp of the [common] people, but everyone is capable of comparing practical results, of the sweetness (*doçura*) of Dona Maria's government with the ferocity of the usurper's, of the order and economy of the former with the dilapidation of the latter."[164] In fact, constitutionalism's alleged benefits had never been demonstrated, whether in 1821–23 or 1826–28, so the populace remained ignorant of the "utility that can result from such a change." Under the brief episodes of constitutional rule, it appeared as if nothing had improved: "agriculture remained hamstrung by obstacles blocking its development; industry failed to receive the necessary protection; and commerce remained stagnant due to ruinous treaties with foreign nations."[165] It seems that such sentiments were more than propaganda (though they certainly served that purpose as well). Mouzinho de Albuquerque described the Regency's "desire to be useful to [future] governments, which, in happier times, will administer Portugal, by establishing in this little enclave some of the institutions indispensable for the *Carta* to flourish and to make palpable to the people the advantages of the principles enshrined therein."[166] But more practical and less enlightened considerations may

---

[163] The *Folhinha*'s treatment of this final theme is discussed in Chapter 5.
[164] *Chronica da Terceira*, no. 17 (July 14, 1830), p. 70.
[165] C. Carvalho 1832b, p. 14.
[166] ANTT, MNE cx. 155, Mouzinho de Albuquerque to Thomas Mascarenhas, December 17, 1830.

have been at play as well. Besides the insufficient military force, which made full-scale invasion impractical, a consensus emerged against the violent imposition of the *Carta* on an already brutalized Portuguese populace. Resende unceasingly counseled Dom Pedro in 1832–33 that he must wait for the *Carta* to "pass from the paper on which it is written into the hearts of men."[167]

The driving force behind the torrent of legislation was Mouzinho da Silveira who had served Dom João faithfully, and competently, after the 1823 *Vilafrancada*. This pedigree endowed him with impeccable royalist credentials, though he became an early adherent of the *Carta* and thus ran afoul of Dom Miguel and his supporters. Mouzinho da Silveira was perfectly aware of the *Carta*'s imperfections. With characteristic acuity, he perceived that the *Carta* was hamstrung because it arrived "without auxiliary laws, but instead found itself mixed together with millions of statutes that conflicted or were inconsistent with it." "Liberty," he argued, "is an exotic plant, and when its growth is blocked, it cannot become acclimatized."[168] There seems to have been universal admiration for Mouzinho da Silveira's erudition and capacity. As Palmela wrote in 1830, "[he] may not have much experience in matters of government, but there is no Portuguese who exceeds him in talent and energy, nor in general learning, and even less in disinterestedness."[169]

The Terceira Regency's reforms were wide-ranging, ambitious, and radical, a Lusitanian "Great Leap Forward." The number of decrees and new laws introduced was dizzying, sixty-two between March and December 1830 alone. These early decrees covered multiple topics, from amnesty for political crimes, to the abolition of monopoly on soap, to the establishment of less regulated trade, to the elimination of duties on the sale of fish. As the *emigrado* side gained the upper hand in the Civil War, the scope of Mouzinho da Silveira's reform project expanded. Deeply influenced by Charles-Jean Baptiste Bonnin's *Abrégé des Principes d'Administration* (1829), a large portion of the introduction to the far-reaching administrative laws of May 16, 1832 was a loose translation, undertaken by Almeida Garrett, of Bonnin's tract.[170] Mouzinho da Silveira's subsequent fiscal reforms essentially dismantled

---

[167] Resende to Dom Pedro, August 4, 1832, reproduced in Resende 1916, p. 432.

[168] Mouzinho da Silveira 1989, vol. II, p. 639. In his 1849 eulogy, Almeida Garrett was more charitable in his assessment of Dom Pedro's handiwork, claiming that the *Carta* could do no more than "proscribe the past, and point to the future." See his "Memoria Histórica de J. Xavier Mouzinho da Silveira" (1849), in L. Neves 2007, p. 181; for a competent biography, see Manique 1989.

[169] Palmela to Abreu e Lima, May 25, 1830, reproduced in Abreu e Lima 1874, p. 39.

[170] França 1974, vol. I, pp. 129–30. Sá 1969 disagreed, claiming that the May 16, 1832, decrees largely derived from Napoleonic administrative reform, p. 201. Bonnin's

the ancien régime's property system, including the abolition of the *forais* (town charters), *morgadios* (entail), tithes, and personal duties, all in an effort to undermine ecclesiastical and seigneurial land-holding and the related systems of privileges, exceptions, and exemptions.[171] The Terceira reforms would become among the most controversial of all Portuguese legislation of the nineteenth century. In the 1850s, Alexandre Herculano declared that "Mouzinho was a genius; but he was a man. He made mistakes … [yet he] overthrew the props of despotism in such a way that the re-establishment of absolutism was made impossible."[172] Almeida Garrett, a close collaborator in, but later a critic of, the legislative program, called it "a great moment, the juncture where the Old Portugal ended and the New began."[173]

It is crucial to neither glorify nor malign the reforms decreed on Terceira. Official documents of the Regency are littered with petitions from the inhabitants of Terceira and neighboring islands lamenting their plight. In late 1831, for example, the *Câmara* of Horta petitioned Dona Maria, complaining that the "absence of public education" was a dire problem in need of redress. In a population of twenty-four thousand, the *Câmara* reported, there was a single chair (*cadeira*) of primary education, one of Latin, and one of moral philosophy. This scarcity of public instruction meant that the populace lived in a "state of almost total ignorance."[174] Nor was the Regency, for all of its salutary reforms, able to solve the riddle of subsistence either in the Azores or in the area surrounding Porto in the wake of its successful 1832–33 invasion and occupation. Porto's municipal delegation bluntly informed Dom Pedro that the city's inhabitants "lacked entirely or had a severe shortage of basic necessities [flour, wheat, meat, and olive oil are enumerated]" or else could not purchase them owing to prohibitively high prices.[175] Such were the limitations of wartime government. After the Civil War, however, the decrees issued at Terceira would be enforced and implemented, as discussed briefly in Chapter 5.

Abrégé was based on the third edition of his *Principes d'Administration Publique*, first published in 1809 in Paris. Interestingly, *Vintista* Soares Franco had published excerpts from this work in Portuguese in Lisbon in 1822, though these translations went unmentioned (and presumably unconsulted) by Almeida Garrett and Mouzinho da Silveira.

[171] Cardoso and Lains, "Public Finance in Portugal, 1796–1910," in Cardoso and Lains 2010, pp. 259–60.

[172] A. Herculano (May 1853), in Monica 1996, p. 149.

[173] Almeida Garrett, quoted in Braga 1903.

[174] ANTT, MR, Regencia em Angra do Heroismo (SC), mç 260/ cx. 345, Câmara da Horta to Queen Maria II, December 24, 1831.

[175] ANTT, MR, mç 260/61, cx. 346, Comissão Municipal to Dom Pedro, November 27, 1832.

Dom Pedro, Brazilian politics, and the shaping of the Portuguese Civil War

Prior to his abdication of the Brazilian throne in 1831, the Terceira Regency recognized that its success hinged on Dom Pedro, "upon whom the fortunes of our cause rest," in Mouzinho de Albuquerque's phrase.[176] Vigorous efforts to persuade him to travel to Terceira were made from March 1830. Yet Dom Pedro's centrality to the Civil War's outcome would have seemed far-fetched several years earlier. After granting his *Carta* and abdicating the throne, the emperor publicly evinced little interest in Portugal's predicament before Dom Miguel's *coup d'état*. There were various domestic reasons why Dom Pedro distanced himself from European affairs between 1826 and 1831, including mounting levels of Lusophobia in Brazil. For their part, the *Carta*'s supporters expected little aid from Dom Pedro or the Brazilian government. Lavradio told Palmela in October 1826 that, given the "difficult and extraordinary" relations with Brazil, Portugal would be served best by "maintaining the status quo"; that is, receiving regular payments from Brazil in accordance with the terms of the still-secret pecuniary convention that accompanied formal recognition of Brazil's independence in August 1825.[177] Even as the Civil War approached, few, if any, partisans of the *Carta* expected the succor of its framer.

There were several interlocking reasons, then, why the Regency suddenly regarded Dom Pedro as a savior, which are seldom easy to disentangle. The first, and most obvious, reason was the emperor's personal connection to what was transpiring, particularly to his daughter, in whose name the Regency justified its existence and armed struggle. The second reason was Dom Pedro's status as titular head of a sovereign state. Unless Dom Pedro recognized the Regency as the legitimate government of Portugal, to which he was linked by "so many titles and blood," and in which he had "direct interest," there was little hope for other governments to do so.[178] Part of the justification for permitting Dom Pedro to nominate the members of the Regency in 1829 was precisely to secure such formal recognition. The third reason for Dom Pedro's pertinence to the *emigrado* cause was his authorship of the *Carta*, though this connection proved more important to the constitutional royalists than to the more radical constitutionalists. Dom Pedro's

---

[176] ANTT, MNE, livro 356, Mouzinho de Albuquerque to Luiz de Vasconcellos e Sousa, "Circular no. 3," March 19, 1830.
[177] ANTT, MNE, cx. 153, Lavradio to Palmela, September 23, 1826.
[178] ANTT, MNE, livro 356, Mouzinho de Albuquerque to Conde do Sabugal, "Circular no. 5," March 22, 1830.

Figure 8 N. E. Maurin. "SMI O Senhor Pedro Restituindo
sua Augusta Filha a Senhora D. Maria Segunda, e a Carta
Constitutional aos Portuguezes" (Porto: J. B. Fontana, 1832).

right to compose and impose a constitution, during his brief tenure as King of Portugal in 1826, became an essential aspect in the defense of the *Carta* as well as of Dona Maria, whose right to rule was derived directly from it.

This mode of defense, however, often forced the *Carta*'s defenders to employ what may be termed "neo-absolutist" arguments, which engendered further friction among the *emigrados*. Against the Miguelist claim that the *Carta* never received the endorsement of, or ratification by, the *Três Estados*, *Cartistas* invoked a different model of kingship which they claimed was derived from Portuguese tradition. "Only the King makes the law," an influential tract declared, because

only he can give it legal form and force; so long as these two essential conditions are missing, the requests of the *Estados* are nothing more than the expression of their wishes, propositions and nothing more ... measures taken or proposals made by the *Três Estados* only possess the force of law when they are approved and sanctioned by the King.[179]

While an effective rebuttal to the Miguelist arguments for the invalidity of the *Carta* without the convocation of the *Três Estados*, such arguments made committed constitutionalists, who embraced the *Carta* as a pact between the representatives of the people (or orders of society) and the monarch, compelled to operate within clearly defined limits, not "above" or "outside" of the law by virtue of being the author of legislation, cringe and blush. Such arguments appeared to sanction the type of despotism they labored to overthrow. Yet the *emigrados* soon discovered that the prevailing, and mutually exclusive, understandings of the ancient constitution left scant room for maneuver. They were forced, or at least found it more convenient, to claim that royal power in Portugal always had been unlimited and undivided, which made Dom Pedro's unilateral imposition of the *Carta* both legal and consistent with national tradition. As Guerreiro observed, the Crown inherited by Dom Pedro in 1826 was characterized by "absolute power, without legal limits, moderated by religion and the monarch's personal sense of justice." Dom Pedro was therefore justified to "bring into existence a new social order; create new institutions; establish new legislative, administrative and judicial forms ... in sum, he was able to do anything and everything (*tudo quanto*) that was not contrary to the dictates of religion or immutable natural law."[180] The *emigrados* thus justified the *Carta* through a depiction of Portugal's "ancient constitution" which several years earlier they, particularly the *Vintistas* in their ranks, would

---

[179] [Guerreiro] 1831, p. 37.   [180] Ibid., p. 52.

have found anathema. They spun the vices of absolutism into liberal virtues.

The recognition of Dom Pedro's Brazilian government was sought for material reasons as well: to obtain the funds needed to keep the almost penniless Regency afloat. As the fledgling Spanish American republics had less than a decade earlier, the Regency plainly understood that international recognition was required to obtain a loan from financiers. With a loan, as previously mentioned, the Regency would obtain munitions and raise a foreign legion, for the number and resources of the *emigrados* were too small to mount an invasion of Portugal.[181] Recognition of the Regency as the legitimate government of Portugal would enable Brazil to either bankroll the Regency directly or serve as the guarantor of its debt (and debt service). Either way, Brazil would supply the funds owed to Portugal by the terms of the 1825 pecuniary convention of the recognition treaty. These funds, of course, were justified officially as compensation for public property lost owing to Brazil's independence, but, in fact, were earmarked to repay the loan taken by Portugal in London in 1823, which underwrote its botched reconquest of Brazil.

This new arrangement, however, could be effected only if the Regency were recognized, first by Brazil and subsequently by other European powers, as Portugal's legitimate government. Throughout 1830, this was the chief aim of the Regency's diplomacy.[182] Recognition, Mouzinho de Albuquerque hoped, would presage robust relations between Brazil and Portugal. He authorized Conde do Sabugal to enter into negotiations in 1830 for a "permanent and reciprocal defensive alliance." Such an alliance would make it incumbent upon the Brazilian government to "declare war on the usurping government of Portugal," suspend commerce between Dom Miguel's Portugal and Brazil, and, finally, supply the Regency with "three or four frigates" with which it could "establish

---

[181] On the desirability of a foreign legion, see Palmela to Abreu e Lima, March 8, 1831, reproduced in Abreu e Lima 1874, p. 43.

[182] ANTT, MNE, livro 356, Mouzinho de Albuquerque to Conde do Sabugal, "Circular no. 4," March 22, 1830; Mouzinho de Albuquerque sought to have the Regency's debt treated "as if it were a loan contracted by the Brazilian government, paid for with the revenues of the Empire until the debt is paid in full." It was hoped as well that formal recognition would enable Dom Pedro to aid more openly and generously the "Portuguese *emigrados*, mired in dire poverty [in Rio de Janeiro]." See ibid., "Circular # 3." Mouzinho de Albuquerque believed that the diversion of funds from repaying Portugal's 1823 debt to supporting the Regency could be justified because "the revenues of Portugal have been usurped by [D. Miguel's] government." See ANTT, MNE, cx. 155, Mouzinho de Albuquerque to Thomas Mascarenhas, December 17, 1830.

its authority throughout the Azores and take control of Madeira, whose possession would provide the Regency with the resources it currently lacks." It was unclear why Mouzinho de Albuquerque believed that the Brazilian government would be tempted into such an alliance, except out of altruism, or what concessions he envisaged the Regency would have to make in order to obtain such favorable terms. But he clearly expressed to Sabugal the urgency of the situation. "We cannot hope," he concluded, "that a serious movement against Dom Miguel will appear in Portugal while the Regency languishes without resources and remains isolated due to the blockade of Terceira."[183]

Yet the Brazilian government never formally recognized the Regency, a source of immense disappointment and cause for endless complaint. In late May 1830, Mouzinho de Albuquerque complained to Abreu e Lima that Dom Pedro defended his daughter's cause "always in an indirect and equivocal manner, which is therefore inadequate to produce a statement not hamstrung by ambiguity."[184] Yet it was the emperor's unambiguous embrace of the Regency, he confided to another correspondent, "upon which [its] hopes are founded, the only thing capable of animating the loyal Portuguese to combat the difficulties, privations, and hardships in order to restore the honor of the Patria."[185] But Dom Pedro did little, even in a private capacity, furnishing those stranded on Terceira with inadequate material support. Palmela and Vila Flor expressed their chagrin directly to Dom Pedro: "our actions on this island are necessarily passive, for the material assistance VM promised has arrived slowly and only in part. It scarcely sustains 4,000 men in great hardship."[186] These pleas did not win the formal recognition they so desperately desired. Nor did they gain material relief, leading Abreu e Lima to curse the "horrible duplicity," "bad faith," and "perfidy" of the Brazilian government, which "paralyzes us" and "forces us into violent and desperate action."[187] He sarcastically asked Brazil's emissary to Britain and France, Marquês de Santo Amaro, whether his government, "by depriving the Regency of all means to sustain itself,"

[183] ANTT, MNE, livro 356, Mouzinho de Albuquerque to Conde do Sabugal, "Circular no. 5," March 22, 1830.
[184] ANTT, MNE, livro 357, Mouzinho de Albuquerque to Abreu e Lima, May 22, 1830.
[185] ANTT, MNE, livro 767, Mouzinho de Albuquerque to Nuno Barboza de Figueiredo, May 22, 1830, fo. 5.
[186] ANTT, MR (Regência em Angra do Heroísmo), livro 451, Palmela and Vila Flor to Dom Pedro, March 20, 1830.
[187] ANTT, MNE, livro 469, Abreu e Lima to Mouzinho de Albuquerque, November 4, 1830.

sought to "oblige [it] to surrender to the Usurper?"[188] In private correspondence, an exasperated Marquês de Santa Iria ejaculated, "it is extraordinary that we have never received a single favorable thing from Brazil ... from wicked Brazil come only bad things which muddle matters further."[189]

Following his 1831 abdication and return to Europe, the *emigrados* struggled to interest Dom Pedro in their cause. After a chilly reception in London, he sailed to France, and his first days in Paris suggested his continued indifference to Portugal's plight. A frustrated Conde do Lavradio, who implored the ex-emperor to take swift action, recorded that "SMI spends his days hunting, or in similar futile diversions, so much so that (incredibly!) he has been in Paris for nine days and he has still not devoted even an hour to important affairs, which he claims he intends to address, but never does."[190] This behavior followed a pattern. In Paris, Dom Pedro reveled in the hospitality extended by Louis-Philippe and the respite from the burdens of public life. He received honorific French military titles and was offered residence at the Mansart-designed Château de Meudon. He regularly played billiards with the French king.[191] Embracing the pleasures of Paris, he seems to have gone out every night. He frequented the Odeon and the Théâtre-Italien in particular and enjoyed use of the royal box at the Opera and Comédie-Française. Most fond of the Théâtre-Italien, then directed by Gioachino Rossini, Dom Pedro was persuaded to have one of his compositions performed there. His "Ouverture à Grande Orchestre" debuted on October 30, 1831, to underwhelming reviews.[192]

---

[188] ANTT, MNE, livro 469, Abreu e Lima to Marquês de Santo Amaro [José Egidio Álvares de Almeida, 1767–1832], December 22, 1830. Santo Amaro evidently felt great sympathy for the *emigrados* and seems to have promised to try to arrange for a new loan or disbursement of the 1825 pecuniary convention funds to the Regency. These efforts earned him a rebuke from Rio, with Francisco Carneiro de Campos claiming that "to enter into such a transaction, given the current circumstances of the Empire, can only give rise to distrust which malcontents [here] seek to spread and, perhaps, involve this country in unforeseeable trouble which [a policy of] strict neutrality seeks to avoid." See AHI 271/4/4, F. Carneiro de Campos to Santo Amaro, March 4, 1831.

[189] Marquês de Sta. Iria to Condessa de Vila Real, December 31, 1830, in Ventura 2000, pp. 69–70.

[190] Entry of August 28, 1831, from Paris, in Lavradio 1933, vol. II, p. 56.

[191] Though it is important not to interpret the hospitality extended to Dom Pedro as a full-throated condemnation by France of the Miguelist regime or an embrace of constitutionalist governments elsewhere. Before the ex-emperor washed up on French shores, Louis-Philippe's government had proposed to Spain's Ferdinand VII in June 1831 that he should unite the Peninsula, offering Dom Miguel rule over the Philippines as a consolation prize. See J. Fontana 2006, p. 315.

[192] Janke 1974, p. 67; Lustosa 2006, pp. 308–9. On Dom Pedro's Parisian period, see D'Albian 1959, an unjustly neglected book.

The ex-emperor's self-indulgent behavior and lavish lifestyle offended the *emigrados* marooned in Paris. They received public assistance amounting to 2½ francs per day. Upon Dom Pedro's arrival, the meagerness of this allowance embarrassed the French government, which increased the subsidy.[193] Dom Pedro's reluctance to support his daughter's cause publicly, even after his abdication and ignominious retreat to Europe, made Lavradio's task of convincing other European powers to recognize the Regency "not merely difficult but also indecorous."[194]

Eventually, with Louis-Philippe's more than tacit, but still unofficial, endorsement,[195] Dom Pedro warmed to the *emigrado* cause. He joined the Regency on Terceira, and was eventually able to maneuver himself to its head. Some *emigrados* were both incredulous and apoplectic: "the Men of 1820 working for the ex-Emperor of Brazil to become King of Portugal? Who would have predicted it! Who would have believed it! The *regeneradores* of the *patria* acknowledging the rights of the man whom they called a foreigner, acceding to the infernal plan of making regent a man whom even the *negros* and *mulatos* of Brazil did not want!"[196] Even to his staunch supporters, Dom Pedro's spasmodic engagement and long stretches of indifferent lethargy were perplexing, his motives far from transparent. Mouzinho da Silveira could not fathom "what caused Pedro to issue the *Carta* or why he later seemed to abandon it and remain in Brazil."[197] Yet the ex-emperor eventually became semi-palatable to most *emigrado* factions, for strategic as well as ideological reasons, so long as he operated within the limits they imposed. As the Passos brothers joked, they supported Dom Pedro because "he was a revolutionary in 1820; he gave the *Carta* to Portugal; he is the father of our Queen; and, besides, without him, the cause of our puny Regency would never stand a chance of gaining a foothold in the *patria*."[198] Furthermore, the fact that Dom Pedro's meddling exasperated the despised Courts of Europe only enhanced his appeal. As

---

[193] Janke 1974, p. 67. Public relief, for foreigners as well as Parisians, appears to have been common: there were more than sixty-eight thousand persons on relief in Paris alone in 1832, or one in every eleven people. See Kramer 1988, p. 24.

[194] Entry of August 14, 1831, from Paris, in Lavradio 1933, vol. II, p. 44.

[195] Though there are few references to it, it seems obvious that Dom Pedro began in Paris to fashion himself after Louis-Philippe. In Orleanist representation, Louis-Philippe was a "citizen king, whose authority derived from his personal merits and past services, rather than from his royal blood," particularly military service. See Sessions 2011, p. 73.

[196] BPMP, MSS. 1916, "Carta a Rodrigo Pinto Pizarro [por hum Emigrado Portuguez em Paris]," October 31, 1831, fos. 43–44.

[197] Mouzinho da Silveira 1989, vol. II, p. 639.

[198] M. Passos 1831a, p. 4.

one of Dom Pedro's champions remarked, with pleasure and a great deal of hyperbole, to one of the ex-emperor's confidants, "His crimes cannot be expiated: he gave two liberal constitutions to two countries in two hemispheres, and thus destroyed the misguided Holy Alliance."[199]

It may be enquired why Dom Pedro hesitated and perseverated, actions at odds with his much-criticized impetuousness at many junctures, both political and personal. There are several explanations, most of which relate to the delicate Brazilian political context in which he operated, where his continued involvement with Iberian affairs rankled the increasingly vocal "nativist" party. Certainly, the precarious and destabilized state of Brazil's finances left him without expendable resources. Some of his behavior must be attributed to the steady stream of information he received from his advisors concerning Portuguese affairs. After the promulgation of the *Carta* yet before Dom Miguel's usurpation, the letters of Resende caused disquiet. In a December 1827 missive, Resende made clear that "ultra-liberals were falsely professing love for VM, draping themselves in the *Carta* for the nefarious end of re-establishing the infernal [constitution] of Fernandes Tomás," whereas the "ultra-royalists" were swapping the banner of Dom Pedro for that of Dom Miguel.[200] Later Brazil's envoy to France informed him that the faction-plagued *emigrados* "shared only their endless complaints against the Emperor, whom they blame for their misfortune."[201] That such intelligence produced an impression on Dom Pedro is evidenced by a revealing anecdote. During the Azorean Regency and the siege of Porto, Dom Pedro routinely met with his generals "without any formality." On one occasion, he reportedly enquired, "You men, you *Vintistas*, you are with me [only] because of the *Carta?*" to which Sá da Bandeira replied, "it is exactly as VE has said: if not for the *Carta*, we would not have any motivation for entering into this matter between you and *Senhor Infante*." To which the emperor responded, "I was certain of it (*Eu bem o sabia*)."[202]

But Dom Pedro, who evidently thrived on adulation, received further entreaties that aroused his interest in European affairs. In a January 1828 letter from Saldanha, who was in communication with Espoz y Mina about a federal (or confederated) Iberian Peninsula, with Dom

---

[199] Silva Carvalho to Gomes da Silva, June 13, 1831, reproduced in *Documentos para a História Contemporanea* 1891, vol. I, doc. 69, p.76.
[200] Resende to Dom Pedro ("Minuta Incompleta"), December 8, 1827, reproduced in Resende 1916, p. 197.
[201] AHI 271/4/4, Santo Amaro [in Paris] to Miguel Calmon du Pin e Almeida, October 20, 1830.
[202] Episode recounted in Luz Soriano 1887, vol. I, p. 428.

Pedro as its constitutional monarch, the General insisted that European Liberals esteemed him: "Is it possible, *Senhor*," Saldanha enquired, "that VM does not prefer to rule fourteen million men, Portuguese and Spaniards, with whose support you might sustain your authority in America, rather than the alternative of ruling over three million men of every color who nurture in their hearts the darkest ingratitude?"[203] Dom Pedro was inclined to listen carefully to Saldanha's overtures.[204] But even Saldanha's sycophantic exhortation failed to move Dom Pedro, who refused to jeopardize Brazil's de facto geopolitical neutrality. Beyond a smattering of proclamations and dispatching diplomats to European courts to generate support for his daughter's cause, Dom Pedro recused himself from direct action. His involvement in the Portuguese Civil War emerged less from commitment to his daughter's cause or liberal ideas, than from his hasty abdication, which left him casting about aimlessly in Europe, bereft of throne and funds.

His failure to act before 1831, however, should not be mistaken for indifference. Dom Pedro allotted much attention to the affairs of Portugal, even if he proved stingy in the material relief of the *emigrados* and withheld explicit, formal recognition of their cause. In his private correspondence, Dom Pedro lamented the fate of "the much compromised Portuguese refugees … martyrs of legitimacy and lovers (*amantes*) of the *Carta*," whereas his proclamations urged the Portuguese to "save the *Carta*."[205] He sought to answer *emigrado* pleas for material assistance. Barbacena suggested that whatever was allocated could be recouped after Dona Maria was installed on the throne by selling Bissau and Cacheu to France or else Timor to the United States.[206] The minutes of the Brazilian *Conselho de Estado* reveal an intense and abiding interest in Portuguese affairs, but also conflicting views concerning the desirable extent of Brazil's interference. In November 1829, the question arose whether the £300,000 still owed to the Portuguese

---

[203] AMI, II-PAN-05.01.1828-Dau.C., Saldanha to Dom Pedro, January 5, 1828; see also Braz Augusto Aquino Brancato, "D. Pedro: Uma Opção Liberal para a Espanha," in Ramos 2001. There is evidence that a group of Spanish exiles recruited Dom Pedro to vie for the Spanish Crown as early as August 1826; see S. C. da Costa 1995, p. 193.

[204] Not only was he a past governor of Rio Grande do Sul, but Saldanha had refused to lead an army of reconquest to Brazil in 1823, and played a key role in Dom João's overthrow of the Cortes later that year. Saldanha resigned from the government in 1827 when it appeared that the *Carta* was undermined fatally, and fought valiantly against the supporters of Dom Miguel.

[205] See AMI, II-POB.1828.Pl.B.do.1–151 (pasta 1), Dom Pedro to Barbacena, December 23, 1828; and Dom Pedro, "Proclamação á Nação Portuguesa" (1828), found in the same pasta.

[206] Barbacena to Dom Pedro, March 6, 1829, quoted in Oliveira Lima 1933, p. 72.

government according to the terms of the 1825 pecuniary convention should be diverted to support the *emigrados* in Brazil. Most members of the *Conselho*, a body composed of devout monarchists, concurred with Marquês de Aracati that the *emigrados* should receive the funds still owed, but Marquês de Paranaguá dissented, claiming that if it were to "compromise the government in any way," the funds should not be dispensed.[207] Evidently, these funds never reached the *emigrados*. In March 1830, Dom Pedro solicited the Council's opinion on three matters: first, whether the succession to the Portuguese throne was a "European or an American question"; second, whether, circumstances permitting, Dona Maria should marry Dom Miguel; and third, whether Dom Miguel's usurpation was sufficient cause for Brazil to declare war on Portugal. The Council tepidly ventured that the matter of succession was a matter of international public law and therefore came under the purview of all hereditary monarchs. They unanimously expressed their opposition to a marriage, after all that had passed, between Dona Maria and Dom Miguel. Most importantly, they resoundingly rejected the suggestion of a declaration of war on Portugal, for it would "compromise the tranquility of the Empire."[208]

At every turn, then, Dom Pedro was discouraged from active intervention in Portuguese affairs. His lack of charity toward the *emigrados* in Rio de Janeiro may be attributed, as previously mentioned, to the fears that their presence stoked in Brazil. The editor of the Recife newspaper *O Constitucional* recognized that there were many "honorable Portuguese, seeking refuge from the Tiberius of Portugal, who [had] washed up on Brazil's hospitable shores, truly free, hard-working men, free of metropolitan resentments." But he added that "no one would dare deny that the term 'emigrado' has come to be understood here as a byword for an adventurer, a title given to soldiers who support the Luso-Brazilian party who are poised to prey like wolves on Brazilians."[209] Sá da Bandeira was keenly aware of this suspicion, arguing that "the general hatred [of Portuguese] is akin to that felt by the freed slave for his master."[210] Overt involvement in the Civil War would have been construed by Brazilian nativists as evidence for a recolonization scheme or the diminishment of independence through an entangling alliance. In his 1830 Speech from the Throne, Dom Pedro

[207] *Conselho de Estado* (Brazil), Session 36, November 30, 1829, in Senado Federal 1973, p. 95.
[208] *Conselho de Estado* (Brazil), Session 39, March 12, 1830, in Senado Federal 1973, p. 101–3 passim.
[209] *O Constitucional* (Recife), no. 157 (December 30, 1830), p. 3.
[210] Diary entry of November 19, 1828, in Sá da Bandeira 1975, vol. I, p. 113.

promised the Brazilian General Assembly to be "true to my word that I will not compromise the tranquility and interests of Brazil due to [my involvement] in the affairs of Portugal." He reserved the right, however, in his capacity as "father, and tutor, to defend the cause of [Dona Maria's] sovereignty."[211]

Dom Pedro's allusion to his paternal duties hints at the personal and dynastic dilemmas complicating his geopolitical calculus. He clearly was disturbed, and personally wounded, by his brother's usurpation, and, by 1829, greatly preoccupied by the fading likelihood of reclaiming the Lusitanian throne for his daughter, by his doubts concerning the viability of monarchy in Brazil, and by the bleak global prospects of the House of Braganza. Canning's 1825 prophecy, that Dom Pedro "cannot so wholly detach himself from Europe ... as to set its goodwill and opinion at defiance," haunted the emperor in 1828–29.[212] He believed that the survival of monarchy in Brazil depended on its intimate, sustained connection to the royal houses of Europe, to which Brazil could appeal for assistance under duress as well as enhancing its prestige. He sought to bolster these connections by marrying another European princess on the heels of Dona Leopoldina's death, but he was refused by the leading dynasties. He eventually married Dona Amélia (1812–76), daughter of the Dutchess of Leuchtenberg, whose late husband was Prince Eugene de Beauharnais, son of the former French Empress Josephine by her first husband. In 1829, he hatched an elaborate plan to travel to Europe, personally arrange for the marriage of his daughters to French princes, and seek new allies. This plan was tripped up because, according to the 1824 Constitution, Dom Pedro could not leave Brazil without the Assembly's permission, which was a remote possibility. Yet Dom Pedro, at least in the moment in which he composed this document, was adamant of the "advantages of such a journey for my descendants, for whom I work." He was willing to abdicate the Brazilian Crown "in order to enjoy the certainty that it will be worn by my children." He felt himself "without support within the Empire, so [he] must search for it outside of it." Otherwise, he grimly remarked, "I am merely seated on the throne, without resources, awaiting my death, which will ruin my family, and the empire."[213] Though Dom Pedro never undertook the

[211] Dom Pedro, "Falla do Throno," May 3, 1830, in *Fallas do Throno* 1977, p. 177.

[212] TNA, FO 128/2, Canning to Chamberlain, January 12, 1825, fo. 17.

[213] [Dom Pedro], "Plano que eu entendo ser necessario seguir-se para felicidade do Imperio, e do qual não posso despersuadir-me" (1829), printed in H. Vianna 1961, pp. 182–84 passim. According to the document, Dom Pedro hoped to marry Dona Maria to the Duke of Nemours, the second son of Duke of Orleans, and Dona Januário to the Duke of Bordeaux, son of the Duke of Berry and grandson of Charles X.

mission to which he passionately pledged himself (and never sought the Assembly's permission to do so), this 1829 document reveals his motivation. First, it indicates that he had nearly forsaken Dona Maria's claim to the Portuguese throne, or at least downgraded his ambitions for her cause considerably, viewing French support as indispensable. Second, he entertained the notion of abdication, viewing it as a strategic measure should the Brazilian monarchy's edifice crumble further. Third, Dom Pedro was convinced that monarchy in Brazil was imperiled and that only a firm connection with Europe could sustain it. Fourth, and most importantly, Dom Pedro continued to strategize in dynastic terms, judging potential actions by their benefit to his heirs and the House of Braganza, operating largely outside of a national frame of reference.

Yet before these events catalyzed the search for a new vocation, his ambivalence toward the Portuguese liberal cause was deepened by the opposition arrayed against it and by his own trying experience with representative institutions after the reopening of the National Assembly in 1826. In 1829, Barbacena conveyed to Dom Pedro some of the "indisposition" in England toward the *Carta*, advising him to disassociate the cause of his daughter from it, and to go as far as to claim for her "full and absolute power." He begged the emperor to consider whether this arrangement, eminently more agreeable to the courts of Europe, would make the "Portuguese nation less free, less happy than it formerly was, and could be, without such a scrap of paper (*tal folheta*)?"[214] Though he failed to act on this advice and disavow the *Carta* publicly, Dom Pedro's receptiveness to the suggestion may be assumed given his authoritarian turn in the late 1820s. Political developments in Brazil left him wary of liberal ideas, skeptical of the efficacy of written constitutions, and almost paranoid in his fear of revolution. In 1826, Dom Pedro felt it incumbent upon him to demonstrate his fidelity to moderate constitutionalism. The *Carta*, written and promulgated just days before the Brazilian National Assembly reopened for the first time since the dissolution of the Constituent Assembly in 1823, served this aim.[215] But his optimism soon gave way to despair. Liberal nativists in the Assembly remained discontent with the extent of executive power Dom Pedro possessed and were convinced that a new statutory base was needed to destroy the Portuguese legal inheritance and place new institutions on a secure footing. They clashed fiercely with Dom Pedro in 1827–30. A new Criminal Code (1830) undermined the emperor's power to prosecute and punish political crimes. Taken together, the

214 AMI, II-POB.1829.Hor.do.1–27, Barbacena to Dom Pedro, May 6, 1829.
215 Oliveira Lima 1925, p. 62.

liberal opposition stripped executive authority of many judicial prerogatives.[216] After the July Revolution in France, they were poised to wrest even greater concessions.

These parliamentary struggles, and defeats, affected Dom Pedro's conception of constitutional government. As a British resident in Rio in 1828–30 noted, "the Emperor's dislike of secret societies is now so great, that he will not sanction the formation of any society, however legitimate and laudable its avowed object."[217] By the late 1820s, he was convinced that the 1824 Constitution, the model of the 1826 *Carta*, required modification. In February 1829, he sought to suspend constitutional guarantees in Pernambuco, a reprise of his 1823–26 tactics. In March, the emperor sent a circular to his confidants, the salient features of which were two questions: first, "would it be possible under the present circumstances to amend the constitution?"; and second, should Dom Pedro issue another constitution, one that would be "truly monarchical (*verdadeiramente monarchica*)?"[218] All of his advisors recoiled at the difficulty of such a plan. The first reply came from Imhambupe, who took the opportunity to rail against freedom of the press and to advocate for its curtailment since it produced only "malcontents" and "delinquents," instead of "truth and decency." He further contended that Brazil's constitution must remain unaffected by the practices of other nations, since it must be adapted to the "peculiar circumstances of each people." As evidence, he noted that Rousseau abstained from offering legislative counsel to the Corsicans since "he did not know the specific genius of that people [*povo*]." He also warned Dom Pedro against "sudden changes," for to issue another *lei fundamental* would provoke fear that Brazil was on the path to absolutism. Paranaguá agreed, maintaining that the reform of the 1824 Constitution was not "presently possible, [and was] overly bold, and too risky." On the issue of a more "monarchical" constitution, Paranaguá gently admonished the emperor, reminding him that an "astute and philosophical prince is aware that he cannot create a solid government except by basing it in the dominant ideas of the time." Frei António disagreed that Brazil's political turbulence was attributable to faulty legislation, but rather pointed to the imperfect execution of existing laws. For him, the path to security was straightforward, consisting in "undivided and strong executive; compliance with the law; good order and discipline in the armed forces; vigilant use of the moderating power; [and] the creation of harmony and

---

[216] Flory 1981, pp. 9, 42, 51, 111.
[217] Walsh 1830, vol. II, p. 466.
[218] This and all quotations in this paragraph taken from the un-folioed documents found in the folder: AMI, I-POB.17.03.1829.PI.B.c.

good faith among the powers." Frei António recoiled at the prospect of a more monarchical constitution, expressed his "horror," and advised the emperor to "burn every paper on which this suggestion is made," warning that if such proclivities became widely known, the empire's "most frightful ruin" would be imminent.

But Dom Pedro remained unconvinced. He formally summoned the *Conselho de Estado* in 1829 in order to suspend constitutional guarantees and take extraordinary, extra-legal measures. There he was persuaded by Santo Amaro and Inhambupe that such steps were inadvisable.[219] By 1830, Dom Pedro was attacked by the Liberal-Nativist press for presiding over a regime less liberal than that of France.[220] As a modern historian observed, "the Emperor was shaken by the total inversion of reality," as the constitutional order gave rise to unanticipated monsters.[221] From the extant documentary record, it is impossible to ascertain his views of the *Carta* before 1831, but his autocratic tendencies may have diminished his esteem for it, and also for the men and women who used it, and his daughter, to justify their revolution.

The deposed emperor, washed up on Europe's shores in 1831, then, was no ardent constitutionalist.[222] Or, at least, his constitutionalism was subservient to other impulses and aspirations. Despite Dom Pedro's impetuous, mercurial disposition, however, it is clear that he was chastened by the ignominious experience of abdication and exile, and keen to change perceptions of his conduct, if not the conduct itself. One of his closest advisors, Resende, offered consolation, assuring him that, "at 33 years old, there is still time to make amends for the past and to resume the honorable, glorious career that the heavens have opened to you."[223] Dynastic priorities, and his very political survival, pushed him into the arms of the only group that needed him, the beleaguered *emigrado* constitutionalist cause. To be sure, Dom Pedro was convinced that Portugal remained unprepared for any type of modern political system. His extant personal correspondence paints a miserable portrait of the Portuguese populace. In 1832, he lambasted their

---

[219] Minutes of the *Conselho de Estado*, Session 35, October 28, 1829, p. 93.

[220] The size and influence of this press, it should be mentioned, was expanding rapidly. In Rio de Janeiro alone, the number of newspapers nearly doubled between 1827 and 1831. See Wisser 2006, p. 8.

[221] Macaulay 1988, p. 248.

[222] At least not until 1832: the Brazilian envoy to Paris reported to his superior that the ex-emperor "refused to admit those known to be constitutionalists to his home." See AHI 225/4/7, José Joaquim de Rocha to Francisco Carneiro de Campos, January 27, 1832.

[223] Resende to Dom Pedro, July 8, 1832, reproduced in Resende 1916, p. 429.

"apathy," "lack of patriotism," and the "absence of love of liberty."
He derisively mocked the common people, who "do not know how to
do anything else except kiss my hands (*beijar as mãos*) four, even eight
times each day, or prostrate themselves before me, among other signs
of servitude, which suggests to me that the free, independent character that distinguished the Portuguese nation of old has disappeared, a
remarkable occurrence in a century in which all nations have managed
to free themselves."[224] Yet however quixotic and failure-bound he considered the Regency, Dom Pedro had exhausted his options, and chose
active, if misguided, heroism over leisured obscurity.

Strange triumph: *emigrado* factional conflict, military victory, and the end of the Civil War

Though they shared experiences and a common enemy, the *emigrados* were riven by factions. Rival groups cherished divergent visions
of Portugal's political future. In exile, they sought to minimize their
incompatible goals, coalescing around Dona Maria, and professing
their loyalty with grandiloquence:

In our exile, she is the only star that guides us, the only angel who watches
over us; the thought of her gives us support and solace. What other mother has
ever been as tender and compassionate? She gave all to the *emigrados*; she even
ordered the expenses of her royal household to be slashed for our sake![225]

Undoubtedly, some of these sentiments were expressed with sincerity,
though such praise seems excessive for a young woman who was but
thirteen years old at the time. Nevertheless, such language was ubiquitous. It would be foolish to deny that fantastical visions of Dona
Maria's youth, vulnerability, and physical beauty were perceived as key
attributes, easing her embrace by the chauvinistic, post-adolescent, and
chivalric *emigrados*.[226] But the identification of Dona Maria as a "guiding
star" had practical implications that hinted at the deep divisions among
them. For some *emigrados*, fervent support of Dona Maria's rights was
a tacit rebuke to those prejudiced against a female head of state, an attitude common among the so-called *Saldanhistas*. For others, the speedy
accession of Dona Maria would imply the eclipse of Dom Pedro and his
unelected, increasingly dictatorial Regency. Some liberals, including
Liberato Carvalho, believed that Dom Pedro's continued presence was

---

[224] Dom Pedro [from Porto] to Resende, July 17, 1832, reproduced in Resende 1916,
p. 502.
[225] [Anon.], *Breve Razoamento* 1832, p. 5.
[226] França 1974, vol. I, p. 134.

a prelude to yet another usurpation, this time with a liberal veneer.[227] For them, Dona Maria's cause and genuine constitutional government were inextricable. More conservatives supported Dona Maria wholeheartedly because she was the only heir to the throne according to the *Carta*. As Mouzinho da Silveira told Lavradio: "The *Emigração* is the party of legitimacy, and not a band of factionalists, who go about choosing and deposing kings and regents."[228]

The *emigrados* were, it must be recalled, a motley crew composed of various political hues. Throughout the Civil War, they continued to bicker, not least because the mistrust with which they regarded one another was well earned over the preceding decade. Many members of the so-called Palmela group, as previously discussed, had served in the upper ranks of Dom João's administration in the immediate aftermath of his restoration in June 1823. Palmela had decried openly the "intolerant, ambitious, avid faction that sought to substitute experience with abstract doctrines, seeking to delude the people with words and exercising de facto tyranny over the people."[229] Though all now professed their unswerving allegiance to Dona Maria and the *Carta*, several contemporaries believed that they were unified only in their fear of, and loathing for, Dom Miguel and his acolytes. Not all of the avowed liberals, a Brazilian in Dom Pedro's service noted in 1833, were constitutionalists by conviction. Many of them, he claimed (without identifying any by name), were "pure royalists, but personal enemies either of Dom Miguel or one of his intolerant ministers." Genuine constitutionalists, he noted, realized that a system of representative government could not flourish in Portugal so long as it was dominated by "friars, clergymen, and *fildalgos*."[230]

At moments of crisis, the latent suspicions each faction harbored for the other rose to the surface, with Saldanha at one point publicly accusing Palmela of having "secretly wished and worked tirelessly to destroy the *Carta*, offered up the *patria* to a tyrannical yoke, and smashed to pieces the legitimate throne."[231] Still, throughout the period of exile, there were strenuous efforts to construct a shared ideology that trumped mutual disdain. In response to one of irascible Saldanha's frequent

[227] Pinheiro 1996, p. 61.
[228] Mouzinho da Silveira to Lavradio, January 11, 1832, reproduced in Lavradio 1933, vol. II, pp. 146–47.
[229] "Circular do Conde de Palmella," June 9, 1823, reproduced in *Documentos ... História das Cortes* 1883, vol. I, p. 775.
[230] Cunha Mattos 1833, vol. I, p. 190.
[231] Saldanha 1829, p. 21; he said much the same thing in a private letter to Dom Pedro the previous year. See AMI, II-PAN-05.01.1828-DAU.C.

public denunciations of his rivals, two conciliatory London-based *emigrados* insisted that "the political faith that we professed in 1820, 1824, and 1826 was the same as the one we now profess: we were, at all of those crucial junctures, friends of a just liberty; we never applauded the triumph of despotism; and we never participated in the destruction of constitutions."[232]

Two brothers, José and Manoel da Silva Passos, were the most vocal representatives of the radical cohort of the liberal exiles. Sometimes mocked for the closeness with which they collaborated on everything, they believed that simple reformism was an inadequate response to the condition in which Portugal found itself.[233] Under ordinary circumstances, perhaps, a "slow, progressive, and steady reform," based on sound theoretical principles, of existing institutions was desirable. But "the people will not be content with theoretical principles of public law, but rather require the betterment of their physical and moral condition."[234] While they never broke ranks with the Regency, they expressed allegiance to Dona Maria using language that under ordinary circumstances would have garnered accusations of sedition. They asserted the right to overthrow an "unjust king" and claimed that Portugal's ancient constitution was republican, not monarchical, which amounted to an implicit repudiation of the *Carta*.[235] Other *emigrados* went further, rejecting the notion of a regency altogether, and arguing that it was a stalking horse to deprive Dona Maria of her rights and authority as sovereign while fatally undermining the *Carta*. It was either a disguise for the restoration of Dom Pedro's absolutist rule or the first step toward the dismantlement of the *Carta*'s provision for representative institutions. "How much money has [Palmela] received from Brazilian authorities in London?" one especially suspicious *emigrado* in Belgium enquired.[236] As late as 1832, another pamphleteer warned that the "parasites" who composed the Regency would seek, through a veritable "orgy of edicts," to destroy popular sovereignty.[237] Palmela's role as head of the Regency before Dom Pedro's arrival raised suspicion. The Paris-based *emigrados*

---

[232] Magalhães and Botelho 1830, p. 57.
[233] Fellow *emigrado* Alexander Monteiro joked that "The Passos brothers are two volumes of a single work bound together." See BPMP, MSS. 1758 [06], [Alexander Monteiro], "Caracteres Copiados em Bruges no 1 de Julho de 1829," #71.
[234] Passos and Passos 1832a, p. 17.
[235] Pinheiro 1996, p. 61.
[236] [Anon.], *Perguntas á Denominada Regencia* 1830, p. 1.
[237] Cabral 1832, p. 4. Of course, the Miguelist pamphleteers saw the matter differently, claiming that Dona Maria had become the "instrument and sorry victim whose name serves as a cover for the revolutionaries and their execrable aims." See [Anon.], *Algumas Palavras em Resposta* 1831, p. 33.

routinely denounced him, questioning why someone of his background and beliefs retained his post. They refused to accept that the Regency should retain all authority for itself, arguing for a representative body, even on Terceira, citing the examples of Belgium and Poland in 1830–31, both of which had convened elected congresses or parliaments while only provisional governments existed.[238]

These fears fueled a major crisis among the *emigrados*. It was exacerbated still further after the Regency demanded, in mid 1830, that all of Dona Maria's supporters must swear their loyalty and obedience to the Regency. *Emigrados* in Belgium and France resisted this request, and protested vociferously. They reaffirmed their loyalty to both the *Carta* and Dona Maria, but balked at the demand to swear allegiance to the Regency. According to the *Carta*, they claimed, Dona Isabel Maria should have become Regent automatically, as her brother, Dom Pedro, was formally excluded by the terms of his 1826 abdication of the Portuguese throne. Furthermore, they contended that their proven allegiance to the *Carta* made a further pledge redundant, especially as the authority exercised by the Regency surpassed that attributed to the executive in the *Carta*. These dissident *emigrados* were dismayed that the Terceira Regency's "dictatorship" was neither of fixed duration nor subject to ratification by the Cortes.[239] Other *emigrados* acquiesced to the Regency's existence, but insisted that there was a major difference between "recognizing" or "obeying" and "swearing" (*jurar*) allegiance to it. After all, allegiance had already been sworn to the *Carta*. They rejected the notion that failure to swear allegiance as stipulated signified "disunion," disloyalty, or insubordination. Rather, they argued, "the Portuguese can disagree on a legal issue, they can love or despise their public administrators, praise or condemn their acts, even undertake legal resistance to them, without in any manner jeopardizing their loyalty to the Queen and the *Carta*; only in these latter areas can unanimity and union be required."[240]

The matter remained a dispute relegated to the fringes until Rodrigo Pinto Pizarro[241] published his *Norma das Regencias de Portugal*, a thinly veiled, widely disseminated, and bombastic accusation of Dom Pedro's allegedly nefarious designs, which popularized the nuanced, arcane, and inaccessible arguments presented in pamphlets authored by figures such as the Passos brothers, Rocha Loureiro, Ferreira Borges, and

---

[238] [M. Passos] 1831b, pp. 4, 6, 10, 12.
[239] Seabra 1830, pp. 52–53.
[240] [Anon.], *Resposta ao Jornal dos Debates* 1830, pp. 4, 7–8.
[241] Rodrigo Pinto Pizarro (1788–1841), later Barão de Ribeira de Sabrosa.

Liberato Freire. Pizarro's pamphlet made clear that the debate over the Regency was primarily a proxy skirmish, the warm-up for protracted disputes over fundamental aspects of constitutional government in Portugal. Everything that radical liberals feared about the *Carta* – indirect elections, the provision of a Council of State, limitations on the convocation of the Cortes – was coming to pass. As punishment for his insubordination, Dom Pedro sentenced Pizarro (in absentia) to imprisonment if he entered territory controlled by the Regency, a decree that momentarily produced an intellectual chilling effect. The Regency then recruited Araújo e Castro and Pinheiro Ferreira to write a juridical apology, published as *Parecer sobre os Meios de Restaurar o Governo Representativo*, a direct rebuttal to Pizarro's tract, though it persuaded none of the discontents.[242]

Hardly ephemeral, this dispute definitively split the *emigrado* ranks. It refused to disappear because Dom Pedro assumed an increasingly active role in the Regency's operations from 1832. Fierce disagreement arose over whether Dom Pedro could serve as Regent, or at least exercise its functions in practice if not in name, in accordance with the *Carta* as well as generally recognized principles of public law. While Araújo e Castro and Pinheiro Ferreira argued that the Regency was legal owing to the nullity of Dom Pedro's 1826 abdication (i.e. his abdication had been contingent on Dom Miguel marrying Dona Maria, which never occurred), the Passos brothers counter-argued that the abdication had been valid and complete, meaning that the ex-emperor, even in his capacity as ex-King of Portugal, could not serve as Regent. Rather, one of his sisters must serve in that capacity.[243] In *Norma das Regencias*, Pizarro put the matter bluntly: "Dom Pedro is prevented [from becoming Regent] by the same *Carta* of which he was the magnanimous author, and by his pure, spontaneous, unambiguous abdication, which was several times repeated, confirmed, and communicated."[244] By abdicating, he argued, Dom Pedro had renounced his status as a Portuguese, forfeiting the attendant political rights as well. However, as Dona Maria's father, he might serve as her "tutor," the attributes of which were comparatively slight, though he could also command his daughter's armies, in his capacity as tutor, since nationality and citizenship were no barriers to military service. But it would be "absurd," they claimed, for "the emperor

---

[242] Vargues and Torgal, "Da Revolução a Contra-Revolução," p. 87. T. Braga's account of this episode differs slightly. He claimed that Dom Pedro only indicated his preference to have Pizarro imprisoned for inciting rebellion in a private letter to Candido-José Xavier, not publicly proclaimed. See Braga 1903, p. 460.

[243] Passos and Passos 1832a, p. 14.

[244] Pizarro 1832, p. 5.

of Brazil to rule over us."[245] Other pamphleteers went further, disputing the claim that Dom Pedro's abdication of his Brazilian Crown meant that he automatically "became again our *concidadão*, because the link that he had with us was broken entirely [by his 1826 abdication of the Portuguese throne], and cannot be mended."[246] Another commentator flatly declared that Dom Pedro was "dead to us politically."[247]

The fear that Dom Pedro intended to ride roughshod over the *Carta*, perhaps retaining the post of regent for his daughter during the years before she reached majority, prompted some *emigrados* to advocate the immediate acclamation of Dona Maria. Otherwise, they warned, Dom Pedro and his supporters might convert a provisional arrangement into a permanent one and to treat the Regency's prior acts as legally binding.[248] Radical *emigrados* argued that "everything that has been done, is being done, and will be done on Terceira [by the Regency], is provisional, subject to the confirmation of the regular [*permanente*] government, which only the *Carta* and the Cortes, once installed in Portugal, can do."[249] As late as 1834, the Passos brothers argued that the Regency was violating the *Carta* because it had failed to seek ratification by the Cortes of its acts.[250]

Given his preeminent and seemingly indispensable position, however, Dom Pedro pressed successfully for his appointment as Regent. Some *emigrados* supported this move. But many argued that, even if he were offered the post, he should decline it, legal niceties aside. Acceptance of the title would "serve as a pretext for all of the enemy parties to engage in more malevolent behavior and deal a setback to the cause of Dona Maria and the *Carta*." Even if his intentions were pure, Pizarro concluded in his famous pamphlet, his "most magnanimous thoughts would be suspect, his most popular measures twisted [by his enemies], and the partisans of the defeated faction would invent a thousand ways of undermining him."[251] Liberato Freire de Carvalho elaborated on this point, claiming that the violation of the *Carta*, even if motivated by the universally understood impulse of paternal love, was a dangerous precedent from which there was no return: "observance of the *Carta* must be superior to all personal considerations, for if it is violated once, its political chastity (*castidade política*) is lost forever."[252] To make an exception, and deviate from the *Carta*, an *emigrado* newspaper in London

[245] Passos and Passos 1832b, pp. 6–7.
[246] Cabral 1832, p. 14.
[247] [Anon.], *Carta de um Portuguez Emigrado* 1832, p. 5.
[248] [Anon.], *Breve Razoamento* 1832, pp. 22–23.
[249] Pizarro 1832, p. 11.   [250] Pinheiro 1996, p. 67.
[251] Pizarro 1832, p. 12.   [252] J. L. F. de Carvalho 1832, p. 8.

remarked, would pave the way for its full-scale revision and permit "sacrilegious hands to rip its pages with impunity, turning law into a mere fiction."[253]

Other *emigrados* sought to reconcile Dom Pedro's ambitions with the rule of law, to prevent his drive for power from causing a permanent schism among the *emigrados* and from fatally undermining the cause of constitutionalism, whether in the form of the *Carta* or some other document. Ferreira Borges asserted that, according to the *Carta*, Dona Isabel Maria was indisputably the Regent, for Dom Pedro had renounced his rights in 1826 and the Portuguese government subsequently never restored these rights to him. Yet, Ferreira Borges claimed, once Dom Miguel was overthrown, the Cortes could bestow these rights upon him, in accordance with the *Carta*, allowing him to serve as regent during Dona Maria's minority "should such an arrangement be deemed in the national interest."[254] In bowing to the inevitable, the pragmatic Ferreira Borges was attempting to ensure that Dom Pedro's regency would operate within the confines of the *Carta*. It was an echo of the old Cortes debate from the first *Regeneração*, as well as Brazilian constitutional debates of 1822–23, discussed in Chapters 2 and 3, concerning whether a constitution was a "gift" from the throne, given freely out of the monarch's generosity and wisdom, or a compact negotiated between, and ratified jointly by, the monarch and the people to which both were bound.

The belligerent phase of the Civil War began officially on July 8, 1832, at Arnoso do Pampelido, near Mindelo, where the Regency's troops disembarked. After taking Porto and surviving a lengthy siege, the Regency exploited its naval superiority, launching an expedition to the Algarve, with the plan to squeeze the Miguelist army from both the north and the south, forcing it to fight on two fronts. The decisive naval battle, fought off the coast of São Vicente, occurred in early July. Thereafter, constitutionalist forces converged on Lisbon, which was taken on July 24, 1833. At this point, however, the conflict threatened to turn into a stalemate. Much of the countryside was still firmly Miguelist-leaning and Miguelist forces controlled strategically important locations, including the hilltop city of Santarém. But those forces were stretched thin. In some places, they were afflicted by hunger and lack of supplies, for supply chains had been cut by the invading army. Morale in the army, and in the populace at large, was low.[255] Cholera

---

[253] *O Portuguez Constitucional em Londres* (1832), no. 1 (March 27), p. 2.
[254] Borges 1832b, p. 32.
[255] ANTT, MR, mç. 442, cx. 553, José António d'__ Lemos [from Évora] to António José Gavião, January 15, 1834.

Figure 9 [Anon.]. "Vista da Praia de Arnosa de Pampelido, onde Desembarcon [*sic*] o Senhor D. Pedro á Frente do Exercito Libertador" (1833).

outbreaks, too, decimated troops and also killed many of Dom Miguel's civilian supports, including the prolific publicist Madre de Deos.

The Civil War was formally ended by the Convention of Évora-Monte (May 26, 1834). By its terms, Dom Miguel was forced to leave Portugal, but a general amnesty was granted to his supporters who agreed to lay down their weapons and swear allegiance to Dona Maria and the *Carta*. As a further inducement, the terms of the Convention kept many Miguelists in public posts.[256] Though Évora-Monte offered political amnesty, it should be emphasized that Dom Miguel's highest-placed partisans suffered dearly. Of the ninety-two *Pares* nominated in 1826–27, for example, only twenty-one were given their seats back in 1834. Mouzinho da Silveira's 1832 Judicial Reform, which abolished the *foros* as well as other rights, was now enforced. The old seigneurial jurisdictions were replaced with units more conducive to the manipulation of a centralized state. All of these policies greatly diminished the nobility's political clout. The extirpation of religious influence from economic and political life complemented these reforms. The abolition of religious houses, and the seizure of their property, meant that over five thousand clergy were expelled from their residences. Lobo lamented that "the Lusitanian Church is persecuted, and its enemies seek to destroy it."[257] These acts precipitated a decade-long break with Rome. All of these acts – their scope, speed, and ferocity – caused great resentment that would fuel resistance to the Lisbon-centered state in the 1840s, particularly north of the Douro River, which would be the site of multiple large-scale insurrections.[258]

Unsurprisingly, many Miguelists refused to accept the terms agreed upon at Évora-Monte. They followed Dom Miguel's example. Upon his arrival in Genoa, the deposed Infante renounced his earlier promise to comply with the Convention and declared Dona Maria's government illegal (and impious). Some chose either chose to follow Dom Miguel into exile or refused to surrender. José Joaquim de Sousa Reis, better known as "Remexido," led a guerrilla band in the mountains of the Algarve which reactivated the struggle in August 1836. In a proclamation issued in November of that year, Remexido claimed he was reacting against "blasphemy of the name of God in the cities and villages of Portugal, the Temples (Churches) profaned, the altars stripped, and

---

[256] This was poorly received by the conquering army, who thought it excessively conciliatory, to say nothing of depriving them of the "spoils" of public offices they expected to gain as a result of their victory. See Silva 1988, p. 101.

[257] Letter dated October 16, 1836, in Lobo 1944, p. 129.

[258] Ferreira 2002, pp. 541, 566; Marques and Serrão 2002, p. 183.

religious images trampled underfoot by heretics."[259] Though Remexido was captured and executed in June 1838, there is some evidence that other, smaller bands loosely affiliated with Miguelism continued the fight against the central government in the Algarve until at least 1840. Yet even after the bands of rebels were subdued, political tranquility proved elusive. As will be addressed in Chapter 5, the passions set to boil during the Civil War would continue to simmer and adversely impact public life for almost two decades.

PART III

The international context of the Portuguese Civil War: British foreign policy, Spanish domestic politics, multinational financiers, and the "Liberal International"

As Parts I and II sought to illustrate, the Civil War was a conflict influenced by political events and actors on both sides of the Atlantic. Such influence was unavoidable, given the exilic itineraries and perpetual motion of the participants, to say nothing of the "post-imperial" moment in which it transpired. But the active participation of foreigners and multinational interests in the Civil War itself deserves treatment, for it figured prominently not only in the conflict's outcome, but also in the rhetoric employed by both Portuguese radical and conservative publicists from 1820 until 1834. In Part I, Miguelist hostility toward foreign involvement and intervention was treated. After the July Revolution in France, Miguelists believed that their regime was the advance guard of the European counter-revolution. They conceived of (and depicted) their struggle as determining the fate of Europe. In 1831, a publicist wrote:

You [Portuguese] are now attempting, with heroic energy, to prevent the outbreak of another revolution in Europe. The destiny of this country will decide that of Spain, and that of Spain will determine that of Italy, Germany, the Confederation of the Rhine, and even Russia.[260]

Dom Pedro was accused of receiving support from "all of the visionary revolutionists and theoretical philanthropists of Europe" and for having made "a formal pledge to afford asylum to all the European adventurers

---

[259] "Proclamação do Remexido," November 21, 1836, cited in Cardoso and Machado n.d., p. 139.
[260] Boccanegra 1831, Carta VIII, p. 10.

who may flock to the Tagus and the Douro, especially the French."[261] In fairness, the Miguelists shared these somewhat paranoid fears with the Chancelleries of the Holy Alliance, and many liberal activists throughout Europe dreamed that Dom Pedro might place himself at the head of a transnational liberal league, as will be discussed subsequently.

Miguelist fear-mongering and diplomatic anxiety aside, many observers abroad took a keen interest in Portuguese affairs after the *Carta*'s arrival. It was greeted by some foreign commentators as a panacea for Portugal's ills. While the 1822 Constitution had been depicted as a frontal attack on monarchy, noble privilege, and the national church, an English supporter believed that the *Carta* would "cement, in firm union, the various talents and interests of these several estates, under such modifications as shall conciliate and guard the young spirit of popular liberty."[262] However, the tremendous popular backlash it garnered was unsurprising to experienced observers. The notion of two great extreme and irreconcilable "parties" led A'Court to fear for the *Carta*'s fate:

The important events, to which the last ten years have given birth, have scarcely left a man in the nation who does not wear the colors of one of the two great parties by which it is divided. There is not an individual of any talent, who has not figured, at some period of his life, either on one side or on the other. An administration without color could not be formed.[263]

To stave off Spanish intervention, not out of any special fondness for the *Carta*'s contents, Lord Liverpool's government sent an expeditionary force to Lisbon, at the request of Regent Dona Isabel Maria, in late 1826. Certainly, the propaganda value of an aggressive foreign policy, particularly in defense of a small, vulnerable country, nominally led by a child queen, should not be discounted. But the future extent of British involvement in Portugal's internal politics was unclear, and many in government desired a connection of limited duration. Canning's premature death in 1827 led to waning interest in Portugal, compounded by the inscrutable nature of the situation there, as Miguelist uprisings and rapidly shifting political alliances produced chaos.

Yet there were several reasons why England could not extricate itself easily from the tumult. One was historical connection and prestige. As the incoming foreign secretary, the Earl of Dudley, informed A'Court's successor in Lisbon, Sir Frederick Lamb, "YE is already well aware of the peculiar nature of the connection that exists betwixt England and

[261] [Anon.], *Dom Pedro's Expedition* 1832, pp. 39, 44–45.
[262] [Anon.], *An Historical View* 1827, p. 348.
[263] TNA, FO 63/308, A'Court to Canning, August 23, 1826.

Portugal … it is not too much to say that Portugal owes its political existence to England."[264] Dom Miguel's coup produced wildly divergent reactions, but the greater fear, as judged from British diplomatic correspondence, was Dom Pedro's vigorous interference in Portuguese affairs. Dudley conveyed this preoccupation with Dom Pedro's unpredictable maneuvers repeatedly in 1827–28. He asked Robert Gordon, "But when this – the natural – order of things is to be reversed, and when the colony, made the seat of empire, exacts even the shew of subordination from the parent state, is it not to be expected that her wounded pride will occasion, first, disgust, and then resistance?"[265] To Lamb, Dudley remarked that

for the sovereign of what was recently the colony, to govern the mother country from the other side of the Atlantic, is obviously impossible … the completion [of the abdication] is necessary to place the authority of Dom Miguel upon a permanent and intelligible basis, by establishing between Portugal and Brazil those relations which were contemplated in the [August 1825 Treaty].[266]

Britain blamed Brazil for meddling in Portugal. After Dom Miguel's coup, Lord Aberdeen chastized Barbacena: "In truth, it may be affirmed that so far from Great Britain having been instrumental in the production of evils which have recently afflicted Portugal, they are mainly to be attributed to the want of frank, consistent and direct course of policy on the part of the Brazilian government itself."[267] Dom Miguel's actions, British officials believed, threatened to renew belligerent relations between Brazil and Portugal. Wellington initially scoffed at such an idea, noting that "[Dom Pedro] has not the means even of conquering the Banda Oriental. How can he find those to reconquer the kingdom of Portugal?"[268] Yet he subsequently acknowledged that the prospect of a Brazilian invasion of Portugal was less far-fetched than previously imagined. "We do not intend," Wellington told Aberdeen, "to allow the Portuguese monarchy in Europe to be further weakened by the seizure of its remaining colonies by the Emperor of Brazil, or by their being revolutionized."[269]

The situation was further complicated by the internal inconsistency between the respective South American and European diplomatic

[264] TNA, FO 63/331, Earl of Dudley [John Ward, 1781–1833] to Sir Frederick Lamb, March 12, 1828.
[265] Dudley to Robert Gordon, December 14, 1827, in Webster 1938, vol. I, p. 322.
[266] TNA, FO 63/331, Dudley to Lamb, March 12, 1828 and March 26, 1828.
[267] TNA, FO 355/1, Aberdeen to Barbacena, January 13, 1829.
[268] Wellington, "Memorandum: Affairs of Portugal and Brazil," July 19, 1828, in Wellington 1973, vol. IV, p. 544.
[269] Wellington to Aberdeen, August 17, 1828, in Wellington 1973, vol. IV, p. 623.

policies pursued by Britain. British politicians were aware of the potentially disastrous repercussions for monarchy's prospects in Brazil if Dom Pedro failed to install his daughter on the throne and thus retain a firm connection to European royal houses. But they found the notion of a puppet state in Western Europe, directed from Rio de Janeiro, repellent in principle and untenable in practice. Dom Miguel's usurpation shifted the terms of the debate dramatically, forcing the issue of whether Britain's treaties with Portugal mandated its intervention. A narrow interpretation of those obligations depicted the dispute between the partisans of Dona Maria and those of Dom Miguel as a civil conflict. Yet the universally acknowledged role played by Spain and Austria in creating conditions propitious to usurpation, and their active support for the rogue regime, made such a construction absurd. Certain British statesmen hoped that Austria would demonstrate flexibility toward the cause of liberal constitutionalism in this peculiar case. As Emperor Francis's granddaughter, the offspring of his prematurely deceased, beloved daughter, Dona Leopoldina, Dona Maria was entitled to special dispensation. Metternich privately acknowledged that she was "alone the lawful queen of Portugal." Moreover, the Cortes of Lamego, invoked by Dom Miguel to justify his actions, was suspected of being a forgery, both inauthentic and invalid. Metternich concluded that "the Cortes of Lamego is the work of a barbarous age, only curious, even if its genuineness were fully proved, as an historical document, but certainly not as a source of law."[270] Earl Grey believed that Metternich favored the resolution of the Civil War through the symbolic marriage of Dom Miguel to his niece, but feared that Palmela, along with most *emigrados*, would reject such a measure. "Surely, [they] cannot expect us to interfere by force to establish the claim of this little urchin queen?" he wrote.[271]

British policy, while pulled into different directions, undoubtedly gravitated toward support for Dom Miguel in 1827–30. Britain, for example, acted as guarantor of the small (£50,000) Rothschild loan to Dom Miguel for the purposes of enabling him to take possession of his

---

[270] Metternich to Emperor Francis I, September 22, 1828, in Metternich 1970, vol. IV, pp. 524–26. Metternich was correct: it was later shown to be a forgery, as discussed in Chapter 2, pp. 138–39.

[271] Grey to Lieven, October 12, 1828, *Correspondence Lieven and Grey*, vol. I, p. 164. But Grey was mistaken on this count, if Brazilian diplomatic documents are considered. According to Brazil's envoy to Vienna in 1831, both Metternich and Francis I were opposed to the notion of Dona Maria marrying "that sort of husband; [they believe] she would be better off living in a convent than risking her life [with Dom Miguel]." See AHI, 232/4/2, Marquês de Maceió to Francisco Carneiro de Campos, January 5, 1831.

office as regent.[272] By 1829, the question of how long Britain could reasonably withhold recognition of Dom Miguel became urgent. Aberdeen advised Strangford, then on a special mission to Brazil, to convince Dom Pedro to acknowledge his brother as the King of Portugal on the condition of his marriage to his daughter. Aberdeen also wanted British recognition of the legitimacy of Dom Miguel's regime to be contingent on his amnesty of political prisoners.[273]

In the interim, the government's de facto acquiescence to Miguelist rule generated outrage among Britons with internationalist commitments. They viewed official inaction and muteness as yet further proof of Britain's perceptible slide toward the legitimist doctrines of the Holy Alliance. Though refusing to recognize Dom Miguel explicitly, the atrocious expulsion of the *emigrados*, followed by the Royal Navy's blockade of Terceira, furnished proof of the government's reactionary predilections. In response, parliamentarians, journalists, and pamphleteers lined up in support of Dona Maria and denounced the usurpation.[274] They were not, they believed, demanding an unreasonably radical policy. After all, only Spain, the USA, Prussia, and the Vatican had recognized Miguelist Portugal officially. Even Russia and Austria remained on the sidelines.[275]

Sir James Mackintosh, both in the House of Commons and in the pages of the *Edinburgh Review*, presented a cogent case that Dom Pedro was the legitimate heir to the Portuguese throne and that he had not forfeited that right prior to 1826. "Nothing could have done this effectively, solemnly, and notoriously but the express stipulation of a treaty," Mackintosh contended, "the silence of the Treaty [of August 1825] is a proof that none of the parties to it considers these rights as taken away or impaired by any previous or concomitant circumstance."[276] Dom Miguel therefore had "waded to the throne through a succession of frauds, falsehoods and perjuries for which any man amenable to the law

---

[272] Ferguson 1998, vol. I, p. 152.
[273] Chamberlain 1983, pp. 233–34.
[274] Though less vociferous, Dom Miguel did not lack support among publicists and pamphleteers in Britain, notably the ubiquitous and prolific William Walton. See Walton 1830, among other pamphlets.
[275] Marques, "As Relações Diplomaticas," in Marques and Serrão 2002, p. 292.
[276] J. Mackintosh, "Statement of the Cause of Donna Maria da Gloria, as a Claimant to the Crown of Portugal," originally published in the *Edinburgh Review*, reprinted in Mackintosh 1848, p. 229. Mackintosh had a long-standing interest in the Ibero-American world: he had served as chairman of the Colombian Association for Agriculture, which sought to encourage British emigration to land provided by the Colombian government. By 1826, the venture had failed. See O'Leary 1989, p. 166.

would have suffered the most disgraceful if not the last punishment."[277] Britain's actions, or inaction, were interpreted as an abrupt reversal from Canning's comparatively defiant recognition of South American states several years earlier and augured poorly for British assistance for supposedly oppressed peoples throughout Europe. In particular, Philhellenes concerned with the authenticity and extent of their government's commitment to the cause of Greek independence, then hanging in the balance, were alarmed by British passivity during the Portuguese crisis.[278] "Sail to Portugal and there you will see that we are hated by all parties, and trusted by none," one pamphleteer charged, "while the thousands exiled from their homes, in consequence of our change of policy, imprecate curses on British perfidy, and serve as a warning to all not to place reliance on British protection."[279] Lord Porchester sarcastically proposed that Britain should henceforth "entirely abstain from interposing in the internal affairs of suffering nations," pointing to the "fatal effects" such interference had wrought in Sicily and Portugal. "The vehement denunciation of arbitrary principles, the eloquent advocacy of national right, and the enthusiastic cheers of an assenting Parliament," he bellowed, "are forgotten almost as soon as they are uttered, while the prayers of thousands, ruined by our vacillating policy, are heard with indifference or rejected with contempt."[280] Such denunciations failed to produce, in the short term, a shift in British policy. The political climate changed decisively only after the eruption of the July Revolution in France.

The tentative, vacillating nature of British and Austrian policy toward Portugal, however, should not be confused with the absence of foreign involvement in the Civil War. This interference must be viewed against the backdrop of three intimately related, yet distinct, contexts. The first context is the recruitment of mercenaries to which the end of the French Revolutionary Wars, the massive decommissioning of soldiers, and Europe's postwar economic slump gave rise. There were obstacles to the recruitment of foreign soldiers, particularly Britain's spasmodically enforced Foreign Enlistment Act, but the precedent for circumventing such restrictions was already well established. English, Irish, and Scottish volunteers, for example, fought in the Spanish American Wars of Independence, whereas many other foreign adventurers became

---

[277] Mackintosh, "Speech on Moving for Papers Relative to the Affairs of Portugal," delivered in the House of Commons, June 1, 1829, in Mackintosh 1848, p. 570.
[278] On British Philhellenism, see St. Clair 2008; on the connection of Philhellenism to British liberalism more broadly, see Rosen 1992.
[279] [Anon.], An Authentic Account 1830, p. 55.
[280] Porchester 1830, pp. 109–10.

enmeshed in the civil conflicts plaguing the post-colonial successor states in the late 1820s and early 1830s.[281] Connected to the recruitment and retention of foreign fighters, whether booty-hungry mercenaries or liberty-seeking internationalists, was the issue of finance. Who would pay their salaries and purchase their munitions? The second context was the structure of Europe's interstate system, with its intricate web of diplomatic alliances, dynastic ties, perceptions of national interest, and ideological preoccupations.[282] This was the backdrop against which political actors of the Civil War operated. It was far from immutable, and the ripple effect of political transformations (e.g. revolution, ministerial change) in other countries, specifically Britain, France, and Spain, exercised an enormous impact on the conflict's outcome. The third context, intimately related to the second, was the burgeoning and far-flung "Liberal International"[283] (and its lesser known "Anti-Liberal," or conservative, counterpart), the hodgepodge network of political exiles of various stripes and their sympathizers in all countries who tracked the progress of, and sought to aid, constitutionalist regimes throughout Europe. Linked to the first and third contexts was political romanticism, whose pertinent manifestations were a cult of adventure and solidarity with struggling liberals everywhere as well as direct action, whether through fundraising, publicizing their plight, or military service.[284]

The notion of launching a military expedition to mainland Portugal from Terceira, comprised of *emigrados* and fellow travelers, that would ignite a broader popular insurrection in Portugal, while far-fetched was not unprecedented. The military *pronunciamiento* was an already well-established tactic in the 1820s and 1830s.[285] Though Rafael del Riego's 1820 revolt was the most famous example, often invoked and imitated by Southern European liberals, they did not exercise a monopoly over the practice. Dom Miguel's *Vilafrancada* and *Abrilada*, to say nothing of the innumerable local uprisings which employed his name, may be understood as conservative variations on a liberal theme. Don Carlos, pretender to the Spanish throne, and his followers resorted to similar tactics with increasing frequency after 1830, too.

---

[281] On the Foreign Enlistment Act, and its (in-)efficacy as a deterrent, see Waddell 1987; on Anglo-Irish-Scottish volunteers in the South American Wars of Independence, see Brown 2006.
[282] Above all, see Schroeder 1994.
[283] Isabella 2009.
[284] Rosen 1992; Paquette 2004; Brown 2006; Isabella 2009; and Ricketts 2011.
[285] Fowler 2010.

For Iberian liberals, however, the model had begun to reveal its limitations by the late 1820s. After Ferdinand VII's second restoration in 1823, there were numerous failed rebellions in Spain that began with *pronunciamientos* uttered by political refugees upon their clandestine return to that country, the most famous being the doomed 1830 expedition of José María Torrijos to Andalusia and its final demise on the beaches of Málaga. Several similar expeditions destined for Portugal were organized, but never set sail, between 1826 and 1828.[286] In 1830–31, the notion of *emigrados* plotting abroad to return at the head of an army to liberate the *patria* remained ubiquitous. Spanish exiles believed that their past failures were attributable solely to the "lack of resources."[287] In the impending "war between kings and nations, between liberty and slavery," they expected to receive aid from other suffering or recently liberated peoples.[288] Spanish *emigrados*, for example, expected material assistance from Mexican and Colombian allies.[289] The abject record failed to deter new conspiracies from being hatched or discouraged foreigners from joining, and in some instances perishing for, the cause.[290] Thomas Carlyle, whose intimate John Sterling was one of many Cambridge students enraptured by Torrijos, described the Spaniard's appeal and the aspirations of his "band carrying fire in its heart." They envisaged that upon arrival in Spain "all inflammable as touchwood, and groaning indignantly under its brutal tyrant, might blaze wholly into flame around [them], and incalculable victory be won ... Here at last shall enthusiasm and theory become practice and fact; fiery dreams are at last permitted to realize themselves; and now is the time or never!"[291] Such aspirations and dreams, often dashed, enflamed the militant wing of the Liberal International.

The Terceira Regency soon realized that it had no option but recourse to foreign soldiers. Of the Portuguese *emigrados*, many either lacked military training or were unfit for reasons of age, infirmity, incapacity, or lack of proclivity. In Dom Pedro, moreover, the Regency possessed a leader accustomed to the employment of mercenaries, the recruitment of which formed part of his wider effort to encourage European settlement in Brazil and to guard his besieged throne. Early nineteenth-century efforts

---

[286] Castells 1989, pp. 29, 128.
[287] CT, Vicente Bertran de Lis y Rives [Paris] to Ignacio López Pinto [London], February 22, 1831.
[288] CT, [?] Hernández [Brussels] to López Pinto [London], January 10, 1831.
[289] CT, Nicolas de Minuissir [Marseilles] to López Pinto [London], December 20, 1830.
[290] The archetype, of course, was Lord Byron.
[291] Carlyle 1851, pp. 88–89.

in this direction, described in greater detail in Chapter 1, yielded several agricultural colonies composed of emigrants from German-speaking lands and Switzerland. Brazil suffered from a shortage of troops to wage its war in the Banda Oriental, to maintain order in the capital, and to serve as a counterweight to stirrings of provincial autonomy and republicanism. At first, mercenaries were a tolerable, stopgap solution to the manpower deficit, offering the further perceived benefit of augmenting Brazil's European population. By 1823, a mercenary regiment, comprised of four battalions, had been raised. In 1824, Barbacena, then in London, was instructed to recruit three thousand more foreign fighters, preferably Swiss.[292] In the second half of the 1820s, Dom Pedro, casting a wider net, sponsored Colonel William Cotter's mission to Ireland to recruit colonists. Employing unscrupulous methods and deception, he advertised widely in Irish newspapers, promising free passage for men and their families, a bursary for clothes, guaranteed wages, and a land grant of forty acres. In January 1828, 2,400 Irish, mainly from Cork and Waterford, arrived in Rio de Janeiro, where 400 men enlisted in the Brazilian army, where they were placed in foreign battalions. Their presence, along with German-speaking recruits, perturbed Brazilians, primarily nativists who feared European meddling in New World affairs. In 1828, a great mercenary mutiny erupted in the capital, mainly in response to unpaid wages and unfulfilled promises; 150 of the foreign soldiers were killed. This debacle foiled Dom Pedro's plans for aggressive recruitment from Ireland and Germany. He was forced to repatriate 1,400 of the 2,400 Irish at the government's expense[293] and to decommission the German mercenaries in 1829.[294] By 1830, the government succumbed to pressure and disbanded the foreign battalions altogether. Anger against foreign fighters was inflamed further when two decommissioned German mercenaries killed radical, Italian-born, São Paulo-based newspaper editor Libero Badero. In response to the backlash, the government withdrew support (temporarily) for subsidized immigration of all types in 1831, with assistance slashed even for recently established agricultural settlements.[295]

The employment of mercenaries, then, was a common practice in the Luso-Atlantic world, even if its record of success was dubious. The Terceira Regency resorted unhesitatingly to foreign troops out of desperation. Most were drawn by the promise of handsome recompense,

---

[292] Browne 1972, p. 77.
[293] Macaulay 1986, pp. 206–8 passim; on Irish recruitment efforts, see Santos Pozo 2010, ch. 3.
[294] Wisser 2006, p. 168.   [295] Browne 1972, pp. 88, 107–8.

including generous land grants. These promises were rarely kept, certainly never for enlisted men, most of whom never even recovered unpaid wages. A small, but highly prestigious, fraction of the foreign fighters were driven by ideology, including Lafayette's grandson and Hyde de Neuville's son, though many with less glittering pedigrees, including many of the Italian volunteers, claimed that the glory of fighting for constitutionalism was sufficient remuneration.[296] Others were motivated by an unstable mixture of both ideology and money.

Many of the British officers were long acquainted with the Peninsula, whether from service under Wellington's command during the Peninsular War or in the British units stationed in Portugal from 1814 until 1820 and again between 1826 and 1828. George Sartorius, who was named admiral of the modest flotilla of fifty ships amassed at Terceira, is an iconic example of such a figure. Thomas Stubbs, another old Wellingtonian who settled in Portugal following the Napoleonic Wars, was involved in resistance to the Miguelist regime beginning with the 1828 *Belfastada* debacle and helped to secure ships for the *emigrados*, as described previously. While numerically inferior, and leaving behind fewer memoirs, the foreign officers in Dom Miguel's service were driven by a similar combination of pecuniary and ideological motives. Marshal Louis-Auguste Victor Bourmont, who assumed command of the Miguelist army in 1833, was a committed absolutist (though he had served Junot in Portugal during 1807–8 and Napoleon in Russia), defecting to the Bourbons in 1815, participating in the Duke of Angoulême's restoration of Ferdinand VII in 1823, serving briefly as Minister of War in 1829, and commanding the expeditionary force that conquered Algiers in 1830, before refusing to swear allegiance to Louis-Philippe. He participated in the uprising associated with Madame du Berry, and fled thereafter to France for Portugal via England, where Lord Beresford extended his hospitality and undoubtedly facilitated the necessary introductions to high-ranking Miguelist sympathizers. The man who replaced Bourmont, a Scot, Ranald McDonnell, had a long career in the Iberian Peninsula, retreating across the border to aid Don Carlos's cause in Spain after the 1834 Évora-Monte Treaty, only to return to Portugal during the Revolt of Maria da Fonte (1846–47) at the head of a Miguelist guerrilla force, which succeeded in temporarily occupying the northern cities of Braga, Guimarães, and Vila Real.[297]

At first, the number of foreign troops in the Regency's army's ranks was small, though comprised of all nationalities: 300 Britons were joined

[296] Bron 2009.
[297] Rodriguez 2009, pp. 61, 89; Lousada and Ferreira 2006, p. 280.

by 550 Frenchmen, Italians, Belgians, Germans, and Poles. Various other regiments were raised abroad after liberal forces occupied Porto in 1832. One thousand men in Glasgow were recruited to form a regiment of "Scotch Fusiliers," led by brothers James and George Bell, but 400 of them drowned off the Galway coast before the remainder arrived in Porto in November 1832. Colonel William Cotter resurfaced, and raised an "Irish battalion" of 400 men. Other units were formed in France, with Lafayette's assistance, and in Belgium. Most of the Italian volunteers (the majority of whom hailed from the north) were recruited in these latter two countries.[298] Of the 14,300 troops defending Porto during the 1833 siege, there were approximately 4,000 foreigners.[299]

Various memoirs suggest that the recruitment and incorporation of foreigner soldiers into the Regency's army was a haphazard, poorly planned enterprise. For example, Sir Charles Napier, who previously had served in the Peninsular War and later would command British forces in India, commented that "this expedition, like all others sent to Portugal, was ill-managed in the details, which led to much inconvenience, loss of men and money, and well nigh to a total failure."[300] Participation contravened the British Foreign Enlistment Act, which key figures such as Lord Aberdeen wanted enforced, though Whigs opposed such a step.[301] Once in Portugal, the wretched conditions and bleak prospects fostered "continual mutinies and desertions," according to a British mercenary.[302] As a consequence of the Regency's precarious finances, foreign fighters were enlisted for a fixed period and then disbanded at the cessation of hostilities. Some volunteers found this policy insulting, believing that their units were the nucleus of a national citizen army, and that their status as liberal militants should have protected them against such shabby treatment.[303] The failure of the Portuguese government after 1834 to pay salaries in arrears, fulfill land grants, or integrate foreign soldiers into the new national army were the chief grievances expressed by demobilized veterans after the Civil War.[304] Not only had they fought for liberty, but they endured countless hardships, particularly those who survived the siege of Porto. In February 1833, a British volunteer, noted that, in addition to enemy

---

[298] Bron 2009, p. 428. Cotter served as Brigadier-General, but was killed in the siege of Porto. See Santos Pozo 2010, p. 82.
[299] Rodriguez 2009, pp. 77–88 passim.
[300] Napier 1836, vol. I, p. 146.
[301] Chamberlain 1983, p. 270; more generally, see Waddell 1987.
[302] Badcock 1835, p. 375.   [303] Bron 2009, p. 434.
[304] C. Shaw, for example, voiced his "deep indignation" that the "Portuguese nation [had] allowed her faith and honor to be tarnished." See Shaw 1837, vol. I, vii.

fire and cholera, "there was neither money, nor wholesome provisions of any kind, excepting a few vegetables. Cats, dogs and asses' flesh were eaten."[305] With the exception of Dom Pedro, whose personal bravery, easy manner, and quick intelligence were eulogized by numerous foreign volunteers, the Portuguese administration was routinely maligned for its "intrigues and follies," which fueled their discontent.[306]

Funding for the military operation was dependent entirely on foreign financiers. Whatever liquid assets the aristocratic *emigrados* might have placed at the Regency's disposal either had been confiscated by Dom Miguel, had been dissipated in the first phase of exile, or else remained inaccessible in Portugal. The obvious solution was a foreign loan, but the absence of recognition by other states scared off potential lenders. Without formal recognition, the Regency was a risky investment. Ideological affinity, therefore, had to trump cold numerical calculus. In Juan Alvarez Mendizábal, a Spanish émigré banker and (later) politician, they found an unwavering supporter. Mendizábal's largesse, dispensed in the form of a £2 million loan on favorable terms, with a waiver of the standard collateral requirement (as Dom Pedro refused to employ his private wealth for that purpose), was inspired by the same vision that terrified conservatives across Europe. He foresaw Dom Pedro rallying liberals everywhere, toppling the infirm Ferdinand VII, reigning as the constitutional emperor of a federated Iberian Peninsula, and converting Madrid and Lisbon into the twin loci of revolutionary movements throughout Europe, bulwarks against the forces of reaction.[307] The importance of the services Mendizábal rendered were recognized by Dom Pedro in 1833,

---

[305] Badcock 1835, p. 200. Not everyone seems to have minded the dismal conditions during the siege of Porto. As the roguish volunteer A. Tolmer recalled, "I can say from experience that a slice of dog, well-peppered, 'devilled,' and fried in a bit of oil or butter on the lid of one of our mess-tins, was a very luxurious repast in Oporto." He also recommended other dishes of domesticated animals: "A young cat stewed is as tender and sweet as a rabbit." See Tolmer 1882, vol. I, pp. 17–18.

[306] The quotation is in Napier 1836, vol. I, p. 152. For praise of Dom Pedro, see Badcock 1835, p. 405; Shaw 1837, vol. I, p. 411.

[307] On the issue of collateral/security, see Janke 1974, p. 59. By September 1835, Mendizábal had been made prime minister of Spain by Maria Cristina, primarily because of his financial acumen and administrative prowess which enabled him to raise funds and soldiers quickly to combat the Carlist menace. In late 1835, he was given a vote of confidence enabling him to rule by decree. By March 1836, he had suppressed all but a few of the religious orders, expropriating and selling off their property. For further details, see Esdaile 2000, pp. 70–72. Yet in the process of pursuing these reforms, he alienated much of his political support. In R. Carr's harsh judgment, "unfortunately, the first modern statesman of Spain turned out to be a second-rate banker to whom energy was a substitute for political talent." See Carr 1982, p. 171. This depiction notwithstanding, a study examining the influence of Mouzinho da Silveira's legislative program on Mendizábal's policies would represent a major contribution to Iberian historiography.

when the Regent rejected a British offer to escort Dona Maria II and the Duchess of Braganza (his wife) to Lisbon after the military victory over Miguelist forces, instead bestowing the honor (and foisting the exorbitant expense entailed) upon Mendizábal. The Spaniard fixed up, in the most luxurious fashion and at the cost of £12,000, four English merchant ships.[308] In the end, Mendizábal never recovered the money he lent to the Regency, but his willingness to lend diminished the trepidation of other financiers, notably Nathaniel and James Rothschild.[309]

The failure of some states to recognize Dom Miguel's government, the desire of most to maintain official neutrality, and the momentum given to the liberal cause by the 1830 revolutionary tumult relegated many interventionist-leaning governments to the sidelines.[310] Certainly, leading figures were unambiguously sympathetic, but such sentiments of solidarity produced no action. Palmerston privately chafed that, "Really, when one reads what is going on in Portugal one feels tempted to throw the principle of noninterference overboard and to send Pedro straight to Queluz. But nevertheless the thing must be done in a decent manner, but done it should be."[311]

But official neutrality became untenable after 1833, when Dona Maria's forces stood on the brink of military victory. As the Regency's victory loomed, however, the *Carta* came to be viewed in European cabinets as an obstacle to a durable peace. This sentiment was ubiquitous. Talleyrand, then France's ambassador to Britain, told the Duc of Broglie in mid 1833 that he believed the Regency should "abandon Dom Pedro's constitution, that great terror of Spain," for such a move would "allay all the irritability of Europe."[312] Moreover, Broglie held that Dom Pedro's direction of the Regency and his *Carta* prevented national enthusiasm from coalescing in Dona Maria's favor, which had become identified with the regent's "follies, freaks, and his idiotic *Carta*." The best outcome, in Broglie's opinion, would be to "adjourn putting the Constitution of 1826 into operation, until more peaceable times will

[308] Janke 1974, p. 91. The ships were the *Royal Tar*, the *Soho*, the *Superb*, and the *City of Waterford*, the last of which sank en route.
[309] Janke 1974, pp. 67, 115. The postwar impact of foreign finance was perceived very early by several Miguelists. One recommended that the government should inform the public how the rebel Regency army was financed, specifically how "the Portuguese people would have to pay for the expenses of the parricide invasion if the Rebels succeeded." He predicted, with notable prescience, that the foreign loans contracted at unfavorable rates of interest by the Liberals could only be repaid by recourse to the Church's property. See ANTT, MR, mc. 356, cx. 476, [unsigned], "Nota sobre os Meios dos Rebeldes," dated Lisbon, March 29, 1832.
[310] Bullen 1977.
[311] Palmerston (1831), quoted in Webster 1951, vol. II, p. 242.
[312] Talleyrand to Broglie, July 30, 1833, in Talleyrand 1892, p. 139.

allow for its revision and adaptation to the customs of Portugal."[313] In Britain, Wellington shared these views. If Dona Maria's cause succeeded, he feared that Britain "shall be instrumental in having placed in Portugal a revolutionary government which will collect around it a band of revolutionists who will from thence plot and intrigue in safety; and under the protection of England will shake to the foundations every government in Europe, including that of France."[314] Palmerston viewed the matter more pragmatically: "As soon as Pedro got to Lisbon by his own means, the constitution became inevitable," he confessed in a letter to Villiers, Britain's ambassador to Spain and chief Iberian specialist.[315] For his part, Villiers was anxious that the radicalization of Portuguese politics would reverberate in Spain, adding further chaos to that unleashed by the succession crisis occasioned by Ferdinand VII's death. He wrote to Palmela that "it is impossible to deny that any very radical reforms in your institutions (unless they accorded with the wishes of the majority of your nation) will give cause for alarm here."[316] For Comte de Rayneval, French ambassador to Madrid, Portuguese affairs had taken "the most vexatious possible turn," warning of the impending "bloody anarchy."[317] By the end of 1833, Villiers considered Dom Pedro an intolerable nuisance. As Villiers argued:

he has taught how little is to be expected from [Dom Pedro's] sagacity or good faith ... I do not wonder that our government should pause and demand some solid guarantees that they are not about to erect a Government which is to violate every engagement and to proceed in a career of despotism similar to that which under Dom Miguel outraged the better part of Europe.[318]

By early 1834, Villiers argued to Howard de Walden, who by then was Britain's ambassador to Portugal, that recognition of, and military support for, Dona Maria's newly installed regime should be contingent upon Dom Pedro's exit from the political scene.[319] Yet the fear of foreign,

---

[313] Broglie to Talleyrand, August 15 and August 17, 1833, in Talleyrand 1892, pp. 154–57 passim.

[314] Wellington to John Wilson Croker, September 30, 1833, in Wellington 1975, vol. I, p. 321.

[315] Palmerston to Villiers, November 15, 1833, in Palmerston 1985, p. 75.

[316] Bod.Ox., MS. Clar. Dep.C. 465/2, Villiers (from Madrid) to Palmela, November 7, 1833, fos. 14v–15. To which he added, "upon this subject I offer no opinion as I know not whether the Portuguese are sufficiently advanced in knowledge to use intensive political rights in a manner beneficial to themselves."

[317] Rayneval to Talleyrand, August 24, 1833, in Talleyrand 1892, vol. V, p. 169.

[318] Bod.Ox., MS. Clar. Dep.C. 465/2, Villiers to Russell, December 11, 1833, fos. 24–24v.

[319] Bod.Ox., MS. Clar. Dep.C. 465/2, Villiers to Lord Howard de Walden [in Lisbon], January 5, 1834, fo. 32v.

particularly Spanish, intervention in Portugal trumped British misgivings about Dom Pedro. As Wellington told Sir Robert Wilson in March 1834, "If Portugal is not entirely independent [of Spain], she cannot be allied with England. England then is no longer certain of the Tagus."[320]

Dom Pedro's premature death in September, after a recurrent illness, probably of tuberculosis, removed his provocative mien from the calculations of British statesmen. The Quadruple Alliance Treaty of 1834 sought to remove Anglo-French competition in the Iberian Peninsula while committing them jointly to sustaining the fragile thrones of Portugal and Spain against the plots of the ultra-reactionary pretenders, Dom Miguel and Don Carlos. "The great object of our policy," Palmerston told Villiers in February 1834:

ought now to be to form a Western confederacy of free states as a counterpoise to the Eastern league of arbitrary governments. England, France, Spain and Portugal, united as they now must be, will form a political and moral power in Europe which must hold Metternich and Nicholas in check. We shall be on the advance, they on the decline; and all of the smaller planets of Europe will have a natural tendency to gravitate toward our system.[321]

With such promises and alliances, the Spanish threat and the Miguelist menace abated, which gave the victors room for maneuver. How they proceeded, and how they fared, will be discussed in the next chapter.

The cessation of military operations (for it could be argued that the Civil War was pursued by other, marginally less bellicose means over the next two decades) revealed Portugal's precarious position, whether judged in economic terms or in its relation to other European states. But the conflict had also demonstrated that Portugal was embedded securely in Europe in a way that its previous Brazilian orientation often had obscured. In 1820, on the eve of the Porto Revolution, a Portuguese diplomat stationed in Central Europe could observe that "it pains me to confess that I am increasingly convinced that the Pyrenees are the frontier of continental Europe, and that the two kingdoms of the [Iberian] Peninsula are considered by most of Europe to be intermediate states between Africa and Europe, which only merit secondary consideration

---

[320] Wellington to Sir Robert Wilson, March 28, 1834, in Wellington 1975, vol. I, pp. 487–88.
[321] Palmerston to Villiers, February 11, 1834, quoted in Webster 1951, vol. II, p. 390. Palmerston had entertained such ideas for some time: in a September 1832 draft for an article later published in *The Globe*, he described the conflict in Portugal as a "struggle between the opposing principles which are in conflict all over Europe, between arbitrary power with all its concomitant abuses, and rational government, tempered by freedom and justice." Quoted in Bullen 1974, p. 11, fn. 36.

in the political affairs of Europe."[322] By 1834, such a claim would have been dismissed as outlandish.

Yet the barriers to starting afresh after decades of constant war, foreign occupation, imperial dismemberment, and civil strife seemed insuperable to some statesmen. They believed Portugal's very survival as a sovereign state remained imperiled. Many commentators concluded that, confined to the resources within its own territory and constrained by its various commercial treaties with wealthier, more powerful states, Portugal's days as a sovereign entity were numbered. It was within this context, as analyzed in Chapter 5, that many urged Portugal to gaze toward its long-neglected territorial footholds in Africa, and to recreate there the tropical empire recently lost in Brazil.

[322] ANTT, APASG, cx. 1, mç. 2, Conde de Oriola [Minister Plenipotentiary in Berlin] to Saldanha da Gama, September 2, 1820.

5 After Brazil, after Civil War: the origins of Portugal's African empire

> What Africa needs is a [new] Marquês de Pombal, who could revive its agriculture in 10 years, just like the [first] Marquês did in Brazil.[1]

Following on the heels of more than two decades of unabated economic decline and incessant civil strife, the Civil War left Portugal in a shambles. Its remaining colonial possessions were moribund, except where a resurgent slave trade further enervated other, already debilitated sectors of the economy. The state of the peninsular economy was desperate. In 1834–36, government revenues covered just 70 percent of expenditures, resulting in an enormous deficit which would balloon to the equivalent of 8.5 years of government revenue by 1852.[2] The absence of revenue from direct taxation or property taxes was reflected in the fact that between 58 and 68 percent of revenue derived from customs receipts. Adding to the sense of insecurity and dependence was the fact that the lion's share of this external commerce was conducted with just two countries: Britain (58 percent) and Brazil (16 percent).[3] Mouzinho da Silveira's only partially implemented reforms were designed to improve this situation by abolishing privileged companies, the *dizimos*, *forais*, seigneural exceptions, *morgados*, and other fiscal relics of the Old Regime. Concurrently, the postwar Portuguese government, cash-strapped and debt-ridden, sold off huge swathes of the Church's landed property, which previously had been taken over by the state (*bens nacionais*), but did not generate the anticipated windfall revenues.[4] The failure to implement the reforms decreed on Terceira,

---

[1] AHU, SEMU DGU (Sá da Bandeira), cx. 2929, Severo Aurelio de Magalhães to Sá da Bandeira, 1841.
[2] Cardoso and Lains 2010, p. 258.
[3] Ibid., p. 258; and Marques and Serrão 2002, p. 137.
[4] Ecclesiastical property came into the state's possession because of a May 1834 decree eliminating all religious houses (convents and monasteries), and incorporating their property into the *Fazenda Nacional*. Five thousand clerics were expelled from 448 religious houses, though many convents survived the assault. The legislation had a non-fiscal impetus as well: it was, in part, retribution for the Church's support of Dom Miguel. See Cardoso and Lains 2010, p. 259; Marques and Serrão 2002, p. 177.

and the imperfect results from those actually put into effect, left the postwar government in a bind. A persistent deficit necessitated borrowing, mainly from abroad, which further eroded Portugal's sovereignty and autonomy of action. Public debt more than doubled between 1826 and 1836. By 1850, debt service alone amounted to the equivalent of at least £500,000 per year, an unsustainable level.[5]

The end of the Civil War did not bring stability. The exile Miguelist organ O Contrabandista prophesied doom, delighting in troubles swirling around "a government established by a foreigner (Dom Pedro), a constitution copied (from France), imposed on the Portuguese by foreign soldiers, paid for with foreign money, controlled by a cabal of foreign Jews, and presided over by a Brazilian 'Queen.'"[6] Dom Pedro's sudden death in late 1834, combined with Dona Maria's youth and inexperience, encouraged the eruption of long-simmering differences within the victorious liberal ranks. Mouzinho da Silveira's reforms were a flashpoint, but so too was the failure of the Carta's restoration to usher into existence the type of political society envisaged by emigrados of all stripes. Each month seemed to provide fresh proof of the Carta's inadequacy, confirming an 1833 British observation that "the persons who are best acquainted with the actual state of Portugal do not consider the Constitution of 1826 as any means suited to it, nor likely to promote the tranquility and repose which it is their first object to secure."[7] Adding insult to injury, the first postwar cabinet, headed by Duque da Terceira (formerly Vila Flor), earned the unflattering epithet "devorista" because of the peculation in which its members unabashedly indulged.[8] The popular classes, most of which had supported Dom Miguel, chafed under the new regime while the deposed Miguelist leadership plotted their revenge and restoration from foreign capitals.

The period 1834–51, then, was marked by acute conflict. Dona Maria maintained her throne, but the rest of the political landscape remained unsettled.[9] The September 1836 Revolution toppled the

---

[5] Sideri 1970, pp. 161–62; on the Portuguese loans of the mid 1830s, especially the 1835 £4 million Rothschild loan, see Ferguson 1998, pp. 356–57.

[6] O Contrabandista, no. 3 (May 15, 1835), p. 13.

[7] TNA, FO 528/25, [Anon.], "Observations on the State of Affairs in Portugal," January 8, 1833, fos. 4–5

[8] Sá 1975, p. 20; more generally, see Valente 1993.

[9] For an overview of this period, see Bonifácio 2009. Limitations of space preclude discussion of the international dimensions of Portuguese politics, particularly the interplay of Spanish and Portuguese history, which was undoubtedly influential. As Britain's ambassador to Spain noted, with some truth, that "Portugal is to Spain as a skiff to the steamer which is towing it, and that the only chance for the former is getting out of the troubled waters in which both are tossing about now." See Villiers

Carta and reimposed the 1822 Constitution.[10] Many contemporary observers, however, saw this substitution as a desperate response to bad government, instead of an upsurge of genuinely radical constitutional sentiment. Lord Holland remarked that "the Queen seems to have provoked the revolution by misgovernment, favoritism, and intrigue; to have met it without courage and dignity; and finally to have submitted to it with duplicity and insincerity."[11] This incipient revolution was harassed from the outset, both from the political right and the center, whose partisans planned palace coups, fomented military mutinies, and instigated popular uprisings.[12]

The resulting solution, predictably, was a compromise. The hybrid 1838 Constitution was "popular" in the sense that it emerged from an elected body, not royal decree, and that it abolished the *Conselho do Estado* and *Poder Moderador*. However, it was accepted by *Cartistas* because it reinstituted a second (upper) legislative chamber and left royal authority intact.[13] The absolute veto, for example, now disguised under the old euphemism *sanção regia*, remained unmitigated, as did the Queen's authority to dissolve the Chamber of Deputies.[14] This uneasy compromise could not long please all parties and the *Cartistas* managed to gain the upper hand, topple the 1838 Constitution, and restore the *Carta* in 1842.

The 1840s were dominated by the polarizing politician Costa Cabral, a master manipulator, and by internal and external threats to the regime, particularly Maria da Fonte and the Patuleia (1846–47), which may be considered new, if short-lived, episodes of Civil War, and even witnessed a heretofore unthinkable coalition between Septembrists and

---

to Palmerston, September 16, 1837, in Wellington 1975, pp. 706–7; see also Bullen 1974 and 1977.

[10] Sá 1975. One of the chief targets of the Septembrist attacks was Mouzinho da Silveira's "dictatorship" on Terceira: this "downpour of decrees and laws served to darken the chaos in which we already found ourselves lost," *A Revolução de 9 de Setembro 1836* (1838), p. 11.

[11] Diary entry of September 27, 1836, in Holland 1977, p. 351.

[12] The conspiracies and plots are too numerous to catalogue here. Among the most important were the pro-*Carta Belenzada* (1836) and *Revolta dos Marechais* (1837), and the Miguelist *Conspiração das Marmotas* (1837). On these upheavals, see Vargues 1985, pp. 544–49; and Silva 1988, p. 35.

[13] Champions of the *Carta* believed that better functioning states – France, England, Belgium, and Brazil – had two legislative chambers as opposed to the one called for under the 1812 Spanish and 1822 Portuguese Constitutions. They argued that "when a single *câmara* decides the fate of a kingdom, it acts arrogantly, and abuses its power like an absolute monarch." See *O Independente*, no. 140 (August 5, 1836), p. 566.

[14] M. M. T. Ribeiro 1985, p. 188; Bonifácio 1993, p. 93; M. H. Pereira 1994, pp. 43–45; Bonifácio 2005, p. 101; Miranda 2001, p. 44.

revivified Miguelists.[15] As early as 1844, the need for wholesale political change was urged. Three of the leading figures of the Terceira Regency, for example, urged Dona Maria II to take drastic action and "remove these counselors, for their presence serves as a pretext for disorder and anarchy; choose instead some moderate men from whom the nation can expect impartiality and justice."[16] Foreign observers, however, perceived no way forward: Lord John Russell in 1847 declared that "the state of Portugal is in every way embarrassing and pitiable," pointing to the "spirit of tyranny and cruelty in the decrees and acts of the Portuguese ministers without parallel in any part of Europe."[17] From Lisbon, Sir Hamilton Seymour lamented that "Portugal has fallen into that morbid state when rebellion has become a chronic disorder."[18]

Finally, in 1851, Saldanha re-emerged and put himself at the head of a new government, ushering in a relatively placid, prosperous period, traditionally referred to as the *Regeneração*. Many of the key figures of the *Emigração*, including Sá da Bandeira and Almeida Garrett, played pivotal roles.[19] Major modifications were made to the *Carta* in 1852, including provisions that mandated the direct elections of deputies, the reduction of suffrage restrictions, the requirement that all treaties would be presented before the *Câmara dos Deputados* for ratification, the creation of special legislation for overseas colonies, and the abolition of the death penalty for political crimes.[20] By August 1853, just months before Dona Maria II's death on November 15, from complications arising from childbirth, Saldanha told her consort, Dom Fernando, that "since 1834, the throne has not been as respected and venerated as it is today."[21]

[15] António Bernardo da Costa Cabral (1803–89), first Marquês de Tomar; more generally, see Bonifácio 1993.
[16] BAj., 54-XI-44, no. 12, Lavradio, José Jorge Loureiro, and Mouzinho de Albuquerque to Dona Maria II, March 18, 1844, fos. 3v., 4, 9.
[17] Lord John Russell, "Memorandum," February 13, 1847, reproduced in *Documentos dos Arquivos de Windsor* 1955, pp. 88–89.
[18] Seymour to Palmerston, April 23, 1851, quoted in *Documentos dos Arquivos de Windsor* 1955, p. 208. Queen Victoria put this position baldly: "We cannot interfere in internal dissensions beyond ensuring the personal safety of the King, Queen and Royal Family. The Constitution may be, and I believe it is, an unfortunate thing in those Southern Countries; but once it is established, the Queen must abide by it." Queen Victoria to King Leopold I of Belgium, November 17, 1846, in Victoria 1908, vol. II, p. 108. For further British views, especially those of Palmerston, see Bullen 1974, pp. 228, 240.
[19] The tenacity, persistence, and longevity of this old guard is notable. As Sá da Bandeira noted in a letter as a new cycle of civil disturbance began, "We are old. We have served the same cause for many years. And we shall continue to devote all of our remaining energy to being useful to our country," AHU, SEMU DGU, Sá da Bandeira, cx. 2922, cod. 2G, Sá da Bandeira to Visconde [?], October 21, 1846.
[20] Miranda 2001, p. 37.
[21] Saldanha to Dom Fernando, August 7, 1853, quoted in Bonifácio 2005, p. 247.

Offsetting the depressing portrait of national decrepitude and political strife in the 1830s and 1840s was the almost paradoxical efflorescence of cultural and civic life. The mid 1830s, for example, were the heyday of political journalism: fifty-four new publications were founded in 1835; sixty-seven in 1836; fifty-nine in 1837; and fifty-one in 1838.[22] Lisbon social life, too, was revivified after the Civil War, as long-separated family members and friends reunited. Marquês da Fronteira recalled in his memoirs that "there were balls every night, the streets were joyous, and the people celebrated the triumph of liberty."[23] Merrymaking was complemented by a burgeoning postwar civil society. There was a proliferation of new organizations which often complemented state initiatives in the pursuit of national goals. *Sociedades promotoras* proliferated, associations multiplied, and literary-political clubs prospered, including Lisbon's influential *Grémio Literario*, founded in 1846.[24]

The vibrancy of public and cultural life gave contemporaries some hope that the enormity of the challenges Portugal faced could be met. Shorn of its major colony, Portugal was left with a mostly derelict *Estado da Índia*, centered at Goa, coastal settlements in modern Angola, Guinea, and Mozambique, and the Eastern Atlantic archipelagos of the Azores, Cape Verde, and São Tomé and Príncipe. A revamped colonial policy for these possessions, several of which were little more than depots for convicts (*degredados*) and staging grounds for the slave trade, and a full-fledged sense of their importance to Portugal's national destiny, would emerge in coherent form during the overhaul of administration, both domestic and ultramarine, in the 1850s.

Historians often stress the hiatus between the demise of the Luso-Brazilian empire from 1808 and the rise of the "third" African empire that would take recognizable shape in the latter decades of the nineteenth century.[25] There is a great scholarly debate concerning the intensity of this late nineteenth-century colonial interest, its underlying causes, and whether it was driven chiefly by economic considerations or "un-economic" factors, such as ideology, humanitarian impulse, or missionary fervor.[26] These debates are Lusitanian analogues of controversies in the imperial historiographies of Britain, France, and Spain concerning the timing of the transition, and the degree of continuity,

---

[22] Tengarrinha 1989, p. 152.
[23] Fronteira 1928, vol. IV, p. 18.
[24] França 1974, vol. I, pp. 154, 183.
[25] Clarence-Smith 1985 popularized this term in the English-language historiography.
[26] For the works that launched the major historiographical schools, see Hammond 1966; Clarence-Smith 1985; Alexandre 1993; and Alexandre and Dias 1998.

between the early modern and modern empires of those states.[27] Yet discussions about the merits of colonialism did not cease between 1820 and 1850, even though policy was formed haphazardly, applied inconsistently, and generated few lasting results. Debates were both fierce and intellectually substantive. Disagreement concerning the utility and advisability of new colonial ventures served to stifle the implementation of policy, to say nothing of the dire state of government finances. Undoubtedly, colonial affairs did not receive the robust attention they had garnered before 1820 and which they would enjoy again in the second half of the nineteenth century. The political upheaval and disruptions that Portugal experienced in the intervening decades diverted attention away from colonial policy, or at least made interest in *Ultramar* spasmodic, uneven, and pulled in mutually exclusive directions. Historians chiefly interested in results, in concrete policy, are prone, perhaps justifiably, to ignore the many unrealized projects that proliferated, the very sort of plans and schemes ignored by intellectual historians at their peril.[28]

This chapter surveys Portuguese ideas about, and aspirations for, empire in the period 1820–50. It argues that revived interest in colonialism did not occur spontaneously in the 1850s, but rather emerged from an earlier series of protracted and often inconclusive debates about political economy, settler colonialism, emigration, slavery and the slave trade, the preservation of national sovereignty, and the mainsprings of geopolitical greatness. Chapter 5 is divided into three parts. Part I summarizes and examines ideas concerning empire from about 1815 until the end of the Civil War in 1834, a period generally held to have been devoid of imperial schemes and dreams. Part I emphasizes the emergence in Portugal of a political discourse that appraised the colonial past in a negative light and remained skeptical about calls to create a new empire, an attitude whose most illustrious exponent was Mouzinho da Silveira. Part II of the chapter then analyzes the more robust efforts to reconceptualize empire in the period 1834–46, focusing on the initiatives of Portuguese statesman Bernardo de Sá Nogueira de Figueiredo (1795–1876), better known by his last ennobled title Sá da Bandeira, and the activities of the Lisbon-based *Associacão Marítima e Colonial*, which published several series of *Annaes* designed to stimulate interest in, and diffuse knowledge about, Portugal's remaining colonial

---

[27] On the transition between eighteenth- and nineteenth-century imperial regimes in other national contexts, see (for Britain) Bayly 1989; (for Spain) Fradera 2005; and (for France) Todd 2011.

[28] An early version of the argument made here may be found in Paquette 2010.

possessions between 1839 and 1846. Part III examines the connections between the slave trade, and British efforts to suppress it, and the direction of Portuguese colonial policy in the period after 1815.

PART I

Visions of Africa in an age of imperial dissolution and abolition

While the various plans, projects, and attitudes concerning overseas empire in the nineteenth century may be studied as a discrete unit, they are better understood in the context of imperial reform initiatives which proliferated in the late eighteenth century. There were discernible continuities, mainly due to the fact that the challenges Portugal faced changed surprisingly little in the eight decades spanning 1770–1850. For the most part, the challenges remained unmet, the obstacles unmoved, the problems unresolved: rampant contraband trade and the inability of uncompetitive Portuguese industry to mount an effective challenge to it; imperfect knowledge concerning the territory claimed which impeded development; a slave trade-dependent economy with little spare investment capital; and the scant number of willing European settlers. As discussed at length in Chapter 1, there were strenuous efforts to overcome these challenges and to incorporate rustic peripheries into an integrated empire, which gave rise to a bevy of initiatives, chiefly in Brazil: state-sponsored voyages of discovery, led by natural scientists and cartographers, were embarked in Amazonia; roads, ports, and fluvial routes were modernized to facilitate the circulation of goods while a new state-run postal system lubricated the flow of information, news, and commercial transactions; agricultural improvement was advanced in innumerable *memórias* published by the Royal Academy of Sciences while botanical gardens were founded in Belém, Rio de Janeiro, and Lisbon with similar aims in mind; and immigration schemes to populate the *sertão* with Europeans and found strategically located settlements were complemented and reinforced by efforts to enlarge the geographical boundaries of the empire, whether through violent dispossession of Amerindians or the conquest of French Guiana.[29] While there were few direct links between earlier initiatives

[29] The literature on these subjects, treated in Chapter 1, is vast and ever burgeoning. For a sampling, see Silva Dias 1968; Maxwell 1973; Jobim 1986; Brigola 2003. L. Souza 2006; Raminelli 2008; Sanjad 2006; Safier 2009a; and Langfur 2006.

and those analyzed in this chapter, it is crucial to recall that Portuguese statesmen did not operate in a vacuum when they reassessed the remaining African colonial territories in the aftermath of Brazilian independence. Instead, they were keenly aware of past precedents: references and allusions to past practices abound. African colonization was not solely an unprecedented project concocted by Portuguese politicians to assuage wounded national pride or to identify fresh sources of state revenue, but rather a smartened-up atavism of policies which percolated in the decades prior to 1808.

Statesmen, however, did not rely exclusively on old formulas borrowed from the era of "enlightened reform," though the solutions they devised bore a strong resemblance to earlier initiatives, primarily because many of the problems faced were strikingly similar. Old challenges remained, though Brazil's independence deepened some while eliminating others. The impending abolition of the slave trade, in particular, discussed at length in the third section of this chapter, generated new dilemmas for which earlier policies were inapplicable. The reluctance to devote much attention to Portugal's African possessions partially stemmed from an inability to envision a colonial economy not dependent almost exclusively on the slave trade.[30] While the Angola–Brazil nexus had been encouraged (by and large) in Pombaline and post-Pombaline legislation, which prioritized Brazil's agricultural development, its undesirable and unintended consequence was the creation of a South Atlantic economy to which Portugal was peripheral.[31] The majority of traffic between the littorals of South America and Central-West Africa, which further absorbed textiles flowing from the Indian Ocean, effectively excluded Portugal. As early as 1770, Mello e Castro lamented that "one could not without great sorrow see how our Brazilian colonies have absorbed the commerce and shipping on the African coast to the total exclusion of Portugal."[32] By 1814, a former governor of Angola had blamed the slave trade for the economic failure of the colony, since all capital, already thin on the ground, gravitated toward it.[33] He was not exaggerating, for between 1790 and 1830 seven hundred thousand Africans landed and were sold into slavery at the port of Rio de Janeiro alone, the lion's share embarking from the Angolan ports of Benguela,

---

[30] The majority of the slaves from Portuguese territory were destined for Brazil, of course, though some were bound for Cuba's plantations. Murray 1980, pp. 103–4.

[31] On the significance of this autonomous South Atlantic economy in the Age of Revolutions, see J. Miller 1988; Alencastro 2000; Ferreira 2003; Adelman 2006; and Candido 2006.

[32] Quoted in J. H. Rodrigues 1965, p. 27.

[33] Porto Santo 1839, pp. 13–14.

Cabinda, and Luanda.[34] Between 1810 and 1823, slaves represented 90 percent of all exports from Luanda.[35]

From Lisbon's perspective, there were many unsatisfactory features in this system, and these would multiply after Brazil's independence. But even prior to that cataclysmic event, Britain's abolition of the slave trade in 1807, followed by Portugal's promise to eradicate such odious commerce by 1825, enshrined in the infamous 1810 Anglo-Portuguese treaty and then compounded by the 1815 convention by which Portugal pledged to abolish the slave trade north of the equator, triggered the reassessment of the economic foundations of the Luso-Brazilian empire. The end of the slave trade, if not slavery itself, appeared imminent, and the economies of both Portuguese Africa and Brazil would have to adjust accordingly, weaning themselves from mutual dependence on the abominable traffic. After all, Britain was leading the effort and Portugal was in no position, binding treaties aside, to challenge its chief ally, the guarantor, at the high price of impaired sovereignty, of its political exist-ence and the territorial integrity of its overseas empire. These issues will be discussed more comprehensively in Part III of this chapter.

The looming abolition of the slave trade was the backdrop for dis-cussions of Portugal's imperial future. As early as the *Cortes* debates of 1821–22, when every aspect of Portugal's public administration was targeted for reform, prominent voices called for attention and public funds to be lavished on Portugal's remaining, though much neglected, overseas dominions in Africa and Asia. Of course, these arguments were made in the ultimately misplaced hope that Brazil could be coaxed into rejoining the empire, even as a member of a loose confederation, as discussed in Chapters 2 and 3. In this sense, the deliberations of the Cortes did not form part of a "post-Brazil" imperial plan, but rather an effort to revive the pre-1808 configuration and hierarchy of territories, with Lisbon at its center. The April 1822 report of the *Cortes*'s special committee for ultramarine affairs proposed that

agricultural societies should be established in each province with the aim of fomenting all the branches of agriculture. It should bring to the government's attention the taxes, monopolies and other exclusions which retard the pro-gress of cultivation ... and alert the government to lands which have not been brought under cultivation ... colonists should be sent to those places to under-take that project.[36]

[34] M. G. Florentino, "Slave Trading and Slave Traders in Rio de Janeiro, 1790–1830," in Curto and Lovejoy 2004, p. 57.
[35] J. Miller 1988, p. 241.
[36] AHU, CU 035, cx. 27, doc. 2219, "Relatório da Commissão d'Ultramar a cerca do Reino do Brasil," April 19, 1822.

New laws and more efficacious administration, it was believed, would produce a beneficent transformation. The deputies to the Cortes were entreated by reports suggesting that only new laws, and more responsible governors, could produce favorable effects. One *memoria* concerning Mozambique, for example, lamented the "indolence and inactivity of the inhabitants," but blamed the irregular system of government for these defects. Captains-general had "observed only those orders most agreeable to them or in which they had a [material] interest." The orders themselves were "purely abstract, [made] without knowledge of the character or customs of these people."[37] Another *memoria* called for "commercial liberty" throughout Portuguese Africa as the best means of fomenting economic development.[38] The Cortes was prepared to extend the constitutional system to the remaining colonies, but this aim was compromised by numerous obstacles, not least the fatal aggravation of relations with Brazil which dashed dreams of a genuine Luso-Brazilian *Reino Unido*. Some deputies to the Cortes continued to demonstrate interest in colonial affairs, though the attention they lavished yielded few concrete results. In the Cortes debates, leading liberals, including Fernandes Tomás, discussed Africa's connection to Portugal's post-Brazilian future.[39] But Dom João's restoration in 1823 deferred indefinitely liberals' plans for metropolitan and ultramarine Portugal.

There was no overtly anti-colonial discourse in 1820s Portugal,[40] though certainly the optimal form and direction that colonialism should take was an object of heated discussion and the prospect of a bleak future without colonies was countenanced. In the early 1820s, José Acúrsio das Neves mocked "those who seek to console us for this disaster [i.e. Brazilian independence] with illusions of the future advantages to be gained from our currently impoverished dominions in West Africa. We should not delude ourselves with such chimeras. Our glorious days are behind us."[41] The national mood fostered such introspection and prompted some commentators, including Mouzinho da Silveira, then a government minister, to blame Portugal's present plight on its reliance

---

[37] BAj. 54-XIII-3, no. 3, José Francisco Alves e Barboza, "Analyse Statistica, Topographica e Política da Capitania de Rios de Senna ..." (December 1821), fos. 60, 90–91.

[38] Sousa Sequeira 1821, p. 55.

[39] See for example, Fernandes Tomás's "Relatório sobre o Estado e Administração do Reino" (1821), in Tomás 1974, p. 62. The attitude of the *Vintistas* toward colonial affairs is analyzed in V. Alexandre, "A Viragem para África," in Bethencourt and Chaudhuri 2000, pp. 61–67.

[40] Alexandre 1993, p. 659.

[41] See Neves, "Carta XII: O Desmembramento da Monarquia," in J. Neves 1989, vol. VI, pp. 95–96.

on the "false and fleeting wealth"[42] which it extracted from Brazil. In a series of unpublished, but widely circulated and influential, assessments written between 1826 and 1830, as well as in numerous parliamentary interventions prior to Dom Miguel's ascendancy, Mouzinho da Silveira observed that Portugal had switched abruptly from being a nation awash in gold to one drowning in poverty, mainly because an overreliance on colonial extraction had distorted its economy, discouraging the development of manufactures while simultaneously permitting the evasion of vexing questions concerning domestic taxation and revenue collection. With the loss of Brazil, Mouzinho da Silveira argued, "Portugal must pursue the path to industry in the manner other European nations have; it must buy and sell instead of what it has done up to this point: [re-]selling the gold of its colonies."[43] In his 1826–28 parliamentary interventions, Mouzinho da Silveira routinely contrasted Iberian colonialism's practices with those of other nations, both ancient and modern. Portugal and Spain had erred by erecting colonies "on the backs of indigenous peoples," an inferior mode of colonialism when compared to that practiced in antiquity, when colonies allegedly were founded solely as a vent for excess population. When a Greek colony was established, it was free, enjoying the same status as the metropole, and entered into association with it. The Iberian powers had perverted this sensible arrangement, he believed. It was unsurprising that nations without colonies had achieved geopolitical greatness and sustainable opulence while those in possession of vast empires had lagged behind.[44] "Look at France, without mines, and Spain with them," Mouzinho da Silveira urged in another parliamentary intervention, "if France were to have had mines, it would be like Spain today; and Spain would be like France if it had not possessed them. He who is born poor learns to work; he who is born rich never works; nations are like this, just like individuals, and it will always be thus."[45]

If Portugal were to retain its remaining colonies (and it must be stressed that Mouzinho da Silveira never proposed divesting Portugal of them), it would have to do so in accordance with the principles of a radically "new system." He enumerated the features of this potentially beneficent system, in privately circulated memoranda and in his unpublished personal notes, as "free trade, the total elimination of all obstacles

---

[42] "Minuta de Informação sobre o Comércio Externo Português" (1823–26), in Mouzinho da Silveira 1989, vol. I, p. 982.
[43] "Fragmentos de um estudo sobre Portugal" (1830), in Mouzinho da Silveira 1989, vol. I, pp. 564–65.
[44] Speech of Mouzinho da Silveira, February 5, 1827, in *DCSDNP*, p. 245.
[45] Speech of Mouzinho da Silveira, February 6, 1827, reproduced in *PBDP*, vol. I, p. 601.

and duties in trade between [Portugal's] colonies, the abolition of duties on exports [from the colonies], and [the elimination of] restrictions on agriculture."[46] It was impractical, as well as unwise, to enforce outdated, cumbersome legislation. Instead, Mouzinho da Silveira argued, simplification through the dismantlement of the colonial trade regime would permit Portugal to begin afresh.[47] Mouzinho da Silveira was momentarily well placed to translate his scattered ideas of the late 1820s into policy in the early 1830s during and just after the Civil War. In an 1833 *relatório*, the anti-colonial tenor of his ideas is clear: "The Portuguese people have tormented, persecuted, and even killed one another for having failed to understand that the kingdom (*reino*), after having achieved its great conquests, lived for more than three centuries off the labor of slaves, and that now it is necessary to find a new vocation, creating value through our own labor."[48] Nor was Mouzinho da Silveira alone in this conviction. Another *emigrado* pamphleteer lamented that colonial wealth was pernicious ("*um verdadeiro mal*") because it had made the Portuguese people lazy.[49] To these social and economic critiques was joined a political diagnosis with Burkean overtones: Portugal's empire had been the handmaiden of the despotism later practiced in the metropole. If a new empire were to be established, it would have to start again on the basis of a new, untainted set of principles. In 1830, Almeida Garrett recoiled at the miserable legacy of Portugal's administration of Brazil for three centuries. "The government was stupid and tyrannical," he wrote in *Portugal na Balança da Europa* (1830), lamenting the "limitless authority of the capitains-general" and concluding that Portugal's rule in Brazil had not only been "the most despotic, but also the most absurd of all [European] colonial administrations."[50] The remaining colonies would be useless to Portugal, the newspaper *Espreitador* warned in an 1826 editorial, until "all of the old and monstrous legislation is thrown out, and abuses are curbed."[51]

Such negative views of Portugal's colonial past and future were not confined to liberals, though their triumph in the Civil War meant that it

---

[46] "Minuta de informação sobre a possibilidade e os meios de desenvolvimento das Ilhas e das Possessões do Ultramar" (August 21, 1826), in Mouzinho da Silveira 1989, vol. I, p. 924. On the relationship between liberalism and empire in this period, see V. Alexandre, "O Liberalismo Português e as Colónias de África (1820–39)," in Alexandre 2000.

[47] "Minuta de Informação sobre os direitos a pagar pelos Navios no Porto de Lisboa e sobre o Comércio Português em geral" (1826–28), in Mouzinho da Silveira 1989, vol. I, p. 935.

[48] Printed in *Chronica Constitucional de Lisboa*, no. 80 (October 26, 1833), p. 429.

[49] Rebello de Carvalho 1832a, p. 5.

[50] Almeida Garrett 2005, p. 35.

[51] *O Espreitador*, no. 7 (September 5, 1826), p. 27.

was ultimately their vision that informed Portugal's policy in the 1830s and 1840s. During Dom Miguel's reign, various negative assessments of colonies circulated. The newspaper *Defeza de Portugal* urged that Portugal look inward in order to foment its agriculture and increase its population. Several specific measures were proposed, including encouraging the return of those Portuguese still resident in Brazil and establishing internal colonies in Portugal for emigrants from Central Europe on the Spanish Sierra Morena model. Further overseas colonization was discouraged, and the memory of Portugal's Brazilian past was disparaged as "demoralizing." It had introduced luxury and laziness, depopulated the metropole through immigration, and resulted in the decline of agricultural production.[52]

The reflections of Neves, Mouzinho da Silveira, Almeida Garrett, and others echoed sixteenth- and seventeenth-century objections that colonies produced harmful distortions and prefigured late nineteenth-century commentators, including Oliveira Martins, who connected Portugal's early modern imperial expansion with its subsequent decadence. A parasitical economy, based on the extraction of natural resources overseas, precipitated the abandonment of commercial activities in the Peninsula and corrupted metropolitan customs.[53] Even those who resisted such well-worn Fergusonian and Burkean tropes realized that they had entered uncharted historical territory. "The loss of Brazil forces us to make changes to our way of living," the editors of *Paquete de Portugal* wrote in 1831, urging Portugal to discover or invent a new equivalent to "gold" in the neglected fields and pastures of the kingdom, thus replacing the mineral wealth that previously flowed from American mines.[54]

Yet in the second quarter of the nineteenth century, doubters, critics, and skeptics were far outnumbered by those who envisaged a resurgent empire as a fundamental pillar of Portugal's economic development and political survival strategy. Included were those from across the political spectrum. Not all of Dom Miguel's counselors neglected colonial affairs. By the opening of the *Trés Estados* in 1828, Neves had come around to the possibility of a post-Brazilian Portuguese empire.

---

[52] *Defeza de Portugal*, no. 81 (November 8, 1832), pp. 11–12; no. 82 (November 15), p. 6. The distinction between those for and against colonies should not be drawn too sharply. One unpublished Miguelist tract, for example, while advocating the increased settlement of the Algarve, noted that this plan was not mutually exclusively with "founding towns in and cultivating the lands of our African possessions." BAj., 54-IX-52 (6), "Lembranças sobre a Felicidade de Portugal" (c. 1828–34), fos. 1, 12.

[53] On Oliveira Martins's influential view, see, most recently, Mauricio 2000.

[54] *Paquete de Portugal* [London], vol. VIII, no. 10 (July 26, 1831), pp. 291–92.

He argued that "no nation in Europe, except Great Britain, possesses as many ultramarine territories as the Crown of Portugal still holds in Asia, Africa, and in the islands of the Atlantic ... with what remains of our empire, we can still make [Portugal] flourish."[55] He subsequently penned a tract on colonial affairs that would resonate well after the Miguelists were supplanted by the supporters of Dona Maria and the *Carta* in 1834. In spite of his firm support for colonization, Neves castigated Portugal, as Mouzinho da Silveira had done several years earlier, for its overreliance on Brazil's wealth, a fact he held responsible for Portugal's present dire state. "It is misguided to strengthen the extremities of the body if the torso lacks vigor. The metropole is the torso and the revolutions that it has endured have turned it into a skeleton." Portugal could not resign itself to becoming again an entrepôt, a point of transit for the re-export of colonial goods to the ports of northern Europe, he contended, but rather needed to conceive of overseas colonies as a spur as well as a buttress to peninsular industry.[56] Neves thus grafted Mouzinho da Silveira's low appraisal of Portugal's previous practices on to a new approach to metropolitan development that leveraged the colonies for the benefit of metropolitan Portugal's industry.

Regardless of the system adopted, the majority of commentators of all political stripes in the late 1820s and early 1830s could not envision Portugal's geopolitical survival without colonies. As a Porto newspaper, *O Imparcial*, noted in 1826, Portugal, "solely considering its territory on the Iberian Peninsula, is one of the smallest and weakest nations in Europe." Without Brazil, the editorial continued, "Portugal's situation is even more precarious. What will become of Portugal without overseas possessions?"[57] The often unstated fear, of course, had been articulated by Souza Coutinho in his famous 1797 *memoria* urging the intensified development of Brazil ("Portugal, reduced to its European possessions, would shortly become a province of Spain"[58]), a view that was, as shown in Chapters 2 and 3, reiterated frequently in the years 1820–25 as Brazil's independence became likely. In 1830, Neves articulated the pervasive doubt that Portugal, shorn of its extra-European possessions, could survive as a sovereign nation:

Certainly, Portugal achieved greatness without colonies. But in which period of history? When no other European nation had colonies, when sugar, tea,

---

[55] Speech of J. A. das Neves, in *Autos de Abertura* 1828, p. 31.
[56] Neves, "Considerações Políticas e Comerciais," in J. Neves 1989, vol. IV, p. 328.
[57] *O Imparcial* (Porto) no. 20 (September 23, 1826), p. 174.
[58] R. de Souza Coutinho, "Memoria sobre o Melhoramento dos Domínios de sua Majestade na América" (1797), in R. de Souza Coutinho 1993, vol. II, p. 48.

coffee and cacao, and other colonial products were entirely unknown ... everything has changed: the moment Portugal loses its [remaining] colonies, it shall forfeit the remainder of its former greatness.[59]

The inevitability of an imperial future was one of the few areas where liberal constitutionalists and Miguelists found common ground.

Contemporary historians, however, differ on the economic impact on Portugal of Brazil's separation independence, with at least one rejecting that it was the principal cause of Portugal's "underdevelopment" in the nineteenth century.[60] Perceptions, fears, and prophecies mattered. It was widely held that Portugal's sole chance of extricating itself from its post-Brazilian doldrums was through renewed colonization efforts. Deputy José António Ferreira Braklami implored his colleagues in the National Assembly in 1826: "But without capital what can we do? Where can Portugal obtain what it needs? ... Where? In Africa. Yes, *senhores*, in our African dominions we can find the means and resources necessary to pursue our ends."[61] Another deputy contended that "Portugal should look toward its African possessions; from this new America great advantages can be taken, if the right methods are used."[62] Parliamentarians heralded the riches to be extracted – especially coffee, cotton, ivory, and iron – which needed but an "active government" to flourish.[63] The notion of substituting an African for an American empire did not appear out of thin air. There were plenty of non-Portuguese precedents for such a shift in focus, the most prominent of which were the late eighteenth-century physiocrat political writers who advocated Africa as a viable alternative to New World colonies, Talleyrand's advocacy of expanding French-controlled territory in West Africa, and British colonization in both Sierra Leone and the Cape.[64] The Portuguese variation on this theme was that it joined the "myth of El Dorado" to a second "myth of national inheritance,"[65] conceiving of African colonization – whether of South or West Africa – as a long-overdue reprise

[59] Neves, "Considerações Políticas e Comerciais sobre os Descobrimentos e Possessões dos Portugueses na África e na Ásia" (1830), in J. Neves 1989, vol. VI, pp. 468–69.
[60] Lains 1989, pp. 98–101 passim. For the Spanish counterpart to this argument, see Prados de la Escosura 1988, pp. 30–31, 93.
[61] Braklami's speech of December 11, 1826, in DCSDNP, p. 155.
[62] Speech of João da Matta Chapuzet, March 4, 1828, reproduced in PBDP, vol. I, p. 623.
[63] Speech of Moraes Sarmento, in DCSDNP, February 8, 1827, p. 275.
[64] For a summary and analysis of the views of Badeau, Roubard, Dupont de Nemours, and Talleyrand, see Røge 2008, pp. 431–43 passim.
[65] V. Alexandre, "A Questão Colonial no Portugal oitocentista," in Alexandre and Dias 1998.

of the military adventurism, martial glory, and geopolitical *grandeza* of Portugal's fifteenth- and sixteenth-century forebears.

From the restoration of absolutism in 1823 until the end of the Civil War in 1834, for all of the rhetoric, ink, and blood spilled, there were few notable, sustained initiatives, though the exceptions deserve to be mentioned in order to dispel the notion that colonial affairs were ignored entirely. Dom João paid some lip service to the creation of an African empire. An 1824 *alvará*, for example, expressed the Crown's intention to foment reciprocal commerce between Angola and Portugal for the "common benefit of all loyal vassals," encouraging the investment of Portuguese capital as a "powerful stimulus to the cultivation of the extensive and rich *sertões* of that vast country."[66] But this declaration was not followed by concrete action. An explanation, perhaps, for this lethargy was the general expectation that relations with Brazil would be normalized and that, as political tensions subsided, commercial relations would resume to Portugal's advantage. Echoing Bentham, the editor of *O Imparcial* argued that "the same language, habits, customs, religion, laws, kinship" would ensure that Portugal and Brazil remained closely linked.[67] While some Portuguese officials and merchants waited contentedly for the resumption of previous relations, others favored more decisive action toward Portugal's African territories. A privileged company for Mozambique exercising an exclusive right over the ivory trade, for example, was formed and approved in these same years.[68] In 1826, the Crown dispatched sugar cultivation experts to Goa, an effort deemed successful and which resulted in the construction of several *engenhos*, though these efforts were quickly, and inexplicably, abandoned.[69] In 1827, the National Assembly endorsed a proposal to establish a Royal Institute for African Affairs at the University of Coimbra, an initiative stalled presumably by the outbreak of the Civil War.[70] In 1828, there were renewed efforts to encourage coffee cultivation in Angola, and the Miguelist government further reduced the customs burden on colonial imports by 10 percent as an inducement to revive a steeply declining trade with *Ultramar*.[71] *Memórias* proliferated in 1829–30 detailing ways to

---

[66] AHU, (Sá da Bandeira), 2929, *alvará* no. 95, December 6, 1824.
[67] *O Imparcial*, no. 36 (November 11, 1826), p. 150.
[68] J. Pedreira, "Sobre os Escombros de um Império: entre o Brasil e África," in Bethencourt and Chaudhuri 1998, p. 239.
[69] AHU, SEMU DGU (Sá da Bandeira), cx. 2922 2G, João de Mendonça Corte Real [Administrador Geral das Alfandegas deste Estado (Goa)] to António Cezar de Vasconcellos, January 15, 1837.
[70] Alexandre, "Liberalismo," p. 127.
[71] Ferreira 2005, p. 169; Alexandre, "Viragem," p. 67.

improve colonial governance.[72] A major scientific-geographical expedition to Mozambique was undertaken in 1831–32, Dom Miguel's ministers expended intellectual energy on the old Souza Coutinho scheme
to forge an overland link between Portuguese East and West Africa,
and somewhat related plans were hatched (though not executed) to
occupy points on the coast of Natal in order to thwart British expansion there.[73]

PART II

Sá da Bandeira, post-Civil War politics, and the drive for African Colonization

Only in the aftermath of the September Revolution of 1836, in many
respects the unofficial coda of the Civil War, did statesmen return in a
consistent and sustained manner to the theme of colonial development.[74]
As noted previously, the preponderance of historiography stresses, even
if tacitly, an "imperial hiatus" between the loss of Brazil in the early
1820s and Portugal's "turn" to Africa in the 1850s. But it would be
misleading to suggest the absence of debates concerning the utility of
colonies and the optimal strategies to achieve colonial development in
those intervening decades. Certainly, the political chaos enveloping
Portugal during the 1830s made its ultramarine appendages somewhat
peripheral to the country's immediate concerns. Declining trade with
its colonies was discouraging to policy-makers in Lisbon. Portuguese
India's share of Portugal's total trade, for example, plummeted from
10 percent in 1816 to 1 percent in 1828.[75] Nor was the debilitated state
of the remaining colonies encouraging. Metropolitan officials received

---

[72] See, for example, Hay, MSS 93.5, Box 4, Folders 4–13, António Nicolau de Moura
Stockler, "Informação sobre as Ilhas de Cabo Verde em 1830."
[73] Alexandre, "A Questão Colonial," pp. 36–37, 47; J. Miller has taken a dim view of
these 1825–30 schemes: "insofar as planners in Lisbon seriously contemplated investment, they resurrected old mercantilist transportation schemes ... [the collection of
ivory and beeswax] admirably filled the main requirement Lisbon imposed on plans
for economic reconstruction after slaving in Angola: minimal commitment of capital." See J. Miller 1986, pp. 643, 646.
[74] In a book published in 1855, Sá da Bandeira confirmed this neglect of Portugal's
dominions in Africa: "The Portuguese government could pay but little attention to
Africa ... because various causes required its energy to be directed to other places ...
it was in 1838 that the Portuguese government turned again to the affairs of its colonies in Africa." See Sá da Bandeira 1855, p. 26.
[75] Clarence-Smith 1985, p. 25.

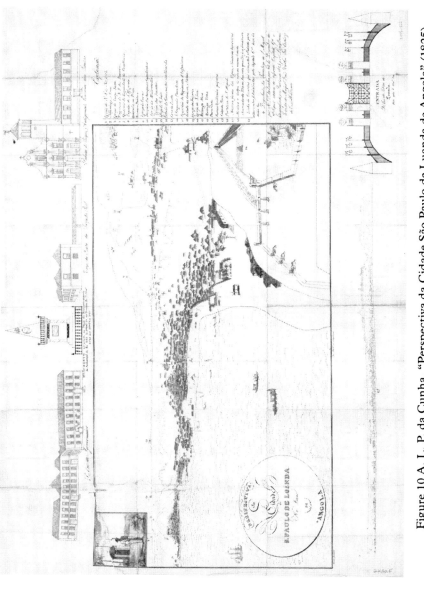

Figure 10 A. L. P. da Cunha. "Perspectiva da Cidade São Paulo de Luanda de Angola" (1825).

reports from Mozambique, for example, describing the most horrifying situation, where "wars have devastated this province and there is widespread hunger, so extreme that it is impossible to find a grain of rice."[76] The situation in São Tomé and Príncipe at the close of the Civil War was little better: "The present state of the administration of this province is the worst imaginable, deteriorated and abandoned in every respect."[77] Between the 1820s and 1840s, São Tomé lacked regular shipping services, credit institutions, commercial houses, and warehouses, while many of its sugar estates were abandoned.[78] Non-economic conditions were equally distressing. The missions, for example, were in steep decline, with the bishopric of São Tomé vacant since 1816.[79] It was amidst these inauspicious, daunting circumstances that the purpose of, and proper approach to, future colonial ventures was debated.

As Portugal's Civil War drew to a close, the victorious liberal regime began to legislate for *Ultramar*. The *Conselho Ultramarino* was abolished in 1833, and support for overseas missions was withdrawn the following year.[80] At first, legislation for overseas territories resembled that of the Peninsula. Assimilation, integration, and legal uniformity were its ostensible goals.[81] The reformers' guiding principle was that the distinction between metropolitan Portugal and *Ultramar* was a false one. They sought to apply constitutional guarantees (and civil and criminal codes) to every part of the Portuguese monarchy. The meaning of citizenship was to be undifferentiated across geographical space. In their legal universalism, they resembled the *Vintistas*, who, in turn, had inherited many of their ideas from the Cortes of Cádiz and also from Joseph Bonaparte's 1808 Bayonne Constitution, which had declared legal equality between Spain and Spanish America.[82] The cause of legal equality received a further boost from the *Carta*, which did not

---

[76] BNL, Reservados, cod. 10648, "Correspondência da Secretaria de Moçambique," ?? to Sebastião Xavier Botelho, July 6, 1826, fo. 30; on early nineteenth-century Mozambique, see Newitt 1994.

[77] AHU, Sá da Bandeira, 825, [Anon.], "Representação sobre o Estado Actual das Ilhas de S. Thomé e Príncipe ...," 1835, fo. 2.

[78] Hodges and Newitt 1988, p. 28. Even though coffee exports would only boom after 1855, 100 tons were produced for export in 1832 and 180 tons in 1842, according to Hodges and Newitt 1988, p. 28.

[79] Alexandre, "A Questão Colonial," p. 148.

[80] Wheeler 1963, p. 19. The extinction of the religious orders was not the only reason for the decline of missionary activity: Pope Gregory XVI withdrew support for the Sé traditionally maintained by Portugal in the Indian Ocean in 1836–38, during the break between Portugal and the Holy See after the Civil War. See Alexandre, "A Questão Colonial," p. 148.

[81] A. C. N. da Silva 2006, pp. 186–87.

[82] A. C. N. da Silva 2009, pp. 52, 57, 87.

distinguish between overseas colonies and metropolitan Portugal, perhaps due to its origins in the 1824 Brazilian Constitution, which did not have to confront such matters. The silence of the *Carta* in this regard emboldened advocates of legal universalism. Of course, the surviving *Vintistas*, and their descendants in the 1830s, differed somewhat from their immediate predecessors: assimilation and integration did not necessarily imply equality in all senses, as would become clear in the late 1830s and 1840s. But this orientation did encourage the removal of some of the most egregious abuses and the reform of institutions that tended to magnify the disparity between Portugal and *Ultramar*. The authority delegated to governors-general, for example, was modified to limit them to military and administrative affairs, stripping them of judicial authority.[83] New *Conselhos do Governo* were created, with the intention of curbing gubernatorial abuses of power and mollifying local elites clamoring for a modicum of self-government. The colonies sent deputies to the *Cortes*, even if representation was calculated on a different basis than in Portugal and thus was not proportional. Several figures from *Ultramar* became robust participants in Portuguese politics in these tumultuous decades. The Goan Bernardo Peres da Silva, for example, was a deputy to the Cortes (1821–23), then fled to Rio de Janeiro during the Miguelist ascendancy, where he wrote pro-*Carta* tracts, before returning to Portugal with Dom Pedro in 1832–34. After the Civil War, he was named Prefect of Goa, the highest post in Portugal's Indian administration.[84]

Yet the aim of erasing differences between metropolitan Portugal and its overseas territories was not realized fully. Many prominent figures opposed it. Poet and politician Almeida Garrett, who briefly served on the Overseas Council when it was resurrected in the 1850s, devoted an 1837 parliamentary speech to denouncing the legal integrationist attitudes then ascendant. He lamented that Mouzinho da Silveira and his supporters, not content to foist "incoherent innovations" on Portugal, sought to extend "this mountain of absurdities overseas, where they became doubly absurd, due to the obstacles, opposition, and local impracticalities encountered there." Other participants in these debates

---

[83] The extent to which governors were deprived of their old powers and privileges is unclear. Numerous petitions denouncing the comportment of governors after 1835 exist. An 1839 petition from Cape Verde maligned the "despotism and violence" of the governor, whose "arbitrary and extravagant conduct inspires horror." See Hay, MSS 93.5, Box 4, Folder 2, "Memorandum d'inhabitants de CV aos Deputados," January 30, 1839.

[84] Though he served for a mere two weeks in this post before returning to Lisbon. On Peres da Silva's career, see Ernestina Carreira, "Índia," in Alexandre and Dias 1998, pp. 666–67; see also Bayly 2012.

went even further. Speaking in the *Pares*, Conde da Taipa argued that colonies were too immature for "modern principles," but required muscular legislation better adapted to their supposedly primitive conditions.[85] These prejudices eventually manifested themselves in "special laws" for the colonies, devised and implemented between 1838 and 1842, which largely curtailed representative institutions and strengthened the military, arbitrary character of ultramarine administration.[86] They also resulted in a more precise, if inconsistently used, terminology to describe and differentiate between overseas territories under Portuguese rule: *"possessões"* and *"estabelecimento"* came into vogue whereas *"provincia"* fell into disuse, though *"colonias"* and *"dominios"* continued to be used regularly. *O Paquete do Ultramar* lamented in 1839 that Portugal "does not want to share with *Ultramar* the blessings of liberty. The government continues to be self-centered, partial, stingy, and deaf to the cries of the Portuguese in Africa and Asia. Ignorant and covetous men continue to govern, deprecators of constitutional government, men guided solely by capricious and ignoble passions."[87]

These arguments gathered adherents after the re-establishment of the *Carta* in 1842. Fourteen of the 156 deputies serving in the lower chamber in 1842 hailed from *Ultramar*. In 1843, Mouzinho de Albuquerque would declare: "Portugal does not have colonies. It has territory spread out in various regions of the globe. But all of these territories are equal before the law, [everyone] has the same rights ... citizens according to the same *Carta*."[88] But the notion that all subjects in an overseas territory could be citizens – in an age in which nation was conceived as an organic community, an assemblage of people with the same language, customs, genealogy, and religion – increasingly fell out of favor. Not all inhabitants of an overseas territory would become citizens, entitled to the same rights or encumbered with the same duties as their peninsular peers. Accordingly, a compromise was reached in the second half of the

---

[85] Almeida Garrett, speech of March 31, 1837, and Conde da Taipa, speech of March 31, 1837, both quoted in A. C. N. da Silva 2009, pp. 52, 389.

[86] The parallels to the contemporary Spanish case are striking. As Fradera demonstrated, "special laws" for the Indies were in place by 1837, which led to the concentration of power in the hands of military officials, the absence of political representation, and the degradation of civilian institutions. See Fradera 1995 and Fradera 2005, esp. pp. 325–26, p. 572; as Javier Alvarado suggested, with reference to the Spanish Caribbean, the term "special" legislation was often misleading, for it left the administrative and legal structures of the Old Regime intact: "the persistence of old uses turned the islands into ... a time capsule, isolated from the [new legal] world surrounding them." See Alvarado 2001, p. 100.

[87] *O Paquete do Ultramar*, no. 1 (July 5, 1839), p. 1.

[88] Mouzinho de Albuquerque, March 81, 1843, quoted in A. C. N. da Silva 2009, p. 399.

nineteenth century: the *Carta* extended to overseas territories, but its implementation could be interrupted, modified, or otherwise changed where local conditions appeared to demand such a deviation.[89] The legal fiction that Portuguese laws applied equally to Portugal and the colonies slowly eroded before it was abandoned completely in 1852.[90] Throughout the nineteenth century, particularly in remote areas of the empire, a systemic dualism prevailed, with Portuguese laws coexisting alongside other legal traditions.[91] The legal universalist vision foundered, then limped along, and finally collapsed.

When the Portuguese Civil War finally drew to a close, yet before concerted government efforts were undertaken, the pace of publications concerning colonial affairs quickened. Predictably, *memórias* appeared, often written by members of the defunct Overseas Council or by former colonial administrators. Perhaps the most influential of these was the former governor of Mozambique Sebastião Xavier Botelho's 1834 tract on East Africa, which opened with a damning indictment of Portugal's colonization efforts since the late fifteenth century:

> To their eternal glory, using the treasure obtained from their conquests, the Portuguese could have established the greatest and most powerful empire in the world. But the vices and ignorance of some their leaders, the profligate use of their new-found wealth, the distance separating the colonies from the mother country, religious fanaticism and political despotism, misunderstandings with the native populations ... the Portuguese brought tyranny in their wake as all of the territory controlled by the Portuguese [overseas] was turned into a theater of perfidy and cruelty ... we did not know how to colonize.[92]

Joaquim António de Carvalho de Menezes, author of a short tract on Angola published in 1834, concurred with Botelho. The chief error of Portuguese colonialism, Menezes asserted, was that the colonies had been kept in "complete subordination" to Portugal, which denied subjects "the proper methods to enrich themselves, basing policy on the false premise that the growth of the colonies would be detrimental to the metropole."[93]

Yet Botelho and Menezes remained optimistic. Acting on the basis of modern principles and following proper methods, Botelho argued

---

[89] A. C. N. da Silva 2009, pp. 15, 408.
[90] Clarence-Smith 1985, pp. 72–73.
[91] Roque 2010, p. 54.
[92] Botelho 1834b, pp. 6–7, 25. Botelho was a fascinating individual. After studying law at Coimbra and pursuing an administrative career, he was forced into exile during Dom Miguel's ascendancy. He was the only colonial governor for whom A. Herculano, the great nineteenth-century man of letters, wrote a eulogy. Herculano praised Botelho as an accomplished poet whose "elegant and fluent" prose animated the otherwise dull subject matter of his *Resumo*. See Herculano 2011.
[93] Menezes 1834, p. 11.

that "in Africa, we can recover much of what we lost with the separation of Brazil from Portugal ... in addition to its metals and precious stones, it is as capable as America of supporting colonies of European settlers."[94] Another ebullient prognosticator claimed that Portuguese Asia and Africa "contained the seeds of great prosperity, if able hands know how to foment it, and develop them, to the extent that one day we might regard the loss of our American possessions with indifference."[95] In the mid 1830s, then, Portuguese political and economic writers, publicists, and public officials began to consider in earnest the notion of harnessing empire to confront the domestic crisis facing Portugal, to alleviate its economic plight while renewing a sense of national purpose. Speaking in the *Pares* in 1835, Palmela argued that while Portugal always had been cognizant of an "obligation to improve the fortunes of its dominions," it had become an "urgent necessity" to extract some advantage from them to "compensate in some way for the great loss that was suffered" with Brazilian independence.[96]

Before the September Revolution of 1836, Sá da Bandeira, then Secretary of State for Naval and Colonial Affairs,[97] sought to devise a more systematic approach to colonial affairs. Among his first acts was the authorization of a monthly periodical, aptly entitled *Memorial Ultramarino e Marítimo*. In the legislation sanctioning its publication, the government declared that "it is of the greatest importance to make the public as well acquainted as possible with the colonies ... far too little is known about them and this lack of familiarity, undoubtedly, is one of the chief reasons why our colonies have fallen into such a state of decadence."[98] The *Memorial* was intended to have two parts: the first would be an "official" section, in which legislative acts or Crown decrees pertaining to colonial affairs would be published. The second would be "unofficial" (*não official*) and would function as a compendium of reports, essays, and other "*memórias*" concerning the conditions in

[94] Botelho 1834b, pp. 27, 42, 84–5. However, Botelho's observations and criticisms should be viewed skeptically. Though the British traveler Alexander included him on the short list of governors "who had conscientiously abstained from" self-enrichment during their gubernatorial tenures, he also noted, with admiration, that the decoration of Botelho's Lisbon palace, where he regularly hosted "the best specimen of a Portuguese party," revealed that "he had collected during his governorship in Africa no small quantity of *poudre d'or*." See Alexander 1834, pp. 199, 212.

[95] AHU, SEMU DGU (Sá da Bandeira), cx. 2924 2G, António José Maria Capelo to Sá da Bandeira, May 13, 1835.

[96] Speech of April 11, 1835, in Palmela 1844, p. 117.

[97] Following the September Revolution of 1836, Sá da Bandeira was promoted to President of the Council of Ministers while Manuel Lopes Vieira de Castro became Minister for Naval and Colonial Affairs.

[98] Quoted in P. F. de Matos 1981, p. 268.

Portugal's overseas provinces. These grand plans amounted to very little, however, as only one issue of the *Memorial* was ever published.

That single issue[99] reveals the government's conception of colonial reform as a means to resuscitate Portugal's economic and political fortunes. It contains the text of Sá da Bandeira's famous February 1836 parliamentary speech which argued that "the poor state in which the colonies are found is not due solely to bad government, but to the fact that [Portugal] had devoted its attention almost exclusively to Brazil." It had therefore failed to exploit the "gold mines, copper, iron and precious stones" of Portugal's African possessions. Echoing Botelho (and others), Sá da Bandeira argued that "in Africa, we can produce the same commodities that we formerly cultivated in Brazil. Cape Verde, Guinea, Angola, and Mozambique have the most fertile soil in which rice, cotton, coffee, and cacao can be grown; in a word, all of the so-called colonial commodities can be grown there."[100]

Sá da Bandeira's interest in colonial affairs was not sudden, but rather the result of long study, sustained over several years. Just after Dom Miguel's coup, he advocated establishing the Regency in Mozambique, not the Azores, suggesting that it could finance itself through trade to Goa and Macao.[101] During his brief exile in Rio de Janeiro in 1828–29, he wiled away the hours by hatching schemes to send Portuguese language specialists to the African colonies in order to "teach the natives to read and write."[102] By December 1829, he was convinced that the Portuguese government should dispatch "able naturalists," such as Humboldt, to Portuguese Africa, insisting that the entire cost be borne by the government.[103] During the Azorean Regency, he gathered information about Portugal's African possessions from his fellow exiles with personal experience in those places, recording their responses in notebooks with characteristic meticulousness. While the content of his interlocutors' responses was not especially illuminating, the questions Sá da Bandeira posed reveal his preoccupations and presage the targets of his later policies. Among other themes, his queries concerned the size and composition of the population of various ultramarine territories, the training and capability of the military force based there,

---

[99] *Memorial Ultramarino, e Marítimo. Publicação Mensal, Redigida pela Secretaria d'Estado dos Negocios da Marinha e do Ultramar*, no. 1 (March 1836). A copy of this document is held at the National Library in Lisbon.
[100] Ibid., p. 11.
[101] Diary entries of February 11 and 13, 1829, in Sá da Bandeira 1975, vol. I, pp. 152–53.
[102] Diary entry for June 17, 1829, ibid., vol. II, p. 75.
[103] Diary entry for December 3, 1829, ibid., vol. II, p. 158.

the "progress of civilization" of the African inhabitants of territories controlled by Portugal, the extent to which Christianity was practiced among them, the relations between governors of São Tomé and Angola, and the possibility of establishing a land connection between Angola and Mozambique.[104]

The information he amassed from the responses he received was incorporated into a hybrid almanac-news compendium-mini encyclopedia, the *Folhinha da Terceira*, which he edited, together with Luz Soriano and José António Guerreiro, between 1830 and 1832.[105] The *Folhinha* lamented the "oppression" and "poverty" prevailing in the "vast provinces that compose the Portuguese monarchy," the "effects of a prolonged despotism."[106] The commentaries on colonial affairs contained in the *Folhinha* were radical, offering recommendations for the reform of every territory. Concerning Bissau, for example, the *Folhinha* blamed Portugal's choice in governors for its lack of economic development, arguing for making its administration entirely dependent on the metropole while opening up its commerce to all nations. In Benguela, the editors claimed, the law was not enforced, a "system of rapine" flourished among the authorities, and the clergy "lived in the most scandalous depravity." In Mozambique, "bad government" was the norm and the *Folhinha* argued for settler colonialism schemes there. Chinese emigration was endorsed. Not only were Chinese "industrious," but it would be less expensive to transport them, rather than European colonists, to Mozambique. Goa was described as a "monument to despotism," and the *Folhinha*'s editors advocated its economic renewal through the production and export of opium. Even distant Timor was "susceptible to great improvements," since it could become a major entrepôt for trade from the Asian mainland to Australia.[107] But the *Folhinha*'s editors were convinced that Portugal's primary imperial future lay in Africa: "there we rule without rivals, over docile nations, who can be civilized easily … if we give the *negros* just laws, propagate European civilization among them, then this oppressed race will be made happy and Portugal will obtain great advantages from them."[108] In order for Portuguese Africa to flourish, however, certain preconditions would have to be met, including the abolition of government monopolies and the establishment of

[104] AHU, SEMU DGU (Sá da Bandeira), cx. 825, "Perguntas do Illmo Bernardo de Sá e Nogueira a que responde, segundo suas pequenas faiças, o seu criado José da Silva" (dated Angra, January 8, 1831).
[105] On his experiences as editor, see Luz Soriano 1891, p. 323.
[106] *Folhinha da Terceira* 1831, p. 84.
[107] Ibid. 1832, pp. 106, 109, 117, 120, 123.
[108] Ibid. 1832, p. 124.

comércio livre to be enjoyed by all nations (including in the trade for ivory, gold, and other high-value products). But the *Folhinha* insisted that all such changes required a transition to free, indigenous labor. Only with free labor could Portugal's envisioned colonial empire outstrip Brazil, for there would be no costs associated with the purchase or transport of slaves: "the *cultivadores* of Africa could fill the markets of Europe with goods and products that now come from America, of the same quality but for a lower price. Portugal could buy from Africa that which it today buys from Brazil," specifically pearls, whale oil, lumber, coffee, sugar, cotton, indigo, tobacco, and rice.[109] Within fifteen to twenty years, the *Folhinha* predicted, a reformed Portuguese Africa would have made "more progress toward a prosperous state than it did in the previous three centuries."[110]

After the constitutionalists' victory in the Civil War, Sá da Bandeira continued to solicit the often brutally honest assessments of experienced individuals through extended correspondence outside of official channels as well as through a life-long collection (and annotation) of older *memórias* concerning Portugal's African colonies, some of which he later used in pressing Portuguese claims for control over territories against the machinations of rival European powers. Even before the September 1836 Revolution thrust him into a position of greater responsibility, Sá da Bandeira had concluded that Portugal's future lay necessarily as a colonial power. In 1835, he drafted a plan to develop the remaining *provincias ultramarinas*. The most salient of his proposals was to make governors responsible for the economic improvement of the territories under their stewardship. Not merely military officials or enforcers of the law, he hoped to transform them into "promoters of agriculture, mining, and settlement." In each province, he imagined, a botanic garden would be founded whose purpose would be to acclimatize plants from other parts of the world to the soil, selecting the most "useful." To the end of creating a colony of European settlement, the government should subsidize the transport of Azorean and Portuguese families, providing them with lands either unclaimed, uncultivated, or those which had fallen into disuse. Finally, he proposed eliminating the distinction, for customs purposes, between colonial and peninsular commodities and manufactures to further ease and encourage their circulation throughout the empire.[111] In all of these proposals, there is more than a faint whiff of the enlightened reform proposals for the

---

[109] Ibid. 1832, p. 125. [110] Ibid. 1831, p. 84.
[111] AHM, DIV/3/18/07/13/04, [Sá da Bandeira], "Projecto da Lei para Promover a Prosperidade das Provincias Ultramarinas," 1835.

development of northern Brazil in the late eighteenth century, though suitably updated and adjusted for a new set of circumstances.

One may detect a certain naïve idealism in Sá da Bandeira's proposals, but it must be observed that these schemes were leavened with the insights he diligently culled from less sanguine "experts." The descriptions which filtered back and flitted across Sá da Bandeira's desk were not encouraging. In confidential correspondence, Lopes de Lima ridiculed the grandiose schemes percolating and the heated debates raging over the niceties of policy in Lisbon, dismissing them as mere *"folhas de papel* which are good for nothing given the present state of our colonies," lacking the basic preconditions for development. What was needed, he informed Sá da Bandeira, was basic yet difficult to obtain: "money, warships, prudent and honorable officials, disciplined soldiers (and not political dissidents or vile convicts), a strong government (without exotic institutions), and laws that can be enforced."[112] A Luanda-based informant warned in 1839 that if contraband trade were not allowed to continue after the formal abolition of the slave trade "it would be impossible to keep this province connected to Portugal."[113] Another Angolan correspondent in the same year warned that if the law abolishing the slave trade were actually enforced the Portuguese merchants would disembark en masse for Rio de Janeiro because there would be no reason to remain once deprived of the "great profits" from the slave trade. No one would choose to remain in a land where "one pays ten *reais* for a loaf of bread worth a penny or where a fever can kill one in less than two hours."[114] The place of the slave trade's abolition in the calculations of Portuguese statesmen is discussed more fully in Part III of this chapter, but it should be noted here how colonial development strategy was energized by this impending event as well as hampered equally by both the persistence of the slave trade and its projected obsolescence.

Perhaps the immediate response, which directly threatened no rival power or entrenched economic interest, and thus was uncontroversial, was the establishment of colonies of white settlement in Angola. Sá da Bandeira was fixated on this project. In a letter to Dona Maria in 1836, he urged Portugal to "promote the colonization of Africa by Europeans, whose industry and capital will, in a few short years, enable us to obtain the advantages we enjoyed in earlier times."[115] This plan,

[112] AHU, SEMU DGU (Sá da Bandeira), cx. 2924 2G, "Apontamentos de J. J. Lopes de Lima," 1836.
[113] Ibid., cx. 825, P. A. da Cunha [in Luanda] to Sá da Bandeira, June 12, 1839.
[114] Ibid., cx. 2929, Paulo Centurim [in Luanda] to Sá da Bandeira, January 9, 1839.
[115] Sá da Bandeira *et al.* to Dona Maria II, December 10, 1836, in *Boletim e Annaes do Conselho Ultramarino*, no. 3 (April 1854), p. 23.

however, was judged by his correspondents with local knowledge to be somewhat far-fetched. Even the generously optimistic pointed out that the indispensable precondition for such a venture would be the active involvement of the government to identify "diligent people," not more than thirty years old, ideally married, from either the Azores or rural Portugal, and to send them in a well-appointed ship at the public's expense.[116] The less charitable, including an anonymous Angola-based writer, argued that inducements and subsidies would achieve little: "Europeans who spend more than two or three years in Angola are infected by inertia and apathy ... and the majority of them are inclined toward the [slave] traffic which is today prohibited and which, according to the letter of the law, should have stopped."[117]

These warnings notwithstanding, increased European emigration and settlement was presented as a key feature in all colonial development proposals in this period.[118] It was a common goal of various administrations between 1836 and 1851. It was considered "lamentable that so many Portuguese had immigrated elsewhere, for if they had come to this colony it would have become rich and flourishing within a few years."[119] Yet there was widespread opposition to turning Angola and Mozambique into mere dumping grounds for convicts. The failure of a settlement of free whites in Angola in 1836, however, prompted a reconsideration of this viewpoint and, in 1839, a royal edict granted free passage to Africa for the wives and children of Portuguese *degredados*.[120] Furthermore, various inducements were offered to encourage Portuguese resident in Brazil to relocate to Angola, but only approximately one hundred had been persuaded to cross the Atlantic by 1839. Before 1840, then, Portuguese presence in the Southern Angola was confined to a "handful of petty traders."[121] What support remained for such a settler scheme coalesced around Moçâmedes, advertised as possessing all of the requisite advantages, including "a good port, the most healthful climate [on the Angolan coast], a rich and well-populated

---

[116] AHU, SEMU DGU (Sá da Bandeira), cx. 825, P. A. da Cunha to Sá da Bandeira, June 4, 1839.

[117] Written by an anonymous correspondent, whose 1840 letter is found in AHU, Angola, cx. 590.

[118] As it was, of course, elsewhere, most notably in Algeria. French preoccupation with population growth, urban overcrowding, and revolution (the "social question" in general) led those across the political spectrum to favor Algeria as a colony of settlement. As Sessions 2011 noted, "Much of Algeria's significance in contemporary eyes lay in the fact that it offered an alternative to the slave colonies of the Old Regime," pp. 191, 201–2.

[119] AHU, Angola, cx. 588, Conselho Junta to Secretario de Estado dos Negocios da Marinha e Ultramar, January 5, 1839.

[120] Bender 1978, p. 64.   [121] Clarence-Smith 1979, p. 14.

sertão, an abundance of fish, and soil magnificently suited for agriculture."[122] Its other virtue was its strategic location for the ivory trade with the interior, part of a broader effort to extend fiscal control southward along the coast.[123] By the mid 1840s, a colony had been established there. It attracted the active interest of the Portuguese intelligentsia, including the ubiquitous Luz Soriano, who served as Angola's *Chefe da Repartição* from 1842 to 1851.[124] The colony received a boost when approximately four hundred refugees from the *Praieira* revolution in Pernambuco (Brazil) joined that fledgling settlement in 1848–49, bringing their sugar *engenho* machinery with them.[125] Yet the enthusiasm for migration to Moçâmedes was never great. Even the forlorn Pernambucans required enticements to settle in Angola. The Portuguese government provided "every possible means of assistance," including subsidized transportation, tools, and other materials considered necessary for the establishment of an agricultural colony.[126]

Sá da Bandeira was not alone in his ambition to substitute a tropical empire in Africa for the one lost in Brazil. There had been murmurings of this sort as early as 1814, when a former governor of Angola (and later prominent diplomat), Saldanha da Gama, urged the cultivation of rice in Bissau and Cacheu to replace that previously received from Maranhão and Bahia, in addition to advocating Angola's future as a cotton emporium.[127] There were also several boisterous, though not especially influential, deputies in the newly opened Chamber of Deputies whose rants carried similar sentiments.[128] The fantasy of an

---

122 Guimarães Junior 1842, p. 27. Other writers concurred with this assessment, calling Moçâmedes a potential "New Luanda," but arguing that any such scheme would require significant government support, including exemption from taxation until the colony was better established. See SGL, Reservados 1, Pasta D, no. 14, [Anon.], "Memórias sobre o Estado Actual d'Africa Occidental, seu Commercio com Portugal e Medidas que Conviria Adoptar-se em 1841," fo. 7.
123 Clarence-Smith 1979, pp. 14, 62.
124 Luz Soriano 1891, p. 397.
125 Naro 2007, pp. 138–39; Alexandre, "Viragem," 82–83; though few of these transplanted Pernambucans were up for the task of settling a colony: Luz Soriano, who observed them, called most of them "useless for this sort of enterprise." See Luz Soriano 1891, p. 415.
126 Visconde de Castro, "Instrucções para o Capitão de Fragata António Sergio de Sousa, nomeado Governador do Estabelecimento da Mossamedes e da Colonia Agricola que do Brazil para ali se acha destinada," April 26, 1849, quoted in Almeida Santos 1978.
127 Porto Santo 1839, pp. 7, 19.
128 In a speech delivered on April 18, 1835, for example, the deputy, L. J. Moniz, argued that "the islands of Cape Verde are an untapped treasure for the nation and it is both necessary and useful that its potential be investigated. In Cape Verde, Portugal will find something of what it lost in Brazil." See the *DCSDNP*, p. 880.

agricultural colony, populated by Portuguese emigrants, an explicit antidote to an economy entirely reliant on the slave trade or mineral extraction, was not easily vanquished. Successive governments thus worked in conjunction with Lisbon's merchant community and related groups with a present or potential stake in the colonies, including naval officers. This effort spawned several collaborations and new initiatives. The Secretary of State for the *Fazenda* sought out advice from Lisbon's merchants in 1837, enquiring into the manufactured products sold in the "the interior of Africa," as well as their provenance, in the hope that non-Portuguese, and especially Brazilian, goods might be substituted with Portuguese ones.[129] There were also attempts to amass greater information about local circumstances through increased communication with colonial administrators, correspondence which exaggerated the likelihood of converting Angola into "another Brazil," replete with "colonial products," in a place "where industry and civilization are unknown."[130]

Nevertheless, in spite of increased attention, it remains an inescapable fact that only a single issue of the much-heralded *Memorial*, the mouthpiece of the government's new colonial initiative, was published and there was no effort to revive it. The proliferation of *memórias*, and the keen interest of high-placed ministers, did not arouse widespread interest, at least not initially. Africa made a scant contribution to Portugal in terms of direct trade, accounting for less than 1 percent of the total until the 1840s and a mere 3 percent in the 1850s.[131] Goa and the other scattered remnants of Portuguese India contributed little more, causing a British official to deprecate them in the mid 1830s as "absolutely valueless, except as shattered and fading memorials of past glory."[132] The decrepitude into which Portugal's empire had fallen was not the sole factor dampening enthusiasm for the government's new initiative. Not all sectors of Portuguese elite opinion were persuaded that the formation of an African empire was advisable or necessary. They did not concur that the severance of the bond between Portugal and Brazil had proven economically deleterious. Porto's merchants, in particular, flaunted the commercial ties with Brazil which had survived

---

[129] Secretario de Estado dos Negocios de Fazenda to the Associação Mercantil de Lisboa, June 16, 1837, quoted in J. Capela 1975, p. 15.
[130] AHU, Angola, cx. 587, "Relatório offerecido ao Imo. e Exo. Visconde de Sá da Bandeira ... por António Manoel de Noronha, nomeado Governador Geral da Provincia d'Angola," August 6, 1838.
[131] Clarence-Smith 1985, pp. 24–25.
[132] Sir Robert Grant, Governor of Bombay, in January 1837, quoted in W. H. C. Smith 1970, p. 135.

independence, boasting that they benefited handsomely from that trade. In 1839, Porto's merchants declared that "Brazil remains the chief target of our small, weak industry and it is from this commerce that we derive our greatest advantage ... at first glance this commerce appears ruinous for Portugal. But it is not."[133] In 1851, the value of trade with Brazil represented 15 percent of all Portuguese commerce whereas the value of its commerce with all territories of *Ultramar* accounted for less than 5 percent.[134] Clearly, merchant networks and circuits of trade, capital, and credit survived, and even thrived during, the formal disaggregation of the Luso-Brazilian empire. The creation of a new African empire, therefore, requiring massive outlays, new levies, and government oversight, was a prospect anathema to many sectors of elite and mercantile opinion.

Furthermore, some commentators, in the tradition of Mouzinho da Silveira, maintained that a national economic growth strategy focused on the colonies would merely prolong, and even exacerbate, Portugal's misery. The solution to Portugal's problems lay in the development of its domestic market. As one commentator contended in the early 1840s, "it is a serious economic error to claim that the whole future of our country depends on the colonies ... It does not. It depends on the development of our domestic production."[135] Some observers continued to blame the colonization of Brazil for Portugal's present economic woes: "because Brazil had provided us with great profits in exchange for little work, we abandoned our agriculture ... it was never considered by anyone that Brazil might one day cease to be a colony ... this chaos has arrived and we are without gold, and, what is worse, without agriculture or industry."[136] The Portuguese government experimented with various measures to solve this problem, including installing a tariff protection regime in 1837.[137] Public works, too, were seen as a means to improve communication and commerce. In 1844, an extensive road-building program was announced, with port facility improvements and the Lusitanian stretch of the Lisbon–Madrid railroad to follow. Such large-scale projects went hand in hand with new taxation and revenue-generation schemes initiated under Costa Cabral's government in the 1840s. But the outbreak of further civil unrest in 1846–47 put these

[133] Statement published by the Associação Comercial do Porto, September 27, 1839, reproduced in J. Capela 1975, p. 18.
[134] Pedreira, "Sobre os Escombros," in Bethencourt and Chaudhuri 1998, p. 243.
[135] Lobo de Ávila, quoted in J. P. Marques 2006, p. 207.
[136] *O Movimento: Periódico Semanal*, no. 11 (January 10, 1836), pp. 84–85.
[137] Lains 2006, p. 249.

projects on hold.[138] The answer to Portugal's woes for these skeptics, then, was not a new imperial scheme. It would entail enormous expense and levels of expenditure far beyond Portugal's limited means for such things as a revived navy. As one pamphleteer warned in 1845, "We must repay our debts and order our finances before we can pursue such projects. Now is not the time to order the construction of steam ships, or *engenhos* for the cutting of wood, among other projects which would waste the money we need for things of more urgent necessity."[139] Such ideas had been expressed by Mouzinho, as well as Neves, in the late 1820s and early 1830s. The relative paucity of legislation concerning Portugal's ultramarine possessions during the reign of Dom Miguel, and Dom Pedro's post-Civil War reform program, may be attributed to this continued skepticism toward the utility of empire. Yet only in the 1840s did such arguments feature prominently in public debate.

Civil society and colonialism: the case of the *Associação Marítima e Colonial*

In spite of Sá da Bandeira's *Memorial*'s short-term failure, and the divided state of public opinion, the notion of an organization and a publication devoted to ultramarine affairs was judged a worthy one. Only the execution had been found wanting. Government backing proved influential in the founding of the *Associação Marítima e Colonial* (hereafter, the Association). The Association was created by two November 1839 royal decrees. The Association was one manifestation of the broader efflorescence of civic culture that blossomed in the 1830s and 1840s. Of the associations founded in that period, the most influential was Lisbon's *Associação Mercantil*, which offered courses on mercantile law from 1835 and political economy from 1837.[140] Undoubtedly, the formation of an institution devoted to ultramarine affairs reflected broader European trends, including Britain's Royal Geographical Society, founded in 1831, and France's *Institut d'Afrique*, founded in 1839, which also published *Annales* on African affairs, ranging from geography to commerce.[141] Based in Lisbon, the Association was endowed with the following responsibility and mission:

---

[138] Mata 2002, p. 34; França 1974, vol. II, p. 349; Cardoso and Lains 2010, p. 261.
[139] [Anon.], *Reflexões ... Estado Financeiro* 1845, p. 12.
[140] Sá, 1964, p. 62.
[141] See Stern 2004, p. 134; and L. C. Jennings 2000. On the British periodicals and pamphlets related to African affairs in the late 1830s and 1840s, see Curtin 1964, pp. 340–41.

to promote the improvement, identify the causes which have influenced, or could influence, the decline of the merchant marine as well as the navy; to suggest methods for its restoration; and to make available to the public all relevant knowledge and all pertinent considerations; in short, everything that seems useful for this important end, while at the same time making ever more intimate the commercial relations between the mother country (*Mai-Patria*) and our ultramarine possessions.[142]

There was a continuity of purpose and method with earlier Portuguese efforts to raise awareness of colonial possessions and to generate support for the government's involvement in (and expenditure on) them. Like the short-lived *Memorial*, the *Annaes Maritimos e Coloniaes*, which the Association was mandated to publish, would have two parts: an "official" part, devoted to the reproduction of government decrees, state reports, and other legislation related to the colonies, and an "unofficial" (*não official*) section, which would contain summaries of the proceedings of the Association as well as reproductions of the reports that were read before it or submitted for the perusal and edification of its members. Colonial matters per se were not the only concern of the Association; indeed, there were three sections (akin to "standing committees") of the Association. The first was devoted to the navy, the second to colonies, and the third to the merchant marine. There was, of course, significant overlap among these three sections.[143]

The *Annaes*, the first number of which was published in November 1840 by the *Imprensa Nacional*, contain the acts of the sessions of the Association, so it is possible to follow the debates and trace the projects undertaken by studying its successive issues, published without interruption until 1846. Membership was open to those who displayed "a recognized zeal for promoting the public good and who combine that with a specialized knowledge of the matters that concern the Association." Judging from the *Annaes*, the principal task undertaken was to ascertain precisely what Portugal possessed overseas, to amass quantitative data, and to collect qualitative descriptions concerning the flora, fauna, demography, and topography of those possessions.[144] The scarcity of available information is suggested by the Association's strenuous efforts to determine the geographical boundaries of Portuguese territory in Africa, including information concerning what

[142] *AMC*, vol. I, no. 1 (November 1840), pp. 9–10.
[143] On the structure of the Association, see Rego 1969, pp. 22–25.
[144] After a great deal of searching in various Lisbon collections in spring 2008, I could not locate the archives of the Association. What appear to be fragments of the Association's records survive in several Lisbon archives, including that of the Sociedade de Geografia.

was contained within those limits. As late as 1834, there was no single depository for material related to the overseas colonies, and pertinent material was scattered. James Alexander, commissioned by London's Royal Geographical Society to obtain permission for a British scientific expedition to Portuguese-claimed Africa in 1834, wasted time in the futile search for "information on Africa." He reported that he searched diligently for "manuscripts," but eventually gave up: "it was difficult to get even a sight of any of them, as from the bad arrangement of the libraries, it is almost impossible for a person to lay his hands on what he wants." Instead he spent hours in fruitful, informative conversation with ex-colonial officials then residing in Lisbon.[145]

For Portuguese politicians and political writers of the late 1830s and early 1840s, of course, interest in the remaining colonies was neither purely academic nor dispassionate. Contemporaries were conscious of the geo-political perils posed by ignorance and inaction. Rival, as well as allied, Powers coveted Portugal's ultramarine possessions, aware of the postwar government's fragility and eager to exploit the undefined boundaries, paltry military presence, and dubious claim to possession. Such fears were long-standing and may have prompted an unofficial policy of secrecy regarding Portuguese Africa. In 1826, for example, British ambassador A'Court apologized to Sir Charles Stuart for failing to send the books that the disgraced envoy had left behind in Lisbon: "I shall be unable to do anything about the journal of 'A Journey from Mozambique to Angola', which is preserved in the archives of the Admiralty – the Portuguese are proverbially jealous in such matters."[146]

But that "jealousy" dissipated somewhat, however briefly, by 1834 when Alexander arrived in Lisbon to solicit permission for his mission. He mixed easily with ministers and past governors, easily obtaining the permission he sought. He praised former officials of Cape Verde and Mozambique as "civil and communicative"; he found Sá da Bandeira ready to "fearlessly expose the incredible abuses which prevailed in Portugal's colonies," while Freire, Minister for Foreign Affairs and War, furnished him with "introductions and recommendations to the Portuguese governors of the colonies, with the present of a map of the Portuguese discoveries in Africa." Furthermore, Dom Pedro "condescended to confer [on Alexander] the rank of Lt-Colonel to facilitate [his] movements in Africa"![147]

---

[145] Alexander 1834, p. 211.
[146] Lill.L., Stuart MSS, A'Court to Stuart, November 26, 1826.
[147] Alexander 1834, pp. 197–99, 214, 246–47.

This brief moment of international scientific cooperation proved ephemeral. Foreign interest in Portuguese Africa again came to be construed as acquisitive and threatening. British insistence on the abolition of the Portuguese slave trade through naval enforcement soured whatever cooperative spirit remained. Portugal, unable to respond militarily to such threats (direct and indirect), resorted to knowledge production to advance its claims.[148] Fear of hostile military action against Portuguese-claimed territories in Africa was pervasive across the political spectrum. From his Paris exile, Visconde de Santarém, wrote an erudite treatise to bolster Portuguese claims to several contested border regions and coastlines in Africa. He sought to prove Portugal's long-standing, continuous, and active presence in such seemingly neglected places.[149] Portugal's apprehension concerning the designs of other European nations was neither misplaced nor paranoid. The actions of British and French merchants and missionaries, backed by their nations' navies, would openly dispute Portuguese sovereignty in the Casamance region of Senegambia, Delagoa Bay in Mozambique, and the Angolan-Congolese coast north of Luanda between 1820 and 1860.[150]

It was the British threat that posed the greatest danger. As early as 1823, some British observers called for Portugal's claims in Africa to be challenged openly. One naval officer with experience in East Africa observed:

In no part southward or northward of the colony of the Rios de Sena have the Portuguese any dominion whatsoever, beyond the muzzles of their guns. In most parts, they are even excluded by the natives ... on what foundation, then, is their claim to dominion built? Merely that they have established themselves on a few points of the coast, have marked the whole continent for their own, and have scarcely been molested, and never had their title questioned by any European nation.[151]

---

[148] As Benton argued, concerning European empires more generally, "sovereignty was not a given ... but would depend on recurring proofs, including mapping, description, the founding of political communities, ceremonies recognizing new vassals, and administrative acts designed to support claims to discovery and possession," Benton 2010, p. 23.

[149] Santarém 1841.

[150] Wheeler 1998, pp. 17–18.

[151] TNA, FO 97/303, Owen to Croker, October 11, 1823, unfol.; Captain Fitzwilliam Owen commanded the "HMS Leven," engaged in anti-slave trade operations off the coast of Mozambique in the early 1820s. An enigmatic if fiery figure, he was originally commissioned by the Admiralty to conduct a grand cartographic survey of the East and West African coastlines, but he preferred clamping down on the slave trade, pursuing this aim with zeal at Mombasa for three years before moving on to sit on the short-lived Mixed Commission established on Fernando Po'. See Rees 2011, pp. 128–30.

Throughout the 1830s, there were attempts by the East India Company, as well as the British Foreign Office, to acquire Goa and Macau. Furthermore, at the height of the dispute over the suppression of the slave trade in 1839, discussed in the next section of this chapter, Palmerston threatened repeatedly to seize Goa as a penalty for Portugal's failure to abide by his government's slave trade policy.[152] Other pretexts for interference and annexation were invented as well. In March 1839, Sá da Bandeira was informed by the British ambassador de Walden that Goa was being used with impunity as a staging area to launch raids into unspecified British-controlled areas of India. De Walden warned that "if such things should happen again, the British authorities in India will be compelled in self-defense to take possession of the settlement at Goa." But he hastened to add that the British government would happily come to an "arrangement to transfer to the British Crown the small possessions which Portugal now possesses on the Coast of India." Britain's offer, however, was more likely to offend than tantalize: "Great Britain will take upon herself to satisfy the pecuniary claims of British subjects upon the Government of Portugal ... and further to relinquish all pecuniary claims which the British government may have upon Portugal for supplies to British troops under the convention of 19 January 1827."[153] Sá da Bandeira declined the "offer," arguing that such a proposal "could never serve as the basis for any transaction" between Portugal and Britain, for Goa (and Diu) were "monuments of national glory, of a degree of perseverance never exceeded by any prince."[154] Two months later, an undeterred de Walden wrote to the recently installed Minister of Foreign Affairs, Ribeira de Sabrosa, reiterating his earlier offer, though sweetening it somewhat by claiming that the "pecuniary equivalent" of Goa would be £500,000. He further insinuated that the Portuguese should consider "the unproductive state of Goa as a source of revenue and the absence of any reasonable prospective hope of amendment in regard to commerce or other elements of prosperity."[155] This proposal, too, was rejected by the Portuguese government, which recapitulated Sá da Bandeira's rationale. Goa was not the sole object of British acquisitive desire. Macau, too, was the target of similar machinations in 1802, 1808, and 1839, dates corresponding to the intensification of the opium trade.[156]

---

[152] Webster 1951, vol. II, pp. 492–93.
[153] AHM, DIV/3/18/07/13/08, Howard de Walden to Sá da Bandeira, March 12, 1839.
[154] Ibid., Sá da Bandeira to de Walden, March 30, 1839.
[155] Ibid., de Walden to Ribeira de Sabrosa, May 21, 1839.
[156] José Vicente Serrão, "Macau," in Alexandre and Dias 1998, p. 729.

These geopolitical factors and incidents formed the backdrop against which the Association was founded and operated. One of the Association's secretaries, António Maria Couceiro, acknowledged these sobering realities in February 1840 when he stated that

among the most urgent tasks that this Association can undertake is to collect all of the data necessary to determine the extent of our dominions, to ascertain the places over which we have the right to rule, whether by virtue of discovery of it or through rights conferred by conquest, and, of these, which places are actually under our control and which ones have been abandoned but not yet ceded to foreign nations.[157]

The first task of the Association, the secretary posited, was to "improve our knowledge of the ultramarine dominions ... it is the absence of such knowledge or the existence of imprecise or erroneous information about the colonies, that prevents them from serving the public good." He argued that one of the ways that the Association could best fulfill the duties outlined in its statutes was through an extensive program of publication.[158] These initiatives, so banal and obvious, may at first also seem belated. It is essential to recall, however, as Sá da Bandeira ruefully noted, that Brazil had occupied the attention of reformers from 1750 until 1825, to the almost complete exclusion of its African and Asian dominions.[159] Moreover, most ultramarine legislation had remained on the books even after Brazil's independence. Portuguese Africa had been administered and treated as if Brazil remained part of the empire, one political writer noted, and as a result "all navigation and commerce is conducted by Brazilians for Brazil," by which he referred to the over-whelming centrality of the slave trade.[160] As a result, astonishingly little was known. What was known, moreover, was terribly out of date, an inadequate basis for policy formulation. Therefore, the fifty-five questions which the Association's secretaries compiled and submitted to the Minister for Colonial Affairs appear almost uninformed, elementary requests for rudimentary data. Among the questions posed by the Association were:

[157] "Proposta para se Conhecer a Estenção e Limites dos Estabelecimentos Ultramarinos" (February 10, 1840), published in a two-page broadsheet held in the library of the Biblioteca Central da Marinha (Lisbon).

[158] AMC, vol. I, no. 1, p. 553.

[159] Sá da Bandeira would repeat this argument well into mid century, perhaps accounting for its persistence in the historiography: "The Portuguese government could only pay slight attention to its African possessions after 1817, because diverse causes necessitated that it devote its attention to other places." See Sá da Bandeira 1855, p. 26.

[160] SGL, Reservados 1, Pasta D, no. 14, [Anon.], "Memórias sobre o Estado Actual d'Africa Occidental, seu Commercio com Portugal e Medidas que Conviria Adoptar-se em 1841," fo. 1.

(question 2) what are the territories overseas where the authority of the Crown is enforced?; (question 14) how is each province administered, and what are the names, salaries, and responsibilities of its employees?; (question 29) what mines have been discovered and [how many] mines are presumed to exist in each province, what metals are extracted there, and are there further possibilities for the development of this branch of public wealth?; (question 35) what institutions of public instruction exist, how many schools are there and where are they located, what are the salaries and responsibilities of the teachers, and what improvements can be made to education?; (question 51) Does the current fiscal system deter and complicate the conduct of commerce, is it possible to improve the manner in which commerce is pursued, and what would these modifications be?[161]

These questions echoed those posed by Sá da Bandeira during the Terceira Regency and sought information similar to that published in the *Folhinha* of 1830–32. Their more distant antecedent was the statistical turn that became fashionable in Luso-Brazilian administration in the early nineteenth century and the Cortes's quest for useful knowledge about ultramarine territories that could serve as the basis for policy. The 1830s and early 1840s were marked by renewed efforts to compile statistics concerning the colonies, not only in Portugal but in other European empires too. The British Colonial Office's compilation of statistics, a historian recently argued, reflected a belief that "statistical information, centrally held, could be used to govern the empire effectively, seen particularly in the implementation of uniform policies on Crown land and the centralization of emigration administration."[162] Similar ideas attracted adherents in Portugal. One of Sá da Bandeira's correspondents, Lopes de Lima, for example, published a six-volume set of essays on Portugal's overseas possessions in 1841. He believed that his enterprise was distinct from traditional historico-philosophical essays produced by earlier generations of administrators and travelers: "I am not writing a historical tome; I am not the editor of a newspaper; [rather,] I am the author of a statistical essay, which does not contain allusions to persons or events, but only hard facts."[163] The production of quantitative and qualitative data, then, became an object of political

---

[161] "Preguntas que para dezenvolvimento das propostas dos Senhores António Maria Couceiro e Joaquim José Gonçalves dirige a Associação Maritima às autoridades do Ultramar" (May 6, 1840), in Biblioteca Central da Marinha, op. cit. document.

[162] Laidlaw 2005, p. 194.

[163] The title of Lopes de Lima's work is *Ensaios sobre a Statistica das Possessões Portuguezas na África Occidental e Oriental* (Lisbon, 1841); a second edition, expanding the analysis to "Ásia Occidental, China, e Oceania," was published in 1846; Hay, MSS 93.5, Box 4, Folder 3, J. J. Lopes de Lima to [General] Augusto Xavier Palmeirim, August 16, 1844.

writers and one of the bases upon which the new colonial policy could be founded.

While the quest for useful knowledge inspired various pursuits, many members of the Association, along with others interested in colonial affairs, believed that colonialism could not be considered solely from the economic point of view. The vice-president of the Association, José Tavares de Macedo, argued that

the question of colonies is much more complicated than it appears in the writings of economists ... for us, the Portuguese, the colonial question cannot solely be understood in economic terms ... our overseas colonies are a bequest of our forefathers, a link to the glorious deeds which have ennobled our history ... the economic aspect of the matter, which in other cases should be the decisive factor in determining our course of action, is of only secondary importance, subordinate to other considerations of a more elevated nature.[164]

Some believed that missionary activity, disbanded in Portugal with the extinction of the religious orders in 1834 and further disrupted as a result of Portugal's tempestuous relations with Rome (1834–41), was preferable to commercial penetration of the African interior. Gazing at Britain's colonies, Couceiro urged in 1840 that "the commerce of England's colonies has increased in tandem with the growth of its missionary activity."[165] Many commentators on colonial affairs were obsessed with the "spread of European civilization," the task of "bringing Africa closer to Europe." As one member of the Association put the matter, "to connect the civilized world to the great portion of the human species that remains barbarous and brutalized."[166] Here Portuguese colonialist ideology shared the broader "progressivist universalism" of European justifications for the abrogation of the sovereignty of indigenous states and increasingly interventionist policies.[167]

By 1841, the Association hosted more sophisticated and better-informed debates concerning the preferred methods for colonization. In an October 1841 session, one of the Association's members, Feliciano António Marquês Pereira, posed a series of questions, the answers to

---

[164] *AMC*, vol. II, no. 2, José Tavares de Macedo, "Noticia do Estado do Commercio de Portugal com as suas Possessões Ultramarinas" (1842), pp. 70–71.

[165] *AMC*, vol. I, no. 1, António Maria Couceiro, "Breves Considerações sobre a Prégação do Evangelho na África" (July 20, 1840), pp. 30–33.

[166] *AMC*, vol. II, no. 2, Joaquim José Gonçalves de Mattos Corrêa, "Relatório dos Trabalhos da Associação" (December 31, 1842), p. 552.

[167] Pitts 2005, pp. 21, 240–54 passim. However, Portuguese commentators did not share the emphasis, discussed by Pitts, of their French and British counterparts concerning the potential conflict between the survival and deepening of liberty at home while simultaneously building an empire abroad; on the handling of this issue in Spain, see Fradera 2005.

which he believed would underpin effective colonization. Among these questions were:

1. Is it possible at the present moment to go against the established principles of political economy by creating a monopoly company for the colonies, assuming that the advantages of doing so outweigh the disadvantages? ... 5. What is the best method of administering the Portuguese colonies? The current system? The English system? The French system? Or a form which takes the most appropriate aspects of the three systems? ... 7. Should the Portuguese colonies continue to be the only colonies in the world that send deputies to the Cortes in the metropole in order to participate in the making of legislation which, for the most part, apply only in Portugal itself and not in its colonies? Or would it be more appropriate to grant legislative councils in the colonies which can draft laws especially for each colony, needing only the approval of the Crown?[168]

The Association searched for replicable models, viewing Portuguese precedent with suspicion. Many aspects of the British colonial experience were held up for emulation, particularly the policies pursued in Britain's Indian Ocean dominions. The British administration of finances, in particular, was presented as "ready for adoption in our colonies."[169] Discussion of the British example necessarily involved the East India Company and the merits (and demerits) of a less-regulated trade policy. The dilemma of privileged trading companies versus less regulated trade had a long pedigree, dating back to the decision to dismantle the Pombaline companies during the *Viradeira* of the late 1770s to early 1780s, as discussed in Chapter 1. The question was revived after 1820 for the same three principal reasons it had occupied the attention of eighteenth-century reformers: first, the relatively undeveloped state of the overseas territories; second, Portugal's incapacity to compete with merchants from other nations under a less regulated trade regime; and, third, the difficulty Portugal faced both in enforcing the terms of colonial monopoly by keeping smugglers out and, when that failed, forcing foreign merchants to adhere to the established terms of trade, compelling payment of customs duties on goods unloaded or embarked. The debate was revived around 1830 by Neves, who was convinced

---

[168] *AMC*, vol. I, no. 11 (supplement), Feliciano António Marques Pereira, "Questões Coloniais," p. 531.

[169] *AMC*, I, no. 2, "Observações acerca do actual systema do Governo dos Estados da Índia ... por José Maximo de Castro Neto Leite e Vasconcellos" (October 20, 1838), p. 87. There was an earlier manuscript version of this article by the same author, one which delved into much greater detail concerning the utility and applicability of British policies in Portuguese territories. See AHU, SEMU DGU (Sá da Bandeira), cx. 2925 2G, "Brevissimo Bosquejo do Systhema por que os Ingleses Governão as suas Colonias no Ramo Administrativo, no Judicial, e no Fiscal," May 14, 1838; on the range of possible British models and anti-models in this period, see Bayly 1989.

that Portuguese Africa could become a "second Brazil" if its development were organized and directed by a privileged trading company. He conceded that it was "impossible not to accept" the arguments against companies then ascendant in Europe, but noted that Portugal's "diminished" and "destroyed" commerce with Goa and its African ports meant that unconventional, even unpopular, measures were required.[170] The severe underdevelopment of Portuguese Africa, which relied almost exclusively on the slave trade, prompted other commentators to reach Neves's conclusions and to contend that companies could "introduce civilization and industry while putting into practice forms of commerce more appropriate to the present system of Europe."[171]

Participants in the debates of the 1830s and 1840s over optimal colonial development strategy promoted privileged companies and/or colonial monopoly, sometimes explicitly making favorable allusion to the "principles of the great Marquês de Pombal," and conceiving of them as a means to exclude foreign traders who undermined Portuguese commerce and whose presence augured the eventual annexation of Portugal's ultramarine provinces by rival powers.[172] Desire to wrest control over trade with Africa, whether by substituting foreign with Portuguese merchants or else by ensuring collection of customs receipts, sparked renewed debates concerning the utility of privileged companies. One political writer attacked the pervasive discourse of free trade, noting that though other nations "flaunted their beautiful treaties on commerce and political economy, they do not follow the lessons that they teach; we should do as they do, and not as they tell us to do." Otherwise, he warned, Portugal would merely repeat the error it committed in Brazil, particularly after the 1808–10 British Treaties, when the Portuguese became "mere assistants to the English as they enriched themselves and then departed, taking with them immense fortunes and leaving us impoverished." It was only with protectionist legislation, and greater regulation, that a sinister fate could be averted.[173]

---

[170] Neves, "Considerações Políticas e Comerciais," in J. Neves 1989, vol. IV, p. 328.

[171] IHGB, DL 39.6, A. Silva Costa, "Reflexões ácerca dos Apontamentos para o Projecto da Companhia das Ilhas de S. Tomé e Príncipe" (July 1826), fo. 54 v. Though this same writer acknowledged that "the terrible climate, the present state of the European market, which is flooded with products from the East Indies similar to those produced in [São Tomé] ... are obstacles that make one less enthusiastic about such a company," fo. 56.

[172] See for example [Anon.], Males que tem Resultado 1840, pp. 18–24 passim.

[173] [Anon.], Resposta Analytica ao Opúsculo 1835, pp. 7, 10–11; compare these Portuguese debates to those in contemporary Spain, where "the Spanish government and Spanish producers used the protected Antillean market as a reserve for

Many of these arguments were accepted by Sá da Bandeira and his collaborators after 1836. There were two trading companies for Portuguese Africa established between 1836 and 1840. The first, a *Companhia de Agricultura e Indústria de Angola e Benguela*, was set up in Luanda in 1836, but soon failed. Its chief advocate, Domingos de Saldanha Oliveira e Daun, argued that "Britain [could not] have achieved its greatness in Asia, an object of universal admiration, had it not deployed the company that raised it to the peak of prosperity."[174] The second privileged company was for Mozambique in 1840, the revival of an ineffectual predecessor established in the late 1820s and dissolved quietly by Mouzinho da Silveira in 1834. The *Companhia de Agricultura e Indústria de Moçambique* was granted an exemption from certain taxes and duties for four years, including the slashing of customs for national and nationalized goods by half.[175] Besides these two companies, numerous proposals for further companies proliferated in the period 1825–40, including those for São Tomé e Príncipe (1826) and Guinea (1839), the latter of which had its statutes approved by the government.[176]

While the arguments for both trading companies and some measure of monopoly were ascendant, they were far from embraced by all. Even during Dom Miguel's reign, a strong case had been made against privileged companies. As Joaquim Bento da Fonseca contended, "the most powerful means to animate and protect our colonial commerce is, undoubtedly, to permit competition and to award prizes for performance and effort."[177] Subsequent commentators maintained that the presence of foreign traders could be advantageous to Portugal's colonies, so long as they unloaded their goods in ports with customs houses and paid the requisite duties. Contraband trade with both Africans and Europeans, however, was deemed "intolerable and ruinous."[178] A good example of this mixed approach – deregulating trade while privileging Portuguese interests – may be found in 1840s legislation for Macau: the

---

uncompetitive Spanish goods and a solution to Spain's chronic trade imbalance." See Schmidt-Nowara 1999, p. 70.

[174] AHU, Angola, cx. 586, March 21, 1836.

[175] AHU, SEMU DGU (Sá da Bandeira), cx. 2922 2G, "Sinopse dos Decretos de Execução Permanente Expedido pelo Ministerio da Marinha e Ultramar, desde 27 de Fevereiro de 1839, sobre Providencias relativas ás Provincias Ultramarinas," October 10, 1840.

[176] For the proposal for a Guinea company, see AHU, SEMU DGU (Sá da Bandeira), cx. 825, Manuel António Martins to Sá da Bandeira, June 22, 1839.

[177] J. B. da Fonseca 1830, pp. 16–17.

[178] AHU, SEMU DGU (Sá da Bandeira), cx. 2924 2G, Lopes de Lima to Sá da Bandeira, November 29, 1836.

declaration of its status as a free port in 1845 followed, in 1846, by the abolition of the Chinese customs house, the expulsion of Mandarins from the city, and the subjection of Chinese residents to taxes from which they were previously exempt.[179] Other publicists argued that exclusive privilege was "always odious and harmful," pointing to the example of the uptick of British trade in India since the partial revocation of the East India Company's special privileges.[180] In spite of the government's encouragement of such measures, through inducements such as tax relief, companies attracted scarce interest in the metropole. As a Lisbon merchants' group noted, "to establish a company in this capital city today is to believe in an illusion."[181] The Association engaged in these debates over less-regulated trade and monopoly as well, though their statements were equally inconclusive. Some members of the Association vociferously opposed efforts to exclude foreign commerce and invoked precedent to bolster their case: "the monopoly of commerce in the Indies that the Portuguese assumed for itself [in the Indian Ocean] was a false move. The government should never again become a merchant."[182] The rather laconic proceedings of the *Annaes*, unfortunately, do not contain greater detail which would reveal the substance of these debates. But both sides – pro-privileged company boosters and their free trade counterparts – demonstrated their knowledge of, and facility with, broader European ideas about free trade, monopoly, and colonial administration.

The description of the Association's debates suggests a broader point about the aims of its members: they were pulled in sometimes mutually exclusive directions. On the one hand, they belonged to a Crown-sponsored body dedicated to the dispassionate search for knowledge about maritime and colonial affairs. On the other, they were keenly aware that the Association was founded as part of an all-encompassing, urgent project of national regeneration and unification. These two purposes often jostled uneasily, as the latter constrained the former. Yet the Association's members would have dismissed those internal contradictions as impertinent. The economic and political circumstances in which Portugal found itself in the early 1840s were recognized, universally, to be dire. In an executive session of the Association, Mattos Corrêa declared that "our generation finds itself in a position not unlike a shipwreck."[183]

[179] Serrão, "Macau," p. 731.
[180] [Anon.], *Refutação a Resposta Analytica* 1836, p. 13.
[181] Quoted in Marques 2006, p. 223.
[182] *AMC*, vol. II, no. 1, Manuel Louzada d'Araujo d'Azevedo, "Sobre as Principaes Causas Remotas da Decadencia dos Portuguezes na Azia" (n.d.), p. 63.
[183] *AMC*, vol. II, no. 12.

PART III

The persistence of the slave trade, the specter of abolition, and the obstacles to Portuguese colonial schemes in the 1830s and 1840s

In 1844, the annual opening meeting of the Association was graced by Dom Fernando II, to whom the president, António Manuel de Noronha, a past governor of Angola, addressed his speech. "Without a flourishing navy, our African possessions are useless," he noted, "without a navy, we must abandon the idea of Portugal having colonies altogether."[184] A robust navy, however, was essential not only to ensure the safe passage of merchant ships threatened by privateers and to defend the African territories from foreign encroachment. It was also coded language alluding to Britain's zealous enforcement of supposedly bilateral anti-slave trade measures. In the first quarter of the nineteenth century, the demise of the slave trade was considered both imminent and unavoidable. Efforts to abolish the slave trade in the Portuguese Atlantic World had a long history, as discussed in Chapters 1 and 3. To recapitulate, the 1810 Treaty with Britain had committed Portugal to eventual abolition in exchange for British guarantees of the integrity of its overseas possessions. At the Congress of Vienna, British insistence was repeated, and the suppression of the slave trade north of the equator was agreed upon in a treaty signed in 1815, though a clandestine trade flourished. In 1817, to diminish violations of the agreement, Britain compelled Portugal to sign an additional convention, granting permission for British cruisers to stop, search, and seize Portuguese ships suspected of engaging in the slave trade north of the equator.[185] If slaves were found on board, the detained ships would be brought to one of two mixed commissions (in Sierra Leone and Brazil, respectively) with judges and arbiters from both nations who would decide whether to condemn or acquit. These 1815 and 1817 agreements did nothing to boost metropolitan Portugal's trade with its African colonies, which plummeted precipitously.[186]

---

[184] *AMC*, vol. III, no. 12, António Manuel de Noronha, "Discurso Pronunciado ...," January 23, 1844, pp. 580–83 passim.

[185] Alexandre, "O Processo de Independência do Brasil," in Bethencourt and Chaudhuri 2000, vol. IV; in general, see Bethell 1970a, pp. 9–18. As Bethell emphasized, mixed commissions had no jurisdiction over the owner, masters, or crew of a detained vessel, but solely over the ship itself and the slaves encountered on board; it also should be noted that the 1817 Anglo-Portuguese Treaty committed Britain to paying the £300,000 it owed to Portugal according to the terms of the 1815 Treaty. See Martinez 2008, p. 577.

[186] V. Alexandre, "As Periferias e a Implosão do Império," in Bethencourt and Chaudhuri 1998, vol. IV, p. 53.

The realization that a major transformation was under way provoked a final flurry of Old Regime *memórias* reconsidering the economic foundations of the Luso-Atlantic world in a post-slave trade
era. The authors of these *memórias* compared Britain's dispossession
of Portugal's "first" Asian empire in the seventeenth century and its
efforts to "establish supreme dominion" in Africa in the nineteenth.
If the slave trade's share of the economy were not replaced with something else, the colonies would collapse and foreign interference, perhaps
annexation, would be unavoidable. To this end, one political writer in
1815 called for the formation of a *Commissão Especial* for African affairs,
presided over by the Minister for the Marine and Colonies, entrusted
with the task of "accumulating all of the information possible concerning the English in Sierra Leone, the laws they have established and the
effects that these have produced," in addition to "enlarging and veri-
fying" the store of knowledge concerning Portuguese Africa. The aim
was to amass knowledge about its natural resources, possible industries, other lucrative enterprises, and the most hospitable areas to "settle and increase the white population." This political writer envisaged
a latter-day episode in the centuries-long Columbian Exchange, with
plants cultivated in Brazil, for both export and domestic consumption,
introduced into Africa. He imagined that families of Brazilian slaves,
under the supposedly benign supervision of Luso-Brazilian capitalists, could be brought to Africa, "whether as journeymen or slaves," to
spread knowledge of agriculture.[187]

Such schemes were not widely known or acted upon, but they did percolate at the highest levels of administration. Maciel da Costa accepted
as a *fait accompli* the end of the slave trade both north and south of the
equator. He proposed turning Portuguese Africa into a "true colony and
governed as such." As part of a scheme to reduce Brazil's reliance on
slave-dependent agriculture and to encourage manufactures, he argued
that Portuguese Africa should transition from a slave trade-based economy to an agricultural one. African ports would be closed to foreigners and the new agricultural products of the hinterlands would be
transported directly to Brazil for either processing or consumption.[188]
These fantastical far-fetched proposals were not only concocted by
ministers in palaces, but by "men-on-the-spot" as well. A governor of
Mozambique heaped praise on its fertile soil, which he claimed was

---

[187] Ambrosio Joaquim dos Reis, "Sobre a situação da Monarquia Portuguesa depois
da Paz de Paris de 1814, indicando algumas providências para a melhorar" (1815),
reproduced in J. V. Capela 1993, doc. 7, pp. 109–12 passim.
[188] Maciel da Costa, "Memoria sobre a Necessidade de Abolir a Introdução dos Escravos
Africanos no Brasil" (1820), reproduced in Salgado 1988, p. 51.

perfect for the cultivation of coffee, indigo, cotton, and sugar cane, lamenting that agriculture had been neglected because all Portuguese inhabitants flocked to the slave trade. However, Mozambique's agricultural potential, if realized, would permit it to flourish after abolition. Export agriculture could substitute for lost revenues from the slave trade, "something perhaps that will not happen with any of our West African possessions."[189]

But this was clearly long-term thinking. In the short term, as Silvestre Pinheiro Ferreira, then Minister for Foreign Affairs, noted in 1822, "the countries that would be irreparably ruined by the immediate abolition of the slave trade are all of the dominions of Portugal on the Coast of Africa, and all those in Asia principally involved in trade with Africa."[190] When the Porto Revolution broke out and the schism with Brazil opened up in the early 1820s, no comprehensive plan for the Portuguese empire's post-slave trade future had been devised, let alone put into place. The enormous profits gained, the number of vested interests involved, the weakness of any enforcement mechanism, and the absence of political will conspired against such action. Brazil's independence and British pressure, however, exacerbated old, and created new, more fearsome, problems for Portugal. The slave trade's continued predominance in the South Atlantic economy meant that the link between Brazil and Portuguese Africa would remain indissoluble even after the former's independence.[191] In the early 1820s there was good reason to fear that Angola and Mozambique, too, would break free of Lisbon and become absorbed into the nascent Brazilian empire, forming a sort of Southern Atlantic confederation. Such a territorial reconfiguration would have reflected the direct traffic enjoyed between Rio de Janeiro and Luanda, a trade, based mainly in slaves, which dwarfed, both in volume and value that between Lisbon and Luanda (and Benguela).[192] Moreover, at most 12 percent of Angola's imports came from Portugal before 1820, with the rest deriving from Brazil.[193] The fear that Mozambique and Angola would ally themselves with independent Brazil was palpable and publicly expressed. An Angolan deputy to the Cortes lamented that the Portuguese in Angola "have persuaded themselves that the bonds

[189] ADB, ACB, SIFAA/ 42, 37, "Copia de hua Memoria Abbreviada da Capitania de Mossambique, feita por hum dos Governadores e Capitães Generaes que foi da mesma Capitania" (n.d., but after 1807).
[190] Quoted in J. P. Marques 2006, pp. 78–79.
[191] In general, see J. Rodrigues 2005.
[192] As J. Miller has observed, "by the end of the eighteenth century, Brazilians virtually controlled Angolan slaving." See J. Miller 1988, p. 501.
[193] Pedreira, "Sobre os Escombros," p. 230.

of commerce matter the most."[194] In Mozambique, the situation was similar: "Brazilians, united with some *nacionaes* and a few Portuguese, are working to declare this province united to Brazil, from which they expect assistance, saying that they no longer enjoy any direct relations with Portugal."[195]

Brazil's pledge not to annex any of Portugal's African possessions, enshrined in the 1825 Treaty, offered little comfort. Stuart called Dom Pedro's promise "a most important step in the abolition of the slave trade."[196] As late as February 1827, however, Dom Pedro insisted on nominating Brazilian consuls to Portugal's African ports, well after his abdication of the Lusitanian crown.[197] Furthermore, his advisors routinely hatched schemes to incorporate parts of African territory claimed by Portugal into the Brazilian empire.[198] Certainly, such schemes would have reflected ever-intensifying trade dynamics. In 1824, it was the provincial treasury of Bahia, not the Portuguese government, which funded the fort at Ouidah.[199] After independence, the slave trade between the Portuguese-claimed Guinea Coast and northeastern Brazil intensified, to the extent that Bahia's slave markets were glutted.[200] Portugal, unable to assert itself and impose its own policy, benefited from British interest in this affair. Echoing Canning, Wellington reminded Lord Aberdeen in 1828: "We do not intend to allow the Portuguese monarchy in Europe to be further weakened by the seizure of its remaining colonies by the Emperor of Brazil, or by their being revolutionized."[201] These sentiments notwithstanding, throughout the late 1820s and 1830s, political conspiracies and small-scale revolts in Angola were construed by Portuguese authorities as plots to secede from Portugal and unite with Brazil.[202]

[194] Castro 1822, p. 2.
[195] IHGB, DL88.4, doc. 26, João Manuel da Silva to M. Gonçalves de Miranda, January 19, 1824, fos. 57–58.
[196] TNA, FO 13/4, Stuart to Canning, August 19, 1825.
[197] Brazilian lobbying for permission to send a consul to Luanda continued well into the 1830s. See, for example, the letter of the Brazilian envoy rebuffed by Palmela: AHI 213/4/1, Sergio Teixeira de Macedo to Manuel Alves Branco, October 25, 1835.
[198] TNA, FO 63/320, A'Court to Canning, February 18, 1827.
[199] Brazilian slavers exercised effective sovereignty over the Ouidah enclave until 1844, when it was reoccupied by Portugal. L. F. de Alencastro, "Continental Drift: The Independence of Brazil (1822), Portugal and Africa," in Pétré-Grenouilleau 2004, p. 106; and Law 2004, p. 169.
[200] Conrad 1986, p. 66.
[201] Wellington to Aberdeen, August 17, 1828, in Wellington 1973, vol. IV, p. 623.
[202] J. R. Dias, "A Sociedade Colonial de Angola e o Liberalismo Português (*c.* 1820–1850)," in M. H. Pereira 1982, p. 272; for a recent treatment of the politics of the Brazilian slave trade in this period, see Parron 2011.

In the short term, British policy provided Portugal with room to maneuver, but Albion's intent to abolish the trade meant that pressure was mounting to revamp a colonial economy in territories in which it enjoyed scant influence, exercised little authority, and competed with better-outfitted rivals. Portugal would be forced to sign another slave trade treaty eventually. Its options were unattractive and its debilitated economic condition in the 1820s further foreclosed imaginative solutions. The absence of clear-cut alternative investments and the paucity of revenue streams beyond export taxes levied on slaving vessels made many observers fear that immediate abolition would be imprudent. According to this logic, abolition would imperil the survival of Portugal's remaining colonies instead of promoting their efflorescence.[203] Policy, therefore, was frozen owing to the absence of feasible alternatives. As Botelho wrote in 1826 from Mozambique, "it is necessary sometimes to keep inveterate customs, even after they are made illegal, due to the extreme difficulty of substituting new ones."[204] An 1829 *consulta* of the Overseas Council acknowledged that "Brazil is now separated from us and should be treated like any other foreign nation," but noted that any attempt to cut Brazil off from its source of slaves or bolster revenue by raising duties on Brazilian alcohol entering West Africa would only further harm Portugal's enfeebled colonies.[205] The editor of *O Imparcial* in the late 1820s went so far as to argue that the survival of Portuguese Asia depended on the traffic, which he described as the "only link that we retain with Goa, Damao and Diu."[206] The survival of the remnants of Portugal's dismembered empire thus depended, paradoxically, on Brazilian slavery. Between 1830 and 1832, only eleven Portuguese ships called at Angolan ports whereas ninety Brazilian ships did.[207] Without them, and foreign interlopers, the economy would collapse. The Miguelist pamphleteer Madre de Deos fretted over the impact of the abolition of slavery and argued that it would be prudent to seek a five-year extension from Britain. If Britain enforced the abolition of the slave trade strictly, according to the terms of the existing treaty, the "colonists will have to emigrate, for lack of subsistence, and

---

[203] IHGB, lata 28, pasta 21, Manoel Patricio Corrêa de Castro, "Memoria sobre os males que impedem o engrandecimento do Reino de Angola" (September 1823), fos. 6–8 passim.

[204] BNL, Reservados, cod. 10648, "Correspondência da Secretaria de Moçambique," Sebastião Xavier Botelho to ?, April 5, 1826, fo. 14v.

[205] AHU, CU, cod. 481, *Consulta* of February 18, 1829, fos. 41–42.

[206] *O Imparcial*, no. 5 (January 11, 1827), p. 20. The editor went on to defend the absurd proposition that the slave trade "must not be as odious as some claim ... among the millions of slaves who have been freed in Brazil, not one has decided to return to Africa," p. 21.

[207] Pedreira, "Sobre os Escombros," p. 239.

Portugal might lose its vast possessions."[208] Clearly, the colonies could not be transformed while this dismal situation persisted and a transitional period, during which the old and new systems would overlap and coexist, was necessary. The Anglo-Brazilian Treaty of 1826, by which Brazil pledged to suppress the slave trade by March 1830, coupled with Brazil's 1831 ban on the import of slaves, temporarily put an end to Portuguese debate on abolition.

But the persistence, if not expansion, of slave traffic, in flagrant contravention of the aforementioned treaties and national legislation, together with Portugal's resolve to revamp its African possessions along different economic lines, combined to resurrect the debate after 1834. Portugal's resolution to suppress the slave trade following Brazil's independence emerged less from a crisis of conscience than from economic and geopolitical necessity. Figures such as Soares Franco, Constâncio, Palmela, and Lavradio had called for the abolition of the trade on these grounds in the early 1820s, but legislation was never brought before the Cortes.[209] In 1836, Sá da Bandeira publicly argued for the abolition (and suppression) of the slave trade on the grounds that "without the abolition of that abominable commerce, it is pointless to legislate for [Angola] and useless to promote agriculture there, because capital will continue to be attracted to the slave trade because it is much more lucrative than any other industry."[210] Sá da Bandeira therefore envisioned an imperial future dependent on the extinction, not the exploitation, of the slave trade. The late 1830s and 1840s thus saw attempts to replace the slave trade with "legitimate commerce," hoping that gold, tortoise shells, palm oil, rice, coffee, ivory, and wax would be most profitable. In the mid 1840s, surprising products gave reformers fresh hope. In Portuguese Guinea, for example, peanuts became the principal export, with peanut oil used in cooking oils, soaps, and candles.[211]

Sá da Bandeira also advocated the elimination of slavery itself, though pragmatic considerations prevented his pursuit of this goal. The December 1836 law he championed prohibited only the export of slaves from Portuguese to non-Portuguese territories, not the slave trade altogether. The decree thus contained two major loopholes: first, slaves could still be imported into Portuguese colonies by land; second, Portuguese colonists could bring up to ten slaves with them when they moved, by any means of transport, from one Portuguese territory to another.[212]

---

[208] BPMP, M-FA-60, F. J. da Madre de Deos, "Tentativa Política," April 1829.
[209] Alexander, "Viragem," p. 67.
[210] *Memorial*, no. 1 (1836), p. 13.
[211] Bowman 1987, pp. 87, 93.   [212] Duffy 1967.

Sá da Bandeira was cognizant that abolishing the slave trade between Angola and Brazil was fraught with difficulties. Angola's governor, Manuel Bernardo Vidal, far from cooperating and enforcing the December 1836 law, blocked its publication. He wrote that "the abolition of slavery and the slave trade in this country would signal the ruin of all of its inhabitants, regardless of color, and would mark the beginning of the end of these possessions."[213] He did not intend, he wrote elsewhere, "to create such a frightful [economic] vacuum" and govern over "ruins" and "extreme poverty."[214] Beyond Luanda, particularly in Benguela, slave traders dominated local administration and metropolitan anti-slave trade legislation hardly perturbed the robust connections with the Brazilian slave market, though British cruisers disrupted some of these links and encouraged clandestine methods.[215] Some colonial administrators, including a governor of Cape Verde, abetted the slave trade, furnishing traders with fraudulent passports.[216] In Mozambique, the governor-general, Marquês de Aracaty, suspended enforcement of the 1836 law.[217] *O Paquete do Ultramar* explained the difficulty of immediate abolition: "the sudden end of the slave trade, without first providing the inhabitants with some means of supporting themselves, would cause the annihilation of those colonies."[218] Entrenched interests proved difficult to extirpate and some officials, including Noronha, believed it impossible to displace them without the creation of a privileged company endowed with "great resources to compete with the slave traders and to foment new types of agriculture and commerce, without which the government must, for lack of resources, tolerate the slave trade."[219] In the absence of such a countervailing force, both individual governors and Portuguese administration as a whole remained dependent on slave traders to stave off fiscal and monetary crisis. When an administrator resisted the prevailing order of things, as Noronha did, his failure was preordained.[220]

---

[213] See the letter in AHU, Angola, cx. 587, February 24, 1838, Vidal to Sá da Bandeira.

[214] Quoted in Alexandre, "Portugal e a Abolição do Tráfico de Escravos (1834–51)," in Alexandre 2000, p. 98.

[215] Ferreira 2008, pp. 317–20.

[216] Farida Shaikh, "Judicial Diplomacy: British Officials and the Mixed Commission Courts," in Hamilton and Salmon 2009, p. 52.

[217] Bethell 1970a, p. 102.

[218] *Paquete do Ultramar*, no. 27 (August 5, 1839), p. 107. For further analysis, see Alexandre 2000.

[219] AHU, Angola, cx. 589, António Manoel de Noronha to Barão da Ribeira de Sabrosa, November 15, 1839.

[220] J. Dias, "Angola," in Alexandre and Dias 1998, p. 374. Noronha was forced to resign several months into his governorship for his refusal to capitulate to slave traders.

Contemporary research corroborates the extent of the slave trade in this period and how reliant Portugal's African possessions were on it: between 1835 and 1839, total exports of slaves reached up to thirty-seven thousand per year.[221] Such bloated figures aggravated Britain's abolitionists and the British government sought to force Portugal to pass and enforce more stringent legislation. Particularly noxious was the fact that the absence of an Anglo-Portuguese convention regarding the slave trade south of the equator meant that merchants of all nations, but especially Brazil, could sail under the Portuguese flag with impunity. The multiple, fluid identities, and murky nationalities, of many of the slave traders created layers of legal complexity: Portuguese-born, naturalized Brazilians used the Portuguese flag as they moved between Bahia, Luanda, Rio de Janeiro, and Lisbon.[222] The existence of the trade south of the equator meant that it continued de facto north of the equator as well. At Ouidah, for example, Portuguese ships trading there regularly carried papers authorizing them to trade for slaves south of the equator – at Malembo, Cabinda, or Luanda – and once those ships crossed the equator, something surreptitiously though easily done, they could not be seized.[223] British cruisers were hamstrung, too, by the language of existing treaties permitting the seizure of a ship only if slaves were on board, even if the intention to trade was manifest. The ships deployed by Britain in its anti-slave trade operations further hampered enforcement, as large, slow-moving frigates with easily sighted masts predominated.[224]

Portugal's financial and diplomatic reliance on Britain forced it to the bargaining table. Sá da Bandeira and the British representative, de Walden, entered into protracted negotiations. The stumbling block was Sá da Bandeira's desire for the British guarantee of military support should the abolition of the slave trade trigger separatist uprisings in Mozambique and Angola or should the colonists there seek to align themselves with Brazil for whatever reason in the future.[225] Frustrated with the slow speed of the negotiations, the British Parliament passed what was popularly known as the Palmerston Bill in 1839, authorizing the unilateral seizure and condemnation of Portuguese ships suspected of involvement in the slave trade. The suspected parties would be tried in admiralty courts, not mixed commissions, thus ending any pretense

---

[221] J. P. Marques 2006, p. 160.
[222] Bethell 1970a, pp. 135–41. Needell argued that, from 1831, most of the Rio de Janeiro merchants involved in the slave trade were Portuguese-born residents of Brazil. See Needell 2001, p. 686.
[223] Law 2004, p. 157.
[224] Bethell 1970a, p. 123.   [225] Ibid., pp. 106–8.

of international cooperation. Finally, after standing at the brink of conflict for three years, an 1842 Anglo-Portuguese treaty closed earlier loopholes and expanded the number of mixed commissions.[226] The 1842 Treaty, which abolished the trade de jure, did not undermine the traffic de facto, particularly because Brazil, which received the majority of the slaves taken from Portuguese Africa, refused to enforce the abolition of the trade until 1850. Britain's Aberdeen Bill (1845), which authorized the seizure of Brazilian slave vessels and extended the web of bilateral mixed commissions championed by Britain, curtailed the trade. The Brazilian government finally relented to complete abolition to avoid, as a recent historian concluded, "a fatal commercial blockade, a catastrophic war with the English, and to gain a free hand in the Rio de la Plata."[227]

Before 1850, Portuguese administrators remained uncomfortably dependent on slave traders. As late as 1843–44, two-thirds of Angola's annual revenue derived from traditional slave trade duties imposed at its ports.[228] Sá da Bandeira's dream of revenue derived from customs duties on commodities and the increased taxation of a subservient local population remained remote. Undoubtedly, some action was taken. Portuguese officials, for example, went on the offensive: of the criminal cases prosecuted in Luanda between 1845 and 1848, approximately 20 percent were for slave trade-related offenses,[229] though many judicial actions against slave traders either never went to trial or the judgments against them were annulled on the basis of purported procedural irregularities.[230]

These efforts aside, Portuguese officials found themselves in a bind. They recognized that the effective abolition of the slave trade (and slavery itself) was the precondition for the deployment of capital in new areas, including agriculture. Yet even a rudimentary grasp of the nature of the existing colonial economy bred inaction and discouraged compliance. Moreover, Britain's pressing for abolition aroused suspicion and nationalist indignation, particularly in the wake of the Palmerston Act.

---

[226] Martinez 2008, p. 622.
[227] Needell 2006, pp. 154–55; British frustration with Brazil had reached a fevered pitch by 1850 when Palmerston wrote that "the plain fact is that nothing can be effected with the Brazilian government on this matter except by compulsion. Arguments have long been used in vain ... it is manifest that the slave traders have been able to exert over the Brazilian government, either by corruption or intimidation, an influence which has overridden all sense of right and wrong and all regard for legal and international obligations." See Palmerston to Hudon, October 15, 1850, in *British Documents* 1991, p. 10.
[228] Wheeler and Pélissier 1978, p. 52.
[229] Ferreira 2008, p. 324.   [230] Dias, "Angola," p. 375.

Britain's perceived threat to Portuguese sovereignty made even practically minded abolitionists, like Sá da Bandeira, indignantly defiant. He denounced Britain's rough methods and contended that punishing slave traders was an attack on the symptom, not the cause, of the problem, which was the continued existence of slavery throughout the Americas. Slave traders merely met this voracious demand.[231] The debate over abolition, moreover, occurred against the backdrop of fierce denunciations of the terms of Anglo-Portuguese trade. Commercial treaties with England were pilloried for threatening industry, artisans, naval strength, and customs receipts. As early as 1834, existing treaties with Britain were considered "advantageous for one nation and onerous for the second." Newspapers almost routinely lamented England's role in the loss of Portugal's empire in the East as well as in America, blaming a succession of treaties (1571, 1642, 1654, and 1703), and holding special disdain for that of 1810, described as an "eternal monument to our misery."[232] Some critics even compared the British role in the 1808–10 Treaties, which opened Brazil's ports to foreign shipping, with Britain's coercive advocacy of abolition in the 1830s and early 1840s. "With that legislation, [Britain] took control of our colonies and we became a conquered country, three million slaves that England could dispose of as she liked." According to this view, abolition of the slave trade and the promotion of "legitimate commerce" amounted to little more than a "pretext" to "control the commerce of our African possessions."[233] Debates over abolition thus became intermingled with those over trade agreements with Britain. As an editorial noted in the lead-up to an (ultimately ratified) 1842 Anglo-Portuguese commercial treaty, "after having heaped insults and having bullied the government of this country, [Britain] now seeks to deprive Portugal of all sources of prosperity and parade the cadaver of our country around Europe as if it were a trophy to its avarice and pre-eminence."[234]

Though Portugal ultimately succumbed to British pressure to abolish the trade, slavery itself lingered in *Ultramar*. There was hardly any discussion of, and certainly no action regarding, the institution of slavery during the Cortes. In the late 1820s and 1830s, prominent voices would condemn slavery, but lofty sentiments did not translate into efficacious policy. In 1842 and 1844, bills were presented to the legislature

---

[231] Sá da Bandeira 1840, p. 8.
[232] *A Aguia*, no. 11 (July 23, 1834), p. 42.
[233] [Anon./Um Portuguez], *Males que tem resultado a Portugal* 1840, pp. 7, 9, 10, 11, 18–19.
[234] Editorial entitled "Mais um Ruinoso Tratado com a Inglaterra," *A Revolução de Setembro*, no. 108 (March 22, 1841), reproduced in Estêvão 1962, p. 90.

to abolish slavery in Portuguese India, but they failed to garner enough votes to pass. The vexing issue of indemnities for slaveholders was a persistent stumbling block. Only in 1856–57 was slavery abolished in Ambriz, Molembo, and Cabinda, while the abolition of slavery within twenty years was promised in 1858. Though slavery was officially outlawed in 1869, forced-labor regimes closely resembling slavery persisted into the twentieth century in many parts of the empire.[235]

By 1846, when civil violence once again marred the Portuguese political landscape, debates concerning colonial affairs were suspended. The Association, for example, ceased to convene, for reasons that remain murky.[236] Though prematurely dissolved after only seven years in existence, it is abundantly clear that the Association's efforts, like those of the government as a whole, yielded few results in the medium-term. Amidst the domestic upheaval that plagued Portugal in the aftermath of its Civil War, colonial development became a second-tier priority. As Vieira de Magalhães noted in 1843, "we have a great deal to do, and we shall be kept busy for many years organizing the branches of administration in Portugal itself. I do not know when we will find the opportunity to concern ourselves with the colonies." Yet even where attention was given and resources allocated, the results were dismal. Indeed, the Minister for Naval and Colonial affairs admitted in 1848 that "all of the methods that we have employed up until now to develop Angola's agriculture have not achieved the results that we imagined that they would."[237] In 1849, a governor of Angola was more direct:

Many recommendations are repeatedly made regarding the improvement of agriculture, and it would indeed be our salvation. But what has been achieved? Nothing or practically nothing ... where then is the capital and where are those white men who want to settle in this wilderness?[238]

This frustration was not misplaced. In the late 1840s, the regular Portuguese military in Angola consisted of a mere sixteen hundred men and the upkeep of this meager force consumed 75 percent of total government expenditure in that unhappy colony.[239] The Lisbon

---

[235] The material in this paragraph is derived mainly from Marques 2008, pp. 39–57 passim, p. 117. On the later period, see L. M. Heywood, "Slavery and Forced Labor in the Changing Political Economy of Central Angola, 1850–1949," in Miers and Roberts 1988.

[236] Even Ribeiro's encyclopedic history of Portuguese associations, clubs, and societies sheds no light on the Association's demise, indicating only that its *Annaes* "even today should be considered as an excellent repository of information concerning *Ultramar*." See J. S. Ribeiro 1876, vol. VI, p. 231.

[237] Quoted in Oliveira 1981, p. 318.

[238] Quoted in J. P. Marques 2006, p. 215.

[239] Pélissier 2006, p. 60.

government was in no position either to seize and hold new territory or to enforce decrees, especially with local populations – both African and Portuguese – averse to metropolitan interference.

Eventually, during the *Regeneração* of the mid 1850s, the government reorganized the administrative apparatus for colonial affairs, re-constituting the *Conselho Ultramarino*, which had been disbanded in 1833, in 1851.[240] A state-sponsored *Colegio das Missões Ultramarinas*, which trained future cadres of missionaries bound for East Asia and Africa, was founded in 1856.[241] The newfound enthusiasm for ultra-marine schemes was reflected in Saldanha's comment that "our African colonies can be very useful to us if we are more generous with them, improving their administration, and showing ourselves to be more scrupulous in the selection of officials."[242] Sá da Bandeira, as chair-man of the *Conselho Ultramarino* from 1851 to 1859 and Minister for the Navy and Overseas Colonies from 1856 to 1859, pursued, under more propitious circumstances, the reform program aborted in the late 1830s.

Even in the 1850s, however, plans for the development of Portuguese Africa proceeded fitfully. In 1856, a French traveler to Mozambique remarked that there was "nothing more than the vestiges of a state ... a cadaver."[243] The young king, Dom Pedro V, acknowledged the slowness of change when he told Visconde de Atouguia that "the development of our rich resources in Africa is impossible as long as capital is invested in the illegal slave trade."[244] More decisive government action was neces-sary to make the colonies viable. As late as 1860, Lavradio informed Terceira that, "without colonies, [Portugal] will have neither a navy nor trade; without a navy and trade, Portugal will be reduced to a wretched condition, and perhaps find itself without the means of preserving [its] independence."[245] This fear would animate the decisions of Portuguese policy-makers in the waning decades of the nineteenth century and, it could be argued, well into the twentieth.[246]

By the mid 1870s, the Geographic Society of Lisbon (*Sociedade de Geografia de Lisboa*) was established and it would achieve much more

---

[240] Caetano 1967.
[241] Alexandre, "A Questão Colonial," in Alexandre and Dias 1998, p. 149.
[242] Boe.C., MS 50.280.7, copy of a letter signed by Duque de Saldanha to an unidenti-fied correspondent, January 1851.
[243] Charles Guillam, quoted in Pélissier 2006, p. 66.
[244] Dom Pedro V to Atouguia, May 26, 1856, in Pedro V 1961, p. 178.
[245] Lavradio to Terceira, March 6, 1860, quoted in W. H. C. Smith 1970, p. 40.
[246] For a summary in English of the Portuguese government's initiatives after 1860, see Marques 1972, ch. 11.

than its forerunner, the Association, ever did to buttress the colonial ambitions of the government. Like the Association, it was founded, in 1876, by royal decree. It was designed to buttress the Ministry for Naval and Colonial Affairs' efforts by "compiling, organizing, and making available, to the benefit of science and the nation, all of the documents that serve to clarify the geography, ethnography, archaeology, anthropology, and natural sciences that relate to Portuguese territory and, especially, to the overseas provinces."[247] But while these initiatives would eventually undergird Portugal's colonization efforts after 1890, they were slow to produce tangible effects in the short term.[248]

This chapter has argued that the ambitions and trajectory of Portuguese colonialism after 1850 cannot be understood without grasping the diverse, often fumbling, ways that Portuguese political writers, politicians, and publicists wrestled with the decolonization of Brazil and negatively assessed Portugal's geopolitical position without colonies. This chapter has contended that the policies pursued during and after the *Regeneração* of the 1850s were not formed spontaneously. Rather, they emerged from the morass of parliamentary debates, pamphlet wars, failed government initiatives, and shifting conceptions of political economy that marked Portuguese political and intellectual life from 1825 until 1850. These debates were themselves the outgrowth of the flurry of reform initiatives undertaken before 1808. While the results of this intensified interest were unspectacular, an appreciation of the continuities and discontinuities, of failed projects and paths not taken, helps to uncover the intellectual impact of Brazilian decolonization in Portugal as well as the underpinnings of Portugal's overseas empire in the late nineteenth and twentieth centuries.[249]

---

[247] February 17, 1876 decree that founded the *Sociedade de Geografia de Lisboa*, quoted in Guimarães 1984, p. 11.

[248] See the problems identified and analyzed by Oliveira Martins 1920.

[249] It remains to be seen whether the Portuguese nineteenth- and twentieth-century fantasy of Angolan wealth ultimately takes a dystopian turn in the twenty-first: Angolan oil money is pouring into debt-ridden Portugal and, as of October 2011, 97,616 Portuguese citizens were registered at Angolan consulates, twice the number registered in 2005. New guidebooks are appearing in Lisbon bookshops for Portuguese professionals flirting with the prospect of leaving stagnant Europe for burgeoning opportunities in Angola. See Mark 2011; Pidd 2011; and H. Santos 2011.

Conclusion: The long shadow of empire in the Luso-Atlantic world

"O historiador não penetra na noite do passado, nessa necropolis venerável das gerações extintas, sem sacudir a poeira das paixões do dia."[1]

This book has challenged the two competing emphases—discontinuity and disjuncture, and seamless transition from one epoch to another— upon which the "Age of Revolution(s)" and nationalist historiographical traditions, respectively, are predicated. It argued that such emphases distort, obscure, or exaggerate crucial aspects of the processes culminating in the disintegration of the Portuguese empire in the period *c.* 1770–1850. By a different route and on a separate basis, it reached a conclusion similar to that of earlier historians, though it employed different types of evidence and drew on sources from both sides of the Atlantic (Portugal and Brazil), concerning the persistence of mutual influence between Portugal and Brazil after the latter's political independence. For the most part, previous historians interested in such surviving connections between the ex-metropole and former colony focused on the economic trajectory or political development of each state during the period following independence (1821–25). Historians working from both "dependency" and "post-dependency" perspectives rightly flagged the "legacies" of colonialism in Brazil, the "heritage" bequeathed by Portugal, and the notable continuities between the colonial and national periods, including Brazil's reliance on slave-driven, export-oriented monoculture, its archaic social structure and perpetuation of deep inequalities (including land distribution), and the post-independence Brazilian government's harnessing (and careful preservation) of the fiscal, administrative, and legal apparatus of the overthrown colonial state. The victory of conservatives, both politically

---

[1] Homem de Mello, *Correio Mercantil*, October 30, 1863, reproduced in Senado Federal 1973, p. 128. This poetic phrase may be translated, very freely, as "the historian cannot enter the darkness of the past, this venerable necropolis of [now] extinct generations, without catching a whiff of the passions of the day."

and ideologically, in many of the states swept up in the revolutionary tumult of 1770–1850, including Brazil, has prodded some scholars to reassess whether there was anything revolutionary about the
revolutionary age and, in the Ibero-Atlantic case, whether independence masked deep continuities with the *ancién regime*.[2] In the case of
Portugal, post-1974 historians, echoing in large part (but with considerably greater sophistication) the lament of their nineteenth-century
forebears, have demonstrated that the economic dislocation, disruption, and devastation, in part exacerbated by the transfer of the Court
(1807–8) and the independence of Brazil, contributed to Portugal's
"underdevelopment" in the nineteenth century.[3] An earlier generation
of historians of European–Latin American relations also pointed to the
creation of "neo-colonial" connections, diverse interactions of varying
intensity and duration, sometimes encompassed by the term "informal
empire," as European financiers and British merchants, with martial
force and other coercive tactics supplied by their lusty and opportunistic governments, stepped into the economic void created by the dismantlement of the Iberian empires.[4]

While engaging with, drawing on, and (deeply) indebted to existing scholarship, this book has avoided recapitulating, concurring with,
or contesting explicitly many of the insights and arguments proffered
by previous historians. This decision was due neither to sycophantic
respect, arrogance, distaste for polemics, nor professional pressures, but
rather a conscious choice to concentrate on aspects of Luso-Brazilian
history which have been ignored, left unexamined, or studied in isolation. The two chief, overlapping insights developed in this book derive
from an abiding dissatisfaction with the distorting prism of the "Age
of Revolution(s)" and the still-blinkered nature of nationalist historiography. The first insight is that the dissolution of the Luso-Brazilian
empire was a highly contingent process in which the role of a handful
of individuals possessing disproportionate amounts of political power
decisively shaped the outcome, thus reversing the reformist and integrationist tendency ascendant between 1760 and 1810, which remained
dominant as late as 1820. Historians should refrain from "post-dictive
assumptions."[5] Imperial collapse was far from preordained. Portugal's
empire was not fated to follow the path just trodden by the Atlantic
empires of Spain, France, and Britain. Recent scholarship has made

---

[2] See the essays in Armitage and Subramanyan 2010; and Paquette and Brown 2013.
[3] Though this view is contested by Lains 1989. Prados de la Escosura 1988 reached a
   similar conclusion with regard to the post-1825 Spanish economy.
[4] The existing literature is surveyed in Brown 2008.
[5] Adelman 2006.

clear that the breakdown of the Atlantic empires was anything but inevitable, but this keen insight has not yet permeated the historiography of the late colonial period. Portugal was not simply the last limping Atlantic empire, bringing up the rear, whose backwardness made it temporarily impervious to the forces eroding the foundations of its defunct counterparts. Through a combination of astute policy, blind fortune, and the opportunistic scavenging of the economic carcasses of rival empires, Crown servants and their collaborators managed to avert, or at least stave off, the forces of disaggregation, diverting or harnessing their energies in a manner that proved advantageous for at least three decades. What in other imperial contexts soon erupted into an "Age of Revolutions," in the Portuguese Atlantic World continued to be an epoch of integration, reform, renewal, renegotiation, and, in some cases and places, devolution. At least until the 1807–8 French invasion and occupation of the Iberian Peninsula, which inverted the political relationship between Portugal and Brazil (but aligned the latter's emerging economic might with a commensurate political primacy), few envisioned imperial collapse – even disgruntled European Portuguese and Brazilian *nordestinos*, who shared a disdain for Rio de Janeiro's parvenu preeminence, strove to reconfigure political authority to gain autonomy and equity, if not primacy, within a revamped order. The spectacular fact of political independence, aided by the generations of historians writing in its wake, served to stifle and counteract the subterranean, imperceptible, subtle forces that converged to sustain the empire. Far from confirming retrospective, teleological assumptions that it was a staggering behemoth destined to collapse, new research suggests the empire's vitality, sturdiness, and late efflorescence. Historians now must explain the longevity of reinvigorated, largely flourishing institutions, not their demise, in a long eighteenth century marked by enlightened reform.[6]

The longevity, late intensification, and dense web of mutually sustaining interconnections (e.g. the myriad and thick links; the multi-continental careers of administrators and merchants) make suspicious a second assumption surprisingly shared by both the "Age of Revolution(s)" and nationalist historiography. The prevailing assumption is that, after independence, Europe and America parted ways. The view presented in this book is that, in the Luso-Brazilian case, at least at first, independence failed to trigger the divergent historical evolution

---

[6] For the case of the Spanish empire's dissolution, see Paquette 2009a; for new approaches to "enlightened reform" in the Southern Atlantic World, see the essays in Paquette 2009b.

of former metropoles (and Europe as a whole) from their ex-colonies. Old connections of various types persisted and new relationships proliferated. Portugal and Brazil continued to affect each other's political and economic development, by both presence and absence. Parallel and sometimes intersecting histories belie the notion of discrete historical epochs and an unambiguous division separating colonial from national, Atlantic from post-Atlantic, European from (Latin) American History. The interpenetration of these histories after formal dominion faded makes clear the fuzziness, wobbliness, ambiguity, and indefinite nature, to say nothing of the inadequacy, of conventional periodization.[7] It is, perhaps, more accurate to speak of "degrees of independence," or "separation," and to emphasize the misgiving, anxiety, trepidation, and ambivalence many historical actors felt toward imperial disaggregation. Few observers, at least in the Luso-Brazilian world, were convinced of independence's irrevocability. Something that appeared both irreversible and inevitable to later historians seemed anything but definitive to contemporaries. The tangled history of the 1826 *Carta Constitucional* is one of the clearest examples of the long-term impact of a generational political imagination that operated unshackled by modern historiography's Balkanized boundaries. If historians were to treat "old-fashioned" political history seriously, especially dynastic considerations, elite projects, and the ways in which these survived the demise of empire, then the neat demarcation between colonial and national history might be recast as an obstacle to historical understanding.

Besides direct influence and active interference, absence exerted great force in the political development of both Portugal and Brazil. While Portuguese history after 1825 may be written without reference to the loss of Brazil, and instead with reference to clashing ideologies, political factions, and pan-European trends (e.g. secularization, restoration and reaction, the decline of the nobility, industrialization, free trade and protectionism, underdevelopment, Romanticism, Liberalism), the political splintering, fragmentation, and constant conflict of that period is illuminated differently when backlit by the supernova of imperial disintegration.[8] The final collapse of the Luso-Brazilian empire left its orphaned subjects on both sides of the Atlantic casting about for new, unprecedented forms of political organization. Far from heroic, they groped their way toward a stable post-imperial order in the shadow of

---

[7] Discussed in the Introduction, p. 14; and in Paquette and Brown 2013.
[8] As Hopkins 1999 argued (in a twentieth-century context), "the big issues of the post-colonial era cannot be understood without acknowledging the extent to which they are a legacy of the empires that dominated the world during the past three centuries," p. 203.

inalienable, and in some cases insuperable, constitutional, economic, and political legacies. Viewed in this manner, Portugal's history "after Brazil" becomes the struggle between partisans of competing visions of how to replace a long-functioning, perhaps unwieldy, but overall resilient system based on inter-continental symbiosis (viewed exclusively from the commanding heights of government administration) which permitted a small state to retain its sovereignty while increasingly outstripped by larger predatory, voracious European rivals. The answers they offered sometimes led away from Brazil (e.g. Miguelism's enthrallment with Portugal's pre-Brazilian colonial expansion in North Africa and the Indian Ocean, to say nothing of its infatuation with Portugal's Reconquest heritage), sometimes toward it (e.g. the Regency of Terceira, dependent on Brazil for funds and political support), and sometimes operated in the long shadow of early modern expansion (e.g. African colonization schemes after 1825, most of which hinged on Brazilian slave trade policy). Regardless, try as they might, Portuguese politicians of the 1820s to 1840s could not escape the unresolved aspects of their broken (but not shattered) relations with Brazil, the persistence of crucial connections, and the inconvenient outcroppings of a now legally extinct, but certainly not fully eviscerated, colonial past.

The ways in which Brazil's political development was alternately stymied by, or indebted to, the legal-cultural-economic-political heritage bequeathed by Portugal has received generous attention from generations of historians, not to mention further, hopefully original, treatment in this book. For example, many historians have recognized the continuities between the colonial reform program and the post-independence state. On the most general level, the ideas and political practices associated with eighteenth-century enlightened reform left an "ample legacy" after independence.[9] Others have discerned unmistakable connections to specific initiatives: the establishment of the *Sociedade Auxiliadora da Indústria Nacional* in 1831, for example, has been interpreted as "suggestive of the pragmatic and progressive orientation" of late eighteenth-century policies and strategies.[10] These continuities, while of the utmost importance, are unsurprising given that the Brazilian political elite remained thoroughly connected to Portugal through the thread of higher education. Coimbra remained the only university in the Portuguese-speaking world at which to study law, the prerequisite for magistracy and judicial appointments, until the founding, in 1828, of law schools in Olinda and São Paulo, themselves

---

[9] Cloclet da Silva 2006, p. 416; L. Neves 1999b, p. 31.
[10] Silva Dias 1968, p. 167; more generally, Silva Dias 1972.

patterned on Coimbra and staffed with Coimbra-trained professors.[11] The impact of this educational arrangement was felt well after independence: every university-trained cabinet minister before 1831 was trained at Coimbra (and two-thirds of the ministers of the *Primeiro Reinado* had been trained at Coimbra before 1799). Of the fourteen individuals to hold the post of Minister of the Empire between 1822 and 1831, twelve were Coimbra graduates. Even as late as 1850, approximately half of all ministers remained Coimbra graduates.[12] The "Generation of the 1790s," and their younger siblings, not only laid the groundwork for imperial reform before 1820, and influenced or orchestrated the independence movement in 1822–25, but actually governed and also shaped Brazil's intellectual development well into the nineteenth century.[13] Historians have identified this common background as responsible for the intellectual homogeneity, statist-orientation, commitment to territorial unity, and insular nature of Brazil's post-independence "mandarin" political elite.[14] Unequivocally pessimistic historians, who argue that independent Brazil largely inherited and reproduced the main institutions of the colonial period, point to the anomalous survival of monarchy in an independent Ibero-America dominated by republics, the power yielded by the "feudal aristocracy," inexorably centralizing policies, and the reinvigoration of old symbolism.[15] As early as the 1970s, an influential historian argued convincingly for understanding Brazilian independence as a "counter-revolution," citing the survival of the Philippine Ordinances of 1603, and most other colonial laws, during the 1822–31 period. "In this way, the archaic structure remained unchanged, anachronistic legislation blocked the process of [legal and

---

[11] Though note that theological seminaries existed in Brazil before 1808 while two medical and military academies were founded soon after the arrival of the Court. The *Seminário de Olinda*, founded in 1798 under the direction of Azeredo Coutinho, played a key role in teaching mathematics, various sciences, and modern languages, not only theology. See Diego Rafael Ambrosini, "'A Interiorização da Metrópole': Atores e Instituições," in C. G. Mota 2006, p. 236.

[12] J. M. de Carvalho 1982, p. 382; L. Neves 1999b, p. 21; Ambrosini, ibid., p. 241.

[13] On this "Generation of the 1790s," see Maxwell 2003; and Safier 2009b.

[14] J. M. de Carvalho 1982, pp. 384, 390; on applicability of the concept of "mandarins" in Brazil, see Pang and Seckinger 1972; on the specific experiences of Brazilian students at Coimbra during the dissolution of Portugal's empire, see Barman and Barman 1976; for a recent view along similar lines, see L. Neves 1999b, p. 31.

[15] Faoro 1958, pp. 196, 225; Mattos 1987 made a similar claim concerning the contradiction of the political elite before 1850, pp. 126, 282. Nor are such assertions solely the domain of *marxisant* historiography. As Needell observed, "the political elite emergent by 1837 was part and parcel of the socio-economic elites presiding over agriculture and commerce associated with African slavery and tropical export staples." See Needell 2006, p. 5; on ceremonial continuities, including the revival of the *beija-mão* ceremony, see Mosher 2008.

political] development," the same historian contended, "there was not a total rupture from the colonial system."[16] While revised criminal and procedural codes would appear in the 1830s, commercial and civil codes would not appear until 1850 and 1916, respectively.

But only recently have historians begun to examine the way that Brazil's political development was shaped by, or contingent on, either events or forces in the former metropole, Europe in general, or the Portuguese-born Brazilians who stayed on in independent Brazil. There has been resistance, to some extent, to historical explanations which transcend endogenous political processes, accept the primacy of European actors and actions, or engage comparatively with Spanish American developments. Such resistance (and anxiety) may be found from Brazil's inception as an independent state. As Bernardo Pereira de Vasconcelos asked the Brazilian Assembly in the late 1820s, "What do we want with Old Europe? America belongs to America; let Europe belong to Europe and all will be for the best."[17] Fortunately, this tendency is falling out of favor. It is an auspicious historiographical moment, then, at which to recognize how Portugal and the Portuguese resident in Brazil continued to shape Brazil's trajectory after 1825. Lusitanian immigrants flocked to Brazil in the 1830s and 1840s: between 1831 and 1842, 18,000 Portuguese registered at Rio de Janeiro alone while at least 26,500 arrived in the capital between 1826 and 1850.[18]

Ignominious 1831 abdication aside, Dom Pedro retained no dearth of allies in Brazil, many of whom entertained fantasies of a restoration until his premature death in 1834. Such support not only percolated at the elite level, but was also ubiquitous among the lower and middle classes. His abdication sparked urban uprisings led by disgruntled troops in Bahia, Pernambuco, and Minas Gerais. Unrest also spread among the civilian population – rural and urban – of the northeast, which had suffered through severe drought in 1824–25 and was afflicted by another protracted drought in 1830–34. The price of manioc flour and other staples reached unsustainably high levels.[19] In the backlands of Ceará, the ex-military official Pinto Madeira fomented a pro-Dom Pedro I revolt. His pro-Portuguese sentiments were well

[16] J. H. Rodrigues 1975, vol. V, pp. 231–32.
[17] Quoted in J. H. Rodrigues 1965, p. 157.
[18] Barbosa 2009, pp. 1, 34; Barbosa demonstrated that between 1836 and 1850, roughly three-quarters of Portuguese immigrants disembarked at Rio de Janeiro; it may be conjectured that the overall number of Portuguese immigrants arriving in Brazil would be somewhat higher than the figures cited if ports besides Rio de Janeiro were included in the tally. Barbosa 2009, p. 51. On the fickle fortunes of the Portuguese in Brazil after independence, see G. S. Ribeiro 2002.
[19] J. J. Reis 1993, p. 15; M. S. Santos 2012, pp. 22–23.

known already, for he led an ill-fated, pro-Portuguese uprising in 1825. Brazilian authorities claimed, accurately, that Pinto Madeira aimed to "re-establish the old system of Portuguese government, and introduce a political schism among the rustic people who cry out for the *rey velho*," using this doctrine as a cover to "rob, murder, and disturb the peace."[20] In 1832, after Dom Pedro's abdication, Pinto Madeira renewed his resistance, determining that the restoration of the deposed emperor was his last, best hope at a regime capable of keeping nativist fury at bay. Though his movement was dismissed as a "crazy insurrection" by an "idiotic *sertanejo*" in the urban press, his actions were heeded as a warning that "fratricide" could "devastate entire cities," reminiscent of the internecine wars then pulverizing the nascent Spanish American polities.[21]

Pinto Madeira's threat dissipated, owing to a combination of brutal repression and weak leadership, but he proved to be a harbinger for more serious, popular threats to the Regency governing Brazil while Dom Pedro II was a child. In April 1832, a coalition of Portuguese-born troops, merchants, and artisans revolted in Recife, aiming to restore Dom Pedro I to the throne. Shouts of "*Viva Dom Pedro, Rei de Portugal, e do Brasil*" echoed in the streets.[22] In rural Pernambuco, planters and Portuguese merchants fomented a rebellion, mobilizing peasants uneasy with the land encroachment of the period.[23] Even when elites withdrew their support, frightened by the social revolutionary turn, the peasant rebellion continued. These revolutionaries became known as "*Cabanos*," after the humble forest huts or shacks, called *cabanas*, in which they dwelled. *Cabano*, of course, was a derogatory term, with negative connotations of backwardness and poverty. By 1832, the War of the *Cabanos*, or *Cabanada*, was raging. A guerilla force composed of Indians, runaway slaves, and other discontents coalesced around the charismatic figure of Vicente de Paula, a former sergeant in the now-disbanded colonial militia, who assumed the rather grandiose title "General of the Royalist Forces." Paula claimed that the "blood-thirsty" Regency and "corrupt, lowly" Assembly jointly had "usurped" Dom

[20] "Officio de José Felix de Azevedo e Sá, Presidente da Provincia do Ceará, ao Ouvidor Interino da Comarca do Crato – Ordenado que se proceda á devassa sobre os crimes de Joaquim Pinto Madeira," July 20, 1825, published in *Publicações do Archivo Público Nacional* 1929, vol. XXIV, pp. 297–98.

[21] *O Harmonizador*, no. 7 (March 12, 1832), pp. 27–29 passim; on Pinto Madeira, see Montenegro 1976; and Mosher 2008, pp. 111–13.

[22] IAHGP, cx. 215, mç. 4, "Oficios do Presidente" (April 25, 1832); APEJE, B. L. Ferreira to Pedro Ara[ú]jo Lima, Sept. 24, 1832, fo. 160.

[23] On elite support for the *Cabanos*, see Ferraz 1996, p. 196; on the *Abrilada* and its connection to rural unrest, see Mosher 2008, pp. 92–93.

Pedro I's throne and were doing the same to his underage successor, thus legitimizing their struggle against the "Jacobins" of Rio de Janeiro, who manipulated the Constitution to pursue their personal ambitions and advance their material interests.[24]

The attachment of the rural poor to royalism, it must be emphasized, was not due solely to sentimental or ideological attachment to the previous regime.[25] As in other Latin American contexts, where pro-royalist and restorationist doctrines circulated among the disgruntled poor, concrete, immediate, and local interests were also in play. Royalism provided a recognized symbolic framework which permitted broader political participation at regional and national levels.[26] The material interests of the Pernambucan royalist-leaning poor had suffered a severe blow following Dom Pedro's abdication. The royal monopoly over the forests was repealed, effectively removing their legal protection and facilitating the seizure of vast swathes of land by the local gentry. The frontier zone between the provinces of Pernambuco and Alagoas became the epicenter of the struggle. It was here that land ideal for sugar cane cultivation remained relatively untapped. Local landlords raised and commanded troops, which sought to evict peasants and Jacuípe Indians from the coveted lands. These subalterns then joined together to oppose the landlords. At the height of the conflict (1833–34), this unlikely multi-ethnic alliance of runaway slaves, peasants, and Indians formed a formidable fighting force.[27] With the blessing of the central government, however, a "scorched earth" policy was adopted, as local landlords utilized the newly formed National Guard to conduct counterinsurgency operations to starve the *Cabanos* out of the forests. This tactic worked, with tragic consequences. In 1834, an army commander reported scenes of "children dying of hunger [and] women reduced to skeletons and dressed in rags" as they stumbled out of the forests.[28] The conflict never formally ended; no truce was ever

---

[24] Vicente de Paula, Proclamation of November 16, 1833, quoted in Andrade 1965, p. 208.

[25] Dirceu Lindoso argued persuasively that the *Cabanada* was a "rebellion of the poor [within] an insurrection of the wealthy." While Lindoso rightly situated the restorationist doctrines the *Cabanos* publicly espoused in broader context, their political doctrines cannot be dismissed as either instrumental or inconsequential. See Lindoso 1983, p. 430; also see Mosher 2008, p. 115.

[26] Méndez 2005, pp. 60, 69, 109, 188; for the fascinating case of New Granada, see Echeverri 2011.

[27] M. J. M. de Carvalho 2012.

[28] Major José Tomas Henriques, May 1834, quoted in Andrade 1965, p. 143. It is clear from documentary records that the authorities were aware of the starvation afflicting civilians and *Cabano* guerillas alike. See AHGAl., doc. 02013, cx. 23, pac. 4, doc. 11, "Officio sobre as noticias do encontro entre o Vice-Presidente de Pernambuco

declared. Vicente de Paula remained at large, if innocuous, until the 1840s. Morever, the *Cabanos* invaded and briefly occupied the city of Maceió, Alagoas, in October 1844 and then again in 1850. At this late stage, however, the ideology of reaction was ascendant and the rebels were referred to only as "anarchists," opponents of the "Holy Roman Church," and "enemies of legality."[29]

Dom Pedro I's 1831 abdication was also greeted throughout Brazil with anti-Portuguese riots, with attacks on Portuguese-owned inns, houses, and stores, accompanied by the ubiquitous cry of *"mata-marotos"* ("kill the rascals[!]").[30] Portuguese-born Brazilians and Portuguese residents were beaten and killed, while stores were looted, ransacked, and burned.[31] Anti-Portuguese attacks in 1831–32, in Bahia at least, often were associated with federalist political sympathies, but most lacked a clearly defined program of social or political reform. The Portuguese were convenient scapegoats, and the notion of expelling them from Brazilian soil, or at least depriving them of civil, military, and ecclesiastical appointments, was an attractive distraction from deep-seated problems.[32] It is difficult to determine whether Lusophobia served to inspire or further inflame such "restorationist" movements or whether the outbreak of rebellion itself generated (or at least brought into the open) fierce anti-Portuguese sentiments. In all likelihood, it was a feedback loop. It is clear that the aftermath of the abdication and the onset of what historians lump together as the early Regency rebellions heightened sentiments which, in turn, made the possibility of Dom Pedro I's return semi-plausible.

As pro-restorationist and Nativist/Lusophobe conflict occurred, the Regency's politicians enacted significant changes. In 1831, the army, long-maligned as a retrograde bastion of Portuguese influence, was

e o Presidente das Alagoas, com relação a novos planos de Guerra, no combate aos insurgentes Cabanos," March 16, 1834, fo.1.

[29] AHGAl., doc. 01434, cx. 20, pac. 01, doc. 01, "Proclamação de Bernardo de Souza Franco, Presidente," October 5, 1844.

[30] In part, the anger was exacerbated by a fresh wave of Portuguese immigration to Brazil after 1825. As one newspaper in Maranhão noted, "the Portuguese who come [to Brazil] are for the most part born in the backward *sertões* of their provinces, and they unite the innate stupidity of country folk in Europe with all of the vices which percolate in the cities of Porto and Lisbon," *O Brasileiro*, no. 3 (September 6, 1832), p. 10.

[31] For Bahia, see J. J. Reis 1993, pp. 22–25; for Minas Gerais, see Bieber 1998. It should be noted that there was animosity on both sides and the Portuguese were not mere passive victims. As the astute British traveler Maria Graham observed in 1823, "the European Portuguese are extremely anxious to avoid intermarriage with Brazilians, and prefer to give their daughters and fortunes to the meanest clerk of European birth than to the richest and most meritorious Brazilian." See Graham 1824, p. 126.

[32] J. J. Reis 1993, pp. 32–38 passim; P. C. Souza 1987, p. 180.

weakened and a national guard, under the control of provincial authorities, was created. The Regency implemented a new criminal code
(previously devised and passed in 1830) and promulgated a procedural
code, establishing the jury system, in 1832. New justices of the peace
were installed. More generally, the 1824 Constitution was amended in
order to decentralize power and dismantle what was vituperated as the
pernicious institutions bequeathed by Portuguese colonialism.[33] An
"Additional Act," *Ato Adicional*, of the Constitution was passed in 1834.
It replaced the weak provincial councils, decried earlier by Frei Caneca
and others, with provincial assemblies endowed with substantial prerogatives, including control over municipal policing, the right to levy
and collect certain taxes, oversight over public works, and responsibility for public education.[34]

It may be argued cogently that many of these policies resulted from
ideas long percolating in Brazil, certainly from 1821, if not from 1808,
as well as endogenous processes and pressures. But the speed, urgency,
and fervency with which they were pursued suggest the pervasive fear
of Dom Pedro's return that existed in Brazil. Some commentators dismissed fears of Portugal and the Portuguese resident in Brazil, disparaging rumors of plots as "fantasies concocted by hyper-active patriotic
imaginations. The Brazilians have more than adequate strength to sustain their independence."[35] Restoration was more than a fantasy, however, though the figure of Dom Pedro was of far greater importance
than some sentimental affinity with Portugal or a nostalgic *saudade* for
the colonial regime. An active *Sociedade Conservadora da Constituição
Jurada do Império* flourished in Rio de Janeiro from 1832, with three
of the Andrada brothers among its charter members. As noted in
Chapter 4, they made overtures to Dom Pedro in 1832–34, to which
he responded evasively and ambivalently. The *Sociedade* was affiliated
with newspapers, including *O Caramurú*. The title became an epithet
for "restorationist" to its detractors. Several of the members of the
Sociedade held positions in the Council of State and occupied Senate

---

[33] Though Flory's negative assessment of the reforms culminating in the *Ato Adicional*
should be kept in mind: instead of the crowning achievement of Brazilian liberalism,
it was the "first institutional expression of this liberal desire to recentralize administration," as many of the "powers delegated to provincial authorities were not previously vested in central government at all, but prerogatives of local government." See
Flory 1981, p. 158.

[34] Also important was the Additional Act's replacement of the three-person regency
with a single regent, chosen by popular election every four years. On these and other
changes ushered in by the 1834 Additional Act, in English, see Barman 1988 and
Barman 1999; Mosher 2008.

[35] *O Harmonizador*, no. 5 (January 16, 1832), pp. 19–22 passim.

seats from which they could not be dislodged except by death, according to the life-terms enshrined in the 1824 Constitution.[36]

The threat, then, was palpable and plausible, but the fear it produced was wildly disproportionate, even hysterical. They confused disaffection with Dom Pedro's abdication with an imminent threat to Brazil's sovereignty, whether blinded by genuine paranoia or motivated by the benefits of intentional obfuscation. "The Portuguese are without doubt the true motors of the disorder which is destroying this province," an official in Pará reported, "they cannot accept that the Brazilians are not their slaves any longer." He alleged that they had "almost confessed to a criminal union with Dom Miguel."[37] When local disturbances occurred, they were blamed routinely on the "Luso-Restorationist club" which sought to return Dom Pedro to his former throne.[38] As Dom Pedro's fortunes in Portugal's Civil War improved, he became the object of reconquest ambition fears. In Recife, *O Carapuceiro* assumed that Dom Pedro would not be "content to retire to England or France and live a quiet, private life. He is ambitious."[39] In Maranhão, one newspaper noted that while the deposed Dom Pedro "recognized the impossibility of conquering all of Brazil," the provinces of the north, upon which "the Portuguese never gazed without *saudades*," remained a target of reconquest owing to their "wealth and proximity to Portugal."[40] There were constant reports in São Luís during 1833–34 of the mysterious machinations of a "restorationist faction" and their legions of shadowy Portuguese supporters.[41] In October 1833, a petition was presented to Recife's authorities, decrying the

homens malvados, who call themselves *Caramurus = Restauradores*, who conspire against the throne of Sr Dom Pedro II, and the government of April 7, seeking the restoration of Duque de Braganza, a hateful objective in the eyes of all good Brazilians, who, if he sat again upon the throne, would destroy the constitutional monarchy at the expense of the lives, honor, and *fazendas* of all those born in Brazil.[42]

Evidently, high-ranking officials expected Portuguese warships to appear on the horizon at any moment. "Duque de Braganza will attempt

---

[36] Kirschner 2009, p. 277; Reinert 1960, pp. 62, 67, 101.
[37] ANRJ, Serie Interior, IJJ⁹, 108 (Pará), Visconde de Goiana to Ministro do Império, August 30, 1831, fos. 328, 332, 338.
[38] IHGB, lata 286, livro 5 (Collecção de Documentos sobre a Cabanagem no Pará, 1834–36), "Decreto de Presidente Bernard Lobo de Souza," October 13, 1834.
[39] *O Carapuceiro*, no. 26 (July 2, 1834), p. 3.
[40] *Echo do Norte*, no. 3 (July 10, 1834), pp. 11–12.
[41] See, for example, *Echo do Norte*, no. 35 (November 4, 1834), p. 139.
[42] ANRJ, IJJ⁹ (Pernambuco), Petition dated October 19, 1833, fos. 111–12.

to invade Brazil to restore his throne," one alarmed Pernambucan official reported, and "we must destroy the miserable horde of slaves [in
Brazil] who support the Duque, who seeks to destroy our liberties and
re-impose the insupportable yoke of tyranny."[43] The impact of these
"recolonization" anxieties and Luso-Restorationist rumors were felt
at many registers of society. On a local level, they spawned grotesque
anti-Portuguese violence. In Rio Negro, Pará, it was reported that "horrible robberies, violence, and massacres were perpetrated against those
who did not have the fortune to be born in Brazil."[44] In the small town
of Arraial do Pilar, in Matto Grosso, Portuguese-born inhabitants were
attacked for allegedly stockpiling weapons for use in the anticipated
war to restore Portuguese rule. The resulting mob violence claimed
the lives of thirty of the town's Portuguese inhabitants.[45] In Maceió, an
official admitted that "adoptive citizens and Portuguese are persecuted
to inhumane extremes by extremist radicals [*exaltados*], to the extent
that commerce here is stagnant, and the city is entirely deserted."[46]
During the *Cabanada*, Pernambuco's provincial government proposed
the transport of all Portuguese-born Brazilians "accused, according to
public opinion," of being restorationists to the island of Fernando de
Noronha, dispensing with legal due process.[47]

At the level of national politics, the Luso-Restorationist "threat"
lent urgency to constitutional and other types of legal-administrative
reform. Such fears were expressed publicly by leading national politicians in the Assembly. Vasconcelos described the likelihood of Dom
Pedro's attempted restoration as "very probable" and a "natural" step.
He observed that the common people were "very frightened" of this
"dangerous" prospect and that "measures must be taken to prevent it."[48]
In 1834, the Assembly voted by a large majority to exclude permanently
Dom Pedro I's return to Brazil, though this measure was defeated in the

---

[43] APEJE, PP[8], José Marciano de Albuquerque e Cavalcanti to Manuel Seferino dos
Santos, August 8, 1833.
[44] APEJE, PP[8], [President of Pará] J. J. Machado de Oliveira to [President of
Pernambuco] F. Paes de Carvalho, October 31, 1832.
[45] Barbosa 2009, p. 80.
[46] ANRJ, IJJ[9] 280 (Alagoas), Presidente Manoel Lobo da Miranda Henriques to José
Lino Coutinho [Ministerio do Império], November 19, 1831, fo. 185.
[47] IAHGP, cx. 215, mç. 4, "Inquerito contra Luis António Vieira" (1834).
[48] Vasconcelos, "Discurso na Câmara dos Deputados, Sessão de 4 de Julho de 1833,"
reproduced in Vasconcelos 1999, p. 213; foreign observers found these fears ground-
less and far-fetched, including the US representative: "There are some who appre-
hend that Dom Pedro I may attempt to regain the throne of Brazil. It does not seem
to me at all probable that he would undertake a scheme so desperate." See Ethan
Brown, Chargé d'Affaires (at Rio de Janeiro), to Edward Livingstone, Secretary of
State, August 1, 1832, in Manning 1932, vol. II, p. 195.

Senate, most of whose members the ex-emperor had appointed personally.[49] As an historian noted recently, the passage of the 1834 Additional
Act was "aided by fears that the former Emperor would succumb to the
siren call of his supporters in Brazil and recross the Atlantic at the head
of an army."[50] Many reforms, therefore, were conceived as safeguards
against the alleged Portuguese menace, which was considered a plausible threat until Dom Pedro's premature death in 1834.

What were Dom Pedro's intentions with regard to Brazil prior to his
death? The record is murky. If Resende's correspondence provides an
accurate glimpse into Dom Pedro's state of mind, the ex-emperor had
not entirely abandoned his aspirations to return to Brazil.[51] Yet in a
September 1832 letter to his son, written from Porto, his careful language cast doubt on that aspiration. He hoped that "Brazil now enjoys
the tranquility, unity, and liberty that are necessary for it to be admired
and respected by other nations, of the Old and New World."[52] A year
later, however, basking in the afterglow of his side's military triumph,
he re-opened the possibility. He was courted by a Brazilian restorationist faction, represented by António Carlos de Andrada Machado. In a
September 1833 letter to António Carlos, he stated that "[his] abdication remains valid [*valiosa*]: [he] never had the urge to nullify it." If the
Brazilian nation, however, following the legal channels established by
the 1824 Constitution, invited him back to Brazil, it would be a different matter altogether. After fulfilling his "obligations" to Portugal,
Dom Pedro explained, he would relish the opportunity "to do the
Brazilians a service of some kind ... I would not hesitate or delay for a
single instant, and I would depart right away for Rio de Janeiro, animated by that sincere love for Brazil which always has been inside of me
and which shall never be extinguished."[53]

---

[49] Reinert 1960, p. 139. Some historians have interpreted "restorationism" as a manifestation of primarily personal squabbles waged by those dislodged from their com-
fortable political perches as a result of Dom Pedro's 1831 abdication. See O. T. de
Sousa 1988.

[50] Barman 1999, p. 60; also see Flory 1981, p. 132.

[51] In July 1832, Resende told Dom Pedro that he should never "lose sight of Brazil,
where you still have the chance to be *grande* and *generoso* ... this [historical] moment
in Brazil, then, belongs to VMI; if you use it well, you will be illustrious; if you fail to
take advantage of it, you will be *desilustrado* in contemporary history and in the eyes
of posterity." Resende to Dom Pedro I, July 8, 1832, reproduced in Resende 1916,
p. 430. It is difficult to ascertain from this letter whether Resende is trying to motivate
Dom Pedro by appealing to his not inconsiderable vanity and sense of self-importance
or whether he was trying to cajole the ex-emperor to revive a formerly expressed, but
now abandoned, ambition.

[52] AMI, mç. 94, doc. 4505, Dom Pedro I to Dom Pedro II, September 28, 1832.

[53] AMI, mç 98, doc. 4820, Dom Pedro (I) to António Carlos de Andrada Machado,
September 14, 1833.

Dom Pedro I's death did not diminish the passion of the parties who used or abused his name, though it did undermine those who manipulated and exploited the vague threat of Portuguese reconquest.[54] It also permitted the eruption of conflicts outside of the shadow of independence. The second half of the Regency (1835–40) was one of the most turbulent periods of Brazilian history, characterized by rebellions, revolts, and conspiracies of all shapes, sizes, and magnitudes of impact, affecting Brazil from the far north (Pará) to the deep south (Rio Grande do Sul).[55] Until recently, these movements of defiance were either dismissed as inconsequential provincial affairs, or depicted as political struggles between regional elites and Rio de Janeiro or intramural bickering within the regional elites themselves. Now historians recognize their radical social dimension, particularly the active participation of slaves, the lower classes, free people of color, and Indians.[56] Political doctrines had been disseminated and absorbed widely, and *Carioca* authorities believed that the extent of their diffusion imperiled the security and tranquility of the distant provinces. Maranhão's *Conselho Geral* noted that "the word 'liberty,' imprudently spoken amongst slaves, has introduced a spirit of insubordination, undoubtedly the precursor of future troubles."[57] The political tide turned irreversibly against violent expressions of discontent and "disorder." Conservatives, weary of the incessant tumult auguring social revolution, concluded that robust, centralized authority was the sole antidote to it.[58] They convinced the electorate of their views in the late 1830s, in a political movement known as the *Regresso*.[59] As a contemporary historian has argued, "the upheavals of the Regency discredited the liberal reforms that decentralized power and provided for greater popular participation."[60] As Regent Feijó summed up the problem facing Brazil in 1836:

[54] Flory 1981, p. 132.
[55] The historiography is rich and complex: among the most important recent works, see J. J. Reis 1993 on the 1835 Revolt of the *Malês* in Bahia; P. C. Souza 1987 and Kraay 1992 on the 1837 *Sabinada* in Bahia; Assunção 1998 on the 1838–41 *Balaida* in Maranhão; Cleary 1998 and Harris 2010 on the 1834–26 *Cabanagem* in Pará; Mosher 2008 and M. J. M. de Carvalho 2012 on the Pernambucan rebellions during the Regency and in the 1840s.
[56] Harris 2010.
[57] BNRJ, MS II-32, 17, 31, "Resoluções do Conselho Geral da Província do Maranhão," February 25, 1833.
[58] On the connection between the former restorationists and the "renegade moderates" who eventually made common cause in the "emergent party of reaction" that would galvanize the *Regresso*, see Needell 2006, p. 58.
[59] On the *Regresso* in general, see Needell 2006.
[60] Mosher 2008, p. 136.

the lack of respect for and obedience to the authorities ... is the gangrene attacking the *corpo social* ... our institutions change frequently, citizens live in constant fear, and the government spends its time making vague recommendations ... the volcano of anarchy threatens to destroy the Empire.[61]

Conservatives thus aimed to insulate political authorities from the vagaries of local politics. Much of the 1834 Additional Act, which had granted the provinces greater autonomy, was nullified, suspended, or repealed. The army was reconstituted, expanded, and improved, no longer subservient to the National Guard. Thereafter, provincial officials were no longer treated as representatives of the local population, but rather servants of imperial government. The criminal procedure code was overhauled and local judicial officials (i.e. judges and prosecutors) were henceforth appointed directly by Rio de Janeiro. The central government's oversight now extended to every municipality and province of the empire.

Support for these new policies gained further momentum when Dom Pedro II's majority was acclaimed in 1840, when he was not yet fifteen years old, three years ahead of schedule.[62] The young emperor made several conciliatory gestures upon his coronation, including the unconditional pardon of all rebels throughout Brazil who surrendered within sixty days. To the unrestrained brute force of the imperial army was now joined the symbolic soft power of monarchy to pacify Brazil. Traditional rituals of court ceremony were revived, including the *Beija-Mão*, or hand-kissing ceremony, which had fallen into abeyance. Larger-than-life-sized portraits of the young emperor were installed in all of the presidential palaces, assemblies, and town halls in the provinces.[63] The *Regresso* had seen off the threat of social revolution, at least partially, through a reinvention of tradition and the revival of older modes of governance.[64]

From the 1840s, in both Portugal and Brazil, the mutual influence that each had exerted on the other waned precipitously, receiving a final blow in the legal abolition, after decades of severe British pressure, of the Atlantic slave trade in 1850. By the late 1830s and 1840s, there were few vocal advocates of a Luso-Brazilian defensive alliance or the

---

[61] Regent Diogo António Feijó, "Falla do Throno," May 3, 1836, in *Fallas do Throno* 1977, p. 261.
[62] On the acclamation and Dom Pedro II's reign in general, see Schwarcz 2000; and Barman 1999.
[63] Mosher 2008, p. 134.
[64] On Brazilian politics in the 1840s and the elites who grappled with the tension between "a slave society governed by liberal institutions ... and an agrarian and uneducated society governed by a cosmopolitan elite," see J. M. de Carvalho 1988, esp. p. 162.

reintegration of Brazil and Portugal into a single political entity.[65] In Portugal, the coming of the *Regeneração* enhanced the country's political stability, permitting some of the turbulence of the preceding decades to subside. New national trajectories were plotted: imperial schemes in Africa, a pan-Iberian union, and more isolationist, narrowly nationalist projects. In Brazil, the Portuguese umbilical cord, now vestigial, gradually withered away.

But not entirely. The immense changes ushered into the Lusophone world from the 1850s did not erase the experiences of the preceding decades, during which the histories of Portugal and Brazil remained entwined, as each grappled, separately and together, with the legacies of enlightened reform, a shared constitutional heritage and political culture, stalled divergence, the survival of myriad atavisms of the Old Regime, and the challenges inherent in breaking old patterns, sliding away from old grooves, and beginning afresh after three hundred years of unceasing interaction.

For these reasons, Portugal and Brazil could never simply ignore each other. Historians did their part to ensure that the older connections did not fade far from public memory, often against the xenophobic and parochial prejudices of the popular historical imagination. Francisco Adolfo Varnhagen, for example, who did more than anybody to shape Brazilian historiography in the nineteenth century, was keenly aware of this indelible mutual influence. A student in Europe in the early 1830s, he enlisted in the Regency's army during the Portuguese Civil War and remained in Europe for long stretches in subsequent decades, collecting documents pertinent to Brazilian History.[66] These experiences contributed, perhaps, to the often-aired complaint that he was excessively charitable to Portugal (and the Portuguese) in his books. As he justified his approach in an 1857 letter to Dom Pedro II, "in general, I have searched for patriotic inspiration without disdain for Portugal, or for *foreign* Europe, from which we received enlightenment."[67]

Varnhagen's opinion, of course, was not an isolated example. New connections and links would be built upon the old, vanquished, yet not razed, foundations of the past. Portuguese immigrants poured into

---

[65] But there were at least some advocates in Portugal. One of them argued that an alliance could be mutually advantageous, permitting Portugal to intervene in Pará, Maranhão, and Paraiba in order to suppress revolts as it was difficult for the Brazilian government to respond promptly for geographical and logistical reasons. See [Anon.], *A Dynastia e a Revolução* 1840, pp. 121, 127.

[66] As recounted in his correspondence. See Varnhagen to Francisco José de Souza Soares de Andreá, February 16, 1843, in Varnhagen 1961, p. 99.

[67] Varnhagen to Dom Pedro II, July 14, 1857, in ibid., p. 247.

Brazil in the late nineteenth century, welcomed not least to meet the labor shortage triggered by the abolition of slavery. The turn of the twentieth century would witness a broader upsurge of Brazilian interest in Portuguese culture and history and vice versa.[68] Brazilian anthropologist Gilberto Freyre's dubious theories of "racial democracy," which held that the supposed racial harmony in Brazil was a direct legacy of Portuguese colonial policies and practices, would be taken up and employed by António de Oliveira Salazar and his accomplices as evidence that the Portuguese empire in Southern Africa in the mid twentieth century was a benign enterprise and that past "achievements" would justify the present debacle and absolve its sins.[69] Luso-Brazilian mutual observation and an awareness of durable, historically forged ties show little sign of disappearing. In early 2011, as Portugal grappled with a deepening debt crisis, the Brazilian president Dilma Rousseff, building on a suggestion made by former president Lula da Silva, floated the idea of Brazil purchasing Portuguese government debt or else giving the Portuguese government a cash injection by buying back Brazilian government debt held by Portugal.[70] The interaction between the two countries has been further quickened by the notable uptick of Portuguese immigration to Brazil. The number of Portuguese living in Brazil leapt from 276,000 in 2010 to 330,000 in 2011.[71]

The historian, however, should not conclude his analysis with a consideration of the present moment, itself so susceptible to sudden changes. In late eighteenth- and early nineteenth-century Portugal, which has been the focus of this study, the prolonged, fecund separation from Brazil, the slow mortification of long-standing Atlantic connections, was marked by false starts, dashed dreams, and misperceived realities. It excited divergent reactions among contemporaries. For Almeida Garrett, writing in 1827, "rarely in History has there been a more important epoch, filled with more extraordinary events and more transcendent results."[72] In 1855, however, the prevailing sentiment was marked by less ebullience. J. F. Henriques Nogueira captured the pervasive despair: "History tells us that we have a glorious past, and of that there is no doubt. But what does History say of our last 50 years? We must be silent. These are painful, sinister, and humiliating years, which are best left unexamined."[73] Yet it is only by excavating

---

[68] Muller 2011.
[69] Dávila 2010, pp. 15–17; on Salazar more generally, see Meneses 2009.
[70] Wearden 2011.   [71] Pidd 2011.   [72] *O Cronista* (1827).
[73] J. F. Henriques Nogueira (1855), quoted in S. P. Matos 1998, p. 281. It should be noted that Nogueira did not share this view; he articulated what he felt to be the general belief about the first half of the nineteenth century held by the Portuguese intelligentsia.

the frustrated ambitions, dead ends, wild schemes, half measures, failures, and ephemeral successes of long-forgotten personages working within long-extinct institutions that historians make comprehensible the scattered fragments bequeathed by an epoch which witnessed the Luso-Atlantic world's simultaneous decomposition, preservation, and reorganization.

Bibliography

PRIMARY

ARCHIVES

Arquivo Central da Marinha (Lisbon, Portugal)
Arquivo Distrital de Braga [Arquivo do Conde da Barca] (Braga, Portugal)
Arquivo Histórico do Itamaraty (Rio de Janeiro, RJ, Brazil)
Arquivo Histórico Militar (Lisbon, Portugal)
Arquivo Histórico Parlamentar (Lisbon, Portugal)
Arquivo Histórico Ultramarino (Lisbon, Portugal)
Arquivo do Museu Imperial (Petrópolis, RJ, Brazil)
Arquivos Nacionais / Torre do Tombo (Lisbon, Portugal)
Arquivo Nacional (Rio de Janeiro, Brazil)
Arquivo Público do Estado do Ceará (Fortaleza, CE, Brazil)
Arquivo Público do Estado do Maranhão (São Luís, MA, Brazil)
Arquivo Público do Estado do Pará (Belém, PA, Brazil)
Arquivo Público Estadual Jordão Emerenciano (Recife, PE, Brazil)
Biblioteca da Academia das Ciências (Lisbon, Portugal)
Biblioteca da Ajuda (Lisbon, Portugal)
Bodleian Library, University of Oxford (Oxford, England)
Boehrer Collection. Spencer Research Library, University of Kansas
    (Lawrence, KS, USA)
Biblioteca Central da Marinha (Lisbon, Portugal)
Biblioteca Nacional de Lisboa [Reservados] (Lisbon, Portugal)
Biblioteca Nacional (Rio de Janeiro, Brazil)
Biblioteca Pública "Benedito Leite" (São Luís, MA, Brazil)
Biblioteca Pública Municipal do Porto (Porto, Portugal)
Hemeroteca do Arquivo Público Estadual Jordão Emerenciano (Recife, PE,
    Brazil)
Hispanic Society of America (New York, NY, USA)
Houghton Library, Harvard University (Cambridge, MA, USA)
Instituto Arqueológico, Histórico e Geográfico Pernambucano (Recife, PE,
    Brazil)
Instituto Histórico e Geográfico de Alagoas (Maceió, AL, Brazil)
Instituto Histórico e Geográfico Brasileiro (Rio de Janeiro, Brazil)
The John Carter Brown Library (Providence, RI, USA)
John Hay Library, Brown University (Providence, RI, USA)
Lilly Library, Indiana University (Bloomington, IN, USA)

The Newberry Library (Chicago, IL, USA)
Sociedade de Geografia de Lisboa (Lisbon, Portugal)
The National Archives (Kew [London], United Kingdom)

PERIODICALS (INCLUDING NEWSPAPERS)

NB: place of publication is Lisbon unless otherwise noted.

A Aguia (1834)
O Amigo do Bem Público, ou a Realista Constitucional (1826)
O Amigo de Dom Pedro (1836)
O Amigo do Povo (Recife [PE], 1829)
Annaes Maritimos e Coloniaes (1840–46)
O Argos da Lei (São Luís [MA], 1825)
O Brasileiro (São Luís [MA], 1830–1832)
O Campeão Portuguez, ou O Amigo do Rei e do Povo (London, 1819–21)
O Carapuceiro (Recife, 1832–34)
O Chaveco Liberal (London, 1829–30)
Chronica Constitucional de Lisboa (1833)
Chronica da Terceira (Angra, 1830–31)
A Cigarra (São Luís [MA], 1829)
O Conciliador Lusitano, ou o Amigo da Paz e União (Lisbon, 1822)
O Conciliador do Maranhão (São Luís [MA], 1821)
O Conciliador do Reino Unido (Rio de Janeiro, 1821)
Considerações do Velho Liberal (1826)
O Constitucional (1828)
O Constitucional (Recife [PE],1830)
O Contrabandista (London, 1835)
A Contra-Mina: Periódico Moral e Político (Lisbon and Coimbra, 1830–31)
Correio Braziliense, ou Armazem Literario (London, 1809–18)
O Correio Interceptado (London, 1825)
O Cruzeiro, ou A Estrela Constitucional dos Portuguezes (London, 1826–27)
O Cruzeiro: Jornal Político, Literario e Mercantil (Recife [PE], 1829)
O Defensor do Throno e do Altar (Coimbra, 1823)
Defeza de Portugal. Semanario Periódico, Político e Moral (1831)
Diário Nacional (Porto, 1820)
O Ecco, Jornal Critico, Litterario, e Politico (1836–38)
Echo do Norte (São Luís [MA], 1834–35)
O Escudo, ou Jornal de Instrucção Politica (1823)
O Espectador Portuguez. Jornal de Litteratura, e Critico (1816–17)
Espelho Político e Moral (London, 1813–14)
O Espreitador (1826)
A Estrela Lusitana (1828)
Folhinha da Terceira (Angra, 1830–32)
A Funda de David Defonte do Clarim Portuguez (1826)
Gaita (1823)
Gazeta Constitucional (1827)
Gazeta de Lisboa (1828–29)
O Harmonizador (Recife [PE], 1832)

O Imparcial (Porto, 1826–28)

O Independente (1821–22)

O Independente (1836)

O Invencivel (1826)

O Investigador Português em Inglaterra, ou Jornal Literario, Político & c. (1818–19)

O Liberal (1820–21)

O Maigo do Bem Público, ou a Realista Constitucional (1826)

Memorial Ultramarino, e Marítimo (1836)

Minerva Constitucional (1820)

Minerva: Folha Política, Literaria e Commercial (São Luís [MA], 1828)

O Movimento (Lisbon, 1835–36)

Novo Correspondente (1837)

O Oraculo (1823)

O Padre Malagrida, ou a Tezoira (Plymouth, 1828–29)

O Palinuro (London, 1830)

Paquete de Portugal (London, 1829–31)

O Paquete do Ultramar (1839–40)

O Patriota (1820–21)

Pavilhão Lusitano (1826)

Periódico para os Bons Realistas (1828)

O Pobre Generoso (1826)

O Popular. Jornal Político, Litterario e Commercial (London, 1824–26)

O Portuguez (London, 1814–17).

O Portuguez Constitucional em Londres (London, 1832)

O Portuguez Constitucional Regenerado (1821–22)

O Portuguez Emigrado, ou Realista Constitucional (Plymouth, 1828)

O Punhal dos Corcundas (1823)

O Realista: Amigo da Observancia da Lei (1826)

Reflexões sobre o Correio Braziliense (1809–10)

A Restauração da Carta (1846)

Reverbero Constitucional Fluminense (Rio de Janeiro, 1821–22).

A Vedeta da Liberdade (1836–39)

O Verdadeiro Liberal (Lisbon, 1821)

PUBLISHED OFFICIAL (GOVERNMENTAL) SOURCES

Actas das Sessões da Câmara dos Senhores Deputados da Nação Portugueza na Sessão Ordinaria de 1828 (Lisbon, 1828).

Actas das Sessões Publicas da Câmara dos Dignos Pares do Reino na Sessão do Anno de 1826 (Lisbon, 1826).

A Amazônia na Era Pombalina. Correspondência Inédita do Governador e Capitão-General do Grão-Pará e Maranhão Francisco Xavier de Mendonça, 1751–1759. Ed. Marcos Carneiro de Mendonça, 3 vols. (São Paulo: IHGB, 1963).

Annaes do Parlamento Brazileiro: A Assembléa Constituinte de 1823. 2 vols. (6 tomos) (Rio de Janeiro: H. J. Pinto, 1879).

Archivo Diplomático da Independência. Vol. VI (Portugal) (Rio de Janeiro, 1925).

Arquivos de Angola (Luanda: Conselho Superior de Estatistica, 1st series. Vol. I (1933), vol. II (1936), and vol. IV (1939)).

Atas do Conselho de Estado, vol. II (1823–34). Ed. José Honorio Rodrigues (Brasília: Senado Federal, 1973).

Boletim e Annaes do Conselho Ultramarino (Lisbon, 1854–67).

British Documents on Foreign Affairs. Reports and Papers from the Foreign Office Confidential Print. Pt I: From the mid-Nineteenth century to World War I. Series D Latin America 1845–1914. Vol. 3: Brazil 1845–93. Ed. George Philip (Bethesda, MD: University Publications of America, 1991).

A Confederação do Equador no Ceará: Manuscritos, 2 vols. Ed. André Frota de Oliveira (Fortaleza: APEC, 2005).

Diário da Câmara do Senhores Deputados da Nação Portugueza (1826–28; 1834–).

Diário das Cortes Geraes e Extraordinárias da Nação Portugueza (Lisbon, 1821–22).

Diário das Cortes da Nação Portugueza (Lisbon, 1822–23).

Documentos para a História das Cortes Gerais da Nação Portuguesa, 8 vols. (Lisbon: Imprensa Nacional, 1883–91).

O Marquês de Pombal e o Brasil. Ed. Marcos Carneiro de Mendonça (São Paulo: Campanhia Editora Nacional, 1960).

Relações de Moçambique Setecentista. Ed. António Alberto de Andrade (Lisbon: Agência Geral de Ultramar, 1955).

Portugal e Brasil: Debates Parlamentares 1821–1836. Ed. Zília Osório de Castro, 2 vols. (Lisbon: Assembléia da República, 2001).

Publicações do Archivo Público Nacional (Rio de Janeiro: Arquivo Nacional, 1912–69).

Relatório Aprezentado á Assemblea Geral Legislativo pelo Ministro e Secretario d'Estado dos Negocios Estrangeiros em a Sessão Ordinaria (Rio de Janeiro, 1833–).

PUBLISHED PRIMARY SOURCES (BOOKS, PAMPHLETS, EPHEMERA, ETC.)

[Abreu e Lima, L. A. de]. *Correspondência Official de Luiz António de Abreu e Lima, actualmente Conde da Carreira, com o Duque de Palmella. Regencia da Terceira e Governo do Porto de 1828–1835* (Lisbon, 1874).

Alexander, James Edward. *Sketches of Portugal during the Civil War of 1832* (London, 1834).

Almeida Garrett, João Baptista da Silva Leitão de. *Discursos Parlamentares* (Lisbon: Typ. da Sociedade Editora, 1904).

Obras Completas, 8 vols. (Lisbon: Editorial Estampa, 1983–92).

Portugal na Balança da Europa (Lisbon: Livros Horizontes, 2005 [1830]).

Alvim, João Carlos, ed. *A Revolta Miguelista contra o Cabralismo: Cartas de António Ribeiro Saraiva e Cândido Figueiredo e Lima* (Lisbon: Assíno e Alvim, 1985).

Andrada e Silva, José Bonifácio de. *Obra política de José Bonifácio (comemorativa do sesquicentenário da independência)* (Brasília: Centro Gráfico do Senado Federal, 1973).

Andrada e Silva, José Bonifácio de. Ed. Jorge Caldeira (São Paulo: Editora 34, 2002).

Andrade, D. G. Lara de. *Reflexões Políticas* (Angra, 1831).

[Anon.]. *A Dynastia e a Revolução de Setembro, ou Nova Exposição da Questão Portugueza da Successão* (Coimbra, 1840).

[Anon.]. *A Facecia Liberal, e o Enthusiasmo Constitucional. Dialogo entre hum Solitario e hum Enthusiasta* (Lisbon, 1822).

[Anon.]. *A Few Words in Answer to Certain Individuals respecting the Present State of Portugal, with Some Observations Concerning the Imposition Practiced upon the Brazilo-Portuguese Bondholders* (London, 1831).

[Anon.]. *A Regeneração Constitucional ou Guerra e Disputa Entre os Corcundas e os Constitucionaes* (Rio de Janeiro, 1821).

[Anon.]. *A Revolução de 9 de Setembro 1836, sua Origem e Effeitos; e a Reacção Cartista em Julho a Setembro 1837* (Porto, 1838).

[Anon.]. *Algumas Considerações Políticas pelo Author de Hontem, Hoje e Amanha* (Lisbon, 1844).

[Anon.]. *Algumas Observações Tanto a Respeito de Estado Actual de Portugal e da Europa* (London, 1831).

[Anon.]. *Algumas Palavras em Resposta ao que Certas Pessoas tem dito e avançado a cerca do Governo Portuguez, com Algumas Observações tanto a respeito de Estado Actual de Portugal e da Europa* (London, 1831).

[Anon.]. *An Authentic Account of Mr Canning's Policy with Respect to the Constitutional Charter of Portugal* (London, 1830).

[Anon.]. *An Historical View of the Revolutions of Portugal* (London, 1827).

[Anon.]. *Analyse do "Projecto de Governo para as Provincias Confederadas"* (Rio de Janeiro, 1824).

[Anon.]. *Analyse e Refutação da Falla de Mr Canning* (Lisbon, 1829).

[Anon.]. *Bazes Eternas da Constituição Política, achadas nas Cartilha do Mestre Ignacio pelo Sacristão do Padre Cura d'Aldea* (Lisbon, 1824).

[Anon./Hum Testemunha Occular]. *Breve Expozição do Esforço Tentado em favor da Carta Constitucional em Portugal em 1837* (Pontevedra, n.d.).

[Anon.]. *Breve Razoamento a Favor da Liberdade Lusitana* (n.p., 1832).

[Anon.]. *Breves Annotações ao Denominado Manifesto do Infante Dom Miguel* (London, n.d.).

[Anon./Um Portuguez]. *Breves Observações de Economia Política em Relação á Inglaterra* (Lisbon, 1845).

[Anon./Hum Liberal e Constitucional]. *Carta ao muito Reverendo Padre José Agostinho de Macedo sobre os Constitucionaes e Liberaes e Alguma Cousa sobre Pedreiros Livres* (Lisbon, 1822).

[Anon.]. *Carta de um Portuguez Emigrado ácerca do ex-Imperador do Brasil e do seu Chamado Manifesto* (Lisbon, 1832).

[Anon.]. *Cathecismo Político para os Bons Realistas* (Lisbon, 1828).

[Anon.]. *Considerações sobre a Constituição da Monarchia Portugueza para as Reformas que se devem Fazer na Carta Constitucional de 29 Abril de 1826* (Lisbon, 1851).

[Anon.]. *Considerações sobre as Cortes do Brasil* (Rio de Janeiro, 1822).

[Anon.]. *Considerações Políticas sobre as Mudanças que Conviria fazer na Constituição Hespanhola a fim de consolidar especialmente em o Reino das Duas Sicilias, escritas em lingua Franceza por Mr Lanjuinais, par de França & c., e publicadas e Paris em Dezembro de 1820* (Lisbon, 1821).

[Anon.]. *Constituição da Grã-Bretanha, ou Principios Fundamentaes do seu Governo Actual* (Lisbon, 1821).

[Anon.]. *Das Sociedades, e das Convencões, ou Constituições* (Rio de Janeiro, 1822).

[Anon.]. *Dialogo entre a Constituição e o Despotismo* (Rio de Janeiro, 1821).

[Anon.]. *Dialogo entre o Corcunda Abatido e o Constitucional Exaltado* (Rio de Janeiro: Imprensa Nacional, 1821).

[Anon.]. *Dom Pedro's Expedition, or Neutrality in Disguise* (London, 1832).

[Anon.]. *Exame da Constituição de D. Pedro, e dos Direitos de D. Miguel, dedicados aos fieis Portuguezes* (Lisbon, 1829).

[Anon.]. *Exposição Genuina da Constituição Portugueza de 1826* (Lisbon, 1828).

[Anon./Lusitano Filantropo]. *Fantasias Constitucionaes, seguidas por algumas Reflexões da Razão, e da Experiencia* (Lisbon, 1821).

[Anon.]. *Golpe de Vista, em que Compendio ... a Legitimidade dos Direitos d'El Rei o Senhor Dom Miguel I no Throno de Portugal* (Lisbon, 1829).

[Anon.]. *Golpe de Vista sobre o Império do Brasil. Escripto por hum Portuguez Curioso que tem por la Viajado* (Lisbon, 1829).

[Anon./JASB]. *Grito da Patria aos Representantes da Nação Portugueza* (Lisbon: Typ. da Gazeta dos Tribunaes, 1845).

[Anon.]. *Investigacoens Politicas de Mr D'Albemireau postas em vulgar com varias ampliacoens pelo author* (London, 1833).

[Anon.]. *Legitimidade da Feliz Regeneração Política de Portugal na Successão do Grande e Immortal Rei o Senhor D. Pedro IV* (Lisbon, 1826).

[Anon.]. *Mais Uma Palavra sobre os Negocios de Portugal em Relação da Europa* (Lisbon, 1832).

[Anon./Um Portuguez, Verdadeiro Amigo da Sua Patria]. *Males que tem Resultado a Portugal dos Tratados de Commercio Celebrados com Inglaterra, a Necessidade de Promover a Nossa Industria Fabril, e Meios de Tirar Vantagem da Navegação e Commercio com as Nossas Possessões Ultramarinas* (Lisbon, 1840).

[Anon.]. *Memoria para a História da Regeneração Portugueza em 1820* (Lisbon, 1823).

[Anon.]. *Monarchia Portugueza Restituida* (Lisbon, 1823).

[Anon.]. *Neutrality; or, Non-Interference of Great Britain in the Present Usurpation of Portugal* (London, 1829).

[Anon.]. *O Conselho da Boa Amizade, ou Projecto de Reconciliação entre os Dous Emisferios* (Rio de Janeiro, [July 29,] 1823).

[Anon.]. *O Constitucional Justificado ás Consciencias dos Anti-Constitucionaes* (Lisbon, 1820).

[Anon.]. *O Liberal Animoso rebatendo a Penultima Pancada Mortal do Liberalismo dada em huma Correspondência Anonima Inserida no Periódico Correio do Porto, no. 173* (Maranhão, 1830).

[Anon./CPC de SM]. *Opúsculo Politica a Facção Revolucionaria de 1820, em Portugal* (Lisbon, 1831).

[Anon.]. *Os Ultimos Recursos dos Antagonistas do Dogma da Legitimidade Reduzidas a Ultima Confutação: Conclusão Política* (Lisbon, n.d.).

[Anon.]. *Perguntas à denominada regencia, seus socios e agentes* (Brussels, 1830).

[Anon.]. *Portugal Antes e Depois de 1846, ou Apontamentos para a História Contemporanea* (Lisbon, 1847).

[Anon./Hum Negociante Portuguez]. *Posição em que se acha Portugal para com Inglaterra segundo os Tratados entre os dois Paizes* (Lisbon, 1834).

[Anon.]. *Quaes são os Bens e os Males que Podem resultar da Liberdade da Imprensa; e Qual he a Influencia que elles Podem ter no Momento em que os Representantes da Nação Portuguesa se vão Congregar?* (Rio de Janeiro, 1821).

[Anon.]. *Reflexões sobre a Necessidade de Promover a União dos Estados de que consta o Reino-Unido de Portugal, Brazil e Algarve nas Quarto Partes do Mundo* (Lisbon, 1822).

[Anon./Hum Cidadão Portuguez]. *Reflexões sobre o Pacto Social, acerca da Constituição de Portugal* (Lisbon, 1821).

[Anon.]. *Reflexões sobre o Partido Apostolico em Portugal* (Lisbon, 1828).

[Anon.]. *Reflexões sobre os Nosso Actual Estado Financeiro* (Lisbon, 1845).

[Anon.]. *Refutação a Resposta Analytica ao Opúsculo intitulado 'Breves Considerações sobre o Commercio, e Navegação de Portugal para a Asia'* (Lisbon, 1836).

[Anon.]. *Refutação da Constituição dos Insurgentes* (Lisbon, 1823).

[Anon.]. *Refutação Methodica das Chamadas Bazes da Constituição Política da Monarquia Portugueza* (Lisbon, 1824).

[Anon.]. *Relação dos Festejos que tiverão lugar em Lisboa nos Memoraveis dias 31 de Julho, 1, 2 de Agosto de 1826* (Lisbon, 1826).

[Anon./Hum Amigo dos Portuguezes]. *Resposta á Carta I de não Sei Quem* (Lisbon, 1830).

[Anon.]. *Resposta ao Jornal dos Debates de 12 D'Agosto e Constitucional de 13* (Paris, 1830).

[Anon./Um Portugues]. *Resposta Analytica ao Opúsculo intitulado 'Breves Considerações sobre o Commercio, e Navegação de Portugal para a Asia'* (Lisbon, 1835).

[Anon.]. *Resumo Histórico do Parlamento de Inglaterra* (Lisbon, 1826).

[Anon.]. *Revolução Anti-Constitucional em 1823, suas Verdadeiras Causas e Effeitos* (London, 1825).

[Anon.]. *Scraps and Stubborn Facts, Refuting the Calumny lately Propagated by the Enemies of D. Miguel, King of Portugal* (London, 1830).

[Anon.]. *Sobre a Constituição da Inglaterra, e as Principaes Mudanças que tem Soffrido* (Lisbon, 1827).

[Anon./Um Perseguido]. *Synchronisms do Reinado de Maria II* (Lisbon, 1848).

[Anon.]. *Verdade Indisputavel. A Carta do Senhor D. Pedro, esse Monumento de Gloria, para huns, e de Infamia para Outros* (Lisbon, 1836).

[Anon.]. *Vozes dos Leaes Portuguezes, ou Fiel Echo das Suas Novas Acclamações á Religião, a El-Rei, e as Cortes destes Reinos*, 2 vols. (Lisbon, 1820).

Arroyo, João Marcellino. *Discursos Pronunciadas na Camara dos Senhores Deputados sobre o Projecto de Reforma Constitucional* (Lisbon: Imprensa Nacional, 1885).

Assento dos Trés Estados do Reino Juntas em Cortes na Cidade de Lisboa (Lisbon, 1828).

[Associação Marítima e Colonial]. *Preguntas que para desevolvimento das Propostas dos Senhores António Maria Couceiro e Joaquim José Gonçalves de Mattos Corrêa dirige a Associação Marítima ás authoridades do Ultramar* (Lisbon, n.d.).

Autos de Abertura e Proposição nas Cortes de Lisboa em 23 de Junho de 1828 de Juramento prestado por el Rei Fidelissimo O Senhor Dom Miguel I (Lisbon, 1828).

Avelar, Felippe Neri Soares de. *A Legitimidade da Exaltação do Muito Alto, e Muito Poderoso Rei, o Senhor D. Miguel Primeiro, ao Throno de Portugal, Demonstrada por Principios de Direito Natural e das Gentes* (Lisbon, 1828).

[Azeredo Coutinho, José Joaquim da Cunha de]. *Obras Econômicas de J. J. da Cunha de Azeredo Coutinho (1794–1804)*. Ed. Sergio Buarque de Holanda (São Paulo: Companhia Editora Nacional, 1966).

Ensaio Económico Sobre o Comercio de Portugal e Suas Colónias (1794). Ed. Jorge Miguel Pedreira (Lisbon: Banco de Portugal, 1992).

[Badcock, Benjamin]. *Rough Leaves from a Journal kept in Spain and Portugal during the years 1832, 1833 & 1834* (London, 1835).

Baillie, Marianne. *Lisbon in the Years 1821, 1822, and 1823* (London, 1825).

Barata, Cipriano. *Sentinela da Liberdade e Outros Escritos (1821–1835)*. Ed. Marco Morel (Editora da Universidade de São Paulo, 2008).

Barboza, António do Carmo Velho de. *Exame Critico das Cortes de Lamego* (Porto, 1845).

Beckford, William. *Italy; with Sketches of Spain and Portugal*. 2nd edn., 2 vols. (London, 1834).

The Journal of William Beckford in Portugal and Spain 1787–1788. Ed. Boyd Alexander (Stroud: Nonesuch, 2006).

Bentham, Jeremy. *Three Tracts Relative to Spanish and Portuguese Affairs with a Continual Eye to English Ones* (London, 1821).

The Correspondence of Jeremy Bentham. Vol. 10 (July 1820–December 1821). Ed. Stephen Conway (Oxford: Clarendon Press, 1994).

Biker, Julio Firmino Judice, ed. *Supplemento á Collecção dos Tratados, Convenções, Contratos e Actos Publicos Celebrados entre a Corôa de Portugal e as Mais Potencias desde 1640*, 30 vols. (Lisbon: Imprensa Nacional, 1872–81).

Boccanegra, Eugenio Bartholomeu. *Voz da Verdade aos Portuguezes* (Lisbon, 1831).

Bollaert, William. *The Wars of Succession of Portugal and Spain from 1826 to 1840; with Résumé of the Political History of Portugal and Spain to the Present Time* (London, 1870).

Borges, José Ferreira. *Autopsia do Manifesto do Infante D. Miguel datado em 28 de Março de 1832* (London, 1832a).

Opinião Jurídica sobre a Questão: Quem Deve Ser o Regente de Portugal Destruida a Usurpação do Infante D. Miguel? (London, 1832b).

Borges Carneiro, Manuel. *Portugal Regenerado em 1820*, 3rd edn. (Lisbon, 1820).

[Borges Carneiro, Manuel/D. C. N Publicola]. *Parabolas Accrescentadas ao Portugal Regenerado* (Lisbon, 1820–21).

Botelho, Sebastião Xavier. *Reflexões Políticas em Julho de 1834* (Lisbon, 1834a).

Resumo Para Servir de Introducção á Memoria Estatistica Sobre os Dominios Portuguezes na Africa Oriental (Lisbon, 1834b).

Escravatura, Beneficios que Podem Provir ás Nossas Possessões d'Africa da Prohibição daquelle Tráfico (Lisbon, 1840).

Bowring, John. *Some Account of the State of the Prisons in Spain and Portugal* (London, 1824).

Brito, Joaquim José Rodrigues de. *Memórias Políticas sobre as Verdadeiras Bases da Grandeza das Nações e Principalmente de Portugal*, 3 vols. (Lisbon, 1803).

Cartas Económico-Políticas sobre a Agricultura e Commercio da Bahia (Lisbon, 1821).

Browne, John Murray. *An Historical View of the Revolutions of Portugal: Since the Close of the Peninsular War; Exhibiting a Full Account of the Events which have led to the Present State of that Country* (London, 1827).

Cabral, Leonel Tavares. *Sobre uma Carta do Snr CJ Xavier ao Snr. Coronel R. P. Pizarro em data de 6 de Janeiro de 1832* (Paris, 1832).

Campos, Benvenuto António Caetano. *Memoria Política sobre a Abolição dos Dizimos: em que se Prova que ella foi Anti-Política, Anti-Religiosa e Prejudicial ao Estado* (Lisbon, 1834).

Caneca, [Frei] Joaquim do Amor Divino. *O Typhis Pernambucano*. Eds. Vamireh Chacon and Leonardo Leite Neto (Brasília: Senado Federal, 1984).

Frei Joaquim do Amor Divino Caneca. Ed. Evaldo Cabral de Mello (São Paulo: Editora 34, 2001).

[Canning, George]. *Corrected Report of Speeches Delivered by the Right Hon. George Canning, in the House of Commons, December 12 1826, on the Motion for an Address to the King in Answer to His Majesty's Message Relative to the Affairs of Portugal* (London, 1826).

Some Official Correspondence of George Canning (London, 1887).

George Canning and his Friends. Ed. Josceline Bagot. 2 vols. (London: John Murray, 1909).

Carlyle, Thomas. *The Life of John Sterling* (Boston: Phillips, Sampson & Co, 1851).

Carneiro, H. J. D'Araújo. *Cartas Dirigidas a SM El-Rey D, João VI desde 1817 a cerca do Estado de Portugal e Brazil* (London, 1821).

Brasil e Portugal, ou Reflecções sobre o Estado Actual do Brasil (Rio de Janeiro, 1822).

Carvalho, Custodio Rebello de. *Bases de todo o Governo Representativo, ou Condições Essenciaes para que a Carta Constitucional da Monarchia Portugueza seja hua Realidade* (London, 1832a).

Da Formação de hum Ministerio Constitucional e da Natureza e Extensão do Direito de Mandar e da Obrigação de Obedecer, precedido de hûa Introducção Histórico-Político sobre Portugal (London, 1832b).

Carvalho, José Liberato Freire de. *Ensaio Político sobre as Causas que Preparão a Usurpação do Infante D. Miguel no Anno de 1828 e com Ella a Queda da Carta Constitucional do ano 1826*, 2nd edn. (Lisbon, 1842 [1830]).

Reflexões sobre um Paragrapho do Manifesto do Senhor Dom Pedro, Duque de Bragança [...] (London, 1832).

Castel-Branco, Joaquim António de Lemos Seixas e. *Memoria Justificativa come que Pertende Provar-se, e com Effeito, Juridicamente se prova a Legitimidade dos Direitos que Assistem ao Serenissimo Senhor Infante Dom Miguel a Coroa e Sceptro de Portugal* (Lisbon, 1831).

Castlereagh, Lord [Robert Stewart]. *Correspondence, Despatches, and other Papers, of Viscount Castlereagh, Second Marquess of Londonderry.* Edited by his brother, Charles William Vane, Marquess of Londonderry. 3rd series, 12 vols. (London, 1853).

Castro, Manoel Patricio Correia de. *Aos Meos Amados Compariotas Habitantes do Reino de Angola e Benguela* (Lisbon, 1822).

Catalogue of the Valuable Library of the Late Honourable Lord Stuart de Rothesay, including many Illuminated and Important Manuscripts ... which will be sold by Auction by Messrs Leigh Sotheby and John Wilkinson ... 31st of May, 1855, & and Fourteeen following days (London: J. Davy and Sons, 1855).

Chagas, Cypriano Rodrigues das. *Compendio do Governo Constitucional* (Lisbon, 1821).

Cleary, David, ed. *Cabanagem: Documentos Ingleses* (Belém: SECULT/IOE, 2002).

Cochrane, Lord [Thomas Cochrane]. *The Life of Thomas, Lord Cochrane, Tenth Earl of Dundonald.* By Thomas, 11th earl of Dundonald, and H. R. Fox Bourne. 2 vols. (London, 1869).

Collecção da Correspondência Official das Provincias do Brazil durante a Legislatura das Cortes Constituintes (Lisbon, 1822).

Collecção de Elogios. Primeiro ao Serenissimo Senhor Infante D. Miguel (Lisbon, 1823).

Collecção Geral e Curiosa de Todos os Documentos Officiaes e Historicos Publicados por Occasião de Regeneração de Portugal desde 24 de Agosto (Lisbon, 1820).

Constâncio, Francisco Solano. *História do Brasil, desde o seu Descobrimento por Pedro Alvares Cabral até á abdicação do Imperador D. Pedro I*, 2 vols. (Paris, 1839).

Leituras e Ensaios de Economia Política (1808–1842). Ed. José Luís Cardoso (Lisbon, Banco de Portugal, 1995).

Corrêa, Elias Alexandre da Silva. *História de Angola* (Lisbon: Editorial Ática, 1937 [1782]).

Correspondence of Princess Lieven and Earl Grey. Ed. and Trans. Guy Le Strange. 2 vols. (London: Richard Bentley and Sons, 1890).

[Cortes of Lisbon]. *As Cortes Geraes e Extraordinarias da Nação Portugueza aos Brasileiros* (Rio de Janeiro, 1821).

Costa, Hipólito José da. *Diário da Minha Viagem para Filadelfia (1798–1799)* (Porto Alegre: Livraria Sulina Editora, 1973).

Costa Almeida, António Lopes da. *Repertorio Remissivo da Legislação da Marinha e do Ultramar Comprehendida nos Annos de 1517 até 1856* (Lisbon, 1856).

Cunha Mattos, Raimundo José da. *Memórias da Companha do Senhor D. Pedro d'Alcantara, Ex-Imperador do Brazil, no Reino de Portugal*, 2 vols. (Rio de Janeiro, 1833).

Daun, José Sebastião de Saldanha Oliveira e. *Diorama de Portugal nos 33 Mezes Constitucionaes* (Lisbon, 1823).

Quadro Histórico-Político dos Acontecimentos mais Memoraveis da História de Portugal desde a Invazão dos Francezes no anno de 1807 até á exaltação de sua Magestade Fidelissima o Senhor d. Miguel I ao Throno dos seus Augustos Predecessores (Lisbon, 1829).

De Staël, Germaine de and Pedro de Souza [Holstein]. *Correspondance.* Ed. Beatrix d'Andlau (Paris: Gallimard, 1979).

[Dias, Miguel António]. *Vozes dos Emigrados Portuguezes* (Paris, 1829).

Documentos dos Arquivos de Windsor. Ed. Ruben Andresen Leitão (Coimbra Editora, 1955).

Documentos para a História Contemporanea. José da Silva Carvalho e o seu Tempo. Ed. António Vianna, 2 vols. (Lisbon: Imprensa Nacional, 1891–94).

Documentos para a História da Independência. Vol. I: Lisbon-Rio de Janeiro (Rio de Janeiro: Biblioteca Nacional, 1923).

Drummond, Ignacio José Correa. *Sonetos em Applauzo ao Feliz Successo da Completa Regeneração da Nação Portugueza. Executado na Praça do Rocio da Corte e Cidade do Rio de Janeiro dia 26 de Fevereiro de 1821* (Rio de Janeiro, 1821).

Estêvão, José. *Obra Política.* Ed. José Tengarrinha, 2 vols. (Lisbon: Portugália Editora, 1962).

Falcão, José Anastacio. *Os Anti-Constitucionaes. Prova-se que são Maos Christãos, Maos Vassallos e os Maiores Inimigos da Nossa Patria* (Rio de Janeiro, 1821).

Fallas do Throno. Desde o Ano de 1823 até o Ano de 1889. Ed. Pedro Calmon (Brasília/São Paulo: Instituto Nacional do Livro, 1977).

Ferreira, Silvestre Pinheiro. *Indicações de Utilidade Pública Oferecidas ás Assembleas Legislativas do Império do Brasil e do Reino de Portugal* (Paris, 1834).

Observações sobre a Constituição do Império do Brasil e sobre a Carta Constitucional do Reino de Portugal, 2nd edn. (Paris, 1835).

Fonseca, Joaquim Bento da. *Memoria Concernente as Companhias de Commercio com Privilegio Exclusivo Dedicada a El-Rei Nosso Senhor* (Lisbon, 1830).

Fonseca, José Maximo Pinto da. *Pernicioso Poder dos Perfidos Validos e Conselheiros dos Reis Destruido pela Constituição* (Rio de Janeiro, 1822).

Fronteira, Marquês de. *Memórias do Marquês de Fronteira e d'Alorna D. José Trazimundo Mascarenhas Barreto. Ditada por êle próprio em 1861* (Coimbra: Imprensa da Universidade, 1928).

[Galvão, Inocencio da Roche]. *O Despotismo Considerado nas suas Causas e Efeitos. Discurso Oferecido a Nação Portugueza* (Rio de Janeiro, 1821).

[Gama, Bernardo José da]. *Memoria sobre as Principaes Causas, por que deve o Brasil Reassumir os Seus Direitos, e Reunir as Suas Provincias, Offerecida ao Príncipe Real* (Rio de Janeiro, 1822).

Gama e Castro, José da. *O Novo Príncipe, ou o Espirito dos Governos Monarchicos,* 2nd edn. (Rio de Janeiro, 1841).

Diário da Emigração para Italia (Lisbon: Typ. Henrique Torres, 1933).

Gorani, José. *Portugal, A Côrte e o País de 1765 a 1767.* Trans. Castelo Branco Chaves (Lisbon: Editorial Ática, 1945).

Graham, Maria. *Journal of a Voyage to Brazil, and Residence There, during Part of the Years 1821, 1822, 1823* (London, 1824).

[Guerreiro, José António]. *Manifesto dos Direitos de Sua Madestade Fidelissima, a Senhora Dona Maria Segunda; e Exposicão da Questão Portugueza,* 2nd edn. (Paris, 1831 [1829]).

Guimarães Junior, António Joaquim. *Memoria sobre a Exploração de Costa ao Sul de Benguella na Africa Occidental e Fundação do Primeiro Estabelecimento Commercial na Bahia de Mossamedes* (Lisbon, 1842).

Guizot, François. *Du Gouvernement de la France depuis la Restauration; Suivi de notes sur les Révolutions d'Espagne, de Naples et du Portugal* (Paris, 1821).

Haller, Karl Ludwig von. *Analisis de la Constitución Española* (Madrid, 1823).

Hemingway, Joseph. *History of the Spanish Revolution, commencing with the establishment of Constitutional Government of the Cortes in the year 1812 and Brought Down to its Overthrow by the French Arms* (London, 1823).

Herculano, Alexandre. "Elogio Histórico de Sebastião Xavier Botelho." In Herculano, *Opúsculos IX* [www.gutenberg.org, accessed October 18, 2011].

A Europa e Nós: Uma Polémica de 1853 (A. Herculano contra A. P. Lopes de Mendonça). Ed. Maria Filomena Mónica (Lisbon: ICS, 1996).

Holland, Lord [Henry Richard Vassall Fox]. *Foreign Reminisces*, 2nd edn. (London, 1851).

Holland, Lord. *The Holland House Diaries 1831–40: The Diary of Henry Richard Vassall Fox, 3rd Lord Holland* (London: Routledge & Kegan Paul, 1977).

Koster, Henry. *Travels in Brazil* (London, 1816).

Lago, Antônio Bernardino Pereira do. *Estatistica Histórico-Geográfica da Província do Maranhão [1822]* (São Paulo: Editora Siciliano, 2001).

Cinco Annos D'Emigração na Inglaterra, na Bélgica, e na França, 2 vols. (Lisbon, 1834).

Lavradio, Marquês do. *Cartas do Rio de Janeiro (1769–1776)* (Rio de Janeiro: Instituto Estadual do Livro, 1978).

Lavradio, Marquês do [Almeida, Francisco José de]. *Introducção á Convocação das Cortes debaixo das Condições do Juramento pela Nação* (Lisbon, 1820).

Lavradio, Marquês do. *Breves Considerações sobre a Necessidade e Meios de Melhorar as Prisões de Portugal* (Paris, 1834).

Memórias do Conde do Lavradio (Coimbra, 1933).

Leitão, António José de Lima. *Arrasoada acerca das Eleições para as Proximas Côrtes em 1834* (Lisbon, 1834).

[Leopoldina, Dona]. *Cartas de uma Imperatriz.* Ed. Angel Bojadsen (São Paulo: Editora Estação Liberdade, 2006).

Lieven, Princess [Dorothea von Lieven]. *The Private Letters of Pricess Lieven to Prince Metternich 1820–26.* Ed. and trans. Peter Quennell (New York: E. P. Dutton, 1938).

Lobo, Francisco Alexandre. *Obras de D. Francisco Alexandre Lobo, Bispo de Vizeu*, 3 vols. (Lisbon, 1848–53).

Cartas do Exílio (Lisbon: União Gráfica, 1944).

Lopes, Joaquim José Pedro. *Reflexões sobre a Necessidade de Promover a União dos Estados de que consta o Reino Unido de Portugal, Brazil e Algarve nas Quatro Partes do Mundo* (Lisbon, 1822). In Raymund Faoro, ed., *O Debate Político no Processo da Independencia* (Rio: Conselho Federal de Cultura, 1973).

Lima, José Joaquim Lopes. *Os Corcundas do Porto. Farça em Verso com o Himno Anti-Corcundas* (Rio de Janeiro, 1821).

Luccock, John. *Notes on Rio de Janeiro and the Southern Ports of Brazil, taken during a Residence Ten years in that Country, from 1808 to 1818* (London, 1820).

Luz Soriano, Simão José da. *Vida do Marquez de Sá da Bandeira e Reminscencia de Alguns dos Successos Mais Notaveis que durante tiveram logar em Portugal,* 2 vols. (Lisbon: Typ. da Viuva Sousa Neves, 1887–88).
Relevações da Minha Vida e Memórias de Alguns Factos e Homens Meus Contemporâneos (Porto: A. Leite Guimarães Editor, 1891).
Macedo, José Agostinho de. *Parecer sobre a Maneira Mais Facil, Simples e Exequivel da Convocação das Cortes Geraes do Reino no Actual Systema Político da Monarchia Representativa e Constitucional* (Lisbon, 1820).
Cartas de José Agostinho de Macedo a seu Amigo Joaquim J. Pedro Lopes (Lisbon, 1827).
A Besta Esfolada (Lisbon, 1828–29a).
[Preface to] *D. Miguel I. Obra Mais Completa e Concludente que tem apparecido na Europa sobre a Legitimidade Direitos do Senhor D. Miguel ao Throno de Portugal* (Lisbon, 1829b).
O Desengano: Periódico Político, e Moral (Lisbon, 1830).
Mackintosh, [Sir] James. *The Miscellaneous Works of the Right Honorable Sir James Mackintosh* (Philadelphia, 1848).
Madre de Deos, Faustino José de. *O Combate Dedicado ao Serenissimo Senhor D. Miguel, Infante de Portugal, ou a Declamação e Protesto das Cortes Extraordinarias* (Lisbon, 1823a).
Epistola á Nação Francesa, na qual se Demonstrão os Subversivos Principios das Constituições Modernas, e se prova que a Maçonaria tem sido a Authora, e Directora da Revolução de Portugal (Lisbon, 1823b).
A Constituição de 1822, Comentada e Desenvolvida na Pratica, 2nd edn. (Lisbon, 1823c).
Os Povos, e os Reis. Opúsculo Offerecida aos Portuguezes (Lisbon, 1825).
Justificação da Dissidencia Portugueza Contra a Carta Constitucional (Lisbon, 1828a).
Notas Pertecentes ao Opúsculo Intitulado Os Povos e os Reis (Lisbon, 1828b).
Annotações ao Artigo Communicado na Gazeta no. 103 (Lisbon, 1828c).
Absurdos Civis, Politicos e Diplomaticos (Lisbon, 1828d).
Justificação da Dissidencia Portugueza contra a Carta Constitucional em Novembro de 1827 (Lisbon, 1828e).
A Facção, e a Contemplação (Lisbon, 1828f).
Poucas Palavras Sobre Garrett (Lisbon, 1829).
A Revolução e Portugal (Lisbon, 1832).
Magalhães, Joaquim António de [with Francisco da Gama Lobo Botelho]. *Analyse das Observacoens do General Saldanha, Publicadas em Paris com a data de 13 de Novembro de 1829* (London, 1830).
Manning, William R., ed. *Diplomatic Correspondence of the US concerning the Independence of the Latin-American Nations,* 2 vols. (New York: Oxford University Press, 1925).
Manning, William R. *Diplomatic Correspondence of the United States/ Inter-American Affairs, 1831–1860.* Vol. II (Washington: Carnegie Endowment for International Peace, 1932).
[Martins, Manoel António]. *Memoria Demonstrativa sobre a Necessidade de Novas Providencias para a Provincia de Cabo-Verde* (Lisbon, 1822).
Mawe, John. *Travels in the Interior of Brazil* (London, 1812).

Melo, Daniel Garção de. *Peças Interessantes relativas á Revolução Effeituada no Pará, a Fim de se Unir a Sagrada Causa da Regeneração Portugueza* (Lisbon, 1821).

Memórias Económicas da Academia Real das Ciências de Lisboa, Para a Adiantamento da Agricultura, das Artes e da Industria em Portugal e Suas Conquistas (1789–1815). Ed. José Luís Cardoso, 5 vols. (Lisbon: Banco de Portugal, 1990).

Mendonça, Marcos Carneiro de, ed. *D. João VI e o Império no Brasil a Independência e a Missão Rio Maior* (Rio de Janeiro: Xerox do Brasil SA, 1984).

Menezes, Francisco d'Alpuim de. *Portugal e o Brazil: Observações Políticas aos Ultimos Acontecimentos do Brazil* (Lisbon, 1822).

Menezes, Joaquim António de Carvalho de. *Memoria Geografica, e Política das Possessões Portuguezas n'Africa Occidental* (Lisbon, 1834).

Metternich, Prince [Klemens von]. *Memoirs of Prince Metternich*. Vol III & IV (1815–29). Ed. Richard Metternich and trans. Alexander Napier (New York: Howard Fertig, 1970 [1888]).

[Miguel, Dom Infante]. *Aos Leaes e Honrados Portuguezes* (Lisbon, 1823).

Miranda, José António de. *Memoria Constitucional e Política sobre o Estado Presente de Portugal e do Brasil* (Rio de Janeiro, n.d.).

Mouzinho da Silveira, José Xavier. *Obras*. Ed. Miriam Halpern Pereira *et al.*, 2 vols. (Lisbon: Fundação Calouste Gulbenkian, 1989).

Napier, [Sir] Charles. *An Account of the War in Portugal between Don Pedro and Don Miguel*, 2 vols. (London, 1836).

[Neuville, Hyde de Neuville]. *Mémoirs of Baron Hyde de Neuville: Outlaw, Exile, Ambassador*. Translated and Abridged by Frances Jackson, 2 vols. (London, 1913).

Neves, José Acúrsio das. *Obras Completas*. Ed. António Almodovar, 6 vols. (Porto: Edições Afrontamento, 1989).

Palma, Joaquim Placido Galvão. *Memorial que Tem Honra de Fazer Subir a Augusta Presença de SM Fidelissima o Senhor D. João Sexto* (Lisbon, 1821).

Palmela, Duque de [Pedro de Souza Holstein]. *Discursos Parlamentares do Duque de Palmella* (Lisbon, 1844).

Despachos e Correspondência do Duque de Palmella, 4 vols. (Lisbon, 1851–69).

[Palmerston, Lord (Henry John Temple)]. *Royal Commission on Historical Manuscripts. Prime Ministers' Papers Series. Palmerston, I: Private Correspondence with Sir George Villiers (afterwards Fourth Earl of Clarendon) as Minister of Spain, 1833–1837*. Eds. Roger Bullen and Felicity Strong (London: HM Stationery Office, 1985).

Passos, José da Silva and Manuel da Silva Passos. *Exame d'Algumas Opiniões e Doutrinas que os Senhores Felipe Ferreira d'Araújo e Castro e Silvestre Pinheiro Ferreira* (Paris, 1832a).

Parecer de Dous Advogados da Caza do Porto (Paris, 1832b).

[Passos, Manuel da Silva]. *Segundo Memorial sobre o Estado Presente de Portugal, e como não ha Razão nem Força para Tirar a Senhora Dona Maria II sua Coroa* (Paris, 1831a).

Memorando para a Ilha Terceira (Paris, 1831b).

Breve Razoamento a favour da Liberdade Lusitana e da Excellente Senhora D. Maria II (Paris, 1832).

Pecchio, Giuseppe. *Anecdotes of the Spanish and Portuguese Revolutions* (London, 1823).

Pedro I, Dom. *Cartas de D. Pedro I a D. João VI Relativas á Independência do Brasil*. Ed. Augusto de Lima Junior (Rio de Janeiro: Jornal de Commercio, 1941).

Pedro V. *Cartas de D. Pedro V aos seus Contemporaneos*. Ed. Ruben Andresen Leitão (Lisbon: Livraria Portugal, 1961).

Penalva, Marquês de [Fernando Teles da Silva Caminha e Menezes, 3rd Marquis]. *Dissertação a Favor da Monarquia, onde se prova pela razão, authoridade e experiencia ser este o melhor, e mais justo de todos os governos; e que os nossos reis são os mais absolutos, e legitimos senhores de seus reinos* (Lisbon, 1799 [1798]).

Dissertação sobre as Obrigações do Vassalo, 3rd edn. (Lisbon, 1945 [1804]).

Pereira, José Maria Dantas. *Escritos Maritimos e Academicos a Bem do Progresso dos Conhecimentos Uteis, e Mormente da Nossa Marinha, Industria e Agricultura* (Lisbon, 1828).

Memoria para a História do Grande Marquez de Pombal, no Concernente à Marinha (Lisbon, 1832).

Pinto, António Joaquim de Gouvea. *Os Caracteres da Monarquia* (Lisbon, 1824).

Demonstração dos Direitos que Competem ao Senhor D. Miguel I (Lisbon, 1828).

Pizarro, R [odrigo] P [into]. *Desembarque do Conde de Saldanha na Ilha Terceira, Impedido pela Marinha Ingleza* (Brest, 1829).

Norma das Regencias de Portugal, Applicada a Minoridade de S. M. a Rainha D. Maria II (Paris, 1832 [1831]).

Pombal, Marquês de [Sebastião José de Carvalho e Melo]. *Escritos Económicos de Londres (1741–1742)*. Ed. José Barreto (Lisboa: Biblioteca Nacional, 1986).

Cartas e Outras Obras Selectas do Marquez de Pombal, 2 vols. (Lisbon, 1822).

Porchester, Lord [H. J. G. H. Carnarvon]. *The Last Days of the Portuguese Constitution* (London, 1830).

Porto Santo, Conde de [Saldanha da Gama, António]. *Memoria sobre as Colonias de Portugal, situadas na Costa Occidental d'Africa, Mandado pelo Antigo Governador do Reino de Angola* em 1814 (Lisbon, 1839).

[Portugal]. *Manifesto da Nação Portuguesa aos Soberanos, e Povos da Europa* (Lisbon, 1820).

Projecto da Constituição Política para a Nação Portugueza, Offerecida ás Cortes que se vão Congregar em Janeiro de 1821 (Lisbon: Typ. Rollandiana, 1820).

Projecto de Constituição Portugueza Accommodada á Hespanhola para ser Offerecido ás Nossas Cortes (Lisbon, 1821).

Ratton, Jacome. *Recordações de Jacome Ratton sobre Occorências do seu Tempo em Portugal de Maio de 1747 a Setembro de 1810* (Lisbon: Fenda, 1992 [1813]).

Reis, Jacinto Rodrigues Pereira. *O Amigo da Razão, ou Carta aos Redactores do Reverbero* (Rio de Janeiro, 1822).

Relatório dos Commissarios enviados por SM Fidelissima ao Rio de Janeiro com os Documentos de sua Correspondencia Official (n.p., dated by JCB as 1824).

Resende, Marquês de [Silva, António Telles da]. "Correspondência do Marquez de Resende (1823–54)," *RIHGB*, 80 (1916), 149–525.

Ribeiro, Luiz José. *Advertencias Uteis Dirigidas ao Soberano, e Augusto Congresso Nacional das Cortes, na Occasião que elle se Constituio em Corpo Legislativo* (Lisbon, 1821).

Rocha, António da Silva Lopes. *Injusta Acclamação do Serenissimo Infante D. Miguel, ou Analyse e Refutação Juridica do Assente dos Chamados Trés Estados do Reino de Portugal de 11 Julho de 1828* (London, 1828).

Rocha, M. A. Coelho da. *Ensaio sobre a História do Governo e Legislação de Portugal para Servir de Introducção ao Estudo do Direito Patrio*, 6th edn. and 7th edn. (Coimbra: Imprensa da Universidade, 1887, 1896 [1841]).

Sá, José António de. *Defeza dos Direitos Nacionaes e Reaes da Monarquía Portugueza*, 2nd edn. (Lisbon, 1816).

Sá da Bandeira, Visconde [Bernardo de Sá Nogueira de Figueiredo]. *O Tráfico da Escravatura, e o Bill de Lord Palmerston* (Lisbon, 1840).

Factos e Considerações Relativos aos Direitos de Portugal sobre os Territorios de Molembo, Cabinda e Abmriz (Lisbon, 1855).

Diário da Guerra Civil (1826–1832). Ed. José Tengarrinha, 2 vols. (Lisbon: Seara Nova, 1975–76).

Saldanha, António de Sousa e Vasconcelos Simão de. *As Cartas de Manuel de Saldanha, 1o Conde de Ega e 47o vice-rei da Índia para Sebastião José de Carvalho e Melo e seus Irmãos (1758–1765)* (Lisbon: Gabinete Português de Estudos Humanísticos, 1984).

Saldanha, Duque de [João Carlos de Saldanha de Oliveira e Daun]. *Exposição Franca, e Ingenua dos Motivos que Decidirão o Brigadeiro João Carlos de Saldanha e Oliveira e Daun a não Aceitar o Commando da Expedição a Bahia* (Lisbon, 1823).

Observações do Conde de Saldanha sobre a Carta, que os Membros da Junta do Porto dirigirão a S. M. o Imperador do Brasil, em 5 d'Agosto de 1828, e mandarão publicar no Paquête de Portugal em Outubro de 1829 (Paris, 1829).

Salgado, Graça, ed. *Memórias sobre a Escravidão* (Rio de Janeiro: Arquivo Nacional, 1988).

Sanctos, P. Luiz Gonçalves dos. *Memórias para Servir a História do Reino de Brasil*, 2 vols. (Lisbon, 1825).

Santa Barbara, [Frei] António de. *Sermão em Acção de Graças pela Desejada e Muito Feliz União da Junta Provisoria do Governo Supremo do Reino com o Governo Interino de Lisboa* (Lisbon, 1820).

Santarém, Visconde de. *Memórias para a História e Theoria das Cortes Geraes, que em Portugal se Celebrarão pelos Trés Estados do Reino Ordenados, Composta neste Anno de 1824* (Lisbon, 1827).

Quadro Elementar das Relações Politicas e Diplomaticas de Portugal com as Diversas Potencias do Mundo desde o Principio da Monarchia Portugueza até Nossos Dias (Lisbon, 1828).

Memoria sobre a Prioridade dos Descobrimentos Portuguezes na Costa d'Africa Occidental (Paris, 1841).

Correspondência do 2o Visconde de Santarém. Ed. Rocha Martins, 8 vols. (Lisbon, Alfredo Lamas Motta & Cia, Lda, 1918).

São Boaventura, [Frei] Fortunato de. *Oração Gratulatoria ... O Senhor D. Miguel I, o Desejado* (Coimbra, 1828).

São José, Francisco de. *Explicação da Nova Palavra Constituição em Forma de Dialogo* (Lisbon, 1830).

Saraiva, A. R. *Cartas Conspiradoras* (London, 1844).

O Miguelista em Londres. Mistiforio Político, Satirico, Litterario, Histórico, Poetico, Documentario (London, 1870).

Diário de Ribeiro Saraiva, 1831–1888, 2 vols. (Lisbon, 1915).

[Seabra, António Luiz de]. *Exposição Apologetica dos Portuguezes Emigrados na Bélgica que Recusarao Prestar o Juramento delles Exigido no dia 26 de Agosto de 1830* (Bruges, 1830).

Serrão, Joel, ed. *Liberalismo, Socialismo, Republicanismo. Antologia de Pensamento Político Português*, 2nd edn. (Lisbon: Livros Horizonte, 1979).

Shaw, Charles. *Personal Memoirs and Correspondence ... Comprising a Narrative of the War for Constitutional Liberty in Spain and Portugal*, 2 vols. (London, 1837).

Silva, Francisco Gomes da. *Memórias Offerecidas a Nação Brasileira* (London, 1831).

Silva, J. L. d'Araújo e. *Disenganos do Liberalismo* (Lisbon, 1851).

Silva Gaio, António de Oliveira. *Mário: Episódios das Lutas Civis Portuguesas de 1820–1834* (Porto: Lello & Irmão, 1981 [1867]).

Silva Lisboa, José da [Visconde de Cairu]. *Principios de Direito Mercantil, e Leis de Marinha, Para uso da Mocidade Portugueza* (Lisbon: 1804).

Refutação das Reclamações contra o Commercio Inglez (Rio de Janeiro, 1810).

Observações sobre a Prosperidade do Estado pelos Liberaes Principios da Nova Legislação do Brasil (Bahia, 1811a).

Memoria Económica Sobre a Franqueza do Commercio dos Vinhos do Porto (Rio de Janeiro, 1811b).

Extratos das Obras Políticas e Económicas de Edmund Burke, 2 vols. (Rio de Janeiro, 1812).

Memoria da Vida Pública do Lord Wellington (Rio de Janeiro, 1815).

Memoria dos Beneficios Políticos do Governo de El-Rey Nosso Senhor D. João VI (Rio de Janeiro: 1818).

Estudos do Bem Comum e Economia Política; ou Ciência das Leis Naturais e Civis de Animar e Dirigir a Geral Industria e Promover a Riqueza Nacional, e Prosperidade do Estado (Rio de Janeiro: IPEA/INDES, 1975 [1820]).

Causa do Brasil no Juizo dos Governos e Estadistas da Europa (Rio de Janeiro, 1822a).

Império do Equador na Terra da Santa Cruz. Voto Philanthropico do Robert Southey (Rio de Janeiro, 1822b).

[Silva Lisboa/signed 'Fiel á Nação'], *Falsidades do Correio e Reverbero Contra o Escriptor das Reclamações do Brasil* (Rio de Janeiro, 1822c).

Roteiro Brazilico, ou Collecção de Principios e Documentos de Direito Político (Rio de Janeiro, 1822d).

Appello á Honra Brasileira contra a Facção dos Federalistas de Pernambuco (Rio de Janeiro, 1824a).

Rebate Brasileiro Contra o Typhis Pernambucano (Rio de Janeiro, 1824b).
Pesca de Tubarões do Recife em Tres Revoluções dos Anarchistas de Pernambuco (Rio de Janeiro, 1824c).
Constituição Moral e Deveres do Cidadão com Exposição da Moral Pública Conforme o Espírito da Constituição do Império (João Pessoa: Editora Universitaria-Universidade Federal da Paraíba, 1998 [1824d]).
Independência do Império do Brasil Apresentada aos Monarchas Europeos por Mr Beauchamp (Rio de Janeiro, 1824e).
Contestação da História e Censura de Mr De Pradt Sobre Successos do Brasil (Rio de Janeiro, 1825).
Leituras de Economia Política, ou Direito Económico conforme a Constituição Social e Garantias da Constituição do Império do Brasil, Dedicadas a Mocidade Brasileira (Rio de Janeiro, 1827).
Espirito da Proclamação do Senhor Dom Pedro I á Nação Portugueza (Rio de Janeiro: Typographia Nacional, 1828).
Cautela Patriotica (Rio de Janeiro, 1828).
Manual de Política Orthodoxa (Rio de Janeiro, 1832a).
Principios da Arte de Reinar de Príncipe Catholico e Imperador Constitucional (Rio de Janeiro, 1832b).
Escritos Económicos Escolhidos: 1804–1820. Ed. Antônio Almodovar (Lisbon: Banco de Portugal, 1993).
Visconde de Cairu. Ed. António Penalves Rocha (São Paulo: Editora 34, 2001).
Silva Maia, Joaquim José da. *Memórias Historicas, Políticas e Filosoficas da Revolução do Porto em Maio de 1828, e dos Emigrados Portugueses pela Hespanha, Inglaterra, França e Bélgica* (Rio de Janeiro, 1841).
[Soares, João Pereira Baptista Vieira]. *A Saudosa Despedida dos Escravos Miguelistas ou, o Ultimo Adeus a seu Senhor D. Miguel* (Rio de Janeiro, 1833).
Soares Franco, Francisco. *Ensaio sobre os Melhoramentos de Portugal e do Brasil* (Lisbon, 1820–21).
Sousa, Maria Leonor Machado de. *Um Ano de Diplomacia Luso-Americana: Francisco Solano Constâncio (1822–23)* (Lisbon, 1988).
Sousa Sequeira, Antonio de Oliva de. *Projecto para o estabelecimento político do Reino Unido de Portugal, Brasil e Algarves* (Coimbra, 1821).
Southey, Robert. *Letters Written During a Short Residence in Spain and Portugal,* 2nd edn. (Bristol, 1799).
History of Brazil, 2nd edn. (London, 1822).
Souza Coutinho, Domingos de [Conde de Funchal]. *Introducção as Notas Supprimidas em 1821, ou Raciocinio sobre o Estado Presente e Futuro da Monarchia Portugueza* (London, 1823).
Souza Coutinho, Rodrigo de. *Textos Políticos, Económicos e Financeiros (1783–1811).* Ed. Andrée Mansuy Diniz Silva, 2 vols. (Lisbon: Banco de Portugal, 1993).
[Talleyrand, Prince de (Charles Mauriced de Talleyrand-Périgord)]. *Memoirs of the Prince of Talleyrand. Edited with a preface and notes by the Duc de Broglie.* Trans. Angus Hall, 5 vols. (New York and London: G. P. Putnam's Sons, 1892).
Tolmer, Alexander. *Reminiscences of an Adventurous and Chequered Career at Home and in the Antipodes,* 2 vols. (London, 1882).

Tomás, Manuel Fernandes. *A Revolução de 1820*. Ed. J. Tengarrinha (Lisbon: Seara Nova, 1974).

Trigoso de Aragão Morato, Francisco Manuel. *Memoria sobre a Successão da Coroa de Portugal, no Caso de não Haver Descendentes de sua Magestade Fidelissima a Rainha D. Maria II* (Lisbon, 1836).

Memórias ... Começadas e Escrever por ele mesmo em Princípios de Janeiro de 1824. Ed. Ernesto de Campos de Andrada (Coimbra: Imprensa da Universidade, 1933).

Vandelli, Domenico. *Aritmética Política, Economia e Finanças*. Ed. José Vicente Serrão (Lisbon: Banco de Portugal, 1994).

[Vasconcelos, B. P. de]. *Bernardo Pereira de Vasconcelos*. Ed. José Murilo de Carvalho (São Paulo: Editora 34, 1999).

Victoria, Queen. *The Letters of Queen Victoria. A Selection from Her Majesty's Correspondence between the years 1837 and 1861*, 3 vols. (London: John Muir, 1908).

Vieira, Feliz Baptista. *Discurso sobre o Estado Religiozo, Político e Diplomatico de Portugal* (Lisbon, 1840).

Vilhena, Luís dos Santos. *A Bahia no século XVIII* ([Salvador]: Editôra Itapuá, 1969).

Pensamentos políticos sobre a Colônia (Rio de Janeiro: Ministério da Justiça, Arquivo Nacional, 1987).

Villa-Garcia, Visconde de. *Analyse e Refutação da Falla de Mr Canning Pronunciada na Câmara dos Comuns em 12 de Dezembro de 1826* (Lisbon, 1829).

Walsh, William. *Notices of Brazil in 1828 and 1829* (London, 1830).

Walton, William. *A Reply to Two Pamphlets* (London, 1830).

[Wellington, Duke of (Arthur Wellesley)], *Despatches, Correspondence, and Memoranda of Field Marshall Arthur Duke of Wellington, K.G.. Ed by his son, the Duke of Wellington*, 15 vols. (London, 1858–72/Reprint Millwood, NY: Kraus reprint, 1973).

Royal Commission on Historical Manuscripts: The Prime Ministers' Papers: Wellington. Political Correspondence I: 1833–November 1834. Ed. John Brooke and Julia Gandy (London: HM Stationery Office, 1975).

SECONDARY

ABBREVIATIONS

AHR	*American Historical Review*
CLAR	*Colonial Latin American Review*
CSSH	*Comparative Studies in Society and History*
EHQ	*European History Quarterly*
HAHR	*Hispanic American Historical Review*
HJ	*Historical Journal*
JLAS	*Journal of Latin American Studies*
JMH	*Journal of Modern History*
LARR	*Latin American Research Review*

LBR   Luso-Brazilian Review
PP   Past & Present
PSR   Portuguese Studies Review
RIHGB   Revista do Instituto Histórico e Geográfico Brasileiro

BOOKS AND ARTICLES

Abreu, J. Capistrano de. *Ensaios e Estudos (Critica e História)*, 3rd edn. (Rio de Janeiro: Livraria Briguiet, 1938).
Actas do Congresso o Marquês de Pombal e a Sua Época (10–12 Nov. 1999) (Oeiras: Câmara Municipal, 2001).
Adelman, Jeremy, ed. *Colonial Legacies: The Problem of Persistence in Latin American History* (London and New York: Routledge, 1999).
Adelman, Jeremy. *Sovereignty and Revolution in the Iberian Atlantic* (Princeton University Press, 2006).
"An Age of Imperial Revolutions," *AHR*, 113:2 (2008), 319–40.
Aguiar, António Augusto de. *Vida do Marquez de Barbacena* (Rio de Janeiro: Imprensa Nacional, 1896).
Albertone, Manuela and António de Francesco, eds. *Rethinking the Atlantic World: Europe and America in the Age of Democratic Revolutions* (Basingstoke: Palgrave Macmillan, 2009).
Alden, Dauril. "The Undeclared War of 1771–1777: the Climax of Luso-Spanish Platine Rivalry," *HAHR*, 41 (1961), 55–74.
Royal Government in Colonial Brazil (Berkeley and Los Angeles: University of California Press, 1969).
"Indian versus Black Slavery in the State of Maranhão during the Seventeenth and Eighteenth Centuries." In Richard L. Garner and William B. Taylor, eds. *Iberian Colonies, New World Societies: Essays in Memory of Charles Gibson* (self-printed, 1986).
Alencastro, Luiz Felipe de. *O Trato dos Viventes: Formação do Brasil no Atlântico Sul, Séculos XVI e XVII* (São Paulo: Companhia das Letras, 2000).
Alexander, Robert. *Re-Writing the French Revolutionary Tradition* (Cambridge University Press, 2003).
Alexandre, Valentim. *Os Sentidos do Império: Questão Nacional e Questão Colonial na Crise do Antigo Regime Português* (Porto: Edições Afrontamento, 1993).
Velho Brasil, Novas Áfricas: Portugal e o Império (1808–1975) (Porto: Edições Afrontamento, 2000).
A Questão Colonial no Parlamento (1821–1910) (Lisbon: Assembleia da República/ Dom Quixote, 2008).
Alexandre, Valentim and Jill Dias, eds. *O Império Africano, 1825–1890* (Lisbon: Editorial Estampa, 1998). [NB: Vol. X of the *Nova História da Expansão Portuguesa*, directed by Joel Serrão and A. H. de Oliveira Marques].
Almeida, Joselyn M., ed. *Romanticism and the Anglo-Hispanic Imaginary* (New York: Rodopi, 2010).

Almeida, Luís Ferrand de. "Aclimatação de Plantas do Oriente no Brasil durante os Séculos XVII e XVIII," *Revista Portuguesa de História*, 15 (1975), 339–481.

Almeida Santos, Mário Márcio de. *Nascimento Feitosa e a Revolução de 1848* (Recife: Universidade Federal de Pernambuco, Editora Universitária, 1978).

Almodovar, António. *A Institucionalização da Economia Política em Portugal* (Porto: Edições Afrontamento, 1995).

Alonso García, Gregorio and Daniel Muñoz Sempere, eds. *Londres y el Liberalismo Hispánico* (Madrid: Iberoamericana, 2011).

Alvarado, Javier. *Constitucionalismo y Codificación en las Provincias de Ultramar. La Supervivencia del Antiguo Régimen en la España de XIX* (Madrid: Centro de Estudios Politicos y Constitucionales, 2001).

Amorim, Maria Adelina and Ana Leal de Faria, eds. *O Reino sem Corte 1807– 1821* (Parede: Tribuna, 2011).

Andrade, Manuel Correia de. *A Guerra dos Cabanos* (Rio de Janeiro: Conquista, 1965).

Andrews, George Reid. *Afro-Latin America* (Oxford University Press, 2004).

Anna, Timothy E. "The Buenos Aires Expedition and Spain's Secret Plan to Conquer Portugal 1814–1820," *The Americas*, 34:3 (1978), 356–80.

Spain and the Loss of America (Lincoln, NE and London: University of Nebraska Press, 1983).

Araújo, Ana Cristina, ed. *O Marquês de Pombal e a Universidade* (Coimbra: Imprensa da Universidade, 2000).

Araújo, Ana Cristina, *A Cultura das Luzes em Portugal. Temas e Problemas* (Lisbon: Livros Horizontes, 2003).

Armitage, David. *The Declaration of Independence: A Global History* (Cambridge, MA and London: Harvard University Press, 2007).

Armitage, David and Sanjay Subrahmanyan, eds. *The Age of Revolutions in Global Context, c. 1760–1840* (Basingstoke: Palgrave Macmillan, 2010).

Armitage, John. *The History of Brazil: from the Period of the Arrival of the Braganza Family in 1808 to the Abdication of D. Pedro the First in 1831*, 2 vols. (London, 1836).

Arriaga, José d'. *A Inglaterra, Portugal e suas Colonias* (Lisbon: Typ. do Comercio, 1882).

História da Revolução Portugueza de 1820, 3 vols. (Lisbon, 1886).

Arruda, José Jobson de A. *O Brasil no Comércio Colonial* (São Paulo: Editora Ático, 1980).

Assunção, Matthias Röhrig. "Elite Politics and Popular Rebellion in the Construction of Post-Colonial Order. The Case of Maranhão, Brazil (1820–41)," *JLAS*, 31:1 (1999), 1–38.

Augello, Massimo M. and Marco E. L. Guidi, eds. *The Spread of Political Economy and the Professionalisation of Economics: Economic Societies in Europe, America and Japan in the Nineteenth Century* (London and New York: Routledge, 2001).

Azevedo, Julião Soares de. *Condições Económicas da Revolução Portuguesa de 1820* (Lisbon: E.C.E., 1944).

Bailyn, Bernard. "The Idea of Atlantic History," *Itinerario*, 20 (1996), 19–44.

Bailyn, Bernard and Patricia Denault, eds. *Soundings in Atlantic History: Latent Structures and Intellectual Currents 1500–1830* (London and Cambridge, MA: Harvard University Press, 2009).

Ball, Terence and J. G. A. Pocock, eds. *Conceptual Change and the Constitution* (Lawrence, KS: University of Kansas Press, 1988).

Barata, Alexandre Mansur. *Maçonaria, Sociabilidade Ilustrada e Independência do Brasil (1790–1822)* (São Paulo: Annablume, 2006).

Barbosa, Rosana. *Immigration and Xenophobia: Portuguese Immigrants in Early Nineteenth-century Rio de Janeiro* (Lanham, MD: University Press of America, 2009).

Barickman, B. J. *A Bahian Counterpoint: Sugar, Tobacco, Cassava and Slavery in the Recôncavo, 1780–1860* (Stanford University Press, 1998).

Barman, Roderick. *Brazil: The Forging of a Nation, 1798–1852* (Stanford University Press, 1988).

Citizen Emperor: Pedro II and the Making of Brazil, 1825–1891 (Stanford University Press, 1999).

Barman, Roderick and Jean Barman. "The Role of the Law Graduate in the Political Elite of Imperial Brazil," *Journal of Inter-American Studies and World Affairs*, 18:4 (1976), 423–50.

Barretto, José. *A Ideologia Liberal no Processo da Independência do Brasil (1789–1824)* (Brasília: Câmara dos Deputados, 1973).

Barretto, José and António Paim. *Evolução do Pensamento Político Brasileiro* (Belo Horizonte: Editora Itatiaia, 1989).

Barretto, Vicente. *Ideologia e Política no Pensamento de José Bonifácio de Andrada e Silva* (Rio de Janeiro: Zahar Editores, 1977).

Barzun, Jacques. *Berlioz and the Romantic Century*, 2 vols. (Boston: Little, Brown & Co, 1950).

Bauss, Rudy. "Rio Grande do Sul in the Portuguese Empire: The Formative Years 1777–1808," *The Americas*, 39:4 (1983), 519–35.

Bayly, C. A. *Imperial Meridian. The British Empire and the World, 1780–1830* (London: Longman, 1989).

The Birth of the Modern World, 1780–1914. Global Connections and Comparisons (Oxford: Blackwell, 2004).

"The 'Revolutionary Age' in the Wider World, c. 1790–1830." In Richard Bessel *et al.*, eds., *War, Empire and Slavery 1770–1830* (Basingstoke: Palgrave Macmillan, 2009).

Recovering Liberties. Indian Thought in the Age of Liberalism and Empire (Cambridge University Press, 2012).

Beales, Derek. *Prosperity and Plunder: European Catholic Monasteries in the Age of Revolution, 1650–1815* (Cambridge University Press, 2003).

Beattie, Peter. "Brazilian History in an Asian Millennium? Reading Dead People's Mail for a Living in a New Global Era," *LBR*, 40 (2003), 31–50.

Beirão, Caetano. *D. Maria I 1777–92. Subsídios para a Revisão do seu Reino*, 2nd edn. (Lisbon: Empresa Nacional de Publicidade, 1944).

Bender, Gerald J. *Angola under the Portuguese: the Myth and Reality* (Berkeley: University of California Press, 1978).

Benton, Lauren. *A Search for Sovereignty: Law and Geography in European Empires 1400–1900* (Cambridge University Press, 2010).

Berbel, Márcia Regina. *A Nação como Artefacto: Deputados do Brasil nas Cortes Portuguesas (1821–1822)* (São Paulo: Editora HUCITEC, 1999).

"A Constituição Espanhola no Mundo Luso-Americano (1820–23)," *Revista de Indias*, vol. 68/no. 242 (2008), 225–54.

Berkeley, Alice D., ed., *New Lights on the Peninsula War. International Congress on the Iberian Peninsula. Selected Papers 1780–1840. The Calouste Gulbenkian Center. Lisbon, Portugal 24th–26th July 1989* (Cacilhas: The British Historical Society of Portugal, 1991).

Bernardes, Denis Antônio de Mendonça. *O Patriotismo Constitucional: Pernambuco 1820–22* (São Paulo/Recife: Editora Hucitec, 2006).

Bernardino, Teresa. *Sociedade e Atitudes Mentais em Portugal (1777–1810)* (Lisbon: Imprensa Nacional-Casa da Moeda, 1986).

Berquist, Emily. "Early Anti-Slavery Sentiment in the Spanish Atlantic World, 1765–1817," *Slavery and Abolition*, 31:2 (2010), 181–205.

Bethell, Leslie. *The Abolition of the Brazilian Slave Trade: Britain, Brazil and the Slave Trade Question 1807–1869* (Cambridge University Press, 1970a).

George Canning and the Independence of Latin America (London: Canning House 1970b).

Bethell, Leslie, ed. *Colonial Brazil* (Cambridge University Press, 1984).

Bethell, Leslie. "The Independence of Brazil." In Bethell, ed., *Brazil: Empire and Republic 1822–1930* (Cambridge University Press, 1989), 3–44

Charles Landseer. Desenhos e Aquarelas de Portugal e do Brasil, 1825–1826 (Rio de Janeiro: Instituto Moreira Salles, 2010).

Bethell, Leslie and José Murilho de Carvalho. "1822–1850." In Bethell, ed., *Brazil: Empire and Republic 1822–1930* (Cambridge University Press, 1989), 45–112.

Bethencourt, Francisco. "Entrevista: Francisco Bethencourt," *Topoi: Revista de História* [Rio de Janeiro], 6 (2003), 165–78.

The Inquisition. A Global History, 1478–1834 (Cambridge University Press, 2009).

Bethencourt, Francisco and Kirti Chaudhuri, eds. *História da Expansão Portuguesa*, 5 vols. (Lisbon: Círculo de Leitores, 1998).

Bethencourt, Francisco and Diogo Ramada Curto, eds. *Portuguese Oceanic Expansion 1400–1800* (Cambridge University Press, 2007).

Bieber, Judy. "Post-Modern Ethnographer in the Backlands: An Imperial Bureaucrats's Perceptions of Post-Independence Brazil," *LARR*, 33:2 (1998), 37–72.

Birmingham, David. *Trade and Conflict in Angola: The Mbundu and Their Neighbours Under the Influence of the Portuguese, 1483–1790* (Oxford: Clarendon Press, 1966).

A Concise History of Portugal (Cambridge University Press, 2003).

Blackburn, Robin. *The Overthrow of Colonial Slavery 1776–1848* (London: Verso, 1988).

The American Crucible. Slavery, Emancipation and Human Rights (London: Verso, 2011).

Blanchard, Peter. *Under the Flags of Freedom. Slave Soldiers and the Wars of Independence in Spanish South America* (University of Pittsburgh Press, 2008).

Blanning, T. C. W. *The Culture of Power and the Power of Culture: Old Regime Europe, 1660–1789* (Oxford University Press, 2001).

Blaufarb, Rafe. "The Western Question: The Geopolitics of Latin American Independence," *AHR*, 112:3 (2007), 742–63.

Bleichmar, Daniela. *Visible Empire. Botanical Expeditions and Visual Culture in the Hispanic Enlightenment* (University of Chicago Press, 2012).

Boehrer, George C. A. "The Flight of the Brazilian Deputies from the Cortes Gerais of Lisbon, 1822," *HAHR*, 40:4 (1960), 497–512.

Boléo, Luísa V. de Paim. *D. Maria I. A Rainha Louca* (Lisbon: A Esfera dos Livros, 2009).

Bonavides, Paulo, "Constitucionalismo Luso-Brasileiro: Influxos Recíprocos." In Jorge Miranda, ed. *Perspectivas Constitucionais: Nos 20 Anos da Constituição de 1976*, vol. I (Coimbra Editora, 1996).

Bonifácio, Maria de Fátima. *Seis Estudos sobre o Liberalismo Português* (Lisbon: Editorial Estampa, 1991).

História da Guerra Civil da Patuleia 1846–7 (Lisbon: Editorial Estampa, 1993).

D. Maria II (Lisbon: Círculo de Leitores, 2005).

Uma História de Violência Política: Portugal de 1834–1851 (Lisbon: Tribuna, 2009).

Borucki, Alex. "The Slave Trade to the Rio de la Plata, 1777–1812: Trans-Imperial Networks and Atlantic Warfare," *CLAR*, 20:1 (2011), 81–107.

Bowman, Joyce L. "'Legitimate Commerce' and Peanut Production in Portuguese Guinea, 1840s-1880s," *Journal of African History*, 28 (1987), 87–106.

Boxer, Charles R. *Salvador de Sá and the Struggle for Brazil and Angola 1602–1686* (London: The Athlone Press, 1952).

The Golden Age of Brazil, 1695–1750: Growing Pains of a Colonial Society (Berkeley: University of California Press, 1962).

Brading, D. A. *The First America: The Spanish Monarchy, Creole Patriots, and the Liberal State, 1492–1867* (Cambridge University Press, 1991).

Braga, Theophilo. *História da Universidade de Coimbra*. Vol. III (1700–1800) and Vol. IV (1801–1872) (Lisbon: Typ. Real das Sciencias, 1898, 1902).

Garrett e o Romantismo (Porto: Casa Editora Livraria Chardon, 1903).

Brancato, Augusto Aquino. "A Carta Constitucional Portuguesa de 1826 na Europa: Um Exame a partir de Documentos Espanhóis," *Revista de História das Ideias* [Coimbra], 10 (1988), 457–73.

Brandão, Ulysses de Carvalho Soares. *A Confederação do Equador* (Recife: IHGP, 1924).

Pernambuco de Outr'óra: A Confederação do Equador (Recife, 1924).

Brazão, Eduardo. *Relações Diplomáticas de Portugal com a Santa Sé: O Reconhecimento do Rei D. Miguel (1831)* (Lisbon: Academia Internacional da Cultura Portuguesa, n.d.).

Breña, Roberto. *El Primer Liberalismo Español y los Procesos de Emancipación de América 1808–1824. Una Revisión Historiográfica del Liberalismo Hispánico* (Mexico City: El Colegio de México, 2006).

Brigola, João Carlos Pires. *Colecções, Gabinetes e Museus em Portugal no Século XVIII* (Lisbon: Fundação Calouste Gulbenkian, 2003).

Brito, Manuel Carlos de. *Opera in Portugal in the Eighteenth Century* (Cambridge University Press, 1989).

Broers, Michael. *Europe under Napoleon 1799–1815* (London: Arnold, 1996).

Bron, Gregoire. "The Exiles of the Risorigimento: Italian Volunteers in the Portuguese Civil War (1832–34)," *Journal of Modern Italian Studies*, 14:4 (2009), 427–44.

Brown, Matthew. *Adventuring through Spanish Colonies: Simón Bolívar, Foreign Mercenaries and the Birth of New Nations* (Liverpool University Press, 2006).

Brown, Matthew, ed. *Informal Empire in Latin America: Culture, Commerce and Capital* (Oxford: Blackwell, 2008).

Bullen, Roger. *Palmerston, Guizot and the Collapse of the Entente Cordial* (London: The Athlone Press, 1974).

"France and the Problem of Intervention in Spain, 1834–1836," *HJ*, 20:2 (1977), 363–93.

Burdiel, Isabel. "Myths of Failure, Myths of Success: New Perspectives on Nineteenth-century Spanish Liberalism," *JMH*, 70 (1998), 892–912.

Burkholder, M. A. and D. S. Chandler. *From Impotence to Authority: the Spanish Crown and the American Audiencias, 1687–1808* (London: University of Missouri Press, 1977).

Butler, Marilyn. *Romantics, Rebels, and Reactionaries: English Literature and its Background, 1760–1830* (Oxford University Press, 1981).

Caetano, Marcelo. *O Conselho Ultramarino. Esboço da Sua História* (Lisbon: Agência Geral do Ultramar, 1967).

Constituições Portuguesas, 4th edn. (Lisbon and São Paulo: Verbo, 1978).

Campanhole, Adriano and Hilton Lobo Campanhole, eds. *Todas as Constituições do Brasil* (Sao Paulo, 1971).

Campinos, Jorge. *Carta Constitucional de 1826* (Lisbon: Decibel, 1975).

Campos, Fernando. *O Frei Fortunato de S. Boaventura: Mestre da Contra-Revolução* (Lisbon, 1928).

O Pensamento Contra-Revolucionário em Portugal (sec. XIX) (Lisbon: J. Fernandes Júnior, 1931).

Campos, Fernanda Maria Guedes de, org. *A Casa Literária do Arco do Cego (1799–1801). Bicentenário* (Lisbon: Biblioteca Nacional/Casa da Moeda, 1999).

Canaveira, Manuel Filipe Cruz. *Liberais Moderados e Constitucionalismo Moderado (1814–1852)* (Lisbon: INIC, 1988).

Capela, José. *A Burguesia Mercantil do Porto e as Colónias (1834–1900)* (Porto: Edições Afrontamento, 1975).

O Tráfico de Escravos nos Portos de Moçambique, 1733–1904 (Porto: Edições Afrontamento, 2002).

Capela, José Viriato, ed. *Política, Administracão, Economia e Finanças Publicas Portuguesas (1750–1830)* (Braga: I.C.S./Universidade do Minho, 1993).

Capela, José Viriato. *A Revolução do Minho de 1846: Os Dificeis Anos de Implantação do Liberalismo* (Braga: Governo Civil do Distrito, 1997).

Cardim, Pedro. *Cortes e Cultura Política no Portugal do Antigo Regime* (Lisbon: Edições Cosmos, 1998).

Cardoso, António Monteiro and António Canto Machado. *A Guerrilha do Remexido* (Sintra: Publicações Europa-America, n.d.).

Cardoso, Ciro Flamarion S. *Economia e Sociedade em Areas Coloniais Periféricas. Guiana Francesa e Pará (1750–1817)* (Rio de Janeiro: Edições Graal Ltd., 1984).

Cardoso, José Luís. *O Pensamento Económico em Portugal nos Finais do Século XVIII, 1780–1808* (Lisbon: Editorial Estampa, 1989).

Cardoso, José Luís, coord. *A Economia Política e Os Dilemas do Império Luso-Brasileiro (1790–1822)*. (Lisbon: Colecção Outras Margens, 2001).

"O Liberalismo Económico na Obra de José da Silva Lisboa," *História Econômica & História de Empresas*, 5:1 (2002), 147–64.

Cardoso, José Luís, ed. *O Tratado de Methuen (1703): Diplomacia, Guerra, Política, e Economia* (Lisbon: Livros Horizonte, 2003).

Cardoso, José Luís. "A Abertura dos Portos do Brasil em 1808: dos Factos á Doutrina," *Ler História* [Lisbon] 54 (2008), 9–31.

Cardoso, José Luís and Pedro Lains, eds. *Paying for the Liberal State: The Rise of Public Finance in Nineteenth-century Europe* (Cambridge University Press, 2010).

Cardoso, José Luís, Nuno Gonçalo Monteiro, and José Vicente Serrão, eds. *Portugal, Brasil e a Europa Napoleónica* (Lisbon: Imprensa de Ciências Sociais, 2010).

Carr, Raymond. *Spain 1808–1975*, 2nd edn. (Oxford University Press, 1982).

Carreira, António. *As Companhias Pombalinas de Grão-Pará e Maranhão e Pernambuco e Paraiba* (Lisbon: Editorial Presença, 1983).

Carvalho, Darcy. *Desenvolvimento e Livre Comercio. As Idéias Econômicas e Sociais do Visconde de Cairu. Um Estudo de História do Pensamento Econômico Brasileiro* (São Paulo: Instituto de Pesquisas Econômicas, 1985).

Carvalho, José Murilo de. "Political Elites and State-building: the Case of Nineteenth-century Brazil," *CSSH*, 24:3 (1982), 378–99.

Teatro de Sombras: A Política Imperial (São Paulo: Edições Vertice, 1988).

Carvalho, Marcus J. M. de. "O Outro Lado da Independência: Quilombolas, Negros e Pardos em Pernambuco (Brazil), 1817–23," *LBR*, 43:1 (2006), 1–27.

"The 'Commander of All Forests' against the 'Jacobins' of Brazil." In John Gledhill and Patience Schell, eds. *New Approaches to Resistance in Brazil and Mexico* (Durham: Duke University Press, 2012).

Carvalho dos Santos, Maria Helena, ed. *Pombal Revisitado: Comunicações ao Colóquio Internacional Organizado pela Comissão das Comemoracões do 2 Centenário da Morte do Marquês de Pombal*, 2 vols. (Lisbon: Editorial Estampa, 1984).

Castells, Irene. *La Utopía Insurrecional del Liberalismo: Torrijos y las Conspiraciones Liberales de la Década Ominosa* (Barcelona: Editorial Critica, 1989).

Castro, Armando, ed. *A Dominação Inglesa em Portugal*, 2nd edn. (Porto: Edições Afrontamento, 1974).

Castro, Zília Osório de. "Poder Régio e os Direitos da Sociedade. O 'Absolutismo de Compromisso' no Reinado de D. Maria I," *Ler História*, 23 (1992), 11–22.

Cavaliero, Roderick. *The Independence of Brazil* (London and NY: I. B. Tauris, 1993).

Centeno, Miguel A. *Blood and Debt: War and the Nation-State in Latin America* (University Park: Pennsylvania State University Press, 2002).

[Centro de História da Universidade do Porto]. *Estudos de História Contemporânea Portuguesa. Homenagem ao Professor Victor de Sá* (Lisbon: Livros Horizonte, 1991).

Cervo, Amado Luiz and José Calvet de Magalhães. *Depois das Caravelas: As Relações entre Portugal e Brasil 1808–2000* (Editora Universidade de Brasília, 2000).

Chamberlain, Muriel E. *Lord Aberdeen: A Political Biography* (London and New York: Macmillan, 1983).

Cheney, Paul. *Revolutionary Commerce: Globalization and the French Monarchy* (London and Cambridge, MA: Harvard University Press, 2010).

Chiaramonte, José Carlos. *Nation and State in Latin America: Political Language during Independence.* Trans. Ian Barnett (Buenos Aires: Teseo 2010a).

"The 'Ancient Constitution' after Independence (1808–52)," *HAHR*, 90:3 (2010b), 455–72.

Church, Clive. *Europe in 1830: Revolution and Political Change* (London: George Allen & Unwin, 1983).

Chust, Manuel, coord. *1808: La Eclosión Juntera en el Mundo Hispano* (Mexico City: Fondo de Cultura Económica, 2007).

Chust Calero, Manuel and Ivana Frasquet. *La trascendencia del liberalismo doceañista en España y en América* (Valencia: Generalitat Valenciana, 2004).

Clarence-Smith, W. G. *Slave, Peasants and Capitalists in Southern Angola, 1840–1956* (Cambridge University Press, 1979).

The Third Portuguese Empire, 1825–1975: A Study in Economic Imperialism (Manchester University Press, 1985).

Cleary, David. "'Lost Altogether to the Civilised World': Race and Cabanagem in Northern Brazil, 1750–1850," *CSSH*, 40:1 (1998), 109–35.

Coelho, Geraldo Mártires. *Anarquistas, Demagogos e Dissidentes: A Imprensa Liberal no Pará de 1822* (Belém: Edições CFJUP, 1993).

Coleman, Deirdre. "Re-living Jacobinism: Wordsworth and the Convention of Cintra," *The Yearbook of English Studies*, 19 (1989), 144–61.

Collingham, H. A. C. *The July Monarchy. A Political History of France 1834–1848* (London: Longman, 1988).

Conrad, Robert. *World of Sorrow. The African Slave Trade to Brazil* (Baton Rouge and London: LSU Press, 1986).

O Constitucionalismo de D. Pedro I no Brasil e em Portugal (Arquivo Nacional de Rio de Janeiro, 1972).

Cooper, Frederick. *Colonialism in Question. Theory, Knowledge, History* (London and Los Angeles: University of California Press, 2005).

Correia, Maria Alcina Ribeiro. *Sebastião José de Carvalho e Mello na Corte de Viena de Áustria. Elementos para o Estudo da sua Vida Pública (1744–49)* (Lisbon: Instituto de Alta Cultura/University of Lisbon, 1965).

Costa, Emília Viotti da. *The Brazilian Empire: Myths and Histories* (University of Chicago Press, 1985).

Costa, Fernando Dores. *A Guerra da Restauração 1641–1668* (Lisbon: Livros Horizontes, 2004).

"Army Size, Military Recruitment and Financing in Portugal during the Period of the Peninsular War 1808–11," *e-Journal of Portuguese History*, 6:2 (2008), 1–27.

Costa, Sérgio Corrêa da. *As Quatro Coroas de D. Pedro I* (Rio de Janeiro: Paz e Terra, 1995 [1940]).

Costeloe, Michael P. *Response to Revolution: Imperial Spain and the Spanish American Revolutions, 1810–1840* (Cambridge University Press, 1986).

Couto, Carlos. *O Pacto Colonial e a Interferência Brasileira no Domínio das Relações Economicas entre Angola e o Reino no Século XVIII* (Marília: Departamento de Educação, 1971).

Os Capitães-Mores em Angola no Século XVIII (Subsídio Para o Estudo da sua Actuação) (Luanda: Instituto de Investigacão Científica de Angola, 1972).

Craiutu, Aurelian. *Liberalism under Siege: The Political Thought of the French Doctrinaires* (New York: Lexington Books, 2003).

Cunha, Alexandre Mendes. "Political Science and Cameralism in Portuguese Enlightened Reformism: Economic Ideas and the Administration of the State during the Second Half of the Eighteenth century," *e-Journal of Portuguese History*, 8:1 (2010), 1–12.

Cunha, P. Penner da. *Sob Fogo: Portugal e Espanha entre 1800 e 1820* (Lisbon: Livros Horizontes, 1988).

Cunha, Rosalina. "Documentos Diversos sobre a Sociedade Marítima, Militar e Geográfica, 1798–1809," *Ocidente* [Lisbon], 72 (1967), 57–66.

Curtin, Philip D. *The Image of Africa. British Ideas and Action, 1780–1850* (Madison: University of Wisconsin Press, 1964).

Death by Migration: Europe's Encounter with the Tropical World in the Nineteenth Century (Cambridge University Press, 1989).

D'Albian, Denyse. *Dom Pedro I, Empereur du Bresil, Roi de Portugal (1798–1834)* (Paris: Librairie Plon, 1959).

Dakin, Douglas. *The Greek Struggle for Independence 1821–33* (Berkeley: University of California Press, 1973).

Dávila, Jerry. *Hotel Trópico. Brazil and the Challenge of African Decolonization 1950–1980* (Durham and London: Duke University Press, 2010).

Davis, John A. *Naples and Napoleon. Southern Italy and the European Revolutions (1780–1860)* (Oxford University Press, 2006).

Davis, Kathleen. *Periodization and Sovereignty: How Ideas of Feudalism and Secularization Govern the Politics of Time* (Philadelphia: University of Pennsylvania Press, 2008).

De Dijn, Annelien. "A Pragmatic Conservatism: Montesquieu and the Framing of the Belgian Constitution (1830–31)," *History of European Ideas*, 28 (2002), 227–45.

"Balancing the Constitution: Bicameralism in Post-Revolutionary France, 1814–31," *European Review of History*, 12:2 (2005), 249–68.

French Political Thought from Montesquieu to Tocqueville. Liberty in a Levelled Society? (Cambridge University Press, 2008).

De Vos, Paula. "Natural History and the Pursuit of Empire in Eighteenth-century Spain," *Eighteenth-Century Studies*, 40:2 (2007), 209–39.

Delaforce, Angela. *Art and Patronage in Eighteenth-century Portugal* (Cambridge University Press, 2002).

Delson, Roberta. "Planners and Reformers: Urban Architects of Late Eighteenth-century Brazil," *Eighteenth Century Studies*, 10:1 (1976), 40–51.

Dias, José Henrique Rodrigues. *José Ferreira Borges: Política e Economia* (Lisbon: INIC, 1988).

Diffie, Bailey. *A History of Colonial Brazil 1500–1792* (Malabar, FL: RE Krieger Publishing Company, 1987).

Disney, A. R. *A History of Portugal and the Portuguese Empire. From Beginnings to 1807*, 2 vols. (Cambridge University Press, 2009).

Domingues, Ângela. *Viagens da Exploracão Geográfica na Amazónia em Finais do Século XVIII: Política, Ciência e Aventura* (Lisbon: Região Autónoma da Madeira, 1991).

"Para um Melhor Conhecimento dos Domínios Coloniais: A Constituição de Redes de Informação no Império Português em Finais de Setecentos," *Ler História*, 39 (2000), 19–34.

Quando os Índios Eram Vassalos. Colonização e Relações de Poder no Norte do Brasil na Segunda Metade do Século XVIII (Lisbon: Commissão Nacional para as Comemorações dos Descobrimentos Portugueses, 2000).

Domingues, Mario. *D. Maria I e a Sua Epoca* (Lisbon: Romano Torres, 1972).

Drayton, Richard H. *Nature's Government: Science, Imperial Britain, and the "Improvement" of the World* (New Haven and London: Yale University Press, 2000).

Droz, Jacques. *Europe between Revolutions, 1815–1848*. Trans. Robert Baldick (New York: Harper & Row, 1967).

Dubois, Laurent. "An Enslaved Enlightenment: Re-thinking the Intellectual History of the French Atlantic," *Social History*, 31:1 (2006), 1–14.

Duffy, James. *A Question of Slavery* (Cambridge, MA: Harvard University, 1967).

Dwyer, Philip. *Talleyrand* (London: Longman/Pearson, 2002).

Dym, Jordana. *From Sovereign Villages to National States: City, State and Federation in Central America, 1759–1839* (Albuquerque: University of New Mexico Press, 2006).

"Citizen of Which Republic? Foreigners and the Construction of National Citizenship in Central America, 1825–1845," *The Americas*, 64:4 (2008), 477–510.

Echeverri, Marcela. "Popular Royalists, Empire, and Politics in Southwestern Colombia, 1809–1819," *HAHR*, 91:2 (2011), 237–69.

Eisenstadt, Shmuel N. "Multiple Modernities." In Eisenstadt, ed. *Multiple Modernities* (New Brunswick and London: Transaction Publishers, 2005).

Elliott, J. H. "Revolution and Continuity in Early Modern Europe," *PP*, 42 (1969), 35–56.

Empires of the Atlantic World: Britain and Spain in America 1492–1830 (New Haven and London: Yale University Press, 2006).

Esdaile, Charles. *Spain in the Liberal Age: From Constitution to Civil War, 1808–1936* (Oxford: Blackwell, 2000).

The Peninsular War: A New History (New York: Palgrave Macmillan, 2003).

Evans, Richard. "Epidemics and Revolutions: Cholera in Nineteenth-century Europe," *PP*, 120 (1988), 123–46.

Fabry, Mikulas. *Recognizing States: International Society and the Establishment of New States since 1776* (Oxford University Press, 2010).

Falcon, Francisco José Calazans. *A Época Pombalina (Política Econômica e Monarquia Ilustrada)* (São Paolo: Editoria Ática, 1982).

"Aspectos Interpretativos da História Político-Administrativa da América Portuguesa nos Séculos XVII–XVIII," *Revista Portuguesa de História* [Coimbra], 31:2 (1996), 411–26.

"As Reformas Ilustradas Pombalinas no Ambito da História Político-Administrativo de Brasil-Colônia." In *Actas do Congresso o Marquês de Pombal e a sua Epoca (10–12 de Novembro* 1999) (Oeiras, 2001).

Faoro, Raymundo. *Os Donos do Poder. Formação do Patronato Político Brasileiro* (São Paulo: Editôra Globo, 1958).

Ferguson, Niall. *The House of Rothschild. Vol. I: Money's Prophets 1798–1848* (London: Viking, 1998).

Fernández Sebastián, Javier, dir. *Diccionario Político y Social del Mundo Iberoamericano. La Era de las Revoluciones, 1750–1850* (Iber-Conceptos I) (Madrid: Fundación Carolina *et al.*, 2009).

Fernández Sebastián, Javier and Juan Francisco Fuentes, dirs. *Diccionario Político y Social del Siglo XIX Español* (Madrid: Alianza Editorial, 2002).

Ferraz, Socorro. *Liberais & Liberais: Guerras Civis em Pernambuco no Século XIX* (Recife: Editora Universitaria da UFPE, 1996).

Ferreira, Manoel Rodrigues. *A Ideologia Política de Independência* (São Paulo: EDANCE, 1972).

Ferreira, Maria de Fatima Sá e Melo. *Rebeldes e Insubmissos: Resistências Populares ao Liberalismo (1834–44)* (Porto: Edições Afrontamento, 2002).

Ferreira, Roquinaldo. "Abolicionismo e fim do Tráfico de Escravos em Angola, séc. XIX," *Cadernos do CHDD* [Rio de Janeiro], 4 (2005), 159–76.

"The Suppression of the Slave Trade and Slave Departures from Angola, 1830s-1860s." In David Eltis and David Richardson, eds., *Extending the Frontiers: Essays on the New Transatlantic Slave Trade Databases* (New Haven and London: Yale University Press, 2008).

Flood, Christopher and Hugo Frey. "Questions of Decolonization and Post-Colonialism in the Ideology of the French Extreme Right." In James D. Le Sueur, ed., *The Decolonization Reader* (London: Routledge, 2003), 399–413.

Florentino, Manolo Garcia. *Em Costas Negras. Uma História do Tráfico Atlântico de Escravos entre a África e o Rio de Janeiro (Séculos XVIII–IX)* (Rio de Janeiro: Arquivo Nacional, 1995).

"Slave Trading and Slave Traders in Rio de Janeiro, 1790–1830." In José C. Curto and Paul E. Lovejoy, eds., *Enslaving Connections: Changing Cultures of Africa and Brazil during the Era of Slavery* (Amherst, NY: Humanity Books, 2004).

Flory, Thomas. *Judge and Jury in Imperial Brazil 1808–1871. Social Control and Political Stability in the New State* (Austin: University of Texas Press, 1981).

Fonseca, Fernando Taveira de. "Scientiae Thesaurus Mirabilis: Estudantes de Origem Brasileira na Universidade de Coimbra (1601–1850)," *Revista Portuguesa de História* [Coimbra], 33:2 (1999), 527–59.

Fontana, Biancamaria. *Benjamin Constant and the Post-Revolutionary Mind* (New Haven and London: Yale University Press, 1991).

Fontana, Josep. *La Crisis del Antiguo Régimen 1808–1833* (Barcelona: Editorial Critica, 1979).

De en Medio del Tiempo: La Segunda Restauración Española, 1823–1834 (Barcelona: Crítica, 2006).

Fowler, Will, ed. *Forceful Negotiations: The Origins of the Pronunciamiento in Nineteenth-century Mexico* (Lincoln, NE: University of Nebraska Press, 2010).

Fradera, Josep M. "Why were Spain's Special Overseas Laws Never Enacted?" In Richard Kagan and Geoffrey Parker, eds., *Spain, Europe, and the Atlantic World: Essays in Honor of John H. Elliott* (Cambridge University Press, 1995), 334–49.

Colonias para Después de un Imperio (Barcelona: Edicions Bellaterra, 2005).

"Reading Imperial Transitions: Spanish Contraction, British Expansion, and American Irruption." In Alfred W. McCoy and Francisco A. Scarano, eds., *Colonial Crucible: Empire and the Making of the Modern American State* (Madison, WI and London: University of Wisconsin Press, 2009), 34–62.

Fragoso, João and Manolo Florentino. *O Arcaísmo como Projeto: Mercado Atlântico, Sociedade Agrária e Elite Mercantile em uma Economia Colonial Tardia*, 4th edn. (Rio de Janeiro: Civilização Brasileira, 2001).

Fragoso, João, Maria Fernanda Bicalho and Maria de Fatima Gouvêa, orgs. *O Antigo Regime nos Trópicos: A Dinâmica Imperial Portuguesa (Séculos XVI–XVIII)* (Rio de Janeiro: Civilização Brasileira, 2001).

França, José-Augusto. *O Romantismo em Portugal. Estudo de Factos Socio-Culturais*, 6 vols. (Lisbon: Livros Horizontes, 1974).

Lisboa Pombalina e o Iluminismo, 3rd edn. (Lisbon: Bertrand Editora, 1983).

Franklin, Robert. *Lord Stuart de Rothesay* (Sussex, UK: Book Guild Publishing, 2008).

Freitas, Caio de. *George Canning e o Brasil*. Vol. II (São Paulo: Companhia Editora Nacional 1958).

Furtado, Celso. *The Economic Growth of Brazil. A Survey from Colonial to Modern Times*. Trans. Ricardo W. de Aguiar and E. C. Drysdale (Berkeley, CA and London: University of California Press, 1971).

Galloway, J. H. "Agricultural Reform and the Enlightenment in Late Colonial Brazil," *Agricultural History*, 53:4 (1979), 763–79.

Games, Alison. "Atlantic History: Definitions, Challenges, and Opportunities," *AHR*, 111:3 (2006), 741–57.

Gash, Norman. *Lord Liverpool. The Life and Political Career of Robert Banks Jenkinson, Second Earl of Liverpool* (Cambridge, MA: Harvard University Press, 1984).

Geggus, David P., ed. *The Impact of the Haitian Revolution in the Atlantic World* (Columbia: University of South Carolina Press, 2001).

Geggus, David P. and Norman Fiering, eds. *The World of the Haitian Revolution* (Bloomington and Indianapolis, IN: Indiana University Press, 2009).

Gil, António Carlos Amador. *Projectos de Estado no Alvorecer do Império* (Vitória, E.S.: Instituto Histórico e Geográfico do Espírito Santo, 2002).

Gil Novales, Alberto. *El Trienio Liberal* (Madrid: Siglo Veintiuno Editores, 1980).

Gildea, Robert. *Barricades and Borders. Europe 1800–1914* (Oxford University Press, 1991).

Godechot, Jacques. *Histoire de L'Atlantique* (Lyon: Bordas, 1947).

France and the Atlantic Revolution of the Eighteenth Century, 1770–1799. Trans. H. H. Rowen (New York: The Free Press, 1965).

The Counter-Revolution: Doctrine and Action 1789–1804. Trans. Salvator Attanasio (London: Routledge & Kegan Paul, 1972 [1961]).

Golove, David M. and Daniel J. Hulsebosch. "A Civilized Nation: The Early American Constitution, the Law of Nations, and the Pursuit of International Recognition," *New York University Law Review*, 85/932 (2010), 932–1066.

Gould, Eliga. *The Persistence of Empire. British Political Culture in the Age of the American Revolution* (Chapel Hill and London: University of North Carolina Press, 2000).

Goycochêa, Castilhos. *A Diplomacia de D. João VI em Caiena* (Rio de Janeiro: Edições GTL, 1963).

Grab, Alexander. *Napoleon and the Transformation of Europe* (Basingstoke: Palgrave Macmillan, 2003).

Grafe, Regina and Alejandra Irigoin. "Bargaining for Absolutism: A Spanish Path to Nation-State and Empire Building," *HAHR*, 88:2 (2008), 173–209.

Graham, Richard. *Patronage and Politics in Nineteenth-Century Brazil* (Stanford University Press, 1990).

Greene, Jack P. *Negotiated Authorities: Essays in Colonial Political and Constitutional History* (Charlottesville and London: University of Virginia Press, 1994).

"State Formation, Resistance and the Creation of Revolutionary Traditions in the Early Modern Era." In M. A. Morrison and A. Zook, eds., *Revolutionary Currents: Nationbuilding in the Transatlantic World* (Lanham, MD: Rowan and Littlefield, 2004).

"Colonial History and National History: Reflections on a Continuing Problem," *William & Mary Quarterly*, 3rd series, 64:2 (2007), 235–50.

Greene, Jack P. and Philip D. Morgan, eds. *Atlantic History: A Critical Appraisal* (Oxford University Press, 2009).

Greene, Jack P. and J. R. Pole, eds. *A Companion to the American Revolution* (Oxford: Blackwell Publishing, 2000).

Griffin, Patrick. *The People with No Name: Ireland's Ulster Scots, America's Scots Irish, and the Creation of a British Atlantic World, 1689–1764* (Princeton University Press, 2001).

Grinberg, Keila and Ricardo Salles, eds., *O Brasil Imperial*, vol. I (1808–1831) (Rio de Janeiro: Civilização Brasileira, 2009).

Guimarães, Angela. *Um Corrente do Colonialismo Português: A Sociedade de Geografia de Lisboa, 1875–1895* (Lisbon: Livros Horizonte, 1984).

Hale, Charles A. *Mexican Liberalism in the Age of Mora, 1821–53* (New Haven and London: Yale University Press, 1968).

"The Reconstruction of Nineteenth-century Politics in Spanish America: A Case for the History of Ideas," *LARR*, 8:2 (1973), 53–73.

Halperín-Donghi, Tulio. *Reforma y Disolución de los Imperios Ibéricos* (Madrid: Alianza Editorial, 1985).

Hammond, R. J. *Portugal and Africa 1815–1910: A Study in Uneconomic Imperialism* (Stanford University Press, 1966).

Hamnett, Brian R. "Constitutional Theory and Political Reality: Liberalism, Traditionalism, and the Spanish Cortes, 1810–1814," *JMH*, 49 ["On Demand Supplement"] (1977), 1071–1109.

Revolución y Contrarrevolución en México y el Perú. Liberalismo, Realeza y Separatismo (1800–24) (Mexico City: Fondo de Cultura Económica, 1978).

"Process and Pattern: A Re-examination of the Ibero-American Independence Movements, 1808–1826," *JLAS*, 29:2 (1997), 279–328.

"Spain and Portugal and the Loss of their Continental American Territories in the 1820s: An Examination of the Issues," *EHQ*, 41:3 (2011), 397–412.

Hanson, Carl A. *Economy and Society in Baroque Portugal, 1668–1703* (Minneapolis: University of Minnesota Press, 1981).

Harris, Mark. *Rebellion on the Amazon: The Cabanagem, Race, and Popular Culture in the North of Brazil, 1798–1840* (Cambridge University Press, 2010).

Hawthorne, Walter. *From Africa to Brazil: Culture, Identity and an Atlantic Slave Trade, 1600–1830* (Cambridge University Press, 2010).

Heinowitz, Rebecca Cole. *Spanish America and British Romanticism, 1777–1826: Rewriting Conquest* (Edinburgh University Press, 2010).

Herr, Richard. *The Eighteenth-century Revolution in Spain* (Princeton University Press, 1958).

"The Constitution of 1812 and the Spanish Road to Parliamentary Monarchy." In Isser Woloch, ed., *Revolution and the Meanings of Freedom in the Nineteenth Century* (Stanford University Press, 1996).

Hespanha, António Manuel, ed. *O Antigo Regime 1620–1807*. Vol. IV of José Mattoso, ed. *História de Portugal* (Lisbon: Editorial Estampa, 1993).

Hespanha, António Manuel, *As Vésperas do Leviathan. Instituições e Poder Político. Portugal. Séc. XVII* (Coimbra: Livraria Almedina, 1994).

Guiando a Mão Invisível. Direitos, Estado e Lei no Liberalismo Monárquico Português (Coimbra: Livraria Almedina, 2004).

"Sob o Signo de Napoleão. A Súplica Constitucional de 1808," *Almanack Braziliense*, no. 7 (2008), 80–101.

"Antigo Regime nos Tropicos? Um Debate sobre o Modelo Político do Império Colonial Português." In João Fragoso and Maria de Fátima Gouvêa, eds., *Na Trama das Redes: Política e Negócios no Império Português, Seculos XVI–XVIII* (Rio de Janeiro: Civilização Brasileira, 2010).

Hesse, Carla. "Towards a New Topography of Enlightenment," *European Review of History*, 13 (2006), 499–508.

Heywood, Linda M. "Slavery and Forced Labor in the Changing Political Economy of Central Angola 1850–1949." In Suzanne Miers and Richard Roberts, eds., *The End of Slavery in Africa* (Madison, WI: University of Wisconsin Press, 1988), 415–36.

Higgonet, Patrice. *Sister Republics: The Origins of French and American Republicanism* (Cambridge, MA: Harvard University Press, 1988).

Higgs, David. "Unbelief and Politics in Rio de Janeiro during the 1790s," *LBR*, 21:1 (1984), 13–31.

Hobsbawm, Eric J. *The Age of Revolution: Europe 1789–1848* (London: Weidenfeld and Nicolson, 1962).

Hodges, Tony and Malyn Newitt. *São Tomé and Príncipe: From Plantation Colony to Microstate* (Boulder and London: Westview Press, 1988).

Holanda, Sérgio Buarque de. "A Herança Colonial – sua Desagregação." In Buarque de Holanda, ed., *História Geral da Civilização Brasileira. Tomo II: Brasil Monárquico*, vol. I (O Processo de Emancipação) (São Paulo: Difusão Europeia do Livro, 1962).

Holmes, Stephen. *Benjamin Constant and the Making of Modern Liberalism* (New Haven and London: Yale University Press, 1984).

Hopkins, A. G. "Back to the Future: From National History to Imperial History," *PP*, 164 (1999), 198–243.

Hoppe, Fritz. *A África Oriental Portuguesa no Tempo do Marquêz de Pombal 1750–1777* (Lisbon: Agência Geral do Ultramar, 1970).

Horward, Donald. "Wellington and the Defence of Portugal," *International History Review*, 11:1 (1989), 39–54.

Howarth, David. *The Invention of Spain. Cultural Relations between Britain and Spain, 1770–1870* (Manchester University Press, 2007).

Hudson, Nora E. *Ultra-Royalism and the French Restoration* (New York: Octagon Books, 1973 [1936]).

Iotti, Luiza Horn, ed. *Imigração e Colonização. Legislação de 1747 a 1915* (Porto Alegre: Assembléia Legislativa do Estado do Rio Grande do Sul, 2001).

Isabella, Maurizio. *Risorgimento in Exile: Italian Émigrés and the Liberal International in the Post-Napoleonic Era* (Oxford University Press, 2009).

Israel, Jonathan. *A Revolution of the Mind. Radical Enlightenment and the Intellectual Origins of Modern Democracy* (Princeton University Press, 2010).

Jacob, Margaret L. *Living the Enlightenment. Freemasonry and Politics in Eighteenth-century Europe* (Oxford University Press, 1991).

Jancsó, István. *Na Bahia, Contra o Império: História do Ensaio de Sedição de 1798* (São Paulo: Editora HUCITEC, 1996).

Jancsó, István, org. *Independência: História e Historiografia* (São Paulo: Editora HUCITEC, 2005).

Jancsó, István and João Paulo G. Pimenta. "Peças de um Mosaico (ou Apontamentos para o Estudo da Emergencia da Identidade Nacional Brasileira)." In C. G. Mota 2000, 129–76.

Janke, Peter. *Mendizábal y la Instauración de la Monarquia Constitucional en España (1790–1853)* (Madrid: Siglo Veintiuno Editores, 1974).

Jardin, Andre and Andre-Jean Tudesq. *Restoration and Reaction, 1815–48* (Cambridge University Press, 1983).

Jasanoff, Maya. *Liberty's Exiles: American Loyalists in the Revolutionary World* (New York: Harper Press, 2011).

Jennings, J. R. "Conceptions of England and its Constitution in Nineteenth-century French Political Thought," *HJ*, 29:1 (1986), 65–85.

Jennings, Lawrence C. *French Anti-Slavery: The Movement for the Abolition of Slavery in France 1802–1848* (Cambridge University Press, 2000).

Jobim, Leopoldo. *Ideologia e Colonialismo* (Rio de Janeiro: Forense-Universitária, 1985).

"Os Jardins Botânicos no Brasil Colonial," *Bibliotecas, Arquivos e Museus* [Lisbon], 2:1 (1986), 53–120.

Júnior, João Feres. *Léxico da História dos Conceitos Políticos do Brasil* (Belo Horizonte: Editora UFMG, 2009).

Kagan, Richard L. *Students and Society in Early Modern Spain* (Baltimore and London: The Johns Hopkins University Press, 1974).

Kantor, Iris. *Esquecidos & Renascidos: Historiografia Acadêmica Luso-Americana (1724–1759)* (São Paulo: HUCITEC/Centro Estudos Baianos, 2004).

Karras, Alan L. and J. R. McNeill, eds. *Atlantic American Societies: From Columbus through Abolition 1492–1888* (London and New York: Routledge, 1992).

Kaufmann, William M. *British Policy and the Independence of Latin America 1804–1828* (New Haven: Yale University Press, 1951).

Kelly, George Armstrong. *The Humane Comedy: Constant, Tocqueville and French Liberalism* (Cambridge University Press, 1992).

Kennedy, John Norman. "Bahian Elites, 1750–1822," *HAHR*, 53:3 (1973), 415–39.

Kirschner, Tereza Cristina. *Visconde de Cairu: Itinerários de um Ilustrado Luso-Brasileiro* (São Paulo: Alameda, 2009).

Klein, Herbert and Ben Vinson III. *African Slavery in Latin America and the Caribbean*, 2nd edn. (Oxford University Press, 2007).

Klinck, David. *The French Counterrevolutionary Theorist: Louis de Bonald (1754–1840)* (New York: Peter Lang, 1996).

Klooster, Wim. *Revolutions in the Atlantic World. A Comparative History* (New York University Press, 2009).

Kraay, Hendrik. "'As Terrifying as Unexpected': The Bahian Sabinada, 1837–38," *HAHR*, 72:4 (1992), 501–27.

Race, State, and Armed Forces in Independence-era Brazil. Bahia 1790s–1840s (Stanford University Press, 2001).

Kraay, Hendrik and João José Reis. "'The Tyrant is Dead!' The Revolt of the Periquitos in Bahia 1824," *HAHR*, 89:3 (2009), 399–434.

Kramer, Lloyd S. *Threshold of a New World: Intellectuals and the Exile Experience in Paris, 1830–1848* (Ithaca and London: Cornell University Press, 1988).

Lafayette in Two Worlds: Public Cultures and Personal Identities in an Age of Revolutions (Chapel Hill, NC and London: University of North Carolina Press, 1996).

Laidlaw, Zoë. *Colonial Connections 1815–45: Patronage, the Information Revolution and Colonial Government* (Manchester University Press, 2005).

Lains, Paulo. "Foi a Perda do Império Brasileiro um Momento Crucial do Subdesenvolvimento Português?" *Penélope* [Lisbon], 3 (1989), 92–101.

Lains, Paulo and Álvaro Ferreira da Silva, eds. *História Económica de Portugal 1700–2000*, 2 vols. (Lisbon: Imprensa de Ciências Sociais, 2005).

Lambert, David and Alan Lester, eds. *Colonial Lives Across the British Empire: Imperial Careering in the Long Nineteenth Century* (Cambridge University Press, 2006).

Lambert, Francis J. D. "The Cortes and the King: Constitutional Monarchy in the Iberian World." Occasional Paper #32 (Glasgow: Institute of Latin American Studies, 1981).

Landers, Jane G. *Atlantic Creoles in the Age of Revolutions* (Cambridge, MA: Harvard University Press, 2010).

Langfur, Hal. *The Forbidden Lands: Colonial Identity, Frontier Violence, and the Persistence of Brazil's Eastern Indians, 1750–1830* (Stanford University Press, 2006).

Larson, Brooke. *Trials of Nation-Making: Liberalism, Race and Ethnicity in the Andes, 1810–1910* (Cambridge University Press, 2004).

Law, Robin. *Ouidah: The Social History of a West African Slaving "Port," 1727–1892* (Athens, OH: Ohio University Press, 2004).

Leite, Renato Lopes. *Republicanos e Libertários: Pensadores Radicais no Rio de Janeiro (1822)* (Rio de Janeiro: Civilização Brasileira, 2000).

Lewin, Linda. *Surprise Heirs, vol. I: Illegitimacy, Patrimonial Rights and Legal Nationalism in Luso-Brazilian Inheritance, 1750–1821* (Stanford University Press, 2003).

Lindoso, Dirceu. *A Utopia Armada: Rebeliões de Pobres na Matas do Tombo Real* (Rio de Janeiro: Paz e Terra, 1983).

Liss, Peggy. *Atlantic Empires: The Network of Trade and Revolution, 1713–1826* (Baltimore: The Johns Hopkins University Press, 1983).

Livermore, Harold. "Cartas de William Walton. O Panfletário Legitimista (1784–1857)," *Anais de Academia Portuguesa da História*, 2 série, 35 (1995), 107–25.

Livesey, James. *Civil Society and Empire: Ireland and Scotland in the Eighteenth-century Atlantic World* (New Haven and London: Yale University Press, 2009).

Llorens, Vicente. *Liberales y Románticos. Una Emigración Española en Inglaterra (1823–34)*, 3rd edn. (Valencia: Editorial Castolia, 1979 [1954]).

Lopes, Maria de Jesus dos Mártires. *Goa setecentista: tradição e modernidade (1750–1800)* (Lisbon: Centro de Estudos dos Povos e Culturas de Expressão Portuguesa, Universidade Católica Portuguesa, 1999).

Losurdo, Domenico. *Liberalism: A Counter-History* (London and New York: Verso, 2011).

Lousada, Maria and Maria de Fátima Sá e Melo Ferreira. *D. Miguel* (Lisbon: Círculo de Leitores, 2006).

Lucena Giraldo, Manuel. *Naciones de Rebeldes: Las Revoluciones de Independência Latinoamericanas* (Madrid: Taurus, 2010).

Lustosa, Isabel. *Insultos Impressos: A Guerra dos Jornalistas na Independência 1821–23* (São Paulo: Companhia das Letras, 2000).

D. Pedro I (São Paulo: Companhia das Letras, 2006).

Luz Soriano, Simão José da. *História da Guerra Civil e do Estabelecimento do Governo Parlamentar em Portugal, Comprehendendo a História Diplomatica, Militar e Política d'este Reino desde 1777 até 1834*, 19 vols. (Lisbon, 1866–87).

Lynch, C. E. C. "O Discurso Político Monarquiano e a Recepção do Conceito de Poder Moderador no Brasil (1822–24)," *Dados* [Rio de Janeiro], 48:3 (2005), 611–54.

Lynch, John. "British Policy and Spanish America, 1783–1808," *JLAS*, 1:1 (1969), 1–30.

Lyons, Martyn. *Post-Revolutionary Europe, 1815–1856* (Basingstoke: Palgrave Macmillan, 2006).

Lyra, Maria de Lourdes Viana. *A Utopia do Poderoso Império: Portugal e Brasil, Bastidores da Política 1798–1822* (Rio de Janeiro: Sette Letras, 1994).

Macaulay, Neill. *Dom Pedro: The Struggle for Liberty in Brazil and Portugal 1798–1834* (Durham: Duke University Press, 1988).

Macaulay, Rose. *They Went to Portugal, Too* (Manchester: Carcaret Press, 1990).

Macedo, Roberto. *História Administrativa do Brasil. Vol. VII: Brasil Sede da Monarquia/Brasil Reino* (Brasília: Editora Universidade de Brasília/ FUNCEP, 1983).

Machado, André Roberto de A[rruda]. *A Quebra da Mola Real das Sociedades. A Crise Política do Antigo Regime Português na Província do Grão-Pará (1821–25)* (São Paulo: Editora HUCITEC, 2010).

MacLachlan, Colin M. "African Slave Trade and Economic Development in Amazonia, 1700–1800." In Judy Bieber, ed., *Plantation Societies in the Era of European Expansion* (Aldershot: Variorum, 1997).

Magalhães, Felix Pereira de. *Apontamentos para a História Diplomatica de Portugal desde 1826 até 1834* (Lisbon, 1871).

Magalhães, Luiz de. *Tradicionalismo e Constitucionalismo: Estudos de História e Política Nacional* (Porto: Chardron, 1927).

Magalhães Godinho, Vitorino de. *Prix et Monnaies au Portugal 1750–1850* (Paris: Librairie Armand Colin, 1955).

Malafaia, Eurico Brandão de Ataide. *António de Araújo de Azevedo, Conde da Barca, Diplomata e Estadista 1787–1817* (Braga: ADB and Universidade do Minho, 2004).

Malerba, Jurandir. *Os Brancos da Lei: Liberalismo, Escravidão e Mentalidade Patriarcal no Império do Brasil* (Maringá-PR: Editora da Universidade Estadual da Maringá, 1994).

A Corte no Exílio: Civilização e Poder no Brasil às Vésperas da Independência (1808–1821) (São Paulo: Companhia das Letras, 2000).

Manchester, Alan K. "The Paradoxical Pedro, First Emperor of Brazil," *HAHR*, 12:2 (1932), 176–97.

British Preëminence in Brazil: its Rise and Decline. A Study in European Expansion (New York, Octagon Books, 1972 [1933]).

"The Recognition of Brazilian Independence," *HAHR*, 31:1 (1951), 80–96.

"The Growth of Bureaucracy in Brazil, 1808–21," *JLAS*, 4:1 (1972), 77–83.

Mandler, Peter. *Aristocratic Government in the Age of Reform. Whigs and Liberals 1830–52* (Oxford: Clarendon Press, 1990).

Manique, António Pedro. *Portugal e as Potências Europeias (1807–1847): Relações Externas e Ingerências Estrangeiras em Portugal na Primeira Metade do Século XIX* (Lisbon: Livros Horizonte, 1988).

Mouzinho da Silveira: Liberalismo e Administração Pública (Lisbon: Livros Horizontes, 1989).

Mansel, Philip. *Paris between Empires. Monarchy and Revolution 1814–1852* (New York: St. Martin's, 2001).

Mark, Monica. "Angola Pours Oil Money into Debt-Ridden Portugal," *Guardian.co.uk*, November 18, 2011 [last accessed March 22, 2012].

Marques, A. H. de Oliveira. *History of Portugal*, 2 vols. (New York: Columbia University Press, 1972).

"A Maçonaria em Portugal na Segunda Metade do Século XVIII." *In Portugal da Revolução Francesa ao Liberalismo. Actas do Colóquio 4 e 5 de Dezembro de 1986* (Braga: Universidade do Minho, 1988).

Marques, A. H. de Oliveira and Joel Serrão, dirs. *Nova História da Expansão Portuguesa*, 11 vols. (Lisbon: Editorial Estampa, 1986-).

Nova História de Portugal. Vol. IX: Portugal e a Instauração do Liberalismo (Lisbon: Editorial Presença, 2002).

Marques, João Pedro. *The Sounds of Silence: Nineteenth-century Portugal and the Abolition of the Slave Trade* (Oxford: Berghahn Books, 2006).

Sá da Bandeira e o Fim da Escravidão. Vitória da Moral, Desforra do Interesse (Lisbon: ICS-Universidade de Lisboa, 2008).

Marquese, Rafael de Bivar. *Administração e Escravidão: Idéias sobre a Gestão da Agricultura Escravista Brasileira* (São Paulo: Editora HUCITEC/FAPESP, 1999).

Marquese, Rafael de Bivar, Marcia Berbel, and Tâmis Parron. *Escravidão e Política. Brasil e Cuba, 1790–1850* (São Paulo: Editora HUCITEC, 2010).

Marshall, Oliver. *English, Irish and Irish-American Pioneer Settlers in Nineteenth-century Brazil* (Center for Brazilian Studies, University of Oxford, 2005).

Martin, Alexander M. *Romantics, Reformers and Reactionaries: Russian Conservative Thought and Politics in the Reign of Alexander I* (DeKalb: University of Northern Illinois Press, 1997).

Martinez, Jenny S. "Antislavery Courts and the Dawn of International Human Rights Law," *Yale Law Journal*, 117 (2008), 550–641.

Martínez Torrón, Diego. *Los Liberales Romanticos Españoles ante la Descolonizacion Americana (1808–33)* (Madrid: Editorial MAPFRE, 1992).

Martins, Ana Canas Delgado. *Governação e Arquivos. D. João VI no Brasil* (Lisbon: IANTT, 2008).

Marx, Karl and Friedrich, Engels. *Revolution in Spain* (New York: International Publishers, 1939).

Mata, Maria Eugénia. "Economic Ideas in Nineteenth-century Portugal," *LBR*, 39:1 (2002), 29–42.

Matos, Pedro Fragoso de. "Oficiais da Armada na Academia das Ciências de Lisboa," *Anais do Clube Militar Naval* [Lisbon], 111 (1981), 251–79.

Matos, Sérgio Pampos. *Historiografia e Memória Nacional no Portugal do Século XIX (1846–1898)* (Lisbon: Edições Colibri, 1998).

Mattos, Ilmar Rohloff de. *O Tempo Saquarema* (São Paulo: Editora HUCITEC, 1987).

Maurício, Carlos M. C. "O falso Portugal de Oliveira Martins," *Ler História*, 38 (2000), 57–86.

Mayer, Arno J. *The Persistence of the Old Regime. Europe to the Great War* (New York: Pantheon Books, 1981).

Maxwell, Kenneth. "Pombal and the Nationalization of the Luso-Brazilian Economy," *HAHR*, 48 (1968), 608–31.

Conflicts and Conspiracies: Brazil and Portugal 1750–1808 (Cambridge University Press, 1973).

"Portuguese America" (Forum on "Atlantic Empires in the Eighteenth Century"), *International History Review*, 6:4 (1984), 529–50.

"The Atlantic in the Eighteenth Century: A Southern Perspective on the Need to Return to the Big Picture," *Transactions of the Royal Historical Society*, 6th series, 3 (1993), 209–36.

Pombal: Paradox of the Enlightenment (Cambridge University Press, 1995).

Naked Tropics: Essays on Empire and Other Rogues (New York and London: Routledge, 2003).

McFarlane, Tony. "Identity, Enlightenment and Political Dissent in Late Colonial Spanish America," *Transactions of the Royal Historical Society,* 6th series, 8 (1998), 309–36.

McMahon, Darrin M. *Enemies of the Enlightenment: The French Counter-Enlightenment and the Making of Modernity* (Oxford University Press, 2001).

Mello, Evaldo Cabral de. *A Outra Independência: O Federalismo Pernambucano de 1817 a 1824* (São Paulo: Editora 34, 2004).

Mello Pereira, Magnus Roberto de. "Brasileiros a Serviço do Império. A África Vista por Naturais do Brasil, séc. XVIII," *Revista Portuguesa de História,* 33:1 (1999), 153–90.

"João da Silva Feijo (1760–1824): Brazilian Scientist in the Portuguese Empire." In Racine, Karen and Beatriz G. Mamigonian, eds., *The Human Tradition in the Atlantic World 1500–1850* (Lanham, MD: Rowman and Littlefield, 2010).

Méndez, Cecilia. *The Plebeian Republic: The Huanta Rebellion and the Making of the Peruvian State, 1820–1850* (Durham, NC and London: Duke University Press, 2005).

Meneses, Filipe de. *Salazar: A Political Biography* (New York: Enigma Books, 2009).

Menezes, Paulo Braga de. *As Constituições Outorgadas ao Império do Brasil e ao Reino de Portugal* (Rio de Janeiro: Arquivo Nacional, 1974).

Mesquita, António Pedro. *O Pensamento Político Português no Século XIX. Uma Síntese Histórico-Crítica* (Lisbon: Imprensa Nacional-Casa da Moeda, 2006).

Miller, Joseph C. *Way of Death: Merchant Capitalism and the Angolan Slave Trade, 1730–1830* (Madison, WI: University of Wisconsin Press, 1988).

Miller, Samuel J. *Portugal and Rome, c. 1740–1830. An Aspect of the Catholic Enlightenment* (Rome: Universitá Gregoriana Editrice, 1978).

Miller, Shawn William. *Fruitless Trees: Portuguese Conservation and Brazil's Colonial Timber* (Stanford University Press, 2000).

Miranda, Jorge, ed. *Perspectivas constitucionais nos 20 anos da Constituição de 1976* (Coimbra: Coimbra Editora, 1996).

Miranda, Jorge. *O Constitucionalismo Liberal Luso-Brasileiro* (Lisbon: Outra Margens, 2001).

Mónica, Maria Teresa. *Errâncias Miguelistas (1834–43)* (Lisbon: Edições Cosmos, 1997).

Monteiro, Nuno G.F. *O Crepúsculo dos Grandes. A Casa e o Património da Aristocracia em Portugal (1750–1850)* (Lisboa: Imprensa Nacional, 1995).

Elites e Poder: Entre o Antigo Regime e o Liberalismo (Lisbon: ICS, 2003).

Dom José: Na Sombra de Pombal (Lisbon: Círculo de Leitores, 2006).

"Liberal-Liberalismo," *Ler História,* 55 (2008), 97–110.

Monteiro, Nuno G. F., ed. *Optima Pars: Elites Ibero-Americanas do Antigo Regime* (Lisbon: ICS, 2005).

Monteiro, Nuno G. F. *et al.*, eds. *Do Antigo Regime ao Liberalismo 1750–1850* (Lisbon: Vega, 1989).

Monteiro, Nuno Gonçalo and Fernando Dores Costa. *D. João Carlos de Bragança 2o. Duque de Lafões: una vida singular no Século das Luzes* (Lisbon: Inapa, 2006).

Monteiro, Tobias. *A Elaboração da Independência* (Editora da Universidade de São Paulo, 1981 [1927]).

Montenegro, João Alfredo de Sousa. *Ideologia e Conflito no Nordeste Rural: Pinto Madeira e a Revolução de 1832 no Ceará* (Rio de Janeiro: Tempo Brasileiro, 1976).

Morelli, Federica, Clément Thibaud and Geneviève Verdo, eds. *Les Empires Atlantiques des Lumières au Libéralisme (1763–1865)* (Presses Universitaires de Rennes, 2009).

Moro, Javier. *El Imperio Eres Tú* (Barcelona: Planeta, 2011).

Mosher, Jeffrey C. *Political Struggle, Ideology & State-Building: Pernambuco and the Construction of Brazil, 1817–1850* (Lincoln, NE and London: University of Nebraska Press, 2008).

Mota, Carlos Guilherme. *Nordeste 1817: Estruturas e Argumentos* (São Paulo: Editora Perspectiva, 1972a).

Mota, Carlos Guilherme, ed. *1822: Dimensões* (São Paulo: Editôra Perspectiva, 1972b).

Mota, Carlos Guilherme, org. *Viagem Incompleta: A Experiência Brasileira (1500–2000)* (São Paulo: Editora SENAC, 2000).

Mota, Carlos Guilherme. *Os Juristas na Formação do Estado-Nação Brasileiro. Vol. I: Século XVI a 1850* (São Paulo: Editora Quartier Latin do Brasil, 2006).

A Idéia de Revolução no Brasil e Outras Idéias, 4th edn. (São Paulo: Editora Globo, 2008).

Mota, A. Teixeira da. "Acerca da Recente Devolução a Portugal, pelo Brasil, de Manuscritos de Sociedade Real Marítima, Militar e Geografica (1798–1807)," *Memórias da Academia das Ciências de Lisboa*, 16 (1972), 237–310.

Murray, David R. *Odious Commerce: Britain, Spain, and the Abolition of the Cuban Slave Trade* (Cambridge University Press, 1980).

Myrup, Erik Lars. "Kings, Colonies, and Councilors: Brazil and the Making of Portugal's Overseas Council, 1642–1833," *The Americas*, 67:2 (2010), 185–218.

Naro, Nancy Priscilla. "Colonial Aspirations: Connecting Three Points of the Portuguese Black Atlantic." In Naro, Roger Sansi-Roca and David H. Treece, eds., *Cultures of the Lusophone Black Atlantic* (Basingstoke: Palgrave Macmillan, 2007).

Needell, Jeffrey D. "The Abolition of the Brazilian Slave Trade in 1850: Historiography, Slave Agency, and Statesmanship," *JLAS*, 33:3 (2001), 681–711.

The Party of Order: The Conservatives, the State, and Slavery in the Brazilian Monarchy, 1831–1871 (Stanford University Press, 2006).

Neely, Sylvia. *Lafayette and the Liberal Ideal, 1814–1824: Politics and Conspiracy in an Age of Reaction* (Carbondale: Southern Illinois University Press, 1991).

Neves, Carlos Agostinho das. *S. Tomé e Príncipe na Segunda Metade do Século XVIII* (Funchal: Região Autónoma da Madeira, 1989).

Neves, Lúcia Maria Bastos Pereira das. "Censura, Circulação de Ideías e Esfera Pública de Poder no Brasil, 1808–24," *Revista Portuguesa de História* [Coimbra], 33:2 (1999a), 665–97.

"Intelectuais Brasileiros nos Oitocentos: A Constituição de uma 'Familia' sob a Proteção do Poder Imperial (1821–1838)." In Maria Emília Prado, org., *O Estado como Vocação: Idéias e Práticas Políticas no Brasil Oitocentista* (Rio de Janeiro: Access Editora, 1999b), 9–32.

Corcundas e Constitucionais. A Cultura Política da Independência (1820–22) (Rio de Janeiro: Revan/FAPERJ, 2003).

Neves, Lúcia Maria Bastos Pereira das *et al.*, eds. *Literatura, História e Política em Portugal (1820–56)* (Rio de Janeiro: Editora UERJ, 2007).

Newitt, Malyn. *A History of Mozambique* (London: Hurst, 1994).

Newitt, Malyn and Martin Robson. *Lord Beresford and British Intervention in Portugal 1807–1820* (Lisbon: ICS, 2004).

Novais, Fernando A. *Portugal e Brasil no Crise do Antio Sistema Colonial (1777–1808)*, 7th edn. (São Paulo: Editora HUCITEC, 2001).

O'Brien, Karen. "Colonial Emigration, Public Policy and Tory Romanticism, 1783–1830," *Proceedings of the British Academy*, 155 (2009), 161–79.

O'Leary, Patrick. *Sir James MacKintosh. The Whig Cicero* (Aberdeen University Press, 1989).

O'Reilly, William. "Genealogies of Atlantic History," *Atlantic Studies*, 1:1 (2004), 66–84.

Oberacker Jr., Carlos H. *A Imperatriz Leopoldina. Sua Vida e sua Época. Ensaio de uma Biografia* (Rio de Janeiro: Conselho Federal de Cultura, 1973).

Oliveira, Mário António Fernandes de. *Alguns Aspectos da Administração de Angola em Época de Reformas (1834–1851)* (Lisbon: Universidade Nova de Lisboa [Press], 1981).

Oliveira Lima, Manoel de. *Dom João VI no Brasil*, 3rd edn. (Rio de Janeiro: Topbooks, [1908] 1996).

O Movimento da Independência (1821–22) (Editora da Universidade de São Paulo, 1989 [1922]).

Dom Pedro e Dom Miguel: A Querela da Successão (1826–28) (São Paulo: Ed. Melhoramentos, 1925).

D. Miguel no Trono (1828–33) (Imprensa da Universidade de Coimbra, 1933).

Oliveira Martins, J. P. *Portugal Contemporaneo*, 2nd edn., Tomo I. (Lisbon: Livraria Bertrand, 1883).

O Brasil e as Colonias Portuguezas, 5th edn. (Lisbon: PAM Pereira Editora, 1920).

Onuf, Peter. "Introduction." In Onuf *et al.*, eds., *Old World, New World. America and Europe in the Age of Jefferson* (Charlottesville and London: University of Virginia Press, 2010).

Paim, António. *Cairu e o Liberalismo Econômico* (Rio de Janeiro: Tempo Brasileiro, 1968).

Palmer, R. R. "The World Revolution of the West: 1763–1801," *Political Science Quarterly*, 69:1 (1954), 1–14.

The Age of Democratic Revolution: A Political History of Europe and America, 1760–1800, 2 vols. (Princeton University Press, 1959–64).

Pang, Eul-Soo and Ron L. Seckinger. "The Mandarins of Imperial Brazil," *CSSH*, 14:2 (1972), 215–44.

Paquette, Gabriel. "The Intellectual Context of British Diplomatic Recognition of the South American Republics, c. 1800–1830," *Journal of Transatlantic Studies*, 2:1 (2004), 75–95.

Enlightenment, Governance, and Reform in Spain and its Empire, 1759–1808 (Basingstoke and New York: Palgrave Macmillan, 2008).

"The Dissolution of the Spanish Atlantic Monarchy," *HJ*, 52:1 (2009a), 175–212.

Paquette, Gabriel, ed. *Enlightened Reform in Southern Europe and its Atlantic Colonies*, c. *1750–1830* (Farnham and Burlington, VT: Ashgate, 2009b).

Paquette, Gabriel. "After Brazil: Portuguese Debates on Empire, c. 1820–1850," *Journal of Colonialism and Colonial History*, 11:2 (2010), e-format only via Project Muse.

"Empire of Exceptions: The Making of Modern Brazil," *History Today* [London], 61:6 (2011a), 39–46.

"The Brazilian Origins of the 1826 Brazilian Constitution," *EHQ*, 41:3 (2011b), 444–71.

Paquette, Gabriel and Matthew Brown. "Introduction: The Persistence of Mutual Influence: Europe and Latin America in the 1820s," *EHQ*, 41:3 (2011), 387–96.

Paquette, Gabriel and Matthew Brown, eds. *Connections After Colonialism: Europe and Latin America in the 1820s* (Tuscaloosa: University of Alabama Press, 2013).

Parron, Tâmis. *A Política da Escravidão no Império do Brasil, 1826–1865* (Rio de Janeiro: Civilização Brasileira, 2011).

Parry, Jonathan. *The Rise and Fall of Liberal Government in Victorian Britain* (New Haven and London: Yale University Press, 1993).

Pedreira, Jorge Miguel. *Estrutura Industrial e Mercado Colonial: Portugal e Brasil, 1780–1830* (Lisbon: DIFEL, 1994).

"From Growth to Collapse: Portugal, Brazil, and the Breakdown of the Old Colonial System (1760–1830)," *HAHR*, 80:4 (2000), 839–64.

Pedreira, Jorge Miguel and Fernando Dores Costa. *D. João VI. Um Príncipe entre Dois Continentes* (São Paulo: Companhia das Letras, 2008).

Peixoto, António Carlos *et al. O Liberalismo no Brasil Imperial: Origens, Conceitos e Prática* (Rio de Janeiro: Editora Revan, 2001).

Pélissier, René. *As Companhas Coloniais de Portugal*. Trans. Isabel Teresa Santos (Lisbon: Editorial Estampa, 2006).

Pereira, Alvaro S. "The Opportunity of a Disaster: The Economic Impact of the 1755 Lisbon Earthquake," *Journal of Economic History*, 69:2 (2009), 466–99.

Pereira, Ângelo. *As Senhoras Infantas Filhas de El-Rei D. João VI* (Lisbon: Editorial Labor, 1938).

Os Filhos de El-Rei D. João VI (Lisbon: Empresa Nacional de Publicidade, 1946).

D. João VI. Príncipe e Rei, 4 vols. (Lisbon: Empresa Nacional de Publicidade, 1953–58).

Pereira, José Esteves. *O Pensamento Político em Portugal no Século XVIII. António Ribeiro dos Santos* (Lisbon: Imprensa Nacional-Casa da Moeda, 1983).

Pereira, Miriam Halpern. *Das Revoluções Liberais ao Estado Novo* (Lisbon: Editorial Presença, 1994).

Pereira, Miriam Halpern *et al.*, eds., *O Liberalismo na Península Ibérica na Primeira Metade do Século XIX*, 2 vols. (Lisbon: Sá da Costa Editora, 1982).

Pereira, Sara Marques. *D. Carlota Joaquina. Rainha de Portugal*, 2nd edn. (Lisbon: Livros Horizontes, 2008).

Pereira da Silva, J. M. *Segundo periodo do reinado de Dom Pedro I no Brazil* (Rio de Janeiro: B.L. Garnier, 1875).

Pétré-Grenouilleau, Olivier, ed. *From Slave Trade to Empire: Europe and the Colonisation of Black Africa 1780s–1880s* (London and New York: Routledge, 2004).

Pidd, Helen. "Europeans Migrate South as Continent Drifts Deeper into Crisis," *Guardian.co.uk*, December 21, 2011 [last accessed March 22, 2012].

Pijning, Ernst. "Regulating Illegal Trade: Foreign Vessels in Brazilian Harbors," *PSR*, 15:1–2 (2007), 321–66.

Pilbeam, Pamela. *The 1830 Revolution in France* (Basingstoke: Macmillan, 1991).

Pimenta, João Paulo G. "A Independência do Brasil e o Liberalismo Portugues: Um Balanço da Produção Acadêmica," *Revista de História Iberoamericana*, 1:1 (2008), 70–105.

Pina, Ana Maria Ferreira. *De Rousseau ao Imaginário da Revolução de 1820* (Lisbon: Universidade Nova de Lisboa, 1988).

"O Resgate de D. Miguel, o 'Príncipe Infeliz'," *Ler História* [Lisbon], 45 (2003), 49–62.

Pinheiro, Magda. *Passos Manuel: O Patriota e o seu Tempo* (Edições Afrontamento/ Câmara Municipal de Matosinhos, 1996).

Pitts, Jennifer. *A Turn to Empire: The Rise of Liberal Imperialism in Britain and France* (Princeton University Press, 2005).

Popkin, Jeremy. *The Right-Wing Press in France, 1792–1800* (Chapel Hill: University of North Carolina Press, 1980).

Portillo Valdés, José M. *Revolución de nación: orígenes de la cultura constitucional en España, 1780–1812* (Madrid: Centro de Estudios Políticos y Constitucionales, 2000).

Crisis Atlántica: Autonomia e Independência en la Crisis de la Monarquía Hispana (Madrid: Marcial Pons, 2006).

Portugal da Revolução Francesa ao Liberalismo. Actas do Colóquio 4 e 5 de Dezembro de 1986 (Braga: Universidade do Minho, 1988).

Posada-Carbó, Eduardo and Iván Jaksić, eds. *Liberalismo y Poder. Latinoamérica en el Siglo XIX* (Santiago: Fondo de Cultura Económica, 2011).

Postma, Johannes and Stuart B. Schwartz, "Brazil and Holland as Commercial Partners on the West African Coast during the Eighteenth Century," *Arquivos do Centro Cultural Calouste Gulbenkian*, 34 (1995), 399–427.

Prado Júnior, Caio. *Evolução Política do Brasil e Outros Estudos*, 4th edn. (São Paulo: Editora Brasiliense, 1963).

Prados de la Escosura, Leandro. *De Imperio a Nación: Crecimiento y Atraso Económico en España (1780–1930)* (Madrid: Alianza Editorial, 1988).

Proença, Maria Cândida. *A Independência do Brasil: Relações Externas Portugueses, 1808–1825* (Lisbon: Livros Horizonte, 1987).

A Primeira Regeneração: O Concerto e a Experiência Nacional (1820–1823) (Lisbon: Livros Horizontes, 1990).

Quijada, Mónica. "Una Constitución Singular: La Carta Gaditana en Perspectiva Comparada," *Revista de Indias*, vol. 68/no. 242 (2008), 15–38.

Racine, Karen. "'This England and This Now': British Cultural and Intellectual Influence in the Spanish American Independence Era," *HAHR*, 90:3 (2010), 423–54.

Raminelli, Ronald. *Viagens Ultramarinas: Monarcas, Vassalos e Governo á Distância* (São Paulo: Alameda Casa Editorial, 2008).

Ramos, Luís A. de Oliveira. *Da Ilustração ao Liberalismo* (Porto: Cello & Irmão, 1979).

Sob o Signo das "Luzes" (Lisbon: Imprensa Nacional-Casa da Moeda, 1988).

Ramos, Luís A. de Oliveira, ed., *D. Pedro, Imperador do Brasil, Rei de Portugal. Do Absolutismo ao Liberalismo. Actas do Congresso Internacional* (Universidade do Porto, 2001).

Ramos, Luís A. de Oliveira, *D. Maria I* (Lisbon: Círculo de Leitores, 2007).

Randall, Robert W. *Real del Monte: A British Mining Venture in Mexico* (Austin, TX: University of Texas Press, 1972).

Rangel, Alberto. *Os Dois Ingleses. Strangford e Stuart* (Rio de Janeiro: Departamento de Impresna Nacional, 1972).

Rees, Siân. *Sweet Water and Bitter: The Ships that Stopped the Slave Trade* (Durham: University of New Hampshire Press, 2011).

Rego, A. da Silva. *O Ultramar Português no Século XIX (1834–1910)*, 2nd edn. (Lisbon: Agencia Geral do Ultramar, 1969).

Reinert, Sophus. *Translating Empire: Emulation and the Origins of Political Economy* (Cambridge, MA: Harvard University Press, 2011).

Reis, António, dir. *Portugal Contemporâneo*. Vol. I (Lisbon: Publicações Alfa, 1990).

Reis, António do Carmo. *A Imprensa do Porto Romântico (1836–50): Cartismo e Setembrismo* (Lisbon: Livros Horizonte, 1999).

Reis, João José. *Slave Rebellion in Brazil: The Muslim Uprising of 1835 in Bahia* (Baltimore and London: The Johns Hopkins University Press, 1993).

Riall, Lucy. *Garibaldi: Invention of a Hero* (New Haven and London: Yale University Press, 2007).

Ribeiro, Gladys Sabina. *A Liberdade em Construção: Identidade Nacional e Conflitos Antilusitanos no Primeiro Reinado* (Rio de Janeiro: Relume Dumará, 2002).

Ribeiro, Gladys Sabina, ed. *Brasileiros e Cidadãos. Modernidade Política 1822–1930* (São Paulo: Alameda, 2008).

Ribeiro, Gladys Sabina. "Portugueses do Brasil e Portugueses no Brasil: 'Laços de Irmandade' e Conflitos Identitários em Dois Atos (1822 e 1890)." In Bela Feldman-Bianco, ed. *Nações e Diásporas. Estudos Comparativos entre Brasil e Portugal* (Campinas: Editora Unicamp, 2010).

Ribeiro, José Silvestre. *História dos Estabelecimentos Scientificos, Litterarios e Artisticos de Portugal nos Successivos Reinados da Monarchia*. Tomos IV and VI (Lisbon: Typographia da Academia Real das Sciencias, 1874, 1876).

Ribeiro, Maria Manuela Tavares. "A Restauração da Carta Constitucional e a Revolta de 1844," *Revista de História das Ideias* [Coimbra], 7 (1985), 183–241.

Ricketts, Mónica. "Together or Separate in the Fight Against Oppression? Liberals in Peru and Spain in the 1820s," *EHQ*, 41:3 (2011), 413–27.

Robertson, John. *The Case for the Enlightenment: Scotland and Naples, 1680–1760* (Cambridge University Press, 2005).

Robinson, Ronald and John Gallagher. "The Imperialism of Free Trade," *Economic History Review*, 2nd series, 6 (1953), 1–15.

Robson, Martin. *Britain, Portugal and South America in the Napoleonic Wars. Alliances and Diplomacy in Economic Maritime Conflict* (London and New York: I. B. Tauris, 2011).

Rocha, António Penalves. *A Economia Política na Sociedade Escravista (un Estudo dos Textos Económicos de Cairu)* (São Paulo: USP/Editora HUCITEC, 1996).

"Idéias Anti-Escravistas da Ilustração na Sociedade Escravista Brasileira," *Revista Brasileira de História* [São Paulo], 20 (no. 39) (2000), 43–79.

Rodrigues, Celso. *Assembléia Constituinte de 1823: Idéias Políticas na Fundacão do Império Brasileiro* (Curitiba: Juruá Editora, 2002).

Rodrigues, Jaime. *O Infame Comércio: Propostas e Experiências no Final do Tráfico de Africanos para o Brasil (1800–1850)* (Campinas: Editora da Unicamp, 2000).

De Costa a Costa: Escravos, Marinheiros, e Intermediarios do Trafico Negreiro de Angola ao Rio de Janeiro (1780–1860) (São Paulo: Companhia das Letras, 2005).

Rodrigues, José Honório. *Brazil and Africa*. Trans. R. A. Mazzara and Sam Hileman (Berkeley, CA and Los Angeles: University of California Press, 1965).

A Assembléia Constituinte de 1823 (Petrópolis: Editora Vozes, 1974).

Independência: Revolução e Contrarevolução. Vol. 5: A Política Internacional (Rio de Janeiro: Livraria Francisco Alves Editora SA, 1975).

Rodriguez, Moises Enrique. *Under the Flags of Freedom. British Mercenaries in the War of the Two Brothers, the First Carlist War, and the Greek War of Independence (1821–40)* (Lanham, MD: Hamilton Books, 2009).

Røge, Pernille. "'La Clef de Commerce': The Changing Role of Africa in France's Atlantic Empire 1760–1797," *History of European Ideas*, 34 (2008), 431–43.

Roldán Vera, Eugenia and Marcelo Caruso, eds. *Imported Modernity in Post-Colonial State Formation. The Appropriation of Political, Educational and Cultural Models in Nineteenth-century Latin America* (New York: Peter Land, 2007).

Roller, Heather F. "Colonial Collecting Expeditions and the Pursuit of Opportunities in the Amazonian Sertão, *c.* 1750–1800," *The Americas*, 66:3 (2010), 435–67.

Roninger, Luis and Carlos H. Waisman, eds. *Globality and Multiple Modernities. Comparative North American and Latin American Perspectives* (Brighton and Portland, OR: Sussex Academic Press, 2002).

Roque, Ricardo. *Head-hunting and Colonialism: Anthropology and the Circulation of Skulls in the Portuguese Empire, 1870–1930* (Basingstoke: Palgrave Macmillan, 2010).

Rosanvallon, Pierre. *Le Moment Guizot* (Paris: Gallimard, 1985).
La Monarchie Impossible. Les Chartes de 1814 et de 1830 (Paris: Fayard, 1994).
Rosen, F. *Bentham, Byron, and Greece: Constitutionalism and Nationalism in Early Liberal Political Thought* (Oxford: Clarendon Press, 1992).
Rosenblum, Nancy C. *Another Liberalism: Romanticism and the Reconstruction of Liberal Thought* (London and Cambridge, MA: Harvard University Press, 1987).
Ruggiero, Guido. *The History of European Liberalism*. Trans. R. G. Collingwood (Boston: Beacon Press, 1959 [1927]).
Russell-Wood, A. J. R., ed. *From Colony to Nation: Essays on the Independence of Brazil* (Baltimore: The Johns Hopkins University Press, 1975).
Russell-Wood, A. J. R., "Iberian Expansion and the Issue of Black Slavery: Changing Portuguese Attitudes, 1440–1770," *AHR*, 83:1 (1978), 16–42.
The Portuguese Empire 1415–1808. A World on the Move (Baltimore and London: The Johns Hopkins University Press, 1992).
"Brazilian Archives and Recent Historiography on Colonial Brazil," *LARR*, 36:1 (2001a), 75–105.
"A Dinâmica da Presença Brasileiro no Índico e no Oriente. Séculos XVI–XIX," *Topoi: Revista de História* [Rio de Janeiro], no. 3 (2001b), 9–40.
"Centers and Peripheries in the Luso-Brazilian World, 1500–1808." In Christine Daniels and Michael V. Kennedy, eds., *Negotiated Empires: Centers and Peripheries in the Americas* (New York and London: Routledge, 2002).
"Sulcando os Mares: Um historiador do Império Português emfrenta a 'Atlantic History'," *História* [São Paulo], 28:1 (2009), 17–70.
Sá, Victor de. *Perspectivas do Século XIX* (Lisbon: Portugália Editora, 1964).
A Crise do Liberalismo e as Primeiras Manifestacões das Ideias Socialistas em Portugal (1820–52) (Lisbon: Serra Nova, 1969).
A Revolução de Setembro de 1836, 3rd edn. (Lisbon: Livros Horizontes, 1975).
Sá da Bandeira e o Liberalismo em Portugal (1795–1910). Actas Comemorações do Bicentenário do Nascimento. 21 a 23 de Setembro de 1995 (Câmara Municipal de Santarém, 1996).
Safier, Neil. *Measuring the New World: Enlightenment Science and South America* (University of Chicago Press, 2008).
"Spies, Dyes, and Leaves: Agro-Intermediaries, Luso-Brazilian Couriers and the Worlds they Sowed." In Simon Schaffer., eds., *The Brokered World: Go-Betweens and Global Intelligence* (Upsala: Science History Publications, 2009a), 239–65.
"A Courier between Empires: Hipólito da Costa and the Atlantic World." In Bailyn, Bernard and Paricia L. Denault, eds., *Soundings in Atlantic History. Latent Structures and Intellectual Currents 1500–1830* (London and Cambridge, MA: Harvard University Press, 2009b), 265–93.
Sanjad, Nelson. "Éden Domesticado: A Rede Luso-Brasileira de Jardins Botânicos 1790–1830," *Anais de História de Além-Mar*, 7 (2006), 251–78.

Santos, Catarina Madeira. "Entre Deux Droits: Les Lumières en Angola (1750–1800)," *Annales HSS*, 60:4 (2005), 817–48.

"Luanda: A Colonial City between Africa and the Atlantic, Seventeenth and Eighteenth Centuries." In Liam Brockey, ed., *Portuguese Colonial Cities in the Early Modern World* (Farnham: Ashgate, 2008).

"Administrative Knowledge in a Colonial Context: Angola in the Eighteenth Century," *British Journal for the History of Science*, 43:4 (2010), 539–56.

Santos, Estilaque Ferreira dos. *A Monarquia no Brasil: o Pensamento Político da Independência* (Vitoria: Editora da Universidade Federal do Espirito Santo, 1999).

Santos, Hermínio. *Trabalhar em Angola: Guia Essencia para Profissionais Portugueses* (Lisbon: Planeta, 2011).

Santos, Martha S. *Cleansing Honor with Blood: Masculinity, Violence and Power in the Backlands of the Brazilian Northeast, 1845–1889* (Stanford University Press, 2012).

Santos Alves, José Augusto dos. *Ideologia e Política na Imprensa do Exílio. O Portuguez (1814–26)*, 2nd edn. (Lisbon: Imprensa Nacional-Casa da Moeda, 2005).

Saraiva, José H. *O Constitucionalismo Monárquico e a Política Ultramarina* (Lisbon: Agência –Geral do Ultramar, 1963).

Schmidt-Nowara, Christopher. *Empire and AntiSlavery: Spain, Cuba, and Puerto Rico, 1833–1874* (University of Pittsburgh Press, 1999).

"After 'Spain': A Dialogue with Josep Fradera on Spanish Colonial Historiography." In Antoinette Burton, ed., *After the Imperial Turn: Thinking with and through the Nation* (Durham: Duke University Press, 2003), 156–69.

The Conquest of History: Spanish Colonialism and National Histories in the Nineteenth Century (University of Pittsburgh Press, 2006).

Slavery, Freedom, and Abolition in Latin America and the Atlantic World (Albuquerque: University of New Mexico Press, 2011).

Schroeder, Paul. *Metternich's Diplomacy at its Zenith 1820–23* (Austin, TX: University of Texas Press, 1962).

The Transformation of European Politics 1763–1848 (Oxford: Clarendon Press, 1994).

Schultz, Kirsten. *Tropical Versailles. Empire, Monarchy, and the Portuguese Royal Court in Rio de Janeiro, 1808–1821* (London: Routledge, 2001).

"The Crisis of Empire and the Problem of Slavery. Portugal and Brazil *c.* 1700–1800," *Common Knowledge*, 11:2 (2005), 264–82.

"The Transfer of the Portuguese Court and Ideas of Empire," *PSR*, 15:1 (2009), 367–91.

Schwarcz, Lilia Moritz. *As Barbas do Imperador: D. Pedro II, um Monarca nos Tropicos* (São Paulo: Companhia das Letras, 2000).

A Longa Viagem da Biblioteca dos Reis. Do Terramoto de Lisboa à Independência do Brasil (São Paulo: Companhia das Letras, 2002).

O Sol do Brasil. Nicolas-Antoine Taunay e as Desaventuras dos Artistas Franceses na Corte de D. João (São Paulo: Companhia das Letras, 2008).

Schwartz, Stuart B. *Sovereignty and Society in Colonial Brazil: The High Court of Bahia and its Judgs 1609–1751* (London and Berkeley: University of California Press, 1973).

Scott, H. M., ed. *Enlightened Absolutism: Reform and Reformers in the Later Eighteenth Century* (London: Macmillan, 1990).

Scott, H. M., "Conclusion: The Continuity of Aristocratic Power." In Scott, ed., *The European Nobilities in the Seventeenth and Eighteenth Centuries*. Vol. II (London: Longman, 1995).

The Birth of the Great Power System 1740–1815 (London: Pearson/Longman, 2006).

Seckinger, Ron. *The Brazilian Monarchy and the South American Republics 1822–31: Diplomacy and State-Building* (Baton Rouge and London: LSU Press, 1984).

Serrão, Joel. *Temas Oitocentistas; Para a História de Portugal no Século Passado* (Lisbon: Edições Atica, 1959).

Sessions, Jennifer E. *By Sword and Plow: France and the Conquest of Algeria* (Ithaca and London: Cornell University Press, 2011).

Shaikh, Farida. "Judicial Diplomacy: British Officials and the Mixed Commission Courts." In Keith Hamilton and Patrick Salmon, eds., *Slavery, Diplomacy, and Empire: Britain and the Suppression of the Slave Trade, 1807–1975* (Brighton and Portland, OR: Sussex Academic Press, 2009).

Shaw, L. M. E. "The Marquês de Pombal (1699–1782): How He Broke Britain's Commercial Ascendancy in Portugal," *Journal of European Economic History*, 27:3 (1998), 537–54.

The Anglo-Portuguse Alliance and the English Merchants in Portugal, 1654–1810 (Aldershot: Ashgate, 1998).

Shepard, Todd. *The Invention of Decolonization. The Algerian War and the Re-Making of France* (Ithaca and London: Cornell University Press, 2006).

Sherwig, John M. *Guineas and Gunpowder: British Foreign Aid in the Wars with France, 1793–1815* (Cambridge, MA: Harvard University Press, 1969).

Shipway, Martin. *Decolonization and its Impact. A Comparative Approach to the End of Colonial Empires* (Oxford: Blackwell, 2008).

Sideri, S. *Trade and Power: Informal Colonialism in Anglo-Portuguese Relations* (Rotterdam University Press, 1970).

Silbert, Albert. *Le Portugal méditerranéen à la fin de l'Ancien Régime, XVIIIe-début du XIXe siècle. Contribution à l'histoire agraire comparée* (Paris: SEVPEN, 1966).

Do Portugal de Antigo Regime ao Portugal Oitocentista, 3rd edn. (Lisbon: Livros Horizonte, 1981).

Silva, Ana Cristina Nogueira da. *O Modelo Espacial do Estado Moderno. Reorganicação Territorial em Portugal nos Finais do Antigo Regime* (Lisbon: Editorial Estampa, 1998).

"Uma Justiça 'Liberal' para o Ultramar? Direito e Organização Judiciaria nas Provincias Ultramarinas Portuguesas do Século XIX," *Revista do Ministério Público* [Lisbon], 27 [no. 105] (2006), 165–200.

Constitucionalismo e Império. A Cidadania no Ultramar Português (Coimbra: Almedina, 2009).

Silva, Ana Rosa Cloclet da. *Construção da Nação e Escravidão no Pensamento de José Bonifácio 1783–1823* (Campinas: Editora da UniCamp, 1999).

Inventando a Nação: Intelectuais Ilustrados e Estadistas Luso-Brasileiros na Crise do Antigo Regime Português 1750–1822 (São Paulo: Editora HUCITEC, 2006).

Silva, Andrée Mansuy-Diniz. *Portait d'un Homme d'État: D. Rodrigo de Souza Coutinho, Comte de Linhares, 1755–1812. Vol II: L'Homme d'État 1796–1812* (Paris: Centre Culturel Calouste Gulbenkian, 2006).

Silva, Armando Barreiros Malheiro da. "O Clero Regular e a 'Usurpação': Subsídios para uma história sócio-política do Miguelismo," *Revista de História das Ideias* [Coimbra], 9:2 (1987), 529–630.

Miguelismo: Ideologia e Mito (Coimbra: Minerva História, 1993).

Silva, José Manuel Azevedo. *Mazagão. Uma Cidade Luso-Maroquina deportada a Amázonia* (Viseu: Palimage Editores, 2007).

Silva, Júlio Joaquim da Costa Rodrigues da. *As Cortes Constituintes de 1837–38: Liberais em Confronto* (Lisbon: INIC, 1988).

Silva, Luiz Augosto Rebello da. *Varões Illustres das Tres Epochas Constitucionaes: Collecção de Esboços e Estudos Biographicos* (Lisbon, 1870).

Silva, Maria Beatriz Nizza da. *Silvestre Pinheiro Ferreira: Ideologia e Teoria* (Lisbon: Livraria Sá da Costa, 1975).

A Repercussão da Revolução de 1820 no Brasil: Eventos e Ideologias (Universidade de Coimbra, 1979).

Movimento Constitucional e Separatismo no Brasil (1821–23) (Lisbon: Livros Horizonte, 1988).

A Cultura Luso-Brasileiro: Da Reforma da Universidade á Independencia do Brasil (Lisbon: Editorial Estampa, 1999).

"A Corte no Rio de Janeiro: o Perigo Francês, o Perigo Espanhol e o Poderio Inglês," *RIHGB*, 169 (438) (2008a), 137–71.

D João, Príncipe e Rei no Brasil (Lisbon: Livros Horizonte, 2008b).

Silva, Maria Beatriz Nizza da, coord. *O Império Cultura e Sociedade no Rio de Janeiro (1808–21)* (São Paulo: Instituto Nacional do Livro, 1977).

O Império Luso-Brasileiro 1750–1822. Vol. VIII of A Nova História da Expansão Portuguesa (Lisbon: Editorial Estampa, 1986).

Silva, Miguel Cicero Peregino da. *Pernambuco e a Confederação do Equador* (Rio de Janeiro: Imprensa Nacional, 1924).

Silva Dias, Maria Odila da. "Aspectos da Ilustração no Brasil," *RIHGB*, 278 (1968), 105–70.

"A Interiorização da Metropole (1808–1853)." In C. G. Mota 1972b, 160–86.

Silveira, João dos Santos Silveira. *Acção Política do Agente e Representante de el-Rei, o Senhor D. Miguel I, em Londres* (Ponte Delgada: n.p., 1985).

Simon, William Joel. *Scientific Expeditions in the Portuguese Overseas Territories (1783–1808)* (Lisbon: IICT, 1983).

Sims, Harold. *The Expulsion of Mexico's Spaniards, 1821–1836* (University of Pittsburgh Press, 1990).

Sked, Alan, ed. *Europe's Balance of Power 1815–1848* (London and Basingstoke: Macmillan, 1979).

Slemian, Andréa. *Vida Política em Tempo de Crise: Rio de Janeiro (1808–1824)* (São Paulo: Aderaldo & Rothschild Editores, 2004).

Smith, E. A. *Lord Grey 1764–1845* (Oxford: Clarendon Press, 1990).

Smith, W. H. C. *Anglo-Portuguese Relations 1851–1861* (Lisbon: Centro de Estudos Histórico Ultramarino, 1970).

Sobrevilla Perea, Natalia. "From Europe to the Andes and Back: Becoming 'Los Ayacuchos'," *EHQ*, 41:3 (2011), 472–88.

Sousa, José Baptista de. *Almeida Garrett (1799–1854), Founder of Portuguese Romanticism. A Study in Anglo-Portuguese Cultural Interaction* (Lewiston, NY: The Edwin Mellen Press, 2011).

Sousa, Octavio Tarquinio da. *História dos Fundadores do Império do Brasil. A Vida de D Pedro I*, 3 vols, 3rd edn. (Rio de Janeiro: Livraria José Olympio Editora, 1957).

Sousa Dias, Gastao. *D. Francisco Inocêncio de Sousa Coutinho: Administração Pombalina em Angola* (Lisbon: Editorial Cosmos, 1936).

Souza, Iara Lis Carvalho. *Pátria Coroada: O Brasil como Corpo Político Autônomo 1780–1831* (São Paulo: Editora UNESP, 1999).

Souza, Laura de Mello e. *O Sol e a Sombra. Política e Administração na América Portuguesa do Século XVIII* (São Paulo: Companhia das Letras, 2006).

"Política e Administração Colonial: Problemas e Perspectivas." In Mello e Souza, Júnia Ferreira Furtado and Maria Fernanda Bicalho, eds. *O Governo dos Povos* (São Paulo: Alameda, 2009), 63–90.

Souza, Paulo Cesar. *A Sabinada. A Revolta Separatista da Bahia 1837* (São Paulo: Editora Brasiliense, 1987).

Sperber, Jonathan. *Revolutionary Europe, 1780–1850* (Longman: London, 2000).

St. Clair, William. *That Greece Might Still be Free: The Philhellenes in the War of Independence* (Cambridge: Open Book Publishing, 2008).

Starzinger, Vincent E. *The Politics of the Center: The Juste Milieu in Theory and Practice, France and England, 1815–48* (New Brunswick, NJ and London: Transaction Publishers, 1991).

Stein, Stanley J. "The Historiography of Brazil 1808–1889," *HAHR*, 40:2 (1960), 234–78.

Stein, Stanley J. and Barbara H. Stein. *The Colonial Heritage of Latin America: Essays on Economic Dependence in Perspective* (Oxford University Press, 1970).

Stern, Philip J. "'Rescuing the Age from the Charge of Ignorance': Gentility, Knowledge, and the British Exploration of Africa in the later Eighteenth century." In Kathleen Wilson, ed., *A New Imperial History* (Cambridge University Press, 2004), 115–35.

Stock, Paul. *The Shelley-Byron Circle and the Idea of Europe* (New York: Palgrave Macmillan, 2010).

Stone, Lawrence. *The Causes of the English Revolution 1529–1642* (London: Routledge, 1972).

Sucena, Eduardo. *Lisboa, O Fado e os Fadistas*, 2nd edn. (Lisbon: Vega Editora, 2002).

Sweet, James H. *Domingos Álvares, African Healing, and the Intellectual History of the Atlantic World* (Chapel Hill: University of North Carolina Press, 2011).

Symes, Carol. "When We Talk about Modernity," *AHR*, 116:3 (2011), 715–26.

Tavares, Adérito and José dos Santos Pinto. *Pina Manique: Um Homem entre duas Épocas* (Lisbon: Casa Pia de Lisboa, 1990).

Temperley, Harold. *The Foreign Policy of Canning 1822–27: England, the Neo-Holy Alliance and the New World* (London: Frank Cass, 1966 [1925]).

Tengarrinha, José. *História da Imprensa Periódica Portuguesa*, 2nd edn. (Lisbon: Editorial Caminho, 1989).

Thompson, I. A. A. "Crown and Cortes in Castile, 1590–1665," *Parliaments, Estates and Representation*, 2 (1982), 29–45.

Thompson, Martyn P. "The History of Fundamental Law in Political Thought from the French Wars of Religion to the American Revolution," *AHR*, 91:5 (1986), 1103–28.

Thurner, Mark. *From Two Republics to One Divided. Contradictions of Post-Colonial Nation-Making in Andean Peru* (Durham, NC: Duke University Press, 1997).

Todd, David. "A French Imperial Meridian, 1814–1870," *PP*, 210 (2011), 155–86.

Tombs, Robert. *France 1814–1914* (London and New York: Longman, 1996).

Torgal, Luís Reis. *Tradicionalismo e Contra-Revolução: O Pensamento e Acção de José da Gama e Castro* (Universidade de Coimbra, 1973).

Torgal, Luís Reis and João Lourenço Roque, eds. *O Liberalismo (1807–1890)*. Vol. V of José Mattoso, dir., *História de Portugal* (Lisbon: Editorial Estampa, 1993).

Torres, João Camillo de Oliveira. "As Origens da Carta Portuguesa," *Revista de Ciência Política* [Rio de Janeiro], 6:3 (1972), 21–28.

Tortarola, Edoardo. "Eighteenth-century Atlantic History Old and New," *History of European Ideas*, 34:4 (2008), 369–74.

[Universidade Católica Portuguesa (Porto)]. *Catolicismo e Liberalismo em Portugal (1820–1850)* (Lisbon: Imprensa Nacional-Casa da Moeda, 2009).

Vale, Brian. *Independence or Death! British Sailors and Brazilian Independence 1822–25* (London and NY: I. B. Tauris, 1996).

The Audacious Admiral Cochrane: The True Life of a Naval Legend (London: Conway Maritime Press, 2004).

Valente, Vasco Pulido. *Os Devoristas: A Revolução Liberal 1834–36* (Lisbon: Quetzal Editoras, 1993).

Varela Suanzes-Carpegna, Joaquin. "O Constitucionalismo Espanhol e Português durante a Primeira Metade do Século XIX (Um Estudo Comparado)," *Historia Constitucional*, 11 (2010), 237–74.

Vargues, Isabel Nobre. "Insurreições e Revoltas em Portugal (1801–1850): Subsidios para uma Cronologia e Bibliografia," *Revista de História das Ideias* [Coimbra], 7 (1985), 501–72.

A Aprendizagem da Cidadania em Portugal (1820–23) (Coimbra: Minerva, 1997).

Varnhagen, Francisco Adolfo de. *História da Independência do Brasil*, 3rd edn. (São Paulo: Edições Melhoramentos, 1957).

Correspondência Ativa. Ed. Clado Ribeiro de Lessa (Rio de Janeiro: Instituto Nacional do Livro, 1961).

Ventura, António. *O Exílio, os Açores e o Cerco do Porto. D. Luis de Sousa Coutinho, Primeiro Marquês de Sta. Iria, nas Guerras Liberais* (Lisbon: Edições Colibri, 2000).

Venturi, Franco. *Utopia and Reform in the Enlightenment* (Cambridge University Press, 1971).

"Il Portogallo dopo Pombal," *Revista Storica Italiana*, 95 (1983), 63–101.

Verdelho, Telmo dos Santos. *As Palavras e as Ideias na Revolução Liberal de 1820* (Coimbra: INIC, 1981).

Vianna, António. *Apontamentos para a História Diplomática Contemporânea. Vol. II: A Emancipação do Brasil* (Lisbon: Typ. do Anuario Commercial, 1922).

Apontamentos para a História Diplomática Contemporânea. Vol. III: A Carta e a Reacção (Lisbon: Gráfico Santelmo, 1958).

Vianna, Hélio. "D. Pedro I de 1829 à 1831: Contribuição à História Final do Primeiro Reinado de Acôrdo com Documentos em grande parte inéditos," *RIHGB*, vol. 252 (1961), 178–97.

Dom Pedro I, Jornalista (São Paulo: Edições Melhoramentos, 1967).

Vidal, Laurent. *Mazagão: A Cidade que Atravessou o Atlântico. De Marrocos para a Amazónia (1769–1783)*. Trans. Manuel Ruas (Lisbon: Editorial Teorema, 2007).

Vidal, Laurent and Tania Regina de Luca, eds. *Franceses no Brasil. Séculos XIX–XX* (São Paulo: Editora EUNESP, 2009).

Vieira, Benedicta Duque. *A Revolução de Setembro e a Discussão Constitucional de 1837* (Lisbon: Edições Salamandra, 1987).

Villalta, Luiz Carlos. *1789–1808: O Império Luso-Brasileiro e os Brasis* (São Paulo: Companhia das Letras, 2000).

Waddell, D. A. G. "British Neutrality and Spanish American Independence: The Problem of Foreign Enlistment," *JLAS*, 19:1 (1987), 1–18.

Walker, Timothy. "Abolishing the Slave Trade in Portuguese India: Documentary Evidence of Popular and Official Resistance to Crown Policy, 1842–1860," *Slavery & Abolition* 25:2 (2004), 63–79.

Wearden, Graeme. "Brazil Considers Helping Portugal Ease Debt Crisis," *Guardian.co.uk*, March 30, 2011 [last accessed March 22, 2012].

Weber, David. *Bárbaros: Spaniards and Their Savages in the Age of Enlightenment* (New Haven: Yale University Press, 2005).

Webster, C. K. *The Foreign Policy of Castlereagh 1815–1822: Britain and the European Alliance* (London: G. Bell & Sons, 1925).

Britain and the Independence of Latin America 1812–1830: Selected Documents from the Foreign Office Archives, 2 vols. (London and NY: Oxford University Press, 1938).

The Foreign Policy of Palmerston 1830–41: Britain, the Liberal Movement and the Eastern Question, 2 vols. (London: G. Bell & Sons Ltd, 1951).

Wehling, Arno. "Estado, Governo e Administração no Brasil Joanino," *RIHGB*, 168 (436) (2007), 75–92.

Wheeler, Douglas L. "Some Aspects of 19th-century Portuguese Thought on Portuguese Africa, 1835–1875," *The Journal of the American Portuguese Cultural Society*, 4: 1–2 (1970), 43–48.

The Empire Time Forgot : Writing a History of the Portuguese Overseas Empire, 1808–1975 (Porto: Universidade Fernando Pessoa, 1998).

"Letter to the Membership: End of the 'Boxer Century' – What's Next? The Current State of the Teaching and Writing of Portuguese and Portuguese Imperial History in North America," *PSR*, 8:2 (2000), 4–8.

Wheeler, Douglas L. and René Pélissier. *Angola* (Westport, CT: Greenwood Press, 1978).

Wheeler, Douglas L. and Walter C. Opello. *Historical Dictionary of Portugal*, 3rd edn. (Lanham: The Scarecrow Press, 2010).

Winch, Donald. *Classical Political Economy and Colonies* (London: LSEPS & G. Bell and Sons, 1965).

Winn, Peter. "British Informal Empire in Uruguay in the Nineteenth Century," *PP*, 73 (1976), 100–126.

Wright, Beth S. *Painting and History during the French Restoration: Abandoned by the Past* (Cambridge University Press, 1997).

Zahler, Reuben. "Liberal Justice: Judicial Reform in Venezuela's Courts, 1786–1850," *HAHR*, 90:2 (2010), 489–522.

UNPUBLISHED DISSERTATIONS AND THESES

Baum, Emmi. "Empress Leopoldina: Her Role in the Development of Brazil, 1817–26," PhD diss., New York University (1965).

Biléu, Maria Margarida Correia. "Diogo Inacio de Pina Manique, Intendente Geral da Polícia: Innovações e Persistências," MA diss., Universidade Nova de Lisboa [Sintra] (1995).

Bonnabeau, Richard F. "The Pursuit of Legitimacy: The Stuart Mission and the Recognition of Brazilian Independence 1824–26," PhD diss., University of Indiana-Bloomington (1974).

Borrêcho, Maria do Céu de Brito Vairinho. "D. Maria I: A Formação de Uma Rainha," MA diss., Universidade Nova de Lisboa (1993).

Brigola, João Carlos Pires. "Ciência e Política: do Pombalismo ao Liberalismo. Francisco Simões Margiochi," MA diss., Universidade Nova de Lisboa, (1990).

Browne, George P. "Government Immigration Policy in Imperial Brazil, 1822–1870," PhD diss., Catholic University of America (1972).

Candido, Mariana Pinho. "Enslaving Frontiers: Slavery, Trade, and Identity in Benguela, 1780–1850," PhD diss., York University [Canada] (2006).

Clayton, Arnold B. "The Life of Tomás Antônio de Vilanova Portugal: A Study in the Government of Portugal and Brazil, 1781–1821," PhD diss., Columbia University (1977).

Davidson, David. "Rivers and Empire: The Madeira Route and the Incorporation of the Brazilian Far West, 1737–1808," PhD diss., Yale University (1970).

Ferreira, Roquinaldo Amaral. "Transforming Atlantic Slaving: Trade, Warfare and Territorial Control in Angola, 1650–1800," PhD diss., UCLA (2003).

Figueiredo, Fernando Augusto de. "Timor: A Presença Portuguesa (1769–1945)," PhD diss., University of Porto (2004).

Gibson, Carrie. "The Impact of the Haitian Revolution on the Hispanic Caribbean, c. 1791–1830," PhD diss., University of Cambridge (2010).

Holub, Norman. "The Liberal Movement in Brazil, 1808–54," PhD diss., New York University (1968).

Lousada, Maria Alexandre Lopes Companhã. "O Miguelismo: O Discurso Político e o Apoio da Nobreza Titulada," unpublished, "Provas de Aptidão Pedagógica e Capacidade," Faculdade de Letras, University of Lisbon (1987).

Monteiro, João Paulo Gomes de Almeida. "As Ideias da Nação, Sociedade e Homem no Pensamento Político de Faustino José de Madre de Deus," MA diss., Universidade Nova de Lisboa (2000).

Morton, F. W. O. "The Conservative Revolution of Independence: Economy, Society and Politics in Bahia, 1790–1840," DPhil diss., Oxford University (1974).

Muller, Fernanda Suely. "(Re-)Vendo as Páginas, (Re-)Visando os Laços e (Des-)Atando Nós: As Relações Literárias e Culturais Luso-Brasileiras Através dos Periódicos Portugueses (1899–1922)," PhD diss., Universidade de São Paulo (2011).

Pintassilgo, Joaquim António de Sousa. "Diplomacia, Política, e Economia na Transição do Século XVIII para o Século XIX: O Pensamento e Acção de António de Araújo de Azevedo (Conde da Barca)," MA diss., Universidade Nova de Lisboa (1987).

Protásio, Daniel Estudante. "Historiografia e Ideologia na Obra do 2o Visconde de Santarém (1791–1856)," MA diss., University of Coimbra (1999).

Reinert, Helen K. "A Political History of the Brazilian Regency, 1831–40," PhD diss., University of Illinois (1960).

Santos Pozo, Gilmar de Paiva dos. "Imigrantes Irlandeses no Rio de Janeiro: Cotidiano e Revolta no Primeiro Reinado," MA diss., Universidade de São Paulo (2010).

Semedo, Victor Manuel Eugénia. "Liberalismo em Cabo Verde (1820–1834)," MA diss., Universidade Nova de Lisboa (2004).

Silva, Pedro Miguel Carvalho Alves da. "O Dispotismo Luminozo: Introdução ao Pensamento de Dom Rodrigo de Sousa Coutinho," MA diss., Universidade Nova de Lisboa (1997).

Sommer, Barbara. "Negotiated Settlements: Native Americans and Portuguese Policy in Pará, Brazil, 1758–1798," PhD diss., University of New Mexico (2000).

Sousa, Ana Madalena Rosa Barros Trigo de. "D. Francisco de Sousa Coutinho em Angola: Reinterpretação de un Governo, 1764–1772," MA diss., Universidade Nova de Lisboa (1996).

Villalta, Luiz Carlos. "Reforma Ilustrado, Censura e Práticas de Leitura: Usos do Livro na América Portuguesa," PhD Diss. Universidade de São Paulo (1999).

Wheeler, Douglas L. "The Portuguese in Angola, 1836–91: A Study in Expansion and Administration," PhD diss., Boston University (1963).

Wisser, William. "Rhetoric and Riot in Rio de Janeiro, 1827–1831." PhD diss., University of North Carolina (2006).

Index

CPSIA information can be obtained at www.ICGtesting.com
Printed in the USA
BVOW05s0918100714

358581BV00001B/7/P